CW00631275

The National Small Press Centre

HANDBOOK

The National Small Press Centre Handbook

General editor John Nicholson
Published by The National Small Press Centre Committee
BM BOZO,
London WC1N 3XX
June 1997
© The Contributors and The National Small Press Centre

ISBN 0 904063 29 1
British Library Cataloguing in Publication Data:
a catalogue record for this book is available from the British Library

Printed in Great Britain by Redwood Books
Kennet House, Kennet Way, Trowbridge, Wiltshire BA14 8RN
(0125 769979)

This book is sold subject to the condition that it shall not, by way of trade or otherwise, be lent, re-sold, hired out or otherwise circulated without the publisher's prior consent in any form or binding other than that in which it is published.

Trade distribution by Turnaround Publisher Services Ltd
Unit 3, Olympia Trading Estate, Coburg Road, London N22 6TZ
0181 829 3000

The Roll of Honour and Gratitude:

Cover

Design: Cecilia Boggis
Illustration: Martin Guderna for the Vancouver Small Press Festival 1991 (while every effort has been made to trace him we would be grateful to contact him)
Origination: Bridget Tisdall

Part One

Features and Confessions solicited and edited by John Nicholson; design by Cecilia Boggis, pictures and graphics scanned by Andy Hopton. Thank you to all of the Contributors to this section.

Part Two

The A to Z was checked in turn by the entire National Small Press Centre Committee. It was revised on screen by John Nicholson. Most of the submitted free listings were input and made rational by Alan Henson of Black Sheep Press. The backlog of entries from Small Press Listings and News From The Centre were isolated by John Nicholson and input (after he got Repetitive Strain Injury) by Lesley and John Dench and Andy Hopton. The entire A to Z was tagged and stylistically revised by Sally Farrimond. Design by Cecilia.

Part Three

The DIY Guide was overhauled and redesigned as The Manual by Cecilia. It was initially checked by the NSPCC then final revisions were made by Andy Hopton and Lesley and John Dench. Extra bits were added by John and Cecilia. The new inputting and revision on screen was done by Cecilia.

Part Four

The Resource Directory was overhauled and re-conceived by John Nicholson, design by Cecilia. Checking and revision was done by the NSPCC with much additional work by Rose Heaword. The on-screen work was done by JN.

Advertising was obtained under the ægis of Cecilia Boggis.
Consultant for software and advice Peter Kettle.
A special thanks to Tony Askew who helped beyond the call of friendship and was instrumental in keeping the lines of communication open after the Centre left Middlesex University.

CONTENTS

7   General Introduction

11   **BOOK 1**

Matters Arising

A

THE STATE OF PLAY

13   **Breaking into Libraries** *Chris Atton*
Small Presses and Libraries

17   **Was it a Ghastly Mistake?** *John Nicholson*
Campaigning for Small Presses

23   **The Penniless Publisher** *Anne Hodkinson*
Using Invisible Assets

25   **Let's Talk Business** *Jim Lavis*
Small Presses and Marketing

29   **What is Happening to Artists' Books?** *John Bently*
Changes in Recent Years

32   **Have Small Presses a Future?** *John Nicholson*
Differences between America and Britain

B

35   HOBBY HORSES!

C

47   CONFESSIONS: 21 SMALL PRESSES CONFESS HOW AND WHY THEY DID IT

95   **BOOK 2**

A-Z Directory of Small Presses

185   **BOOK 3**

Manual — How To Publish Yourself in 26 Simple Steps

211   **BOOK 4**

A Directory of Resources

INTRODUCTION

They tried to put us out of business but – we're back!

Remember the Small Press Group of Britain's Yearbooks? Every year from 1988 to 1993 this 'bible' helped to change lives and bank balances for hundreds. They also transformed morale for thousands all over the world. The books were huge money-spinners too. Invaluable resource and reference tools and inspirational.

Then it stopped.

The SPG who published the Yearbooks was destroyed internally. It was said, by the sensible money-minded, that the books could not be produced because there was no capital.

Well, we're here to show how wrong this was and is. How the Small Press spirit is the opposite of that outlook. How a small press exists *despite* lack of money. How it creates the money, the 'capital'. It has faith in its abilities and imagination.

For three years there has been no equivalent. So the gap still exists as does the need.

Although this is the first 'Handbook' we learned from those six Yearbooks. Times have changed in the intervening four years and the situation has become unrecognisable from the first edition, worked on in Summer 1988.

It has been a good moment to take stock and see how things have changed since that first step in the dark.

One of the moving spirits of that first edition, Ed Baxter, writes in his Confession about his own small press, Aporia, how all he had painfully learned ten years ago was shared but how it is now all out of date!

Others who were on the original team producing the Yearbooks have been instrumental in this Handbook. Three veterans and three newcomers. Another explanation for the silence is the toll the work took, personally. A couple of days after the 1994 edition had been completed its typesetter (and advert seller and designer and general anchor) collapsed suddenly and her life would have ended except for the efforts of a passing doctor and others with enough first aid knowledge. As it was her life hung in the balance. Today she has an implanted defibrillator which is designed to recover her from such episodes. Her life changed as did mine. Although she returned to her day job three months later and was full-time in 5 months, she shed most of her other commitments, including the Chair of the Group in January 1994.

An entirely new Board took over with the exception of non-elected Officers. Unhappily by the Spring all but two of this Board had been ousted or resigned and the final act came in the Autumn with a fiasco of a fair and the cessation of the Ltd Co in November. This news filtered out to members the following Summer.

There was no 1995 Yearbook and none since. Because nothing else has filled the gap the Centre, which had survived the debacle of the Group, began work on a totally different book in 1996.

How does the Handbook differ from the Yearbooks? There are many similarities. The Yearbooks had got so many things right it would have been pointless to change for change's sake. However we totally overhauled the Resource Directory because we believe this is a way the Centre and the Handbook will develop. We believe there must be closer co-operation between the Services and the presses and that the Centre is the only agency through which this can be made to happen. Both parties cannot exist without each other and need a neutral ground to meet – the Centre.

We have revised the DIY Guide as explained in its introduction. It has been re-designed to be more user-friendly ie accessible. Wherever possible the information has been updated with the standard caveat that any such enterprise is governed by the fluidity of events ie always check!

But there are changes in the outside world which are relevant. The biggest change is how the technical processes differ from those we described ten years ago! Then small pressers were getting used to Amstrads. Today a new generation has no concept of a world which is unable to function without web sites, e-mail and modems. Mobile phones are only an outward sign of the revolution in communications. Put together, these technical changes are transforming not only our lives but specifically the notion of publishing. In particular the collapse of the book was foreseen by 'zines. 'zines were a natural for the Web. Even in 1988 we were prophesying the obsolescence of bookshops as we know them. This has not yet become visible but it is only a matter of time. The ending of the Net Book Agreement is a distraction, just a step on the way.

Stockbroking in department stores and banking in supermarkets are already here. Look how pubs and betting shops have changed! How long before a hybrid emerges? Possibly amalgamating Cyber cafes? In New York a famous

Deli has the stockmarket figures on a display over your head. In Las Vegas you can gamble while you sleep. Why, even in England banks look like pinball games parlours.

These are changes which affect how we expect to live. Therefore they will inevitable change how we communicate and the nature of 'publishing', of sharing information.

How else is the situation different? Nearly every town has its quickprint shop and freelance origination studio. How is it possible to document all of these? Certainly it is beyond the scope of this Handbook. And it would be almost worthless. Events change so quickly, the directory would cost more than £100 and you only use it about six times.

Or the would-be publisher has their own DTP system. Ten years ago we dealt in terms of bedsit publishing. Now it is on the web or the net. It has gone deeper, become more untraceable. Electronic publishing. Compiling the A to Z is even more strange. Then we hunted, today we surf. We are still seeking the invisible. But does it want to be found?

Much small press activity wants to be remain unknown and untraceable. A paradox? If you are trying to communicate, through printed matter or on the web, can you claim to be a hermit? True you can omit any identity, disguise any address. But that prevents any dialogue. It reduces your publication to a harangue.

There are laws of data protection which prevent the storage of information and its dissemination. Fine. Tell that to the people who batter you with junk mail!

There is a middle path, the P.O. Box or the similar firms who promise to protect your privacy. If you do publish your details you cannot object to them being publicised. Besides you can be sure you got on the files of the thought police a long time ago.

The most important difference about the Centre's Handbook is that all of it is under the Centre's control so it is a living, growing, breathing process. We can revise the information continually and send it out continuously. Every three months *Small Press Listings* contains details of some 60 imprints while every other month *News From The Centre* is packed with news and information - about grants, Short Run Printers and other services, distributors, fairs, developments etc.

So plug in at once and help each other and everybody, including yourself.

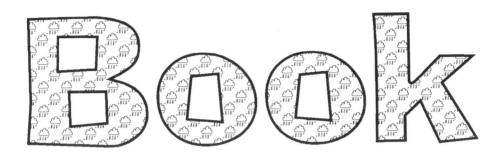

Failed to get a distributor? Can't get stocked in bookshops? At least you could sell a copy to your library.

BREAKING INTO LIBRARIES

WHY BOTHER?

Chris Atton

After ten years as a professional librarian, I finally cracked. I'd been a reader and a supporter of small presses (even an occasional publisher) for all that time, and where opportunities arose, I'd attempted to acquire small press material for the libraries in which I'd worked.

I was only one person working in one library at a time. But if I could do it, why shouldn't others? What was needed was something bigger. So I wrote a guidebook to small presses and alternative literature, specifically aimed at librarians. This was published in 1996. Despite its publication by a mainstream publisher, I had doubts as to how successful it would be. After all, the absence of small press material in libraries is well-known.

There's a guide book

Yet the reviews the book has received confounded my expectation. The subject of the book was clearly exciting to many people. Their knowledge of the field was limited, but they were enthusiastic. A year later, and I'm hopeful that the dozen or so positive reviews I've had will translate into a few thousand librarians actively seeking out small press material for their shelves. This is important not for reasons of self-publicity, but because libraries should be of immense value to small presses.

This value is twofold.

First: libraries may act as archives, as repositories, ensuring that at least a vestige of small press enterprise remains for the future. In Britain, the six legal deposit libraries perform this function, along with a tiny group of specialists such as the collection of little magazines at University College London. Of course those small presses that don't send copies to the Big Six, for whatever reason, don't get to be archived. And in these days of clawback those libraries are hardly likely to come knocking on your door demanding their rights. I'd guess that most small press material goes uncollected by the legal deposit libraries.

At a local level, libraries hardly collect it at all. What's worse is that even the means to discover what is available (including the book you're reading now) are largely uncollected by local libraries, what we might call the 'meta-archives' of yearbooks, directories and indexes. From a total of 13 university libraries in Scotland, for instance, only one takes *The Left Index*, only one (another) the *Alternative Press Index*. Both are in the country's capital city. Of the national libraries of the UK, only the British Library subscribes to *The Left Index*; none subscribes to *Alternative Press Index*.

Even were these publications acquired it is hardly likely to make a dent in the ignorance of librarians towards small presses. And it certainly doesn't help sales. A collection such as New York State Library's archive of Factsheet Five, the meta 'zine which was itself an archive, is – as its own librarian admits – difficult to store, difficult to access and therefore of limited value to the here and now. The archetypal roomful of cardboard boxes might be of inestimable worth to scholars of publishing history fifty years but does nothing for the small presses of the present. The small press publisher, like the small press author, usually has an urgent message. If you have the key to preventing Doomsday you may be disappointed when, instead of allowing your warning to save the world, the librarian puts it into a time capsule. How ironic to bury such ephemeral and topical material for cultural archaeologists.

What small presses need are librarians who are not only actively engaged in purchasing their publications for use in the here and now; but who are also actively engaged in promoting them. What is needed is more than an archive. The publications need to be seen, handled and read. But first the librarians have got to know the small presses exist.

Here is the second value: libraries which do more than store, they encourage readers.

According to the standards expected of professional librarians, librarians are expected to know about all types of publications. In its 1989 Policy Statement on Censorship, the Library Association expects librarians to provide *'as far as resources allow*, all books, periodicals and other materials, *except the trivial*, in which its readers claim legitimate interest.' Unfortunately, those two phrases I've highlighted are crucial to many acquisition policies. The plea of 'not enough money' has been used by librarians unwilling to consider stock beyond their standard repertoire. The designation 'trivial' (read: unpopular, unreadable, whatever) may be used to keep the shelves free from 'subversive' or otherwise 'marginal' writings.

Duty of librarians
More hopefully, the Library Association's *Code of Professional Conduct* insists that all its members 'have an obligation to facilitate the flow of information and ideas and to protect and promote (that word again) the rights of every individual to have free and equal access to sources of information without discrimination and within the limits of the law.' But how many do it?

I think I'm in the minority (of one?), as a librarian working in a general (university) library who regularly orders small press material. I do this not on principle, but simply because I've taken the trouble to discover just how much material is out there, so I can choose from as wide a range as exists. That's what 'collection development' in libraries is all about; not lazily picking best-sellers from the 'top ten' lists of a favoured library supplier. It means more work, it means dealing with dozens of small publishers and distributors. And it seems that not many librarians are interested in doing that.

But there are signs that librarians are starting to cast their nets a little wider. Cumbria County Heritage Services (which includes libraries) are currently collaborating with Northern Arts to promote 'all writers and poets who are published by independent presses.' So if you live or work in Cumbria, get in touch via your local library. Do remind them that 'independent press' should include small presses of all sizes, because some libraries have a hazy definition of what's 'independent'. Take our second project, this time covering Berkshire, Buckinghamshire and Oxfordshire and involving Southern Arts. This aims to improve library provision of literature 'under-bought' by libraries, though it includes literary fiction from mainstream publishers as well as poetry 'from small or large publishers' and 'books from established independent presses.'

These are two drops in the ocean, but at least they're drops. Yet they won't have any impact unless they are accompanied by promotion of the material in the libraries and an educational project amongst the librarians. There's hope here too. Cumbria promise an independent press book fair and 'mini-festival.' The southern project has a specific aim of educating librarians about wider practices of stock selection. Librarians are good at promoting literature, it's true. They run children's story times and get thriller writers in to brighten those long dark evenings. To be seen to actively promote one part of the publishing industry, however, even though it's small, non-profit making and generally ignored is seen as 'political.' The big boys (sic) will get upset; the library suppliers will fell left out. Yet it's those very library suppliers that fail those of us who wish to collect small press materials for our libraries.

What about the suppliers?
Library suppliers simply don't buy – or even promote – small press publications as a mater of course. But they don't see that as *their* failure.

Duncan Turner of James Askew & Son believes it is the "sales and marketing failures" which prevent small press titles from being identified and acquired by library suppliers. He is confident that such failures represent only 'a few titles by obscure experimental publishers' and that his company in fact is able to identify and acquire almost all small press titles. Do you believe him? 1

The sales and marketing manager of Greenhead Books, Nigel Lancaster, does not go so far as to claim that his company are aware of the majority of titles published in the UK, but he has said that Greenhead are 'willing and able to supply any available publication, whatever the source.' Do you believe him? 2

Turner surely misreads the publishing situation in the UK drastically, if he believes there are 'only a few' missed by his or any other library supplier. Lancaster's assertion raises the question of availability linked with accessibility: how do you know a title exists? Even if you do, how do you know where to get it from? Where do you get *The Bug* from? Where do you get *Fatuous Times* from?

If we are sceptical of such library suppliers what can we do about it? By 'we' I speak to both librarians and small presses. I've already offered one strategy: librarians dealing with a multiplicity of small publishers and distributors. I do it and I can vouch for its success. But the trend in library supply is towards greater centralisation, not towards pluralism. Some libraries are considering contracting out library *stock selection* to a single commercial company. In these cases the librarians won't even choose the books any more.

Building bridges

What hope for small presses? Turning against that tide might be worthwhile, but it's going to exhaust all but the strongest. What is needed instead – and what is possible, I believe – is for the library suppliers to form the bridge between the librarians and the small presses. You can still try to sell your wares direct to libraries and try to convert every librarian to small presses; just don't be too hopeful.

That is one side of what can be done. More importantly small presses should educate themselves too. They should learn how the libraries work. As a group small presses need to approach library suppliers. The latter are only interested if there's a demand for what you're selling, so librarians also need to be approached to stimulate that demand. Let's build on the projects in Cumbria and the South; find some advocates within the library profession. Link up with other committed support bureaucracies such as the regional Arts Councils. After all they are already paying public money to support some small presses.

But there is another practical way small presses can build bridges to librarians and their suppliers. What about small press fairs that explicitly welcomed librarians and their suppliers with a programme of educational and orientation events? For instance 'talk tables' where librarians, suppliers, publishers and distributors could sit down and learn about each other. This would be at once a pragmatic and a radical first step.

I've heard that an even more ambitious idea was mooted a few years back. With the stimulus of one visionary librarian, the organiser of the huge Small Press Group's fairs was discussing a scheme to approach a handful of library suppliers. The idea was to ask the suppliers to sponsor a the SPG's prestigious fair. This would have begun the bridge-building and mutual education. It would have been of inestimable value to the suppliers by educating them in one day. Would they still have been able to make such confident claims of omniscience and accessibility? It would have encouraged suppliers to distribute small presses *en masse*, rather than one here and one there every few years.

Now the Small Press centre is beginning a new series of fairs in the prestigious Royal Festival Hall perhaps the scheme could be dusted of? Given the attention that small presses are beginning to enjoy amongst librarians, this could be a venture worth pursuing. I'd support it, certainly.

Notes

1 D. Turner 'Stock Selection, the library supplier's view'. Scottish Libraries Journal, May/June 1993 p10-11.

2 N. Lancaster letter to 'Assistant Librarian', August 1992 p121.Chris Atton's book 'Alternative Literature, a practical guide for librarians', is available from Gower @ £39.50. ISBN 0 566 076659

Chris Atton's book 'Alternative Literature, a practical guide for librarians', is available from Gower @ £39.50 ISBN 0 566 076659

How do the circumstances in 1987 differ from those in 1997? Did the Small Press Group make any difference during its seven/eight years? Is there a need for a new group catering for small presses? How should such an organisation function? And the old refrain, 'What is a small press?'

WAS IT A GHASTLY MISTAKE?

TEN YEARS, BEFORE AND AFTER

John Nicholson

In the beginning

In the formative months of the group the founding members planned two projects: to put on a small press fair and to publish a joint catalogue. After the official formation of the Group at the end of January 1988 the number of small presses who came out of the woodwork made the notion of a joint catalogue impossible. It would have been sensible, if we had begun with a couple of dozen members. But the membership shot passed the 50 mark within three months and, following our exhibiting at the London Book Fair in March 1988, which generated a piece in The Guardian, we received more than 200 enquiries. Had we identified a need! Suddenly we faced a third job: to organise and administer a group.

At once we met the chant 'What is a small press?'

The Question

To deal with that problem first. After all the answer will clarify whether a new group is needed or possible.

It is a valuable as asking what is a fish? What a futile waste of time. Clearly The Question is meant to annoy and cause trouble. No answer satisfies such questioners. We had come together to get on, not waffle. We were practitioners not commentators.

Answer 1: a small press is somebody who isn't the least interested in definitions but wants results.

As we described it the term was inclusive rather than exclusive. It covered all forms of publishing which was not reliant on commerce - minuscule eclectic publishers (MEPs).

Answer 2: small presses are obsessives, serial offenders.

He, she, he & she or he/she will persevere until they die. They may go through times when they are short of cash but they are rarely short of ideas. Watch how they produce something with no money!

Small Presses are not ruled by money.

It was inevitable that our cheek in creating a new organisation, just doing it, (copyright J Rubin) annoyed those who had been soldiering for more than 20 years, as they saw it, answering that need. But this is not our fault. The enquirers simply did not know of the existing organisations, (how was that our fault?) or their needs were not met. What is wrong with that? Weren't the founding members of the Small Press Group in exactly the same position? We knew there were organisations out there but we also knew they were as irrelevant to our small presses as the Publishers' Association.

What made us wonder, as the SPG swelled and we achieved more ambitious programmes, was why we were told the SPG was all a ghastly mistake and we should pack up and join the other organisations.

Here is one of the inevitable prices of success. The more we succeeded the more the work ballooned. Of course we were all volunteers. Of course we never foresaw what we were creating. Of course we ended up relying on a core of less than ten volunteers. Of course the demands became intolerable.

Instead of asking The Question it is more interesting to ask 'Where does the term originate?' 'Small Press' is an American term. We learned it in May 1987 when we discovered a small press fair and a small press center in New York. The term was not in currency in Britain, indeed it was hardly known.

The concept, as we saw it, applied to our own efforts for nearly 20 years. Efforts which, because they were inexplicable, emphasised and aggravated my existence in outer darkness. Admittedly we knew we were not alone. Others lurked in the murk. We each admired each others work. We were invigorated by each other's nerve and obstinacy. We did not overlap so we felt no difficulty in helping each other. An example: we swopped tips - we told each other if we found a cheap printer, how to cut corners, any possible stockist, warnings against hostile shops. We might include each other's bumf in our mail-outs. Without knowing it we were acting as an unofficial group or association. We shared what can be described as a small press spirit. In other words we were small presses without realising.

So there is another answer. Small Press probably don't know themselves they are small

presses.

But there was more to the concept. What was also unknown in Britain was the ethos of small press. The unquestioned belief that being a small press was nothing to be ashamed of but was, on the contrary, considered admirable. It was the essence of the Spirit which created America: entrepreneurial, independent, based on free speech and opposed to authoritarianism. No wonder it was unheard of in England.

The irony is that at the moment we saw the concept and brought it back to Britain it was starting to implode in America. The May 1987 New York small press fair had received good coverage. We were introduced to it by an article in the New York Times. (How different. Small Presses are treated like any other initiative in America, particularly in New York. They are cherished and are encouraged with publicity. Hard to imagine automatic press coverage in London for an event which has no celebs or free-loading.) In retrospect I realise this report harked on definition in an oblique way. The participants were wondering what happened when a small press succeeded? How did it deal with growth and money? Of course the response to such quandaries differs vastly in America and England.

By the time the New York small press fair had become an offshoot of the New York Small Press Centre the disintegration was advanced. Mike Gunderloy wrote about this battle to claim the term 'small press' after he had moved on from his masterpiece, Factsheet 5. In his day Factsheet 5 exhibited the same all embracing eclectic approach. When his readers rebuked him for listing Nazi nutters he obliged and left them out. Promptly he was rebuked again. 'Please include every nutter, regardless. No censorship. Where else can we find out what is going on, in all areas?'

This was the spirit to which we responded and brought home. That at the very moment there was turmoil is an irrelevant paradox. As I have shown we only discovered all that much later. Indeed it only emerged in America some time afterwards. What is relevant here is how the spirit fired us and how we relayed our excitement. And how others responded to the idea. The excitement and enthusiasm caught fire.

What next? To 'come out.'

It means realising there is no need to accept being treated in this way. That is passive. There is an active face too. It means that we are perfectly capable of organising collectively. After all every one of us has organised individually. Put these tow faces together and what do you have? It means we do not need to wait for permission or grants collectively any more than we did individually.

Here is another answer: a small press doesn't realise it is sitting on a goldmine of potential.

What was the landscape in 1987?
The final turning point was our meeting with a small press distributor. Could we finally get somebody else to do the trudging? I can swop tales of tramping cities and towns for 20 years trying to get my publications stocked. As we sat in their office for an hour, they were personal friends, at least 6 calls came in from other small presses asking the same question. All of us down were turned down routinely. It made sense. How could any commercial firm cope with hordes of financial incompetents, all raving, all singing from different song-sheets? We left exhilarated. We had a demonstration of how many small presses were out there, lost. We all shared the same problems but the biggest problem was we were all isolated. None of realised

the others existed!

Here was an answer to 'what is a small press?' A lost soul.

If you like the first decision had been taken without us. We were forced to come together or perish.

Those of us who were already in touch, in a disorganised way, met for the first time. Accepting the term 'small press' we knew we could relate to thousands of small presses - in America. By the simple use of the term we plugged into a vast world! What of Britain?

Another characteristic of small presses is we all know a few others.

From half a dozen you rapidly leap to thirty six. We agreed to alert them to the concept. What we didn't waste a second discussing is 'What Is A Small Press?' We had seen it ourselves. The moment the concept is made visible small presses recognise themselves. All others shy away.

People who ask the question are not small presses.

They are usually commentators, media persons or grant givers. By contrast small presses are practical and have no time to get bogged down.

Small presses are in the business of solving problems, not creating them.

Those founding six pooled their knowledge of organisations theoretically available: the Association of Little Presses and the Independent Publishers Guild. None of the founding six saw any way to relate what they did to either organisation. We fell between them. One was too commercially minded, the other not enough.

We saw the two organisations as being the opposite ends of the scale to the ALP: one loathed money the other loved it. Untrue but a starting point. 'Small presses' fall between the extremes. In our first days a member of the IPG gave us a definition which still helps.

'Small publishers dream of becoming big publishers. Small Presses don't give a damn.'

The differences were there from the start. It was never hidden from the SPG side. This makes a nonsense of any suggestion we are the same and should join existing organisations. The ALP criticises the Centre as 'commercial'. The small presses we saw in America would not understand this quaint English attitude. They don't even see themselves as hobbies. Why do the English have this suspicion of financial reward? It's a long story and here is not the place. Suffice it to say small presses do not regard making money as a fault. Small presses have no ethical hostility to money. We have to pay our bills. By the same token we do not see why we should go unpaid for all the work we do. Most small presses are the work of one or two people who are not only the authors but also the typesetters, designers, marketing and publicity, promotions, book-keepers and bankers. And this should not be reflected in the pay out? What an English phenomenon.

There you have another reason why the new concept was instantly accepted, it *was* different. It provided a home. Besides the original six were appropriately diverse. This meant we had no rivalry. The accusation that small presses are pathological non-joiners is correct. But only a tiny few refuse to help themselves even if it means others benefit. All we needed to do was set things up in such a way that nobody's independence was threatened.

Small presses are not short-sighted.

So much for identifying small presses. What did they want? Primarily to get better treatment. This comes before making money because one is not possible without the other. The example was America where bookshops had been dealing happily with small presses for years. They did not ask the Question. In Britain a tiny number of small presses had managed to establish individual relationships with a few shops. But that merely emphasised the problem. British bookshops were, and are, unaware of any need to do business with small presses. *They do not even know the Question.*

From this attitude stem the excuses: it is too difficult, it would loose the bookshops money, and so on. If course these are not reasons but excuses. They are indefensible with the available technology.

A perfect example is this Handbook. It is indistinguishable from books produced by mainstream publishers. It has all the trimmings: bar code, ISBN etc. *If the customers are not interested in who published the book why should the shop staff care?* Collectively small presses can produce a product which surprises both the customer and the trade. The con trick is many bookshops, including some chains, stock this book. Yet most of them are unaware of 90% of the imprints listed in our A/Z. *This means the customers know more than the bookshops!* Of course the customers can buy directly from the publishers which means the bookshops really are losing money…

Here we can digress a moment. A good example of the changes during the ten years is the difference in bookshops. Or is it? Bookshops have altered superficially but from the perspective of small presses they are still dinosaurs. I sometimes think they have got worse. The more choice of paperbacks disguises the reality. These smart new imprints belong to a consensus of outlook. Perhaps that is why it can be profoundly depressing to browse through the fifty new novels which seem to come out every week. Each screams how it is the most amazing ever. Commonsense contradicts this. It makes you query the need for lying. If they are all so good then they are on the same level. Until you dismiss not one but the lot in faint distaste. I long for one book which admits it is a mess! It would gain my sympathy. I think most people know they too are messes and unbalanced so they would give it a try!

I don't intend to rehearse all the SPG went through instead I offer a quick sketch of the context. What a change in banks. Ten years ago they were like churches, cathedrals even. Their atmosphere was hushed, reverential. Your banker was like a father confessor. A fantasy to those who only know the playgrounds that are today's banks. Even the staff behave like the jolly amateurs hosting a quiz show. Perhaps that explains why your statements are hit and miss. Easy come, easy go. The amounts make anybody from the old ways blanch. It was a standard joke to ridicule people who reminisced about how prices used to be. But that meant the 1920s. Now it means ten years ago. The decade has created a gulf.

The same applies to computers. Our first Yearbook talked in terms of cut and paste using glue. Quaint. Today's children see the Web as a part of everyday life.

This atmosphere, of slick, quick glossiness - has reached books. More than ever before in more bookshops and sold in a jazzy way. But it is also more ruthless. Shelf-life rules. Authors have joined the game. They ask for the cash and status of stars. Martin Amis and his dentures, Rushdie and his goons. In 1988 we banged on about how ordering would cut out bookshops.

What is the web doing to them? Small presses are their own bookshops now.

Finale
Which brings me back to where I started. In Britain my small press still has no home. It still has a struggle because people regard it as an indulgence, worse than vanity press. I still have no stockists. I am luckier than many because some of my titles are listed in Counter Production's mail order catalogue. But this is only a superior version of what the small presses used to do for themselves. Or a better organised sales tool than this Handbook. In other words I still see the problem as a failure of awareness. Let us hope the Centre can help to change this.

Although this article first appeared in Small Press World in 1993 we feel it contains much wisdom which is valid today.

THE PENNILESS PUBLISHERS

HOW TO CAPITALISE ON INVISIBLE ASSETS

Anne Hodkinson

In the world of publishing, we of the Small Press brigade tend to jump in where angels fear to tread. Yes we know all about "building lists", "forward planning" and all the other headings designed to make us more efficient and successful. Yet where does the money come from to enable us to go forward?

Many of you know exactly the routes you take to achieve publication of your treasured author or text and I hope that the following remarks will help to expand some of the avenues you might not have tried already.

One example

I was most fortunate (as a Penniless Publisher) to be invited at the cost of my particular association, to attend the world conference of that association where we heard of the various methods employed by the larger publishers in the group in getting their publications to a wider audience. What surprised me most was that there were systems currently in place which I had not noticed or even thought about and the powers that be at The Small Press Centre thought you might be interested in hearing about some ways to raise finance and publish your title(s).

Imagine the scenario – a group of people pay their annual subscription/ membership fees to their association, which in turn spreads the income over the various departments of the association. Any large organisation whether it is the World Wildlife Association, the Church, local history groups or Trade Associations may have a publishing department. The finance committee has budgeted for each department according to the overall income and the publishing department or person will know how much there is to work with for the following year.

It is quite possible that last year, the department knew what it was going to produce for the following year and made the appropriate arrangements in the hope of getting a similar if not larger budget this year. So already the money we have put into our association is being earmarked for one title or another. The outcome is that not only do we contribute to the publishing arm of our favourite charity, church or association but we then proceed to buy the books which that department has produced.

Double indemnity

We are paying twice for our books but in a way we are helping to keep publishers in business. Not a bad thing if our money is wisely used and provision is made for proper distribution, which unfortunately is not always the case.

However, here is one possible avenue for marketing our manuscript. Do you belong to or are you associated with a body which would welcome the opportunity to publish or sell for you or even consider co-publishing? This is especially true of world-wide associations and it would pay you to research any association to which your title(s) would appeal on a world-wide basis. As a result of the conference I attended, I can list 6 forthcoming titles which will appeal to three other publishers in my association. The resultant reduction in costs is well repaid for the research and time needed.

Author as asset

The next real bonus we have is our author(s). The same applies to them. They are members of all sorts of clubs and associations. Don't forget to use a marketing questionnaire with your authors (see in the next section). Find out as much as you can about them and more importantly get them 'on tour' if you can. For example, I have one author who will speak to many organisations about her work in Israel over the past ten years. Not only is she wishing to raise funds for her association but her book will help. First we are preparing a series of visits to raise the necessary production costs by talking to those who often wish to hear this author speak. By taking your author around you can pre-sell your publication and for those who have paid for the book prior to publication, you merely run-on those extra copies to your original print run. We all know that run-on prices are very very good so it is well worth the effort. On the co-publishing side of things, it is useful to consider a barter arrangement with an overseas publisher. You produce the CRC and they print and freight free to you. This often saves the overseas publisher the cost of the copyright licence to produce in their country. Full use should be made of any overseas exhibitions and book fairs to talk to other publishers and perhaps do the same in reverse.

Share and reduce

Lastly, all of us should seriously consider forming specialist subject areas where we can rep for each other around the country. The SPC Handbook is full of information on each of us, we should make contact and offer the same discount and terms so that our efforts are not relying on the amount of books we sell. For every book placed in a bookshop we have achieved success because not all of us are acceptable to the distribution companies.

We are now becoming a large enough body to form area groups despite our subject specialisation and for those who work alone or in very small teams, the opportunity to share ideas and talk through problems is very valuable. For those of you who are already putting into practice some or all of these ideas – forgive the lecture. For those about to try them out – Good Luck!

Anne Hodkinson runs The Friendly Press in Bristol

A breath of cold air amongst the idealism reminds us we are in business.

Let's talk business

DISTRIBUTOR'S SERVICES — ARE THEY SUITABLE FOR THE SMALL PRESS?

Jim Lavis

For today's smaller – and often specialist – publisher, the distribution function is no less important than other key functions in the publishing cycle, e.g., editorial, design, marketing, selling and finance. Alas, historically it has often rated a lesser vote in the overall scheme of things, with predictable consequences. Fortunately this situation is now changing and distribution is foremost in many people's minds.

INTRODUCTION

Although the role has not changed in basic principles, it *is* changing in perception and is gaining more exposure in today's ever changing publishing industry, perhaps more so since the demise of the Net Book Agreement. There is continuing controversy over the roles and supply routes of publishers, library suppliers and wholesalers, all of whom are not only trying to reach shrinking traditional markets, but also creating new markets to meet the continuing demands of an ever increasing output of new titles. Distributors, large or small, have a significant contribution to make to the success of the book trade of the future.

However the term is defined, or however it is accomplished, doing it well can and will improve your sales revenue and hopefully the quality of your list. Having it done badly will undoubtedly have an equally adverse effect. So how do you decide whether or not to undertake the activity itself – how do you evaluate your needs – who do you approach – what questions do you ask – and of course not least of all, how much will it cost?

Not surprisingly there are no simple answers to these questions. I nevertheless hope that the overall content of this article will enable you to gain a deeper understanding of some of the issues involved, if distribution features in your plans for the future. The ultimate decision is of course yours, and a little inside knowledge will not come amiss. It is also worth pointing out that decisions on distribution can rarely be made in isolation and that marketing, selling and promotional activities should also form part of your discussions.

For the purposes of this article my comments relate to books and books in series. There are those (aliens from other industries) who would argue that selling books is no different to selling shoes, jewellery or even baked beans, therefore distribution is a mere function of the manufacturer. That books have to move from point A to point B by road, rail, sea or air in boxes, accompanied by an invoice/delivery note to fulfil a customer's demand, is as close a statement to the similarity in the other products that I can agree with. It is the intrinsic nature of the product and the complex demands of the market place that make books "different".

While large organisations tend to think generally in terms of globalisation, centralisation, mergers, take-overs and acquisitions, smaller organisations can think – and act – more positively in terms of specialisation, operational detail and genuine personal services. However, they need to contact like-size companies in the distribution areas, companies who understand their needs and related problems and who can offer advice and guidance. Although your reputation might be enhanced if you are distributed by a major company, what losses are sustained if they are not up to standard ? Of course the same argument applies to smaller organisations – but they have more to lose if their performance deteriorates.

In general terms a distributor's range of services should include the following – the italicised paragraphs are intended to be your guidance notes.

1 WAREHOUSING
Pallet or bin storage in dry conditions of printed stocks for current and back list titles. A forward picking area to satisfy daily orders and a bin for returns and soiled stocks where books are not in mint condition. Month end reports of opening and closing stock levels with movements should be supplied. Stocktaking should be at 12 month intervals.

Define ownership & insurance conditions, not only of stocks in the warehouse for loss damage or theft, but also of stocks in transit to customers. Replacement values for warehouse losses could be based on printing costs, while losses in transit could be expressed as net invoice values. You have to balance the costs of insurance – if it is charged separately – against the cost of supplying replacements. Establish whether storage and insurance charges are separate or part of an inclusive deal. Pallet storage charges usually consist of two elements – one charge to accept the pallet and place it on racking and the other charge is the weekly pallet rental (usually regardless of the quantity of stock held on it.)

2 CREDIT CONTROL & ACCOUNT MANAGEMENT
The distributor should be able to demonstrate effective credit control and cash collection procedures, particularly for overseas accounts in difficult areas. These include issuing pro-forma requests where credit is risky, activating credit card orders and seeking credit references for new accounts. There is also an element of discretion for the distributor to decide which non-trade orders to accept on open credit terms. In general the distributor will have his own rules and procedures on levels of trade discounts, small order surcharges and a returns policy.

Victims of the recent recession, within the industry, have been booksellers, wholesalers and library suppliers. You may well need to discuss how to assess the credit risk on non-trade orders e.g. from local government departments, schools, businesses or corporations – where pre-payment routines may be difficult – if your list attracts such buyers.

Your sales income is really no more at risk with a small distributor than with a larger organisation, if a trade account becomes insolvent. A smaller distributor is less exposed – partly because his turnover is less – but partly because he has a greater chance of spotting a trend of delayed payments and acting on them more immediately. His philosophy is slightly different –

he has no room (financially) to consider the plight of others, therefore his "stop credit" rules may be quicker, whereas a large company might be more generous and provide more leeway to a company in difficulties. They will still only get their 5p in the pound in the long run, so you can guess what your proportion will be. Some publishers – often in the face of conflicting advice – may want to take a risk in certain areas. The distributor will rightfully want such transactions identified in writing.

3 ORDER FULFILMENT

Rapid and reliable invoicing routines are essential, not only to service same-day "hot-line" orders but also to service all orders within 48 hours – an industry aim – but far from being achieved. In addition it is vital that reports for books not currently available are issued within the same time framework. This should be followed by equally efficient and accurate order picking routines, so that orders are in the delivery cycle within 72 hours. An order routing audit trail is necessary to track claims.

Accurate, reliable and well managed order picking routines are as important to the distributor as they are to the client publisher and of course the customer. Familiarity of the titles by order picking teams is vital, whether the stocks are arranged by ISBN, author, title, series or imprint.

Publishers selling direct to customers are sometimes reluctant to hand over that stream of business to a distributor – and in fact some larger distributors will not even handle direct sales. The basic functions of picking and packing are the same, so you might try to negotiate a different rate – or different procedures eg., just send them your own dispatch note or label after you have received payment from your customer.

4 DISTRIBUTION FACILITIES

Distributors use a variety of carriers to deliver goods to customers depending on weights, location, speed of service and cost. If rates are quoted, they are likely to be cheaper than if you went direct to the carriers, with the exception of packets weighing up to 750g, where Royal Mail has the edge. Large distributors providing services for high volume publishers, would provide very good contract rates and are often able to quote a percentage figure for carriage against invoice values. Smaller distributors may want to recover the carriage costs they have incurred on your behalf because they have a higher proportion of smaller units to send out.

For a distributor to assess his service charges for your account he will need to know how many titles you plan to publish, when, their prices, your actual and expected turnover, ratio of trade to direct sales, a sales area breakdown and some idea of invoice frequency and average packet/carton weights. If a percentage figure is quoted, check that against what you are currently paying. Remember – it is normal trade practice for the publisher to bear the cost of delivery to the bookshop in the UK and Northern Ireland (or the UK freight forwarding address where European or other overseas booksellers have that facility – otherwise it is charged out to them) and for the non-trade customer to have the cost of carriage added to his invoice. Claims for non-deliveries can best be dealt with by "track-back" services, so it might be worth selectively paying that little bit extra. In contrast, some smaller specialist publishers may not only charge out carriage to trade accounts, they also provide low discounts – and have done for some time.

5 SALES INFORMATION (domestic clients)

Sales information should be shown by sales area or region on a monthly basis with year to date figures for each title, totalled for all titles, or by pre-determined group. Some analysis of type of sale – whether generated by a trade representative, mailing response, or particular promotion may be available depending on client turnover. Monthly turnover by account with details of what has been sold to that account should also be produced.

It is possible that any sales information you have has been compiled in more detail than the distributor can provide from his standard system. However there is no harm in continuing to gather such information if you can from some of the detail the distributor provides. Basically you need to know how many copies of all your titles you are selling, to whom and which are the best sales regions. If you are selling to different types of purchaser – trade account, library, institute, private buyer, etc., then those sales may be identified at month end by a code, or perhaps sub-totalling by that code. One thing to bear in mind is that distributors work for several publishers, so they have to adopt a position of economic commonality of computerised reports and information.

5a SALES INFORMATION (international clients)
Sales information should be shown by national region on a monthly basis with year to date figures for each title expressed in units.

It is generally accepted (although there are exceptions) that the detailed customer based sales information as shown in para 5, is not reportable to the overseas publisher on the basis that international sales data is best expressed in terms of units.

CONCLUSIONS
Probably the major benefit of appointing a distributor is the ability to be able to sell your titles into trade accounts that would otherwise not wish to trade with you. Another benefit, particularly if you have an expanding list, is that it may well free up your time enabling you to concentrate on other key functions. With the right distributor you may find that you are linked up with a national trade sales team visiting key booksellers in all areas, that would otherwise be difficult to achieve. The level and detail of sales information may also be enhanced.

The downside ? Well of course there has to be one – at least – and it affects your most important function, cash flow. If you decide to appoint a company look very carefully at the effect it has on your money – not only the lesser proportion for each sales transaction, but also the delay involved in receiving that lesser amount. Distributors will account for sales in various ways, the two most popular being A) within 5 to 30 days of when *they* are paid and B) within 90 to 120 days of raising an invoice. The service charge for that month's processing is usually levied at the end of the month, either by deductions from revenues or by issuing a service charge invoice.

If possible, try to seek an opinion on service quality and costs from a similar sized publisher, rather than a major imprint from the portfolio of your intended distributor. He should not mind being asked to do this.

One final point. Your publications need not only to compete with or complement other publications on the market, but also with all the other demands for personal or business disposable income. If you have a commercially viable list, then distributors will be interested and should be able to discuss a reasonable solution to your needs.

28   *Jim Lavis runs a family based distribution, promotional and marketing business, established in 1982, providing services for a range of international scholarly, academic, educational and specialist publishers. Before that he had three years experience with a scientific publisher, preceded by more than twenty-five years with Blackwells International Library Services*

The ultimate non-commercial end of the Small Press spectrum — or the outer edge of the Art world and its vast sums?

ARTISTS BOOKS

WHAT HAS CHANGED RECENTLY?

John Bently

In the three years or so that have passed since I last wrote something about Artists' Books for this Handbook's lamented predecessor, the Small Press Yearbook, there has undoubtedly been a larger than usual avalanche of activity to report, too much for me to even begin to skim the surface without resorting to the use numbered lists accompanied by incomprehensible diagrams. I shall leave this to future academics and briefly pose this question: Is all this activity the quickly burning tail of yet another hype-fuelled comet passing briefly through the tangled skies of the late 20th century Art solar system?

The craze

In 1995 there emerged something of a congestion of Book Art 'survey' exhibitions. The Collins Gallery in Glasgow mounted a commendably wide-ranging consensus featuring artists young and old in as sympathetic a surround as glass-cases can provide.

Artists considered of importance were exhibited in little arranged sections with a selection of representative works. The show toured to Rochdale and the Shetland's and introduced a huge new audience of sheep to the possibilities inherent in an ancient and supposedly threatened species.

Simultaneously, back in London, the Tate Gallery held a miniature retrospective of their own Artists Book Collection. So unexpectedly successful was this, audience wise, that they had to extend the show for over a month, and a conference held in the Clore Gallery lecture theatre was sold out months in advance.

I wonder why they didn't think to produce even the merest hint of a catalogue? A different species of sheep, me included, were denied their grazing rights, I think.

The ever conspicuous Les Bicknell curated two ground-breaking shows, at the Minories, Colchester and the Glynn Vivian Art Gallery, Swansea, in which his own eclectic tastes provided a cunning contrast to the more bookishly-correct selections of the Tate and Collins shows.

In these two exhibitions his personal selections of favourite contemporary books ('Mapping Knowledge') sat alongside a further exhibition which on both occasions gave six artists their own environment to expand their ideas from book to wall and back again. The Swansea show, 'Beyond Reading', was financed as part of the UK Festival of Literature and featured specially commissioned work which in most cases strove to extend the boundaries of both 'the Book' and its gallery setting.

In 'Beyond Reading', you could touch the books. Books, when alive, are meant to be handled. With this very much in mind, over in Ireland, Andi McGarry was busily instigating the Annual Wexford Artists Book Exhibition, a vibrant salon of Book Art drawn from across national boundaries, all displayed in jumble-sale heaps for instant perusal, handling and purchase.

Again, this show toured extensively - to Dublin and North Shields among other places. Next year, Poland and New York are on the itinerary, so send for details now.

So many other shows came and went like bright bubbles on a summer's day. The Site Gallery's Jeffrey Archer extravaganza, organised by Joanna Lee and Tony Kemplen in Sheffield and containing a multitude of 'altered' biographies of Jeffrey Archer, was wacky and enjoyable; a K-Tel compilation to offset the Tate's Deutsche Gramaphon.

Other shows deserve more of a mention than they're going to get – Chris Taylors, Dean Clough (Halifax) melding of tradition and innovation, ('Change the Contect: Change the Text'), Sophie Artemis' mini-retrospective at the Pearoom Arts Centre, Sleaford; Ron Kings maxi-retrospective at the South Bank, in late 1996. The Hardware Gallery, the Eagle Gallery and workfortheyetodo continued to support the creation and exhibition of Book Art. All held numerous important exhibitions and helped keep the comet sparkling.

The fair flourishes

We have also witnessed the firm establishment of the London Artists Bookfair, now permanently uprooted from the Festival Hall to the Barbican. Last year the usual eclectic mix of attitudes and artists conjoined with the throng in our annual chance to meet old and new friends and steal their ideas. In contrast to the sorely missed Small Press Fair, a stall at the LABF costs about £300 (for the best part of four days, admittedly), but for most Book Artists, this remains their biggest marketplace.

Another unarguable high point of the last few year (I'm biased – I'm one of the editors) has been the emergence of the *Artists Book Year Book,* the 2nd edition of which was targeted to coincide with the Bookfair.

Largely commanded by its tireless editor-general Tanya Peixoto, aided by a team of brave sergeants, the ABYB provides a solid platform for the often violently differing opinions flying about in the Artist Book ether.

If the first two books seemed too fair-mindedly inclusive in content, the third edition, due out in 1998, will provide a committed, controversial and argumentative alternative. Please send us your suggestions for inclusion now!

The sinking of Stephanie

Ever the optimist, but echoing the inevitable gloom that resides in every Englishman's soul, I must end this piece with darker news.

For many years the champion of Artists Books and other small press delights, through her learned and unmissable column in *Artists Newsletter*, the indomitable Stephanie Brown, has been removed from office.

Apparently, a survey of the magazine's readers revealed that nobody ever read her column. This is most odd, because every review I ever had therein led to extensive orders for my famously unsellable books. On one occasion I sold 30 copies of a book in an edition of 100 directly as a result of a review by Stephanie Brown in her column.

Always succinct, often sharply witty, and comfortingly lucid, the coverage we received, the people it introduced us to; the inexpensive additions to our collections, will be sorely missed.

Only Stephanie Brown and Cathy Courtney have written regularly about Artists Books in a nationally distributed organ, and their contribution to the growth of this particularly unpublicised form of Art has yet to be properly recognised. Considering how many people are currently making Art in Book-form, and these numbers are both being swelled and reflected by the current plethora of Degrees in Book Art available in British Arts schools (to name but a few: BA BookArt, Croydon College of Art, MA Book Art, Camberwell College of Art etc), Cathy Courtney's 10 columns a year in *Art Monthly*, unmissable though they remain, is scant coverage indeed.

Perhaps we are returning to the underground, to consort anew with worms and moles, where we belong...some of us...

Ed to Author: in the tail of the comet flies the ufo for those hopping on board to Heaven's Gate

Address list

Art Monthly
Cathy Courtney
Suite 17
26 Charing Cross Road
London
WC2 H0DG
0171 240 0389

Artists Book Yearbook
Editor in Chief Tanya Peixoto
1 Hermitage Cotage
Clamp Hill
Stanmore
Middlesex
HA7 3JW

Artists Newsletter
Editor Angela Kington
P O Box 23
Sunderland
SR4 6DG

Camberwell College of Art
M A Book Art
Eileen Hogan
Peckham Road
Camberwell
London
SE5

Collins Gallery
University of Strathclyde
22 Richmond Street
Glasgow
G1 1XG
(Morag Davidson)

The Eagle Gallery
Emma Hill
159 Faringdon Road
London
EC1 3AL
0171 833 2674

Glynn Vivian Gallery
Alison Lloyd
Alexandra Road
Swansea
SA1 5Dz
01792 655 006

Hardware Gallery
Diedre Kelly
162 Archway Road
London
N6 5BB
0181 341 6415

London Artists Book Fair
Marcus Campbell
St James Art Books
Picadilly Arcade
London

W1
0171 495 6487

Site Gallery
Tony Kemplen & Joanna Lee
1 Brown Street
Sheffield
S1 2BS
0114 272 5947

The Tate Gallery
Meg Duff, Librarian
The Library
Millbank
London
SW1

Wexford Artists Book Collection
Andi McGarry
SUN MOON & STARS PRESS
Donkey Meadows
Wexford
Eire
053 23764

workfortheeyetodo
51 Hanbury Street
London
E1 5JP
0171 426 0579
(Maggie Smith)

John Bently describes himself above. His imprint is Liver and Lights.

31

Completing the circle we examine how Small Presses present their case to sympathetic librarians.

HAVE SMALL PRESSES A FUTURE?

DIFFERENCES BETWEEN AMERICA AND BRITAIN

John Nicholson

The first article in the inaugural issue of COUNTERPOISE magazine is about Small Press: 'Literature: Culture's Most Valuable Resource'.

Counterpoise is a quarterly published by a section of the American Libraries Association. 'The alternative library review journal' Counterpoise aims to put before librarians a wealth of material they would otherwise miss. It is therefore a very exciting venture and a gauge. It will help to mold the opinion of a crucial element, the conservators of printed matter.

The author of the essay on small press, Elaine LaMattina, the managing director of White Pine Press, argues strongly for the need to conserve small presses as the safeguards of literature. She takes the view that the small press is the only refuge for a multitude of ignored material.

The Doomsday scenario

She contrasts the golden vision of the early 1990s with the crisis of the late 1990s. Then small presses were booming. The changes in re-structuring of the book trade meant publishers were shedding authors who were a 'goldmine'. Major bookstores were welcoming small press titles as never before. Funding was coming in. How could it go so wrong?

As 1997 opens LaMattina reckons around half the American small presses are dead or doomed.

The seeds of the boom contained the harvest of the bust. The bookstore chains are ruthless businesses. They work on shelf-life. Very few small press titles have shelf-life. They are not designed to sell within the necessary 2/3 months. Consequently they are returned. Often they are returned as 'damaged' which means they do not get full worth. Then there was a side effect of the new market. The chain bookstores, with the help of the new policy, squeezed the independent bookstores. They went bust or struggled and could be less helpful to small presses. This destroyed an old relationship built on empathy. Then the funding was seriously squeezed. So all the trends which should have brought blessings brought curses.

I have problems with this. I do not disagree with her analyses. However I see it as a cause for rejoicing not for concern.

LaMattina mentions what first attracted her to small presses, a tactile pleasure at handling a chapbook of poems in the library. My introduction was different. I was excited to see the wildness of small presses. The determination not to be trammelled. Not to be prevented from doing it. The sheer imaginative power which put money on one side. So although both of us share the exhilaration we have different experiences.

The opposite view

All the processes LaMattina describes as ushering in a golden age I deplore. So it is no surprise I rejoice to see the betrayal which I foresaw. Because I regard all LaMattina describes as being sucked into the game of pretending we are proper publishers. That we are businesses. For her to complain of 'a subtle form of economic censorship' makes me smile. From where I sit this happened long ago when they believed in the game. Once you accept the rules you cannot complain when you are caught by them. All the trends she describes I see as ways the small presses were sucked into surrendering their independence. They thought things were predictable. They relied on grants. They expected buinesses to behave in a non-businesslike manner. They related to The Market. They made their case. They became supplicants. This is not how I see small press!

Of course I am a fox without a tail. The experiences recounted by LaMattina are unimaginable in Britain. We can hardly sympathise as we have no conception of being taken seriously. In Britain no new small presses grew out of the wreckage of the publishing conglomerates. No chain bookstores changed to welcome small press publications. No large funding poured into small presses. The processes she outlines are a foreign country.

Sure a minuscule number of new independent publishers started up. But they belonged inside the game. Sure their titles went into bookstores but they always would have done because they were perceived as ordinary publishers. Sure there was a stab at funding. But the Arts Council made £5,000 available to about half a dozen small publishers. The terms ruled out any firm who would not play by the rules of the publishing world. Some cash could be squeezed out of foundations, but again, on terms which proved you believed in Business. You can see all these are mutually sustaining to the exclusion of the true small press. There is the real censorship.

Closing in

Granted the ethos is different between Britain & America. The small presses in America takes it as a given they will make a financial reward. The British small press does not ever expect to cover more than expenses. The small press in America expects to make a living. I do not know one small press in Britain which makes a living and I speak from intimate experience of nearly forty years. It is almost a definition that if you are making a living in Britain you are no longer a small press. The only ones who make any money have all sorts of sidelines and dodges too.

There is another way I part company from LaMattina. She mentions new horizons such as the internet. She does not mention how small presses have taken to it. So far the attempts to control the internet are few and unimportant. Clearly this will not last. However that is another issue.

Technology is only a means, like offset litho or telephones. In the meantime 'zines in particular flood the internet. They are the most adaptable to it. But they are only a metaphor for small press, small press at its most basic. At its wildest. It is not surprising 'zines are on the Net. Small press is a byword for exploring formats and has more in common with Artists Books than glossy paperbacks. Rather than shy away from technology small press pushes it further.

LaMattina wonders if it will be possible in the future to repeat her anaugural thrill? In a library journal it may be more relevant to ask if there will be any libraries as we know them. How will we preserve our culture? What is culture? Big ones. We are living through a time of change as wide-reaching as the invention of printing. Isn't that stupendous?

LaMattina takes the view that small presses are important because they provided a starting point for authors. Doesn't this contain a paradox? An author becomes famous after graduating to proper publishers and leaving the small presses. This condemns small presses to an eternal kindergarten. They take all the risks and get none of the rewards, acting as unpaid, unofficial adjuncts to proper publishing.

Finally I even disagree with the notion that small presses provide an invaluable role in culture. I see this as another form of justifying small presses, of showing they are a part of Society. I come from the opposite end. I see small presses as refusing to accept *any* role, even the conscience of the world. In the same way I hate any notion that writers are 'responsible'. That they have a relationship to Society. That way lies a Committee. Am I arguing for perpetual revolution? I am not advocating *anything*. I am asking questions, that is all. Other people can deal in answers.

John Nicholson can't shut up, can he?

HOBBY HORSES!

Number One:
A COLLECTION OF COMMENTS:

VANITY PUBLISHING AND VANITY PRESSES

These terms are interchangeable. A Vanity Press is not a publisher in any accepted sense of the word ie a publisher is responsible for selling the titles.

Defining a Vanity Press is tricky because Vanity Presses are tricky. That is understandable as they are in business. Probably this is the main thing to remember. They exist to make money, like any business. They are not there to provide a service.

What do Vanity Presses do? They produce copies of a work, usually in book form. By produce we mean they may take responsibility for everything from the handwritten manuscript to the sending out of copies for review or to potential stockists. Already you can see how the definition in the previous paragraph blurs. But there is a test. Every part of this process is paid for, by the customer. The customer is the person who is being 'published'. The 'publishing' is done by a firm, the Vanity Press.

The point is that publishers, which includes small presses, want to see as many copies sold as possible. A Vanity Press does not have this concern. After the Vanity Press has discharged its obligations the copies belong to the author. So you finish up in the same position as if you had merely had it printed.

> **The main victim of the Vanity Publisher? The gullible! If anybody has more ways of detecting a VP please tell us so we can pass them on. A Vanity Press and a Small Press live in opposite worlds...**

At once you can see the gulf between Vanity Press and small press. The small press may be a one person operation to publish that one persons work. But any vanity is a side issue. It has no commercial aspect.

There is another side to the accusation of vanity. Small press authors laugh bitterly at the accusation they are vain because they self-publish. They are automatically denied any of the trappings taken as basic by the authors of regular publishers. The self-publishing small press looks at the publicity and promotion lavished on authors by regular publishers, the window displays and full colour posters, the signing ceremonies, the dump bins and stacks on tables, the interviews on tv and radio, the profiles of the characters of authors, plenty of reviews in all papers and magazines, the battle for bigger advances ...and this is not vanity? This is simply marketing. None of that is available to small presses. It is rare for small presses to carry a photo of the author on the back cover and many forget to put a potted biography, such is the low importance they attach to the cult of personality.

We mentioned the blurring. That is quite deliberate. As more questions and pressure are brought to bear on Vanity Presses they shift their ground. Originally Vanity Presses were basically printers seeking customers. There is nothing wrong with that. However they became clever. They realised how many authors are out there who will never be published by regular publishers. So they set up an attractive shop front. Instead of saying 'pay us to knock out your book' they presented themselves as Publishers.

Of course they are correct, there is a huge pool of would-be published authors. This is exactly the same audience addressed by small press. But small press comes from the opposite end. A small press keeps responsibility and is aware of that responsibility. It does not expect somebody else to do the job. The moral is that any small press which is lazy or inefficient can be similar to a Vanity Press in superficial ways. But the fundamental difference remains. The Vanity Press makes money, the sloppy small press does not.

The blurring has practical applications too. Ever since the early 1960s, with the invention of cheap printing on offset litho, printing has been accessible to anybody. A job can be done quickly and cheaply. Hence there has been a huge new scope for Vanity Presses. Many authors do not want all the hassle of negotiating with printers. The Vanity Press will shoulder the worry. For money.

Has nobody questioned Vanity Presses? Certainly. But not in any concerted way. After all why should they? Vanity Presses are doing nothing illegal. That they may present themselves in a somewhat misleading way you may be sure is carefully covered by their legal advisors. And they shift and blur.

Besides the regular publishing world has a grey edge. We hear of practices which are considered standard. For example look back at that Questionnaire to authors. You may feel, like us, that it is unpaid research. Of course it makes sense for both parties, publisher and author, to maximise sales. However we feel there is a shift. The author is effectively doing a job which otherwise would be done by somebody on salary. Then we hear how university presses, including the most respectable, require their authors to submit their work on disk, not manuscript or typescript. Again it is sensible. But it only takes a second to think: hey, if it is on disk the slog has been done. The publisher can manipulate the text, edit and proof-read. Hang on. Some of these presses also require the authors to follow a style sheet, ie do some of those jobs too. Obviously

this streamlines things. Yes, but it is work which used to be done by the publisher and paid for. You see how little bits are being shaved off and passed back to the author?

In any business one of the most eagerly sought things is how to make small savings. The tiny saving, when multiplied, amounts to serious money. Now put together a lot of small savings, each of which makes some money, and you can see how it adds up! Also how it reduces the wage bill. And where did this money come from? It is work now done by the authors. It can be seen as a subsidy for the publisher. Is the author paying the publisher?

The fine line is - does the author actually pay out any money from their own pocket? Not in subsidy but in cash? Here again there is a blur. It may be that some sort of deal is made with a regular publisher whereby the author does not take full royalties on all the first copies sold. So no money has actually been paid out, merely withheld. Is this verging on Vanity Press? By now we are deep in the blurred area. All that can be said is - what is the intent? Is the reason genuinely to assist the author or is there a customer relationship, however blurred?

Now you can see why no organisation has campaigned actively against Vanity Press. This is not to say that there has not been a consensus of disapproval. A measure of the lack of effect is that the most respectable newspapers happily carry display adverts for Vanity Presses. Yet the papers are, as is their right, unhappy about similar adverts for a book attacking Vanity Press.

Should Vanity Presses be stopped? Why? They make some people happy. If you want to spend your savings to see yourself in print and are aware that is all you are doing - so be it. Other people find equally harmless pleasure in buying phoney degrees and titles, having distant stars named after them or becoming the laird of a clod of Scottish earth. It's their money.

In recent years individuals have campaigned against Vanity Press. We mentioned one such book, produced by a small press. Here the story gets interesting, complicated and instructive.

The treatment of that book highlighted the difference between Vanity Press and small press, witness the hypocritical behaviour of the newspapers. Then The Poetry Society decided to take up the cudgels. After all poetry is probable one of the most vulnerable areas for Vanity Press. The Society carried a review of the book which attacked Vanity Press. So far so what? But they went a bit further. They included in the list of names one firm which seriously objected to being labelled a Vanity Press. This firm claimed it was a small press which had a number of imprints and published a huge number of poets who would otherwise never get published. So the small press complained to The Poetry Society.

Here we can only go on the version given in the Court account. Because The Poetry Society did not withdraw the small press's name from its list of Vanity Presses. On the contrary The Society repeated and increased this accusation by now putting this accusation on its web page. Obviously the small press was sore. It took the mighty Poetry Society to Court. Before the case came to Court The Society removed the offending piece from its web page. The matter ended on 20 February 1997 with an out of Court settlement in favour of the small press. The Poetry Society agreed to apologise – in their magazine and on their web page.

What does this tells us? To beware of small presses. To be careful about making accusations. That the line between Vanity Press and small press may blur. Probably most of all that the Court heard a comment about Vanity Press distinguishing it from self-publishing or small press.

'Vanity publishing is a process, regarded as disreputable, by which an author pays to have his work published. It is quite distinct from self-publishing.'

So you have been warned. Again we qualify. 'Disreputable' does not mean illegal, otherwise something could be done about Vanity Press. We have argued that there is no need to put them out of business. But we do say that the customer ought to understand what they are paying money for. If they seriously want to publish their own work they can do it much cheaper for themselves. They can become their own small press. It will mean they take responsibility and worry. But the financial risk is less. And the rewards can be greater.

Number Two: CASUALTIES

Presses vanish in a blink. But people? So many of the stalwarts of 1988 have gone. Some have died. J.L. Carr died still fighting. More of a shock because they were scarcely 50 or younger went Tony Roberts (Zodiac House), Chris Challis and Jonathan Zeitlyn. Charlene Garry of Basilisk Bookshop.

That's the sad news, now the good news. A decade is long enough to make a difference. So in Part One we offer not just case studies which prove the Small Press spirit is irrepressible but also some recollections and surveys of the decade.

The Vanity Press is a scourge on the Small Press scene. We can only go on issuing the warnings and make people appreciate just what they are letting themselves in for when they clip out that little newspaper advert.

ALL IS NOT VANITY!
John Dench

The adverts are slick. They appear regularly in the National Press and wide circulation magazines and every year, hundreds if not thousands of people, fall into the trap of believing that eagerly answering the plea of 'Authors Required' or 'Publisher seeks Manuscripts' will set them on the road to fame and fortune. Of course it's more likely to leave them in obscurity and penury (well, out of pocket to the tune of several thousand pounds anyway).

In the past I have had people pass me such ads in the sincere belief that they are being helpful. It's sometimes hard to explain to the uninitiated that their help is in vain and why. These days everyone knows about the Vanity Presses and how they operate, don't they? Clearly not. The gullible still allow themselves to go on being legally conned while the Vanity Presses seek ever more devious ways of extorting money from people under the pretence of providing a service. It seems that no matter how many warnings are issued, people cannot resist the temptation. Quite often they are just ignorant of how the unscrupulous 'presses' work and only find out too late, after they have signed the 'contract'.

Vanity Presses thrive on the fact that the mainstream publishers still operate a blinkered and somewhat hard–nosed system of considering work from 'unknowns.' No doubt some of what they receive ranges from the downright awful to the mediocre. Every publisher has a 'slush pile.' The mainstream is concerned with promoting 'products' with names on the covers that will sell.

But, what's this? Publishers who **want** you to send them your work. That's great...isn't it? Well, of course it isn't, because the golden rule is that no publisher has to advertise (I will challenge this belief later). The golden rule should be that no publisher should be able to lead people up the proverbial garden path.

But if they don't attempt to get you by the 'normal routes' then there's always the good old device of the competition circuit. It has been coming to my (and thankfully others) frequent attention that the likes of 'The International Society of Poets' (aka The Poetry Library of America), 'The Poetry Guild' and 'The Poetry Council of Great Britain' are yet further means of persuading people that they are only a few steps away from the Laureateship. My advice is to forget it...and them. They don't understand the term 'editorial discretion' and the term integrity is an alien one in these circles. They accept everything that is submitted to them. Then they hound you to buy the anthology which only the contributors will see.

Come on, have you ever seen these poetic gems reviewed anywhere? Ever seen the anthologies on sale?

I recall some years ago attending a series of seminars which dealt with the Romantic Poets and which was held at a local Adult Education Centre. Each week about half a dozen of us

> **Some points to bear in mind:**
> **(a) Almost everyone who submits a poem will get it published.**
> **(b) Almost the only people who read these anthologies are those people whose work appears in them!**
> **(c) You are paying an extortionate price for an anthology to have one poem published.**

would dutifully turn up, listen to the tutor and then after the seminar, fall into an informal discussion over coffee about poetry (our own and other people's) and the vexed question of getting it published. One particular fellow – let's call him Alfred – expounded at some length about the long, hard struggle he had undertaken to have his own particular masterpiece recognised, but that... (and at this point Alfred adopted a sickly grin and turned rather smug) "...actually, I've had my work accepted by a publisher and I'm bringing out a collection later this year!" Alfred beamed.

The surrounding company, including the tutor, were astounded and then delighted for Alfred. I can't deny that, at the time, I felt some kind of sneaking admiration for him too. We heaped praise upon Alfred's by now ever–swelling head. He received the adulation willingly and continued to bleat. From that moment on, Alfred's presence at the seminars became almost unbearable. People now hung on his every word. Alfred was, after all, a 'published author.' Alfred appropriated some kind of credibility. He was an authority, and make no mistake he loved every minute of it. Perhaps we should all have picked up on the "I'm bringing out a collection" aspect. We didn't.

A few weeks later, the local paper ran a sizeable article about our 'poet' and trumpeted his 'achievement'. There, in black and white, was the name of the publisher. To most, if not all the readers, the name meant little. But it meant a good deal to me. I recognised the company concerned as a vanity publisher. Our 'great man' had, without doubt, paid a tidy sum for the few copies of his slim volume. Once again, I witnessed the awe with which people read the article and heaped praise on the 'local author.' No one, except me (and of course our celebrity), knew the truth which belied his 'wonderful achievement'. Anyone, who had sufficient funds could have had paid to have had their work published by the company concerned. The illusion of 'success' persisted. Alfred was An Author. Presumably his outlay was worth it in feeding his vanity.

My aim in relaying this story is simply to highlight that all too common facet in humans which even now, in these so–called enlightened times, persists: gullibility. The Vanity Presses trade on that facet for all they are worth.

However, I would take issue with those who hold the view that 'proper publishers never advertise'. My own Press (Providence) is this year launching a new publication, called 'Scriptor' – a magazine of regional writing for the South–East. How else are we to encourage people to send us their work for consideration if we don't 'advertise' – or publicise – the fact that we, and the new publication, exist?! No, we don't use the National Press, but the existing writers mags and directories.

Here are the ways our project differs from a VP. Unlike the VPs, taking out a subscription to our new magazine is a matter of choice, not a condition of acceptance. Because this is a new venture we can't offer payment but we are not asking people to pay us to have their work published! If the work we are sent isn't suitable, either because in our opinion it is poorly written or it ignores the Contributors Guidelines we offer, it doesn't go in.

You have been warned!

Number Three: MARKETING QUESTIONAIRE

Here is a typical research tool used by publishers, large and small. It will help you in many ways, not least because it concentrates your mind. Also you may have second thoughts by the time you have answered it. If you are effectively providing the basis of the sales strategy then what is the publisher doing? Of course they bring their experience and expertise – and their money. However you may consider after answering this questionnaire that the gamble is not such a gamble. That you might as well take the gamble yourself. After all if you believe in the product, your title, you presumably believe it will sell. Therefore you believe you will recoup most if not all the outlay, sooner or later. There, you see? you are beginning to wonder if you could do just as well, if not better, by publishing it yourself. You are contemplating becoming a small press.

MARKETING QUESTIONNAIRE

At your earliest convenience, would you kindly complete this questionnaire and return it to xxxxxxx. The information you provide is extremely helpful to us in promoting and selling your book.

DATE:

TITLE OF BOOK:

YOUR NAME AS IT WILL APPEAR ON TITLE PAGE:

HOME ADDRESS AND TELEPHONE NUMBER:

OFFICE ADDRESS AND TELEPHONE NUMBER:

TITLES OF PREVIOUS BOOKS (including publisher, date and sales figures if available). Please indicate any which have been serialised or book club selections.

HAVE YOU BEEN ASSOCIATED WITH ANY MAGAZINES OR JOURNALS AS EDITOR OR CONTRIBUTOR? Please give titles and dates of recent articles.

HAVE ANY SECTIONS OF THIS BOOK APPEARED IN PERIODICALS?

COMPETING BOOKS:

PLEASE LIST ANY PROMINENT PEOPLE (scholars, government officials, authors) WHO MIGHT GIVE US A COMMENT TO USE IN PROMOTION. Indicate with an asterisk beside the name you know personally and please include addresses if you have them.

NAME AND ADDRESSES OF ANY ORGANISATIONS OR ASSOCIATIONS OF WHICH YOU ARE A MEMBER OF WHICH YOU FEEL WILL HAVE A SPECIAL INTEREST IN YOUR BOOK. WHOSE MEMBERSHIP LISTS MIGHT BE AVAILABLE FOR DIRECT MAIL USE AND/OR AT WHOSE MEETINGS WE MIGHT EXHIBIT.

AWARD FOR WHICH YOU FEEL YOUR BOOK MAY BE ELIGIBLE:

TEXTBOOK POSSIBILITIES (Please give us the names of individuals teaching courses for which your book might be used).

REVIEW MEDIA Copies of your book will be sent to appropriate newspapers, magazines and scholarly journals. Please list any professional periodicals, college papers or magazines that should receive information on your book. Suggestions about USA and European publications will also be helpful.

NAMES AND ADDRESSES OF BOOKSTORES WHERE YOU ARE KNOWN PERSONALLY:

WHICH DO YOU FEEL ARE THE THREE OR FOUR MOST APPROPRIATE JOURNALS IN WHICH TO ADVERTISE YOUR BOOK?

PLEASE LIST LOCALITIES WHERE YOU HAVE LIVED: (Local interest publicity might be appropriate).

ARE YOU WILLING TO DO RADIO, TV AND PRESS INTERVIEWS IF THE OPPORTUNITY ARISES?

INDIVIDUAL BOOK BUYERS. Can you supply us with a list of individuals who would be particularly interested in buying your book?

PLEASE GIVE A CONCISE DESCRIPTION OF YOUR BOOK, INCLUDING IMPORTANT POINTS TO EMPHASISE IN PROMOTION (about 200 words). How does it doffer from other books in the field? Does it present new information? Is it controversial or especially timely?

PLEASE LIST ANY SPEAKING ENGAGEMENTS PLANNED FOR THE NEXT 18 MONTHS, INCLUDING DATE AND PLACE WHEN POSSIBLE.

PLEASE WRITE A BRIEF BIOGRAPHY OF YOURSELF AS YOU WOULD LIKE IT TO APPEAR ON THE BOOK JACKET (about 50 words)

IMPORTANT:
PLEASE SEND A RECENT PHOTOGRAPH OF YOURSELF. A clear snapshot will suffice. Photographs are not always used on book jackets, but are often needed for publicity purposes. If one is not available now, please indicate when we may expect to receive it.

Number Four:
HOW IS IT DIFFERENT TEN YEARS LATER
– OR WHO IS IN THE ROOM?

Fine

Presses❖

Association

of Little

Presses❖

Independent

Publishers'

Guild❖

INK❖

Author

Publisher

Enterprise❖

Author

Publisher

Network❖

Artists'

Books❖

When the SPG began there had been occasional fairs for **Fine Presses** but they became fewer and further between. In its heyday many fine presses exhibited at the SPG fairs. Also we introduced the idea of having trade services exhibiting, years before the International Book Fairs in London and Frankfurt.

The **ALP** is still there and is still the same. It produces a newsletter, a quarterly sampler and an annual directory of its members. It runs fairs which some have described as 'mainly glorified poetry readings'. It shuns Commerce.

The **IPG** has grown. However it doesn't seem to have changed its outlook either. It is a flourishing trade association. But it still relates to the Publishers Association. It holds an annual conference/agm. It produces no directory or aid books. It offers no courses or advice. It has a bulletin for members. The cost of membership was staggered to help newcomers who were small. It is the dominant presence in the 'Small Press' Area at the London Book Fair. It runs similar joint displays at the Frankfurt and American Book Fairs. It lives by Commerce.

But there have been changes. The SPG provided a home for nearly a thousand members in its short life. Inevitably its example encouraged more people to organise.

Another organisation used the same acronym, **IPG,** but with a slightly different title: The **Independent Periodicals Group.** Members were magazines which had established themselves and wanted to make the next leap. They faced the problem of newsstands. So many magazines chasing so limited space. The pace was cutthroat.

We have recently heard of another grouping, **INK**. This is an independent news collective for magazines. Members include The Big Issue, Resurgence, Peace News Green Events, Ethical Consumer and so on. They are not so concerned about getting space in WH Smith's.

Some members of the SPG saw areas not served by the group and set up **Author Publisher Enterprise.** This included writers as well as publishers – a wide brief. The name has now changed to **Author Publisher Network** which indicates they also shifted. Like most groups they produce a newsletter and other items to keep in touch. However their main excursions into the outside world seem to be seminars etc. To date they have not run any major fair. They see their chief endeavour as improving sales.

Another measurable change has taken place in the world of **artists books.** In recent years they have found a community spirit. A fair is held annually and for two years there has been a

Yearbook which gives details of the new titles as well as discursive essays.

This year sees the second edition of the **Small Press Guide.** A useful tool although its title is misleading. It is really a directory of some 500 small presses. There is no other information.

What of **the Small Press Group**? In its many incarnations it ended. However a ghost lives on as the national Small Press centre in so far as 1. the ethos is the same 2. the aim is the establishment of a Centre. The SPG was different from all others if only because – it behaved like a small press. How?

It was erratic, unpredictable, unreliable and had its highs and lows. It astonished and appalled. It rarely knew there were rules. As an organisation it was nuts but it delivered the goods and it invigorated. When it earned cash it spent the lot on projects to benefit small presses. When it was broke it invented ways to generate some, schemes and scams. That is the small press spirit. While it was around it was impossible to stop watching. Sad though it is to see it vanish, the spirit is unquenchable.

A small press never gives up.

And how is the world outside?
Every other year the city of **Mainz** sponsors a small press fair, a mini-presse messe. The organisation comes under the Gutenberg Museum. For more than three days 360/400 of us gather in tents beside the Main in glorious sunshine with sky and water and beer. Of course the language barrier trips up those publications which rely on words but there are plenty of weird and wonderful items too.

In America the Small Press Centre in New York has acquired another title: **The Centre For Independent Publishing.** It continues to run its fair but links it to Book Week. In March 1997 it is trying a new initiative: Small Press Week. An exercise in consciousness raising this has the support of the Publishers Association, the bookshops and the media. It remains to be seen what the results are.

At the London Book Fair 1997 we learned of new alignments etc. Chief of these is the new team **International Titles in Association with Harry Smith.** This glorious title comprises Harry who not only was the Chairman of COSMEP but also won a Poor Richard Award for services to small presses, and the mover and shaker of COSMEP, Loris Essary. The ITIAWHS operates from: 931 East 56th Street, Austin, TX 78751-1724, USA. Tel +512 451 2221. fax +512 467 1330. e mail: laint@eden.com

Independent Publishers Alliance contains small and independent members who cooperate to help each other and themselves. IPA, 9200 Sunset Boulevard, Suite 404, Los Angeles, CA 90069, USA

Small Press Guide❖
Small Press Group❖
Small Press Centre❖
Mainz Mini Press Fair❖
New York Centre for Independent Publishing❖
COSMEP❖
Independent Publishers' Alliance❖

Dustbooks❖ Small Press Magazine❖ Independent Publishers' Network❖ Small Press Week❖ The British Small Press Centre❖

The warhorse of American small presses is Len Fulton. He has produced directories for some 30 years. Not only of the presses and magazines but also of other relevant outfits. Len is at **Dustbooks** (see Resource Directory).

Two magazines are essential. As well as **Small Press**, now in yet another stable, there is **Publishing Entrepeneur**. Both come from Jerrold Jenkins. Mardi Link is editor of the second and Executive editor of the other. The slant to small prees is throughout. Of course The Question as well as the differences between Britain and America mean tread carefully, however what the. Read them. Here is stuff garnered from their current issues. A two page spread about Online Bookstores with addresses; The IPN Independent Publishers Network (more from the Jenkins stable); the International Small Press Publishing Institute; there's news about small press events and fairs, short run printers, software designed for small presses... what a different world.
Jenkins Group, 121 East Front Street, Fourth Floor, Traverse City, MI 49684, USA. Tel +616 933 0455 fax +616 933 0488

Although this round up is hit and miss, either way it indicates the way forward and reminds us how far small presses have to travel in Britain. We were overwhelmed in 1987 to see the gulf between America and Britain. The SPG ran very hard and caught up in some ways and overtook in others. For a while we set the pace. Our Yearbooks inspired the New York Center to produce its Directory. We ran courses which inspired the New York Center. Our fair was in some ways more ambitious. It was already established not only as a national event but had made its impact internationally. In 1994 it was set to move into a larger hall and move on to a new level of public awareness which would have ensured small presses could never be overlooked again. However the gulf has widened again. Not only Small Press Week but so many new initiatives put American small presses at the forefront once more. There are new organisations, new trade magazines, new structures. It will take a huge effort to catch up this time. And where will the impulse come from if not the new British Small Press Centre?

Number Five:
A TEST CASE AND A WARNING!

The old warning remains valid. Nobody can do the job for you. Your own mistakes are the best teachers. As any child knows who ignores warnings and gets hurt, you don't do it again.

Charlotte Soares was inspired to go into print following her Open University course in Family and Community History. She would publish the history of her family. She described the pitfalls in 'Family Tree Magazine', October 1996. If Charlotte was generous with her clan, her generosity now extends to a wider readership. Her case history of a long, punishing learning curve is a valuable guideline for anyone contemplating, for the first time, producing an illustrated publication with wide overseas distribution. Charlotte realised some of her relations/readers, being elderly, would have poor eyesight. Her original idea plan was to design the book 'big, A4, with large print and large illustrations'.

How to pay for it?
Her first mailout soliciting orders to a family scattered throughout the world went well BUT. If only she

had added to 'send money with order' a request for payment in sterling. 'I didn't realise that the banks took commission of £7 or £8 from every £15 of foreign currency. So be warned!'

What to put in it?

Her editorial skills were fine but inexperience emerged in the handling of illustrations. Real costs of repro ended with a bill double the original estimate which had been based on single-sided copying only. 70 of the pages were double sided.

Trials at the Printers

She rejected the xerox option for her typescript and decided to go for computer typesetting using the disc from her Amstrad PCW 9512. A Printer gave her a quote for 150 copies, perfect bound with embossed cover. 'All collating of illustrations was to be done by me, as I was extraordinary in providing my own.' The production of a draft was supposed to take three weeks BUT> The Printer went on holiday and then it took over five drafts to get the text correctly printed. Each draft had some mistakes corrected 'and a crop of new ones'. Had nobody advised her that transfer from typescript to Caslon does change the spacing? Or that putting extracts from letters into smaller point can throw out spacing, page numbering and the matching of illustrated pages with corresponding text? This could have been picked up from the original mock-up of the intended publication complete with illustrations. Instead the Printer charged her for extra work. Rather than accept this penalty, she negotiated for 140 copies instead of the 150 copies originally planned.

Tribulations of collating

The matching of illustrations to text, a tedious task, took endless checking. 'One mistake makes nonsense of the final book, so it's boredom fraught with tension...' and on top of this Open University exams...

Postage

This cost more than £400. An expense not reckoned in the feasibility plan. Very few of the family in receipt of the book reimbursed Charlotte's postal costs. Where possible such costs should be considered in the general price of the book.

Was it worth it?

The final product was indeed very handsome, with burgundy leather-look covers and a gold embossed thistle celebrating Scots heritage. In her delight Charlotte Soares generously let pass damaged copies as well as two bound backwards! She finished with 300 saleable copies out of the 140 copies ordered. She sent out 108 copies. However she remains philosophic, quoting the words of the Scottish Himalayan Expedition: 'Until one is committed there is hesitancy, the chance to draw back, always ineffectiveness...the moment one commits oneself then Providence moves too. All sorts of things occur to help one that would never have otherwise occurred'. One aunt was very generous during a particular cash-flow problem. So the book made it. It made many family members happy, even if the author-publisher ended up still out of pocket. But her family will have been forever transformed by her act, and for such a huge reward, what a small price to pay. Her story also provides a warning for others.

Number Six:
SUBMITTING

Writers submit their manuscripts for consideration, hoping to find a publisher. This book will not explain how to submit, how to send your mss. There is enough advice around for writers. Some authorities worry about writers because they believe them valuable. Not so publishers. We are addressing publishers and there is not a glut of advise for them or any esteem. This is doubly true for small presses. Of course there is a cross-over. Frustrated writers become self-publishers. Then they cease to be writers and become businessmen and women. Watch the change in how they are treated!

This cross-over has long been true of poets. Recently new genres have sprung up, new forms of self-expression: the 'zine and the comic. Literary magazine, 'zine or comix – all experience the same mechanics.

For example the traditional appearance of literary, especially poetry, magazines was technically awful. This was not some punk statement nor some aesthetic fashion. It was pure gormlessness. As Peter Finch has noted 'there is no excuse anywhere for not looking good'. By 'good' we assume he simply means competent. He is not advocating a sort of short back and sides standardisation. Just that presenting the goods carelessly is either deliberate or doubly gormless.

This was not always the case. I remember amazing items. Publications which could scarcely qualify as magazines they were such bundles of surprises. Brighton head Freak Mag was one such. There were other weird and wonderful ones. So out of step they were not mistakes. There were intelligences behind these.

In the era of the 'zine on screen there can be even less excuse for technical silliness. On the contrary the inventiveness which goes into making these productions unique and – yes, beautiful – gives a boost. Here is the refusal to submit. To be forced into a formula. Here is the raw spirit which has to be swallowed and take the consequences. Intercourse of the mind.

Number Seven: HELPING

A generous volunteer who shall be nameless had a recent spell of typing up the pink slips which the National Small Press centre sends out to interested presses. He had originally been inspired by a visit to the SPG's fair at Victoria - the quantity and the quality and , above all, the diversity. he realised he could become a small press. What he hadn't realised, until he typed up some 200 free replies, was just how few presses bother to reply. More than that he was amazed at the standard of their replies. He was expected to turn them into sane copy for this Handbook's A to Z. He had volunteered in the spirit of comradeship. he began to wonder who were his comrades. Here is his requiem.

'Why do it? Run a small press that is. Is it a desire to communicate or is it just an ego trip?

'I was surprised by the slips that came back. The idea is to let others know about your press. But some slips were so illegible that I can only suppose the presses wanted to keep their publications a secret. Did they only publish for their own satisfaction? Others lacked critical information, like how much the publication cost or what it was about. Was this out of embarrassment or modesty? Some rambled on at length, ignoring all guidance on how much to write about the press and its publications. Would their publications be equally self-indulgent? These invited savage editing by the tired and, by then, unsympathetic typist.

'There were presses though that clearly saw the possibility of telling others about their books, 'zines or whatever. Communication was what they wanted to do, and they did it. Succinct descriptions of their publications and all the necessary details of the press and its titles.

'What are the details sought by the Centre?
1 Name of Press: imprint.
2 Address and, if possible, contact person, phone/fax/email/website.
3 Two lead titles, with author, publication date, number of pages, whether illustrated, hard/paperback, ISBN, price, postage & packing and a brief description (30 words maximum).
4 Method of ordering or how to get a catalogue. More relevant information.
5 Method of payment.

'Is it really so hard? But these were the few who bothered to reply at all. There were hundreds who didn't even take that much trouble. How can you help people like that?'

Number Eight:
SELF-HELP, MUTUAL AID, NETWORKING

Once they have crossed the line and become their own publishers small presses often stray further. They may, willingly or not, set up as their own distributors. Then they may become watering holes – they take on distribution for other titles of a similar interest. (Starting with friends they know.) The book is full of such cases eg Counter Productions/Distribution grew from Aporia, Enabler and Hignell's Apple Press are others.

The best example of a watering hole is a small press fair. Networking – the exchange of ideas, tips, contacts – can be as valuable as the selling. After all if you learn of a way to save hundreds of £s, or how to increase your market, that is a huge boost in cash as well as morale.

Even more common is the 'sale' of surplus experience as expertise. They learn how to publish for themselves, how to word-process, edit, proof-read, design, print-buy, manage production, publicise – all skills which they can offer to sell to others, for a fee. After all how many titles can they publish in a year? Those skills would otherwise lie idle, loosing income. Pretty soon they turn into another firm selling origination services. Examples: Words and Images, Hi-Resolution, Counter Productions.

It sometimes happens that the small press finds these supplementary activities more profitable that then publishing. In rare cases small presses have been known to become their own printers or to run their own bookshops, even both. Example: The Land of Cokaygne in the 1970s.

They may even gather all their knowledge into a primer which they publish:

Example: New Caxton Press, Providence Press (Whitstable) for the Centre. This Handbook grows out of precisely such a background. It began as bringing together the experiences of many small presses. In all these cases you are listening to the voice of experience, not teachers. But the best teacher is your own mistakes.

Number Nine:
JUST A THOUGHT...

ALTHOUGH I AM RELUCTANT TO MENTION IT THERE IS ANOTHER DIMENSION TO SMALL PRESSES. INDEED TO THE NONSENSE ABOUT WHAT IS A SMALL PRESS?

SMALL PRESS FAIRS ARE MORE THAN TRADE EVENTS. THEY ARE GLORIFIED MEETINGS, EXCHANGES - NOT OF STOCKS AND SHARES AND FUTURES – BUT OF IDEAS AND CONNECTIONS. THEY INSPIRE. THEY FORM FRIENDSHIPS. THEY OPEN MINDS TO COMPLETELY NEW WAYS OF SEEING. IF YOU HAVE THE TASTE FOR GOING INTO SUCH MATTERS THEY ARE, AS ONE PUNTER OBSERVED OF THE FAIR FOR JOHN MICHELL, 'GOOD ENERGY'.

RHETORIC CERTAINLY, POSSIBLE JARGON, BUT THERE IS A GRAIN. BECAUSE THE CONCENTRATION OF SO MANY MINDS AT ONCE WHILE THEY ARE HIGHLY STIMULATED INEVITABLY RELEASES A NEW TWIST ON REALITY. IT CAN NEVER BE THE SAME AGAIN. THIS RELATES TO THE KIND REMARKS MADE BY LIVER AND LIGHTS AND OTHERS ON HOW THE SPG, AND ITS FAIRS, (VIDE BLACK SHEEP) CHANGED THEIR LIVES.

I AM NOT EQUATING THESE EXPERIENCE WITH ANYTHING LIKE A RELIGIOUS CONVERSION. HOWEVER I DO BELIEVE THERE WAS A TRANSFORMATION WHICH IS ERADICABLE.. SO THE LOSS OF THE FAIRS, EVEN OF THE GROUP, WAS DAMAGE TO MORE THAN A FEW BANK BALANCES. FOR THERE WAS A DIMENSION FAR MORE PROFOUND AND IMPORTANT THAN MAKING MONEY. IF YOU WANT TO USE EXTRAVAGANT LANGUAGE, THE HARM DONE WAS PSYCHIC, OR AT THE LEAST SPIRITUAL. OF COURSE IF YOU REJECT SUCH COMFORTS THERE WAS AESTHETIC WRECKING, ALMOST A CULTURAL CRIME.

IT IS NO SURPRISE THAT THE WRECKING SHOULD HAVE BEEN DONE IN THE NAME OF SENSIBLE BUSINESS, PROFIT AND PROPER BOOK-KEEPING.

KEEP THEM.

Slim Smith

CONTENTS

Anglo Saxon Books
Aptoria
Black Sheep
Bozo
Earthright
Gonibs
LM
Footmarks
Frontier
IMP
Krax
Liver & Lights
Neil Miller
Oleander
Orange Blossom Special
Providence
Pythia
Quince Tree
Roslyn
Runetree
Wave Guide

What is a small press?

This question is guaranteed to enrage a true small press. However we felt it might help to give some answer if we asked a random cross-section of small presses to explain themselves.

We felt it would be more helpful to devote the bulk of Part One to these confessions rather than to weighty discussions on issues which define small presses. Maybe another time?

We also think that this is an invaluable exercise for another reason. We concluded *our* question to them differently: Why did you do it? Here you have more than 20 reasons why people set up as small presses. Often they didn't realise that is what they had done until afterwards.

We sent out a letter soliciting the Confessions including suggestions to start them off:
"Here are a few points you may wish to cover:
* frustration at not getting titles published which you felt valuable
* how you realised you were allowed to publish eg were you inspired by another sp?
* how you went about it
* was the fear of no money an obstacle?
* what were the pitfalls or the pleasures?
* have you any tips?"

We cast our net widely. Here is a brief guide to the subjects covered by these 20 odd presses. Anglo-Saxon studies, speech therapy, whacko patriotism, campaigning, poetry, a walk, travels, a literary magazine which takes many forms, artists books, horror stories, monthly packets of history, women's writings, classic poetry in wallet-size booklets, a novel, plays, microwave ovens— and a fiercely independent publisher covering the waterfront from his house.

Can we discern any pattern? Some break formats rejecting the book: BOZO, Liver & Lights, Pythia, Quince Tree, Orange Blossom Special. Even a magazine itself is a change. Perhaps small presses are strongly aware of what they would like to buy and turn out publications in that image.

Some are mini publishers with a list reflecting an ordinary publishing house: Oleander, Frontier, Runetree. Some publish as offshoots of campaigning. Some specialise (niche marketing): Black Sheep, Anglo-Saxon, Orange Blossom, Black Cat (Neil Miller). Some have only one title: Footmarks. One exists to publish the writer's only novel and nothing more. However like Pythia most realise they are infected with a bug they will never shake off. It lasts a life-time. Sooner or later they will offend again.

All are their own bosses and can suit themselves.

Put together these many reasons not only provide a fascinating snap shot but they could also inspire anybody who wondered or doubted if they could do it themselves.

This series originated in our newsletter, News From The Centre where it continues. In gathering together these accounts we were aware of how many more we wanted. So if you would like to send in your Confession we will publish it eventually, if not in NFTC we hope to anthologise the Confessions as a separate volume. There's another reason to do it.

ANGLO-SAXON BOOKS

Anglo-Saxon Books was started in 1990 with the publication of *The Battle of Maldon*. It is still on our list and consists of manuscript text in Old English, edited text, literal translation, verse translation, and a helpful introduction. It is not wildly exiting. It took us about 14 weeks to prepare for publication. The main difficulty was in creating an Old English font and typing to disk the Old English text. We ordered 500 copies and when it arrived from the printer we went through the trials that face every publisher. The first thought was who is going to buy this book?

Creating a font to enable the spread of an ancient language is all in a day's work when you are dedicated…

The answer seemed quite obvious when it was started but now there were doubts. We opened a box and took out two copies to check for mistakes. It is a great wonder that, when printer's copy is proof-read by three people obvious mistakes go unnoticed but, as soon as you open a book freshly delivered from the printer your eye immediately falls on an error. In that case it was a whole section that had a $ sign in place of an Old English character. It is not a pleasant feeling to own 500 unsaleable books and know that you have to pay to have another 500 printed. That book has since been revised and reprinted several times.

Why we entered the world of publishing we really cannot say. I suppose we had a feeling that something should be done to let more people know that English history did not start in 1066 and that the greatest defeat in the history of the English was not something to celebrate – as was done in 1966. There are still members of the governing elite who insist that the victory of William was a wonderful thing, and there are still those who refer to the English of that time as Saxons, but we are working away at dispelling such ignorance and feel that we are having some success, modest though it may be.

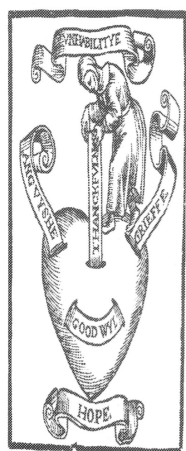

Perhaps it is necessary when starting a small press to have a message that you feel needs to be spread. Or perhaps that is the worst reason from a financial point of view. To earn a living from a small press it is necessary to publish books that a reasonably large number of people want to buy. Publishing books that you think they ought to buy makes a good hobby but usually an expensive one. The other thing to bear in mind is that books have to be sold. Publishing is easy, selling is difficult.

We are still in publishing to spread the good word about early English society and will shortly bring out a language course, First Steps in Old English, but we have also recently published English Martial Arts which for us is a 'popular' book. It has had lots of publicity in martial arts magazines and has sold well at £25 a copy. Although the book is concerned with 16th century martial arts there is still the English history link and, with luck, it will sell reasonably well. It has also resulted in us being offered another martial arts manuscript which looks promising. We know very little about martial arts except what we learned from our own book. Despite that we believe that the earlier lessons we learned can be applied in a new area of interest. Perhaps it is better from a financial point of view to publish books on subjects that can be treated in a dispassionate way.

It is probable that all publishers be they big or small, old or new, make mistakes. The reason for our survival, other than determination, is that we had enough capital to carry us over our learning period. We are still a small press but we want to get bigger; not for the sake of it but because it will better enable us to achieve our primary aim.

APORIA PRESS

I forget just when Aporia Press came into being.

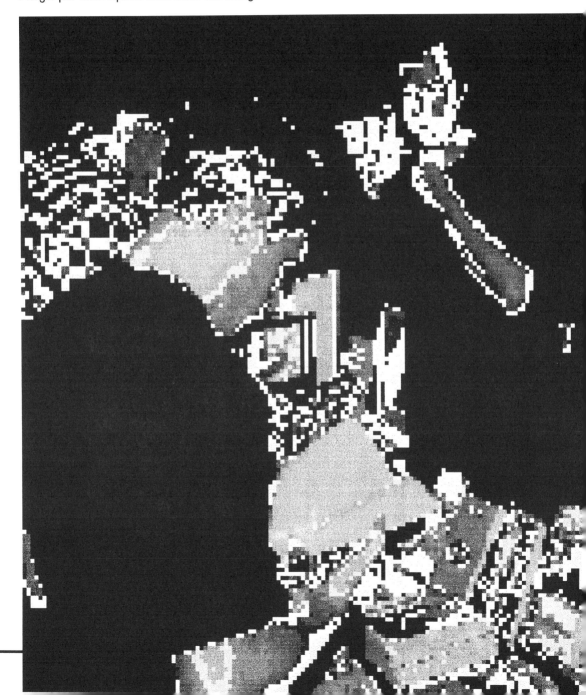

I think that, when I was studying English at university in the early '80s I found that, while the theoretical element of literature was covered in depth, there was little attempt to relate it to the world of practicalities. The student union magazine was closed down because of an article I wrote – for a few days there was heated talk of a libel trial. After this, there was no easy way to learn how to get into print, to learn what worked in terms of design, what could or could not be printed.

I helped out with a friend's music magazine as a means of resting my brain while I pursued a PhD course, and by trial and error learned how to paste-up properly, how to present work to a printer and so on. Eventually, this kind of odd-job, and distributing books – which meant taking my own stuff and those of my mates round the shops on my bike – became my main source of income. Most of my paste-up skills have become, in ten years or so, strictly speaking, obsolete. Nowadays even high street printers are asking for work on computer disks, so I suppose I will need to acquire a whole set of skills if I want to continue.

For reasons I can't recall, while still at university, I thought of publishing a book. I think I was bored stiff with my studies and felt they were leading nowhere. (About seven years after starting my PhD, a book eventually appeared, published by a reputable academic publisher who made little effort to sell it. The remainder copies, purchased at a knock down price, now sit in my bedroom, waiting for the revolution).

The little pamphlet I published myself at this time suffered under the pressure of ignorance. Used to writing, and having the finished product with me in a few hours, if it were something personal, (or ten days, if it were an article for *City Limits* or some other magazine). I wasn't quite prepared to spend all the time it required to produce a book. I suppose that I blundered into it. In retrospect, while I got an ISBN and had a friend draw a nice cover illustration, and while the volume had only one typo in it, I did everything wrong, in a hurry. The advice I received from the few people who offered it was pretty useful. I can't imagine now why I didn't retire to lick my wounds straight away. Instead I did what so many others have done, and put the surplus stock in my bedroom and then set out doing another.

Gradually, by producing other books, many with more typos than I care to mention, I figured out how to do things properly. The bare bones of my experience formed the basis of the DIY Guide in the editions of the Small Press Yearbook, a title which grew over the years in a way which reflected the skills acquired by those involved (mostly amateur enthusiasts) – from the first issue, which is crude and at best provides a snapshot of unfocused activity by many discrete publishers – to the last, which remains a handsome and comprehensive guide to a thriving, fitfully coherent scene.

The *Yearbook* seemingly asserts that there was and is a formal set of relations which one can grasp, even buy into – something which had never occurred to me when I started publishing.

Distribution never entered my head: I thought it was a matter of calling at shops and having them take a dozen or so books in a fit of enthusiasm. This was not always the case. Nor did I have any notion of how other publishers, proper or otherwise, operated. My contacts were mostly people in independent music. Knowing nothing, I suppose I couldn't really go wrong, or if I did I had no one to answer to but myself.

I'm still not sure I know anything about how publishers are meant to function. Publication to me is the broadcasting of text and I don't much mind how it gets done – so although I have a personal bias towards books and towards trying to do things coherently and efficiently, my tastes extend to publications that make no effort to compromise with the market or, in some cases, with so much as a single imaginary reader. I particularly enjoy discovering enigmatic, anonymous and untraceable publications – single broadsheets, crazy manifestos, flexidiscs, containing magic psychobabble, whatever. It's the spirit of urgency, of total evacuation, that appeals to me and which perhaps forms the secret link with my own efforts.

Certainly Aporia Press never had any fixed direction or sense of over-riding purpose. It published what we found interesting at the time, what we wanted to do for one reason or another: an "artist's book", a forgotten tale by De Quincey, a guide to The Festival of Plagiarism, a horror story by Hieronymous Kitsch…

The aim of the imprint emerged from the titles we published…

Only when we began the Tracts and Rants of the Interregnum series, edited by Andy Hopton, did it start to become coherent. There are now half a dozen of these, which received some acclaim from big guns like Christopher Hill and Paul Foot and from many less prominent but equally enthusiastic readers, many fired by the vision of writers dead three hundred years or more. They still sell steadily: works by Winstanley are still read by green activists; the writings of Coppe, Crab and others are perceived as more eccentric, yet I am entirely convinced that they'll be people wanting to read them for as long as they are in print. Most of these writings were published in some-thing resembling the contemporary small press scenario, written in a spirit of enthusiasm and circulated in small edi-tions. Their effect has been profound and allows me to think that my own publishing activities, intermittent as they are and hedged around by the banal problems that afflict anyone who has to work to live, yet constitute a vigorous element in a multifaceted resistant body.

The Press, then, always had several functions. First, it gave us something to do with our time, excess knowledge and ener-gies. Secondly, it could respond to unforseen events, to friends wanting to get something into print. Thirdly, it had a social dimension. My guess is that most independent publishers have an evangelical streak and want to improve the quality of their lives, if not to improve the lives of others. The last twenty years, has seen a shift to the right politically that at times has seemed impossible to resist. Publishing libertarian ravings from three centuries ago may seem an indulgent and ineffectual form of protest, but in any age of dismay and disillusion with politics, it's essential. I'd encourage anyone to do it.

BLACK SHEEP PRESS
Out of the Fold and into the Press

Black Sheep Press has now been going for about five years. It publishes photocopiable work sheets for speech therapists, teachers and parents to help improve the speech and language development of young children with communication problems.

We started because my wife, a speech and language therapist, was saying that a lot of the commercial material available was expensive and, in the case of American products, often unusable. Whereas a friend she worked with was producing lively, useful work sheets for use amongst her colleagues. For my part I wanted to do something vaguely creative with my computer. (I really wanted to emulate William Morris and the Kelmscott Press!)

The first hurdle to overcome was the *"can we become publishers?"* question. This was answered when a friend showed me a copy of the 1992 Small Press Yearbook. Our impressions were re-inforced by a visit to the Small Press Fair in the Autumn. Both the Handbook and the Fair were a celebration of creativity. Encompassing everything from crudely copied zines to beautifully bound works of art, from anarchists to poets, from teachers to transvestites, the yearbook and the fair especially were like a "hard copy" information super highway. The road to publishing was open.

This left the *how* question. We all had day jobs, so although this meant limited time, it also meant that we did not have to run a business which earned us a living. Making the decision to stop watching "soaps" helped with the time! So the "Press" started off as an unpaid "hobby". Fortunately we found the work intrinsically interesting. There was satisfaction each year seeing the catalogue expand and when we spoke to customers we were getting positive feedback about the usefulness of our material. We were able build our mailing list gradually, so avoiding any liquidity problems through overtrading. Because we knew the whereabouts of our primary market, i.e. Health Authorities, we were able to send out catalogues directly without costly advertising

Living in a rural community we try and use local resources as much as possible. This has resulted in a good network of local support. A local printer was able to give us a reasonable price on short runs. We sell by mail order, so a good relationship with the village post office has helped us negotiate our way through the increasingly complicated postal rates. A local computer dealer/reseller has provided advice and support. He helped to update the computer, minimising some of the problems of obsolescence.

Where are we five years on? In a commercial sense we are still extremely small. But our range has increased in size and quality. The illustrator has now been paid for the work she has done in the past and no longer has to wait for payment when she does new work. I've improved my computer hardware and software. As I'm now retired from my main job, I can now devote more time to expanding and improving what we do, answering the phone and talking to customers (always enjoyable) and even occasionally draw some money for my work!

What of the future? We would like to expand into providing resources for schools, particularly reception classes, learning support and S.E.N. units ...and the ghost of William Morris continues to beckon!

Things that helped us and might work for you:
•Before spending a lot of money on software, checkout what is available free on magazine cover discs. We managed for quite a while with free accounting, database and DTP software.
•See if you have a local computer dealer, who can give advice and loan you equipment in an emergency.
•Find a printer who will talk to you as an equal. One who will explain the pros and cons of different papers and processes etc.
•If you need a business bank account shop around. Some banks are not only cheaper but more sympathetic and interested in small businesses.
•If you get to the stage of setting up a full time business, talk to your local Business Link (usually part of your local Training and Enterprise Council) for advice and your local authority (economic development unit) for start up grants, we got half the cost of a photocopier.
•Network.

Alan Henson

The epiphanies flow. The realisation there is a 'gap in the market', that 'there is nothing stopping us,' that 'it works'...

BOZO

It was decades before I knew I was a small press. Also it was not really a desire to publish which started me off. I learned the entrepreneurial spirit another way. I suppose there are some similarities in the sense that you decide to offer the world something nobody else can.

In the late 1950s and early 1960s there was nothing unusual about actor/managers. On the contrary they were the accepted tradition for centuries. We were a distance from the new toads, the director/managers. I was slightly unusual because I was barely out of my teens and I hadn't turned professional. The catch twenty-two of getting your Equity card seemed pointless when I was taking productions around and earning money. I could have engineered my card on the strength of doing it but I didn't need it. Why ask for abstract permission? If the public was prepared to pay who cared?

Wild, free, funny
and dangerous?
Can this be a
publisher? Not
from where John
Nicholson sits...

I was putting on productions and taking them to a range of small
halls and spaces, and selling out. Without realising it I was an
impresario.

It was not a huge leap for me to 'diversify.' When friends talked
of publishing a magazine I had the get-on-with-it approach. The
magazine? Another story. Anyhow I discovered offset-litho. I
saw its capabilities. That was 1962 and it seemed a lifetime
later, at the end of 1968, I offered my services to another new
venture, an alternative newspaper. My contribution was not in
the writing or editorial but, again, my get-on-with-it approach.

By 1972 I had wound up with an empire. Two bookshops
including a headshop and tiny poster gallery, a printing works
with a design studio and a publishing house. We did everything
in-house. Wrote, illustrated, typeset, printed – and sold. In our
spare time we produced
the city's weekly what's
on.

But we were scorned. It
was another ten years
before I found others
who appreciated our
efforts. Sure, along the
way we met a few
isolated idiots like us
who managed to put
new and different
material into the world.
But they were not as
common as you might
think. Offset litho, like
DTP, empowered oceans
of bilge. Political and
Causist pamphlets,
burbling poets ...hun-
dreds rotted in a few
devoted outlets. You
could count these on two
hands. The public
managed to survive
without any of it. This
was different from my
experience in theatre
where you made a
profit!

Back from lying-low in Europe I began my own small press,
although I didn't think of it in those terms. Previously I had
published and edited, rarely written. Now I was prepared to self-
publish. I saw it in this way: a long time had gone passed and
nobody else was speaking up. After twenty years I felt entitled. I
had a clear idea of what I wanted to do and the limitations. I
had ideas about design of the publications and how to achieve
these technically. In other words I knew how to produce a few

things for almost no expenditure. I had no cash so I had to bluff, it was an echo of the old actor/manager days. I recall tricks like taking artwork to printers, getting their approval and running. The printer would have to make good with cowgum, free. The bits were held on by spit.

BOZO was born with a tiny A6 booklet, 28 pages ie three and a half sheets! A card cover ie 2 per sheet. An Elementary Programme for the Salvation of the English Monarchy Whereby it will prove of immediate benefit to the HEALTH and WEALTH of all concerned whilst meriting the lasting GRATI-TUDE of future generations Also containing historical explana-tions of a SINISTER PLOT against the crown and people! These odd items quickly earned a reputation. Apart from what they were about, people liked to handle them. They were unlike anything else. They clearly had their own integrity and validity. They didn't look in any way amateur or silly.

As printers we had made such stuff as John Michel's Radical Traditionalist Papers. I would give his formula my own twist, Patriotic English Tracts. Although the idea was derivative I felt confident enough to branch out in my own directions which I knew were different.

Soon there were enough to be treated as an oeuvre. A tiny profit enabled us to spend more, produce more and be more substantial. We always kept production so miniscule we never lost money. Soon the booklets had grown until we risked a spine. That was the excuse given by bookshops for refusing to stock us. I cherished the endless excuses. The spine wasn't done properly! Somehow they always found something wasn't quite right to fit into their world. We were doing something right! It confirmed our feeling and still does.

I think that is one of the marvellous things about being a small press: it is infinite. The more you have to listen to the lectures about all your mistakes the more you are determined to persevere and be more wrong! You have no time-table. You are not imprisoned in a publishing schedule. No new seasonal titles. No remainders – your 'stock' is always fresh, saleable, (or unsaleable). Also so much of your 'product' is not even a publication in any conventional sense. It may be netted by this dreadful term 'artists books' but BOZO's isn't! BOZO produces ephemera which doesn't date or die because it retains its spark and its ability to delight, inspire and enrage.

Money doesn't count. Plenty of times there has been NO money. NO typesetting so NO text. As if that stops you! There is a galaxy of graphics you can use, lawfully or not. Manipu-late them so they are new and yours. Then there is always an unguarded photocopy machine where you can print enough copies to last you until you do another run or 'edition.' A dozen? Enough to slip into your pocket and walk out. If you design imaginatively you can get a publication out of a sheet of A4. I've done at least half a dozen like that. There is a huge other prospect for the penniless publisher: reprints of out of

copyright stuff. Can't afford any thing original? Reprint! There are masses of tiny things which deserve another run around the park. The Testimony of Wonba, a Waterman on the River Cam. Gems. Who knows, one day somebody may rediscover BOZO's stuff and let it out for another airing?

Final tip. Catalogues. They are versatile, if you rescue them from Publishers. I remember ours, a tiny booklet which was a treasured curiosity in many pockets for years. None of the items inside were bought by these fans, but then we hadn't published them. Or written them. Forget the message, love the medium. You have cheered up somebody. It's 'publishing' a feeling. In an age of internet publishing such artifacts will become even more rare and more precious. I see no reason to shut up. Ever.

EARTHRIGHT PUBLICATIONS

Earthright Publications published its first title in December 1980 and an eleventh will appear on May 1st 1997. It is still very much a small, one-woman endeavour, although there are plans to increase the output and possibly to convert it into a small workers' co-operative.

I have realised that at the current scale of operations Earthright Publications will not provide a consistent income. I think that small publishing has potential but I recognise that I have reached the limit in terms of size of book that I can produce on a one-woman basis.

I did not write, or even conceive, Earthright Publications' first title. *Food: Need, Greed and Myopia* grew from notes that a local man had produced for an adult education course he taught. Some mutual friends showed me the manuscript which the author thought might be worth duplicating and I decided that I would have a go at publishing it as a 'proper' book, not duplicated notes. I was already familiar with the small-scale production of leaflets and newsletters by offset-litho, through my involvement in community groups and with the local community press. Thus Earthright Publications was born.

Food: Need, Greed and Myopia was a modest success and having enjoyed converting a manuscript into a book I decided to continue publishing, with the hope that eventually it might provide a living. I gave up my dull clerical job and began juggling publishing with freelance research work, temping, and occasional periods with part-time work. Sometimes the publishing has been a major strand, at other times it has languished in the background.

From the start I was clear that publishing was about communication. In particular I wanted to relate my publishing to my concerns for peace and environment and my campaigning activities. I wanted to publish books linked to topics of social concern and I wanted to publish good quality books making good use of modern technology, which at that time was offset-litho.

From experience in producing leaflets and newsletters Monica Frisch felt she could 'publish'. She saw it as 'an extension of communicating...'.

Earthright's second title, *Nuclear Fragments* (1982), was very different. It was something I conceived and edited, though the result – an anthology of anti-nuclear poetry with some prose and illustrations – was somewhat different from the original idea. Neither it, nor *Credo and other Poems* by Helen Hawley (1983) were a great success and Earthright is very unlikely to publish any more poetry books.

However the third title, *What's Where in Newcastle* (1983), was much more successful, and was supplemented by *Map Guide to Newcastle upon Tyne* in June 1987. This also sold well and Earthright's third guide will be published in May 1997. *Alleycat's Tyneside: the radical guide to Newcastle* will be a mixture of practical information, maps, contacts and campaigns and will be in a wire bound pocket diary format.

By 1986 the first edition of *Food: Need, Greed and Myopia* was out of print and I agreed to do a revised edition. The text was completely rewritten, the book designed from scratch – about all that didn't change was the concept, the title and the market. Like the first edition, it did well and is now out of print.

The success of the two guides to Newcastle led to *Newcastle upon Tyne: a view* (1988) which was meant to meet a need for an inexpensive souvenir of Newcastle with good black and white photos, informative captions and accompanying text. For various reasons, partly timing, partly poor marketing, this was not the success that was anticipated.

In 1990 I was approached by a local workers' co-operative, who run a wholefood bakery, shop and cafe, which led to a very rewarding co-publishing project. *Food out of Chile* was produced in quite a short period with no hiccups, amazingly, and sold very well, quickly covering its costs and making a healthy profit. I began to feel that I had mastered the art of publishing!

I was wrong. *Generating Pressure*, published late in 1991, is a well written, lively, informative, illustrated book about local opposition to a proposed nuclear power station. But sales tailed off very quickly and it has yet to cover its costs. Perhaps now the campaign has achieved its objective and the nuclear power station will not be built, interest in the book will revive.

The failure of *Generating Pressure* and the financial implications of that, led to a lull in publishing activities for a few years and sales of all titles tailed off. Earthright had published nine titles; three were out of print and another two had covered their costs. I wondered whether to let Earthright wind down and devoted more time to other activities including part-time work.

Then in 1996 the Red Herring Workers' Co-operative, with whom I'd co-published *Food out of Chile* announced that they would like to publish a book to mark the tenth anniversary of their cafe. *Cordon Rouge: vegetarian and vegan recipes from the Red Herring* was a much larger production than the previous one: 176 pages; and much more work. It got done but only just in time for the launch; the printer had started printing some of the pages before the artwork for others was finished! Nevertheless the launch went brilliantly, we got the timing right and over 1000 copies were sold in the first three months and it is making a very satisfactory profit.

This success that has encouraged me to continue publishing, to create, research and edit *Alleycat's Tyneside*, and to consider turning Earthright Publications into a workers' co-operative.

Monica Frisch

EGONIBS
The Altruism of Small Press Publishers

Nobody, but nobody, produces a Small Press publication in anticipation of making money out of it.

I've edited five quarterly editions of our magazine, Fingertips, so I reckon I've earned my place in heaven. The power!, I thought at the beginning. The stupidity!, I sometimes think now. And yet I still enjoy most of the work.

Common problem

Want to sacrifice your life? Your days and nights? Your marriage? Your dog? Your sanity? It's easy — become the editor/publisher of a little literary magazine!

Recently I spent a day at the National Poetry Library studying other Small Press publications, and was mollified to discover from numerous editorials that our problems are common. We are Small Press because we have insufficient capital to invest in production and marketing, so we have to rely on core sales to fellow writers. If we get their support, we reason, we can build a turnover which will allow us to advertise in appropriate media, which will increase our income to the point where we can pay our contributors at least a token sum, assuming we maintain a quality to justify our existence.

Whenever I've explained this policy to writers, I always get the same reaction. They are usually surprised, more often than not polite, but always at least slightly cynical at our naivety. (Or are they perhaps suspicious?) Small Press magazines are not expected to pay their contributors even a token sum. Some even ask writers to pay for a copy of the issue that features their work.

No thanks!

We now know that any announcement we make to fellow writers will result in more work being submitted than subscriptions taken out. What else is disappointing? Having to send rejection letters. The power I mentioned earlier is an unpleasant burden. We decided at the beginning that a curt 'no thanks' wouldn't do. We would always give our reasons when work is rejected. After all, in common with most of our ilk, our raison d'etre is to encourage new writers. It is not easy to be nice without also sounding condescending when you say 'no.' We try to be forthright rather than diplomatic because we prefer that approach when we ourselves are on the receiving end, but there is a narrow line between saying no, because-of-such-and-such-but-thanks-very-much, please-try-again, and appearing pompous.

So, what's involved in producing a Small Press magazine?

* Dedication.
* Equipment: a word processor with suitable software, a decent printer (preferably not dot-matrix) and a long-reach stapler.
* Time: about one hundred and twenty unpaid hours per issue. How is this spent? Accepting and refusing submissions, editing, transposing into correct layout, proof-reading, collating and binding, aftermath correspondence. And that's just the admin.
* Printing: the average home/small-office printer would be too hard-pressed to produce hundreds of copies. It is preferable to have them photo-copied at between eight and ten pence per double-sided sheet, having first run off one complete magazine on the office printer. Once circulation exceeds, say, three hundred and fifty, it is cheaper to hand it over to a proper Printer.
* And the greatest of these is dedication.

So, what are the compensations? There are compensations, aren't there? Yes. First and foremost are the nice people who write and telephone and butt into conversations to hand out compliments after reading the magazine. They add enormously to the secondary pleasure of one's own feeling of having achieved something worthwhile. Then there is the reaction of first-time authors at reaching an audience; the optimism that one day we will read a review in The Independent, or wher-ever, and remember how we were the first to recognise the talent. The support from established writers, who are generally generous with praise and occasionally allow us to publish their work, offers our work status which we are proud to exploit. It is also enormously satisfying to see each issue taking shape. From diverse sources, a mixture of styles coming together to form an entertaining magazine gives great pleasure.

Hobby
Treated as a hobby, and enjoyed as such, Small Press publish-ing has many compensations, and, when successful, provides a fillip to the producers' self esteem as well as to its contribu-tors', which is why we unashamedly call our own partnership EGONIBS. We must be doing something right to have survived a year with renewed enthusiasm for the future.

Ian Lang

ELM

In 1977 I started work as a Lecturer in Library Management at Ealing College of Higher Education. Burdened with work preparing for lectures I asked my new colleague Albert

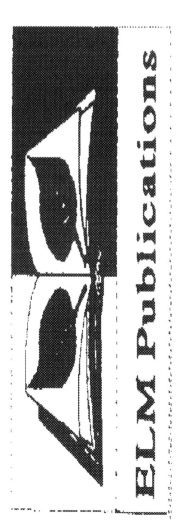

ELM Publications

Standley 'and what is the textbook for this course?'. There wasn't one and he suggested we should write one together.

Finding a publisher was time consuming and we weren't getting appreciative noises from those we approached. I decided to found a company and do it myself. So, E.L.M. (Ealing Library Management) Publications was born, with one book to its credit. The first edition of 1,000 sold out within seven months. We reprinted 1,500 and those lasted a further 18 months.

For four years I did nothing other than sell our one book.

Then in 1981 two colleagues offered to write a book on managing people at work which would deviate from the norm by treating trade unions as responsible organisations and workers as sensible people. (A little to the Left of thinking at the time, especially in a textbook aimed at business and management students.) The book did well (it's now in its fifth edition) and I began to think that this publishing hobby might become a business.

After developing the list for a further five years part-time, I left lecturing to develop ELM full-time.

Staff were acquired, premises bought (freehold office and warehouse, big mistake and expensive overhead) and expansion took place for some five years. We developed a strong business management list, including a good number of tourism and leisure titles. We also branched out into History looseleaf, attempting to fill the gap left by Jackdaw, but aiming the product at teachers in schools (motto 'One pack goes a long way') and addressing the new core curriculum. We moved into GNVQ by producing a set of curriculum guides in looseleaf and on disk.

Unfortunately the recession hit (1987-92). Sales dropped. Our new History for the core curriculum suffered so many changes (on the part of the curriculum designers) that we could hardly alter the products fast enough. Even the looseleaf GNVQ series could not manage with all the changes made By BTEC and the NCVQ. At one point we were making weekly changes to some of the list. Buying a building proved to be a bad idea (if you're in publishing, don't go in for property speculation) as business rates and expenses soared and the capital value of the building fell. Shedding staff and overheads resulted in a slimmed-down and subdued ELM during 1994 and 1995.

Luckily I had kept up my management training skills and used these to find work running short courses which paid a lot of the overheads. Selling the building made a good case study in negotiating – a possible future booklet?

Then followed The Wandering, for three years. We rented a cheap warehouse (but the owner who had been mad keen for me to sign a long lease as he had been 'let down before', asked us to move after we had been in his premises for three days. During this time we moved warehouse four times and offices

She wrote the instructional manual she needed while she did a course. As a librarian she spotted more 'gaps'. Soon there was a business, with ups and downs…

twice.

Now we are more settled. With a small staff (trade counter open 10-4 Mon-Fri), a small office and rented warehouse nearby, we do our own despatch. Three different distributors over the years have convinced us that it is best to do your own. The business management and tourism titles are selling well; the History sales are recovering, the curriculum seems to have consolidated (until the next time), and we are looking forward to a buoyant end of century. Our new line is training resources and materials in business and management (Management Skills like Negotiation, Group and Team Work, Motivation and Performance, Discipline, Interviewing and other personnel skills). We have software and multi-media packs in production and are looking for good ideas for joint ventures.

If you want to reach colleges, libraries and schools with any of your books we would be interested in hearing from you for joint marketing and direct mailing. We mail every three months and often share with other publishers to do this. It keeps the costs well down without seeming to affect response rates.

FOOTMARKS

Quite how the idea of producing a London walking guide (*Walking London's Royal Parks* ISBN 0-9524618-0-3) arose is mysterious – and the decision to research, write, design, illustrate and publish it entirely ourselves even more so! To an extent it is explained by the fact that we both live in London, both have had experience in publishing and enjoy walking – having done many walks together in this country and abroad.

Much of our walking is done in London and perhaps this is the key to it – we wanted to make an urban walk which we both really enjoyed, and which brought together what we consider are London's most open, interesting and accessible features, the Royal Parks. We were also motivated by a *Royal Parks Review Group* report (chaired by Dame Jennifer Jenkins) which suggested that a route connecting the central Royal Parks would "make a magnificent walk".

Our basic idea was to create one circular route that allowed the walker to experience the varying flavours of each Park, and offered connections between the Parks which were direct, safe and interesting. The general route was surprisingly easy to settle – quite independently of each other we mapped out practically the same route, and reached the same decisions on where to split it into six sections.

The main design decision was to have the maps for each section in the same scale and orientation, and with the description of each section's route fitting onto one double page spread of the finished product. This, we felt, would make the the guide very easy to use. We also limited the commentaries on interesting historical and other features to one double page

One enthisiasm turned into another...

spread, and deliberately kept them separate from the descriptions of the route.

Although the whole 12 month project, from the initial idea to receiving 2000 freshly printed copies, was enjoyable and satisfying, it did require much greater attention to detail than we anticipated. We each walked over the route at least a dozen times - checking directions and our description of them, continually improving the route (particularly along the roads and canals connecting the Parks), and ensuring the accuracy of our list of places for refreshment and lavatories.

We established a schedule of deadlines, a system of very regular minuted meetings, and the simplest of financial controls (both of us periodically deposited equal sums into a joint bank account, and paid the expenses from this account with joint cheques). All this not only ensured the smooth transition of our ideas and whims to completed copy, art work and the final product, but also helped us manage the myriad of difficulties that arose – like the cussedness of word-processing programmes; the nightmare of getting good quality typesetting and finding a suitable printing company.

Having a personal computer, Apple with ClarisWorks in our case, was essential. It allowed the project to be financially feasible and to be under our direct control. For instance it was simple and cheap to produce three different mock-ups of the guide (complete with cover and photographs) to show various people for their invaluable comments and criticisms before the final printing.

The maps were particularly time consuming and irksome, in spite of their apparent simplicity. We used a somewhat tortuous combination of tracing, photocopying, freehand and word-processing techniques to create them, but they were based on Ordnance Survey mapping – for which we gladly paid them a royalty!

But this is only half of it – the rest is in the marketing, selling and distribution! We feel, however, that we have been successful in getting the guide accepted by the Royal Parks Agency and most of London's major retail outlets only because of the time and trouble we took in achieving a high quality product.

FRONTIER
Another true-life confession
I had been building up to it for years. I'd edited a couple of small magazines. I'd worked in advertising and I had generally dropped out.

Richard Barnes converts his catalogue into a manifesto...

Even after a really good photographic course in London all I could do was buy an old horse, tie on my pots and pans and start travelling. The horse kept walking, the rain kept falling and gradually the metaphysical pain of turned into the need for a cup of tea and a wide roadside to park the horse.

We went for miles and when I reached the end of the journey in 1977 I began the author's road. A story, a sort of William Cobbett meets George Borrow, began to appear on my desk. A little later a wannabe writer finds himself knocking on the doors of established London Publishers.

Of course it was too much for them. After the book had been with one publisher for 15 months before the Sales Director pulled the stops on my editor the book was back with me. And going nowhere else.

I had spent some time imagining how these publishers might have arranged the book, which photos they would have chosen, and now it seemed over...

A few years later, because I had kept up with the photography, and because the region (East Anglia) had been at the creative forefront of promoting fairs, (not necessarily festivals – for closer definition send £10 for *The Sun in the East* ISBN 0 950870102) it was suggested that I put together a book about them. This would obviously be too marginal for publishers and so, because I had a backer, I went for it myself, publishing in the name of my photographic company and putting the money through the business.

I felt quite at home in the editing, casting up and promotional side of bringing the book out and even managed to turn around the printer's bill of £4,500 and a bit more.

That was in 1983 after which I carried on with the photography until 1986 when a poet, Dominic Sasse, came to me with his work. A little cautiously, still not admitting that I was a pathological type for publishing, I set up Frontier Publishing. I was ready for the game, vocation, addiction, business and folly of publishing.

The book, *Broken China*, was good looking, nobody asked for their money back and I was away. So was the poet who produced another collection for Forward Publishing.

Frontier's next book was the travel piece, *Eye on the Hill, horse travels in Britain*, ISBN 0950870137 @ £14. Now ten years old but undated, except that it originated from a time before the recent politicization of Britain which began in 11979. The book was received well and put to bed the ghost of that would-be writer. Almost straight away another book proposal had arrived and Frontier's next title was entirely photographic. With a captive market, Steven Wolfenden's *To the Town*, a portrait of a Southwold, covered its £6,000 costs before we had even printed. For once the bank manager was impressed.

Following this came a small and unusual work from John Michell entitled *Euphonics – a poets's dictionary of sounds*. ISBN 0950870161 @ £5.95. This was brilliant and funny and

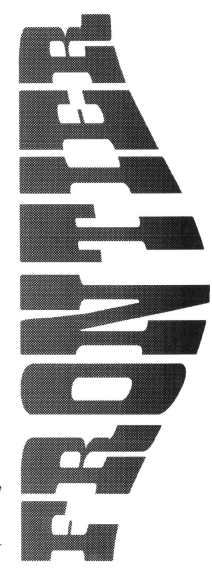

magically resonant with the Platonic view of word pictures described in Plato's 'Cratylus' two thousand years ago. In this instance here was a genius author, with a name, quite an ambitious print-run, and high hopes of sales. Publication day, and some drinking of wine at our launch at the Poetry Society's old headquarters, was followed by a month's national post strike. This completely flummoxed our publicity and sales campaign. By now the 'why I did it' was tempered by 'should I have done it?' I had experienced a serious setback.

This was the second turning point, when caution and self-pity invade the publisher's heart and sap the courage that is needed to go on. The horse died. I accidentally rammed a car with an uninsured tractor, which further drubbed the thinning wallet. But, as I've hinted in this confession, I was hooked. There was so much involved: my ego, loyalty to authors, the out-of-towner's war on London's literary spin doctors, the competition with the larger publishers, the need for money. What clinched it, and still does, is the idea of publishing the next book. In 1990 I continued with our little travel list, publishing *Calling from Kashgar – a journey through Tibet*, by Rod Richards (not the Tory M.P.) as well as a fiction title. The following year I published a round-the-world cruise book aimed at the sailing fraternity entitled *Travellers on a Trade Wind* by Marca Pirie ISBN 1872914063 @ £14.95 which sold out in a year.

Even better was the return to poetry in *The Green Book of Poetry* edited by Ivo Mosley, firstly in hardback @£14.95 then in paperback in 1994 @ £8.95 ISBN 1872914063. This has been - and I wouldn't lie to fellow small pressers - one of the very best and most successful poetry books of all time. Recognition? Not really, except we are known for this book in every bookshop. Letters come in, one from Hungary this morning, saying 'Thank you for publishing this book.' Riches? Not really, we've been flying by the seat of our pants all the way. During the ten years of Frontier you've seen Bloomsbury start up with £18 million capital. You've seen Fourth Estate and Piatkus get their sales to over a million p.a. and yet they are called small publishers. My bank manager thinks I'm more than a small press. In fact a V.S.P.

I look at BOZO's confession where JN (my respect and admiration) says that money doesn't count. I think it does especially when a printer is printing a quantity of a 300pp book. But that's a publisher's hang-up, to be responsible. If the book is good that's WHY I KEEP DOING IT!

INDEPENDENT MUSIC PRESS

It's a long way from carrier bags in Dudley to hand-made supercars in Detroit. Sadly, the carrier bags are mine and the supercars are not.

The bags came in handy for the self-distribution of the first book I wrote and published, entitled 'The Eight Legged Atomic Dustbin Will Eat Itself', a biography of three indie bands I followed. As luck would have it, that title sold 5,000 copies with the help of a

Some four years ago Martin wrote wry accounts of producing and selling his first ever book – on pop groups. Today he makes a living from his writing and publishing. Does he qualify as a small press...

National Express coach pass and a dog-eared map of the UK, and so persuaded me to leave my near chart-topping death metal band The Chocolate Speedway Riders (what, you haven't heard of us?) for a life in publishing.

The first three years after that starting point were, as Smashy and Nicey would say, grim-tastic. In that time, I put out another six books, all self-financed, all self-written, and struggled to bridge that horrendous millennium-stretching gap between the print bill being paid and the fat cheque for the 27 copies that have actually sold coming in. Along the way I travelled to New York where I spoke on 40 underground radio shows about various books, as well as being mugged, literally (a smelly man with metal teeth, 42nd Street) and metaphorically (a dubious distributor with rotten scruples, Upper New York State), but surviving none the less.

The biggest problem at first was one of momentum – getting bands to trust me enough and then convincing the public, that they wanted a book on what were very often fairly obscure acts. The trick was to pick acts I knew had a cult following on the underground scene. As a result, in those first three years, I never remaindered any stock but never reprinted either. It was a thin line.

Then almost to the day after I had been trading three years, things started to get a little easier. I was approached to write books for other publishers, which I now do as often as possible (17 so far) and my own label Independent Music Press gathered momentum as it became more well known, helped by a fortunate spate of best sellers including Ian Hunter's 'Diary of a rock n roll star', two official Prodigy books, The Buzzcocks, and an Oasis biog. Inevitably as a slave to fashion I had logged on and tuned in to the Net by now although sales so far for my rather eye-catching site, are to use the Internet lingo, bollocks.

My first trip to Frankfurt International Book Fair was an eye-opener for me and the multitude of publishers who apparently had never seen anyone with bright green hair and body pierces at the fair before. One foreign licence later, I published my first photo-only book which luckily went on to sell in twelve countries. The launch party for that ended with a famous pop star chasing after my terrified wife in Stringfellows and me and an old school friend guzzling the house champagne and copping off with life membership– I haven't been back since…

The start of 1997 saw a new company, Twisterella, running in parallel to my music label. Its aim is to publish two kinds of books – ones that appeal to me and ones that sell shitloads. It is like starting all over again, as I know few contacts in the non-music side of the game but it is a wholly refreshing experience to have to start from scratch. Look out for that tacky Christmas best-seller that you only read once – it could be me.

The problem now is one of trying to expand whist trying to

stay small — I still work from home, use the Net virtually non-stop for research and business, and hungrily consume any new technological development that will make my companies more efficient. However, writing four or five books a year and publishing another five can be difficult.

I do not need the carrier bags any more, thanks to an excellent distribution deal for both labels, but the supercars are some way off yet — the only one I've been near is that of a well-oiled American mega-star. I can dream...

KRAX

I don't think we could start it in the same way now. We've rather reached the stage of taking the easy option these days, but after all we don't get the same thrill from sex, sport or ice-cream either. Back at the beginning there was three unemployed old school friends who decided to celebrate the ending of their teenage years by producing 'A Magazine'. There were snags: no money, no printing equipment and no contents. With a rather anorakian arrogance we ignored this as being irrelevant at the time. It still proves to be the case today.

Ideally we would have had articles, fold-out pages and all the stuff that twenty-year olds wanted to know about but was never on the shelves of W.H. Smiths. So we wrote the articles and prepared the fold-out pages and only then considered the practicalities. We found we could 'borrow' a screen-printing frame if we paid for the inks and materials but there was no other option for typesetting other than to do it ourselves. This was where the articles went out of the window and the poetry came in — impatient Youth couldn't face typing lengthy articles several times on typewriters with wonky letters. Photocopying was not accessible and at .02p a sheet far too expensive anyway! So we lashed out £5 on card for the covers, appropriated a very mixed bag of assorted paper and, over a couple of weeks, produced about 60 good copies for a work of art.

That was the first edition, fold-out and all. Total cost with bus fares about £7.50.

The second edition *was* properly litho printed but by that point we had beat the Catch 22 situation — we did have someone we knew who could do illustration rather than art, we did know of a cheap printer (not cheap enough as one of the original three departed at this point), we did have a weird, if skeletal distribution in a handful of shops, we were promised some help from a rep — which only fell through because our prices were too low. We had got something very wrong though. We assumed we'd be selling to students but our customers were considerably older than ourselves. We should have known that students only 'borrow' things never 'buy' them.

We had the time and enthusiasm to do this — and vitally we had one or two supportive friends. (Rule number one: always have at least two supportive friends). Each issue was vastly different to the one before and always a compromise on the material left out because it was either too expensive to reproduce or too lengthy. We stuck rigidly to the budget as only (*only?* how naive we were) editions one and three had sold out. By issue six reality had set in. Some of the shops complained about the lurid nude centre spread despite the commonplace Page 3 by then. We started to include reviews as other small presses had begun to pick up on us. We were loath to give over space to these. As in other publications we'd found that 20 pages of opinionated reviews were only monotonous but discouraging to the potential reader (whatever that was?) So we did imitate the recently departed Second Aeon magazine by cramping them into tiny print at the back - giving scope for a lot without it becoming a platform for pretentious criticism. This is always said to be the first hurdle for any publisher – the six publication (magazine, novel or whatever) – when the initial enthusiasm has reached the 'we've done that' point and the time factor of two years has thrown up domestic changes and, with a group of people, internal frictions.

By issue 8 we'd left the Harrogate base, got another printer, cut down on shop distribution. It had become wearisome trying to get shop-keepers to pay up. I recall one making every excuse from being too busy to a desperate 'we only settle-up at the end of the month'. I pointed out that it was Saturday 27th February and got the money. I sympathise with publishers of larger volumes as we found that we were only dealing with sums of around £4 but had to have slagging matches to get that amount.

Fortunately by now having a sizeable subscription list we started doing interviews. So-called controversial newspaper interviews have nothing on interviewing poets. Some issues have not included an interview because either the interviewee got the wrong end of the stick (thought I was trying to chat them up for a date, assumed they had to be technical and rambled on about grammar and syntax or spent the whole time slagging off other writers) or the interviewer became
- too drunk to recall it the following day
- engaged to the interviewee (once)
- or too confused to make any sense of the conversation.

The ones that were printed received the usual feed back of
- 'I never said that'
- people disparaged complaining that 'They would never have said that'
- and assorted milder threats of pouring water over my head.

All of which does make book publishing look more inviting!

This is where we have remained ever since: same number of copies produced at periods of between 9 months and a year with a gradual swing towards more United States contributors and customers. Without asking for any advice along the way we keep going through a naive enthusiasm and, without getting involved in any financial wheeling and dealings, the

Krax magazine has been publishing for 25 years and is still run by the same people who started it, Andy Robson and Dave Pruckner. At the 28th National Poetry Festival, Andy Robson was honoured with a new award 'for services to poetry publishing...'.

publishing was never threatened as, luckily, by using personal funds for extraneous things like travelling, general correspondence, promotion badges, etc, the magazine covered its costs. (Apart from two editions which we appreciated later as being a mistake). On one of the magazine we produced a card game, a series of back pocket booklets (originally done to ease the losses from the two failed mags) which had two titles run to two editions, and some one-off booklets which have all failed to achieve their potential – much to our disappointment.

All these other publications have come at intervals when we've been prepared to gamble the money. We've been disappointed by being unable to follow up the Subraman/Lifshin booklet with another despite have the material for it (since used by another publisher in the US). The reasons for lasting is by not trying to do too much, too soon. By trying to balance what two or three people agree to be good writing and by not including anything else. By not chasing 'name' writers and being fobbed off with second rate material. By not pandering to a supposed audience - as we still don't know who they are!

John Bently claims to be innocent: he isn't really a publisher. He's a painter, a poety, a performer? Will it wash?

LIVER AND LIGHTS
A Rabid Mongrel

When the dust settles, it is the garish uniform of the visual Artist that I am most likely to be caught wearing; an artist whose work, increasingly in the last ten years, has taken the form of the Book.

I trained as a painter. This is an activity, sadly unfashionable, that I still practice and continue to feel passionate about, in all its multi-faceted emanations, and not merely the narrative strand from which I frequently draw in order to claim my personal antecedents.

However, from long before the education system had attempted to squeeze me into an increasingly narrow specialisation, I had other, equally passionate enthusiasms: writing, making, performing and history, to name but a few.

Attempts to incorporate these other interests into my paintings had frustratingly gone the way of all idiocies, when, inspired by the American poet and artist Kenneth Patchen, the inimitable William Blake and a record by the *Desperate Bicycles* ('it was easy, it was cheap, go and do it') which had contained on the sleeve advice for self-motivated punks on how to manufacture and distribute their own records, I struck on the not particularly original idea of making a book. This was 1978.

The resulting ordeal, culminating in an unwieldy heap of 50 copies of a litho-printed, curtain-bound visual-verbal naively called "Jewel", a collaboration with my friend Stephen Jaques which we gave away to disappointingly less than delighted chums, who used them unfailingly as door-steps or to roll joints on.

I knew, while I was struggling with all the unmastered processes, as yet again we fucked up the printing or the registration or got glue everywhere, that somehow my life had changed. I had found a home.

By the early '80s, Jaques, myself and our fellow conspirator James Blundun had been unceremoniously puked out of Art School and found ourselves impoverished and ensconced in various hovels abounding in the Great Smoke. We had innocently come to consider ourselves a sort of three-man Movement, united in the Great Toilet by our mystical belief in the power of Art, with so much to say and nobody to listen.

Inspired in no small part by Wyndham Lewis' *BLAST* and the Blue Rider Almanac of Kandinsky and Marc, we decided to publish an annual journal celebrating our inner world – a Manifesto!

The resulting publication, launched to coincide with an exhibition of our pictures in salubrious Peckham, in an edition of 210, made entirely by hand with a hard cover made of scavenged shirt boxes, each drawing lovingly hand-coloured, was called, for reasons too labyrinthine to describe here, *Liver and Lights No. 1.*

Nearly 15 years later, I am currently making Liver and Lights No's 23 and 24 for publication next year. No longer the organ of a slightly gastric group but of an individual (Me! Another long story...) my adoration of, and dependence on the simple machine that is the turning page by now has contrived to stimulate my creative juices for nearly 20 years.

For me now, my own books are a rabid mongrel art-form drawing all the disparate silks of my curiosity into one shining (hopefully. I've had my failures) web.

Each new book I make acts as a foundation from which so many other ideas and activities can be constructed. In the last four years, in particular, books designed by installation in galleries have been accompanied by performance of

their texts, usually in collaboration with the wondrous musical landscapes of the cellist and composer Mr Harvey Eagles.

From the rarefied ivory tower world of the contemporary Art Gallery we have tentatively ventured into the live poetry circuit, pubs, rock clubs, cabaret nights, exorcisms and schools to recreate a version of our world for an often incredulous audience, some of which occasionally purchase my books as if they were Dr Scratschit's patent Cure All Tonic & Wart Remover; some of whom hurl tomatoes.

These are only a few of my reasons for making books, and if I am still here in twenty years time and asked to write this piece again, be sure, I'll tell you twenty more, at least.

John Bently

Ed: *In twenty years time we expect you to be keeping us all in vegetables.*

NEIL MILLER PUBLICATIONS

I started this minuscule press six months ago after writing tales of the unacceptable for some ten years, without success.

Before the advent of the computer I was busy sending my misspelt and mispunctuated tales into such unknown publishers

as MacMillan, Pan and Anthony Goff esq. Naturally, they were rejected with a slip of paper saying 'Don't try again.'

I didn't give up, not me. I stumbled across a magazine called 'Fear' and sent them a tale but they said "Not for us." but they sent me some addresses of the small presses. Through this I managed to find out about some markets in the USA.

A local paper took one of my tales and serialised it; when asked if they wanted more they said " Yes please." but there was no pay. I sent tales to magazines within the small press and Hey Presto!, I was published… no pay. How do we get paid? I tried going to functions attended by famous people like Joan Killings etc…no luck.

So, like a fool, I decided to publish myself, to hell with 'em!

Then I bought 'Acclaim' which had a list of small presses in it and I sent for some of the magazines, and why not? – it was a cheap way of finding out what was going on in this weird world. The books came and they weren't bad, at least they were trying to have a go. I continued to have a go at the USA, without success although one company liked one of my attempts and wanted it edited; I did that but got no reply. A very expensive postal trap to get into, the only people making money were the Post Office!

I went back to my original, stolen, idea of doing my own book. Then a flash idea came; why not get some other poor fools together and make an anthology similar to the old Pan Books of Horror which I had always admired? I remembered writing to the then editor, Herbert Van Thal and him writing a scrawled note saying "Couldn't make an offer for it." I phoned him and he spoke in a far off voice, as if coming from the grave; "Send another in." Then he died.

I didn't give up; I sent my tale of an antiques dealer *Proudfoots Possessions* to peter Cushing and he wrote back, 'May God be with you always, Peter.' then he died.

So I put some ads in amongst the Small Presses for authors and away I went.

I meant to start this press off as a business venture, making money for me and the authors. I thought, naively, that authors would be keen to help launch a publication with themselves in it. WRONG!

Authors, it seems, need to see their names in lights; never mind the money, give them the front page splash. Money, it appears to authors, is a filthy word. It's OK if Jeffrey Archer makes a bundle but it isn't art. If authors send in money to the Ian St. James Awards and get a rejection slip that's OK, to be expected. But if a new press needs some sales to keep it in action that's sacrilege. Also any punctuation mistakes, spelling errors, etc. are to be ridiculed, how dare a small press make

An author gets sick of rejection slips. He 'gets on his bike'. Soon he wonders at the behaviour of other writers…

HORROR

BLACK CAT TALES

mistakes – it's OK if you are a giant like *The Times* with a hundred proof-readers and sub-editors but a small press, never!

After spending weeks ploughing through reams of stories I picked what I considered to be the best of the bunch. Then I phoned dozens of printers for the best deal. The best deal, that was a joke. I fond a nice printer who is on the verge of a nervous breakdown, because of the deadlines, now he has me to contend with.

The first cover was to have no title, it was meant to be to be intriguing but the booksellres didn't like it – it was too weird for their customers, apparently. The authors didn,t understand it either, it was far too unconventional for them. What are we deaing with here? Conventional authors writing Horror and Mystery?

It was getting costly. The computer broke down in a temperamental fit. I had already bought one machine; a laptop, for £1300 and now this one needed fixing – eighty quid down the chute.

Not to mention the time, what with authors ringing me to say " Are you publishing my excellent tale or not?"

When the booklet was finshed and authors were presented with a copy, out of six authors including myself (vanity); One wrote back to say that my tale was drivel and the others no better – his was the best. Unbeknownst to him I had had edited a major error out of his story.

One said he was proud to be involved in the book and that my tale was great and the previous author's tale; the one who complained, was childlish.

One sent in a new tale without comment. So, three out of did not reply to my letter and copy of the booklet, they are clearly awaiting royalties!

I put ads in *Private Eye* and have had many phone calls from prospective authors but none were willing to part with £2.25 for a copy to find if their style was suitable and to help me keep the press going.

I contacted the BBC for an interview, no reply. TV South, no reply. SKY said they were interested, no reply. All this to launch the booklet and hopefully make a profit from which we can all benefit. If the authors had tried as much as I had the booklet would have sold out. I have sold by word of mouth (in pubs etc.) over seventy copies, had this figure been mulitiplied by the other five authors 350 would be the total and the proposition would be near to viable.

I have received over three hundred enquiries concerning the booklet from budding authors; I sent mail shots to them all and gained 35 sales. These people wrote back with some encouraging comments which boosted my flagging ego.I have also been on Local Radio trying to push the booklet.

A large newsagent network wanted the booklet in all their branches, subject to management approval. They have 9000 outlets but don't want to fork out even a percentage of the cost; sale or return only, Thank You!

I will be publishing a new booklet shortly with some dead authors featured in it, so no rude replies from the grave expected! Unless Bram Stoker can write from the grave!

This is a taster of the way I feel and write at the moment; when I've sold a million copies maybe I will change my attitude!

THE OLEANDER PRESS
37 years as a small publisher

When I began publishing in 1960, I aimed to remain without staff, buildings, vehicles, computers and such paraphernalia (the fax, e-mail, Internet and mobile phone fads have similarly passed us blissfully by), to disrupt family life as little as possible. A couple of typewriters, yes, a telephone, and desks separated for reading, writing and publishing, but no thudding, buzzing or parping machines such as photocopiers or pagers.

We sit on the mountain that Gutenberg and his successors nobly scaled first, with the book at the centre of all we do. The idea was, is and always shall be to fill in the gaps (and they are constantly increasing) that commercial publishers do not choose to fill. So that rules out gardening and cookery, expensive colour art books, 'best-selling' novels as seen at every airport bookshop and W.H. Smith high street store, and major long-term reference books involving collaborators.

I wrote one such long-term book (*The Oxford Companion to Spanish Literature*) but on condition that I wrote every work myself and checked the proofs myself. I also wrote and published a major medium-term reference book (*A Dictionary of Common Fallacies*) but it took no more than five years of my life, and I did other things at the same time – though not very many.

Audrey (my wife) and I identified an evolving sequence of series in which to specialise as 'niches'. This was together with opportunities given by contacts in the media, the Royal Society of Arts, the Royal Geographical Society, and odd, occasionally very odd, submitted manuscript from authors who had tried the big name presses but had been rejected. For example Professor Alfred Steers of Cambridge, whose *Coastal Features of England and Wales* we

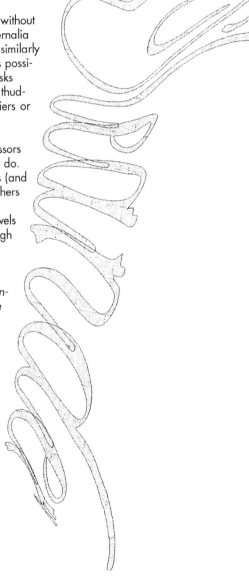

Philip Ward must
be reckoned one
of the giants of the
British small
publishing
movement.
Fiercely
independent he is
still out there.
Learn from him...

were lucky enough to publish, with his distinguished pupil Clifford Darby's *Medieval Cambridgeshire*, and Darby's distinguished pupil Richard Grove's *The Cambridgeshire Coprolite Mining Rush*. It is perhaps unique for a small publisher to produce work by three successive generations of Cambridge scholars in the same illustrious department.

Our first series was poetry, which by and large has not broken even. This appeared while we subsidised our publishing from two salaries in librarianship. Only *Swansongs* by Sue Lenier (which made the *Daily Mirror* because the attractive poet has beautiful legs) made a substantial profit which enabled us to produce her second book, *Rain Following*, which lived up to its name with a damp reception.

Our second series which made our reputation, was devoted – in all senses – to Libya. In this country we were married, and spent the wondrous first 7 years of our marriage, during which our daughters were born in Tripoli. Some of these books have been reprinted, and the most successful seven are currently in print. While working in Libya, I wrote not only about Libya (three books for Faber & Faber, for whom I also wrote guides to Lebanon and Iran), but began a career as a travel writer which has taken me to more than fifty countries. Of my fifty-plus books as an author, more than half have been devoted to travel. I began a travel books series which has been financially our flagship, and has attracted other authors on the list such as the great actor Michael Pennington (on Siberia) and the New Zealand doctor G.E. Moloney (on Saudi Arabia). This third series continues to prosper.

The fourth series derived from my travels in Saudi Arabia and my long-term interest in the Middle East, includes classic reprints such as Sir Richard Burton's Midian trilogy, Neil Innes' brilliant account of his career as *Minister of Oman*, and the first translation of Didler's *Sojourn with the Grant Sharif of Makkah (1854)*.

Our fifth series was devoted to "The Language of Literature" and centres on the scholarship of the late Douglas Gregor. No sensible commercial publisher would invest in his scholarly grammars and anthologies of Romagnol and Friulan, major regional languages of Italy though they are. No Italian sponsor came forward to help him or us, so we assumed the risk, and over 20 years made a modest profit on both titles, which enabled us to publish his phenomenal comparative study of the six Celtic languages (*Celtic*). As far as he knew, he was one of only two men then living to acquire familiarity with all six, and now both he and Kenneth Jackson are dead. The language series blossomed with the appearance of *French Key Words*, and important revision tool for students, to be followed at roughly annual intervals by similar coverage of Italian, Spanish, German and Arabic key words.

By this time our family had moved from Libya by way of Malta and Indonesia to Cambridge, and with the Librarian of the Cambridgeshire Collection of the county library service, Michael

Petty, we created a local studies publishing list ranging from *Cambridge Newspaper and Opinion* and *Varsity Rags and Hoaxes* to *Cambridge College Walks* in English, French and Spanish and *Roman Cambridgeshire*, twenty-nine volumes that set out to fill gaps in the existing local literature.

Then in 1979 our manual *The Small Publisher* appeared, with case histories from fifty small presses both similar to us and totally different, across the whole spectrum from the one-man press to the Oxford Polytechnic Press (from the institution now called Oxford Brooks University) and the Hakluyt Society based at the British Library. This work became a standard text for examinations by the Booksellers' Association and the Publishers' Association and has never been out of print. Its reputation led to our being approached by authors whom we should never had dared to approach directly, like Raymond Lister, the authority on Blake and Samuel Palmer, whose autobiography *With My Own Wings* we lucky enough to secure; and the distinguished medical librarian the late John Thornton, whose short history of *Medical Book Illustration* proved equally successful, as well as prestigious.

Our series of Oleander Dramascripts found find additions in Carey Harrison's radio plays *A Suffolk Trilogy* and *From the Lion Rock*, both in signed, limited editions.

In the last year we have published a humorous volume of stories called *English is a Foreign Language* by V.J. Prasad; the sensational discoveries made over the last four years by Dennis Baron proving that *De Vere is Shakespeare*, my own worldwide illustrated directory of *Contemporary Designer Bookbinders*, an attempt never previously made; and William Whallon's extraordinary reconstruction of Aeschlyus' tetralogy, *The Oresteia*, including a pornographic satyr play which Greek playwrights regularly introduced into their tragic cycles to reduce the tension in the audience, a relief lost in modern interpretations all over the world. Each of these books, in its own idiosyncratic way, represents a triumph of the small press in a crowded marketplace, and each has achieved reviews, sales and respect for both content and presentation.

Altogether, the future looks as bright as the past for the small publisher willing to respond to known gaps with intelligent market research by visiting libraries and bookshops and target groups such as clubs, interest societies, and commercial companies with information requirements. *Cultural Trends* published in March 1997 reported that the British people are reading more books and watching less TV than they did in 1991. In 1990, 77% of the population bought at least one book and this figure has been maintained throughout the succeeding period, and visits to national museums and galleries increased from 23.4 million in 1985 to 26.7 million in 1994. The average weekly TV viewing dropped by 24 minuets *per diem* between 1993 and 1995, and theatre audiences rose from 9.1 million adults in 1986-7 to 9.7 million adults in 1994-5, with a corresponding advance in ballet attendance.

Although 80% of British homes have at least one video cassette recorder, books have not suffered in real terms since the advent of the CD and the video, and each 'advance' in technology (the term is a curious one, though understandably used for purposes of propaganda) seems only further to reinforce the value of the high quality private press, such as The Old Stile Press or Libanus Press; the dedicated poetry publisher, such as Peter Jay's indispensable Anvil Press and Michael Schmidt's valuable Carcanet Press; and the general or specialised independent publisher, such as Nick Hern's drama house, and Tarquin's brilliant educational series of mathematical and related books, many of then ingenious in production terms.

More than 100,000 new titles appeared from the British publishers in 1996, that is to say almost double the total emanating from USA houses: an indicator of the spread of democracy, the defeat of censorship, and the vitality and depth of our cultural and artistic life in most communities and most ethnic groups. Of these 100,000 titles, a vast proportion is due to small publishers, and this is cause for (if no complacency, then) great and perpetual celebration.

Philip Ward

ORANGE BLOSSOM SPECIAL

As one carries out some intention, one's perspective of one's original reasons for having started it, invariably change. It becomes hard to remember with any clarity the actual reasons why anything was done. The only certain recollection I have was that I knew it would entail a great deal of work, that it would probably never pay, and yet that it would be on its own terms, a substantial success. All of which convictions have been borne out.

The facts of my case are that about two and a half years ago I decided to publish a serial magazine or pamphlet for youngsters, say between 12 – 16, who like to read, and who are interested in History. I was at that stage in my life where I realised I would have to do something, having spent years laying around. Want of cash was extreme, the needs of my family growing, and even though the project would hardly be remunerative, it would keep me occupied and give me the sensation of making an effort to earn, I being one of those people who have tried their hands at many things, and yet seem never to be able to bring a penny home.

The particular idea was borne upon me when – for some forgotten reason – my two boys expressed a desire to have read to them a history of Spain. We talked and read a lot about all sorts of things. When I sensed they were beginning to grow interested in any subject I would go to the library, or bookshop and look for a suitable book. This 'history of Spain' for intelligent, literate young minds seemed never to have existed. I spent days in Foyles and up and down the Charing Cross Road, in libraries – all to no avail. I looked for a book on any other European country – the same. It became apparent that schoolbooks of the very lowest sort, and the sort of history by caption that Dorling Kindersley have made their speciality, comprised the whole range of what was available. The dull, bland books of my childhood began to appear more lustrous.

And so, I decided to supply the remedy, and begin publishing a partwork – each month dealing with a different subject about which kids would hardly otherwise have a chance of learning. I decided I would try to maintain a high standard, however this might limit the popularity of the magazine. Though I try to keep them from being dull, there are at least ten thousand words each issue, so that they only appeal to those kids who are genuinely interested and love reading. It appears that no one else considers catering for these people. Knowing from the outset that my greatest difficulties would be in distribution to such a scattered market, and that it would be a long time before I was able to sell enough to support the venture, I undertook to do as much as I could for myself.

The research and the writing, was my chief interest and pleasure, but otherwise – because I had to – I grew to love the typing, layout, designing, collating, binding, finishing, distributing, envelope stuffing. The only work I paid for was the printing. I see no other way round this approach without having large financial resources. In some ways, want of funds can be an advantage. Had I been able to pay others to do what I did I might have had more leisure, but I would've given up sooner. Sweat is the only resolute investment.

Recently I sent out my 25th issue, having sold something in the region of 12,000 copies. To give an idea of what I have covered here is the list of every issue so far:

Barbary Corsairs
The Mongol Invasion of Japan
Elizabethan Rogues and Vagabonds
Indians of North America

Reading to his son Charlie Boxer found the inadequacies of published histories. Soon he woke up committed to a monthly 'jackdaw'. In Spring 1997 he sleep-walked through organising his first small press fair…

Ozymandias King of Kings
The Risorgimento
Speculative Booms and Crashes
St. Paul's and the Fire of London by Frank Graham
The Albigensian Heresy
Vikings in the Hebrides
Wild Children
The Ottoman Siege of Vienna by Jason Goodwin
The Great Sahara
The Quakers & the Civil War
Science & Technology in Old China
Minority of William the Bastard by Paula Fletcher
The Romanian Revolution, 1989
The Authorship of Shakespeare by John Michell
American Gangsters
The Peloponnesian War
Border Raids of Lowland Scotland
The Golden Age of Piracy by Rob Morgan
The Alps
Russia before the Revolution by Rose Baring
Terra Australis Incognita & other tales of the South Seas.

PROVIDENCE PRESS (WHITSTABLE)

For John Dench, the motivation to turn to self-publishing is simple to explain, and easy to understand, particularly if like him, as an aspiring writer, you have journeyed the same route and endured the same disappointments in trying to interest mainstream publishers in your work. It's a familiar story, but it took quite some time to realise that work which had been laboured over for nearly ten years was inevitably doomed to remain filed away, never to reach a wider public unless a totally new direction was found.

Disillusionment grew along with the piles of manuscripts; novels, short stories, poetry, drama scripts, essays... they deserved a better fate! Arrogance? Maybe. Vanity, No! The belief in the work, not a search for an ego massage, was the key. Thus the Providence Press (Whitstable) began its life in 1989 in the humble and somewhat cramped surroundings of the proverbial spare room.

An old manual typewriter, a dinosaur of an old, battered (freely donated) office photocopier and bags of enthusiasm, along with 20 plus years experience as a printer were the vital ingredients that led John to publish five modest, homespun publications which appeared in the course of just over a year.

These consisted of an essay, 2 slim volumes of poetry, a long prose poem and not least of all a work entitled *A Parable of Providence* from which the Press derived its name.
The ambition had been realised, and John felt very pleased with the results, but then the disillusionment returned, this time in the guise of effective marketing or rather the lack of it. Rejection slips were now replaced by disdainful grimaces and shaking heads from smug bookshop owners and snooty librarians and it looked as if Providence was set to be a 'one-year wonder'. This was, it has to be said, due in part to impulsiveness... a nice idea, but fraught with problems from the outset, technical and otherwise, not least of all a non-existent budget. And so for the next couple of years, the Press remained in a state of limbo. The once pristine coloured covers faded as did the enthusiasm.

But things rapidly changed when John met and formed a relationship with Lesley which eventually led to the Press being thoroughly reappraised in 1992 and relaunched in 1993.

Reappraisal was certainly needed, but it was undertaken with a revived sense of commitment to see the Press succeed as an efficiently run venture with a future. Lesley's enthusiasm and practical support in getting things going again was immensely valuable. Hard work was certainly required to re-establish the Press on more stable and 'professional' lines and sacrifices had to be made. Nevertheless, we agreed to continue with the arrangement of producing everything literally 'in-house' – giving us total control of everything from original idea to finished product.

The inevitability of having to dump those first edition booklets was heart-rending but necessary. But, as part of a much-discussed 'Press Policy' we decided to re-design and re-publish those first five works. We were very pleased with the results and this time the spectre of how to market them was countered by a much more carefully considered approach. Involvement with Small Press associations, specialist book-shops, poetry events, Small Press Fairs, writing magazines with their mail-order routes have helped tremendously, as has observing the way other SPs operate. There is no doubt that Small Presses are, by their nature, diverse, as are the people that run them! It's a whole other world which makes compari-sons with the mainstream and the scurrilous vanity outfits, irrelevant. Involvement in the Small Press scene has brought its rewards, and its demands, which we regard as impetus. The new look Providence has also enabled Lesley to bring some of

The poet owns-up. Everything goes into the bin. Then the publishing house is re-born. But he keeps committing Poetry...

her work to fruition.

Of course there are still set-backs, we make mistakes and hopefully learn by them. We overstretch ourselves occasionally and there is tension when self-imposed deadlines approach. This situation is sometimes exacerbated by our both having demanding full-time jobs elsewhere. Providence is therefore, and always has been, an evenings, weekends and whatever-time can-be-spared-activity.

Finance, or rather the lack of it, is as much a problem for Providence as it is for most SPs. The Press is entirely self-financed and has never received any kind of 'arts funding'. We don't think or talk in terms of substantial profit margins. So long as we make enough to cover the costs associated with production and administration, with a little surplus for the next project, then we are happy.

The dedication remains, with an ever-growing Catalogue and new areas continually being explored, including the recent decision to publish other writers in a new magazine for the South-East, as well as a Newsletter on behalf of a local wildlife group. For all of this, we are still very much on a learning curve, but we have a strategy and we strive to adhere to it; a positive approach even when things aren't always going the way we had intended!

We remember once being asked by a media student 'How do Small Presses become Big Presses?' Our answer was simple. With a few notable exceptions, they don't...because they don't want to. The questioner, however, was persistent. 'But surely you want to make lots of money from what you are doing, don't you?' This suggestion was just as easily countered by a belief which has always been uppermost in our minds: being independent, and thus in control of every stage, brings a reward of its own. It is one that perhaps only other Small Press Publishers fully understand.

John and Lesley Dench

PYTHIA
My name is Celia. I am a small press
Pythia Press was an offshoot of friendship. Through *Women in Publishing* I had met a number of other women who were wary of

the standard line. Indeed, I was introduced to WiP by Val Stevenson. She was the partner of Paul Sieveking, co-editor of *Fortean Times*. While he was at Cambridge University Paul had been led astray by John Nicholson, and was a visitor at the bookshop John and I ran in the city. Val and Paul – and Bob Rickard, founding editor of *Fortean Times* – were among the nine who met in John Michell's flat in Autumn 1987 to consider creating a Small Press Group.

In 1988 the Small Press Group was founded and JN and I were swamped! But Val and I kept in touch as part of another unofficial grouping of the WiP women I mentioned. About six of us would meet every so often and disrupt a cafe in Soho. The management asked in what name to book our table – we were strikingly valuable customers. When the clamour died down in response, the obvious reply was "The Shy Women". (An applicant was turned down when she expressed concern about the noise.)

Another link came, again, via John Michell. His current partner, Christine Rhone was eager to learn how to publish. Rather than spend hours lecturing – why not do it?

Soon I found myself piggy in the middle.

At what point did we consciously decide? We chose a name and an idea of what we were trying to do: *"reprints of rare writing by remarkable women"*. Christine designed a logo and Val chose our first titles. We would publish two – at the same time, on Bastile Day 1989.

We saw ourselves as continuing, reviving, the tradition of the early Women's movement. The SCUM manifesto was a classic piece of waste paper! By the late 1980s Wimmin's Studies were on every academic list and most mainstream publishers had a list of Wimmins titles. Wimmin publishing was big, big business. We had confirmation very soon. You can imagine how we reacted when we had our mistakes listed by a Wimmin's small publisher? The wimmin's bookshops wouldn't stock our titles. They were booklets, they weren't *books*. They committed the first offense: they were spineless.

Both our first pair would be A5 booklets. The card for the covers was carefully sought and chosen. In my lunch hour I went to Paperpoint in Covent Garden and discovered two odd but complementary colours. The book by Margaret Fell, the Quaker, was bound in a grainy grey reminiscent of a dour puritan dress material; the Olympe de Gouge in textured clotted-blood red! I designed the plain front covers, drawing on my experience as the typesetter for Fortean Times, John Michell and others.

The choice of the first pairing was excellent. The Fell *Women's Speaking Justified...* appeared at the height of the controversy about ordination of women in the Church of England. Olympe de Gouge's *Rights of Women* coincided with the 200th

Friendship? Disasified with the boom in feminist publishing Celia Boggis goes back to the roots – only to be criticised, by Feminist Publishing!

anniversary of the French Revolution, our chosen publication date. De Gouge had castigated the revolution as dealing only in the Rights of Man and ignoring the Rights of Women. She was guillotined as a result.

Neither work was unknown, but neither was available in a simple edition. Clearly the pairing was inspired!

Word spread. We repped the books ourselves where possible, or with the help of the best repper then in the business: Clare Baker of Cambridge University Press. Through the Small Press Group we found a distributor perfect for the style and subject matter of the books: Counter Productions. We had enough mentions and reviews, even in Quaker literature and American University publications, to build up a sizeable mail order market. The booklets sold. Steadily. We were able to pay back the stake money which Christine had found in some obscure feminist literary fund.

Most of all the idea of Pythia took off: a new, independent Women's Press, entirely without dogma or structure. We attracted everything, including offers of money from genuine patrons.

We exhibited at the Small Press Group's 1989 fair. It made us seem real. It justified all the work I had put into the SPG. However, Pythia was never an organised business. During the fair I was busy with the SPG admin. Val had a new baby, which would reduce her role in WiP as well as Pythia. Christine had adapted one of John Michell's customs. late rising, and set up our Pythia stall after lunch – missing half the fair! A pity as she had hand-coloured a drawing of Olympe. Intended for publicity it drew many enquiries from would-be purchasers. A spirited rendering of the Olympe text was performed in the adjacent small hall to an appreciative audience.

But Pythia had all the characteristics of a classic Small Press. It had not been set up as a business. It had no real centre. No office. It relied on friends. By definition this changed the meetings of friends into business meetings. It was becoming too serious. Months after Val moved house a batch of correspondence came to light, unopened. It included orders, enquiries, cheques and even dollar bills. By then we were selling out of copies and we couldn't handle the admin. None of us had the time or inclination to run Pythia. We had done what we set out to do. We owed nobody anything – in any sense. On the contrary we had made a very valid point which anybody else could implement, as I emphasised when I lectured on self-publishing at the WiP Conference the following year.

In 1991 I attended the International Feminist Book Festival in Barcelona. It confirmed all I felt about Women's mainstream publishing. It was a world I didn't want to join. On the other side I saw into the world of small presses via the Small Press Group. As the SPG grew it swallowed more of my life. Somehow time passed and the moment passed too.

It is only later, looking back that you see that you have stopped. There was no conscious decision to pack up Pythia. We never had a meeting to hammer out 'What Now?'. Indeed I do not really regard it as over. Even now, 5 years later, it flickers. I still get offers – of help, of titles and of money. It is all still there, all still viable. Nobody else has done it and nothing has got better! When the next Pythia title appears the gap will merely have been an interval.

Cecilia Boggis

QUINCE TREE - J.L. CARR

Pause here – Rose Heaword describes that most special of Britain's small presses…

Would that Jim Carr had been writing this! Unhappily he died on 26th February, 1994 but that was not the end of his Quince Tree Press, as you will see in the A-Z Section of this Handbook. His son, Robert and daughter-in-law, Jane continue to distribute the publications of this unique small press and they intend to continue publishing under the Quince Tree imprint.

What was so remarkable about Jim Carr was that – although recognised nationally, and internationally, with two Booker shortlistings, and two novels adapted as major TV films – he still found most satisfaction in being his own publisher.

What turned a school-teacher into a full-time writer/publisher? A Workers' Educational Association class on 'Modern Writers of Significance' and the success of his novel, 'A Day in Summer' (1963) were catalysts. He and his wife Sally, a former Red Cross nurse, having a house and capital of £1,600, decided to give the project two years. They just managed to go into profit at the cut-off point. And the back room at 27 Mill Dale Road, Kettering, Northamptonshire had become the printing house which would later be known as The Quince Tree Press.

They had started with hand-drawn historical maps of the English counties and the highly distinctive little 'Carr's Pocket Books'. These were, in his own words, 'made to fit a handbag or a pocket (or a cuff) to be read in a hot bath, a cold bedroom, a dull sermon, or a tedious speech'. Most of these minature booklets are miniature anthologies. They contain distillations from poets with the kind of illustrations JL enjoyed. Others were very unusual 'dictionaries'. Since the series kicked off in 1964, over 500,00 booklets have been sold.

Cobbett features in this series and there is the memorable 'Poor Man's Guide to the Revolt of 1381.' The mannerisms of modern journalism jolt us into looking at these events afresh: under the heading 'Media Commentators, Conjectural Speculators and Pop Prophets 'we find Chaucer 'pop poet and (had the post been invented) Laureate' who only mentions the Rising with 'cynical brevity'. Langland is the 'hard-liner…who strips the Fancy Dress from the Middle Ages'. Events are presented

> *"This is a Printing Office,*
> *Cross-roads of Civilisation,*
> *Refuge of all the Arts against*
> *the Ravages of Time.*
> *From this place words may fly*
> *abroad*
> *Not to perish as Waves of*
> *Sound but fix'd in Time,*
> *Not corrupted by the hurrying*
> *Hand but verified in Proof.*
> *Friend, you are on Safe*
> *Ground:*
> *This is a Printing Office."*

THE QUINCE TREE PRESS

There are 61 books in this collection. They fit a common envelope, go for minimum postage, are comfortable bedside books, (only one hand need suffer exposure) and can be palmed from the cuff during tedious speeches and overlong sermons.

in a terse diary with the final observation 'Neither historian, philosopher nor even TV professional pundit can totally explain the inspiration which fired these Englishmen into brief, exuberent, explosive energy' but the speculation which follows presents a superb spectacle of anger finely channelled by a scornful wit, as well as historical awareness. As he once remarked (in a letter to the present writer), '1381 was a blow for Liberty. The little book I mean..'.

The eye as well as the mind is delighted, as woodcuts take the reader almost by surprise, so accustomed are we now to the relentless motorway of mere typography, and typography of the most basic functionality in its haste to get from A-B. For readers who relish a different pace, these visual interruptions cause a moment to enjoy the view and maybe mull over what has gone before, whether these be the small decorations and colophons beloved of earlier printers, full-page illustrations or end-papers. Not surprisingly, JL celebrates the art of Thomas Berwick in his pocket booklet series. Yet it is not all nostalgia: the gritty end-papers for "What Hetty Did" show a CND march against a wintry landscape and an urban riot.

Carr even found time and space to remind us that Baskerville is not a technical term but a human being. The dedication in his Hetty novel include 'to the Memory of John Baskerville of Birmingham who designed this type-fount, invented wove paper

and lost money cheerfully on particular books which he published'.

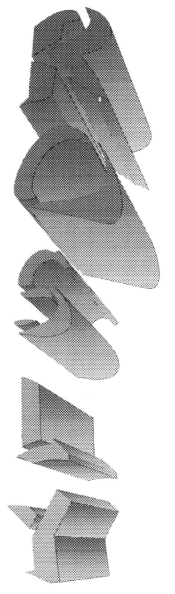

If the prevailing atmosphere is gentle, somewhat wryly humourous, it can be deceptive. Anyone who has experienced the range of JL Carr's output can sense the under-lying exaperation at the injustices inflicted on our society and the sheer brute stupidity, the boring waste of it all. If injustice or violence is not in the here and now of his own narratives, it is present in the characters' memory. 'A Day in Summer' (1963) is a classic tale of revenge with an unexpected ending. The horrors of the '14-'18 War continue to dog the two protagonists in the incomparable 'A Month in the Country' (1980) which transferred so effectively to cinema in Pat O'Connor's film (UK,1987). Apart from such hints at his feelings you need only check the list of the other authors whom he selected to publish from the 'classics'.

JL Carr belongs to a robust tradition of 18th and 19th century writer/publishers who were characterised by their independence in thought and action. As a writer he knew from experience that commercial publishers are good at producing books and the initial launch, but that they are not so good at getting books over to a further reading public. Independent publishers side-lined and pushed aside by current distribution practices would agree on this. His novel 'Harpole & Foxberrow: General Publishers – a Business History (with Footnotes)' is about a small publishing business. Sheer delight, it debunks some highly debunkable aspects of this scene and it only costs £5.95. We hear that booksellers are buying it for themselves!

ROSLYN

Writing it
I felt I had something to say and was egocentric enough to think other people would want to read it.

Over the subsequent years I wrote down thoughts, ideas and experiences, sometimes with an eye to using them in my novel. I had poems and articles and short stories published in little magazines but I always planned to keep my original promise to myself.

In the mid-'80s, living in Johannesburg with my South African wife, Roslyn, I found the time to develop a structure to hang my ideas on, and my actual novel-writing began. I used weekends, primarily, until 1988. Then, while my wife continued to work, I took off a year and a half to work full-time on my novel.

I used a newly purchased computer to do a lot of the rewriting and the occasional first draft of a paragraph, but most writing was done with a pen. I wrote about 100 drafts and

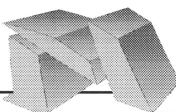

In 1971 Jeff
Probst was living
in San Fransico.
He decided he
would write a
novel. That was
only the start of his
adventures.
Quarter of a
century later he
published it...

the novel of 70,000 words boiled down to a novella of about
30,000 words. I read every book I could find on How To Write
A Novel. Then on How To Write A Novella – when I realised that
was what I now had. I read parts of my book at writers' groups
and received valuable feedback. A London agent phoned me,
told me he'd heard (from the writing group's leader) that I was
writing a novel and to send it to him when I'd finished.

We moved to London in 1990. Getting the manuscript out of my
suitcase was like seeing an old friend again after an enforced
break, and I continued to work on the book, with a scarf over
my head in our Edgware Road bedsit, and made use of the
computers in the Holborn library on Theobalds Road.

I changed the name of the book's characters, locales and the
title, and eliminated any allusions to the real places or people or
events.

In July 1991 I 'finished' the book. At least I felt that 'this will have
to do,' in the words of Anthony Burgess. I was lucky to have had
the time, the support and quiet to experience the making of an
attempted work of art. 30,000 words were all I had to get
published. It wasn't *so* few.

Who will publish it?
I took the manuscript to the agent's house in Camden and
dropped it through his mail slot. I fantasised that he would phone
the next day. 'I've read it. It has the makings of a minor cult
classic. It will be hard to get published but I will do my best.' He
wrote back that he had enjoyed it but it wasn't for him.

I began to read books on marketing. What was the book?
Speculative fiction? Science fiction? Literary fiction? I sent the
manuscript to numerous other agents and none were interested.
On the phone, one asked what it was about and who my
influences were. I thought about these questions then prepared a
synopsis and sent it with sample manuscript pages to about
fifteen publishers. No luck. I thought about taking the sex and
drugs out of for the younger reader, but the book wouldn't work
with out either.

I did some more rewriting, some rearranging of events and felt,
again, by August 1993 that I was 99% satisfied with the book.

I will!
I had to see my 'quips and sentences and... paper bullets from
the brain' between covers! I decided to publish it myself. My
sister-in-law had the slide of a painting she had done which
fitted the book well. It became the front cover illustration. A
friend with more technical know-how than I, and sophisticated
computer equipment, printed out the pages of the book in page
lay-outs. I contacted the Publishers' Association and they
recommended a mid-sized, fifteen person printing firm near
Finsbury Park. I arranged to have my book printed and bound
by this firm called SPIDER'S WEB.

They were good to work with and had many helpful ideas on all aspects of the printing process, including the recycled paper I wanted to use and the look and feel of a small, colour-jacketed book from the '60s. They printed and bound six hundred copies for me, fifty hardback, for about £2,500.

On 22 July 1994 the book was published – by Roslyn Press.

Boxes of it
I had forgotten to put a blurb on the book so I had an insert printed. I took the book around to a number of local book-shops, all of whom took some copies to sell. I sold copies to Foyle's and Waterstone's on Charing Cross Road. Of the ten bookshops that took books (some on sale or return – others, including the local W H Smiths, purchased them outright) seven currently hold copies. I've sold fifty copies so far through bookshops and some to work colleagues. I have sent about twenty five copies to reviewers and national and local libraries (six borrowings so far in the Hornsey branch). Forty five went free to friends and family. (As John Nicholson said to me when I admitted not all had been read: 'Why didn't you just post them a £5 note?') The family got hardbacks. Marketing score: all told, I've given away more copies than I've sold.

I got a local paper to do a feature on me, from the self-publishing angle. I met a Sunday Times reviewer one evening at an ICA discussion about how books do, or don't, get reviewed. My book was subsequently reviewed in that paper. A newspaper I used to work on, in California, reviewed my book.

Wiser?
Now, a year and a half after publication, I'm preparing a leaflet about my book. This is one of the results of my con-sultation with the NSPC – a priceless hour packed with many gems of marketing advice. I hope to follow these ideas, between the work I need to do as an English teacher at a secondary comprehensive.

I look forward, too, to the next small press fair the Centre organises. The one last November became the impetus for my current ideas and plans for my book, 'Bachelor Butterflies.'

THE RUNETREE PRESS
Should anyone, a few years ago, have said 'You're going to be a publisher', I'd have laughed. Yet that's what I became, almost by accident, in trying to help a small special interest group which was agonising over its PR. I offered a low-cost, effective publishing package (with plenty of hidden subsidies – mine!). The potential for information dissemination seemed to elude them. So why should this go to waste? Experience in handling short-run material taught me the viability of such publications when readers' interests are understood. Elements in any promotional strategy include meetings and book fairs. The SPG annual fair (in its *original* format) at the Royal

Suddenly you have boxes of stock in your warehouse a.k.a. under your bed. How to sell them? How to sleep again?

Horticultural Hall clinched my decision to go into print, alongside other small publishers I was promoting.

The name "Runetree" was suggested by the logo I designed. My main concerns whilst working as an information consultant had

been environment and appropriate technology. Earlier training in historical disciplines was, however, a reminder of past dimensions. These ancient landscapes, local history, the uses and abuses of history (particularly in the growth or loss of personal identity) and how, in consciousness, past and present interact. Trees have always figured strongly, particularly the OAK, ASH and THORN. Together, how they resonate! My interest in Old English (the rootstock of what we speak today) linked this greenwood trinity to their Runic selves which seemed to sprout as branches of a great tree, a mediator between things past and what may lie ahead. May that future be sustainable !

First steps were tentative and with reason. It's great fun to do your own thing but who, in their right mind, wants to end up with heaps of unsold, unsaleable stock under the bed or otherwise causing endless storage problems? A bad case of DIY vanity publishing? So my earliest attempts were very short-run (with possible re-runs, if needed) and with a target readership in mind. This included a facsimile of a well researched, highly readable but out of print monograph, the authors of which were happy to see someone else taking on reprinting and distribution. This publication is a

modest success story, finding regular outlets in the Wessex region, as well as satisfying those studying King Alfred's campaigns from the viewpoint of local topography.

Runetree's Dramascript series was prompted by other needs. Like the Oleander Press I have a strong commitment to radio drama. Time and again people say that such and such a play was terrific, 'parts of it I'd love to mull over again...' Some radio plays are so good that they deserve wider recognition. However, getting hold of transcripts is seldom easy, often expensive. Let's have them in print! (After all, think how *Under Milkwood* started..) During the Maldon Millennium in 1991, I came across *The Battle of Maldon*, a radio play by the Scottish writer Menzies McKillop. The resulting Runetree publication led to further discovery of this writer's work in radio, both in Canada and the UK. I combined three plays in one volume. His treatment of Columba, Cuthbert and Caedmon is not hagiography. His plays are original in form, full of light and darkness, of wry humour, fired by a decency that has nothing to do with rules and regulations – and what a feeling for language !

Dramascript's latest is a reprint of Robert Gittings' play, *The Makers of Violence*. Originally commissioned by the Friends of Canterbury Cathedral in 1951, it is still a play for today. Through hostage-taking during the 11th century Danish invasion of England, it explores the roots of violence at a much deeper level. Other Dramascripts are under consideration dealing with 19th century events.

Also relating to performance are Runetree's audiotape cassettes. To help those who want an introduction to spoken Old English, *Saxon Voices* is a professional recording which has been edited and read by Bill Griffiths, a scholar/poet/small publisher with long experience in adult education. It is interesting to note that an audiotape of this kind can apply for an ISBN.

Oh, to be more proactive and commission new work! However, much has to be learnt before substantial resources can be invested in original publications. Still, the usefulness of timely reprints is not to be scorned. In observable cycles of communication they have a role. (Where would many readers be without Llanerch, which brings out inexpensive paperback facsimiles of texts otherwise only available through expensive dealers or libraries of difficult access?) My imprint also has a strong commitment to mutual support amongst small and specialist presses. We must ensure the survival of independent publishing against the oppressive onslaught of market forces. Last year Runetree collaborated with Paul Watkins to ensure a reprint of this publisher's brilliant presentation of a European historical symposium. Its first printing had sold out like hot cakes with orders still coming in! The Runetree catalogue will list publications from other small presses with similar

interests, a practice I have noted in the listings of others, where a certain reciprocity operates. This is not only good practice in terms of information dissemination, it also shows the heartening co-operation to be found in some parts of our constituency.

Switching from interplays of past and present to thoughts of a sustainable future, people ask about my updating a directory I edited in the '80s (now o/p) dealing with appropriate technologies for the British Isles. Rigorous revision is needed, since the AT scene is so volatile, its sources of information having likewise seen radical shifts. If resources could be gathered for this project, I would not use a commercial publisher again. With advances in DTP this is a 'must' for Runetree, hopefully in co-operation with one or more organisations which understand the imperatives of sustainable development and the real needs of AT information dissemination.

WAVE GUIDE
Get Tuned In

It was microwave ovens that made me a publisher. I first used one in the Sixties, twenty years after they were introduced. It was called an oven, so I expected it to do oven work. It wouldn't – any more than a Bombay Duck would quack. Millions of people must since have been disappointed by these ovens which are not ovens. Even the Companies who make them cling to conventional concepts – bent a little.

Before long, I was eating and sleeping microwave ovens. Putting them into the shops by the hundred, training people to demonstrate them, and repairing them if they went wrong. I enjoyed solving user problems. 'You should write a book about it', they said. 'What you've told us is nothing like what we've heard before'. So I did - if that's what you can call sweat-stained typescript.

The Consumers' Association were the first to see my dummy. They couldn't fault its content, and even said they were optimistic about publishing it. It needed endorsing with some famous name, but most big Companies ruled against such things. That was when Korean giant GoldStar was beginning to make its mark in the UK, so I approached them, and endorse it they did.

'It needs recipes', they said. 'It's not that sort of book', I replied – but gave in, and contacted old colleague cookery writer Annemarie Rosier. She had to read it ten times to see things my way, and then insisted I changed nothing. So recipes it has – but with a big difference. They don't need timings.

The best I got from publishers was from a hardback firm. They said it would make a good paperback. Publish-it-yourself was the answer, so in 1990, it was set out by a costly computer program and printed, by a small firm here on the Isle of Wight. The typesetting was awful. I had to show an operator how to avoid whole lines compressing to look like one long word – and lines with but a single word.

We certainly proved the Contrarian Law, which says you'll get the opposite of what you might reasonably expect. The book, now called *Microwave for Certain*, was to help retail staff among others. A trade magazine said every shop should have a copy for reference - but with no effect. We feared repercussions from the oven manufacturers, because of the way I had spilled the beans – exposing their fallacies. In the event, they welcomed it. Several bought it and used it to train their own staff.

Consumers (those who read it) loved it, including little old ladies in bed-sits. Book shops I called at bought it quite well, but then didn't sell many. Microwave owners needed it right enough, but it wasn't what the big publishers had trained them to buy. In short, 'Microwave for Certain' was a great success, but a small seller. However, after publishing it, I had magazine articles accepted instantly, and was asked to write a regular feature for a trade newspaper. That was called 'Up the Microwave'. It ran for two and a half years.

We published *The Caterers' Microwave Bible* last year, by which time we were equipped for typesetting and illustrating. The huge advantage an author has in doing this is the ability to edit the text to fit every line, paragraph, and page. Leave it all to a computer, and you'll have sentences which begin with a solitary A at the end of a line, and ugly gaps which could easily be filled by knocking a word over from a previous line. If there's one thing I can feel proud about with my *Bible*, it is its gracefully sculptured right hand margins on every page.

According to the microwave oven trade, the book is just what's needed. 'Should have been written years ago', said one man. Caterers tend to neglect thier ovens, site them badly, and think they are faulty (or make them faulty) through using them wrongly and that's not the half of it. Now the Catering Managers' Association say they like the book, so let's see what happens.

Catering students who study it will surely be better informed than their teachers. They could really get the ball rolling. The catering industry is strongly prejudiced against microwave as a cooker. Only a tiny number of chefs have discovered where it is superior in that role. Most have never taken the trouble to learn the techniques. Little of the book is about cookery, but what there is would be of value to a great number of top end caterers – if only they'd read it and believe what it says.

The encouraging news is that one shop which bought it has re-ordered, and re-ordered, and re-ordered, and re-ordered. Could this herald the catering student jackpot?

He couldn't make his microwave oven work. He taught himself. Before long he saw others needed to learn how to work their microwave ovens. He wrote a guide. Then he published it. He came a Small Press...

IT'S GOT THE LOT.

Of course it hasn't. But it has got everything we could find. However we make no claim to omniscience. Also nobody knows more than the compilers of such information how speedily it goes out of date. Likewise we are well aware how out of date information lingers. The Centre receives enquiries about the SPG, the Small Press Group of Britain Ltd – which ended in 1993/4 – or Small Press Monthly – which ended in Spring 1991. The Centre's office at Middlesex University ended in February 1996. We field all these enquiries as best we can.

What can be done to prevent this? Absolutely nothing. Firstly we update our own information in other directories. But they usually solicit around the middle of the year at the latest. Consequently if you have to move after the Autumn it is inevitable you will be unable to update until the next edition. That means you must make contingency arrangements to cover more than a year. Secondly there is the matter of reference sections in libraries. Clearly every library wants to have the latest edition of every directory on its shelf. But that is impossible in a time when they are strapped for cash. Consequently we get enquiries from SPG Yearbooks dating back at least to 1991. That makes the information seven years old. Isn't it reasonable to expect such plainly old information to be treated with caution? Not everybody is reasonable.

Which brings us to this book. Given the problems you might wonder if it is worth producing a directory. Well, it needs common sense. If you bear in mind the caveats just mentioned and treat the information as an aid not a bible then the book is incredibly useful. Because the vast majority of the information is valid. Just because a % is obsolete does not negate the exercise. Our score of correct hits is a good start and provides a base line. Besides this book contains so much more.

We want to improve our % every bit as much as our readers. To do that we need resources. What you hold is what was possible with no money.

Nor does this Handbook claim to be an exhaustive list of everybody and everything. If it was easy everybody would do it. It is almost an impossibility even if we had the resources. We don't. The Centre has never received any funding or grants. All of this work is done by volunteers in their spare time. We do our best. The response to the Yearbooks showed we filled a need and raised the game. It is some reward to know your work has made a valuable difference. But that doesn't make it any easier to do the work.

> Such is the nature of small presses, almost a definition? that many have tiny life spans. Yet, like the dragonfly which lives in splendour for a day, they are replaced by many more. The moral is persevere.
>
> We take every reasonable effort to keep our records up to date. We also consider that any publication in the public domain wishes to sell. Therefore the dissemination of knowledge about that publication can only be helpful, especially when no cost is involved for the publishers.
>
> Every time we issue the same caveat: don't take any information as gospel. Every directory issues the same warning. It is the nature of information to go out of date quickly. Check for yourself.

HOW DO WE GET THE INFORMATION?

a It comes to us. We process it and regurgitate it.

b We seek it. In other directories. Some refuse to let you help yourself. That doesn't stop you getting in touch with the entries and inviting them to have an entry in your directory. But we also seek it in all sorts of places, many unlikely. Lifeboats? One of our team subscribes to a newsletter about life-boats. All kinds of kind people monitor for us. \if you know better, or about somebody we missed, tell us!

c We solicit it. This is a limited operation. Here is where money would make the difference. Think about it. Our A/Z contains some 2,500 entries. Our other directory sections have more than 500 other addresses. How much will it cost to send an update form to all of them? To produce the form, the stamps, the envelopes and the labour? You are looking at more than £1,000. The Centre cannot justify such expense, even if it had the cash.

In the days of the SPG it was different. We did try to send to all the presses. That was when the SPG was seeking bookings for its fair, display adverts, sales of the Yearbook, and subscriptions. Also it was publicising the fair, the Yearbook and its existence. Every Summer 'The Big Push' cost the SPG more than £500 in stamps alone but the return justified the outlay. The Centre has no equivalent sources of revenue. In return we might pick up a dozen subs and a few sales. Together they would amount to around £200/300. Then there is always the hidden subsidy. Why should those who work incredibly hard go unpaid?

> This is a transitional edition. We have cleared away the backlog of the SPG and reclaimed the data from the control of the firm who ran their computerised administration. So much for the Past. Looking forwards we hope to be installed in a new premises with a host organisation supplying helpers who wish to participate in our activities. This will enable us to create our own new database under our direct control. It means we can revise continually, on a daily basis. Our records will be upgraded and responsive eg Small Press Listings will come into its own. The Resources Directory will become three-dimensional as we form links with firms. This will encourage sponsorships for a variety of programmes.

Of course all this is leading up to a touch for money. There could be no better proof of how badly a Centre is needed than the need to run this updating properly. The Centre should be able to update continually. To collect, process and revise. And to disseminate. For this work it needs not only the facilities and equipment but also the staff. It needs database workers, proofreaders and people to produce the Listings and the Handbook. In an ideal world the work would be done in premises paid for, on machinery paid for, by workers paid for. That is how it should run, properly.

Even then it will be impossible to guarantee accuracy.

But what a difference we make.

USE THIS DIRECTORY:

Go through it and note down anything interesting, useful or daft. Highlight it in day-glo so you can find it quickly. Contact people who you like the sound of. Ask them for advice. You can soon build up a mailing list of potential sympathisers or, hopefully, friends. Always put your name, imprint and return address on the mail you send to each other. You may build up a network of people who agree to mutual publicity if only at the level of exchanging free adverts or listings in each others publications. Use the directory as a huge publicity resource. But use your common sense. You waste your time and money, and upset others, if you do blanket mailings. Not everybody is sympathetic.

BUY FROM THIS DIRECTORY

There must be something in here you want – and can't get anywhere else. Send the cash (and p&p). (If you are sending an SAE for a catalogue, make sure it is C5 or C4 – not a tiny envelope, nor an enormous one). If you don't buy from each other why should others buy from you? And please mention this Handbook.

A & L PUBLICATIONS
c/o 25 Poplar Road
Herne Hill
LONDON
SE24 0BN
Poetry.

A & M PUBLISHERS
7 Flax Close
Helemshall
ROSSENDALE
BB4 4JL

A-2 PUBLICATIONS
7 Hart Street
EDINBURGH
EH1 3RN

AARD Press
D. Jarvis
Aardverxus
31 Mountearl Gardens
LONDON
SW16 2NL
*Artist's Bookworks, ephemera,
cards, T-shirts, badges, artistamps,
mailart doco & alternative sort of
stuff.*

AARDVARK PUBLISHING
11 Cobbins Way
HARLOW
CM17 0LU

ABBEY BOOKS
P.O. Box 29
UTTOXETER
Poetry

Rick ABBOT
58 South Street
BRAUNTON
EX33 2AN
Travel.

ABBEY PRESS
72A Green Lanes
LONDON
N16 9EJ
Business Book Publisher.

ABCADO PUBLISHERS
Wayne Browne
20 St. Mary's Meadow
Wingham
CANTERBURY
CT3 IDF
Tel 01227 722 391

*Book Publishers - of academic
books on History Geography
Religion Art Poetry Medicine and
Australian History.*

ABC BOOKS
P.O. Box 189
LEIGH-ON-SEA
SS9 1NF
Occult.

ABERYSTWYTH ARTS CENTRE PUBLICATIONS
University College of Wales
Penglas
ABERYSTWYTH
SY23 3DE
Art.

ABLE CHILDREN
(see Pullen Publications)
9 Station Road
KNEBWORTH
SG3 6AP
School Textbooks.

ABSOLUTE PRESS
14 Widcombe Crescent
BATH
BA2 6AH
Food and Drink. Plays.

ABSTRACT
1A Elm Row
LONDON
NW3 1AA

ACAB Press
BM 8884
LONDON
WC1N 3XX
*Publisher of a series of anonymous
accounts of the Polltax riot of 31st
March 1990 presenting 'the other
side of the story.'*

ACADEMY BOOKS
35 Pretoria Avenue
LONDON
E17 7DR
*Cars. Classic Cars. History of Cars.
Welsh History.*

ACCENT EDUCATIONAL PUBLISHERS
17 Isbourne Way
Winchcombe
CHELTENHAM
GL54 5NS
School textbooks. Literature.

ACCESS COMMITTEE FOR ENGLAND
35 Great Smith St
LONDON
SW1P 3BJ

ACCORDIA RESEARCH CENTRE
Queen Mary and Westfield College
Mile End Road
LONDON
E1 4NS

ACE OF RODS
BCM Akademia
LONDON
WC1N 3XX
Mysterious and esoteric.

ACL COLOUR PRINT AND POLAR Publishing (UK)
2 Uxbridge Road
Belgrave

LEICESTER
LE4 7ST
Sport.

ACORN PUBLISHING
Spindlewood
Watery Lane
Lower Westholme
Pilton
SHEPTON MALLET
BA4 4EL
Tel 0157 284 200

ACTIVITY DIGEST/PRINTFORCE
David Saint
Westmead House
123 Westmead Road
SUTTON
SM1 45H
Tel 0181 770 1100
*Activity Digest publishes books for
adults working with children
particularly on games activities and
things to do. Printforce publishes
books for adults working with
children particularly in youth group
and schools.*

ACUMEN PUBLICATIONS
Patricia Oxley
6 The Mount
Higher Furzeham
BRIXHAM
TQ5 8QY
Tel 01803 851 098
*Press developed out of magazine;
devoted to producing good poetry
in an aesthetic setting. Each fully
illustrated book is printed on high-
quality paper with wrap-round
cover. Acumen magazine (bi-
annual, £5.50pa) publishes best
poem available plus reviews
articles and the Acumen Interview.*

ADAMANTINE PRESS
3 Henrietta Street
LONDON
WC2E 8LU
0171 836 4975
Studies on the 21st century.

ADARE PRESS
White Gables
Ballymoney Hill
BANBRIDGE
BT32 4DR
Local History.

AD HOC PUBLICATIONS
PO Box 850
LONDON
W14 8EW

ADOLPHUS PUBLICATIONS
Sharnden Old Manor Farm
MAYFIELD
TN20 6QA
Children's Fiction.

ADULT LITERARY AND BASIC SKILLS UNIT
Kingsbourne House
229-231 High Holborn
LONDON
WC1V 7DA
Education. Mathematics.

ADZINE
Jane Ellicott
43 Brooksbank House
Retreat Place, Hackney
LONDON
E9

*Quarterly listing of fanzines,
conventions, fan clubs, ads - sale
or wanted.*

AEDIFICANMUS PRESS
113 The Ridgeway
Northaw
POTTERS BAR
EN6 4BG

AEGIS PRESS
14 Herdson Road
FOLKESTONE
CT20 2PB
Tel 01303 251 762
*Poetry Anthologies. Edited by
David Shields, John Rice and
Michael Curtis with front cover
illustration by Sara Wicks, 'The
Scarpfoot Zone' is a major new
anthology of poetry by
contemporary Kent writers. 35 of
the County's leading poets have
contributed work in a diverse array
of forms, styles and subjects.
Included are poems about art,
sport, history, travel, love and loss.
Many poets chose to write about
Kent, a county undergoing immense
change. The work both builds on
the rich tradition of poetry in Kent
and, as we approach the end of the
century, points boldly to the future.
£5.95 ISBN 0 9519777 3 3*

AFTER THE BATTLE MAGAZINE
Church House
Church Street
LONDON
E15 3JA

AFRICA BOOKS
3 Galena Road
LONDON
W6 0LT
Biography. History of Africa.

AFRICA ARTS COLLECTIVE
3 Myrtle Parade
Myrtle St
LIVERPOOL
L7 7EL
Source books

AGENDA
William Cookson
5 Cranbourne Court
Albert Bridge Road
LONDON
SW11 4PE
Four p.a. Arts council support.

AGOG
Mr Ed Jewansinski
116 Eswyn Road
LONDON
SW17 8TN
*Poetry-based mag. Available on
disc.*

AGRICOLA TRAINING
Ryelands
Stouw
LINCOLN
LN1 2DE
Stockbreeding.

A.H.A.S.
Mike Williamson
10, Brockenhurst Road
ALDERSHOT
GU11 3HH
Tel 01252 26589
*Our press is based on desk top
publishing.*

Our two best sellers are:-
"The Crimea Roaders". The story of Ismena Smith's childhood in Aldershot during the 1930's and her life of happy poverty.
Volumes 1 & 2, £4.00 together inc P & P
"Twixt Common & Copse". Tim Childerhouse's latest book, the story of the ancient and common lands of Aldershot. 100pp, card cover, £7.74 inc P & P

AIM HIGH PRODUCTIONS
280 Liverpool Road
ECCLES
Manchester
M30 0RZ

AIRE PRESS AND PUBLISHING
Roger Ratcliffe
PO Box HP 36
LEEDS
LS6 3RN
Tel 01532 789 618
Former Sunday Times Northern Correspondent Roger Ratcliffe publishes the only guides to Leeds and Bradford praised for their design and described by the Guardian as 'encyclopedic, free of advertising.' Libraries/ Bookshops without stock titles on these cities can order direct.

AIREINGS
Jean Barker
24 Brudenell Road
LEEDS
LS6 1BD
A poetry magazine. Published twice a year. emphasis is on women's work, but we accept work from men too. We want good poetry on many & varied subjects. Cost £2.00 per copy. Sub. £4.50 pa (inc p&p)

AIRFIELD PUBLICATIONS
18 Ridge Way
Wargrave
READING
RG10 8AS
Military Airfields.

AIR RESEARCH PUBLICATIONS
34 Elm Road
NEW MALDEN
KT3 3HD
Second World War

AIRSTRIP, APT & BRAQUE
88 High Street
Bildeston
IPSWICH
IP7 7EA
Underground comics, black and white, sometimes with coloured wraparound cover. Usually produced on photocopier. themes are sci-fi, fantasy and flying.

AIRTIME PUBLISHING
13 The Hollows
Long Eaton
NOTTINGHAM
NG10 2ES
Railways.

A.J.F. DESK TOP PUBLISHING
Tudor Mint
Vulcan Road
SOLIHULL
B91 2JY
Fiction. General.

AK PRESS
Alexis McKay
PO Box 12766
EDINBURGH
EH8 9YE
Tel 0131 5555165 fax 0131 5555215
e-mail:ak@akedin.demon.co.uk.
Publishers of radical political writings: anarchism, philosophy, situationism, politics.

AKLO
50 St John Street
OXFORD
OX1 2LQ

AKROS PUBLICATIONS
18 Warrender Park Terrace
EDINBURGH
EH9 1EF
Poetry.

ALBA PUBLISHING
78 Weensland Road
HAWICK
TD9 9NX
Family History.

ALDA PUBLISHERS
3A Beaufort Close
REIGATE
SY

ALDEN PRESS
Mr T S Steptoe
Osney Mead
OXFORD
OX2 0EF

ALDERSHOT HISTORICAL AND ARCHAEOLOGICAL SOCIETY
10 Brockenhurst Road
ALDERSHOT
GU11 3HH
Tel 01252 26589.
* The Crimea Roaders - The story of Ismena Smith's childhood in Aldershot during the 1930's and her life of happy poverty. Now in its 5th Edition. £1.95p including postage and packing.
* Tim Childerhouse's latest book, Twixt Common & Copse, the story of the ancient common lands of Aldershot. 100pp, card cover, £6.95 plus 79p p&p, cheques payable to above.

G.L.D. ALDERSON
Canny Hill
Pool Lane
Brocton
STAFFORD
ST17 0TY
Military History.

ALECTO HISTORICAL EDITIONS
46 Kelso Place
LONDON
W8 5QG
History of Art.

THE ALEMBIC PRESS
Claire Bolton
Hyde Farm House
Marcham
Abingdon
Oxfordshire
OX13 6NX
Tel 01865 391 3391
A private press printing limited edition books by traditional letterpress methods. Books bound by hand, mainly at the press. Also

run letterpress workshops. B&B available. Send for hand printed prospectus of current titles.

ALF SUPPORTERS GROUP
BCM 1160
LONDON
WC1N 3XX
The ALF Supporters Group helps with the expenses incurred when people are arrested fined and imprisoned for ALF activities; helping towards defendant's expenses solicitors' fees, fines and compensation orders and also towards animal rights prisoners' needs while imprisoned. 'The SG Newsletter.' Reports from Britain and around the world on the welfare of those arrested on trial or imprisoned for animal rescue or ALF-type activities such as criminal damage (within the ALF policy of non-violence).

ALICE PUBLICATIONS
Richard Hull
2 Co-op Buildings
Pecket Well
HEBDEN BRIDGE
HX7 8QP
Dedicated to the memory of Radio Alice, Bologna, Italy, 1974-77. One person business, part time using Acorn Archimedes DTP facilities. I am attempting to provide greater access to publishing resources.

ALICE IN WONDERLAND
Rikki Hollywood
62 Stanhope Road
GREENFORD
UB6 9EA
Tel 0181 578 7114
Alice in Wonderland comic - Hippy/Gothic version!! Double issue Pt 1+2 collectors (includes Postage + packing) payable to Rikki Hollywood. Alice in Wonderland. 48pp. Out now! £2.00 per copy.

Keith ALLARDYCE
Ingledene
Wansbeck Road
ASHINGTON
NE63 8JE
Photography.

ALLARDYCE BARNETT PUBLISHERS
14 Mount Street
LEWES
BN7 1HL
Literature, Art and Music.

ALLBOROUGH PRESS
15A Vinery Road
CAMBRIDGE
CB1 3DN

ALLEN & TODD
9 Square Street
Ramsbottom
BURY
BL0 9BE

BENJAMIN ALLEN PUBLICATIONS
1 Carnhill Avenue
NEWTONABBEY
BT36 6LE
Artists Books, postcards, badges, ephemera.

ALLENHOLME PRESS
10 Woodcroft Road

WYLAM
NE41 8DJ
Bibliographies.

Anne ALLINSON
33 Cranemoor Avenue
Highcliffe
CHRISTCHURCH
BH23 5AN
Poetry.

Helen ALLINSON
34 Woodstock Road
SITTINGBOURNE
ME10 4HN
* Borden: A History of the Kentish Parish - Recently reprinted. A comprehensive account of the village through the ages, 200 pages, A4 size, 8 pages of plates and maps. £10 plus £2.15 p&p.

ALMA PUBLISHERS
18 Evelyn Road
Ham
RICHMOND
TW10 7HU
History of Education.

ALMERIA PRESS
127 High Street
TEDDINGTON

ALOES BOOKS
69 Lancaster Road
LONDON
N4 4PL
Poetry.

ALO-WA
c/o Southwark Women's Centre
2-8 Peckham High Street
LONDON
SE15 5DY
Biography.

ALPHA CHART Ltd
6a High Street
Aldreth
ELY
CB6 3PQ

ALSRATH PUBLICATIONS
263 Station Road
Balsall Common
COVENTRY
CV7 7EG

ALTERNATIVE ARTS
49-51 Carnaby Street
LONDON
W1V 1PF
Art.

JOURNAL OF ALTERNATIVE & COMPLEMENTARY MEDICINE
53A High Street
BAGSHOT
GU19 5AH

ALTERNATIVE TENTACLES
Ms Elaine McIntosh
61-71 Collier Street
LONDON
N1 9BE

Alick ALTMAN
118 Bilton Lane
HARROGATE
HG1 3DG
General Fiction.

ALUN BOOKS:
Goldleaf Publishing
2nd Floor Royal Buildings

PORT TALBOT
Poetry.

ALWYN PRESS
14 Alwyn Avenue
LONDON
W4 4PB

AMANUENSIS
12 Station Road
DIDCOT
OX11 7LL

AMAR PUBLICATIONS
31 Watling Street
BURY
BL8 2JD

THE AMATE PRESS
Robin Waterfield
St. John's Lodge
14A Magdalen Road
OXFORD
OX4 1RW
Tel 01865 722 091
Founded in 1973 we have published over 60 volumes of biography poetry and religious with contributions by Iris Murdoch, Graham Greene, Anne Ridler, AM Allchin & Bishop John Taylor Aldwinckle.

AMAZING AMAZING AMAZING
BCM Amazing
LONDON
WC1N 3XX
Amazing stuff from whatever comes off the top of my head when I do a multi-media thing. Any girls out there into multi-media: poetry kite-flying Psu Chi (healing through gentle poking with a stick) Film: Cobbing nose picking with rice paper etc. 'Amazing Things: The Final Thingy'. Magazine published when we've got enough stuff and we can use the copier at the Poly. Send your stuff and things and let's interlock in a global networkthingy. Anyone want an Ian Curtiss autographed picture disc of Love will Tear us Apart ?

AMAZING COLOSSAL PRESS
18 Hind Street
RETFORD
DN22 7EN

AMBIT
17 Priory Gardens
Highgate
LONDON
N6 5QY

AMCD PUBLISHERS LTD
PO Box 102
PURLEY
CR8 3YX
0181 668 4535
Chinese Japanese Russian - as well as French German & Spanish. More eclectically it publishes material on Croydon's history as well as that of Surrey.
* English - Japanese Dictionary of Finance (1992).

TORR A'MHULLAICH BOOKS
5 Kirkton Muir
Bunchren
INVERNESS
IV3 6RH

AMIGO BOOKS
Ken Sheldon
18 Summerhill Road
LAUNCESTON
PL15 7DU

AMMONITE BOOKS
58 Coopers Rise
GODALMING
GU7 2NJ
Health and Hygiene.

AMOEBA PUBLICATIONS
Lakeside Manor Farm
Crowland Road
Eye Green
PETERBOROUGH
PE6 7TT
Education.

AMPERSAND PRESS
Firedog Mothers
c/o #8
89 Lancaster Road
Ladbroke Grove
LONDON
W11 1QQ
Tel 0171 792 0341
A visual arts magazine intended to embody the best of, respectively, artists books and poetry/literature magazines. A bi-yearly publication in limited edition, featuring artists prints and exploiting the particularity of experience anything that lies flat concidered, no poems about Woodpeckers! Multiples preferred.

AMRA IMPRINT
21 Alfred Street
SEAHAM
SR7 7LH
Amra Imprint is the successor to Bill's 'Pirate Press' of the 1970s. It publishes booklets on Anglo-Saxon culture, local history and some modern poetry.

AMSKAYA
25 Albert Road
Addlestone
WEYBRIDGE
KT15 2PX

AMY JOHNSON APPRECIATION SOCIETY
Local History Unit
Park Street Centre
Hull College
Park Street
HULL
HU2 8RR
The Society has been founded to celebrate the memory of Amy Johnson (1903-1941). Newsletter. Issue number 2 now available. Subscription £5 cheques payable to H Purkis.

A.N. PUBLICATIONS
PO BOX 23
SUNDERLAND
SR4 6DG
Economics for Artists. Law for artists. Organising exhibitions.

ANANKES'S WOMON PUBLICATIONS
P.O. Box 1348
Madison Square Station
New York 10159
USA
New title: Poems of feminist intelligence officer.

ANARCHO PRESS
Stan Trevor
'Briagha'
Badninish
Donorch
SUTHERLAND
IV25 3JB
Aimed to extend consciousness to bring about a rational society. Method - publishing poetry etc.

A N C
P O Box 38
28 Penton Street
LONDON
N1 9PR

THE ANCIENT
82 Hythe Road
BRIGHTON
BN1 6FE
The Bi-monthly Review of Antiquity. ISSN 0953 2978. Published by George Lambor, edited by Ward Rutherford. The only publication devoted to the ancient and classical worlds. Read by all, with an interest in the distant past, whether as scholars or laymen. Typical articles: Jersey's La Hougue Bie, a monument older than the pyramids; Why Nero wasn't all bad; Mummy labels, how the dead were identified. £1.80 per issue. Subscriptions for one year (6 issues): £10.00 in the UK; £12.00 in Europe; £15.00 elsewhere abroad; £21.00 to the rest of the world. Payment by VISA accepted.

ANDERSON FRASER PUBLISHING
230-232 Holloway Road
LONDON
N7 8DA
Recycled Papers.

ANDIUM PRESS
Haut du Mont
La Haule
JERSEY
Channel Islands

ANDRED PUBLISHING
Pennies
Church Lane
Sheering
BISHOP'S STORTFORD

CHRIS ANDREWS PHOTOGRAPHIC ART
1 North Hinksey Village
OXFORD
OX2 0NA
Local Travel Guides.

Sue ANDREWS
17 Manor Road
Bildeston
IPSWICH
IP7 7BG
Brett Valley Histories feature aspects of Local History from the towns and villages through which the River Brett flows in South Suffolk. Latest No. 16 Working on the Land: Farming in Bildeston 300 years ago. Booklets under £1 plus p&p.

AND WHAT OF TOMORROW
(see Woodmans Press)
Editor Jay Woodman
14 Hillfield
SELBY
YO8 0ND

ANGLICA PRESS
18A Lake Road
Hamworthy
POOLE
BH15 4LH
Poetry.

ANGLO-SAXON BOOKS
Tony and Pearl Linsell
Frithgarth
Thetford Forest Park
Hockwold-cum-Wilton
NORFOLK
IP26 4NQ
Tel/fax 01842 828 430
We specialise in Old English Texts and things Anglo-saxon from monastic sign language through Old English verse to runes. Future publications are planned on Anglo-Saxon Herbs and Anglo-Saxon Plants and Food. Catalogue available.

ANIMALS
Jonathon Rooks
Selborne Agencies Limited
25 Selborne Road
SIDCUP
DA14 4QP
Tel 0181 302 1629
Publish bi-monthly colour conservation magazine reporting on captive breeding programmes, information on events at zoological gardens, reviewing activities of the Zoo world.

ANOMALOUS PHENOMENON REVIEW
Nottingham UFO Investigation Society
443 Meadow Lane
NOTTINGHAM
NG2 3LF

ANPAR BOOKS
11 South Park Gardens
BERKHAMSTED
HP4 1JA
Animals.

AN POST
General Post Office
DUBLIN 1
Republic of Ireland
Stamps.

Robin ANSELL
Yeovil Library
King George Street
YEOVIL
BA20 1PY
Batten's South Somerset Villages (1894) has been reprinted, charting the history of 10 villages surrounding Yeovil. Includes details of families, houses, churches and rare early photographs. New introduction by Robin Ansell ALA. £12.50 + £1.50 p&p (cheques payable to Somerset County Council).

ANTI ANTI INFORMATION NETWORK
37 Pamplins
BASILDON
SS15 5RN
In the run up to Armageddon we will be concentrating on publishing experimental writing and poetry. We will be specifically trying to push the boundaries of the written

word to its limits and beyond. We will use any means available to us in this quest. Send sase.

ANTI COPYRIGHT
PO Box 368
CARDIFF
CF2 1SQ
Worldwide distribution for agit/ scuril. fly-posters/art. Subversion and supercessionist.

ANTIQUE ATLAS PUBLICATIONS
31A High Street
EAST GRINSTEAD
RH19 3AF
Antique Maps.

ANVIL BOOKS LTD
45 Palmerston Road
DUBLIN 6
Ireland

ANVIL PRESS POETRY
69 George Street
LONDON
SE10 5BX
Recently published work by E.A. Markham, Anthony Howell, Michael Hamburger, Ivan V. Lalic, Tony Connor, Luis de Gongora.

ANYTHING GOES
Steve Langton
39 Oswald Crescent
ASHBOURNE
DE6 1FS
Cross genre zine – cinema, video, lazer disks, books.

APORIA PRESS
308 Camberwell New Road
LONDON
SE5 0RW
Aporia Press publishes a variety of titles, ranging from 17th century TRACTS to contemporary polemic. MSS NOT solicited. Distributed by Counter Productions (qv). Write for our full list of numinous wonders.

APOSTLE PRESS
Mr Theo Fossel
119 Station Road
BEACONSFIELD
HP9 1LG
Book on walking-sticks has sold thousands. Sticks available too.

APOSTROPHE
Mrs Diana Andersson
41 Canute Road
FAVERSHAM
ME13 8SH
Apostrophe, is a poetry magazine now in its sixth year, welcomes poems in translation & well crafted poetry on any topic. Published in March & September. Annual subscription £4.50

APPROACH POETS
28 Grosvenor Wharf Road
LONDON
E14 3EF
Poetry.

APRA PRESS
S.W. Honley
443 Meadow Lane
NOTTINGHAM
NG2 3GB
Tel 01602 874 615
Local History and Folklore Publishing research into both. Short

run publications for groups individuals and societies. Typesetting Graphic design etc.

A.P.T. Books
Bryntirion
Llanfair Caereinion
WELSHPOOL
SY21 0BZ
Air Transport.

ANTIQUARIAN ARROW
BCM Opal
LONDON
WC1N 3XX

ARBOR VITAE PRESS
Jonathan M. Wood
BM Spellbound
LONDON
WC1N 3XX
Distinctive & modest press producing limited edition pamphlets & books on romantic, rural, anachronistic & mystical themes. Latest title: 'Chedworth and Other Sights,' by Annabel Thomas. September 1995. A volume of poems on the Cotswolds. £4.99 unsigned. £6.99 signed. 125 copies perfect bound.

AQUARIUS
6th Floor
The White House
111 New Street
BIRMINGHAM

ARAMBY PUBLISHING
1 Alanbrooke Close
KNAPHILL
GU21 2RU
Poetry booklets.

ARC PUBLICATIONS
Nanholme Mill
Shaw Wood Road
TODMORDEN
OL14 6DA

ARCADIAN
(Gothic Garden Press)
Mike Boland
30 Byron Court
HARROW
HA1 1JT

ARCHANGEL PRESS
6 Sluvad Road
Panteg
PONTYPOOL
NP4 0SX

D. ARCHER
The Pentre
Kerry
NEWTOWN
SY16 4PD
Maps. Bibliography.

ARCHETYPE PUBLICATIONS
31-34 GORDON SQUARE
LONDON
WC1H 0PY

ARCHITECTURAL ASSOCIATION GRADUATE SCHOOL
34-36 Bedford Square
LONDON
WC1B 3ES
Tel 0171 636 0974 fax 0171 4140782 & 6360996.
List of other publications available; mail order only, distributed by

SCHEMA, 401 1/2 Workshops, 401 Wandsworth Road, London SW8 2JP.
* 'Design of Educational Buildings,' 1995, Primer £20, Examples £20, Set (Primer, Examples, Database, Bibliography & Posters) £65.
* 'Solar Energy and Housing Design,' 1994, 2 vols £15 each, Set £25.

ARCHITECTURAL PUBLICATIONS
182 Ralenhill Road
BELFAST
BT6 8EE
Local History.

ARCTURUS BOOKS
I. Hayes
The New House
East Grafton
MARLBOROUGH
SN8 3DB
Mail-order service for esoteric and occult. Same address for the Blue Angel imprint.

ARDO PUBLISHING COMPANY
Methlick
ELLON
AB41 0HR
Fiction General.

ARESTOS PUBLICATIONS
11 Redhill Crescent
Wollaston
WELLINGBOROUGH
NN9 7SX
Literature.

ARGO PRESS
The Ruins
32a Dale Street
YORK
YO2 1AE
Offer quality works in the following areas; fiction; autobiography & biography; history; mythology and psychology; childrens books and music publishing.

ARIADNE PUBLICATIONS
56 Whiting Road
GLASTONBURY
BA6 8HR
British Mythology.

ARK PUBLICATIONS
PO Box 150
PLYMOUTH
PL1 1AX

ARKEN BOOKS
108 Aviemore Way
BECKENHAM
BR3 3RT

ARLEN HOUSE
1 Middle Street
GALWAY
Ireland

ARMA PUBLICATIONS
PO Box 2299
BARNET
EN5 5PN
Education.

ARNCLIFFE PUBLISHING
Roseville Business Park
Roseville Road
LEEDS
LS8 5DR
36 Books.

ARNISTON RANGERS F.C.
73 Hunterfield Road
GOREBRIDGE
EH23 4TS
Football History.

Christopher J ARNOLD
Bronawel
Green Lane
ABERMULE
SY15 6LB
Self-publisher.

ARTENN MAAT
Dr B J Cocksey
PO Box 197
EPSON
KT17 1YJ
Books and booklets on psychic research, coincidence, inspiration and evidence of intelligence beyond current ideas of space and time. The emphasis is on rigorous genuinely open-minded scientific enquiry. Artenn Maat would like to hear from anyone with relevant experience.

ARTIQUE PRESS
Edwards Centre
Regents Street
HINCKLEY
LE10 0BB
Customs and Folklore.

ARTISAN
45 Kew Road
Failsworth
MANCHESTER
M35 9LB
Historical Biography.

ARTISTS' COLLECTIVE GALLERY
166 High Street
EDINBURGH
EH1 1QS
Art.

ARTMUSIQUE PUBLISHING COMPANY
31 Perry Hill
LONDON
SE6 4LF

ARTRAGE
28 Shacklewell Lane
LONDON
E8 2EZ

ART SALES INDEX
1 Thames Street
WEYBRIDGE
KT13 8JG
Art.

ARTSCAPE
Orrel
Fish Street
SHREWSBURY
Folklore.

ASSET BOOKS LTD
Dr A W Holmes
1 Tanners Dean
LEATHERHEAD
KT22 8RU

ASHBRAKEN
14 Cropwell Road
Radcliffe-on-Trent
NOTTINGHAM
NG12 2FS
Geography.

ASHBY LANE PRESS
Mr B K Foster
Ashby Lane
BITTESWELL
LE17 4SQ

ASHDOWN PUBLISHING
104 High Street
STEYNING
BN4 3RD
Art. Handicrafts.

ASH TREE PUBLICATIONS
Ash Tree Close
Baghill Road
West Ardsley Tingley
WAKEFIELD
WF3 1DF
School Textbook.

ASHWATER PUBLISHING
68 Tranmere Road
TWICKENHAM
TW2 7JB

(The) ASIAN WEEKLY
Cross Lances Road
HOUNSLOW
TW3 2AD

**ASIAN WOMEN'S WRITING
FORUM MAGAZINE (AWWF)**
c/o 1 Ferndown Street
BRADFORD
BD5 9QT

ASIA PUBLISHING HOUSE
45 Museum Street
LONDON
W1

ASIAN WOMEN'S NETWORK
c/o London Women's Centre
Wesley House
4 Wild Court
LONDON
WC2B 5AU

ASPECT
33a High Street
Thatcham
NEWBURY
RG13 4JG

ASSET BOOKS LTD
Dr A W Holmes
1 Tanners Dean
LEATHERHEAD
KT22 8RU

**ASSOCIATION OF LITTLE PRESSES
(ALP)**
111 Banbury Road
OXFORD
OX2 6XJ
*Publishes PALPI, a newsletter and a
year book. ALP was formed in
1966 to bring together and assist
small presses of all types and
persuasions. (See entries in
Resource Directory and DIY Guide.)*

ASTON PRESS
Joan Selby-Lowndes
22 Church Lane
Aston Rowant
OXFORD
OX9 5SS

ASTRA PRESS
20 Candleby Lane
Cotgrave
NOTTINGHAM
NG12 3JG
ASTRAPOST

7 The Towers
STEVENAGE
SG1 1HE

ASYLUM MAGAZINE
Mr Bob Haynes
7 Walmersley Road
New Moston
MANCHESTER
M10 0RS
*Magazine 'Chimera' uses strips
and short stories*

ATD PUBLICATIONS
10 Wykeley Road
Wyken
COVENTRY
CV2 3DW

ATELIER BOOKS
4 Dundas Street
EDINBURGH
EH3 6HZ
Biography.

AT THE EDGE
Editor/proprietor: Bob Trubshaw
2 Cross Hill Close
Wymeswold
LOUGHBOROUGH
LE12 6UJ
Tel/Fax 01509 880 725
*Quarterly magazine 'exploring new
interpretations of past and place in
archaeology, folklore and
mythology,' £2 per issue, ann.sub.
UK £7, Europe £8, rest of world
(air mail) £11; ISSN 1361-0058.*

ATHOL BOOKS
10 Athol Street
BELFAST
BT12 4GX
*Local History. Education. Irish
History.*

**ATLANTIC EUROPE PUBLISHING
COMPANY**
86 Peppard Road
Sonning Common
READING
RG4 9RP

ATLANTIS PRESS
Michael Dainiell
1 Wolvercote Court
Wolvercote Green
OXFORD
OX2 8AB

ATLAS PRESS
BCM Atlas Press
LONDON
WC1N 3XX
*Emissions of the anti-tradition.
Specialists in surrealism,
'pataphysics and logorrhoetics of
surprising virulence. Trade editions
(distributed by Airlift) and the
limited edition series 'The Printed
Head'.*

ATMA ENTERPRISES
Christopher Gilmore
13 Bull Pitch
DURSLEY
GLU 4NG
Tel 01582 405 354
*Talking books of family fables four
illustrated by gifted teenagers
stories written and read by
Christopher Gilmore. 'At once
funny fantastic exciting
andenchanting...filled with light*

*and laughter.'Artswest. Books and/
or tapes: telling tales. Snow Ghosts.
Horace Hedgehog etc.*

ATTIC BOOKS
The Folly
Rhosgoch
BUILTH WELLS
LD2 3JY
Biography.

AUGURIES
Editor N Norton
48 Anglesey Road
Alverstoke
GOSPORT
PO12 2EQ

A.U.L. Publishing
Queen Mother Library
Meston walk
ABERDEEN
AB9 2UE
Photography.

AULTON PRESS
Aulton Croft
Ardallie
PETERHEAD
AB4 8BP
Poetry.

AURORA
Unit 9C
Bradley Fold Trading Estate
Radcliffe Moor Road
Bradley Fold
BOLTON
BL2 6RT
* Cargreaves, Kate. 'Journey to
Our Children.' £8.95. True story of
infertility treatments and adoption
maze.
* Nicklin, John. 'Trawling With the
Lid Off.' £9.95. The lives of
trawlermen, the hardships of fishing
vessels, the injustices. B&W photos
including images of the eruption of
Surtsey Island.

AURELIUS BOOKS
Diane Balshaw
116 Slater Lane
Leyland
PRESTON
PR5 3SE
*Aurelius Press, publishes the novels
of Frances Aumerle. It has
published one title so far:
"Richelieu and the Power Factor" a
story of intrigue at the court of
Louis XIII.*

AUSSTEIGER PUBLICATIONS
8 Back Skipton Road
BARNOLDSWICK
BB8 5NE
Tel 01282 812 741
*Through the medium of an
enjoyable day's walking we aim to
bring to the fore the economic and
social history of the Pennine and
Dales region that all can gain from
- truly journeys of exploration.*

Matthew D. AUSTIN
22A Chief's Street
ELY
CB6 1AT
Photographic Record Local History.

AUTHORS' PUBLISHING GUILD
Peter Gilles
Spoods Farm
Tinkers Lane

Hadlow Down
UCKFIELD
TN22 4ET
Tel 01825 830 319

AUX
64 Beechgrove
Brecon
POWYS
LD3 9ET
Tel 01874 625 725
*AUX serves as a clearing house for
flyers, maverick information,
incendiary artwork, eclectic
paraphernazia and specializing in
autonomous publishing. Many
items are not intended for sale and
are only avaliable on an exchange
basis or for a substantial cash
incentive.*

AVEC DESIGNS
PO Box 709
BRISTOL
BS99 1GE
*Education for the Deaf. Education
for the Disabled. Books.*

AVENUES PRESS
117 Park Avenue
HULL
HU5 3EX
Local History.

AVERNUS
35 Fishers Lane
LONDON
W4 1RX

AVERT
PO Box 91
HORSHAM
RH13 7YR
*Avert is an Aids charity producing
publications on Aids and HIV
infection. Current titles include:-
Prisons, HIV & Aids; A Survey of
Aids Education in Secondary
Schools; Positively Primary (a book
for primary school teachers).*

AVES PUBLICATIONS
5 Athol Street
DOUGLAS
Isle of Man
Art.

AVON POETRY NEWS
(see PENNYFIELDS PRESS)

AWAY PUBLICATIONS
PO Box 2173
BATH
BA1 3TJ
Tel 01225 338 269
*A small independent press
specialising in creative fiction and
non-fiction. Two titles in 1997.*

aw-Ra BOOKs
Ms Heather Haig
BCM aw-Ra
LONDON
WC1N 3XX
*Reporting the cause and effect of
growing irresponsibility towards
domestic animals. "Action for
animals" series has eight titles
including 'Chasing Shadows.'*

AXLETREE COMMUNICATIONS
10 Merebank Lane
CROYDON
CR0 4NP

AYLESFORD PRESS
158 Moreton Road
UPTON
Wirral
L49 4NZ
Poetry.

David AYRES
11A Batford Road
HARPENDEN
AL5 5AX
Poetry

B4 PUBLISHING
3 Tyers Gate
LONDON
SE1 3HX

B & B PUBLISHERS
31 St Martin's Road
CAERPHILLY
CF8 1EF

B & W Publications
7 Sciennes
EDINBURGH
EH9 1NH

Ann BABER
22 Lawrence Close
WESTON-SUPER-MARE
BS22 9EX
Food and Drink.

BACK BRAIN RECLUSE MAGAZINE
16 Somersall Lane
CHESTERFIELD
S40 3LA
*A Magazine that aims to expand
the literary taste of readers by
publishing the more experimental
forms of speculative fiction; by
moulding an outlet for new writers
and artists and by reviewing/
publicising other magazines in this
field.
Back Brain Recluse Magazine. ISSN
0269-9990. Published quarterly. 4
issue subscription £6.30. Writers'
guidelines available for sae.*

BACKGAMMON
61 Dunsmure Road
LONDON
N16 5PT

D.H. BACON
3 The Glade
Crapstone
YELVERTON
PL20 7PR
Industry.

BACSA
76.5 Chartfield Avenue
LONDON
SW15 6

**BAD PRESS
(see Breakfast All Day)**
Chisenhale Works
64/68 Chisenhale Road
LONDON
E3 5EZ
*Breakfast All Day Magazine/comic
publications.*

BADGERS BOOKS
Charles Walker
Flat 1
12 Western Place
WORTHING
BN11 3LU
*Look to publish material relating to
ongoing occult activities and
exposure of satanic/macabre
groups throughout UK. Occasional
newsletter "Mysteries" also
available (free with sae).*

BADGER PUBLISHING
Unit 1
Parsons Green Estate
Boulton Road
STEVENAGE
SG1 4QG
School Textbooks.

BAD TASTE PUBLICATIONS
John Seager
24 Hartham Road
LONDON
N7 9JG
*Specialists in contemporary adult
and not so adult humour that hasn't
been hijacked by cartoon-strip
merchants, at the expence of
scribblers.*

BAD WRITER'S PRESS
c/o Artworks
Barrow Borough Council
Piel View House Abbey Road
BARROW-IN-FURNESS
LA13 9BD
Poetry.

THE BAETYL PRESS
98 Fairfoot Road
Mile End
LONDON
E3 4EH

DUNCAN BAIRD PUBLISHERS
6th Floor
Castle House
75/76 Wells Street
LONDON
W1P 3RE

Lesley BAIRSTOW
5 Chelsea Manor Court
Chelsea Manor Street
LONDON
SW3 5SA
*Paradise Walk - Chelsea: 88
pages, A5, many illustrations,
photos, maps. A comprehensive
historical account of Old Paradise
Walk near the Royal Hospital*

*1796-1994. Also contains general
Chelsea history. Available from
above at £5.49 incl postage.*

BALANOSTER PRESS
P.O. Box 67
CARLISLE
CA4 9DE

BALCOMBE BOOKS
PO Box 101
EPSOM
KT19 9GY

BALDER
60 Elmhurst Road
READING
RG15 5HY

JIM BALDWIN PUBLISHING
Graham Pooley
11 Smith Lane
FAKENHAM
NR21 8LQ
Local History.

Mark BALDWIN
24 High Street
Cleobury Mortimer
KIDDERMINSTER
DY14 8BY
Tel 01299 270110
*Transport; particularly inland
waterways and local history and
topography.*

BALLINAKELLA PRESS
WHITEGATE
County Clare
Republic of Ireland
*Small publishing house producing
mainly Irish and European
historical and topographical books.
Three main series: People & Places
(of Irish clans), Houses of Irish
Counties, Biographies. Also
Ballinakella paperbacks of
International interest and
Bell'acards, post and greeting
cards of high quality.*

BAM Books
159 Warwick Road
SOLIHULL
B92 7AR

Frank BAMFORD
9 Malvern Drive
ALTRINCHAM
WA14 4NQ
Local History.

BANK PRESS
8 Bank House
Grains Road
OLDHAM
OL2 8JG

BANNATYNE BOOKS
R. Court
6 Bedford Road
LONDON
N8 8HL

BANNERWORKS
1st Floor
Kings Head Buildings
Cloth Hall Street
HUDDERSFIELD
HD1 2EF
*Yorkshire based community arts
group. Banners, murals,
photography, fabrics and graphics.*

BANTON PRESS
75 Nelson Street
LARGS
KA30 9AB
*Customs and Folklore. Occult.
History of Religion. Archaeology.
Place Names. Philosophy. All
facsimile editions.*

BARE BONES
16 Wren Close
FROME
BA11 2UZ
*The bare bones press is devoted to
Haiku and other forms of poetry in
miniature. A quarterly magazine
and occasional chapbooks are
published. A mail order booklist of
haiku titles from the USA and
Japan is available.*

David and Jocelyn BARKER
47 Sayes Court
ADDLESTONE
KT15 1NA
Local History.

**RICHARD ALAN BARNES
PUBLICATIONS**
118 Watling Street
Grendon
ATHERSTONE
CV9 2PE
Tel 01827 713360
*Publisher of scholarly books on
historic organs and historic
instruments in historic places. Also:
other interests include music of a
general nat ure and music in
education.*

BARN OWL BOOKS
Westowe Farmhouse
Lydeard St Lawrence
TAUNTON
TA4 3SH
*Reference book for collectors of
detective fiction.*

BARNS PUBLICATIONS
14 High Elm Road
Hale Barns
ALTRINCHAM
WA15 0HS

BARNY BOOKS
The Cottage
Hough-on-the-Hill
GRANTHAM
NG32 2BB

BAROS BOOKS
Edwin Banfield
5 Victoria Road
TROWBRIDGE
BA14 7LH
Tel 01225 752915
*Publisher of books on barometers
and meteorological instruments.*

BARRINGTON BOOKS
Bartle Hall
Liverpool Road
Hutton
PRESTON
PR4 5HB
Tel 01772 616816
*We aim to promote the new
movement of experimental,
sociopolitical Science Fiction, by
publishing an annual collection of
original short stories by new and
established writers. High standards*

of writing and production. Writers please send S.A.E. for our manifesto.

Louis BARROW
184B Wisbech Road
MARCH
PE15 8EZ
General Fiction

Mr G P BARTLETT
Adams Farm, The Street
North Warnborough
BASINGSTOKE
RG25 1BL
Publishers of 'How to...' advice books and educational cassettes.

BARTLETTS PRESS
39a Kildare Terrace
LONDON
W2

THE BARTON PRESS
30 Broomy Hill
HEREFORD
HR4 0LH

David BARTON
45 Wellmeadow Road
Hither Green
LONDON
SE13 6SY
Tel 081 698 3392
Self-publisher collections or drawings in related sequences. Artists Books. Mainly line drawings with occasional texts. Also a number of books in collaborationwith poets comprising line drawings and poems/prose all relating to the human figure.

BARTON HOUSE PUBLISHING and Datacraft Publications
9 Barton Orchard
BRADFORD-ON-AVON
BA15 1LU
We publish new age (Barton House) and new age titles, selling them through the book trade and direct mail. We are now moving into audio and combined print/audio.

THE BASEMENT PRESS
Peter Gould
Basement Flat
29 Burrell Road
IPSWICH
IP2 8AH
The Basement Press is a one -man show specialising in small books & broadsides printed by letterpress, with wood-engraved illustrations. Titles: "A Southwold Alphabet" "Sir Thomas Browne: On Dreams"

BASEMENT WRITERS
Sally Flood
23 Mount Terrace, Turner St
Tower Hamlets
LONDON
E1 2BB
Tel 0171 247 1854
We publish new writers. Have been meeting & publishing since 1973, & are a non profit making group.

BASSET PUBLICATIONS
60 North Hill
PLYMOUTH
PL4 8HF

BAST'S BLEND PUBLICATIONS
P.O. Box 9600
OBAN
Argyll
PA34 4BP
Also publish books on paganism, Gaian theory, social chaos, parapsychology and related topics. Newly self-published title:
* *Spence, Iain. The Sekhmet hypothesis. ISBN 0952536501, £2.00 + £1.00 p&p.*

BATSTONE BOOKS
Aurobindo Ashram
12 Gloucester Street
MALMESBURY
SN16 0AA
Biography. Philosophy.

BATTLE OF BRITAIN PRINTS INTERNATIONAL
Church House
Church Street
LONDON
SE15 3JA

BAULKING TOWERS PUBLICATIONS
David Caldwell
Baulking Towers
UFFINGTON
SN7 7QE
Local sports, local authors, rural satirical magazine.

BAVERSTOCK BOOKS
50 Westbury Leigh
WESTBURY

C. BAXTER PHOTOGRAPHY
Unit 2/3 Block 6
Caldwellside Industrial Estate
LANARK
ML11 6SR
Biography. Mammals. Birds.

BAY FOREIGN LANGUAGE BOOKS
19 Dymchurch Road
St. Mary's Bay
ROMNEY MARSH
TN29 0ET
Language.

BB Books
A. Shaw
1 Springbank
Longsight Road
Copster Green
BLACKBURN
BB1 9EU
Poetry pamphlet & literary magazine publishers. Specialising in innovative & creative writing. Post-Beat poetics & counter-culture theoretics, iconoclastic rants & anarchic psycho-cultural tracts.

BBNO
Tapping Well Farm
Burrowbridge
BRIDGWATER
TA7 0RY
Food & Drink.

BBR DESIGN
Chris Reed
16 Somersall Lane
CHESTERFIELD
S40 3LA

BEACON BOOKS
Malvern
23 Worcester Road
MALVERN

WR14 4QY
Walks Books.

BEAMSCAN
20 Vaughan Avenue
LONDON
NW4 4HU

BEAN PRESS
5 Vauxhall Crescent
Castle Bromwich
BIRMINGHAM
B36 9JP

BEAUCLERK PUBLISHING
29 The Gilberts
Sea Road
RUSTINGTON

BEAUFORT PUBLISHING LTD
PO Box 22
LIPHOOK
GU30 7PJ
Tel 0142 876 588
A specialist publisher of reference books in the field of military architecture - hillforts castles fortifications - from architectural archaeo logical historical and military points of view. 'Fortress' - The Castles and Fortifications Quarterly edited by Andrew Saunders. 64pp. 70 illustrations. £18.00 per annum. Leading journal with professional and lay enthusiast readership. 'Military Architecture' by Quentin Hughes. 256pp. 400 illustrations. £25.00. A broad survey of the art of defence from earliest times to the second World War. 'Fortress Britain' by Andrew Saunders. 256pp 255 illustrations. £20.00. A history of fortification in the British Isles and Ireland since the introduction of artillery.

BECCON PUBLICATIONS
75 Rosslyn Avenue
Harold Wood
ROMFORD
RM3 0RG

BECK BOOKS
29 St. Mary's Mount
Station Road
COTTINGHAM
HU16 4LQ
Hull Jazz.

Richard BECK
49 Curzon Avenue
STANMORE
HA7 2AL
Mathematics.

Stan BECKINSALE
4 Leazes Crescent
HEXHAM
NE46 3JX
Archaeology.

BECKSIDE DESIGN
18 Willowfield Avenue
Nettleham
LINCOLN
LN2 2TH

BEDFORD TO BLETCHLEY RAIL USERS ASSOC.
23 Hatfield Crescent
BEDFORD
MK41 9RA

Newsletter for members, outings on old trains to nationwide destinations, exhibitions.

BEDLAM PRESS
Church Green House
Old Church Lane
Pateley Bridge
HARROGATE
HG3 5LZ
Publishes only long poems or sequences of poems informed by some political consciousness.

J. BEE
Computer Bureau
Carlton House
Whassett
MILNTHORPE
LA7 7DN
Short Stories.

BEECH PUBLISHING HOUSE
15 The Maltings
Turk Street
ALTON
GU34 1DL
Poetry. Stockbreeding. Pets.

BEECHES PRESS
John Pitt
44 Marsala Road
LONDON
SE13 7AD
Fine Printer.

Robert BEECH
11 Springwood View Close
SUTTON-IN-ASHFIELD
NG17 2HR
Family History.

BEESWAX SCORPION PRESS
154 Blake Road
West Bridgford
NOTTINGHAM
NG2 5JZ

BEIHIREYO BOOKS
Mrs AK Turya
60 St. Fabians Drive
CHELMSFORD
CM1 2PR
Tel 01245 261079
Publishing medical, nursing and heath care books and manuals; and handbooks for secondary school level subjects on heath issues; and communication skills.

BELAIR PUBLICATIONS
PO BOX 12
TWICKENHAM
TW1 2QL

BEL-AIR PRESS
7E Sharp Street
GOUROCK
PA19 1UL
Sport.

BELFRY BOOKS
118 St. Pancras
CHICHESTER
PO19 4LH
Short Stories.

BELHAVEN PUBLISHERS
8 King's Saltern Road
LYMINGTON
SO41 9QF

BELLCODE BOOKS
10 Ridge Bank
TODMORDEN

OL14 7BA

BELLEROPHON
Manchester House
Church Hill, Slindon
ARUNDEL
BM18 0RD
Fiction, aviation history, psychology and paranormal investigation.

BELLEVIRE PUBLISHING TRUST
8/5 Ehrickdale Place
EDINBURGH
EH3 5JN

PETER BELL (Bookseller)
4 Brandon Street
EDINBURGH
EH3 5DX
Bibliographies.

BELLY-LAUGH BOOKS
18 Sefton Press
LEIGH
WN7 1LX
Children's Fiction.

BELTANE FIRE
Kevin & Ingrid Carlyon
16 Cross Street
ST LEONARDS ON SEA

BELVOIR BOOKS
The Chapel
Redmile
NOTTINGHAM
NG13 0GA

BEMERTON PRESS
9 Hamilton Gardens
LONDON
NW8 9PO

BENET BOOKS
Sunnyside
Derrythorpe
SCUNTHORPE
DN17 8EY

BENEVENAGH BOOKS
89 Springfield Road
New Elgin
ELGIN
IV30 3BZ
History of Local Aviation.

BENJAMIN PRESS
69 Hillcrest Drive
BATH
BA2 1HD
Poetry.

Benjamin RUTH
384 Barks Drive
Norton
STOKE-ON-TRENT
ST6 8EU
Produce the Journal of the Astrological Research Gabriel Order. Publish own ideas on Occult Mechanisms of Manifestations.

BENTOS PUBLISHING COMPANY
52 Melville Road
Stillorgan
BLACKROCK
County Dublin
Republic of Ireland
Historical Biography.

Jacob J BERGER
174 Plum Lane
LONDON
SE18 3HF
Philosophy. Russian Literature.

BERKS BUCKS & OXON NATURALISTS' TRUST
3 Church Cowley Road
Rose Hill
OXFORD
OX4 3JR
Wild Life.

BERKSHIRE, PROVINCIAL GRAND LODGE OF
Berkshire Free Masonic Centre
Mole Road
Sindlesham
WOKINGHAM
RG11 5DR

BERKSWELL PUBLISHING
PO Box 420
WARMINSTER
BA12 9XB
Books on Wessex, field sports, or what is broadly called our heritage. Lead titles include: 'History of Fox Hunting in South West Wiltshire.' ISBN 0904631 08 7. 'Walking in Lesser Known Mendip.' ISBN 0904631 10 9.

BERNICA BOOKS
11 The Ridge
RYTON
NE40 3LN
Local History.

BERRYDALES BOOKS
5 Lawn Road
LONDON
NW3 2XS
Food.

BERTRAND RUSSELL PEACE FOUNDATION
Bertrand Russell House
Gamble St
NOTTINGHAM
NG7 4ET

BERWICK PUBLISHERS
Argosy Libraries
96 Haddington Road
DUBLIN
Republic of Ireland

BESSACARR PRINTS
Historic Scotland
20 Brandon Street
EDINBURGH
EH3 5RA

BEST PUBLISHING COMPANY
High Gillerthwaite
Ennerdale
CLEATOR
CA23 3AX

BETE NOIRE
Editor John Osborne
American Studies Dept
The University
Cottingham Road
HULL
HU6 7RI

BETJEMANIAN
c/o Mr E Griffin
Manor Farm House
Queen Catherine Road
STEEPLE CLEYDON
MK18 2QF

BETTER PUBS
Old Chapel
Bottreaux Mill
SOUTH MOLTON

Trevor Allen BEVIS
28 St Peter's Road
MARCH
PE15 9NA
The Westrydale Press publishes studies of the Fens. Trevor has written more than 80 titles.

BEWICK PRESS
132 Claremont Road
WHITLEY BAY
NE6 3TX

BEYOND THE RISING SUN
530 Great Western Road
Kelvinbridge
GLASGOW
G12 8EL
Art.

BEYOND THE PALE PUBLICATIONS
7 Winetavern Street
BELFAST
N Ireland
BT1 1JQ

BHASVIC Resources
c/o Brighton Hove and Sussex
Sixth Form College
Dyke Road
HOVE
BN3 6EG
Social Sciences.

Mr Les BICKNELL
18 Fleets Road
Sturton By Stow
LINCOLN
LN1 2BU
Minimal environmental bookworks looking at the form from a sculptural perspective.

Mr Joe BIDDER
33 Queensdown Road
Hackney
LONDON
E5 8NN

Lawrence BIDDLE
The Woods
Leigh
TONBRIDGE
TN11 8NA
Local History.

JOSEPH BIDDULPH PUBLISHER
32 Stryd Ebeneser
PONTYPRIDD
CF37 5PB
Amazing selection of living and historic languages and other dialects rating as endangered species. Ask for latest additions. J.Biddulph also found under imprint 'Languages Information Centre' which publishes magazine 'Hrafnhoh,' an amalgam of genealogy, heraldry, poetry and review.

(THE) BIG ISSUE
4 Albion Place
Galena Road
Hammersmith
LONDON
W6 0LT
Tel 081-741-8090
(Fax 081-741-2951)

Ms Karen BILLING
Bindells Bookshop
20a North Street
SKIBBEREEN

West Cork
Irish Republic

BILLIONTH PRESS
45 Handforth Road
LONDON
SW9 0LL

BIOPRESS
The Orchard
Clanage Road
BRISTOL
BS3 2JX
Botany. Historical Biography.

BIRCH BOOK PRESS
P.O. Box 81
Delhi
NEW YORK 13753
USA
Hand crafted books. Popular culture, fascinating fiction, passionate poetry.

HINTON BIRD
Rushen Vicarage
PORT ST. MARY
Isle of Man
History of Education.

BIRDS HILL PUBLICATIONS
Maurice Sturgeon
24 Goldfinch Close
Birds Hill
CHELSFIELD
BR6 6NF
Tel/Fax 01689 850 859
'Half A Mo!' by Maurice Sturgeon. 44pp. £6. ISBN 1 900894009. A collection of stories and rhymes. The anecdotes and accounts relate to true events. The poems were mostly written to amuse, provoke and occasionally infuriate the author's family and friends. Author's acknowledgement of encouragement from Granville Writers. Also available on tape cassette at £5.00.

BIRDWORLD
Holt pound
FARNHAM
GU10 4LD
Birds.

BIRMINGHAM & MIDLAND INSTITUTE
9 Margaret Street
BIRMINGHAM
B3 3BS

BIRMINGHAM POLYTECHNIC
Department of English
Franchise Street
Perry Barr
BIRMINGHAM
Anthology by the writer in residence.

BIRMINGHAM PUBLISHING COMPANY
P.O. Box 1779
Quinton
BIRMINGHAM
B32 3AZ
Looking for business books - using USA marketing methods to promote titles.

BIRMINGHAM, UNIVERSITY OF
Faculty of Education
P.O. Box 363
BIRMINGHAM
B15 2TT

BISHOPSGATE INSTITUTE
230 Bishopsgate
LONDON
EC2M 4QH
History of Education.

BITTER EXPERIENCE PUBLISHERS
P.O. Box 10006
INVERURIE
AB51 5WX
NORRIS, D., 'Perils of the Policy, a layman's guide to the pitfalls of insurance,' 1995, 64 pp.pbk, £5.75. Frank report on marine insurance hazards. Publisher invites others to share experiences of dealings with insurers good or bad for next year's updated edition.

BLACK ACE ENTERPRISES
Mr Hunter Steele
Ellemford Farmhouse
DUNS
TD11 3SG
Publishing modest print runs of high quality editions.

BLACK ARTS IN LONDON
28 Shackewell Lane
LONDON
E8 2EZ

BLACKBOARD REVIEW
Unit 25 Devonshire House
High St
Deritend
BIRMINGHAM
B12 0LP

BLACK BOX PUBLISHING LTD
Ray Languedoc
11 Broadfield Close
Tong Street
BRADFORD
BD4 9SJ
Horror, Fantasy, Politics, Sci-Fi, Religion and Wildlife.

BLACK CAT BOOKS
Neil Miller
Mount Cottage
Grange Road, St. Michaels
TENTERDEN
TN30 6EE
'Tales of Horror,' & 'Tales of the Unexpected.' Editor Neil Miller. £2.25 each, £4.00 for two. October edition features R. Chetwynd-Hayes. We published two books last year. This year we are running a competition, 5000 words: mystery/ horror/crime/ comedy/unexpected. Do not send unsolicited mss. SAE for details.

BLACKCURRENT STAIN
Burdett Cottage
4 Burdett Place
HASTINGS
TN34 3ED

BLACK ECONOMY BOOKS
Dept. 8
1 Newton Street
Piccadilly
MANCHESTER
M1 1HW
Latest title is 'From Colditz to Bangladesh' a mixture of poetry, story, fairy-tale and graphics with the common theme of Childhood often to do with poverty, misery and the fun found despite all that.

52pp paperback, ISBN 1-901178 00 5, price £2.00. Also have a catalogue of previous publications.

BLACK FROG PRESS
14 Ramsey Close
Manton Heights
BEDFORD
MK41 7NE
Occult.

BLACKHEATH PUBLISHING
14 Greenwich Church Street
LONDON
SE10 9BJ
Plays.

MATT BLACK PUBLICATIONS
51 Pearson Place
SHEFFIELD
S8 9DE

BLACKOUT
c/o Jason Cobley
47 Borough Meadows
CATTERICK VILLAGE
DL10 7NX

BLACK PENNELL PRESS
Thomas Rae
36 Margaret Street
GREENOCK
PA16 8EA

BLACK SHEEP PRESS
Alan Henson
Coast Cottage
Donna Nook
LOUTH
LN11 7PA
Tel 01507 358 669
Email: alan@nook.netkonect.co.uk
Publications to assist children's speech & language development. Designed by speech & language therapists for use in school, home & clinic. Work sheets can be photocopied. Catalogue available. 'Language in Pictures,' 6 issues, from £4.75.
'Consonant Work Sheets,' 20 issues, from £4.50.

THE BLACKSMITH
Swords into Ploughshares
7 Plum Lane
LONDON
SE18 3AF

THE BLACK SWAN PRESS
28 Bosleys Orchard Grove
OX12 7JP

BLACKWATER BOOKS
45 Approach Road
LONDON
E2

BLACK WOMANTALK
Box 32
190 Upper Street
LONDON
N1 1RQ

BLACKWOODS PUBLISHERS
12A Crane Court
Fleet Street
LONDON
EC4A 2EJ
Tel 0171 583 3328

Brian BLAIR-GILES
Norbury Hall
Norbury Hall Park
55 Craignish Avenue

LONDON
SW16 4RW
Biography. Poetry.

Lewis BLAKE
Gordon Dennington
62 Park Hill Road
Shortlands
BROMLEY
BR2 0LF
Tel 0181 464 9260
Detailed factual accounts of south east London under air attack in World War II. Original research of unpublished material. Illustrated with original photos. Absorbing reading. Red Alert - Lewis Blake. Paperback 192pp revised 1992 £7.50 including postage). Bolts from the Blue - Lewis Blake. 94pp 1990 £4.00 (including postage). Covers V2 rock campaign.

R. BLAKE
Regent Cottage
13A Regent Parade
HARROGATE
HG1 5AW
Historical Biography.

Trudy BLAKE
25 Aked Close
Longsight
MANCHESTER
M12 4AN
Poetry.

BLANK PAGE
B4 Westminmster Business Square
Durham Street
LONDON
SE11 5JH
Limited editions of artists books. Signed prints.

ROB BLANN PUBLISHING
349 Tarring Road
WORTHING
BN11 5JL
Tel 01903 246587
Carefully researched and written by Rob Blann two fascinating books expose the joys and traumas of Victorian and Edwardian fishermen in a seaside resort - action-packed with daring lifeboat rescues colourful town parades civic events and some curious occurrences.
A Town's Pride: Victorian Lifeboatmen and Their Community. £9.95. ISBN 0 9516277 0 8. A4 soft cover 174pp 110 authentic photos.
Edwardian Worthing: Eventful Era in a Lifeboat Town. ISBN 0 9516277 1 6. A4 hardback 194pp 210 period photos.

ROYAL NATIONAL INSTITUTION FOR THE BLIND
224 Great Portland Street
LONDON
W1N 6AA

BLIND SERPENT PRESS
Brenda Shaw & John Glenday
65 Magdalen Yard Road
DUNDEE
DD2 1AL

BLORENGE BOOKS
3 Holywell Road
ABERGAVENNY
NP7 5LP

BLUE WINDOW BOOKS
53 Elderfield Road
LONDON
E5 0LF

BLUNTISHAM BOOKS
23 Priory Road
NEWCASTLE
ST5 2EL
Walks in the Falkland Islands.

BLUNT SLUG COMIC
Rikki Hollywood
62 Stanhope Road
GREENFORD
UB6 9EA
Tel 0181 578 7114
'If David Lynch wrote a comic - this would be it!' Sublime! (Speakeasy). When you were sperm you beat the rest of your batch to the egg - with that same enthus iasm. Send cheque/po £1.50 payable to R J Hollywood for double issue (1 and 2).

BLYTH SPIRIT
11 The Ridgway
FLITWICK
MK45 18H

BOB
3 Maidstone Street
Victoria Park
Bedminster
BRISTOL

BODY SHOP INTERNATIONAL
Hawthorn Road
Wick
LITTLEHAMPTON
BN17 7LR
Art.

BOGG (U K address)
George Cairncross
31 Belle Vue St
FILEY
YO14 9HU

BOGGART'S PRESS
3 Sutton Street
BLACKBURN
BB2 5ES

BOGLE L'OUVERTURE
52 Chignell Place
LONDON
W13 0TJ

BOJANGLES PRESS
J Bigotto
The Cosmic Centre
25 Acacia Avenue
ROMFORD
IG25 4GH
The truth is you can only be what you are and it can only be what it is. 'The It'. Quarterly Writings - Ed. Swami Nythanis (formerly Frank Nulty) £3.00 on rice pape; handwritten in the Psu Cha style.

BOLAND PUBLISHING
Bondway Business Centre
71 Bondway
LONDON
SW8 1SQ

THE BOLD PRESS
Kelvin Smith
7 Minster Road
OXFORD
OX4 1LX
Tel 01865 243095

The Bold Press was established in 1992 to bring to Europe writings from the Western States of America particularly works by Native American and Hispanic American writers.

THE BOLO PRESS
7 Mister Road
OXFORD
OX4 1LX

BON ACCORD PRESS
2 Park Crescent
STAFFORD
ST17 9BQ

BONAVENTURA PRESS
Janet Sloss
Scrubbetts
Bagpath
TETBURY
GL8 8YG
Dual-language Menorcan books. Bonventura Press opened in 1995 to publish author/owner's historical biography, after ten years of research, writing and vainly searching for a publisher.

BOOK ART PROJECT
Paul Johnson
30 Queenstown Road
MANCHESTER
M20 8NX
Paul Johnson is director of the Gulbenkian Foundation-funded BAP, based at Manchester Polytechnic, which aims to develop children's literacy through the book arts. He is also a successful book artist exhibiting widely.

THE BOOK CASTLE
Paul Bowes
12 Church Street
DUNSTABLE
Tel 01582 605670
Local interest titles primarily on Bedfordshire Herefordshire and Buckinghamshire walks autobiography History photographic country-side folklore childrens also retail bookseller. Changes in our Landscapes: Aspects of Bedfordshire Buckinghamshire and the Chilterns: Eric Meadows: 176pp 29.10.92 ISBN 1 871199 31 X £19.95 Leafing Through Literature: A4 hb colour/b-w photographs. Writers Lives in Herts and Bedfordshire: David Carroll: 208pp 3.9.92 £7.95 A5 p.b ISBN 1 871199 01 8. Swans in My Kitchen: The Story of a Swan Sanctuary: Lis Dorer: 88pp 29.9.92 £4.95 A5 pbk ISBN 1871199 16 6

BOOKMARQUE PUBLISHING
John Rose
26 Cotswold Close
Minster Lovell
WITNEY
OX8 5SX
Tel 01993 775179
Publishes approx. 8 titles a year, predominently filling gaps in motoring history although other titles as diverse as poetry & dieting!

BOOKS FOR KEEPS
6 Brightfield Road
Lee
LONDON

SE12 8QF
Bibliography.

BOOK HOUSE
Kirkby Stephen
Grey Garth
Ravenstonedale
KIRKBY STEPHEN
CA17 4NQ

BOOK TRUST
Scotland
15a Lynedock Street
GLASGOW
G3 6EF

BOOK SHOP (Home Counties)
20 High Street
Princes Risborough
AYLESBURY
HP17 0AX
Local History.

BOOKS UNLIMITED
Leslie Waller
69 Onslow Square
LONDON
SW7 3LS

BOOKWORKS
19 Holywell Row
LONDON
EC2A 4JB
Tel 0171 247 2536 fax 2540
Has been publishing artists' books since 1987 and has established itself as a leading independent publisher over recent years. Titles include works by Susan Hiller, Brian Catling, Chris Newman.

BOOTH-CLIBBORN EDITIONS
18 Colville Road
LONDON
W3 8BL

BORDER PRESS
The Outdoorsman's Bookstore
Llangorse
BRECON
LD3 7UE
Sport.

BORDERLINE PRODUCTIONS
P.O. 93
TELFORD
TF1 1VE
Music.

Henry BOSANQUET
22 Stanhope Road
DARLINGTON
DL3 7AR
Author of the legendary 'Walks Round Vanished Cambridge' series, which now can't be got for love nor money. His magnus opus is still in the card-index.

JOHN BOSWORTH PUBLICATIONS
8 Folly Field
BISHOP'S WALTHAM
SO3 1EB

BOTANICAL SOCIETY OF THE BRITISH ISLES
B.S.B.I. Publications
24 Glapthorn Road
Oundle
PETERBOROUGH
PE8 4JQ
Botany.

BOTTON BOOKSHOP
Botton

WHITBY
YO21 2NJ

J. BOUDRICOT PUBLICATIONS
Ashley Lodge
Rotherfield
CROWBOROUGH
TN6 3QX
(Mostly translated from the French): Industrial History. Military Ships History.

BOUNDARY MAGAZINE
The King's Road Writers
23 Kingsley Road
RUNCORN
WA7 5PL

THE BOURNE SOCIETY
Mr J Tyerman
60 Onslow Gardens
SOUTH CROYDON
CR2 9AT
Tel 0181 657 1202
The Way We Were: A Bourne Society Book of Days by John D Matthews - a composite year of daily items spanning the centuries (from written sources). East Surrey area. Price £4.50 plus 50p p&p, cheques payable to 'The Bourne Society'.

BOURNEMOUTH LOCAL STUDIES PUBLICATION
40 Lowther Road
BOURNEMOUTH
BH8 8NR
Historical Biography.

Simon BOWLANDS
see SJB Publishing

MEGAN BOYES
49 Evans Avenue
Allestree
DERBY
DE3 2EP
Biographies of the Byron family.

BOYS AND GIRLS' WELFARE SOCIETY
57A Schools Hill
CHEADLE
SK8 1JE
Social Welfare.

BOYS' GRAMMAR SCHOOL
Cambridge House
Cambridge Avenue
BALLYMENA
BT42 2EN

BOYZ
77 City Garden Row
LONDON
N1 8EZ

BOZO
John Nicholson
BM BOZO
LONDON
WC1N 3XX
We have risen more times than Christ. Our ever-popular water-walking act will be seen again this year. The miracle happened. The fourth Patriotic English Tract, first since 1984, was published the day the election was announced. Costs £1 sterling. The next on the skids: *Women Who Go Bump In The Night - a topography of murder, lies and sex; John Nicholson; £9.99 pb; (1993,) 0904063 28 3.

*Invisible Crimes, the life and times of Rosemary West; John Nicholson; 1997, £24.99; case bound only.
*Scared Shitless - the sex of horror; John Nicholson; 1998; Price t.b.a.; 0904063 27 5.
*An Elizabethan Lady's Missal of Shrunken Head Arrangements. Due to popular demand we have retained this title.

BRACKEN PRESS
Byways
Low Street, Scalby
SCARBOROUGH
YO13 0QS
Limited editions. Intaglio, silk screen and wood-engravings.

B. Bradbury
21 Westaway Park
Yatton
BRISTOL
BS19 4JU
Yatton Local History Society have published their latest book Yatton at War 1939-1945, which includes memoirs, reminiscences, home guard stories and facts about a Somerset village life during W.W.II. Price £2.50 from local newsagents or £3.00 including p&p from above.

BRADFORD & ILKLEY COMMUNITY COLLEGE
Great Horton Road
BRADFORD
BD7 1AY

BRADFORD POETRY
Editor Clare Chapman
9 Woodvale Way
BRADFORD

BRADFORD, UNIVERSITY OF
Disaster Planning and Limitation Unit
Department of Industrial Technology
BRADFORD
BD7 1DP

BRADHILL BOOKS
Frances Ball
16 Poplar Farm Close
Milton-under-Wychwood
CHIPPING NORTON
OX7 6LX

BRADLEY PRESS
7 Durham Road
Wolviston
BILLINGHAM
TS22 5LP
Handicrafts.

BRADPEAK INTERNATIONAL
110 Bellingham Road
Catford
LONDON
SE6 2PR
Tel 01 697 3864

Mr James BRADSHAW
Natural Friends
15 Benyon Gardens
Culford
BURY ST EDMONDS
IP28 6EA

E.F. BRADFORD
Orchard House
Castleton
WHITBY

YO21 2HA
Historical Biography.

BRAID BOOKS
c/o 69 Galgorm Road
BALLYMENA
BT42 1AA

BRAINWAVE
33 Lorn Road
LONDON
SW9 0AB

Dean BRAITHWAITE
see Strange Matter

BRAMCOTE PRESS
27 Seven Oaks Crescent
Bramcote Hills
NOTTINGHAM
NG9 3FW
General Fiction.

**BRAMPTON PUBLICATIONS/S.B
PUBLICATIONS**
5 Queen Margaret's Road
Loggerheads
MARKET DRAYTON
TF9 4EP

Leonard BRAND
Woodside Junior School
Morland Road
CROYDON
CR0 6NF
History of Education.

BRANDON BOOK PUBLISHERS
Cooleen
DINGLE
Co Kerry
Ireland

CHARLES BRAVOS
H S Gibbons
35 Lamont Road
LONDON
SW10 0HS

BRAWDY
Plas yr Wregin
Brynhyfryd
Dinas
NEWPORT
SA42 0YH
Tel 01348 811 450
JONES, The late Major Francis,
'Historic Houses and Families of
Pembrokeshire,' the last book by
the distinguished Welsh historian
and genealogist, and Welsh Herald
Extraordinary. Published by the
Executors. 1996, £25 to
subscribers, ask p&p. More re-
issues planned so ask for details.

BREAD AND CIRCUSES
71a Westward Road
STROUD
GL5 4JA
*Occasional booklets on social
science topics, especially economic
and educational. (Special interest in
Rudolf Steiner's social science.)*

BREAD 'N ROSES
Tenants Corner
46a Oval Mansions
Vauxhall Street
LONDON
SE11 5SH

BREAKAWAY PUBLICATIONS
The Old Vicarage
Newchapel

STOKE-ON-TRENT
ST7 4QT
*Publish Rouge, a lesbian and gay
socialist quarterly. Some books,
pamphlets and packs.*

**BREAKFAST ALL DAY
(see BAD Press)
Chisenhale Works
64/68 Chisenhale Road
LONDON
E3 5EZ**
Magazine/comic publications.

BREAK/FLOW
89 Vernon Road
Stratford
LONDON
E15 4DQ
*Idiosyncratic and meticulous
underground magazine covering
literature, philosophy, dance music,
underground resistance &c. Issue 1
covers amongst others Trocchi &
Project Sigma, Anti-Oedipus - Price
£3.00.*

BRENTHAM PRESS
Margaret Timms
40 Oswald Road
ST ALBANS
AL1
Tel 01727 835731
*Small publications of literary and
social value outside the commercial
market: poetry local history essays
occasional criticism and reprints.*

BREWIN BOOKS:
Alton Douglas
371 Rednal Road
Kings Norton
BIRMINGHAM
B38 8EE
Local History.

BREWERS QUAY
Hope Square
WEYMOUTH
DT4 8TA
Historic Local Walks.

BRIDGE PUBLICATIONS
2 Bridge Street
Penistone
SHEFFIELD
S30 6AJ

(THE) BRIDGE
James Mawer
112 Rutland Street
GRIMSBY
DN32 7NF

BRIDGE BOOKS
61 Park Avenue
WREXHAM
LL12 7AW

BRIDGE HOUSE PUBLISHERS
Burdett Cottage
4 Burdett Place
George Street Old Town
HASTINGS
TN34 3ED
Literature.

BRIDGE STUDIOS
Kirklands
Scremerston
BERWICK-ON-TWEED
TD15 2RB

BRIDGEWATER BOOKS
Bridgewater House

Langford
LECHLADE
Gl7 3LN
Fiction General.

THE BRIEF & BLYTH SPIRIT
British Haiku Society
Sinodun
BRAINTREE
CM7 5HN

BRIGHT BOOKS
Carpenters
Moor End
Great Sampford
SAFFRON WALDEN
CB10 2RQ
Children's Fiction.

BRISTOL BROADSIDES
108c Stokes Croft
BRISTOL
BS1 3RU
*A publishing co-op running writers
workshops. Books by local people
including autobiography, peotry,
history.*

BRISTOL JUNIOR CHAMBER
16 Clifton Park
BRISTOL
BS8 3BY
Secret Underground Bristol.

BRISTOL TEMPLAR
Julian Lea-Jones
33 Springfield Grove
Henleaze
BRISTOL
BS6 7XL

BRISTOL, UNIVERSITY OF
Department of Politics
12 Priory Road
BRISTOL
BS8 1TU

**BRITISH ASSOCIATION FOR LOCAL
HISTORY (BALH)**
Michael Cowan
24 Lower Street
SALISBURY
SP2 8EY
Tel 01722 320115
Fax 01722 413242
*Local historians range from
interested individuals & members of
local societies to the professionals
in the field such as archivists and
university lecturers. The British
Association for Local History is the
national body that exists to serve
them all.
'Writing Local History : A Practical
Guide' by David Dymond (18988)
96pp £6.95 The classic book
written by an expert. Essential
reading for all local historians,
newcomers or experienced.
'From Chantry to Oxfam: A short
history of Charities & Charity
Legislation,' by Norman Alvey
80pp 30 illus. £6.95. A succinct
account of the tangled history of
charities, how they evolved, were
defined & regulated.*

BRITISH BIKE MAGAZINE
48 Union Lane
CAMBRIDGE
CB4 1QTS

BRITISH COPYRIGHT COUNCIL
29-33 Berners Street
LONDON

W1P 4AA

**BRITISH EARTH MYSTERIES
SOCIETY**
David Barclay
40 Stubbing Way
SHIPLEY
BD18 2EZ
*Magazine for flying saucers and
similar. Cups.*

BRITISH FANTASY SOCIETY
15 Stanley Road
MORDEN
SM4 5DE
*Began 1971. Newsletter for
members. Magazines, conference
and awards.*

BRITISH HUMANIST ASSOCIATION
14 Lamb's Conduit Passage
LONDON
WC1R 4RH
Customs. Philiosophy.

BRITISH INSTITUTE IN PARIS
Senate House
Mallet Street
LONDON
WC1E 7HU
Poetry.

**BRITISH INSTITUTE OF MENTAL
HANDICAP**
Wolverhampton Road
KIDDERMINSTER
DY10 3PP
Education.

BRITISH LEISURE PUBLICATIONS
Windsor Court
EAST GRINSTEAD
RH19 1XA

BRITISH MAHABODHI SOCIETY
London Buddhist Vihara
5 Heathfield Gardens
LONDON
W4 4JU

**BRITISH NATIONAL CARNATION
SOCIETY**
3 Canberra Close
HORNCHURCH
RM12 5TR

**BRITISH ORGANIC FARMERS AND
THE ORGANIC GROWERS
ASSOCIATION**
Lowsonford Farm
Henley-in-Arden
SOLIHULL
B95 5HJ
Agriculture.

BRITISH PRINTING SOCIETY
BM/ISPA
LONDON
WC1N 3XX

**BRITISH PRINTING SOCIETY
PUBLISHING GROUP**
c/o Alfred Jones
14 Penrose Arc Aest
LIVERPOOL
L14 6UT

BRITISH ROMANY UNION
The Reservation
Hever Road
EDENBRIDGE
TN8 5DJ
*Children Fiction. Poetry. Social
Sciences.*

BRITISH SHINGON BUDDHIST ASSOCIATION
58 Mansfield Road
LONDON
NW8

BRITISH SMALL ANIMAL VETERINARY ASSOCIATION
Kingsley House
Church Lane Shurdington
CHELTENHAM
GL51 5TQ
Pets. Beekeeping.

BRITISH SOCIETY OF MASTER GLASS PAINTERS
The Ridings
Singleborough
BUCKINGHAM
MK17 0RF
Stained Glass.

BRITISH TRUST FOR ORNITHOLOGY
Beech Grove
Station Road
TRING
HP23 5NR

BRITISH UFO RESEARCH ASSOCIATION
1 Woodhall Drive
BATLEY
WF17 7SW

BRIXTON POETS
2 Lorn Court
Lorn Road
Brixton
LONDON
SW9

BRIXTON SOCIETY
Ken Dixon Archivist
139 Herne Hill Road
LONDON
SE24 0AD
The Brixton Society is the amenity group covering the whole Brixton area from Stockwell to the South Circular active in environmental and community issues acting as Planning Watch-dog and a focal point for local history research.
* Brixton Memories - the latest publication by the Brixton Society, recollections of local life from 1920s to 1950s (52 A4 pages with 16 illustrations). Copies available at £5.49 including postage.

Richard BROAD
Tencery Cottage
Dunkeswell
HONITON
EX14 0QZ
Dunkeswell - Parish and People by Richard Broad 1994 Social Study of Devon Village in Blackdown Hills including connections with Abbey, Canada and United States Navy. Part of mainstream English history and apart from it. A5 172pp 21 photos 3 maps £7 inc p&p.

BROADCAST BOOKS
Pitt House
Chudleigh
NEWTON ABBOT
TQ13 0EL

BROADFIELD PUBLISHING
71 Broadfield Road
MANCHESTER

M14 4WE
Tel 0161 227 9265
The fourth edition of the Manchester Guide, 'A Year in The Theatre' - of greater Manchester is the biggest and best yet. More pages, more - you name it. Only the price hasn't increased. 'Less than a penny a play.' £6.99. ISBN 08521502 3 9

BROADHEAD PUBLISHING
Broadhead
Castleshaw
Delph
OLDHAM
OK3 5LZ

BROAD LEYS PUBLISHING COMPANY
David and Katie Thear
Buriton House
Station Road
Newport
SAFFRON WALDEN
CB11 3PL
Tel 01799 540 922 fax: 01799 541 367
Highly successful as publisher and distributor in niche market of small publishing. Second illustrated catalogue of books and videos: good for small/specialist publishing in this area, as well as for books from larger commercial sources. Books & monthly magazine, 'Country Garden & Smallholding.'
NEW: 'The Smallholding Plan,' a checklist and guide for those thinking of embarking on this venture, £2.15.

BROADSIDE
Peter Johnson
68 Limes Road
Tettenhall
WOLVERHAMPTON
WV6 8RB
Tel 01902 753047
Birmingham and Black Country History Folklore Photographs EZ and English folklore and folksong books.

BROADSTREET PRESS
33 Grasmere Avenue
COVENTRY
CV3 6AY
'Representational Practice, a newsletter dedicated to exposing society's hidden workings and the involvement, in that concealment, of academia and the media.' Per copy £1 or sub £5 for first six issues. This imprint's name celebrates the removal of the handle on the pump in Broad Street. Instead of an act by legendary vandals it ushered in a public health programme. Lots happening at the press. The begetter is John Linsie who also seeks funds to translate the Works of German philospher Wil Wundt, founding father of experimental psychology.

BROCKWELL BOOKS
64 Selsdon Road
LONDON
SE27 0PG

BROKEN PENCIL MAGAZINE
P.O. Box 203
Stn P Toronto
ONTARIO M55 2S7

Canada
e-mail: halpen@io.org
hclark@inforamp.net
homepage: http://www.io.org/-halpen/bpencil.html
Guide to Alternative Publications in Canada, ISSN 1201-8996, $4.95 per issue.

BROMPTON PUBLICATIONS
16 Trebovoir Road
LONDON
SW5 9NH
Library Science.

J. BROOKE
Guildford
53 Chantry View Road
GUILDFORD
GU1 3XT
Poetry.

Henry C G BOOTHROYD BROOKS
Harroway Edge
Keppel Road
DORKING
RH4 1NG

BROOKS BOOKS
23 Sylvan Avenue
Bitterne
SOUTHAMPTON
SO2 5JW
Biography.

BROOKSIDE PRESS: KETTERING BOOKS
14 Horsemarket
KETTERING
NN16 0DO

BROOKSIDE BOOKS
28 Colesbourne Road
Bloxham
BANBURY
OX15 4TB

R. BROOMHEAD PUBLISHING
P.O. Box 219
STOCKPORT
SK4 1LL
'Robin Hood: ancient poems, songs and ballads.' 356 pp, hardback, £14.99. Please order from your local bookshop or enquire direct from publisher sending SAE.

Mr Angus BROWN
c/o New River Project
Unit P8
Metropolitan College of Craftsmen
Enfield Road
LONDON
N1 5AZ

C.E. BROWN
Jackson's Drive
Charlecote
WARWICK
CV35 9EW
Biography.

D BROWN
TPAS
48 The Crescent
SALFORD
M5 4NY

John W BROWN
316 Green Lane
Streatham
LONDON
SW16 3AS
Reprints of 18th and 19th century local histories of south London and

north-east Surrey available. Includes works by Lysons, Brayley, Walford and others covering Battersea, Croydon, Putney, Streatham, Tooting, Wandsworth and other areas. For full list send SAE.

R. & S. BROWN
13 Goppa Road
Pontarddulais
SWANSEA
SA4 1JN
Customs and Folklore.

BROWN & BROWN PUBLISHING
Keepers Cottage
Westward
WIGTON
CA7 89Q
Tel/Fax 016973 42915
Publications for improvement in the skills of reading, spelling and maths. Publishes: A Speller's Companion, a lively introduction to word origins and the history of English spelling. ISBN 1870596250, 64 pps, £2.25.

BROWN WELLS AND JACOBS
2 Vermont Road
LONDON
SE19 3SR
Children's non-fiction.

BROWNES PUBLISHERS
17 Gainsboro Road
BOGNOR REGIS
PO21 2HT

BROWSE PRESS
10 Highcroft
STEVENAGE

BRUNDALL BOOKS
12 Belgrave Mount
WAKEFIELD
WF1 3SB
Short Stories.

Alan BRYAN
c/o 36 Tower Road North
Warmley
BRISTOL
BS15 2YR
Historic Guide.

BRYNGLAS PUBLICATIONS
23 Durham Avenue
BROMLEY
BR2 0QH
Autobiography.

BRYNMILL PRESS
Professor John Pick
Willow Cottage
20 High Street
Sutton-on-Trent
NEWARK
NG23 6QA
Poetry and novels. Literature. 'Twenty years of ... works of literary criticism, philosophy and theology - always of the first quality' - Salisbury Review.

BSDR & D
13A The Bull Ring
WAKEFIELD
WF1 1HB
Education.

B.S.M.W. Books
50 Ceres Road
LONDON

SE18 1HL
Biography.

BUCEPHALUS PRODUCTIONS
Flat 4
3 Hornsey Lane Gardens
LONDON
N6 5NY
Poetry

BUCHAIR UK
Wellingtonia 8
Raglan Road
REIGATE
RH2 0DP
Air Transport.

BUCKINGHAM PRESS
25 Manor Park
MAIDS MORETON
MK18 1QX

Mr Paul BUCK
4 Bower Street
MAIDSTONE
Good for a ruck.

BU-COMP PUBLISHERS LIMITED
Andrew Fairclough
25 Durmford House
LONDON
SE6 2TA
*Mnemonics, lateral thinking, jazz,
Japanese culture, organice
farming, history of radical
movements, body-building - just a
few of our subjects - not in the
same book.*

(THE) BUDDHAPADIPA TEMPLE
14 Calonne Road
Wimbledon Parkside
LONDON
SW19 5JH

**(THE) BUDDHIST PUBLICATION
SOCIETY**
58 Eccleston Square
LONDON
SW1

BUDDY BOOKS
Tomkin-Hill
543 Victoria Road
SOUTH RUISLIP
Poetry.

BUFO
3 Elim Grove
BOWNESS-ON-WINDERMERE
LA23 2JN

BUGS AND DRUGS
Bear Hackenbush
P.O. Box 960
BRISTOL
BS99 5QU
*Britain's sickest fanzine dedicated to
the destruction of youth culture and
beer-induced stupidity.*

**THE BULLETIN OF THE VINTAGE
SPORTS-CAR CLUB**
24 Eaglesfield
Hartford
NORTHWICH
CW8 1NQ
*A heavy glossy 100 pages packed
with info, pics and ads. The Club:
121 Russell Road, Newbury, Berks
RG14 5JX.*

BULLFINCH PUBLICATIONS
245 Hunts Cross Avenue
Woolton

LIVERPOOL
L25 9ND
Fiction General.

Walter Henry BULLOCK
35 Forest Road
BURTON-ON-TRENT
DE13 9TW
Historic Architecture.

Basil BUNTING POETRY ARCHIVE
Durham University Library
Palace Green
DURHAM
DH1 3RN
Pretty self-explanatory

THE BUNYAN PRESS
Brian Maunders
34 Park Hill
AMPTHILL
MK45 2LP
*I have a Vandercook press which
allows me to print letterpress as
well as a variety of relief printing
methods. I concentrate on
producing limited edition works
(poetry, broadsheets and books).
These I illustrate mainly with wood-
engravings.*

BUNYAN STUDIES
The Administrator
Raman Selden Centre for Textual
and Cultural Studies
Dept of English Studies
University of Sunderland
Forster Building
Chester Road
SUNDERLAND
SR1 3SD
*Academic journal: Articles on
Bunyan and the history and
literature of the seventeenth century.*

**BURBURY CREATIVE WRITERS
CIRCLE**
Burbury Park Complex
Wheeler Street
Newtown
BIRMINGHAM
B19 2UP

BURDA
Mr Fred Schulenburg
Swan House
37/39 High Holborn
LONDON
WC1V 6AA

BURDEN AND CHOLIJ
Faculty of Music
12 Nicholson Square
EDINBURGH
EH8 9DF

Philip L. BURKINSHAW
Davis Brothers
The Courtyard
School Lane
LEOMINSTER
WR6 8AA
Biography.

THE BURRELL PRESS
P.O. BOX 168
IPSWICH
IP2 8AQ
*We hope to publish travel writing,
fiction, poetry. Not deliberately
revolutionary or avant-garde; some
empasis on attractive printing &
good book production, also on
illustration.*

Fred H. BURTON
17 Davenport Fold Road
Harwood
BOLTON
BL2 4HA
Historical Biography.

BURY LIVE LINES
The Derby Hall
Market Street
BURY
BL9 0BN
*Writers workshops in the arts and
crafts centre. Into computers.
Performance group available.*

Donald William BUSFIELD
2 Purley Knoll
PURLEY
CR8 3AE
Local History.

BUSINESS ARCHIVES COUNCIL
185 Tower Bridge Road
LONDON
SE1 2UF
Biography.

**BUSINESS EDUCATION
PUBLISHING**
Leighton House
10 Grange Crescent
Stockton Road
SUNDERLAND
SR2 7BN

BUSY BEEVER
Mark Beevers
Glenside Cottage
SALTBURN
*One man and his demon press -
photocopied booklets of own works
poetry epigrams humorous &
serious (26 to date)
'Both Barrels Blazing' by Mark
Beevers 12pp. £0.50 (poetry)
'Double Edge Sword' by Mark
Beevers 20pp playlet. 0.50p
'Jesteryears II' by Mark Beevers
20pp £1.00 (poetry) P&P free.*

Chris BUTCHER
96 Dovecroft
New Ollerton
NEWARK
NG22 9RQ
History.

BUTLER SIMS
55 Merrion Square
DUBLIN 2
Republic of Ireland
Travel in Ireland.

BUTTERBUR & SAGE LTD
B J Hepburn
99/101 St Leonards Road
WINDSOR
SL4 3BZ
*Proper recipes for proper living.
Catalogues.*

Ralph BUTTLE
28A Church Fields
WELLINGTON
TA21 8SE
Historical Biography.

BYRGISEY
Tanzy Cottage
Rimpton
YEOVIL
BA22 8AQ
Second World War History.

**CACTUS GRAPHIC DESIGN/
NETWORK**
P.O. Box 587
LONDON
SW2 4HA
*Produce a contributor magazine
and other wierdities. Hot on
networking.*

CADENZA PRESS
Gilbert Beale
4 James Close
BLANDFORD FORUM
DT11 7PQ
Fine Press

CAERDROIA
53 Thunderdsley Grove
Thundersley
BENFLEET
SS7 3EB
Labyrinths, mazes etc.

Michael CAINE
12 rue Marie et Louise
F 75010 PARIS
FRANCE
Artists books.

CAIRNS PUBLICATIONS
47 Firth Park Avenue
SHEFFIELD
S5 6HF
*Books and cards of meditations,
prayers, reflections on sexuality,
gender, healing, church. Reshaping
of psalms, language of prayer etc.
Exploratory, liberal, radical
perspective.*

CAKEBREADS
Brenda Fuller
Ford End
Clavering
SAFFRON WALDEN
CB11 4PU
*'Quiet Heroines' by Brenda
McBryde, the story of the nurses of
the Second World War. Paperback
246 pages. Retail £6.95 UK
(hardback Chatto, 1985).*

CALABRIA PRESS
15 Calabria Road
LONDON
N5 1JB

CALCRE
Mr Roger Gaillard
Boite Postale 17
F-94404 VITRY-SUR-SEINE CEDEX
FRANCE

CALEDONIAN BOOKS
Slains House
COLLIESTON
AB4 9RT

CALTON PROMOTIONS
P.O. Box 9
EXETER
EX1 2AQ

CALUMET PRODUCTIONS
6A Fairbourne Road
LONDON
N17 6TP
Poetry.

CAMBERWELL PRESS
Camberwell College of Arts
Peckham Road
LONDON
SE16 6RR

CAMBRIDGE CONTEMPORARY CLASSICS
Bridge House
Hildersham
CAMBRIDGE
CB1 6BU
Romantic Fiction.

CAMBRIDGE HOUSE BOYS' GRAMMAR SCHOOL
Cambridge Avenue
BALLYMENA
BT42 2EN
Local History.

CAMBRIDGE INSTITUTE OF EDUCATION
Shaftesbury Road
CAMBRIDGE
CB2 2BX
Bibliography.

CAMBRIDGE POETRY WORKSHOP
10 Fulbrooke Road
CAMBRIDGE
CB3 9EE
Poetry.

CAMELOT BOOKS
3 Grange Road
Bishopsworth
BRISTOL
BS13 8LE

CAMERON AND HOLLIS
P.O. Box 1
MOFFAT
DG10 9SU
Second World War History.

CAMOMILE PRESS
Claybourne
91 Stannary Road
Stenalees
ST AUSTELL
PL26 8ST
Camomile is a low cost/low volume imprint - publishing local interest authors & minority circulation newsheets. Also DTP etc.

CAMPAIGN FOR REAL EDUCATION
18 Westlands Grove
Stockton Lane
YORK
YO3 0EF

CAMPAIGN LITERATURE
Adelaide College
3 Nineyard Street
SALTCOATS
KA21 5HS
Biography.

CAMPDEN AND DISTRICT HISTORICAL SOCIETY
Westington Corner
CHIPPING CAMPDEN
GL55 6DW
Memories of an Old Campdonian by F W Coldicott xix + 210 pp, 24 illustrations, 5 maps, £7.50. Reminiscences of rural life from the early part of this century: childhood, early manhood, war service etc.

CAMPHILL PRESS
Botton Bookshop
Botton
WHITBY
YO21 2NJ

Peter J. CAMPION
Myrtle Cottage
Gretton
CHELTENHAM
GL54 5EP
Local Industrial History.

CANDELABRUM
9 Milner Road
WISBECH
PE13 2LR

CANFORD PUBLISHING
C S Wright
53 Canford Lane
BRISTOL
BS9 3NX

CANIMPEX PUBLISHING
BCM-Canimpex
LONDON
WC1N 3XX

CANNON POETS
Prof K Mahadva
Century House
Erdington
BIRMINGHAM
B23 5XN

CANTERBURY RESEARCH SERVICES
David Wright
71 Island Wall
WHITSTABLE
CT5 1EL
'East Kent Parishes: A Guide for Genealogists, Local Historians and Other Researchers.

CANTO PRESS
Chris Stewart
2 Cricklewood Park
BELFAST
BT9 5GW

CAPABILITY BOOKS
Stowe Bookshop
Stowe
BUCKINGHAM
MK18 5EH

CAPALL BANN PUBLISHING
Freshfields
CHIEVELEY
RG20 8TF
Tel/Fax 01635 46455
Independent British publishing house owned and run by 'people involved in areas in which we

publish.' Earth mysteries, folklore, holistic living, Shamanism, Wicca, Divining. Detailed catalogue available on request. Eight new titles include:
GALE, Jack, 'Goddesses, Guardians and Groves, Awakening the Spirit of the Land.' £10.95.
PENNICK, Nigel, 'Secret Signs, Symbols and Sigils,' £10.95.

CAPITAL GAY
38 Mount Pleasant
LONDON
WC1X 0AP

Tony CAPLAN
Durrus
CORK
Ireland

CAPPRICCIO PRESS
Barry Turner
28 Beaulieu Place
Rothschild Road
Chiswick
LONDON
W4 5SY

CAPRICORN PUBLISHER
1 Hill House
38 Park Street
OLD HATFIELD
AL9 5AZ

CARA
c/o London Lighthouse
178 Lancaster Road
LONDON
W11

CARCANET
208 Corn Exchange Buildings
MANCHESTER
M4 3BQ
Veteran paper oddity and subsidised.

CARDOZO KINDERSLEY EDITIONS
152 Victoria Road
CAMBRIDGE
CB2 3DZ
Art.

CAREER CONCERN
P.O. Box 75
CHESTERFIELD
S40 1NZ
Careers.

CAREL PRESS LTD
18 Chertsey Bank
CARLISLE
CA1 2QF

CARGO PRESS
34 St Pauls Road
BEDFORD
MK40

CARIAD BOOKS
28 Oaten Hill
CANTERBURY
CT1 3HZ
Short Stories.

CARING & SHARING
Lana Davies
Cotton's Farmhouse
Whiston Road
COGENHOE

CARMINA PUBLISHING
Flat 1
33 Knowle Road

Totterdown
BRISTOL
BS4 2EB

CARMINE PINK
4 Dashwood Road
OXFORD
OX4 4SJ
Non-profit making venture for creative women. Make notepaper, cards and posters. Newsletter. Contact lists.

CARNEGIE PRESS
18 Maynard Street
Ashton
PRESTON
PR2 2AL

CARNEGIE DUNFERMLINE TRUST
Abbey Park House
DUNFERMLINE
KY12 7PB
History of Manufacturing.

CARNIVOROUS ARPEGGIO
329 Beverley Road
HULL
HU5 1LD

CARNTYNE HOUSE PUBLICATIONS
14 Graystane Road
Invergowrie
DUNDEE
DD2 5JQ

CAR NUMBERS GALAXY
Noel Woodall
16 Boston Avenue
BLACKPOOL
FY2 9BZ
Listing 67500 Historical car number registrations many with owners. Plus all D.V.L.A. auction prices. Hundreds of photographs Car Numbers. Compilation of Personalised Registrations.

THE CARPATHIAN PRESS
Richard & Andrew Dolinski, Peter Nagy
46 Campell Road
WOODLEY
RG5 3NB
Tel 01734 505 641
Founded 1977. Specialise in fine limited edition letterpress printing and publishing. Books are both hand and machine type set and printed on high quality mould papers. On average two major titles each year.

CARPHOLOGY COLLECTIVE
16 Wiverton Road
Forest Fields
NOTTINGHAM
NG7 6NP
Poetry.

CARTERPRINT ENTERPRISES
26 Crinton Road
Hartburn
STOCKTON-ON-TEES
TS18 5HE

CARTY/LYNCH
Dunsany
NAVAN
Co. Meath
Republic of Ireland.
Castles.

CASCANDO PRESS LTD
P.O. Box 1499

LONDON
SW10 9TZ
Tel 0171 267 5899 fax 0171 209 2438
The National Student Literary Magazine. Readership 35,000; good reviews from M. Bradbury, Arts Council and TLS.

CASDEC
22 Harraton Terrace
Birtley
CHESTER-LE-STREET
DH3 2QG

CAST PUBLICATIONS
18 Haverbearks Place
LANCASTER
LA1 5BH

CASTLE BOOKS AND PUBLISHERS
6 Bank Street
CASTLETOWN
Isle of Man
European History.

CASTLE BAILEY PRESS
West Dean
SALISBURY
SP5 1JL
Local History.

CASTLEBERG
18 Yealand Avenue
Giggleswick
SETTLE
BD24 0AY

CASTLEDEN PUBLICATIONS
11 Castlegate
PICKERING
YO18 7AX
Tel 01751 76227
Publisher of local history and guide books. Printing done 'in house'. Page origination. Letterpress. Latest books litho printed.

CATALOGUE OF CRAP
Ian Shield
40 Bingfield Gardens
Fenham
NEWCASTLE UPON TYNE
NE5 2RX
Self-published comic featuring strips entitled "The Skidding Whippet", "Catalogue Woman", "Bonk faced Bishop & His Bouncing Bisexual Boob Bugs" and "Removable Buttock Wolf Boy" amongst others. Price £2.00.

CATCHROSE
Brampton Bridge House
12 Queen Street
NEWCASTLE-UNDER-LYME
ST5 1ED
Biography.

CATHAIR BOOKS
1 Essex Gate
DUBLIN 8
Republic of Ireland
Historical Biography.

CATH TATE CARDS
39 Kingswood Road
LONDON
SW2 4JE

Catholic Rectory
Hills Road
CAMBRIDGE
CB2 1JR
Our Lady and the English Martyrs,

Cambridge. New edition of church guide, including early history of mission and parish. 48pp, A5, with 8 full page illustrations and laminated colour cover. A quality production, £2 each incl p&p.

CATS TRUST
3 Alexandra Road
Heaton
NEWCASTLE-UPON-TYNE
NE6 5QS
Education.

J. CATT
Great Glemham
SAXMUNDHAM
IP17 2DH
Education.

CAUSE FOR ALARM
http://www.teleport.com/~richieb/cause/
Online mag monthly. Electronic freedom issues.

CAVALIER HOUSE
35 Sandiway
KNUTSFORD
WA16 8BU

CAXTON AND HOLMESDALE PRESS LTD
c/o 31 Braeside Avenue
SEVENOAKS
TN13 2JJ
Literature.

C.B. PUBLISHING
18 Lochlann Terrace
CULLODEN
Inverness
IV1 2DU

C BOOKS
P.O. Box 11
REDCAR
TS10 1PY

CELCAKES
Springfield House
Gate Helmsley
YORK
YO4 1NF

THE CELTIC CROSS PRESS
Rosemary Roberts
The Old Vicarage
Collingham
WETHERBY
LS22 5AU
Fine Printer.

CENCRASTUS
Unit 1 Abbeymount Techbase
8 Easter Road
EDINBURGH
EH8 8EJ

CENTAUR PRESS
J Kingsley Cook
72a Marquis Road
LONDON
NW1 9UB

CENTERPRISE
136 Kingsland High Street
LONDON
E8 2NS
See Resource Directory under Resources.

CENTRE FOR ALTERNATIVE TECHNOLOGY Publications
David Thorpe

Machynlleth
POWYS
SY20 9AZ
Tel 01654 702 400 fax 01654 702782
Email: cat@gn.upc.org
Web: http://www.foe.co.uk/CAT;
Expert advice for green living. Practical resources to help everyone acheive sustainable lifestyles with renewable energy, organic growing, energy conservation, ecological sewage treatment and environmentally sound building. Superb, comprehensive 60-page catalogue 1996-97 (16th ed.) out now. A bargain at .95p if sustainable futures matter to you. Mail order service, phone for catalogue.

CENTRE PUBLISHING
Cuilleann
Wester Galcantray
CAWDOR
Nairn
IV22 5XX
Literature.

Century House
Erdington
BIRMINGHAM
B23 5XN

CENTURY PRESS (Sussex)
2 East Meadway
SHOREHAM-BY-SEA
BN43 5RF
Asian History. Biography. Short Stories.

CERBERUS PRESS
24 Fairmount Drive
LOUGHBOROUGH
LE11 3JR

THE CEREALOGIST
George Wingfield
Heron House
North Wotten
SHEPTON MALLET
BA4 4HW
Tel 01749 890 257
The journal for crop circle studies, published three times a year.

CERTAINTY MAGAZINE
85 West Ealing Broadway
LONDON
W13 9BP
Adult fetishism. Magazine.

CERVERA PRESS
Language of Dance Centre
Flat 4
17 Holland Park
LONDON
W11 3TD
The Cervera Press publishes dance materials on specialized dance styles; Historical, Classical and Contempory. These are made more explicite and educationally valuable through use of Labanotion (the universally based dance notation system) Together with background history and study/performance notes.

CERVERA PRESS
Labanotation Institute
University of Surrey
GUILDFORD
GU2 5XH
Operatic dances.

CETOS PUBLISHING
75 Beattyville Gardens
ILFORD
IG6 1JY
Geology.

CHAPTER TWO
199 Plumstead Common Road
LONDON
SE18 2UJ

CHALICE
16 Blenheim Rd
Beechwood
NEWPORT
NP9 8JL
New Age Networking magazine

Barrie CHAMBERS
21 Bonet Lane
Brinsworth
ROTHERHAM
S60 5NE
A Mexborough Scrap Book. Turn of the century Mexborough from newspaper articles, school log books etc. A4 paperback, 98pp text, 24 photos, dozens 'period' letterheads. Features potteries, glass-works and mining, canal and railways. £5.90 incl p&p.

Jill CHAMBERS
4 Quills
LETCHWORTH
SG6 2RJ
Rebels of the Fields tells the story of the 1830 'Swing Riots' and the men, mainly from Wiltshire, Hampshire, Berkshire and Dorset, who were tried and sentenced to transportation to New South Wales after the riots. Price £11 incl p&p.

CHAMELIUS BOOKS
1 Merewood Cottages
Ecclerigg
WINDERMERE
LA23 1LH

CHAMPION PRESS
Anfield House
89 Days Lane
SIDCUP
DA15 8JP
Publishing sports books by self and other writers.

CHANGE
P.O. Box 824
LONDON
SE24 9JS

CHANGING PERSPECTIVES LIMITED
Riverside House
Winnington House
NORTHWICH
CW8 1AD

CHANGING PERSPECTIVES: PROTECTION THROUGH PREVENTION
Ashfield Nursery School
Elswick Road
NEWCASTLE-UPON-TYNE
Child Protection.

CHANGING PLACES PUBLICATIONS
23 Crossvale Road
Huyton
LIVERPOOL
L36 0UY
Biography.

CHANNEL TUNNEL ASSOCIATION
44 Westbourne Terrace
LONDON
W2 3UH
Bibliography.

CHANSITOR
St. Mary's Works
St. Mary's Plain
NORWICH
NR3 3BH
School Textbooks.

CHANTRY PRESS
Rose Cottage
The Street
Eastcombe
STROUD
GL7 7DN
Local History.

C.H.A.O.S. INCORPORATED
Edd A Hillier Pizza Research Centre
148 Humber Road South
Beeston
NOTTINGHAM
NG9 2EX
*Another member of a network of
incoherence. Sometime publisher of
Lobster Telephone and exchange of
ideas and information and the
number II. Dedicated to confusion.
Interested and interesting. Truth is
no obstacle. Write...The means is
the end.*

CHAOS INTERNATIONAL
BCM Sol
LONDON
WC1N 3XX

CHAPMAN MAGAZINE
80 Moray Street
BLACKFORD
PH4 1QF
Tel 0131 557 2207
*Promotes Scottish writers.
Magazine and books.*

CHAPMAN
4 Broughton Place
EDINBURGH
EH1 3RX
*Literary publisher specialising in
poetry and in promoting new
writers and experimental work. The
central commitment is to Scottish
lierature and culture in Scots as
well as English.*

CHAPTER TWO
95 Genesta Road
LONDON
SE18 3EX
Tel 0181 316 5389
*Chapter Two concentrates on
publishing Christian literature of a
conservative Evangelical nature.
Dispensational and fundamental
books are stocked and a catalogue
listing all the books is available on
request. Chapter Two operate a
very efficient mail order
department.*

CHAPTER & VERSE
Granta House
96 High Street
Linton
CAMBRIDGE
CB1 6JT

CHAPTER AND VERSE
Heather Seddon
2 Jubilee Retreat

Bury Road
LONDON
E4 7QJ
*New title: Gonzalez, Carmela and
Seddon, Heather: The bitter fruit of
a broken tree. ISBN 0951992317,
228 pps, £7.95.*

CHARLEWOOD Press
Gerald Ponting
7 Weavers Place
Chandlers Ford
EASTLEIGH
SO53 1TU
*Charlewood Press publisher local
history material on the
Fordingbridge area (Hants) written
by the partners Anthony Light &
Gerald Ponting.
"Tudor Fordingbridge"
"Breamore - a short history &
guide"
+ five smaller publications.*

CHASE PUBLICATIONS
The Chase
Hinton Martell
WIMBOURNE
BH21 7HE
Sport.

CHB PUBLISHING
123 Pemros Road
PLYMOUTH
PL51LU
*Publications of Railway and Bus
books, and also poem and general
interest books.*

CHENARA PUBLICATIONS
P.O. Box 267
CHELTENHAM
GL51 0UY
Occult.

CHERRY GARDENS PUBLICATIONS
Cherry Gardens
Groombridge
TUNBRIDGE WELLS
TN3 9NY
Countryside.

CHERUB PUBLICATIONS
19 South Quay
GREAT YARMOUTH
NR30 2RG

CHERUB PRESS
David and Kim Butcher
18 Hargrave Road
Shirley
SOLIHULL
B90 1HX
Fine Printers.

CHESTER CITY RECORD OFFICE
Town Hall
CHESTER
CH1 2HJ
*Transport History Source Guide. A
guide to local sources for canals,
railways, trams, buses, roads and
motor cars. Includes useful dates,
booklists, addresses. Price £1.50
(incl p&p). Cheques and postal
orders payable to Chester City
Council. Details Ring (01244)
402110.*

THE CHEVERELL PRESS
Hamilton House
66 Upper Richmond Road
LONDON
SW15 5PQ
Theatre books. How to become a

*working actor. Writing and
Managing your own One Man
Show. Fiction - no.*

CHEVINGTON PRESS
D R Wakefield
Triangle
SALTMARSHE
Near Howden
DN14 7RX

**CHIAROSCURA
(also Curious Press)**
88 Laurence Court
NORTHAMPTON
NN1 3HD

CHILDWALL WRITERS
Leybourne Close
Gateacre
LIVERPOOL
L28 4SP

CHILFORD HALL PRESS
Chilford Hall
Linton
CAMBRIDGE
CB2 6LE

CHIMAERA PRESS
Michael and Helen Hutchins
16 Oakhill Road
BECKENHAM
BR3 2NQ

CHINA CAT
20 Perry Road
Great Barr
BIRMINGHAM
B42 2BQ

CHRISTIAN FOCUS PUBLICATIONS
Geanies House
Fearn
TAIN
IV20 1TW
Children non-fiction. Religion.

D D CHRISTIE
18 St John's Road
POOLE
BH15 2NB
Tel 01202 679891
*An octogenarian hobby publisher
of self-produced books. 'The
Horace cricket sagas' illustrated by
the author. 'A Bumpy Wicket' by
Donald Chrisie.*

PAX CHRISTI
9 Henry Road
LONDON
N4 2LH

CHTHONIOS BOOKS
7 Tamarisk Steps
HASTINGS
TN34 3DN

CHUDLEIGH PUBLISHING
45 Chudleigh Crescent
ILFORD

CICATRIX
Eamer O'Keeffe
BM/Cicatrix
LONDON
WC1N 3XX
Fiercely feminist.

CICERONE
2 Police Square
MILNTHORPE
LH7 7QE
Tel 01539 562 069

*A leading guidebook company
specialising in outdoor activities
and in general books about the
North. Approach with a synopsis in
first instance. No fiction or poetry.*

CINNABAR
38 St Pauls Road
BEDFORD
MK40 4NT

CIRCLE PRESS
Ronald King
26 St Lukes Mews
Notting Hill
LONDON
W11 1DF
Tel 0171 792 9298
*First formed in 1967 by a group of
printmakers interested in publishing
limited edition artist's books. Since
then the press has produced more
than 150 classic and
contemnporary titles; letter press;
litho; intaglio and silk screen;
ranging in price from £5 to £1000.*

CIRUS ASSOCIATES (S.W.)
Little Hintock
Kington Magna
GILLINGHAM
SP8 5EW

C.I.S.S. Publishing
63 Ravensbourne Gardens
Clayhall
ILFORD
IG5 0XH
Stamps. Postal History.

CITY PUBLISHING
Regent House
291 Kirkdale
LONDON
SE26 4QE
Local Travel Guides.

CITY WOMEN'S NETWORK
30 Essex Street
LONDON
WC2R 3AL

CIVIL-COMP PRESS
10 Saxe-Coburg Place
EDINBURGH
EH3 5HR
Engineering.

CIVIL SERVICE AUTHOR
c/o Iain R McIntyre
Burnside
Station Road
BEAULY
IV4 7EQ

C.K.D. PUBLICATIONS
61 Highfield Road (South)
CHORLEY
PR7 1RH
Local History.

CLAIBORNE PUBLICATIONS (UK)
36 High Street
SAXMUNDHAM
IP17 1AB

CLAIRE PUBLICATIONS
Tey Book Craft Centre
Brook Road
Great Tey
COLCHESTER
CO6 1JE
School Textbooks.

CLAM PUBLICATIONS
13 Pound Place
Shalford
GUILDFORD
GU4 8HH

CLARINETWISE
Jacqueline Browne
Pengribyn
Cilrehdyn
LLANFYRNACH
SA35 0AA
Tel 01239 698 601
Clarinetwise magazine is a new commercial-looking glossy for the clarinet world. A must if you have anything to do with clarinets. Subs £12 pa. Unclear how many issues this gets you or the price of a sample copy. Ring to check.

CLARION
Neatham Mill
ALTON
GU34 4NP
Illustrated poetry booklets. Also the Prospero imprint.

CLARK AND HOWARD BOOKS
4 Merridale Garden
WOLVERHAMPTON
WV3 OH4
Tel 01902 22715
Small publisher run as a hobby. Books typed by Hilary Clark commercially printed (offset litho or similar) paperbacks.
'Horse and Cart Days. Memories of a farm boy' by A.B. Tinsley. 'The Greens of Grasmere.' A Narrative by Dorothy Wordsworth 1808'. 60pp. 8 illustrations and map.

B.R. CLARKE
11 Penn Gardens
BATH
BA1 3RZ
Railways.

Joseph CLARKE
37 Grafton Way
LONDON
W1P 5LA
Mainly bibliographies on down-to-earth subjects, eg "Proportional Representation"; "Sick Building Syndrome"; "Viticulture in England"; "Perfume Manufacture". Also "Where to Look for Job Vacancies" - a survey of job vacancy adverts in UK press. Even small presses can be boring!

NIGEL J CLARKE PUBLICATIONS
Unit 2 Russell House
Lym Close
LYME REGIS
DT7 3DE
Tel 012974 ~~3669~~ 42513
We publish Walking Guides/ Historical Town Guides/Booklets on Local West Country attractions/ Fossil booklets/Local speciality Maps/Tide Tables. We wholesale postcards and touring maps. Our market is mainly the West Country and we sell 25,000 titles annually.

CLAUDIA PRESS
C.S. Walton
BM Claudia
LONDON
WC1N 3XX
"Little Tenemet on the Volga", £5.99

*"I, Claudia - Feminism Unveiled",
£3.30
Ethnography/individualism.*

CLAYHANGER BOOKS
The Old Rectory
Clayhanger
TIVETON
EX16 7NY
Anthropology.

Mr Christopher CLAYTON
The Print Business Limited
91 Church Road
LONDON
SE19 2TA

CLEARWATER COMMUNICATIONS
77a Fountainhill Road
ABERDEEN
AB2 4EA

CLEARWELL CAVES
Clearwell
Coleford
FOREST OF DEAN
GL16 8JR
Children's Fiction.

CLEVELAND KEY
8 Worcester Close
STANFORD-LE-HOPE
SS17 8AL

CLEVER MAP COMPANY/ AGAMA LTD
6 Old Town
Clapham Common
LONDON
SW4 0JY
Tel 0171 498 1679
SAUNDERS, Rupert, 'The Tube Hopper,' 18 pp. booklet, ISBN 1-897828-06-3. Beautifully designed wallet-size, advice on how to cut down journey time on London tube. £2.50.

CLIFTON PRESS
P.O. Box 100
MANCHESTER
M20
Publishes educational study guides for students and teaching materials for tutors.

CLOCKTOWER PRESS
Duncan McLean
17 West Terrace
SOUTH QUEENSFERRY
EH30 9LL
Our aim is to produce small cheap booklets of new writing mostly Scottish and almost all short stories. All feature high quality illustrations. 3 or 4 produced per year. Order direct from the above address.

CLOUD
48 Biddlestone Road
Heaton
NEWCASTLE-UPON-TYNE
NE6 5SL

CLUANIE DEER FARM PARK
Beauly
IV4 7AE
Scottish Red Deer.

Hilary Anne CLUTTEN
Rose Farm
North Green
Pulham St. Mary
DISS
IP21 4XX

Local Food.

C.M.R (Constance Rover) PUBLICATIONS
Flat 1
4 Clifton Crescent
FOLKESTONE
CT20 2EW

CND PUBLICATIONS
162 Holloway Road
LONDON
N7 8DG
Law.

C N P PUBLICATIONS
Dr James Whelter
Roseland
Gorran
ST AUSTELL
Tel 01726 843501
Publishes a quarterly Cornish magazine, The Cornish Banner/An Banir Kernowck, and occasional booklets that develop from that: viz. political essays, poetry, celtic design, history etc. ISSN 0306 9079.

COALVILLE PUBLISHING COMPANY
Springboard Centre
Mantle Lane
Coalville
LEICESTER
LE6 4DR

COBTREE PRESS
Anthony Smith
Little Preston Lodge
Coldharbour Lane
Aylesford
MAIDSTONE
ME20 7NS
Fine Printer.

COBWEB
57 William Morris House
Margravine Road
LONDON
W6 8LR

COCKBIRD PRESS LIMITED
P.O. Box 356
HEATHFIELD
TN21 9QW

COCK AND BULL PRESS
Andy G.
P.O. Box 612
CARDIFF
CF2 4XS
Currently producing my own work: cheap queer fiction.

CODIL Language Systems
33 Buckingham Road
TRING
HP23 4HG
<The London Gunners come to Town examines the life in a temporary WW1 garrison town (Hemel Hempstead) as seen by a child, the borough surveyor, and the London Territorials (47th Division). 288 pages, profusely illustrated, bibliography, extensive index, £9.95 p&p £1.50.

COLLECTORS' BOOKS
Bradley Lodge
Kemble
CIRENCESTER
Gl7 6AD

COLLINDIST PUBLICATIONS
Robert Corfe
6 Southgate Green
BURY ST. EDMUNDS
IP33 2BL
Tel 01284 754 123
Publishing arm of the Campaign For Industry and The Collindist Association. The CFI is the only U.K. organisation promoting the productive economy within the constraints of social and environmental responsibility. The CA is the philosophical think-tank for the CFI.

COLLINS AND BROWN
Mercury House
195 Knightsbridge
LONDON
SW7 1RE

John Hugh COLLINS
15 Oakenbrow Sway
LYMINGTON
SO41 6OY
Family History.

COLOPHON PRESS
18A Prentis Road
LONDON
SW16 1QD
Bibliography.

COLOUR GROUP (G.B.)
17 Castlebar Road
LONDON
W5 2DL
History of technology.

COLT BOOKS
9 Clarendon Road
CAMBRIDGE
CB2 2BH

COMMUNITY OF POETS PRESS
Philip Bennetta
Hatfield Cottage
CHILHAM
CT4 8DP
Produces themed quarterly A5 poetry magazine with an emphasis on community and organisational life and learning.

COMPART
7 The Maltings
Grove Green
MAIDSTONE
ME14 5UF
Have published 'The Competitors Handbook of Slogan and Tiebraker Information' by Mervyn Coverdale.

COMPOSERLINK
Mr Richard Lauder
18 Ashwyn Street
Hackney
LONDON
E8 3D

COMMON GROUND
45 Shelton Street
Covent Garden
LONDON
WC2H 9HJ

COMMON SENSE
16 Keir Street
EDINBURGH
EH3 9EU
A journal of new ideas.

COMMONWORD
21 Newton Street
MANCHESTER
M1 1FZ

COMMON GROUND: WORLDLY GOODS
Unit G. Arnos Castle Estate
Junction Road
Brislington
BRISTOL
BS4 3JP
'Apple Source Book'.

COMMON SENSE
Richard Gunn or Brian McGrail
P.O. Box 311
SDO
EDINBURGH
EH9 1SF
Journal of Edinburgh Conference of Socialist Economics publishes political analysis, philosophy, fiction, poetry and reviews.

COMPACT SERVICES
29 St Helen's Road
Sandford
WAREHAM
BH20 7AX

COMPASS PUBLICATIONS
191 Field Avenue
CANTERBURY
CT1 1TS

COMPOSITIONS BY CARN
10 Laburnam Grove
EASTLEIGH
SO5 4DJ

COMPUPRINT PUBLISHING
1 Sands Road
Swalwell
NEWCASTLE-UPON-TYNE
NE16 3DJ
Political Science.

COMPUTER PROFESSIONALS FOR SOCIAL RESPONSIBILITY
(Berkeley Chapter)
http://www.cpsr.org/dox/
program/workplace/index.html
Newsletter.

COMTAL PUBLICATIONS
K. Goodwin
87 Queens road
TEDDINGTON
TW11 0LZ
"Cathars - country, customs and castles", by Simon de Vries: 20pp + map. £2.25 inc P+P
In preparation:
"Wines of the Cathar Country"
"Food of the Cathar Country"
"In the Footseps of History 1- The de Montforts".

COMUNN NA CLARAICH
(The Clarsach Society)
65 Mount Vernon Road
EDINBURGH
EH16 6JH
Poetry.

CONCATENTION
44 Brook Street
ERITH
DA8 1JQ

A.T CONDIE PUBLICATIONS
Merrivale
Main Street
CARLTON

CV13 0BZ

CONDOR BOOKS
3 Broadway
Earlsdon
COVENTRY
CV5 6NW
Tel/Fax 01203 714 359
GRANA, Alvaro, 'How to make and play Pan-pipes.' Splendid manual & music book, good review in Times Ed. Suppl., 9 Feb.'96. 1995, 40 pp. A4 pbk, ISBN 0-9526729-0-1, £8.95. Special rates for educational establishments.

CONNECTIONS
c/o Jeanne Conn
165 Dominic Drive
New Eltham
LONDON
SE9 3LE

CONNOLLY ASSOCIATION
c/o Four Provinces Bookshop
244-246 Grays Inn Road
LONDON
WC1X 8JR

CONSIDER
Dr Charles Harvey
58 Keyford
FROME
BA11 1JT
Etymology: L. considerare, (sidus - eris, a star) originlly, and still amongst those who know, 'to examine the stars'. CONSIDER has been set us to publish consid ered works on all aspects of astology, especially in relation to psychology, philosophy, and world affairs.

Robert CONSTANT
17 Droxford Crescent
Tadley
BASINGSTOKE
RG26 6BA
Children's Fiction.

CONTEXT
18 Winnipeg Drive
Lakeside
CARDIFF
CG2 6ET
Tel/Fax 01222 753 162
News Magazine of Family Therapy & Systemic Practice. Membership journal for Association of Family Therapy. Quarterly; single issue £4; ISSN 0969 1936.

CONTRA FLOW
56a Info Shop
56 Crampton Street
LONDON
SE17
Info 'zine. Donation for dose.

F COOK TRAVEL GUIDES
8 Wykeham Court
Old Perry Street
CHISLEHURST
BR7 6PN

COOPER PUBLICATIONS
24 Pelham Road
Clavering
SAFFRON WALDEN
CB11 4PQ
Local Walks Books.

COPPER BEECH PUBLISHING
11 Martyns Place
EAST GRINSTEAD

RH19 4HF

Dave COOPER
5 Kingsgate Drive
BLACKPOOL
FY3 8HB
Biography.

R.A. COOPER
Butterhill House
49 Old North Road
Wanstord
PETERBOROUGH
PE8 6LB
Family History.

Victor COOPER
20 Lynwood Chase
BRACKNELL
RG12 2JT
A Dangerous Woman - Life and Times of Lady Deborah Moody (1586-1659?) of London and Wiltshire, Founder of Gravesend, Brooklyn, NY. Celebrates 350th anniversary of first 'Freedom of Conscience' charter - 'A unique contribution to the cause of freedom' - Rudolph Guiliani, NY City Mayor. Price: £11.40 incl p&p.

COORLEA PUBLISHING
West Lodge
Taverham Hall
NORWICH
NR8 6HU

I.S. COPINGER
J.W. Dickenson
44 St. Monica Grove
DURHAM
DH1 4AT
Local History.

COQUELICOTS PRESS
Fovant Elm
Tisbury Road
SALISBURY
SP3 5JY

CORBIE PRESS
11 River Street
Ferryden
MONTROSE
DD10 9RT
Art. Poetry.

CORDEN OF CAMBRIDGE PRESS
47 Newham Road
CAMBRIDGE
CB3 9EY
Little Press. The Historic River by S M Haslam. Rivers and culture down the ages. Outdoor Games for Brownies in Built-Up Areas by S M Haslam.

CORNER HOUSE PUBLISHING
70 Oxford Street
MANCHESTER
M1 5NH

THE CORNUCOPIA PRESS
10 Curzon Street
LONDON
W1Y 7FJ

CORNWALLIS PRESS
24 Linton Crescent
HASTINGS
TN34 1TJ
Literature.

CORPORATE LINK
Swale View

Low Row
RICHMOND
DL11 6NE

CORRIB CONSERVATION CENTRE
Ardnasillagh
OUGHTERARD
County Galway
Republic of Ireland
Archaeology.

CORYLUS PRESS
Hazel Harvey
53 Thornton Hill
EXETER
EX4 4NR
Tel 01392 54068
Exeter local guides to parks and gardens. 'Secrets of a Garden City' by G. Levine 40 pages £4.50. ISBN 0 951571508. 'Exeter Park Leaflets' by G. Levine 50p each.

THE COSMIC ELK
Heather Hobden
68 Elsham Crescent
LINCOLN
LN6 3YS
Tel 01522 691 146
Books, booklets, leaflets & posters on HISTORY, SCIENCE & the HISTORY of SCIENCE. New authors & ideas welcome. Books in print. Prices include postage in UK: "John Harrison and the Problem of Longditude", ISBN 1-871441-13-X, £10
"Life and Death in the Traditional Beliefs of the Yakuts", ISBN 1-871443-12-1, £2
"The Telescope Revolution", ISBN 1-871443-10-5, £3
"First Scientific Ideas on the Universe", ISBN 1-871443-05-9, £2 A4 card & comb binding.

MS CATHERINE COT
c/o L'Autre Journal
2 rue du Colonel Drint
F-75001 PARIS
France

COTHILL HOUSE SCHOOL
Niche Marketing and Publishing Service
The Dovecote
6 Turville Barns Eastleach
CIRENCESTER
GL7 3QB
History of Education.

COTHU
The Business Council for the Arts
Irish Management Institute
Sandyford Road
DUBLIN 16
Republic of Ireland
Art.

COTSWOLD MUSIC
Bridge Cottage
Beckford
TEWKESBURY
GL20 7AN
Music.

COTTAGE BOOKS
1 Higher Hill Lane
CULLOMPTON
EX15 1AG
Poetry.

COTTAGE GALLERY PUBLICATIONS
Husilar Cottage Studio/Gallery
South Yorkshire Buildings

Moorend Lane Silkstone Common
BARNSLEY
S75 4RJ
Art.

COTTAGE LOAF
The Coppers
Scothern Lane
Sudbrooke
LINCOLN

COTTAGE PUBLISHING
Norton Cottage
Station Road
Letterston
HAVERFORDSWEST
SA62 5RZ
Food.

COUNTER INFORMATION
p/h CI
11 Forth Street
EDINBURGH
EH1
*Broadsheet reporting resistance
activity worldwide.*

COUNTERPOISE
Chris Atton
Dunning Library
Napier University
10 Colinton Road
EDINBURGH
EH10 5DT
e-mail: c.atton@napier.ac.uk
*NEW JOURNAL to be published in
Jan. 1997 by Alternatives in Print
Task Force of the American Library
Association. Chris Atton is
Associate Editor for UK. He is also
'Information for Social Change.'
(see Librarians at Liberty.)*

COUNTER PRODUCTIONS
P.O. Box 556
LONDON
SE5 0RL
*Publisher and Mail Order sales of
UK and overseas small press
publications. Specialising in
radical, dissident, surreal, outre,
anarchic, visionary, fortean, anti-
authoritarian books, magazines
and pamphlets. Send sae for
descriptive catalogue.*

COUNTYVISE
(Birkenhead Press)
John Emmerson
1-3 Grove Road
Rock Ferry
BIRKENHEAD
L42 3XS
*Local biography. Local History.
Historical Biography. History of
History of the Port of Liverpool and
its Docks. Merseyside Port Folios.*

COVENTRY CHURCH CHARITIES
c/o Godfrey-Peyton and Co.
Hill Street
COVENTRY
Local History.

COVEROPEN: A.G. (NORTHERN)
138 Albert Road
Farnworth
BOLTON
BL4 9NE
Humour.

John COWELL
52 Lon-y-bryn
MENAI BRIDGE
LL59 5LL

Local History.

C.P.I. PRESS
Science House
Winchcombe Road
NEWBURY
RG14 5QX
Agriculture.

C.R Publishing
35 Thorn Grove
CHEADLE HULME
SK8 7LP

CRABFLOWER PAMPHLETS
Jeremy Page
18 Nevill Road
LEWES
BN7 1PF
*Distributed by the Frogmore Press -
published pamphlet collections by
new (Michael Paul Hogan, Sophie
Hannah, Giles Goodland) and
established (Geoffrey Holloway,
Robert Etty, David Lightfoot) poets
in addition to several significant
anthologies.
"Objects on Hills" by Giles
Goodland (1996)
"Second Helping of your Heart" by
Sophie Hannah (1994).*

CRABTREE PRESS
4 Portland Avenue
HOVE
BN3 5NP
Historical Biography.

CRABWELL PUBLICATIONS
2 The Ridgeway
River
DOVER
CT17 0NX

CRACKED BELL PRESS
51 York Avenue
Great Crosby
LIVERPOOL
L23 5RN

CRAKEHILL PRESS
5-7 Sowerby Road
THIRSK
YO7 1HR

CRANBOURN PRESS
7 Cecil Street
LONDON
WC2N 4EZ
*Subjects: Art.
Books July to December 1991 - 1*

CRANE PRESS
30 South Street
ASHBY-DE-LA-ZOUCH
LE6 5BT
*Subjects: Local History. Books
January to June 1991 - 1*

Nico CRAVEN
The Coach House
Ponsonby
SEASCALE
CA20 1BX
Tel Beckermet 841256
*A book on cricket published each
spring by the author - mostly about
the character and characters of
county and village cricket.*

CREATION BOOKS
83 Clerkenwell Road
LONDON
EC1R 5AR

Tel 0171 430 9878 fax 0171 242
5527
*Spring 1996 catalogue contains:
Hammer of the Gods, apocalptic
texts for the criminally insane.
Authored by Nietsche but describes
their other titles which range from
studies of murderers to sexfilth. As
they put it: 'Dedicated to the
extremes of the imagination, to
publishing violent and beautiful
literature. To blast the citadels of
enlightenment and immolate
"proper" literature in a pyre of
Fahrenheit 451 intensity.'*

CREATIVE MIND
Lark Lane Community Centre
80 Lark Lane
LIVERPOOL
L17 8UU

CREATIVE MONOCHROME
20 St Peters Road
CROYDON
CR1 1HD

CREEK PUBLISHERS
Tarn Hows
Wyre Road
Skippool
Thornton-Cleverleys
BLACKPOOL
FY5 5LF
Local History.

CREMER PRESS
26 Whalley Bankes
King Street
BLACKBURN
BB2 1NU
*Established over forty years in
printing, letterpress and offset litho.
Now specialising in short run
books of poetry etc.*

CRESCENT MOON
Jeremy Robinson
18 Chaddesley Road
KIDDERMINSTER
DY10 3AD
*We publish books on poetry,
media, literature, feminism and the
arts. We publish two literary
magazines: "Passion"(UK) and
"Pagan America" Lead titles.
"Andy Goldsworthy" by William
Malpas, £12.99, a critical
appreciation of the popular British
contemporary sculptor.
"The Best of Peter Redgrok's
Poetry", by Peter Redgrok, £12.99,
a collection of poetry from one of
the most powerful of British poets.*

**CRICKET STATISTICIANS,
ASSOCIATION OF**
3 Radcliffe Road
West Bridgford
NOTTINGHAM
NG2 5FF
Cricket.

CRITICAL WAVE PUBLICATIONS
Steve Green & Martin Tudor
33 Scott Road
Olton
SOLIHULL
Tel 0121 706 0108
*'Critical Wave'- The European
Science Fiction and Fantasy Review
- is the Genre's leading showcase
for news reviews features and art
portfolios. Founded in 1987
Michael Moorcock has called it*

*'The most consistently interesting
and intelligent review on the SF
scene'.*

CRITIQUE
Dean Braithwaite
Rhyd-Dderwen
Hebron
WHITLAND
SA34 0XX
*Critique is an independent review
supplying to the printed and
broadcast media in general, with
special emphasis on 'alternative'
and small press publications. All
submissions and publicity material
welcome.*

CROCHET DESIGN
17 Poulton Square
MORECAMBE
LA4 5PZ
Handicrafts.

CROCUS
Cathy Bolton
Commonword
Cheetwood House
21 Newton Street
M1 1F2
Tel 0161 236 2773
*We are a community publisher. We
publish a variety of work by North
West Writers. In particular we seek
to give a voice to people who
traditionally have been denied or
lacked access to publication.*

CROFTSPUN PUBLICATIONS
Catherine Gill
Drakemyre Croft
Cairnorrie
Methlick
ELLON
AB41 0JN
Tel 01651 4252
*Pocket sized booklets with card
cover desk-top published for
individuality and up to the minute
accuracy. The Birthday Book is
specially written for the client's birth
date and the Cottage Guide is
being continually updated.*

CROLKERNE BOOKS
95 Westward Drive
Pill
BRISTOL
BS20 0JS

CROMWELL EDITIONS
43 Manchester Street
LONDON
W1M 5PE
Art. Biography.

CROOKED STARE
Flat 2
47 Shortlands Road
BROMLEY
BR2 0JJ
*Publishers of poetic and quirky
art.zines including:
"Diving for Aliens", the story of an
outsider.
"Kids of Delusion", an offbeat zine
for winsome poets.
Send 50p for a sample issue.*

CROSBY'S BOOK PROMOTION
14 Highmead
FAREHAM
PO15 6BM
Romantic Fiction.

Phyllis CROSSLAND
Trunce Farm
Greenmoor
SHEFFIELD
S30 7DQ
Second World War.

CROSS-TALK
Editor Martin Spellman
P.O. Box 803
HARROW
HA3 6UH
An irregular publication which describes itself as 'A Trade Union Zine of Commentary and Analysis for the Communications Industry'. Price 50p per issue or £2.00

CROW'S ROCK PRESS
c/o A McHugh
The G.A.A. Centre
CAHERLISTRANE
Galway
Republic of Ireland

CROYDON NATURAL HISTORY AND SCIENTIFIC SOCIETY
CHNSS Ltd
20 Queenhill Road
Selsdon
SOUTH CROYDON
CR2
Croydon in the 1940s and 1950s an illustrated history edited by John Gent. 64pp, £6.45 incl p&p, cheques to above.

C.R.S. RECORDS
26 Crosland Road North
LYTHAM ST. ANNES
FY8 3EP
Children's Fun Books.

CRUCIFORM PRESS
2 Southview Close
SOUTHWICK
BN42 4TX

CRUITHNE PRESS A.P.G.
10 The Square
GLASGOW
G12 8QQ
European History.

CRUSE
Cruse House
126 Sheen Road
RICHMOND
TW9 1UR

CRYPTOZOOLOGY NEWSLETTER
Huntshieldford
St Johns Chapel
BISHOP AUKLAND
DL13 1RQ

C S PUBLISHING
P.O. Box 8186
NICOSIA
Cyprus
Tel 357 2 333069

C.T.A PUBLICATIONS OFFICE
Generation Centre
Dame Street
ROCHDALE
OL12 6XB

C.T.W PUBLICATIONS
75 High Street
SPENNYMOOR
DL16 6BB

CUBE PUBLISHING
Croydon College Company
College Road Croydon
CR9 1DX

Poetry.

CUBE PUBLICATIONS
Local Heritage Books
6 Pound Street
NEWBURY
RG14 6AB

CUCKOO PUBLISHING
40 Hayward Avenue
LOUGHBOROUGH
Children's non-fiction.

CUCKOO HILL PRESS
David Chambers
Ravelston
South View Road
PINNER
HA5 3YD
Fine press.

CULLABINE BOOKS
11 Pound Close
RINGWOOD
BH24 1LR

CULVA HOUSE PUBLISHERS
A. Whitworth
The Carrs
Briggswath
WHITBY
YO21 1RR
Local History.

CURIOUSLY STRONG
Bateman Street
CAMBRIDGE
CB2 1NB

CURVED AIR
8 Sherard Road
LONDON
SE9 6EP
Model yachts.

CWM MORLAIS BOOKS
K. James
2 Brecon Rise
MERTHYR TYDFIL
CF48 2BW
Established in 1992. Publishes own work only, ranging from drama to sf/fantasy.

CYPHERS
3 Selskar Terrace
Ranelagh
DUBLIN 6

D.A.C. PUBLICATIONS
12 South Bank
Staplehurst
TONBRIDGE
TN12 0BD

DAEMON PRESS
35 Kinnard Way
CAMBRIDGE
CB1 4SN
Biography.

Henry DAGNALL
30 Turner Road
Queensbury
EDGWARE
HA8 6AY
Astronomy.

DAGON MAGAZINE
Carl T Ford
11 Warwick Road
TWICKENHAM
TW2 6SW
Journal of eldritch lore and fantasy fiction inspired by Lovecraft.

DAINICHI(ACADEMIC)PUBLICATIONS
c/o P.O. BOX 556
LONDON
SE5 0RL
Independent Academic publisher specialising in philosophy. Titles include primers and speculative works.

Alan DAKERS
Ragdon
CHURCH STRETTON
SY6 7EY
Local History.

DALE HOUSE PRESS
John Crook
18 Keere Street
LEWES
BN7 1TY
Tel 01273 472 007
'The Ladies of Miller's' by Diane Crook. The book tells the story of two remarkable, eccentric sisters who in 1939 purchased the former home of a miller in Lewes High Street and promptly set about turning it into an arts centre! With help from nearby Charleston, the two sisters were able to maintain the artistic impetus through the war and went on to set up the influential Millers Press. The book provides an interesting glimpse of pre and post-war cultural life in the area. Price £7.50.

DALPHINIS PUBLICATIONS
7 Birling House
Graveney Grove
LONDON
SE20 8XA
Poetry.

DALRIADA
2 Brathwic Place
BRODICK
Isle of Arran
KA26 8BN

DALTON WATSON FINE BOOKS
14 Highfield Road
BIRMINGHAM
B15 3DU
Military History.

DAMIER BOOKS
5 Waterloo Street East

TIPTON
DY4 8NG

DANDELION ARTS/MAGAZINE (Fern Publ's)
Ed. J Gonzales-Marina
24 Frosty Hollow
EAST HUNSBURY
NN4 0SY

DANIELS PUBLISHING
38 Cambridge Place
CAMBRIDGE
CB2 1NS
Tel 01223 467 144 fax 01223 467 145
Publishes ring-bound photo-copiable resources concerned with health issues, health education, social welfares issues, stress management, etc. Resource sheets for use in conjunction with seminars/conferences.

DARK DIAMONDS PUBLICATIONS
Andrew Cocker
P.O. Box HK31
LEEDS
LS11 9XN
*Independent publisher established 1988.
"Dark Diamonds Magazine", essays and art on environmental and related issues.
"A Riot of Emotions Fanzine", art/illustrations poetry zine/music reviews.*

DARK LILY
BCM Box 3406
LONDON
WC1N 3XX

DARK PEAK DESKTOP PUBLISHING
63 Warley Town Lane
Warley
HALIFAX
HX2 7SA
Tel 01422 839 899

DART
13 Prince of Wales Terrace
LONDON
W8 5PG

PER PRO DATNOW LIMITED
Thames View Business Centre
ABINGDON
OX14 3LF
Tel 01235 555 506

DAUPHIN PUBLISHING
118A Holland Park Avenue
LONDON
W11 4PA
Art.

Kay DAVENPORT
1 Cannon Flynn Court
Minrow Road
ROCHDALE
OL16 5DP
Local History.

David BARTON
45 Wellmeadow Road
Hither Green
LONDON
SE13 6SY
71 books published since 1978 plus 8 in collaboration with poets. Line drawings which do not illustrate but create the narrative; concerned with the predicament of the human figure.

"Stunt 3", 32 pages A5 (500 copies)
"Telling", 176 pages A5 (500 copies)

L. DAVIES
14 Larkhill Lane
Freshfield
LIVERPOOL
L37 1LX
Poetry.

Leonard DAVIS
82 Brightfield Road
LONDON
SE12 8QF
Music.

DAWES PUBLISHING
Oaklands
Elm Grove
WORTHING
BN11 5LH

JOHN DAWES PUBLICATIONS
12 Mercers
HAWKHURST
TN18 4LH
Swimming pool and energy efficiency technologies and aplications, handbooks and directories to inform the specifiers and the user. Proprietor is leading light in APN. (see Resources Directory under Membership Organisations)

DAWN PUBLICATIONS (BAR HILL)
84 The Spinney
Bar Hill
CAMBRIDGE
CB3 8SU
Sport (Soccer).

G. DAWSON
7 Rockland Road
LONDON
SW15 2LN
Careers.

DAY DREAM PRESS
39 Exmouth Street
SWINDON
SN1 3PU

N. DAY PUBLISHING
Clematis Cottage
Church Walk
THAMES DITTON
KT7 0NN
Travel.

DAYTON'S PUBLISHING
Homend House
15 The Homend
LEDBURY
HR8 1BN
Fishing Vessels.

DEAD PAN
Richard Lanyon
Polcrebo Moors
Nancegollon
HELSTON

DEAR SIR
Editor: John Johnson
54 Frant Road
TUNBRIDGE WELLS
TN2 5LJ

DEBORAH CHARLES PUBLICATIONS
173 Mather Avenue
LIVERPOOL

L18 6JZ
Tel 0151 724 2500
Specialist press for academic legal publications. Journals include international journal for the semiotics of law, law and critique, feminist legal studies. Monograph series in legal semiotics. Also custom typesetting including Hebrew and Greek.

DEBUT BOOKS
20 Aragon Lodge
Boleyn Court
Epping Road
BUCKHURST HILL
IG9 5UE
Tel 0181 924 3720
WINNER, Tolleck, 'Pushed to kill,' thriller described in flier as 'domestic horror,' 1996.

DECADE
26 The Meadway
BUCKHURST HILL
IG9 5PG
Local History.

DEDALMS
Langford Lodge
St Judiths Lane
SAWTOY
PE17 5XE
Tel 01 487 832 382

THE DEDALUS PRESS
John F. Donne
24 The Heath
Cypress Downs
DUBLIN 6W
Republic of Ireland
Tel Dublin 902582
New poetry by Irish poets and poetry in translation; the emphasis is on widening the horizons of Irish poetry producing work that stimulates challenges and delights.

DEERHURST PUBLICATIONS
Kevin Law
17 Frenchgate Road
EASTBOURNE
BN22 9EU
We publish low cost consumer guides. We specialise in medicine and health.

DEFIANT PUBLICATIONS
190 Yoxall Road
Shirley
SOLIHULL
B90 3RN

DELECTUS BOOKS
27 Old Gloucester Street
LONDON
WC1N 3XX
Publish books on Sadeian interest. Deal in decadent literature as a mail order bookseller.

DELHI LONDON POETRY QUARTERLY
50 Penywern Road
LONDON
SW5 9SX

DELOS PRESS
11 School Road
Moseley
BIRMINGHAM
B13 9ET

DEMI ARTS
The Business Village

Broomhill Road
LONDON
SW18 4JQ

DEMI-GRIFFIN PRESS
74 Victoria Road
OXFORD
OX2 7QE

DENVIL PRESS
1 Marlborough Road
EXETER
EX2 4TJ

DEORWENTA PUBLICATIONS
Westgarth
Edmundbyers
CONSETT
DH8 9NQ

DEOSIL DANCE PROJECTS
Keith Morgan
14 Littlemoor Lane
Balby
DONCASTER
DN4 0JZ
Publishers of unique pagan/new age & occult literature works on witchcraft runes spells & other magickalities. Publishers of modern grimoires & much much more!

DEPTFORD FORUM PUBLISHING
Jess Steele
110A New Cross Road
LONDON
SE14 5BA
Our publications aim to uncover, promote and celebrate SE London in general and Deptford in particular. At present we work within the local community producing publications about Deptford's history, helping to fill the scandalous gaps of a century of neglect.

DEPROVENT PUBLISHERS
71 Havelock Close
Commonwealth Avenue
White City
LONDON
W12 7NQ
Tel 0181 740 5160
Publisher of academic computer books and manuals. Accept contract jobs from self-publishers. Provide general printing services, runs self-publishing training workshops to aid interested writers from start to finish.

DERBY TV/TS GROUP
c/o Derby CVS Self Help Team
Temple House
Mill Hill Lane
DERBY
DE3 6RY

DERG HOUSE
St. Conlan's Road
NENAGH
Co. Tipperary
Republic of Ireland
Poetry.

DERWENTSIDE CULTURAL ASSOCIATION
Old Miners Hall
Delves lane
CONSETT
DH8 7EY

DESERT ISLAND BOOKS
Dr Clive Leatherdale

31 George Street
BRIGHTON
BN2 1RH
Quality books on Far Eastern travel, Dracula and vampirism and soccer histories.

DESKHAT
Seema Jena
90 Dunstable Road
LUTON
LU1 1EH
South Asian literature journal committed to publishing poetry, fiction, literary criticism and book review by writers from the Indian sub-continent, British Asian writers and writes from the rest of the Indian diaspora.

DESKTOP PUBLICATIONS
6 Silver Street
Winteringham
SCUNTHORPE
DN15 9ND

DESKTOP PUBLISHERS JOURNAL
listserve@DTPjournal.com
or try: http://
www.dtpjournal.com/ezine.htm
Free newsletter. Send message. Subscribe.

DESNE PUBLISHING
14 Sweetacres
Hemsby
GREAT YARMOUTH
NR29 4NR
Low cost - First Time publishing.

DESTRONIC
57 Tyndale Street
West End
LEICESTER
LE3 0QQ
Electronic publishing, graphic design, psyklops.

DETONATOR PUBLISHING
Steve Ainger
33 Damask Way
WARMINSTER
BA12 9PX
Tel 01985 212 871
Detonator is a sporadically published fanzine concentrating on new strips by upcoming writers and artists. Features and reviews on the British and American comics scene and a desire to inform and entertain.

THE DEUCALION PRESS
D S Savage
67 Church Street
Mevagissey
ST AUSTELL
PL26 6SR
Publishers of works on religious philosophy by the late Revd E F F Hill (1896 - 1954). Apocalypse and Other Essays. The Church and Unity, a pamphlet on the true nature of the church. A Theory of Sex.

DEVELOPMENT EDUCATION CENTRE
Selly Oak Colleges
Bristol Road
BIRMINGHAM
B29 6LE
Education.

DEVIZES BOOKS PRESS
Handel House
Sidmouth Street
DEVIZES
SN10 1LD

DEVON BOOKS
Wheaton Publisher
Hennock Road
EXETER
EX2 8RP

DEWDNEY PUBLISHING
Cairngorm Cottage
Treluswell
PENRYN
TR10 9AN
Hunting.

DEXTRAL BOOKS
P.O. Box 52 South D.O.
MANCHESTER
M20 8PJ
Education.

D.F.G. PUBLISHING
15 Park Lane
Duston
NORTHAMPTON
NN5 6QD

DIAL 174 MAGAZINE
Editor Joseph Hemmings
21 Mill Road
WATLINGTON
PE33 0HH
*Poetry, Short Stories and Essays.
Published four times a year in
seasonal cycle. Autumn issue
includes 'U-Judge-It' poetry
competition results. As mss are
received, anything outstanding or
topical is placed in a file for 'next
issue consideration'. Publishing
Policy is available from the editor.*

THE DIAMOND PRESS
5 Berners Mansions
34/36 Berners Street
LONDON
W1P 3DA

DIAMOND PUBLISHING GROUP
73 Princes Gardens
LONDON
W3 0LR

DICKENS PUBLISHING
Stoneleigh
North Cadbury
YEOVIL
BA22 7DJ
Fiction, General.

DIDSBURY PRESS
7 Darley Avenue
DIDSBURY
M20

DIEHARD LETTERPRESS
3 Spittal Street
EDINBURGH
EH3 9DY
Theatre History.

DIGITHURST
Newark Close
ROYSTON
SG8 5HL
General Fiction.

DIHEDRAL PUBLISHING
P.O. Box 3
HAVERSHILL

CB9 8DJ
Mathematics.

DILETTANTE PUBLICATIONS
44 St David's Hill
EXETER
EX4 4DT

John DILLEY
84 Barton Avenue
PAIGNTON
Railways.

JOHN DILNOT BOOKS
11 Harrowby Road
LIVERPOOL
L21 1DP
Art. Handicrafts.

DINOSAUR PRESS
Emma Hill
c/o The Eagle Gallery
159 Farringdon Road
LONDON
EC1
*Established in 1991 to publish
limited edition artists books and
encourage the collaboration
between artists and contemporary
writers.*

DINGO PRESS
150 Hardy Crescent
WIMBORNE
BH21 2AS

DINING TABLE PUBLICATIONS
22 Warleigh Road
BRIGHTON
BN1 4NT

DIONYSIA PRESS
(see Understanding)

DIRECT CLAIM
86 Freston Road
LONDON
W11 4BH

DIRECT EXPERIENCE
18 Anglesea Road
IPSWICH
IP1 3PP
*Lectures and workshops for
primary schools based on our
book, A Tool for Learning.*

**DISABILITY ARTS MAGAZINE
(DAM)**
10 Woad Lane
Great Coates
GRIMSBY
DN37 9NH

DISABILITY WRITES
2 Temple Square
MANCHESTER
M8 8UP

DISCUSS
c/o DISC
Trinity Community Centre
Middle St
LANCASTER

THE DITCH
P.O. Box 587
LONDON
EC2
*Community arts mag for Borough
of Shoreditch: 'Don't treat the
community here like the plastic
figures on an architect's model.'*

PETER DIXON BOOKS
30 Cheriton Road
WINCHESTER
SO22 5AX

DO-DO MODERN POETS
Patric Cunane and Sue Johns
108 Sheldrick Close
LONDON
SW19 2UK
Poetry.

Bob DOBSON
3 Staining Rise
Staining
BLACKPOOL
Tel/Fax 01253 895 678
*Really Lancashire: A magazine for
the Red Rose County. First issue
May 1996, £6 per year (4 issues).
Free pilot edition available from
above.*

DODMAN PRESS
Roger Burford Mason
26 West Hill
HITCHIN
SG5 2MZ

DODONA RESEARCH
Dalkeith House
8 Central Avenue
LEICESTER
LE2 1TB
Economics.

DOG
Editor: David Crystal
99 Wallis Road
LONDON
E9 5LN

DOG HOUSE PUBLICATIONS
18 Marlow Avenue
EASTBOURNE
BN22 8SJ
Tel 01323 29214
*State of the art How To publications
for companion dog owners.*

DOG ROSE PRESS
Peter Howell
26 Bell Lane
LUDLOW
SY8 1BN
*A new press specialising in 19th
century memoirs, architectural
monographs and publications on
disability and access.
"Memories" by Luke Ionides, pub.
July 1996.*

T DONOVAN PUBLISHING
52 Willow Road
LONDON
NW3 1TP

DOORS IN AND OUT OF DORSET
(Words & Action Dorset Ltd)
43 Avenue Road
BH21 1BS

DORCHESTER PRESS
69 Strathalmond Road
EDINBURGH
E14 8HP

DORNOCH PRESS Ltd
Barry C. Turner
Station Square
Dornoch
SUTHERLAND
IV25 3PG
Tel 01862 810 153; Fax 01862
810 608

'My Mi$tak£s: how to succeed
without making mistakes,' a 'how
to' book by printer turned
publisher, authentic hands-on stuff.
His 'Kwikbooks' series are fast
moving short story books which
give opportunity to new writing
AND DISTRIBUTION of selected
mss., which sets him apart from
vanity publishers. 1994, 2nd ed.,
76 pp. pbk, ISBN 1-86028-015-3,
£9.95.

DORSET WISE/GLOSA
Wendy Ashby
P.O. Box 18
RICHMOND
TW9 2AU
*'Dorset Wise' A5 magazine: Peace;
Environment; 3rd World.*

DOT PRESS LIMITED
54 Sandford Industrial Estate
Kennington
OXFORD
OX1 5RP

DOUDLE WAND LTD
c/o 15 Collier Street
GLOSSOP
SK13 8L3

DOUGLAS BARRY PUBLICATIONS
21 Laud Street
CROYDON
CR0 1SU

DOUGLAS ELLIOT PRESS
2A Denmark Terrace
Fortis Green
LONDON
N2 9HG

DOVECOTE HOUSE PRESS
Dovecote House
Wadenhoe
PETERBOROUGH
PE8 5SU
Poetry.

**DOVETAILS EDUCATIONAL
SERVICES**
James Aroowsmith
58 Flag Lane
CREWE
CW1 3BG

C J DOVEY
173 Chaldon Way
COULSDON
Surrey
CR5 1DP
Tel 01737 555 157
Educational Books.

DOWER HOUSE PUBLICATIONS
7A Westminster Street
YEOVIL
BA20 1AF

DOWNHOLLAND PUBLICATIONS
2 Southern Heys Cottage
Moss Side
Formby
LIVERPOOL
L37 9BE
Poetry.

DRAGONBY PRESS
Richard Williams
15 High Street
Dragonby
SCUNTHORPE
DN15 0BE
Tel 01724 840 645

Bibliography (crime fiction and mass market paperbacks).

DRAGONFLAIR
P.O. Box 5
CHURCH STRETTON
SY6 6ZZ
Computers.

DRAGONFLY PRESS
2 Charlton Cottages
Barden Road
Speldhurst
TUNBRIDGE WELLS
TN3 OLM
Tel 01892 862 395
Small press with a literary bias. Sporadic output. We do not welcome unsolicited manuscripts. The Writer's Guide to Self-Publishing by Charlie Bell. 24 page booklet.

DRAGONHEART PRESS
Mr. S. Woodward
11 Menin Road
ALLESTREE
DE22 2NL
Dragonheart Press harbours the voice of artists able to transform their perception into powerful new poetry. Using DTP and high definition copiers it is able to produce affordable new works. Past collections include zemgeist by Sunday Times story winner Paul Heapy.

DRAGONS BREW
50 Hookland Road
PORTHCAWL
CF36 5SG

DRAGONWHEEL BOOKS
Sandcott
Rectory Lane
PULBOROUGH
RH20 2AD

LAURENCE & PAMELA DRAPER
Laurence & Pamela Draper
Cnocnigan Culbokie
DINGWALL
IV7 8JH
Tel 034 987 559
Social and technical story of the mine worked in World War I mainly by German POWs. Recipient of the prestigious Lloyds Bank Award for Independent Archeologist.

DREADFUL WORK PRESS
Cora Greenhill
9 The Windses
Upper Padley
GRINDLEFORD
S30 1HY

DREAM PUBLICATIONS
4 Bradstock House
Harrowgate Road
LONDON
E9 7BS
Pyschology.

DREAMTIME BOOKS
21 Portland Road
OXFORD
OX2 7EZ

DREWFERN
83 St Helen's Road
LEAMINGTON SPA
CV31 3QG

DRIFFIELD
41 North Road
LONDON
N7 9DP
Driff's Guide to All the Second-hand and Antiquarian Bookshops in Britain.

DRUM FROAICH
Garrie View
Conon Bridge
DINGWALL
IV7 8HB
Children's Fiction (in Gaelic).

DRUMLIN PUBLICATIONS
Nure
MANORHAMILTON
Co. Leitrim
Republic of Ireland
Biography.

DRUNKEN DRAGON PRESS
84 Suffolk Street
BIRMINGHAM
B1 1TA

D SQUIRREL PRESS
12 Willow Corner
BAYFORD
SG13 8PN
Children's puppet show/story, verse sessions. Workshop for puppetry. Magazine of unpublished authors.

DUNCEITHERN PUBLISHING
111 Mussenden Road
Castlerock
COLERAINE
BT51 4TU

J DUNNING PUBLICATIONS
20 Riverside Gardens
ROMSEY
SO51 8HN

DUNNOCK PRESS
J.F. Haines
5 Cross Farm
Station Road
Padgate
WARRINGTON
WA2 0QG
Produces a single sheet A4 newsletter, HANDSHAKE, which is devoted to news and information about science-fiction poetry.

Ruth DUNSTAN
102 Redlands Road
SOLIHULL
B91 2LU
Poetry.

DURHAM ACADEMIC PRESS (ZNS)
1 Hutton Close
BISHOP AUCKLAND
DL14 6XB
Tel 01388 776 555
New academic imprint. Books, theses and monographs in various disciplines. Book proposals welcome. Catalogue available.

DYKE PUBLICATIONS
Ernest Ryman
38 Bankside
BRIGHTON
BN1 5GN
Tel 01273 552 241
Since 1984 this one-man band has concentrated on producing booklets and cards of local interest and usually of nostalgic flavour.

DYLLANSOW PENGWELLA
2 Chapel Terrace
Trispen
TRURO
TR4 9BA

DYNAMIC FORCES
James Hill
12 Russell Square
BRIGHTON
BN1 2EE
We provide a choice of imperishable scriptures whose unifying theme is no more persistent than a waxy quantity of atoms built up in the space between two objects.
"Everyday Fallacies Exploded"
"Encyclopaedia Immensus" both by Rev. William Lurk

EAGLETRIM PUBLISHERS
16 Kingsmill House
Kingsmill Terrace
LONDON
NW8 6AA

E.A.H.
1 Thompson Drive
THATCHAM
RG13 4FJ
Civil Aircraft.

EARLYBRAVE PUBLICATIONS
P.O. Box 3165
BRENTWOOD
CM13 1TL
DEIGHAM & HITCH (eds.), 'Clinical effectiveness from guidelines to cost-effective practice.' 1995, ISBN 1-900432005.

EARTH
Paul Bennett
20 Stonegate Road
BRADFORD
BD10 0HF
Magazine dedicated to Jonathan Seagull's magical mystery tours, Forteana, UFOs.

EARTH FIRST
Box 152a
Info Shop

56 Crampton Street
LONDON
SE17

EARTHGIANT
35a West Street
Abbotsbury
WEYMOUTH

EARTHLINES
7 Brookfield
Strichley
TELFORD
TF3 1EB

EARTHQUEST NEWS
19 St Davids Way
WICKFORD
SS11 8EX

EARTHRIGHT MAGAZINE
Burnfoot Lodge
Barskinning
MAUCHLINE
KA5 5TB
Scotland's only journal of radical economics/geonomics.

EARTHRIGHT PUBLICATIONS
Monica Frisch
8 Ivy Avenue
RYTON
NE40 3PU
Tel 0191 413 7972, E-mail mfrisch@gn.apc.org
Social, environmental and local issues. Latest publication got splendid review in 'BBC Vegetarian Good Food Magazine.' (Feb. 1997). Attractive distillation of experience by Red Herring which runs a wholefood shop, bakery and restaurant.
Red Herring Workers' Co-op, 'Cordon Rouge: Vegetarian and Vegan Recipes.' 176pp, pbk, illus, ISBN 0-907367-10-0, £7.50(p&p incl.)

EARTHWISE
498 Bristol Road
Selly Oak
BIRMINGHAM

M. EARWICKER
34 Marisfield Place
Selsey
CHICHESTER
PO20 0PD
Biography.

EAST END PUBLISHING
44 Oxted Road
SHEFFIELD
S9 1BP

EASTERN RAINBOW
Paul Rance
17 Farrow Road
Whaplode Drove
SPALDING
PE12 0TS
Tel 01406 330242

EASTFIELD PRESS
140 Boundary Road
NEWBURY
RG14 7NX
Local Travel Guide.

EAST LONDON HISTORY SOCIETY
13 Abbotsbury Close
Stratford
LONDON
E15 2RR

East London Record No. 17, articles on Old Canning Town and Hackney Schoolboy Football in the thirties, Youth Service in Tower Hamlets, Family Builders' Merchant Business, Whitechapel Burial Ground, Victorian College for Unorthodox Medicine - £2.90 incl postage.

EATON PUBLISHING COMPANY
5 Hatfield Road
Westbrook
MARGATE
CT9 5BL

EAVESDROPPER
Mr Philip Woodrow
15 Mount Pleasant Crescent
LONDON
N4 4HP
Monthly poetry broadsheet.

(THE) ECHO ROOM
c/o 45 Bewick Court
Princess Square
NEWCASTLE-UPON-TYNE
NE1 8EG

ECOBASE DIRECTORY ON DISK
Peter Berry Associates
Pwllyfan
Llansadwrn
LLANWRDA
SA19 8LS
Tel 01550 777 661
New revised version January 1997. Over 10,500 continuously updated records of statutory, voluntary and commercial organisations active locally, regionally, nationally or internationally in environmental field, UK and Ireland. £95 + VAT. (50% discount for existing users).

ECO ENVIRONMENTAL INFORMATION TRUST
10-12 Picton Street
Montpelier
BRISTOL
BS6 5QA
Tel 0117 942 0162 fax 0117 942 0164
Titles include:
* *Surviving the computer jungle, uses and abuses of computers in environmental information provision. £5.50 (p&p incl. in UK); 32 pp. [seminar report]*
* *Norman, Deborah The green maze, environmental information and the needs of the public. £7.50 (p&p incl); 68 pp. [research report]*
* *New title: ECO directory of environmental databases. (2nd ed) ISBN 1874666016. £40 (£25 concessionary rate). "A major reference work," the Library Association.*

Ross EDWARDS
Flat 17
Annaty
Upper Springland
Isla Road
PERTH
PH2 7HQ
Poetry.

THE EDGE
Magazine/Distribution for Savoy Comics
The Edge
P.O. Box 1106
CHELMSFORD

CM1 2SF
Magazine of imaginative past-SF writing (mostly). Writers of fiction include Shirley, Moorcock, Bertheht, Dr. Filippo Kilworth etc. Also use interviews.

Brian EDGE
48 Woodside Avenue
Wistaston
CREWE
CW2 8AN
Numismatics.

EDGE CREATIONS
P.O. Box 7
South Delivery Office
MANCHESTER
M20 0BR
General Fiction.

THE EDGELEY PRESS LIMITED
Molys House
39 Moscow Road
Edgeley
STOCKPORT
SK3 9QB
Tel 0161 477 0744
Takes a look at and comments on the Arts, consumer affairs, and where to dine in the North-West of England.

EDIT
22 Moorway Lane
Littleover
DERBY
DE3 7FR

EDITIONS
Bluecoat Chambers
School Lane
LIVERPOOL
L1 3BX

EDITORIAL MATTERS
Mr Peter Muir
P.O. Box 61
LONDON
SE21 7HS
Produces business magazines, books and newsletters. Also included in specialist music publications.

EDLINGTON PRESS
163 Walton Road
WALTON-ON-THE-NAZE
CO14 8NE
Second World War History.

EDUCATIONAL HERETICS PRESS
(see Education Now)
113 Arundel Drive
Bramcote
Beeston
NOTTINGHAM
NG7 3FQ
Tel 01602 257 261
Education. The group is a non-profit making research, writing and publishing co-operative devoted to developing the mainstream press. It reports posit more flexible forms of education and educational diversity through such initiatives as flexischooling, minischooling and democratic learning.

EDUCATIONAL PUBLISHING SOCIETY
Dr George West
27 Cavendish Road
Hazel Grove
STOCKPORT

SK7 6HY
Tel 01625 878 604

EDUCATION FOR DEVELOPMENT
7 Westwood Row
Tilehurst
READING
RG3 6LT
Education.

EDUCATION NOW
(see Education Heretics)

EDUCATION SERVICES
364 Woodstock Road
OXFORD
OX2 8AE

EGERTON PRESS
5 Windsor Court
Avenue Road
LONDON
N15 5JQ
Short Stories.

EGONIBS
see FINGERTIPS

EGOTIST PRESS
John MacKay
BM Egotist
LONDON
WC1N 3XX
Tel 0181 556 2293
Egotist Press publishes avant-garde literature and intellectual theory.

EIGHTFOLD PRESS
Fiona Beckett
c/o 1 Cage Lane
Great Stoughton
HUNTINGDON
PE19 4DB

ELANOR & HEREMOND LIMITED
Nantissa House
69 Leaside Road
ABERDEEN
AB2 4RX
Tel 01224 625574

ELDORADO COMMUNICATIONS
17 Condor Close
Garston
LIVERPOOL
L19 5NU
Soccer.

ELECTRIC FIREFLIES
41 Oxford Road
SOUTHPORT
PR8 2EG

ELECTRICK SKIZOO
Left Hand Productions
c/o AK Press
P.O. Box 12766
EDINBURGH
Anarchist 'zine which has features on the London Psychogeographical Association, Anarchist Computer Net, Anticopyright Network, Survivalists &c. plus listings. No price given.

ELECTRIC SHOCK TREATMENT
see EST

ELECTRONICK MEDIUM
126 Cleveland Street
LONDON
W1P 5DN
Parapsychology

ELEPHANT EDITIONS
BM Elephant
LONDON
WC1N 3XX
Anarchist pocket books.

ELF PUBLISHING CO
Langton Villa
Langton Green
TUNBRIDGE WELLS
TM3 0BB
Is independent author Michael Birch's self-publishing imprint. He produces his own paperbacks to a high commercial standard using an SPS Book-Builder system.

ELITE Words & Images
P.O. Box 24
SHERBORNE
Humour.

ELLENBANK PRESS
The Lathes
Selby Terrace
MARYPORT
CA15 6LX
Tel 01900 817 773
Based in Cumbria. Specialises in high quality hard backs and paperbacks on the Lake District, walking, climbing, conservation and natural history.

ELLERTON PRESS
Michael Brown
20 Ferndown Drive
Clayton
NEWCASTLE-UNDER-LYME
ST5 4NH
Poetry.

ELLIOT MANLEY ASSOCIATES
Tilford Reeds House
FARNHAM
Surrey
GU10 2DJ
Tel 025 125 2555
Software Quality Management, published five times a year.

ELLISONS' EDITIONS 4
1 High Street
Orwell
ROYSTON
SG8 5QN
Biography. Australian History.

ELM PUBLICATIONS
Seaton House
Kings Ripton
HUNTINGDON
PE17 2NJ
01487 773238
Ealing Library Management Publications.

THE ELMETE PRESS
22 Beck Lane
Collingham
WETHERBY
LS22 5BW

ELVENDON PRESS
The Old Surgery
High St
Goring-on-Thames
READING
RG8 9AW

ELVET PRESS
9 Crofters Green
WILMSLOW
SK9 6AY
Biography. Poetry.

ELVISLY YOURS
107 Shoreditch High Street
LONDON
E1 6JN

EMBERS HANDPRESS
Roy and Eve Watkins
16 St Leonard's Road
NORWICH
NR1 4BL

EMERGENCY BOOKS
c/o Central Books
99 Wallis Road
LONDON
E9
Magazine featuring work by names.

EMJAY
17 Langbank Rise
Rise Park
NOTTINGHAM
NG5 5BU

EMPRESS
C & P Devereux
P.O. Box 92
PENZANCE
TR18 2XL
Tel 01736 65790
Used to publish The Ley Hunter. Runs its own specialist book service.

ENCOUNTERS PRESS
Box 1
5 Freemount Street
LONDON
E9 7NQ

ENDEAVOUR PUBLISHING
Doreen Farrand
42 Stoke Road
Ashton
NORTHAMPTON
NN7 2JN
Tel 01604 864 346
We publish work which support our philosophy: 'Life should be simple improvable practical and above all enjoyable'. Childrens books, Alternative energy, Small businesses, Self improvement, Anything that feels right.

ENGLANG BOOKS
P.O. Box 240
SOUTHAMPTON
SO9 7RJ
Languages.

ENITHARMON
40 Rushes Road
PETERSFIELD
GU32 3BW

ENABLER PUBLICATIONS
Alan Dearling
3 Russell House
Lym Close
LYME REGIS
DT7 3DE
Tel/fax 01297 445 024
Aims to provide an interesting and innovative range of titles designed to explore freedom of spirit and movement. Areas of special interest include Travellers, independence and alternative lifestyles. Titles include:
* Merrifield, Jeff & others: The perfect heretics, Cathars and Catharism.

* Rawle, Sid: The right to roam, autobiography (as told to Jeremy Sandford).
* Dearling, Alan: The Sigil. A novel about journeys in several dimensions.

ENSIGN PUBLICATIONS
226 Portswood Road
SOUTHAMPTON
SO9 4XS

ENSLOW PUBLISHERS
US P.O. Box 38
ALDERSHOT
GU12 6BP
Children's non-fiction.

ENTERPRISE PUBLICATIONS
2A Southmoor, Buckleigh Road
Westward Ho!
BIDEFORD
EX39 3PU

ENTERPRISE AVIATION
42 Claygate Road
LONDON
W13 9XG
Aviation.

ENTERPRISE FIRST
FOA Jim Prettyman
47 Queen Charlotte Street
EDINBURGH
EHJ6 7EY

ENVOI
Roger Ellein
44 Rudyard Road
Biddulph Moor
STOKE-ON-TRENT
ST8 7JN

EN WRITING AND MUSIC
Carl Tinfield
P.O. Box 10553
LONDON
N1 1GD

EON PUBLICATIONS
(see Issue One/The Bridge)

EONTA
27 Alexandra Road
Wimbledon
LONDON
SW19 7JZ

EOTHEN PRESS
7 Bridge Street
Wistow
HUNTINGDON
PE17 2QA

E.P.A.
Blythburgh House
Wendens Ambo
SAFFRON WALDEN
CB11 4JU
Historical biography.

EQUINOX PRESS
Sinodun House
Shalford
BRAINTREE
CM7 5HN
Tel 01371 851097
For the present; minimalist poetry (such as haiku) only; in English or another language with English translation.

ERRAN PUBLISHING
Nick Clark
8 Dale Road

CARLTON
NG4 1GT
Publishes 'Poetry Hours' for Dreamland Poetry Group.

ESCAPE FROM GRAVITY
Association of Autonomous Astronauts
BM Jed
LONDON
WC1N 3XX
The irregular bulletin of the AAA who plan to leave this planet by any means necessary and have a five-year plan to establish a world-wide network of local, community-based AAA groups dedicated to building their own space ships. Send 4 first class stamps for the next 4 issues. Also available 'Here comes Everybody - the First annual Report of the AAA' for £2.50 postpaid - payable to J. Skeet.

ESCARGOT PRESS
Old Park Cottage
Woodbury Lane
AXMINSTER
EX13 5TL
Formed in 1991, self publishing poetry and later, it's hoped, stories. Texts are lettered by hand, then photocopied or printed on fine paper; binding was also hand done until orders increased. Our name indicates slowness, succulence and determined silvery track.

ESCREET PUBLICATIONS
Moe Sheerard-Smith
Garthend House
Millington
YORK
YO4 2TX
Small press set to establish a name in the field of writing tuition and advice. 'Write a Successful Novel' by Frederick E Smith and Moe Sherrard-Smith.

EST
Electric Shock Treatment
Brian Duguid
41a Bedford Hill
Balham
LONDON
SW12 9EY
Irregular music 'zine dealing with experimental/ industrial music. Latest issue, No. 7, concentrates on American Minimalist Music (Tony Conrad, Charlemagne Palestine, Rhys Chatham) plus the usual massive review section. Also reviews other publications and provides a directory of suppliers &c. (not all dealing with music). Price £3.00 - payable to B. Duguid.

ESTAMP
204 St. Albans Avenue
LONDON
W4 5JU
Reflects interest in professional involvement in printmaking and papermaking. The books are about the making of books and their materials.

E.S.T.
(see Electric Shock Treatment)

ESTUARY PRESS
11 Clare Close
Waterbeach

CAMBRIDGE
CB5 9PS
Poetry.

ETHNIQUE
42 Mackay House
Australia Road
LONDON
W12 7PB

ETHNOGRAPHICA
19 Westbourne Road
LONDON
N7 8AN
Nigerian Traditional Architecture. Vegetarian Cooking. Art. Photography.

Eileen EVANS
c/o Social Services
The Grove Rax Lane
BRIDPORT
DT6 3JL
Children's Fiction.

K. Jane EVANS
7 Seafield Court
51 South Road
WESTON-SUPER-MARE
BS23 2LU
Biography.

Roger D.C. EVANS
Brook House
Kirklands Road
Nailidon
SHIPLEY
BD17 6NS
Military History.

EVENSFORD PRODUCTIONS
Evensford
Little Chart
ASHFORD

EVERGREEN
P.O. Box 52
CHELTENHAM
GL50 1YQ
Tykes Dumplings and Scrumpy Jacks by Bryan Waites. An entertaining and instructive examination of 25 distinctive regions of Great Britain into the behaviour of people in the localities. Hardback, 240 pp, £9.95 inc. p&p.

EVERGREEN
P.O. Box 147
WALTHAM CLOSE
EN7 6BZ
Tel 01992 632 250
A bi-monthly maglet whose core function is to be a clearing-house for 'lonely hearts.' It has grown to include extra material such as info about various social activities (at which you can meet) or ideas for presents (which you can give) even odd anecdotes (which you can recount). Display ads offer even wider interests including free internet advertising, good food and home brewe centre, vegetarian society of Ireland and discrimination in sport.

EVERY CHANCE AT THE LAST PUBLICATIONS
18 Owthorpe Grove
Sherwood
NOTTINGHAM
NG5 2LX
National Hunt (Sport).

EVERYWOMAN
34 Islington Green
LONDON
N1 8DU

EXCALIBUR PUBLICATIONS
13 Knightsbridge Green
LONDON
SW1X 7QL

EXECUTIVE PUBLICATIONS
Spring Valley Industrial Estate
Braddan
DOUGLAS
Isle of Man

EXILE PUBLICATIONS
38 Emerald Street
SALTBURN-BY-THE-SEA
TS12 1ED
*Poetry magazine, accepting poems
from the North East and other
regions.*

EX LIBRIS PRESS
1 The Shambles
BRADFORD ON AVON
BA15 1JS
Tel/Fax 01225 863 595
*Small publisher specialising in
history, biography, walking guides
and landscape, mainly in West
Country, incl. four titles by the late
Ralph Whitlock. Free copy of
illustrated catalogue of up to 50
books.*

EXPERT BOOKS
18 Rawlins Close
Woodhouse Eves
LOUGHBOROUGH
LE12 8SD

EXPRESSIONS
10 Turfpits Lane
Erdington
BIRMINGHAM
B23 5DP

EXPERT PUBLICATIONS
Jill Jackson
Sloe House
HALSTEAD
CO9 1PA
Tel 01787 474744

EXTRA PUBLICATIONS
82 Trinity Road
LONDON
SW17 7RJ

EXTRAORDINARY PEOPLE PRESS
Katherine Butler
Suite 412
Triumph House
185-191 Regent Street
LONDON
W1R 7WB
Tel 0171 734 3749
*'We are a new small press which
has just published our first title
'Trans-x-u-all, the naked
difference.' We are dedicated to
publishing books by or about
'extraordinary people.' Our
publications are non-fiction. Our
second book is due out late 1997
on the subject of stage hypnosis.'
'Trans-x-u-all' costs £11.99. ISBN 0
9529482 0 6.*

EXUBERANCE
c/o Jason Smith
34 Croft Close
CHIPPERFIELD

EYEBROW EDITIONS
82 Sinclair Road
LONDON
W14 0NJ

FAIR WAY PUBLICATIONS
1 Fairway
TIVERTON
EX16 4NF
Education.

**FAME PUBLISHERS
INTERNATIONAL**
Samuel Agyepong
88B Morley Road
Leyton
LONDON
E10 6LL
*Publishing of books paperback &
hardback, fiction & non-fiction,
specialist, scientific, technical &
non-technical, works of
scholarship, science, religion,
literature, etc.
"Systems Approach to Organised
Life, Anatomy of a Nation at Ease,
Political Systems". Vols 1 & 2.*

FAMEDRAM PUBLISHERS
School Road
Gartocham
ALEXANDRIA
G83 8RT

FAMILY TREE MAGAZINE
Michael Armstrong
61 Great Whyte
Ramsey
HUNTINGDON
PE17 1HL
Tel 01487 814 050
*Monthly. Single copies UK £1.90;
subs. UK £21.50. ISSN 0267-1131*

FAMILY WELFARE ASSOCIATION
501-505 Kingsland Road
LONDON
E8 4AU
Education.

**FANCLUB & FANZINE
DIRECTORIES**
c/o Simon Wade

236 Kingsway
Huyton
LIVERPOOL
L36 9UF

FANNAG PRESS
P.O. Box 100
PORT ERIN
Isle of Man

FANTASY ASSOCIATION
15 Stanley Road
MORDEN
SM4 4DE

FAR COMMUNICATIONS
5 Harcourt Estate
Kibworth
LEICESTER
LE8 0NE
Pyschology.

T.C. FARRIES
Irongray Road
Lochside
DUMFRIES
DG2 0LH
Animals.

Michael FARR
40 Lillywhite Crescent
ANDOVER
SP10 5NA
Railway History.

THE FARTHING PRESS
Three Cottages
Short Green
Winfathing
DISS

FATCHANCE
Lake Cottage
South Street
Sheepuash
BEAUWORTHY
EX21 5ND

FAULKNER PUBLISHING
28 Fairhaven Close
Lode
CAMBRIDGE
CB5 9HG
Literature. Ancient History.

FAUST PUBLISHING COMPANY
Thorneyholme Hall
Roughlee
BURNLEY
BB12 9LH

FAVERSHAM SOCIETY
Fleur de Lis Heritage Centre
13 Preston Street
FAVERSHAM
ME13 8NS.
*Blackpowder Manufacture in
Cumbria detailed account of seven
factories, which between them
operate from 1764 to 1937. A4
format, 54pp with factory plans.
Faversham Papers No. 42. £4.95
post-free.*

FAX-PAX
Bowling Green Studio
Norfolk Road
FALMOUTH
TR11 3NT

FEASIBLE PRODUCTS
Alasdair Johnson
118 Dunbar's Close
Canongate
EDINBURGH

EH8 8BW
Tel 0131 557 1863
*A mantelpiece press for writers and
readers - send for catalogue!*

FEATHER BOOKS
Revd. John Waddington-Feather
Fairview
Old Coppice
Lyth Bank
Bayston Hill
SHREWSBURY
SY3 0BW
Tel 01743 872177
*We specialise in religious poetry;
primarily Christian, but any poetry
which tries to explore the mystery
of Godhead and life. Also publish
the Quill Hedgehog Clubs booklets
newsletter and poems written by
members of Quill Hedgehog
novels' fans.
"Death Came for the Archbishop
and other poems" by Maurice
Irvine (March 1995) ISBN 0
947718 22 2, £2.50
"Flowers From the Hill" by Bruce
James (August 19950 isbn 0
947718 25 7, £2.50*

FELPHAM PRESS
Kathy Kidd
6 Crescenta Walk
BOGNOR REGIS
PO21 2YA

FELTHAM PRESS
111 Station Road
NEW MILTON
BH25 6JP

FEMINIST ARTS NEWS
P.O. Box CR8
LEEDS
LS7 4TD
Tel 01532 629023
*Radical arts magazine for the 90s
relevant to womens lives.*

FEMINIST AUDIO BOOKS
52-54 Featherstone Street
LONDON
EC1Y 8RT

FEMINIST REVIEW
11 Carleton Gardens
Brecknock Road
LONDON
N19 5AQ

Robert FERGUSON-GRANDE
17 Kingsbury Road
LONDON
NW9 7HY
Poetry.

FERN PRESS
(see Words and Images)

FERARD-REEVE PUBLISHING
Greenfields Farmhouse
Kings Barn Lane
STEYNING
BN44 3YG
Plays.

FERRY PUBLICATIONS
Miles Cowsill
12 Millfields Close
Pentlepoir
KILGETTY
SA68 0SA
Tel 01834 813991
*Ferry Publications produces
specialist books on the history of*

ferries and ferry companies. Ferry Publications also produces a quarterly ferry magazine on the British ferry scene.

FESTIVAL EYE
38 Stanmer Street
LONDON
SW11 3EG
For the new-age traveller and Stonehenge fan

FICEDULA BOOKS
P.O. Box 10
LLANDRINDOD WELLS
LD1 5ZZ
Birds.

FIELDER GREEN ASSOCIATES
294 Tadcaster Road
YORK
YO2 2ET

FIELDS & FRAMES Productions
Corshellach
Bridgend
DUNNING
PH52 0RS

FILM WORDS
London House
243 Lower Mortlake Road
RICHMOND
TW9 2LS

FINE PUBLISHING
Priory Lane
Toft Monks
BECCLES
NR34 062

FINGER PRESS
27b Daventry Street
LONDON
NW1 6TE
Poetry and postcards.

FINGERTIPS
Ian Lang
7, Knights Croft
New Ash Green
LONGFIELD
DA3 8HT
Egonibs is a partnership of three writers intent on encouraging fellow writers. We publish Fingertips quarterly. The magazine contains essays, short fiction & poetry. No restrictions on subject, but pornography & offensive material is not welcome.

FIREFLY PUBLICATIONS
J Hart
7 Millward Road
RYDE
Isle of Wight

FIRE RAISERS
Alistair Fitchett
64 Lugar Place
Troon
STRATHCLYDE
KA10 7EA
Tel 0292 314057
Blending media and music fiction and the politics of dissent Fire Raisers is a magazine of contemptible writingof the '90s. The intention; to engender hope through action ... take a risk!

FIRST CLASS PUBLICATIONS
P.O. Box 1799
LONDON
W9 2BZ

FIRST RESOURCE
Paul Cowell
43 Vyner Street
YORK
YO3 7HR
Tel 01904 638 721
Religious publishers with a special interest in Mysticism, music worship, Dionysius.

FIRST TIME MAGAZINE
Josephine Austin
4 Burdett Place
George St.
HASTINGS
TN34 3ED
"First Time", ed Josephine Austin (LCSM), a bi-annual magazine designed to encourage first time poets. Poems not exceeding 30 lines are invited. Poems must not have been published elsewhere & must be author's original work. Name & address must be printed on each sheet. Manuscripts cannot be returned unless s.a.e. enclosed. Editor's decision is final. No correspondence can be entered into regarding choice for publication. UK subscription £6.00 pa + £1.00 postage US subscription $13.00 pa include. surface postage. Back copies £1.25 + postage, current issue £2.50 + postage.

FIRST TIME PRESS
4 Penswick Grove
Coddington
NEWARK-ON-TRENT
NG24 2QL
Interested in one act playscripts only, that may or may not have been performed, but have never previously appeared in print. No playscripts concidered without a preliminary letter.

FIRST WORLD PUBLISHING
Richard House
30-32 Mortimer Street
LONDON
W1N 7RA
Holidays. European Travel.

FIR TREE PRESS
Connie Stranks
Fir Tree House
Warmington
BANBURY
OX17 1BU

FISHER PRESS
P.O. Box 41
SEVENOAKS
TN15 6YN
Biography.

M FITTER
6 Avon Road
Keynsham
BRISTOL
BS18 1LJ
The War Over Keynsham (WW2). Foreword by Leslie Crowther CBE; Hard backed 350 page book; 137 photos/documents. £15.95 + £4.00 p&p. WW2 recollections of Keynsham residents; bombing, evacuees, plane crashes, American soldiers in Keynsham, ARP, Fire Service, Home Guard, local men in the Services.

FITZGERALD PUBLISHING
Tim Fitzgerald
89 Ermine Road
LONDON
SE13 5JJ
Specialist entomological and arachnological company producing books about spiders and stick insects for the university and hobbyist market.

FIVE LEAVES PUBLICATIONS
P.O. Box 81
NOTTINGHAM
NG5 4ER
Tel 0115 960 3355
Gender concern publications.

FIVE SEASONS PRESS
The Butts
Shenmore
Madley
HEREFORD
HR2 9NZ

FIVE STAR PUBLICATIONS
4696 West Tyson Street
Chandler
AZ 85226-2903
USA
Tel (602) 940-8182, fax (602) 940-8787
e-mail fivestar@ix.netcom.com
New title: Radke, Linda Foster: The economical guide to self-publishing. Foreword by Dan Poynter. 1996, 196 pps, pbk, ISBN 1877749168, $19.95 + $3.50 p&p (first class air mail $7.50).

FLAIR
5 Delavall Walk
EASTBOURNE
BN23 6ER

FLAMBARD PRESS
4 Mitchell Avenue
Jesmond
NEWCASTLE-UPON-TYNE
NE2 3LA
Poetry.

FLAUNDEN PRESS
Old Town Books
94 High Street
STEVENAGE
SG1 3DW
Set up 1991. Co-operative venture drawing on profesional skills of a small group of colleagues with high standards.

FLEECE PRESS
Simon Lawrence
1 Grey Gables
Blacker Lane
Netherton
WAKEFIELD
WF4 4SS
Fine Printer. Historical Biography. Book Binding.

FLEETING MONOLITH
62 Langdon Park Road
LONDON
N6 5QE

FLEMING PRESS
P.O. Box 662
SHEFFIELD
S10 1DU
Humour.

FLICKS BOOKS
29 Bradford Road

TROWBRIDGE
BA14 9AN
History of Cinema. World Cinema.

FLORENCE NIGHTINGALE MUSEUM TRUST
Stansgate House
Lambeth Palace Road
LONDON
SE1
Tel 0171 620 0374

THE FLORIN PRESS
Weavers Cot
Cot Lane
Biddenden
ASHFORD
TN27 8JB

FLOWERS EAST
199-205 Richmond Road
LONDON
E8 3NN
Art.

FLYING SAUCER REVIEW
P.O. Box 162
HIGH WYCOMBE
HP13 5DZ

FLYING SUGAR PRESS
Yaron
18 Beaumont Court
38/40 Beaumont Street
LONDON
W1N 1FA
Flying Sugar Press fulfils a childhood dream of self-publishing, and brings tog-ether my skills in drawing and writing. I discovered the techniques of etching, and the dream crystallised into Flying Sugar - my misnomer for the sugar lift process. Finely-crafted artists' books in small hand-printed editions, illustrated with my own etchings and text.

FLYLEAF PRESS
James Ryan
4 Spencer Villas
GLENAGEARCY
Co Dublin
Republic of Ireland
+ 280 6228
Specialises in Family and local history of Ireland.

FOCAL POINT PUBLICATIONS
81 Duke Street
LONDON
W1M 5DJ
Second World War.

FOCUS PUBLICATIONS
9 Priors Road
WINDSOR
SL4 4PD

FOLENS
Albert House
Apex Business Centre
Boscombe Road
DUNSTABLE
LU5 4RL

FOLK DANCE ENTERPRISES
Lambert's Hall
Kirkby Malham
SKIPTON
BD23 4BT

FOLKLORE FRONTIERS
Paul Screeton
5 Egton Drive

Seaton Carew
HARTLEPOOL
TS25 2AT

FOLLOW, FOLLOW
P.O. Box 539
GLASGOW
G11 7LT

FOLLY PUBLICATIONS
Folly Cottage
151 West Malvern Road
MALVERN
WR14 4AY

FOOD & FUTURES
Sue Mellis
49 Halifax Road
LONDON
NW3 2HX

FOOLSCAP & What Poets Eat
Judi Benson
78 Friars Road
East Ham
LONDON
E6 1LL
Tel 0181 470 7680
*"Foolscap" - twice yearly magazine
of poetry & prose, 80 pages, A4,
£3.00 or £6.00 subs.
"What Poets Eat" - collection of
food related poems & recipes. 120
pages, wire-bound, with black &
white illustrations. Includes : Ken
Smith, Mathew Sweeney, John
Harvey, Ruth Padel etc. £6.50 incl.
postage.*

**FOOTBALL SUPPORTERS
ASSOCIATION**
P.O. Box 11
LIVERPOOL
L26 1XP
Football.

FOOTMARK PUBLICATIONS
Robert Rose
12 The Bourne
FLEET
GU13 9TL
Tel 01252 621 431
*A series of local walks books,
giving directions and maps,
suitable for families Walsks
between two to seven miles. Most
take about two hours to walk.*

FOOTMARKS
Roger Jones
17 Holland Park Gardens
LONDON
W14 8DZ
*Presently a one person publisher
undertaking all research, writing,
illustration, design, marketing &
distribution. Leisure activities,
particularly walking, established
1995 with the printing of "Walking
London's Royal Parks".*

FORELAND Publishers
Foreland Fields Road
BEMBRIDGE
PO35 5TP

FOREST
Chris Tame
2 Grosvenor Gardens
LONDON
SW1W ODH
Tel 071 823 6550
*Freedom Organisation for the Right
to Enjoy Smoking Tobacco.
Publishes a wide range of leaflets,*

*pamphlets and monographs
relating to the general case for
individual liberty and free choice
and against social authoritarianism
and medical paternalism.*

FOREST BOOKS
20 Forest View
Chingford
LONDON
E4 7AY

FOREST PUBLISHING
Woodstock
Liverton
NEWTON ABBOT
TQ12S 6JJ
Railways.

FORMIL MODEL ENGINEERING
12 Oak Tree Close
BEDALE
DL8 1UG

John H. FORREST
64 Belsize Park
LONDON
NW3 4EH
Travel (South America).

FORTH NATURALIST & HISTORIAN
L. Corbett
Biological Sciences
University of Stirling
STIRLING
FK9 4LA
*To promote environment & heritage
- central Scotland. Annual - current
volume 18, "Central Scotland -
land , wildlife, people", 230 page
authoritive survey.Price £5 +£2
p+p.
"Introduction to Cahil Hills with
walks". £3.50.*

T.E.L. FORTY
22 Annesley Road
Iffley
OXFORD
OX4 4JQ
Poetry.

FORUM BOOKS
Little Heath Road
Chobham
WOKING
GU24 8RL

FORUM FOR SOCIAL STUDIES
53 Kinlet Road
LONDON
SE18 3BZ

Mr Anthony Peers FOTHERGILL
Pilgrims Bell
7 Janice Drive
Fulwood
PRESTON
PR2 4YE
No Unsolicited Poems/Prose.

**FOUNDATION FOR NATIONAL
PROGRESS**
P.O. BOX 58249
Boulder
CO 80322
USA
*Founded in 1975 to educate and
empower people to work toward
progressive change. The non-profit
FNP publishes Mother Jones
Magazine which covers world
issues, not just USA.*

THE FOUNDLING PRESS
Jim McCue
Birchetts Mead
Langton Road
Langton Green
TUNBRIDGE WELLS
TN3 0EG
*The Foundling Press exists to rescue
literary orphans and to print them
in fine limited editions. Titles
include: Letters from Henry James
to Bruce Richmond. Limited edition,
350 numbered copies, £20.
New title: The book, film and
theatre reviews of William Empson.
Originally printed in the
Cambridge magazine Granta, and
now collected in a limited edition of
300 copies, £18.*

FOUR OAKS PUBLICATIONS
4 Oaks Road
Shiplake
HENLEY-ON-THAMES
RG9 3JH
General Fiction.

FOURTH WORLD REVIEW
Rev John Papworth
24 Abercorn Place
St Johns Wood
LONDON
NW8
*Media star for his recent views on
the morality of 'stealing from
superstores'.*

THE FOX PRESS
Oak Tree
Main Road
Colden Common
WINCHESTER
SO21 1JL
*Poetry, animal welfare, natural
history, local publications,
magazine and booklets.*

FOXLINE PUBLISHING
32 Urwick Road
Romiley
STOCKPORT
SK6 3JS
Railways. Buses.

FOX PUBLICATIONS
31 St Andrewgate
YORK
YO1 2BR

Derek FOXTON
15A Commercial Street
HEREFORD
HR1 2DE
Local History.

FRACTAL REPORT
West Towen House
PORTHTOWAN
TR4 8AX
*Details of the production of Fractal
images on home computers. Most
makes covered. Free sample.*

FRAGMENTE
8 Hertford Street
OXFORD
OX4 3AJ
Magazine of contemporary poetics.

FRANCHISE PUBLICATIONS
32 Sutton Road
BOURNEMOUTH
BH9 1RN

KEVIN FRANCIS PUBLISHING CO.

85 Landcroft Road
LONDON
SE22 9JS

Mervyn E. FRANKLIN
61 Chelsworth Avenue
IPSWICH
IP4 3BB
Handicrafts.

FRASER PRESS
203 Bath Street
GLASGOW
G2 4HZ
Architecture.

FREEDOM PUBLISHING
Charmiene and Scott Leland
P.O. Box 4
Topsham
EXETER
EX3 0YR
Tel 01976 213181

FREELANCE FOCUS
7 King Edward Terrace
BROUGH
HU15 1EE

FREE RADICAL
Mr Steve Green
33 Scott Road, Olton
SOLIHILL
B92 7LQ
*Topics as diverse as religious
fanaticism and the author's
experience as a newspaper
jounalist.*

FREE RANGE PUBLISHING
Bilton Road
CHELMSFORD
CM1 2UJ

FREE SUN PUBLICATIONS
16 Viewbank
HASTINGS
TN35 5HB

FRESHWATER
Ferry House
Far Sawrey
AMBLESIDE
LA22 0LP

FRIAR'S BUSH PRESS
24 College Park Avenue
BELFAST
BT7 1LR

FRIENDLY PRESS
Anne Hodgkinson
300 Gloucester Road
Horfield
BRISTOL
Tel 01272 429 142
*We work with primary children and
teachers. Our courses offer
complete training kits, tapes, books
aids. Send for catalogue of many
items including Friendly Press,
Quaker imprint.*

FRIEZE
21 Denmark St
LONDON
WC2H 8NE

FROGLETS PUBLICATIONS
Mrs Fern Flynn
Froglets
Brasted Chart
WESTERHAM
TN16 1LY
Tel 01959 562972

Specialising in environmental historical and weather books mainly pictorial.

THE FROGMORE PRESS
Jeremy Page
42 Morehall Avenue
FOLKESTONE
CT19 4EF
The Frogmore Press publishes the bi-annual "Frogmore Papers" & occasional anthologies & pamphlets by individual poets. The annual Frogmore Poetry Prize was founded in 1987.
"Genius Loci" by W.H. Petty & Robert Roberts, £2.95+30p p+p
"Second Helping of Your Heart" by Sophie Hannah £2.95 + 30p p+p.

FROGMORE PAPERS
(see Crabflower)

FRONTIER PUBLISHING
Richard Barnes
Windetts
Kirkstead
NORWICH
NR15 1BR
Tel 01508 558 174 fax 01508 550 194
Titles from unusal travel to photographic studies. Next: Ancient Egypt.

Allan FROST
1 Buttermere Drive
Priorslee
TELFORD
TF2 9RE
Priorslee remembered by Allan Frost. Life in an industrial, mining and farming area before it became merged into Telford New Town. £4.95 from above or from bookshops.

FROSTED EARTH
Ian Currie
77 Rickman Hill
COULSDON
CR5 3DT
Tel 01737 554869
Frosted Earth initiated the Country Weather Book Series documentary in a pictorial record the main events to affect the South East back to Caesar's invasion. Everybody talks about the weather. This is a unique way to read about it.

THE FRUSTRATED WRITERS SOCIETY
12 Harrisons Court
Myers Lane
LONDON
SE14 5JR
Tel 0171 635 8170
'Peckham Cry' by Janice Cooke. An innovative approach to raising funds for the prevention of child abuse. This is the story of a child growing up in London during the 1950's. 'Unless people like me who were abused can tell the world, and in telling help them to understand the problems that child abuse brings through all of the child's adult life, children will continue to be abused. Public awareness of the problem is the only solution.' £6.99 (post-free). Send a SAE A5 envelope with your remittance.

FTT
Joseph Nicholas
5a Frinton Road
Stamford Hill
LONDON
N15 6NH
We published their letter in our 1994 edition. We don't know if they still exist. However this is such a brilliant description of a small press that we have repeated it.
"Dear People, We don't know how FTT came to be added to your mailing list, but for the past couple of years or so we've received invitations from you to advertise in your yearbook, appear at Small Press Fairs, and so on. I'm writing to suggest that it might not be worth your while to continue sending us such invitations, since our aims would appear to be somewhat different from those of the majority of small press publishers. We publish two or three issues of FTT a year, in a print run of 150-180 copies, for an active response from those prepared to write us letters of comment, provide contributions for future issues, or send us their own publications in exchange, and we aren't particularly interested in expanding our readership base much beyond this. We may indeed be missing out on a great deal by not doing so, but we publish FTT principally for its own sake, and if it were to involve us in any more work than at present it would rapidly cease to be a hobby and become instead a deadly chore. So I think it might perhaps be best if we didn't advertise in your yearbook, appear at small press fairs, or indeed remain on your mailing list!"

Mr Alan FULTON,
City of Aberdeen
Arts & Recreation Division
Libraries Section, Central Library
Rosemont Viaduct
ABERDEEN
AB9 1GU
Tel 01224 634 622
A Printing and recording section which mainly concentrates on the heritage of North East Scotland.

FUN AND LEARNING PUBLISHERS
24 North Road
LEADENHAM
LN5 0PG
Children's Fiction.

FUCHSIAPRINT
122 Northumberland Avenue
STAMFORD
PE9 1EA

F.W.H. TRANSPORT MONOGRAPHS
Bishop's Castle
High Heaton
NEWCASTLE-UPON-TYNE
NE7 7QF
Railways.

GAILLET PRESS LIMITED
Jeremy Irwin
16 The Moors
Pangbourne
READING
RG8 7LP
Fine Printer.

GAIRFISH
9 Pankhurst Court
Caradon Close
LONDON
E11 4TB
Publishing anthologies on all aspects of Scottish culture. Literary criticism, polemic, shorter fiction and cutting edge poetry.

GALACTIC CENTRAL PUBLICATIONS
'Imladris'
25a Copgrove Road
LEEDS
LS8 2SP
Publisher of SF and SF-related reference works specialising in author bibliographies.

THE GALDRAGON PRESS
136 Byres Road
GLASGOW
G12 8TD
Small poetry publisher, established 1991. Also typesetting + printing services.

GALE CENTRE PUBLICATIONS
Whitakers Way
LOUGHTON
IG10 1SQ
Social Welfare.

Joan GALE
Brackenrigg Cottage
Rothbury
MORPETH
Local and personal.

GALLERY PRESS
70-71 High Street
LAVENHAM
CO10 9PT
Fine Press.

GALLIARD PUBLISHERS
21 Hillside Crescent
EDINBURGH
EH7 5EB

H. GALLOWAY
39 Nutwell Road
Worle
WESTON-SUPER-MARE
BS22 0EW
Family History.

THE GAMECOCK PRESS
11 Park Road
RUGBY
CV21 2QU
Fine Press.

Richard GANDER
20 MSB House
The Mall
BROMLEY
BR1 1TT
Local History.

GANYMEDE
P.O. Box 421
SWINDON
SN1 5AU

GARBONZA BEANPRESS
128 Centenary Road
GOOLE
DN1Y 6PE
Poetry.

John Mitchell GARDNER
2 North Campbell Avenue
Milngavie
GLASGOW
Biography.

GARGOYLE'S HEAD PRESS
Chatham House
Gosshill Road
CHISLEHURST
BR7 5NS
Historical Biography.

GARNETT
Susan Garnet
Holme Lee
Longsight Road
Copster Green
BLACKBURN
BB1 9EU
Education.

GARRARD AND CO.
112 Regent Street
LONDON
W1A 2JJ
Garrard and Co., history of.

GATEHOUSE BOOKS
St Lukes
Sawley Road
MANCHESTER
M10 8D
Tel 0161 9522
Gatehouse is unique in that its writers are adults who are developing their reading and writing skills. Gatehouse books are especially popular in Adult Basic Education; schools and the prison service.

GATES OF ANNWN
Mr C E Bradwood
395 Broxburn Drive
SOUTH OCKENDON
RM15 5PJ
Pagan contact magazine dedicated to the Old Religion.

GATEWAY BOOKS
Alick Bartholemew
The Hollies
Wellow
BATH
BA2 8QJ
Tel 01225 835 127 fax 01225 840 012
New title: republication of Sir George Trevelyan's classic anthology of poetry, 'Magic

Casements: the use of poetry in the expanding of consciousness,' ISBN 1-85860-047-2; £5.95. Video to accompany book: George reading and commenting on eleven of his favourite poems; £12.95, running time 34 mins. Check with Gateway for p&p and special offers. Excellent 1996 catalogue.

GATEWAY GUIDES
235 Queens Road
Penkridge
STOKE-ON-TRENT

GAY AUTHORS W/S NEWSLETTER
c/o Kathryn Byrd
Gemma
BM Box 5700
LONDON
WC1N 3XX

GAY MEN'S PRESS
P.O. Box 247
LONDON
N17 9QR

GAY TIMES
Millivres Ltd
Ground Floor
Worldwide House
116-134 Bayham St
LONDON
NW1 0BA

GAYWRITES! (R.I.P.)
Andrew Gatheridge
11 Whitchurch Place
Cathays
CARDIFF
CF2 4HD
Gay Writes! was a one-off and after a third edition of 'Bedsitter Boys' I decided to jack it all in. I encourage everyone to produce at least one book. You've got nothing to lose and may learn a few new things about your life. 'Bedsitter Boys' is photocopy Gay-Art.

G.C BOOK PUBLISHERS
10 Bank Street
WIGTOWN
DG8 9HP

GCCR
1 Robin Close
Ingleby Barwick
STOCKTON-ON-TEES
TS17 0TD

G C S
Dave Gilbert
Waterdene House
Water Lane
LEIGHTON BUZZARD
LU7 7AW
Tel 01525 371 324
GCS publish guide books and offer a typesetting service to publishers. Our guaranteed 'delivery on time' has proved invaluable to some of the country's foremost publishers.

Barbara GEERE
15 Stamford Drive
BROMLEY
BR2 0XF
Education.

GEFN PRESS
Flat b
7 Elmwood Road
LONDON
SE24 6AQ

GEISER PRODUCTIONS
Sidney Du Broff
7 The Corner
Grange Road
LONDON
W5 3PQ
Tel 081 579 4653
Geiser Productions are producers of sponsored and commissioned works creators of books on the outdoors and fiction. We will do an article or an encyclopedia or anything else in between. Work emanating from Geiser Productions has appeared in twenty-three countries.

JOURNAL OF GENDER STUDIES
Humberside Poly
Inglemire Ave
HULL
HU6 7LU

GENERATION X
Adrian F.
1 South View
MEXBOROUGH
S64 9NE
Tel 01709 890116
Covers the worldwide fanzine scene (100s reviews/contacts every issue). Music, strange films, personalities and associated subjects like comics. Heavily into promoting DIY projects (music press and film etc).

GERHARD AHN
Bonstorfer Str 7.
29320 Hermannsburg
Germany
New European small press. Contact the publisher for more details. 'Letter from the Australian Jungle'.

GERSHOM PUBLICATIONS
1 Daisy Road
LONDON
E18 1EA
Poetry.

G.G. PUBLISHING
26A Park Road
Cheveley
NEWMARKET
CB8 9DF
Poetry.

G.G.A. International Publishers
Gavin Green
G.G.A. Int.
Greenacres
Santa Eugenia
MALLORCA
07142 Baleares
Spain
G.G.A. publishes novels and non-fiction books. UK cheque to G.G.A. "How to Win at the Casino" (Roulette), £9.95
"New Songs for Recording Artists & Song Book" with cassette, £5.95.

GHOST PUBLISHING
12 Seager Road
SHEERNESS
ME12 2BG

GHOSTS & SCHOLARS
Rosemary Pardoe
Flat One
36 Hamilton Street
Hoole
CHESTER

CH2 3JQ

J.P.GIBSON & CO, ART PRODUCTIONS
80 Hillcrest Rise
Cookridge
LEEDS
LS16 7DL

GIEBELS PUBLISHING
10 Martello Manor
Strand Road
BRAY
Co. Wicklow
Ireland
Publish 'Evolution in Life Beyond Death' by Henk Giebels. Which promises new insights into evolution beyond Earth from before the Big Bang to the Apocalypse and Beyond. 192pp paperback, ISBN 0-9525980-1-9, Price £8.99.

Cornelius A. GILLICK
Moderne Shoppe
6 Hulme Hall Lane
MANCHESTER
M10 8AZ
Education.

GIMELL RECORDS
4 Newtec Place
Magdalen Road
OXFORD
OX4 1RE
History of Music.

Anne GITTINS
14 Victoria Road
Fleet
ALDERSHOT
GU13 8DN
Biography.

GK Books
George Lawson
74 Goldstone Road
HOVE
BN3 3FH
Tel 0273 208049
Publishers of books on Travel, Humour, True Crime, and Childrens Books. Appreciate hearing from people who have researched their market and have a sound sales base. Synopses rather than MSS. S.A.E for reply.

THE GLADE
62 Hook Rise
NORTH TOLWORTH
KT6 7JY
Archaeology.

GLENIFFER PRESS
P.O. Box 56
PAISLEY
PA2 6AT

GLENVIL GROUP
Salisbury Hall
Park Road
HULL
HU3 1TD
Russian History.

GLEVUM PRESS
2 Honyatt Road
GLOUCESTER
GL1 3EB

GLIDDON BOOKS
Skeetshill Farmhouse
Sotesham St Mary
NORWICH

NR15 1UR

GLOBAL EGO NETWORK
Ego 1
Global HQ
New Street
BIRDSALL
BM31 4RG
The self-zine! Happening thingies spurting outa your mind in a mega med ia sort of way with film video rantings scribblings poetic sequences or just anything you like... All contributions considered. Anything legal or not; so long as it's easy and never has to actually get done.

GLOBAL TAPESTRY JOURNAL
Dave Cunliffe
Spring Bank
Longsight Road
Copster Green
BLACKBURN
B1 9EU
Tel 01254 249 128
A manifestation of exciting creativity. Innovative prose writing and novel extracts. Contains PM Newsletter - reviewing small alternative networks and the large publishing house releases. Bohemian, post-beat, counter-culture orientation.

GLOSA
Ron Clark and Wendy Ashby
P.O. Box 18
RICHMOND
TW9 2AU
Tel 0181 948 8417
Plenty of studies of this language tool.

G.M.S. ENTERPRISES
67 Pyhill Bretton
PETERBOROUGH
PE3 8QQ
Air Transport. Military Aircraft. Air Force History.

GNOSIS PRESS
Mary Nolan
P.O. Box 2
Lochboisdale
SOUTH UIST
Outer Hebrides
HS8 5UE
Tel 01878 700 375
BUDD, Vincent, 'The Human Mythus,' an exploration of some current delusions about the human condition. 1995, 474 pp, pbk, ISBN 0-9526136-1-1, £12 (+ £1.50 p&p).

GOLDEN APPLE PRODUCTIONS
Hinton House
Hinton
CHRISTCHURCH
BH23 7EA

GOLDEN BELL PRESS
1 Hungate Lane
Aylsham
NORWICH
NR11 6UD
Local History.

GOLDEN-EYE MAPS
The Cottage
Mill Street
Prestbury
CHELTENHAM
GL52 3BG

Travel Guides.

GOLDEN FLEECE PRESS
63 Barshaw Road
Penilee
GLASGOW
G52 4EE
Poetry. Established 1991 by Charles E Stuart the sole proprietor. Golden Fleece Poets are either previously published or, in many cases, previously unpublished the press acting as a stepping stone for new poets.

GOLDFINCH BOOKS
P.O. Box 2414
LONDON
N12 0NG
Art.

GOLDMARK
Orange House
14 Orange Street
UPPINGHAM
LE15 9SQ

GOLDSMITHS' GALLERY
Lewisham Way
LONDON
SE14 6NW
Art.

GOODALL PUBLICATIONS
Larchwood House
274 London Road
ST ALBANS
AL1 1HY

GOODAY PUBLISHERS
P.O. Box 60
CHICHESTER
PO20 8RA

John M. GOODIER
15 Rectory Lane
LYMM
WA13 0AJ
Walks Books.

GOOD-READ BOOKS
30 Spen Valley Road
DEWSBURY
WF13 3EZ
Children's Fiction.

GOOD STORIES MAGAZINE
(see Oakwood Publications)

GOOD TIMES
The Elephant House
Hawley Crescent
LONDON
NW1 8NP

GOODWINS BOOKSELLERS
28E High Street
LEIGHTON BUZZARD
LU7 7EA
Local History.

GOON SHOW PRESERVATION SOCIETY
3 Flotterton Gardens
Fenham
NEWCASTLE-UPON-TYNE
NE5 2DS

GORSE PUBLICATIONS
P.O. Box 214
Shamley Green
GUILDFORD
GU5 0SW
'Pigeon Grounded' a new collection of poems by Pat

Earnshaw. Contains a medley of poems in differing styles and content. Signed copies at £6.99 (post free). Back list of books on lace: history, fashion, identification, and technique of both hand and machine laces.

GOSTOURS
29 Marchwood Road
SHEFFIELD
S6 5LB
Birds.

GOTHIC PRESS
Managing editor Robin Crisp
P.O. Box 542
Highgate
LONDON
N6 6BG
History biography supernatural and occult non-fiction is the essence of material published by Gothic Press. Poetry and gothic romantic fiction are planned. Unsolicited manuscripts are not welcome at present.
* *'The Highgate Vampire' by Sean Manchester.*

GOTHIC GARDEN PRESS
Mr Mike Boland
30 Byron Court
HARROW
HA1 1JT

GOTHIC IMAGE
7 High Street
GLASTONBURY
BA6 9DP
Publisher & Bookshop. Tours of mystic sites. Send for details.

GOTHIC SOCIETY
Ms Jennie Gray
Chantham House
Gosshill Road
CHISLEHURST
BR7 5NS

Mervyn GOULD
29 Blackbrook Court
LOUGHBOROUGH
LE11 0UA
Cinema History: Mercia Cinema Society publishes solely on this, concentrating on the buildings. For list and membership information send an SAE to above. Latest book Loughborough's Stage/Screen. including Coalville and the Deeming Circuit, £15.50 incl p&p. Cheshire & Essex next. Bioscope magazine quarterly, back numbers available.

GOWER PRESS
G Daniel
19 Gwynant Place
Lakeside
CARDIFF
CF2 6LT

GOWLAND & CO
93 Bedford Road
Birkdale
SOUTHPORT
PR8 4HT

F. GRAHAM
10 Blythswood
North Osborne Road
Jesmond
NEWCASTLE-UPON-TYNE
NE2 2AZ

History Atlases.

GRAINLOFT BOOKS
Grainloft
Ansty
HAYWARDS HEATH
RH17 5AG
Poetry.

GRAND PRIX SPORTIQUE
Upton
TETBURY
GL8 8LP

GRANT BOOKS
Victoria Square
DROITWICH
WR9 8DE
Tel 01905 778155
Limited edion golf books with the emphasis on history, architecture and the early players. Also bibliographies of golf books.

GRAPHICOM EXPRESS
2A Comeragh Road
West Kensington
LONDON
W14 9HP

GRAPHICON AD
Ian Pyper
4 Mirefield Street
Kensington
LIVERPOOL
L6 6BD
Since early 1991 the main activity has been to produce artists limited edition bookworks by Ian Pyper. Inspired by surrealism, dream language and an interest in so-called Primitive Cultures.

GRAVE ORC INCORPORATED
George N. Houston
The Cottage
Smithy Brae
KILMACOLM
PA13 4EN
George Houston is the founder of Grave Orc and the Editor of Midnight in Hell (Weirdest Tales of Fandom). Established in 1990. Ambitions in 1993 were to publishe Pulp magazine (all fiction fan magazine) and Ultimate Cult Video Collector's Price Guide.

Andrew GRAYSON
56 Piercy End
Kirkby Moorside
YORK
YO6 6DF
GRAYSON, Andrew, 'The Horseflies of Yorkshire,' 1995, 48 pp, pbk, 16 distribution maps, 1 table, 36 figures, ISBN 0-9521201-0-0, £3 (incl. p&p).

Jane GREATOREX
Wash Farm House
Hedingham Road
HALSTEAD
The Saville Family and Colne Engaine connections, recently published by local historian specialising in manorial and oral history of Essex. This, my fifth book, traces the Savilles over three hundred years, using manorial records and surveys. Details from above. £4.00 post free.

GREAT WEN PUBLICATIONS
P.O. Box 1500

LONDON
SW5 0DA
Travel Accommodation.

GREEN ANARCHIST
Box H
34 Cowley Road
OXFORD
OX4 1HZ
Magazine.

GREEN BAY PUBLICATIONS
72 Water Lane
Histon
CAMBRIDGE
CB4 4LR

GREEN BOOKS
Foxhole
Dartington
TOTNES
TQ9 6EB
Publisher and distributor including 'green' titles from America.

GREEN BOOK LTD
2 Sydney Place
BATH
BA2 6NF

GREEN CIRCULAR
c/o Quest
BCM-SCL-QUEST
LONDON
WC1N 3XX

GREENCROFT BOOKS
Trefelin
Cilgwyn
NEWPORT
SA42 0QN
Local Folk Tales.

ROBERT GREENE PUBLISHING
John Coutts
1 Cirrus Crescent
GRAVESEND
DA12 4QS

GREEN EVENTS
14 Curzon Road
LONDON
N10 2RA
Tel 0181 365 2958
Independent current awareness bulletin, networking editions targeted specifically at N.London, S & W.London, Oxfordshire, S.Devon and Leeds. Can be found at certain distribution points as freebies. Ann.sub. £6 secures regular mailing of 10 issues p.a.; £10 for 20 issues for next two years.

GREENGATES PRESS
Itchenor
CHICHESTER
PO20 7DA
Alternative memoirs by John Hasted.

GREEN INK PUBLICATIONS
c/o Green Ink Bookshop
8 Archway Mall
LONDON
N19 5RG

GREEN LEAF BOOKSHOP
82 Colston Street
BRISTOL
BS1 5BB

GREENLEAF
96 Church Road

Redfield
BRISTOL
BS5

GREENLIGHT PUBLICATIONS
Ty Bryn
Coomb Gardens
Llangynog
CARMARTHEN
SA33 5AY
School Textbooks.

GREEN PRINT
10 Malden Road
LONDON
NW5 3HR

GREENSWARD PUBLICATIONS
Charles Westaway
116 Wessex Oval
WAREHAM
BH20 4BS
Tel 01929 554 838
Guide books: particularly walking guide on county basis.

GREEN REVOLUTION
P.O. Box 845
BRISTOL
BS99 5HQ
Obvious + women.

GREEN WATER PRESS
Hazelwood
Waters Green
BROCKENHURST
SO42 7RG
Tel 01590 23915
Cottage industry making of books. Personal experiences philosophy psychology in essays prose poetry or visual imagery. Ideas welcome for consideration.

GREENWAY WOMEN'S PRESS
Greenway Women's Centre
19 Greenway
Cregagh
BELFAST
BT6 0DT
Poetry.

GREENWICH EXCHANGE
161 Charlton Church lane
LONDON
SE7 7AA
Literature. Education.

GREENWICH GUIDE-BOOKS
72 Kidbrooke Grove
LONDON
SE3 0LG

GREVATT & GREVATT
Dr. S.Y. Killingley
9 Rectory Drive
NEWCASTLE UPON TYNE
NE3 1XT
Publishes books in the following fields: language and linguistics; poetry; religion and philosophy; society in India. Small print-runs; no royalties for first 500 copies. Proposals accompanied by S.A.E. only considered.
"Sound, Speech, and Silence: Selected Poems". Siew-Yue Killingley 0-947722-08-4, £7.50 net(UK), £9.75 (overseas). xii, 80pp, 1995
"Where no Poppies Blow; Poems of war and Conflict". Siew-Yue Killingley 0-9507918-5-7, £4.50 net (UK); £5.85 (overseas), viii, 55pp. 1983

GRH PUBLICATIONS
2 Wayne Close
Gunton
LOWESTOFT
NR32 4SX

Mr V L GRIFFITHS
See Pericles Publications

GRILLE
c/o Simon Smith
53 Ormonde Court
Upper Richmond Road
Putney
LONDON
SW15 5TU

GRIM HUMOUR (magazine)
Richard Johnson (editor)
P.O. Box 63
Herne Bay
CT6 6YU
Magazine devoted to the innovative experimental and provocative end of our counter-culture whether music film or literature/graphics. Also open to intelligent inspired and thought-provoking fiction besides as much related review material as it can possible get.

GRINDLE PRESS
Ms K G Holroyd
P.O. Box 222
IPSWICH
IP9 1HE
Publishes 'Arthritis at your age?' Late teens to early 50s. A friendly handbook for young and youngish adults with a rheumatic disorder.

GRITT AND WITT PUBLISHING
5 Wolffe Gardens
Stratford
LONDON
E15 4JJ
Publishers of general interest books including childrens stories.

GROCER'S HALL PRESS
33 Glenrandel
Eglinton
LONDONDERRY

Graham GROOM
23 Meadow Street
DARWEN
BB3 2QL
The History of Darwen Cricket Club Volume One: The Etrurians Years 1901-1910. A5, 56pp, photographs, scorecards, newscuttings, full averages of all players. £3.50 inc. p&p. £1.00 per book (50% of profits) donated to the Cricket Club.

GROVER BOOKS
Peter Andrews
10/12 Picton Street
BRISTOL
BS6 5QA
Tel 0117 942 0165
Grover books publish books that provide practical solutions to environmental problems, sustainable living and Agenda 21 issues.
"LETS Work", a study of local exchange trade systems.
"The Seed Saver's Handbook", how to preserve our valuable vegetable heritage.

GRUFFYGROUND PRESS

Anthony Baker
Ladram
Bristol Road
WINSCOMBE
BS25 1PW
Tel Winscombe 2285
The Press publishes finely printed limited editions, on handmade or mould-made papers, of (mostly new) English poetry, usually with an original wood-engraved illustration. Unsolicited manuscripts are not considered.
"Aquamarine" by Lawrence Sail (1988)
"Even the Flowers" by Freda Downie (1989)

John GRUNDY
59 Finglaswood Road
Finglas
DUBLIN 11
Republic of Ireland
History of Irish Republic.

GRYFFON PUBLICATIONS
The Close
Barnsley
CIRENCESTER
GL7 5EE

GRYPHON PRESS
4 Orchard Road
St Margarets
TWICKENHAM
TW1 1LY

GSSE
11 Malford Grove
Gilwern
ABERGAVENNY
NP7 0RN
Applications of psychology to education especially small businesses.

Jan GUICE
12 Whitehall Mansions
121 Elderfield Road
LONDON
E5 0LD
Poetry.

GUILDHALL PRESS
Paul Hippsley
41 Great James Street
LONDONDERRY
Northern Ireland
BT48 7DF
Tel 0504 264413
Community Book Publisher Specialising in Local History publications associated with Derry Donegal and the North West of Ireland. Typesetting and design Facilities available for external clients using In-House Desktop publishing system. Third party Publishing considered.

Norman GUNBY
31 Falmouth Gardens
Redbridge
ILFORD
IG4 5JU
Local History.

GUITAR RESEARCH MONOGRAPHS
Graham Wade
34 Holmwood Avenue
Meanwood
LEEDS
LS6 4NJ
Publishes monographs concerning

the history and repertoire of the classical guitar. The European Guitar Teachers' Association (UK) (EGTA UK) Journalis also published at this address.

GUNGARDEN BOOKS
Gungarden Lodge
RYE
TN31 7HH
Children's Fiction.

GWASG GREGYNOG
David Esslemont
Newtown
POWYS
SY16 3PW
Fine printer

GWASG PRIFYSGOL CYMRU
Gwennyth Street
Cathays
CARDIFF
CF2 4YD
Welsh Customs and Folkore (in Welsh).

GWELFRYN PUBLISHERS
Llandiloes Road
NEWTON
SY16 4HX
School Textbooks.

GWYDYR MINES PUBLICATIONS
78 Oakenshaw Lane
Walton
WAKEFIELD
WF2 6NH

HAGGERSTON PRESS
38 Kensington Place
LONDON
W8 7PR

(THE) HAIKU QUARTERLY
Day Dream Press
39 Exmouth Street
SWINDON
SN1 3PU

HALFSHIRE BOOKS
6 High Street
BROMSGROVE
B61 8HQ

HALLMARK BOOKS

42 Tennyson Road
PENARTH
CF6 1RZ
Mystery Fiction.

HALSTEAD PUBLICATIONS
13 Queens Road
HARROGATE
HG2 0HA

HAMBLEDON PRESS
102 Gloucester Avenue
LONDON
NW1 8HX
Used to publish cricket books, now we publish academic history books.

HAMPUS BOOKS
P.O. Box 227
FOLKESTONE
CT20 1GB

HANBOROUGH BOOKS
The Foundry
Church Hanborough
OXFORD
OX7 2AB
Now Previous Parrot. Fine Printer.

HANDPOST BOOKS
84 Llanthewy Road
NEWPORT
NP9 4LA
Travel.

HANDSAW
Mr Felix Prior
20a Maclise Road
LONDON
W14 0PR

HANDY PRESS
Box 79
WOODFORD GREEN
IG8 0QZ

HANGMAN BOOKS AND RECORDS
Kyra de Coninck
32 May Road
ROCHESTER
ME1 2HY
Poetry Publishing. Have published poetry, prose and artists books. The work of Billy Childish, Celine, Sexton Ming and others.

HAPPY LEARNING
Una Dowding
18 Trevor Road
Hucclecote
GLOUCESTER
GL3 3JL
Tel 01452 618 828
Happy Learning Series.

HARDIE PRESS
35 Mountcastle Terrace
EDINBURGH
EH8 7SF
Music.

Peter HARDING
Mossgiel
Bagshot Road
Knaphill
WOKING
GU21 2SG
Railway publisher.

HARDWICK PRESS
Mr Brian Lunn
Aircraft Down
36 Darrington Road
East Hardwick

PONTEFRACT
WF8 3DS

HARE'S EAR PRODUCTIONS
9 St Paul's Gate
WOKINGHAM
RG11 2YP

HARMONY PUBLISHING LIMITED
Elaine R Abraham
14 Silverston Way
STANMORE
HA7 4HR

HARMOR BOOKS
Foxwell
Wendlebury
BICESTER
OX16 8PW
Education.

HARPIES & QUINES
P.O. Box 543
GLASGOW
G20

Alma HARRIS
9 Grazingfield
Wilford
NOTTINGHAM
NG11 7FN
In Days of Yore: Queen Isabella and Sir Roger Mortimer by Alma Harris 1325–1330. The bloodless invasion and deposition of Edward II. The mystery surrounding his alleged murder. Mortimer's rise and fall. History of Nottingham Castle. 40 pp. £3.95 inc. 35p postage.

HARRY GALLOWAY PUBLISHING
39 Nutwell Road
WESTON-SUPER-MARE
BS22 0EW
Tel 01934 514443
or 01823 282267
Publisher of new & reprinted genealogical source material for Somerset, Devon, & Cornwall, in microfiche/hard copy format, sometimes both for some titles.

HARVENNA BOOKS
Leo Alison
Barton Lane
Fraddon
ST COLUMB
Tel 01726 860 413
Cornish local history.

HARVEY PRESS
Ward 23/20
Royal Hospital
Chelsea
LONDON
SW3 4SR
Biography.

Elizabeth HARVEY-LEE
1 Belton Road
LONDON
NW2 5PA
Printmaking.

John HASTED
1 Eton Court
Pemberley Avenue
BEDFORD
MK40 2LH
Biography.

Scott HASTIE
24 Coniston Road
KINGS LANGLEY
WD4 8DU

Poetry.

HASTINGS ARTS POCKET PRESS
25 St Mary's Terrace
HASTINGS
TN34 3LS

Peter B. HATTON
27 Church Road
Hale
LIVERPOOL
L24 4AY
Local History.

HAUNTED LIBRARY
Ro Pardoe
Flat One
36 Hamilton Street
CHESTER
CH2 3JQ
Tel 01244 313685
Publishes twice-yearly magazine "Ghosts & Scholars", containing fiction in the tradition of M. R. James and articles, etc., on Jamesian writers. also related single-author booklets. "Ghosts & Scholars 20", £4.00 ($7.00) including P+P.

HAUTEVILLE PRESS
1 Hauteville Court Gardens
Stamford Brook Avenue
LONDON
W6
Translations and commentaries of classical texts; English literary comment, unusual incidents in history.

HAVERS' DIRECTORIES
Elsdon Mailing Unit
16 Nonsuch Industrial Estate
Kiln Lane
EPSOM
KT17 1EG
Bibliography.

HAWKER PUBLICATIONS
13 Park House
140 Battersea Park Road
LONDON
SW11 4NB
Social Welfare.

Denise HAWRYSIO
108 Crampton Street
LONDON
SE17 3AE
Artists books of a truly remarkable quality.

HAWTHORN PRESS
Bankfield House
13 Wallbridge
STROUD
GL5 3JA
Music. Occult.

HAWTHORNE EDUCATION
17 Guillemot Close
Hythe
SOUTHAMPTON
SO4 6GJ

Lorna HAYCOCK
41 Long Street
DEVIZES
SN10 1NS
How Devizes Won the War — the effect of the war on a west country market town. 96pp with maps and 46 illustrations by Devizes Local History Group £6.50 plus 50p postage.

HAYDEN PRESS
Hayden Lodge
Gloucester Road
Staverton
CHELTENHAM
GL51 0SS
Artists Books.

C. HAYES
2 Undercliff Gardens
VENTNOR
Isle of Wight
PO38 1UB
Music.

HAYLOFT PRESS
99 Oakfield Road
Selly Oak
BIRMINGHAM
B29 7HW

David HAYNS
Stoke Cottage
Church Street
MALPAS
SY14 8PD
Centenary facsimile reprint of 'Malpas Parish, Town and Church' by William Kenyon (1895). £2.00 (inc postage). Cheques to 'Malpas Field Club'.

HAY THREE
29/30 Warwick Street
LONDON
W1R 5RD

HAZELWOOD
122 Sunningfields Road
London
NW4 4RE

HAZLEWOOD PUBLISHING
Staverton Court
Staverton
Dartington
TOTNES
TQ9 6NU

HEAD PRESS
David Slater
P.O. Box 160
STOCKPORT
SK1 4ET
Tel 0161 476 0592
Sex Religion Death is the mastiff for Headpress Magazine a Quarterly exploration of bizarre culture deviant conceptions and cinematic extremes. Each issue kind of a psychotic dip a platform for criticism, interviews, reviews and anecdotes. Headpress encourage correspondence from writers and groups.

HEADLAND POETRY PUBLICATIONS
Wirral
38 York Avenue
WEST KIRKBY
Wirrall
L48 3JF

HEADSTART HISTORY
P.O. Box 41
BANGOR
LL57 1SB

HEADWAY PUBLISHING
44 Yew Tree Close
Lordswood
CHATHAM
ME5 8XN
*FRAZER, K.J., 'The Bullsh**ter's*

Guide to Wealth and Success,' high spirited self-help. Good reviews in The Standard and The Businessman. 172 pp., pbk, ISBN 0-9526278-0-9, £5.99.

HEARING EYE
Box 1
22 Torriano Avenue
LONDON
NW5 2RX

HEART OF ALBION PRESS
Bob Trubshaw
2 Cross Hill Close
Wymeswold
LOUGHBOROUGH
LE12 6UJ
Tel 01509 880725
bobtrubs@gmtnet.co.uk
Self-publishing venture and distributor for other small presses with similar interests (ancient landscapes, folklore, Leics. & Rutland history) Send s.a.e. for superb current catalogue.
* Forthcoming publication early 1997 Jeremy HARTE: 'Research in Geomancy - 1990-1994, Readings in sacred space: a bibliography.' Published on floppy disc for reading on any wordprocessor (files in Windows Write format and duplicated in plain ASCII); by using 'Find' specific topics can be readily located in text. On request a print-out can be supplied with disc. Provisional price £5.95 (disc only) £9.95 (disc and print-out).

HEATHROW PUBLICATIONS
7 Palace Business Estate
Bircholt Road
Parkwood
MAIDSTONE
ME15 9XU

HEDGEHOG PRESS
Alan Brignull
33 Heath Road
Wivenhoe
COLCHESTER
CO7 9PU
The Hedgehog Press is a collection of small letterpress equipment operated for fun.
Latest production is "The Speculators", Thackeray's tale of railway mania (£3.50).
Still available, "Charles Clark", an illustrated biography of a Victorian farmer-printer (£7.50).

THE HEDGEHOG PRESS
23 Gladstone Avenue
LOUGHBOROUGH
LE11 1NP

HEDGEROW PUBLISHING LIMITED
Mr T M Hale
325 Abbeydale Road
SHEFFIELD
S7 1FS
Tel 01742 554 873
Photographers and publishers of high quality photographic greetings cards and post cards.

HEINDESIGN STEMPELSPASS
Diana Arseneau
Eiper Strase 76
5800 Hagen 1
Germany
Tel 0049 2331 72211, fax 0049 2331 72292

With a rubber stamp in your hand, you're a one-person print shop! Create works of art, statements of love. Amaze your friends, confuse your enemies. Over 700 designs, write for free catalogue. Artists/designers: always seeking new ideas. Write us!

HELM INFORMATION
The Bank
Mountfield
ROBERTSBRIDGE
TN32 5JY
Literature.

HELSFELL PRESS
235 Windermere Road
KENDALL
LA9 5EY

N HENANDEZ
252 Victoria Road
RUISLIP MANOR
HA4 0DW
Publishes small magazine.

HENDERSON-ROBERTSON PUBLISHING
Struan
Toberonochy
OBAN
PA34 4UG
Children's Fiction.

HENDON PUBLISHING
Hendon Mill
Colne
NELSON

HENHOUSE PUBLISHING
Pyramid
Hawerby Hall
NORTH THORESBY
DN36 5LL
01472 840278
Women's writing. Anthologies and courses.

HENRY SWEET SOCIETY
Mark Atherton
21 Girdlestone Close
OXFORD
OX3 7NS
The Society was founded in 1984 to promote and encourage the study of the history of all branches of linguistic thought, theoretical and applied, including non-European traditions. They are holding a colloqium at the university of Luton 10-13 September. The above address is for correspondence. Other depts should funnel off. An academic newsletter is produced.

CLIVE HERBERT WILDLIFE PUBLISHING
67A Ridgeway Avenue
EAST BARNET
EN4 8TL
Tel 0181 440 9314
Publisher of wildlife and natural history booklets/leaflets relating directly to the North London area only. Specifically local material and topics which would not find publication elsewhere.

HERCULANEUM PRESS
Joel Biroco
BM Utopia
LONDON
WC1N 3XX

HERE AND NOW
P.O. Box 109
LEEDS
LS5 3AA
and
c/o Transmission Gallery
28 King St
GLASGOW
G1 5QP
Magazine from collectives in Scotland and West Yorkshire. 'Emerging from the barricades of the left to view the wreckage and the wasteland sold to us as paradise. Is the choice between Pepsi and Coke?'

HERGA PRESS
7 High Street
HARROW-ON-THE-HILL
HA5 2EH
Historical Biography.

HERITAGE MAGAZINE
2 The Courtyard
WOKINGHAM
RG11 2LW

HERITAGE PRESS
1 St James Drive
MALVERN
WR14 2UD
Tel 01684 561755
The first of Heritage's Art Travel Guides on Burne-Jones and William Morris appeared in 1991 with 50 illustrations, 16 in colour. Other titles on these artists and on other topics including Armour, Hereldry and Costume followed, some in Limited Editions.

HERMAFRODUX LIMITED
Anthony Christie
14b Elsworthy Terrace
LONDON
NW3 3DR

HERMETIC JOURNAL
P.O. Box 375
Headington
OXFORD
OX3 8PW

HERMIT PRESS
Anthony Christmas
15 Robertson Road
BUXTON
SK17 9DY
Fine Printer.

HERMITAGE PUBLISHING
Chris Street
P.O. Box 1383
LONDON
N14 6LP
Tel 0181 886 1414
Began as publisher of 'Earthstars' a book which suggests there's nothing straight -forward about ley-lines. It reveals that London's ancient sacred sites form precise geometric patterns - a vast landscape temple groundplan. New items, send for Catalogue.

Chris D. HEWITT
1 Coleswood Road
HARPENDEN
AL5 1EF
Cycling History.

HEYFORD PRESS
R Dennis
The Old Chapel

Shepton Beauchamp
ILMINSTER
TA19 0LE

H.G.B. SERVICES
32 Dudley Street
GRIMSBY
DN31 2AB
European Travel.

HIDCOTE PRESS
33 Hidcote Road
Oadby
LEICESTER
LE2 5PG
Geography.

HIDDEN DETAIL
61 Fir Street
NELSON
BB9 9RQ
Film fanzine, especially Chinese.

HIGHFIELD PRESS
224 Coast Road
Ballygally
LARNE
BT40 2QQ

HIGHFIELD PUBLICATIONS
Vue Pointe
Spinney Hill
Sprotborough
DONCASTER
DN5 7LY
Hygiene.

HIGH FORCE PUBLICATIONS
12 Edinburgh Drive
DARLINGTON
DL3 8AW
Tel 01325 468 390
Booklets of local history and geographical and architectural interest.

HIGHGATE PUBLICATIONS
24 Wylies Road
BEVERLEY
HU17 7AP

HIGHLAND PRINTMAKERS WORKSHOP & GALLERY
Ms Nina Ashby
20 Bank Street
INVERNESS
IV1 1QE
We generally edition original prints. In 1993 we produced our first loose-leaf book: 'The Sea', a collection of six Haiku poems by Irene Irvine, set in Albertu s 18 pt and illustrated by six wood engravings by Ross-shire artists; calico bound slip cover - sponsored by Ross & Cromarty District Council. Edition size of book - 12 copies.

HIGNELL'S APPLE PRESS
Sarah Campbell (Miss)
550 Berridge Road West
Hyson Green
NOTTINGHAM
NG7 5JU
Two titles in print. Send for details.

Brian Merrikin HILL
Ingmanthorp
Hall Farm Cottage
WETHERBY
LS22 5EQ
Tel 01937 584674
Poetry magazine with reviews.

HILLINGDON MIND NEWSLETTER
c/o MIND
Sterling House
276A High St
UXBRIDGE
UB8 1LQ
Tel 01895 271 559

PETER HILL PUBLICATIONS
2 Lovap Way
Great Oakley
CORBY
NN18 8JL
Local History.

HILLSIDE PUBLICATIONS
11 Nessfield Grove
KEIGHLEY
BD22 6NU

HILLTOP PRESS
Steve Sneyd
4 Nowell Place
Almondbury
HUDDERSFIELD
HD5 8PB
Founded 1965. Specialist in science fiction & other genre poetry, including reprints & bibliographical material, including regular Data Dump Series & individual chapbooks. Also booklets on castles, local history/curiosa. "Spaceman" by Dave Calder "AE- The Seven Wonders of the Universe" by Mike Johnson.

HINGTON ASSOCIATES
Westlands House
Tullibardine
AUCHTERARDER
PH3 1NJ
Travel.

HINTON BOOKS
26 Clare Avenue
Hoole
CHESTER
CH2 3HS

HIPPOPOTAMUS PRESS
R. John
22 Whitewell Road
FROME
BA11 4EL
Tel 01373 466653
Publisher of full poetry collections. Publisher of Outposts Poetry Quarterly.

HI RESOLUTION
4 Smallbridge Cottages
Horsmonden
TONBRIDGE
TN12 8EP

HISARLIK
4 Catisford Road
ENFIELD LOCK
EN3 6BD
Tel 01992 700 898 fax 0181 292 6118
Spring Catalogue 1997 contains details of books, journals, electronic publications on folklore, medieval studies, local history.

THE HISTORICAL PRESS
160 Kennington Road
LONDON
SE11 6QR

HISTORIANS' PRESS
9 Daisy Road
LONDON

E18 1EA
Historical Biography.

HISTORICAL PUBLICATIONS
Highgate Literary and Scientific Inst
11 South Grove
LONDON
N6 6BS
Local History.

HISTORIC ROYAL PALACES
Marketing Department
Hampton Court Palace
EAST MOLESEY
KT8 9AU
Historic Palaces.

HISTORY ON YOUR DOORSTEP
15 Welbeck House
ASHTON-UNDER-LYNE
PL6 7TB
Local History.

Roy William HOBB
8 Bacon Avenue
NORMANTON
WF6 2HR
Railways.

HOBBY PUBLICATIONS
11 Walton Heath Road
Walton
WARRINGTON
WA4 6HZ

HOBLINK NEWSLETTER
Morrigan
Box 1
13 Merrivale Road
STAFFORD
ST1 79GB
The Hoblink Newsletter is for lesbian gay and bisexual Pagans Witches and Occultists. It is produced 6 or 8 times a year and includes articles opinion news and contacts.

HOLCOMBE PUBLISHING
1 Raylees
Ramsbottom
BURY
BL0 9HW
Coastal Shipping.

Margaret HOLDERNESS
10 Holwick Court
Off Summer Lane
BARNSLEY
S70 2PE
Short Stories.

HOLDSOME PRESS
Barnwood
West Hill Park
Titchfield
FAREHAM
PO14 4BT
Poetry.

HOLLIES PUBLICATIONS
69 Hawes Lane
WEST WICKHAM
BR4 0DA

HOLOCAUST EDUCATIONAL TRUST
BCM Box 7892
LONDON
WC1N 3XX

HOLY GRAIL
P.O. Box 542
LONDON
N6 6BG

Illustrated exposure of present day witchcraft and satanism.
* *Highgate Vampire, from Satan to Christ.*

HOME BASE HOLIDAYS
Lois Sealey
7 Park Avenue
LONDON
N13 5PG
Tel 0181 886 8752
Publishes three directories of home exchange offers world wide each year. Also publishes annual guide: "Bed & Breakfast in the United States & Canada", A5 ISBN 0 9510866 8 5, line drawings, 100 pages, £6.50. Published Jan. 1996 (10th edition).

HOMEMADE BOOKS
Broadacres
Southwood
GLASTONBURY
BA6 8PG
Historical Biography.

HOMER, THE SLUT
24a Inglethorpe Street
Fulham
LONDON
SW6 6NT
"Homer, the slut": Quarterly Bob Dylan fanzine with a yearly bonus issue for subscribers. A mixture of news from around the world and serious analysis of work from his entire career. "Analytical but understandable" for even the most in-depth critiques.

(THE) HONEST ULSTERMAN
Editor Ruth Hooley
159 Lower Braniel Road
BELFAST
BT5 1NN

HONNO
Ailsa Craig
Heol-y-Cawl
DINAS POWYS
CF6 4AH
Books by women living in Wales or with a Welsh connection in English and Welsh.

David HOOK
125 Folly Lane
ST ALBANS
AL3 5JQ
Literature.

HOPE VALLEY PRESS
Unit 15
Vincent Works
Brough Bradwell
SHEFFIELD
S30 2HG
Sporting History.

V & A HOPKINSON
27 Metcalfe Avenue
Killamarsh
SHEFFIELD
S31 8HW
Killamarsh Chronicle: Killamarsh Comes of Age 1770-1900. 66pp, fold-out map. £4.50 plus 50p postage. Bygone Killamarsh, 76 old photographs. £3.50 plus 50p postage.

JONATHAN HORNE PUBLICATIONS
66c Kensington Church Street

LONDON
W8 4BY
Tel 0171 221 5658
Specialist monographs on antique ceramics.

HORSEHOE PRESS
c/o D. Heather
Eight Ash House
Eight Ash Green
COLCHESTER
CO6 3PX

Barbara HORSFALL
87 Brookhouse Road
FARNBOROUGH
GU12 0BU
Now running Concordat poetry folio.

HORNSEY HISTORICAL SOCIETY
The Old Schoolhouse
136 Tottenham Lane
LONDON
N8 7E
•*The Little School by Dr Joan Schwitzer outlines the fortunes of a church infant school built 1848 used until 1934, now the headquarters of Hornsey Historical Society. The changing educational provision of the period is described. £2.20 including p&p.*
•*How Bounds Green Tube was Bombed in 1940 killing 19 is among subjects covered in Hornsey Historical Society's Bulletin No 36.*

HORUS COMMUNICATIONS
67 Duesbury Street
Princess Avenue
HULL
HU5 3QE

HOUSE OF THE GODDESS
33 Oldridge Road
LONDON
SW12 8PN

HOUSE OF MOONLIGHT
Mr John Howard
15 Oakwood Road
Bulbrook
BRACKNELL
RG12 2SP
Poetry leaflets.

HOUSE OF RAINBOWS
14 Post Horn Place
Fords Farm
READING
RG3 5QE

RICHMOND HOUSE PUBLISHING
1 Richmond News
LONDON
W1V 5AG

HOUSMANS
5 Caledonian Road
Kings Cross
LONDON
N1 9DX
Publisher and bookshop.

HOVERCLUB
12 Mount Pleasant
Bishops Itchington
LEMINGTON SPA
CV33 0QE

Frances HOWARD
38, Humped Road
HITCHIN
SG4 0LD

The works of Anthony Bates. Biblical teachings based on soul memory of eye witnesses, reincarnated. Compassion for all creatures and people essential to the process of world peace. "Symbolic Painting" "Holocaust or World Change"

HOWARD PUBLICATIONS
Keenans Mill
Lord Street
LYTHAM ST ANNES
FY8 2DF

D HOWELLS BOOKS
57 The Dene
WARMINSTER
BA12 9ER

HRAFNHOH
Publisher & Editor Joseph Biddulph
32 Stryd Ebeneser
PONTYPRIDD
CF37 5PB
Dialects and languages, heraldry and surname studies, mostly in English. Various numbers of Hrafnhoh contain a new Africana supplement, 'Black Eagle,' dealing with the languages, social, economic, religious and cultural life of Africa and its Diaspora. Irregular intervals, 3-4 times p.a. UK £5.25 post incl. Single copies UK £2 post incl. Please make all monies payable to Joseph Biddulph. ISSN 0952-3294

H S B PUBLICATIONS
68 Lincoln Road
Leasingham
SLEAFORD
NG34 8JT
Tel 01529 305 787
Books on life in a Lincolnshire village in the early part of this century.

K. HUGHES
Royal Crescent Road
SOUTHAMPTON
SO9 1WB
Astronomy.

HULME VIEWS
9 Otterburn Close
Hulme
MANCHESTER
M15 5HB

HUMAN POTENTIAL
3 Netherby Road
LONDON
SE23 3AL
Magazine.

HUMAN RIGHTS FORUM
2 Eaton Gate
LONDON
SW1

HUME SCOTT FRASER PUBLISHING LTD
4 North Several
LONDON
SE3 0QR
Financial and business books for professionals and students.

W. HUNT
Stourton View
East Stour
GILLINGHAM
SP8 5JZ

Printing and Printers.

David HUNT
54 Priory Road
RICHMOND
TW9 3DH
Historic Gardens.

C HUNTER
Shore House
Lerags
OBAN
PA34 4SE
Zoology.

HUNTER HOUSE
4 Thiepval Avenue
BELFAST
BT6

HUTTON PRESS LTD
130 Canada Drive
Cherry Burton
BEVERLEY
HU17 7SB

HYBRID
42 Christchurch Place
PETERLEE
SR8 2NR

HYDATUM
P.O. Box 4
ROSS-ON-WYE
HR9 6EB

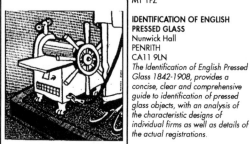

IAN HENRY PUBLICATIONS LTD
20 Park Drive
ROMFORD
RM1 4LH
Tel 01708 74119
Local history, transport, fiction and miscellaneous. Details in catalogue.

ICELAND INFORMATION CENTRE
P.O. Box 434
HARROW
HA1 3JE

ICON PRESS
Philip Brown
71 Northbourne Road
EASTBOURNE
BN22 8QP
Tel 01323 645 081

Produce art handbooks for full and part-time students by international artist and tutor Philip Brown who has exhibited widely in France England Spain and recently Japan. His paintings are in private collection in many countries.

ICONOCLAST PRESS
c/o Fulbeck Cottage
Sudthorpe Hill
Fulbeck
GRANTHAM

ICPA
11 Dale Close
Thames Street
OXFORD
OX1 1TU

IDAF PUBLICATIONS LTD
Canon Collins House
64 Essex Road
LONDON
N1 8LR

IDEAS UNLIMITED
P.O. Box 125
PORTSMOUTH
PO1 4PP

IDENTITY MAGAZINE
Cheetwood House
21 Newton Street
MANCHESTER
M1 1FZ

IDENTIFICATION OF ENGLISH PRESSED GLASS
Nunwick Hall
PENRITH
CA11 9LN
The Identification of English Pressed Glass 1842-1908, provides a concise, clear and comprehensive guide to identification of pressed glass objects, with an analysis of the characteristic designs of individual firms as well as details of the actual registrations.

IGNATOR
20 Livingstone Road
DERBY
DE3 6PR

IJATI PRESS
19 Chantry Road
Moseley
BIRMINGHAM
B13 8DL
Poetry.

ILLUMINATI PUBLISHING
119 Wellesley Road
CLACTON-ON-SEA
CO15 3PT
Children's Fiction.

IMAGE
Suite 310
Blackfriars Foundry
156 Blackfriars Road
LONDON
SE1 8EN

IMAGE DIRECT
P.O. Box 4011
LONDON
W9 3XW
In 1993 we offered an informative new book packed with over 65 superb rare previously unpublished

B/W photographs documenting the rise of Joe Strummer. Are we still going? Check.

IMAGES
Peter and Anne Stockham
The Staffs Bookshop
4/6 Dam Street
LICHFIELD
WS13 6AA
We closed our shop in Cecil Court moved to Lichfield and purchased a very large Staffs bookshop. The reprint of 'Joyful Newes' a 17th century chapbook celebrated this. We still specialise in illustrated children's books and dolls books but now include other subjects. We plan some local studies and have a long list of chapbooks in print which we can send you.

IMAGES PUBLICATIONS
Wood Lane
Barley Green
WOOLPIT
IP30 9RP

IMAGE THREE DESIGN
37 Pamplins
BASILDON
SS15 5BN
We have a list of audio and visual material.

IMAGING SERVICES
Gable End
Hall Street
Long Melford
SUDBURY
CO10 9JT
Local History.

I.M.O. PUBLICATIONS
82 Woodhall Drive
BATLEY
WF17 7TE
Poetry.

IMPACT BOOKS
Jean-Luc Barbanneau
151 Dulwich Road
LONDON
SE24 0NG
We publish reference books, practical guides, illustrated books, children's books, travel writing and fiction (under the "Olive Press" imprint).

IMPERIAL PUBLICATIONS
P.O. Box 5
LANCASTER
LA1 1BQ
Military Science. Manufacture of Guns. First World War History. Second World War History.

IMPRESS
7 Burghley Road
BRISTOL
BS6 5BL
Poetry.

IMPRINT PUBLISHING
117 Waterside
Pear Tree Bridge
MILTON KEYNES
MK6 3DF

IMPRINTS
53 Aragon Tower
Longshore
Pepys Estate
LONDON

SE8 3AH

INDELIBLE INC
Roberta McKeown
BCM 1698
LONDON
WC1N 3XX
Defying categorisation Indelible Inc. continues to hurl charming and fascinating books at the uncaring public. Words which have never been used to describe the imprint include: chinless, flouncy, gelatinous and marsupial. Please write for a catalogue, enclosing an SAE and bubble gum.

INDEPENDENT BOOKS
3 Leaves Green Crescent
BROMLEY
BR2 6DN
Tel 01959 73360
A war biography from the Luftwaffe. Prisoner of war escape story from the German side.

INDEPENDENT MUSIC PRESS IMP)
Martin Roach
PO Box 14691
LONDON
SE1 3ZJ
0171 357 8007
Publishers of UK No.1 seller "The Eight Legged" book and official biographies of The Mission, Ned's, Napalm Death and The Prodigy. Distributed by Omnibus Press, IMP is one of Britain's biggest selling small presses, available in 15 countries worldwide.

INDEPENDENT PUBLISHING CO
c/o Soma Books Ltd
38 Kennington Lane
LONDON
SE11 4LS

CENTRE FOR INDEPENDENT TRANSPORT
RESEARCH IN LONDON (CILT)
3rd Floor Universal House
88-94 Wentworth Street
LONDON
E1 7SA
Women and Transport; Town Planning.

INDIA STUDY CIRCLE FOR PHILATELY
1:1 Boston Court
Brownhill Road
Chandler's Ford
EASTLEIGH
SO5 2EH

INDIGO PUBLICATIONS
72 Anmore Road
DENMEAD
PO7 6NT
Poetry.

INFOBASE PUBLICATIONS LTD
Dr A P Harris
Westgate
West Common
GERRARD'S CROSS
SL9 7QS
Tel 01753 893089, fax 01753 891360

INFORMATION
North Quaker Meeting House
1 Archobold Terrace
NEWCASTLE-UPON-TYNE

NE2 1DB
Bibliography.

INFORMATION FOR SOCIAL CHANGE
14 Hugh Miller Place
EDINBURGH
EH3 5LG
Promotes alternatives to the dominant paradigms of library and information work, publishes journal 'Information for Social Change.' Associated with 'Counterpoise,' journal by and for US radical librarians - see above.

INFORMATION ON IRELAND
P.O. Box 958
LONDON
W14 0JF

INFORMATION SOUGHT
Paul Todd
36-42 Southern Row
LONDON
W10 5AN

INGLETON PUBLICATIONS
8 Halifax Road
Briercliffe
BURNLEY
BB10 3QH

INGRAM PUBLISHING
The Lodge
Wardle Old Hall
WARDLE
CW5 6BE

INIS GLEOIRE PUBLICATIONS
14 Fitzwilliam Avenue
BELFAST
BT7 2HJ

INK INCLUSIVE
2 Hinge Farm Cottages
Long Drive
Waterbeach
CAMBRIDGE
CB5 9LW

INKLING
45 Enfield Cloisters
Fanshaw Street
LONDON
N1 6LD
Tel 071 729 5569

INKSHED
387 Beverley Road
HULL
HU5 1LS

INK STONE
Sean Burningham
1D Powis Circle
ABERDEEN
AB2 3YT
Tel 01224 276810
Poetry pamphlets.

INKWELL PUBLISHING LTD
Brian James
Tameside Service Centre
Waterloo Road
STALYBRIDGE
SK15 2AU
Tel 0161 338 4132

INNER BOOKSHOP
34 Cowley Road
OXFORD

INNOVATIVE PUBLISHING CO
19 Forest Street

Shepshed
LOUGHBOROUGH
LE12 9BZ
Adventurous publishers - Modern Day pamphleteers - Information should be broadcast - If it's written, it should be read.

IN PRINT PUBLISHING
Alastair Dingwall
9 Beaufort Terrace
BRIGHTON
BN2 2SU
Tel 01273 682 836, fax 01273 620 958
Series 'Literary Travellers,' and three academic journals.
NEW: 'Dickens in France,' selection of his writings, 136 pp, hbk, ISBN 1-873047 76 2; £9.95.
'Journal of a Tour to Corsica,' Boswell's account 1768, 120 pp, hbk, ISBN 1-873047 71 1; £9.95.

INSIDER PUBLICATIONS
43 Queens Ferry Street Lane
EDINBURGH
EH2 4PF
Accommodation.

INSIGHT PUBLICATIONS
Kevin D. Harper
P.O. Box 49
CAMBERLEY
GU16 5FZ
Publisher of poetry and lyric booklets paperbacks and other books by young people. Part of the EMKH Arts business involved with music and art among students. Humour poetry music novels short stories Christian interests write for a catalogue.

INSTANT LIBRARY
P.O. Box 15
LOUGHBOROUGH
LE11 2RR
Libraries.

INSTITUTE OF THIRD WORLD ART & LITERATURE
16 Windemere Road
LONDON
W5 4TO

INTEGRATION NEWS.
c/o Integration Alliance
132 Wimbledon Park Road
LONDON
SW18 5UG

INTEGRITY WORKS
47 Marloes Road
LONDON
W8 6LA

INTELLECT BOOKS
Adrian Healey
Suite 2
108/110 London Road
OXFORD
OX3 9AW
Fax 01865 865 115
Books for people who work with words. New technologies of computing artificial intelligence hypertext and multi-media offer novel ways of working with language. We cover these and more radical as pects of language and its use by people and computers.

INTER-ARTS
62 Broughton Street
EDINBURGH
EH1 3SA

INTERBEING
Leeds Network of Engaged Buddhists
c/o Alex White
91 Clarendon Road
LEEDS
LS2 9LY
Tel/Fax 0113 244 4289
e-mail:
101726.3420@compuserve.com
You don't have to be a Buddhist to subscribe to, and enjoy this magazine which is very much engaged in the here and now. ISSN 1356-840X. Ann.sub.(3 issues) UK £6.00, Europe (incl. Eire) & World surface £8.00(20 IRCs), World air £10(25 IRCs); distributed free to Buddhist prisoners through Angulimala Chaplaincy.

INTERFACE
Larry Watson
Newtown Community House
117 Cumberland Road
READING
RG1 3JY
Tel 01734 351 116
Not a press Interface help community publishers with advice training but most of all support and encouragement. We work with all kinds of community groups in response to their needs and requirements aiming to make publishing accessible to everyone.
* Newtown Diamond Community magazine. Published in Urdu Punjabi and English for and by the community of New Town.
* St Stephens quarterly put together by elderly people for the sheltered housing project - St Stephens Court.
* GO: Girls Only. A comic made by and for girls in Reading.

INTERFERENCE
Michael Gardiner
Wadham College
Parks Road
OXFORD
OX1 3PN

INTERLINK DESIGN GROUP
Unit 2, Hartshorn House
Neath Road, Maesteg
BRIDGEND
CF34 9PG

INTERMEDIA GRAPHIC SYSTEMS LTD
Lewes Business Centre
North Street
LEWES
BN7 2PE

INTERPERSONAL
Martin J.S Briercliffe
BM Interpersonal
LONDON
WC1N 3XX
Tel 01733 314758
Ever thought you'd like some help to deal with your personal problems but haven't been able to ask then this book is for you. A straight forward guide to help you identify and deal with the problems in your life.

How To Deal With Your Inner Personal Problems Martin J.S. Briercliffe 128 16/9/92 ISBN 1 874769 00 1 £5.99 Psychology Self help.

INTERZONE
David Pringle
217 Preston Drove
BRIGHTON
BN1 6FL
Tel 0273 504710
No longer small our circulation is thousands but we began as a small press. Britain's premier sf mag. Same team branched out with another newstand magazine. Send for details.

INTYPE
Input Typesetting Limited
See Quadrant House
Low cost short run book service. Books book proofs reprints manuals on-demand publishing in house magazines fanzines programmes slow sellers. Runs of 25 up to 1000 copies. Fast delivery competitive pricing help and advice. Price scale available on request.

IOLO
Mr Dedwydd Jones
38 Chaucer Road
BEDFORD
MK40 2AJ
The 'Black Books On The Welsh Theatre' series reached No. 6 in 1996 with 'Wild West Stages'. The scourge continues. Couldn't care less about the topic? Buy them for a bloody good laugh then.

ION PRESS 23
56 Mulben Crescent
Crookston
GLASGOW
G53 7EH
New poetry with a major emphasis on good design. Desirable limited editions.

IOTA
David Holliday
67 Hady Crescent
CHESTERFIELD
S41 0EB

IPS Publishing
8 Woodland Avenue
Hagley
STOURBRIDGE
DY8 2XQ
Food & Drink.

Alastair IRELAND
23 Pinnacle Hill Park
KELSO
TD5 8HA
The Leadhills and Wanlockhead Light Railway.

(THE) IRISH IN BRITAIN HISTORY CENTRE
76 Salisbury Road
LONDON
NW6 6NY

IRISH PEATLAND CONSERVATION COUNCIL
3 Lower Mount Street
DUBLIN
Republic of Ireland
Subjects: Local Travel Guides. Books January to June 1991 - 2.

IRISH WOMEN'S PERSPECTIVES
c/o 123 Lavender Sweep
LONDON
SW11 1EA

IRON PRESS
Peter Mortimer
5 Marden Terrace
Cullercoats
NORTHSHIELDS
NE30 4PD
Tel 0191 2531901
Veteran poetry mag with spin-off books.

WORSHIPFUL COMPANY OF IRONMONGERS
Ironmongers' Hall
Barbican
LONDON
EC2Y 8AA
Subjects: History of the Ironmongers' Company. Books January to June 1991 - 1.

IRWELL PRESS
3 Durley Avenue
PINNER
HA5 1JQ

I.S ENTERPRISES
P.O. Box 379
Clarkston
GLASGOW
G76 8AD

Robert ISAACS
40 Bath Road
Bridygate Common
Warmley
BRISTOL
BS15 5JW
Tel 01272 672995

C.J. ISAACSON
7 Golds Pightle
Ringstead
HUNSTANTON
PF36 5LD
Biography.

ISIAN NEWS
F O I
Huntingdon Castle
Clonegal
ENNISCORTHY
Wexford
Ireland

ISLF HANDPRESS
Andy English
10 Matthew Wren Close
Little Downham
ELY
CB6 2UL
My books focus on image more than text, ranging from small editions and wood-engravings to unique volumes, often prompted by found objects. Commisions for engravings and single books undertaken. Send S.A.E. for more information and to join mailing list.

THE ISLINGTON POETRY WORKSHOP & ISLINGTON WRITING FORUM
Bruce Barnes
19a Marriott Road
LONDON
N4 3QN
Tel 071 281 2369
A Writing workshop that produces occasional anthologies.

I.S.O. PUBLICATIONS
137 Westminster Bridge Road
LONDON
SE1 7HR
Humour. European Naval History.

ISSUE
Jeremy Nuttall
24 Eastwood Road
BIRMINGHAM
B12 9NB
Tel 0121 440 1739
Issue magazine is a magazine devoted to discussion of all types on all subjects; especially morality faith religion politics and music. The Victory point Gazette is devoted to interactive fiction and postal games.

ISSUE ONE
(Eon Publications)
2 Tewkesbury Drive
GRIMSBY
DN34 4TL

ITINERANT PUBLICATIONS
Ronald McNeil
13 Albert Road
GOUROCK
PA19 1NH
Tel 01475 34999
Publish writers from West Central Scotland, also public performances.

I.T.M.A. - INFOTEXT MANUSCRIPTS
A Baron/T.D. Man
c/o 93c Venner Road
LONDON
SE26 5HY
Tel 0181 659 7713

IT'S A SMALL WORLD
92 Hornsey Lane
LONDON
N6 5LT

IVANHOE PRESS
Kings Meadow
Ferry Hinksey Road
OXFORD
OX2 0DP

I-WAS
BCM Utopia
LONDON
WC1N 3XX

AC PUBLICATIONS
Mr John Vasco
28 Bellomonte Crescent
Drayton
NORWICH
NR8 6EJ
Tel 01603 861 339
Publication of books relating to the activities of the Luftwaffe in World War 2.

JACKSONS ARM
P.O. Box 74
LINCOLN
LN1 1QG
The small press with a spiky, subversive feel, Jackson's Arm specialises in short-run, high quality productions - mainly first collections or work by new poets. Unsolicited MS are not required. Founded 1985.

JADE PUBLISHERS
10 Madeville Road
AYLESBURY
HP21 8PA

JAMES & JAMES
75 Carleton Road
LONDON
N7 0ET

GOVERNORS OF JAMES ALLEN'S
Girls' School
East Dulwich Grove
LONDON
SE22 8TE
History of James Allen's Girls' School.

David Bryan JAMES
Dolhuan
Llandre
Bow Street
DYFED
SY24 5AB
Local History.

Elizabeth JAMES
61 Crofton Park Road
LONDON
SE4 1AF
General Fiction.

Trevor JAMES
36 Heritage Court
LICHFIELD
WS14 9ST
Croydon Harriers 1920-1970 fiftieth anniversary booklet, 36 pages with photographs £2.00 incl p&p. Obtainable from above.

JANE PUBLISHING
Adrian Spendlow
23 Bright Street
YORK
YO2 4XS
Tel 01904 647 086
As a performance poet Adrian is committed to this early medium. Looking always for opportunities to share with writers and listeners particularly in the field of vocal and drama poetry. LET IT LIFT UP FROM THE PAGE! Send s.a.e. for reply. Pomes.

Jennie JANES
29 Pynchon Paddocks
Little Hallingbury
BISHOPS STORTFORD
CM22 7RJ
Crosswords.

JANUARY BOOKS
18 Amberley Grove
CROYDON
CR0 6ND

JANUS PUBLISHING COMPANY
Duke House
37 Duke Street
LONDON
W1M 5DF
Co-partnership publishers.

JARDINE PRESS
James Dodds
2 Clipt Bush Cottage
Polstead Street
Stoke-by-Nayland
COLCHESTER
CO6 4SD

JAY BOOKS
c/o Good Book Services
The Street
CHARTMOUTH
DT6 6PU
Etiquette.

John W.T. JEFFERIES
57 Weston Crescent
Aldridge
WALSALL
WS9 0HA

JEMA PUBLICATIONS
40 Ashley Lane
MOULTON
NN3 1TJ

JENKINS MAIL ORDER
121 Lent Rise Road
SLOUGH
SL1 7BN
Photocopiers and How to Win.

JERSEY ARTISTS
P.O. Box 75
Normandy House
ST HELIER
Jersey
Channel Islands

JERSEY WILDLIFE PRESERVATION TRUST
Les Augres
MANOR TRINITY
Jersey
Channel Islands
Zoology.

JESUS LA PRODUCTS
Christopher
c/o 15 Belegrove Close
WELLING
DA16 3RG
"Destroying Xerox infinity since 1983, we now have a new printer for our low-tech, lo-fi creations. Beyond the smallpress world for a terminally ephemeral and free one!"
"Bike-Not" - bike magazine for people who don't.
"I Don't care About ..."

JIGSAW BOOKS
Stephen Hancock
Jigsaw Box
111 Magdalen Road
OXFORD
OX4 1RQ
Publishing and distributing house of Jigsaw nonviolent perspective. A radical nonviolence perspective.

J.M.F. BOOKS
Llanerch

Felinfach
LAMPETER
SA48 8PS
Local History.

JMK CONSULTANCY
39 Balgreen Road
EDINBURGH
EH12 5TY
Customs and Folklore.

JOE SOAP'S CANOE
Mr Martin Stannard
30 Quilter Road
FELIXTOWE
IP11 7JJ
Stalwart lit mag.

Marion JOHNSON
199 Victoria Avenue
Borrowash
DERBY
DE72 3HG
South Derbyshire - number six in the Ockbrook and Borrowash Local History Series: Walking Round Borrowash - discover the past from what can be seen today. £3 plus 40p p&p from author, above.

JOHNSONS PUBLISHING
James Street West
BATH
BA1 2BU

JOHNSTON AND BACON
P.O. Box 1
STIRLING
Loch Ness Monster.

JOINT PUBLICATIONS
8 Priestly House
Old Street
LONDON
EC1V 9JN

JONATHON PRESS
16 Poplar Grove
Flint Hill
STANLEY
DH9 9BE
Poetry magazine.

JONES-SANDS PUBLISHING
10 Startin Close
Exhall
COVENTRY
CV7 9NA

Brian JONES
32 Myers Avenue
BRADFORD
BD2 4ET
Second volume of Index of Indexers which lists around 200 indexes for consultation (usually by post). Use to family historians. Copies cost £2.25 incl UK postage or £2.65 by overseas surface mail. Parts available individually. "Pre-1841 West Riding Census Transcriptions". SAE for details.

Doris JONES
89 Linwood Drive
COVENTRY
CV2 2LZ
Short Stories.

Philip JONES
40 Regina Crescent
Ravenshead
NOTTINGHAM
NG15 9AE
Newstead Abbey: A Portrait in Old Picture Postcards by Philip Jones &

Michael Riley. Paperback, 44pp, 56 postcards of the Abbey and grounds dating mainly from before WW1, £2.95 plus 50p p&p.

JORDAN PUBLICATIONS
1 Ashfolds
Horsham Road
RUSPER
RH12 4QX
Children's Fiction.

(THE) JOURNAL
18-20 Dean Street
NEWCASTLE-UPON-TYNE
NE1 1PG

J.S.B PUBLICATIONS
14 Moorfield Place
Shepshed
LOUGHBOROUGH
LE12 9AW

JUMA
Martin Lacey
44 Wellington Street
SHEFFIELD
S1 4HD
Tel 0742 720915,
Book publishers - principal subject football. Book and fanzine mail order. Also litho printers specialising in small press work: books, magazines, publicity material &c. Low prices. Here's some back hits edited by M. Lacey.
* El Tel Was a Space Alien. ISBN 1 872204 00 7
* Get Your Writs Out! Compilation of Fanzine Writing. ISBN 1 872204 02 3
* Where's the Bar. ISBN 1 872204 03 1
* Non-league Football Yearbook.

JUST WOMEN
3 Holway Hill
TAUNTON

J.W.B. PUBLICATIONS
(John White Brown)
5 Hambledon Close
Ladybridge
BOLTON
BL3 4ND
Poetry.

KABET PRESS
John Hort
239 Bramcote Lane
NOTTINGHAM
NG8 2QL
Tel 01602 283 001
Shakespeare for children.

KADATH PRESS
The Hermitage
East Morton
KEIGHLEY
BD20 5UJ

KADU BOOKS
6 Ivy Avenue
BLACKPOOL
PY4 3QG
European Travel.

KAIROS PRESS
552 Bradgate Road
Newtown
Linford
LEICESTER
LE6 0HB
Leicestershire and Rutland Woodlands Past and Present by Anthony Squires and Michael Jeeves. 160 pages, 49 photographs, 29 maps, 15 tables, 5 drawings. The History of Woodlands in the Two Counties and their wildlife, management and conservation needs. £9.95 post-paid.

R.M. KAMARYC
43 Broomfield
HARLOW
CM20 2JZ
Military Science.

KARRERA
Foxworthy
Lotton
IVYBRIDGE
PL21 9SS

KATABASIS
Ms Dinah Livingstone
10 St Martins Close
LONDON
NW1 0HR
Tel 0171 485 3830
Publishes English poetry and bi-lingual editions of poetry in translation mainly Latin American.

THE KATES HILL PRESS
Carol Stokes
126 Watsons Green Road
DUDLEY
DY2 7LG
Fiction and social history from the Black Country and West Midlands.

KAWABATA PRESS
Knill Cross
Millbrook
TORPOINT
PL10 1DX

RICHARD KAY PUBLICATIONS
80 Sleaford Road
BOSTON
PE21 8EU
Tel 01205 353 231
New catalogue for 1996 already out, with forthcoming titles on Lincolnshire life, vernacular history and dialect, plus topics of general interest (Essays of Dissent). One of the best regional lists available.
Leicestershire Entertainments:

History of the Deeming Cinema Circuit in Loughborough, Coalville, Cannock, Sutton Coldfield and Rugeley is in 'Loughborough's Stage and Screen' Mercia Cinema Society: £14.25/£1.50 p&p from Mervyn Gould, 29 Blackbrook Court, Loughborough LE11 0UA. Coming soon: Boston/ Spalding/ Howden Fairground bioscope.

Dennis KEEN
51 Warren Road
RUGBY
CV22 5LG
Sport.

KEEPSAKE PRESS
2 Park House Gardens
TWICKENHAM
TW1 2DE

Andrew KELLY
19 Cumberland Street
EDINBURGH
EH3 6RT
Tel 0131 556 8673

KELSEY PUBLISHING
Kelsey House
77 High Street
BECKENHAM
BR3 1AN
Cars. Car restoring.

KELTIA PUBLICATIONS
Kaledon Naddair
P.O. Box 307
EDINBURGH
EH9 1XA
Tel 0131 666 2822
Produce books monographs and Journals by Kaledon Naddair and other writers on all aspects of Keltic Culture e.g. Art-Symbolism Poetry Language Megalithic Sites Nature-Reservoirs Mythology and Pagan-Spiritually. We produce the Real McCoy - pioneering research is our speciality.

H.M. KENDALL
20 Mortimer Close
Orelton
LUDLOW
SY8 4PG
Historical Biography.

KEN FERGUSON PRESS
Ken Ferguson
20 Lanercost Park
CRAMLINGTON
NE23 6RU
Tel 01670 733 927
Hand made limited edition books of poetry, printed letterpress. Illustrations, designed, plates hand cut, printed, hand coloured, then hand bound by Ken Ferguson. "Trip to the Seaside", 10 poems by Anne Jones. 10 relief prints - 60 copies, £55.00 p+p £2.50 "Day at the races", 12 poems by Newcastle & Tyneside Cymrodorion Society, 11 relief prints, 60 copies, £75.00, p+p £3.00.

KENRIC
BM Kenric
LONDON
WC1N 3XX

KENSINGTON WEST PRODUCTIONS
338 Old York Road

LONDON
SW18 1SS
Sport.

KERNOW POETS PRESS
18 Frankfield Rise
TUNBRIDGE WELLS
TN2 5LF
Tel 01892 539 800
* 'Postcards from Occupied Lands' by Bill Headdon is a collection of poetry written from the aspect of exile, wherever exile might be, the land which exists both as concrete reality and the shifting, treacherous quick-sands of memory. £2.95 plus 50p p+p.
* 'Cornish Links' is an anthology of poems arranged in the context of a Cornish travelogue. £4.95 plus 60p p+p.
* 'Links' a new poetry magazine to be launched this year.

KEROUAC CONNECTION
76 Calderwood Square
East Kilbride
GLASGOW
G74 3BQ

Tom KERR
1 Winsor Avenue
Holywood
BELFAST
BT18 9DG
Poetry.

Pamela KETTLE
Sutton Court
Sutton Scarsdale
CHESTERFIELD
S44 5UT
History of Hardwick Inn.

Frank KEY
103 Cavendish Road
Highams Park
LONDON
E4 9NG
After a two year silence the Hooting Yard calendar returns. All those who have had no idea what day it was can now live again. The 1997 edition rejoices (c M Thatcher) in the title 'Planet of the Crumpled Jesuits.' Mr E informs customers, 'Instead of the usual cack-handed drawings you get a dozen photographs culled from an old encyclopedia, each one doctored and crumpled - or possibly crumpled and doctored.' Each copy is signed, (by whom is not mentioned) numbered and individually dedicated (your decision). For all this you only give money? A simple £5 or cheque to the same value made payable to some 'P J Byrne.'

KEYHOLE PUBLICATIONS
BCM Keyhole
LONDON
WC1 3XX

KHABS
Box TR 24
LEEDS
LS12 3QU

KIBLAH PUBLISHING
Park House
CERNE ABBAS
DT2 7BG
Equinox magazine.

KIMBO INTERNATIONAL
P.O. Box 12412
LONDON
SW18 5ZL
'Lochs magazine is a new quarterly uniting some of the best comedy writers around.' The title comes from Lairds Of Camester Highlanders Society. Vol 1 Issue 1 available. Single copy .90p. Sub special £15 pa.

KINDRED SPIRIT
Room T
Foxhole
DARTINGTON
TQ9 6EB

Simon KING
(see SIMON KING PRESS)

THE KING'S ENGLAND PRESS
Steve Rudd
37 Crookes Lane
Carlton
BARNSLEY
S71 3JR
Tel 01226 722 529
The Press is reprinting the entire 'King's England' series of guidebooks to each of the English counties first published in the 1930s. In addition we also do distribution for other small Local History Publishers and run Local History bookshop.

KINGSLEA PRESS
137 Newhall Street
BIRMINGHAM
B3 1SF
General knowledge.

KINMEL PUBLISHING
Kinmel Hall
St George
ABERGELE
LL2 9DA

KIPPER PRESS
39 George V Avenue
LANCING
BN15 8NQ
Tel 01903 753315
Publisher of children's books.

KISSING THE SKY
Miss Sharon Elton
23 Southwark Close
LICHFIELD
WS13 7SH

THE KIT-CAT PRESS
Kenneth Hardacre
10 Fosseway Drive
MORETON-IN-MARSH
GL56 0DU
Fine printer.

KITES
The Highgate Society
10A South Grove
LONDON
N6

KITHEAD
De Salis Drive
Hampton Lovett
DROITWICH
WR9 0QE

KITTIWAKE
David Parrott
Darowen
MACHYNLLETH

SY20 8NS
Tel 01650 511 314 fax 5116
Truly helpful pocket-sized guide books based on personal research; carefully designed and fully mapped and illustrated.

K.M.S. BOOKS
Market Place
BOSTON
PE21 6LY

F. KNIGHT
11 Church Cottages
Stopham
PULBOROUGH
RH20 1EG
Local History.

KNIGHTSBRIDGE PUBLICATIONS
Newcastle Road
Newsham
BLYTH
NE24 4AG

KORVET PUBLISHING AND DISTRIBUTION
Sarah Garrett
P.O. Box 115
Old Post Office Gallery
ROYAL LEAMINGTON SPA
CV31 1GH
Tel 01926 315 262 fax 01926 450 973
Militaria.

KOZMIK PRESS
David Ryan
134 Elsenham Street
LONDON
SW18 5NP
Tel 0171 935 5913
*Kozmik Press exists to promote progressive new poetry & fiction. While large publishers are enslaved purely evaluating profitability, Kozmik Press beleives in that old fashioned precept, "art for art's sake".
"Taboo". A novel by David Stuart Ryan. A probe into the secret heart of Germany as a clandestine romance is analysed.
"John Lennon's Secret". One of the first and still the most accurate descriptions of the extraordinary life - and death -of one of the 20th century's great influences.*

THE KQBX PRESS
James Sale
16 Scotter Road
Pokestown
BOURNEMOUTH
BH7 6LY
Tel 01202 42155
Committed to promoting poetry in the south and to publishing high-quality collections from any region.

KRAX
Andy Robson
c/o 63 Dixon Lane
LEEDS
LS12 4RR
Main publication is nine-monthly Krax magazine - a light-hearted poetry selection, interview with writer or artiste & large review section. Mini-booklets plus occasional oddities also.

KRINO
The Paddocks
Glenrevagh

CORRANDULLA
Co Galway
Ireland

KRIS PUBLICATIONS
Chris Wilson
239B Preston Road
WEMBLEY
HA9 8PE
*Literate TV Fiction and cartoons.
Send for details*
* Playing with Words. Play rhymes
for pre-school children.
* Hell! it's Heaven. Cartoons of the
after life.

KRISTALL PRODUCTIONS
71B Maple Road
SURBITON
KT6 4AG

KK KRISTO PRODUCTIONS
31 Thistle Grove
WELWYN GARDEN CITY
AL7 4AD

**KROPOTKIN'S LIGHTHOUSE
PUBLICATIONS**
Jim Huggon
Box KLP
Housemans Bookshop
5 Caledonian Road
LONDON
N1
*Anarchist-pacifist press specialising
in poetry, posters, pamphlets from
within that tradition.*

K-SLAW INC.
P.O. Box 375
Belmar
NJ 07719
USA
*OKULICZ, Karen, 'Try ! A survival
guide to unemployment,' 1995, 73
pp., pbk, ISBN 0-9644260-0-5,
$10.00.*

KSL
BM Hurricane
LONDON
WC1N 3XX
*The bulletin of the Kate sharpley
Library, an archive of anarchist
publications.*

K.T. PUBLICATIONS
Editor: Kevin Troop
16 Fane Close
STAMFORD
PE9 1HG
Magazine.

KUDOS
Graham Sykes
78 Easterly Road
LEEDS
LS8 3AN

KUMA COMPUTERS LTD
12 Horseshore Park
Pangbourne
READING
RG8 7JW
Tel 0734 844335
*Specialise in publishing quality
computing books. Topics include
DTP programming an usage of
microcomputers portable
computers and their software.*

Z KWINTNER BOOKS
6 Warren Mews
LONDON
W1P 5DJ

LAAM
P.O. Box 249A
SURBITON
KT6 5AX

Peter van LAARHOVEN
Patersstrat 96
B 2300 Turnhout
Belgium
Fax +.32.14/42.88.29.
*Belgian society promotes comics/
bandes dessinees/strips of all
kinds. Publishes FORMALINE, a
who-does-what-and-where network
for the small press comic book
world. A CD-ROM version is
available. FORMALINE is
distributed by Het Raadsel,
Amsterdam, The Netherlands, Fax:
+.31.20/682.32.86.*

LAECE BOOKS
T.R. Leach
3 Merleswen
Dunholme
LINCOLN
LN2 3SN
Tel 01673 860 637
*Publishes a series of books on
Lincolnshire country houses and
other material relating to local
history in Lincolnshire.*

**LAGAN PRESS
/ANNA LIVIA PRESS**
21 Cross Avenue
DUN LAOGHAIRE
County Dublin
Republic of Ireland
Literature.

Mary LAKER
Chantry
Church Road
Kennington
ASHFORD
TN24 9QD
Poetry.

LAMBOURN PRESS
The Old Forge
7 Caledonian Road
LONDON
N1 9DX

LAMBOURN PUBLICATIONS
12-14 High Road
LONDON

N2 9JP
Biography.

LAME DUCK PUBLISHING
71 South Road
Portishead
BRISTOL
BS20 9DY
Education.

THE LAMP PUBLISHING HOUSE
BM Follower
LONDON
WC1N 3XX
*Dedicated to publishing works
which present a moderate, non
fundamentalist approach to religion
and human spirtuality. More
specifically, publishes literature
based on philosophy of first
Galilean followers of Jesus of
Nazareth, emphasising his
humanity, and his teachings on
Kingdom of God.*

LANCITIE LTD
Harbour Road
LYDNEY
GL15 4EJ
*PRICE, Bill, 'So you want a boozer,'
a satire by journalist and former
MP who was Parliamentary adviser
then consultant to Licensed
Victuallers organisations. £6.50
p&p incl.*

LANDFALL PUBLICATIONS
Bob Acton
Landfall
Penpol
Devoran
TRURO
TR3 6NW

LANDY PUBLISHING
Bob Dobson
Acorns
3 Staining Rise
Staining
BLACKPOOL
FY3 0BU
Tel/Fax 01253 886103
*Publisher and book dealer.
Publishes Lancashire local history &
dialect books, also a quarterly
magazine for the red rose county
"Really Lancashire". .*

LANGDON PUBLISHING
Acorn Workshops
250 Carmarthen Road
SWANSEA
SA1 1HG

LANGTRY PRESS
23 St Marks Road
HENLEY-ON-THAMES
RG9 1LP

**LANGUAGES INFORMATION
CENTRE/CANOLFAN
HYSBYSRWYDD IEITHYDDOL**
Joseph Biddulph
32 Stryd Ebeneser
PONTYPRIDD
CF37 5PB
*Send SASE for this publisher's
amazing list with international
coverage of languages and
dialects you don't often find
elsewhere. 'Biddulph's Concise
Versemaker: some reflections on
traditional English metre, and how*

*to shape it for yourself.' 28 pp,
ISBN 0-948565-48-9, £4.00.
Postage free in UK.
JUST OUT 'Biddulph's Handbook of
West Country Brythonic.'This is the
quest for the lost Celtic language of
South West England. ISBN 1-
897999-06-2, UK £4.00. All
monies payable to Joseph
Biddulph.*

LAPIN BLANC
Elizabeth Rudd
55 Warwick Square
LONDON
SW1C 2AJ
High quality children's books.

LARK PUBLICATIONS
68 Lamble Close
Beck Row
BURY ST. EDMUNDS
IP28 8DB
Botany.

LARKS PRESS
Ordnance Farm House
Guist Bottom
DEREHAM
NR20 5PF
*Memoirs of a Thatching Family
1860-1968 by B S Reeve (£4.95
incl p&p). The story of a Breckland
thatcher whose grandfather, father
and brother thatched with Norfolk
reed, sedge and straw especially in
Norfolk and Suffolk, but also as far
away as Kent and Yorkshire.*

LAST DITCH PRESS
22 Evesham Road
STRATFORD-UPON-AVON
CV37 9AA
*Trash teen-mags and postcards with
poems.*

LATHAM PRESS
9 Latham Avenue
RUNCORN
WA7 5DS
Betting Shops.

**LATIN AMERICAN WRITERS
PUBLICATION**
107 Gorefield House
Gorefield Place
LONDON
NW6 5TB
Tel 0171 328 2895

LAUNDRY PRESS
41 Bryony Road
LONDON
W12 0LS
Poetry.

LAWRENCE POLLINGER LIMITED
18 Maddox Street
Mayfair
LONDON
W1R 0EU

Barbara LAWSON
1 Elverlands Close
Ferring
WORTHING
BN12 5PL
Poetry.

LAWTON HERITAGE SOCIETY
17 Brattswood Drive
Church Lawton
STOKE ON TRENT
ST7 3EJ
The Lawton Chronicles Volume 1

1995 contains articles and a number of other items relating to the Parish of Church Lawton in Cheshire. Price £2.50 plus 50p p&p.

Thelma LAYCOCK
34 Jacques Close
Queenswood Drive
LEEDS
LS6 3NQ
Poetry.

R J LEACH & CO
38 Inglemere Road
Forest Hill
LONDON
SE23 2BE
Mainly military publishing producing up to six titles per year, both reprints and new books.

LEADER BOOKS
MFPA 9
Inverness Place
LONDON
W2 3JF
Art.

LEADING EDGE PRESS
B Swann
The Old Chapel
Burtesett
HAWES
UL8 3PB

LEAF PUBLISHING
9 Lock Road
RICHMOND
TW10 7LQ
Travel.

LEARNING STYLES
P.O. Box 1071
ANDOVER
SP10 1YN
Careers. British History. School Textbooks.

LEARNING TOGETHER ABC
Dorothy Dowling
18 Blackstock Drive
SHEFFIELD
S14 1AG
A finger spelling alphabet book, with signs, for deaf and hearing children. Also: game, finger spelling cards,large chart, manual,alphabet. All full colour.

LEATHERHEAD AND DISTRICT LOCAL HISTORY SOCIETY
72 Culverhay
ASHTEAD
KT21 1PS
Tel 01372 275 542
A History of Ashtead, editor J C Stuttard, Autumn 1995 publication. Roman times to present, more detailed account of 19th and 20th centuries. 264 pages, 70 b&w photos, drawings, maps. £9.99 p&p £2 UK. Obtainable from bookshops or Sales Secretary, above. Cheques to Society.

LEAVES/SCALES
P. Holman
14 Ropery Street
LONDON
E3 4QF
Poetry.

LECHLADE PRESS
89A Allport Lane

Bromborough
WIRRAL
L62 7HL
Sport.

Jonathan LEDBURY
40 Bunyan Road
LONDON
E17 6EY
Tel 0181 527 0247

Kitty LEE
13A New Street
CROMER
NR27 9HP
Social Welfare.

LEECHWELL PRESS
Leechwell Cottage
TOTNES
TQ9 5SY

LEE DONALDSON ASSOCIATES
14 Pall Mall
LONDON
SW1Y 5LU
Town Planning.

LEEDS POSTCARDS
P.O. Box 84
LEEDS
LS1 4HU

LEEMAN PRESS
227A High Street
NORTHALLERTON
DI7 8LU

LEEWAY PUBLICATIONS
185 Baring Road
LONDON
SE12 0LD
School Textbooks.

LEITH HEENAN PUBLISHERS
Barney Leith
24 Gardiner Road
Abingdon
OXFORD
OX14 3YA
Tel 01235 535 224, fax 01235 529 137

LEMAITRE KELLY PUBLISHING
Corene Lemaitre
19 Cumberland Street
EDINBURGH
EH3 6RT
Tel/Fax 0131 556 8673

John LE MESURIER
Radipole
Les Hibits
St. Martin's
GUERNSEY
Channel Is
Short Stories.

LEO PUBLISHING
31 Callis Street
Clare
SUDBURY
CO10 8PX

LEOMANSLEY PRESS
16 Leomansley Road
LICHFIELD
WS13 8AW
General Fiction.

LEONARDO PUBLISHING
22-26 Paul Street
LONDON
EC24 4JH

LEONINE PRESS
8 Burnfield Drive
RUGELEY
WS15 2RH
Current title: Millington, Gordon. Alien encounters. ISBN 0952317605, pbk, £9.95 + £1.50 p&p. Cheques payable to Simon Moore. Limited first edition in hardback.

LEO'S PUBLISHING SERVICE
29 Fardale Road
Streatham
LONDON
SW16 6DA

LESBIAN & GAY CHRISTIAN MOVEMENT
Oxford House
Derbyshire Street
LONDON
E2 6HG
Journal.

LESBIAN & GAY FREEDOM MOVEMENT
BM Box 207
LONDON
WC1N 3XX
Newsletter.

LESBIAN INFORMATION SERVICE
P.O. Box 8
TODMORDEN
OL14 5TZ
Newsletter.

LIBANUS PRESS LTD
Rose Tree House
Silverless Street
MARLBOROUGH
SN8 1JQ

LIBERTARIAN ALLIANCE
Chris Thame
1 Russell Chambers
The Piazza
Covent Garden
LONDON
WC2E 8AA
Tel 071 821 5502
Publishes a wide range of leaflets pamphlets and monographs on all aspects of economic, political, social, moral and sexual freedom from classic liberal, libertarian, free market and anarcho-capitalist perspectives.

LIBRA
Miss Norton & Mr Day
3 Hall Terrace
CROOK
DL15 0QN

LIBRARIANS AT LIBERTY
Editor: Charles Willett
1716 SW Williston Road
Gainsvill
FL 32608-4049
USA
Tel + 352/335-2200
e-mail: willett@afn.org
Radical magazine. Also editor of Counterpoise qv. Also CRISES Press.

LIFEWISH PRESS
6 Springlawn Drive
Blanchardstown
DUBLIN 15
Republic of Ireland
HALL, James J., 'University Degrees by Mail,' covers 'from the phoniest

to the most genuine universities in the world.' 1991, 123 pp., A4 comb-binding, no ISBN.

LIGHT'S LIST OF LITERARY MAGAZINES
Dr John Light
The Light House
29 Longfield Road
TRING
HP23 4DG

LILBOURNE PRESS
Nicholas Reed
26 Hichisson Road
Peckham Rye
LONDON
SE15 3AL
Tel 0171 732 7778
We specialise in books on Local History and Art History.

LILLIPUT PRESS LTD
4 Rosemount Terrace
Arbour Hill
DUBLIN 7
Ireland

LIMELIGHT PUBLICATIONS
M P Wilkinson
P.O. Box 8
MARKFIELD
LE67 9ZT
Tel 01530 244 069
Involved with Leicestershire Writers' Monthly.

LIMITCODE
Tatton Buildings
6 Old Hall Road
Gatley
CHEADLE
SK8 4BE
Languages in Business.

LINDEN HALL
H. McNichol
Liberten Park Court
1-4 Lasswade Road
EDINBURGH
E16 6JH
Biography.

LINDEN ENTERPRISES
Old School
Wormshill
SITTINGBOURNE
ME9 0TR

LINGUASIA
45 Museum Street
LONDON
WC1A 1LR
Language.

LINGUAVIVA CENTRE
Eason and Son
Brickfield Drive
Crumlin
DUBLIN 12
Republic of Ireland
General Fiction.

LINK PRESS
35 Elizabeth Walk
READING
RG2 0AW
Asian History.

LINK UP
51 Northwick B Centre
Blockley
MORETON-IN-MARSH
GL56 9RF

Magazine for those who care about the future of the planet.

LISEK PUBLICATIONS
58a Comerford Road
LONDON
SE4 2AX
Historic Biography. Second World War.

LISIEUX HALL
Whittle-le-Woods
CHORLEY
PR6 7DX
Social Welfare.

LITTLE BIG BOOKS
Number Six
4th Avenue
BIRMINGHAM
B29 7EU
Plan the first part of an evolving series of teacher aids titled the 'User's Guide to the Brain' by Peter Scott and Grant Jesse. A net bulletin board will be set up to follow the second stage pilot scheme in Spring. More info from e-mail: ugh@grant-jesse.com

LITTLE CHERUB PUBLICATIONS
19 South Quay
GREAT YARMOUTH
NR30 2RG
Tel 01493 842637
'Guess the Question!' An original quiz book compiled by quiz wizard Valerie Jordan. You are given the answers and have to supply the Question. The questions are printed in the back of the book. The only reversible Quiz Book!

LITTLE PEOPLE BOOKS
6, 4th Avenue
BIRMINGHAM
B29 7EU
Publishes Eddy Champion Comic which seeks to highlight environmental issues. Covers food, the future, recycling, sustainable development, energy efficiency, transport, life conservation, waste minimalisation, communications, community, soil and water. Produced and purchased to provide support for the registered educational children's charity, World of Water. £1.25p.

LITTLE PRESSES (ASSOCIATION OF)
Membership Secretary
89a Petherton Road
LONDON
N5 2QT
Annual and bi-monthly for members. (see Resource Directory: Membership Organisations.)

E.R. LITTLER
St. Andrew's Vicarage
65 Electric Avenue
WESTCLIFF-ON-SEA
SS0 9NN
Architecture.

LITTLEWOOD PRESS
Nanholme Centre
Shaw Wood Road
TODMORDEN
OL14 6DA
Littlewood Arc publishes 10-12 titles per year including prizewinners of the Annual Northern Short Stories Competition.

Poetry predominates, although occasionally prose considered. Unsolicited MSS. not encouraged.

LIVER AND LIGHTS
John Bently
The Scriptorium
101 Upland Road
East Dulwich
LONDON
SE22 0DB
Tel 0181 693 1362
Liver and Lights is the collective title for series of books made by John Bently since 1984. Since 1987 the series has increasingly concentrated on depicting an invented parallel world inhabited by vivid eccentric characters.

LIVING ARCHIVE PUBLISHING
3 Stratford Road
Wolverton
MILTON KEYNES
MK12 5LJ
Individual and collectives of reminiscences from the Milton Keynes area; documentary arts hour-to-do-it manuals; documentary play scripts; teachers' packs based on local archive material.

LIZZIE BOOKS
Rutland Road
TWICKENHAM
TW2 5ER

LLANERCH PUBLISHERS
Derek Bryce
Felinfach
LAMPETER
SA48 8PJ
Tel 01570 470 567
NEW paperbacks: RODRIGUES, Louis J., 'Anglo-Saxon Didactic Verse,' seventh in series 'Anglo-Saxon Verse Specimens rendered into Modern English,' ISBN 1-897853-99-8, £8.95.
JACKSON, Kenneth, 'Studies in Early Celtic Nature Poetry,' facsimile reprint of Cambridge U.P. 1935 ed., ISBN 1-897853-79-3, £7.95.
GRANT, Paula transl., 'Aldfrith's Beowulf,' historical interpretation first published in 'Open History,' journal of the Open University History Society in 1994, now with full text of epic. ISBN 1-897853-98-X, £5.95.

LLANGEITHO TIMES
Derlwyn Fach
Langeitho
TREGARON
SY25 6QU
Community Journalism. Children's Fiction.

LLANGORDA PRESS
40B Jessop Road
WALSALL
WS1 3AS
Local History. Historical Biography.

LOBSTER TELEPHONE
148 Humber Road South
Beeston
NOTTINGHAM
NG9 2EX
'Zine.

LOCAL HISTORY PRESS

Susan & Robert Howard
3 Devonshire Promenade
Lenton
NOTTINGHAM
NG7 2DS
Tel 0115 970 6473
Publish Local History Magazine six times per annum - A national review & listings periodical with news, articles & free 50 word noticeboard for all subscribers. Also run a mail order bookshop & history-into-print service for self-publishing authors.

LOCAL HISTORY MAGAZINE
3 Devonshire Promenade
Lenton
NOTTINGHAM
NG7 2DS
Tel 0115 970 6473
Published by the Local History Press. The warhorse of the movement which has provided unrivalled help for myriad small presses in the genre. Always packed with articles and news. Subs £13.50 for 6 issues, (includes p&p) bi-monthly. Earn them a new subscriber and you get an extra issue free!

LOCAL HISTORY PUBLICATIONS
John W Brown
316 Green Lane
LONDON
SW16 3AS
Tel 0181 677 9562
A non-profit-making publisher producing a range of reprints of books that are now out of print and unavailable as well as contemporary local history publications. Titles include:
"A Guide to the Medieval Manor", £4.20, including p+p
"Sherlock Holmes in Streatham", £4.20 including p+p

LOCAL HISTORY PUBLICATIONS for FRIENDS OF NORWOOD CEMETERY
316 Green Lane
LONDON
SW16 3AS
GRAHAM, Paul, 'West Norwood Cemetery: the Dickens Connections,' 1995, booklet, All profits from sale go to restoration work at cemetery.

LOCAL HISTORY UNIT
Park Street Centre
Hull College
Park Street
HULL
HU2 8RR
Tel: 01482 329 943 ext 2806
* Victorian Letter Boxes: From Pillar to Post. A study of victorian letter boxes in Hull by David Litten, £4.00 inc. p&p.
* Waterworks: The History of Dunswell Waterworks by Sylvia Ranjon, £3.00 inc. p&p. Cheques made payable to Hull College. Phone for further details.

LOCHAR PUBLISHING
8 The Holm
MOFFAT
DG10 9JU

T. LOCKE MEMORIAL FUND
Great Glen Foods

P.O. Box 10
Old Ferry Road
North Ballachulish
FORT WILLIAM
PH33 6RZ
Health.

Herbert Hope LOCKWOOD
10 Alloa Road
Goodmayes
ILFORD
IG3 9SP
A Happy Thought - The story of Barking and District Historical Society 1934-1994 by Herbert Hope Lockwood. Price £2.50. This is a story of those who extended the frontiers of knowledge to create the history of Barking.

LODDEN VALLEY BOOKS
Rex Hora
108 Chilcombe Way
Lower Earley
READING
RG6 3DB

LOGASTON PRESS
Andy Johnson
Little Logaston
WOONTON ALMELEY
HR3 6QH
Tel 01544 6344
Started with books on Herefordshire and surrounding area covering walking history local people folklore etc. Now encompassing natural history cookery South Wales photography. Essence is to take on books with people with whom we enjoy working.

THE LOMOND PRESS
R L Cook
4 Whitecraigs
Kinneswood
KINROSS
KY13 7JI
Poetry.

LONDON ARCHITECTURAL PRESS
37 Alfred Place
LONDON
WC1E 7DP
Architecture.

LONDON CARTOON CENTRE
14 Conlan Street
LONDON
W10 5AR
Set up in the 1980s, the Centre offers womens' groups juniors, master classes etc in a 10 week vocational qualification (the only in Europe). Courses in all aspects of cartooning skills (finished art, life drawing, scripting, colouring, humour, comic book, comic strip, editorial cartoons and marketing self-publishing projects.

LONDON CYCLIST
London Cycling Campaign
28 Great Guildford Business Square
30 Great Guildford Street
LONDON
SE1 0HS
Tel 0171 938 7220

LONDON EARTH MYSTERIES CIRCLE
P.O. Box 1035
LONDON

W2 6ZX

LONDON ICOM
18 Ashwin Street
LONDON
E8 3DL

J. LONDON
Coomless
Broughton-in-Tweeddale
BIGGAR
ML12 6QH
History of Education.

LONDON LIGHTHOUSE
178 Lancaster Road
LONDON
W11 1QT

LONDON MAGAZINE
30 Thurloe Place
LONDON
SW7

LONDON VOICES
70 Holden Road
LONDON
N12 7DY

**LONDON VOLUNTARY SERVICE
COUNCIL**
68 Chalton Street
LONDON
NW1 1JR
*History of Voluntary Service in
London.*

LONG BARN BOOKS
Susan Hill
Longmoor Farmhouse
Ebrington
CHIPPING CAMDEN
GL55 6NW
*Susan HILL, 'Listening to the
Orchestra.' Four short stories. Pbk,
£3.99.*

LONGDALE PRESS
23/23 Ward
Royal Hospital
Chelsea
LONDON
SW3 4SR

LONGEVITY REPORT
West Towan House
J de Rivaz
Porthtowan
TRURO
TR4 8AX
*Debates the use of science to
extend human lifespan. Free
sample. Authors get free
subscription to following volume.*

(THE) LONGSTONE
37 Lowtherville Road
VENTNOR
Isle of Wight
PO38 1AR

LORACLE ENTERPRISES
BCM Loracle
LONDON
WC1N 3XX
*Spreading knowledge of occult
traditions.*

LORN HOUSE PUBLICATIONS
80 Jane Street
EDINBURGH
EH6 5HG

LOST DREAMS
Box 184

52 Call Lane
LEEDS
LS1 6DT

BILLIE LOVE COLLECTION
3 Winton Street
RYDE
PO33 2BX
Poetry.

LOVELY JOBLY (LJ)
75 Lambeth Walk
LONDON
SE11 6DX

LOVERSEED
48 Flowery Field
Woodsmoor
STOCKPORT
SK2 7ED
*Gasworker Ancestors: How to find
out more about them. A4, 64p
guide to gas industry genealogical
sources, with a gas industry history,
gasworks plan and description,
tables of occupations and wages,
lists of biographies and histories
and of undertakings etc. £5.50
including postage.*

LOWLANDER PUBLICATIONS
592A Chatsworth Road
CHESTERFIELD
S40 3JX

LOWNDES PUBLICATIONS
17 Lowndes Park
DRIFFIELD
YO25 7BE
Local History.

LRO BOOKS
The Hollies
Botesdale
DISS
IP22 1BZ
*Military Road Vehicles. Humour.
Civil Road Vehicles.*

LUATH PRESS
BARR
KA26 9TN
*Publishers of Scottish books of all
types in the three languages of
Scotland.*

LUNDIN LADIES GOLF CLUB
Woodielea Road
Lundin Links
LEVEN
KY8 6AR
Lundin Ladies Golf Club 1891.

LYFROW TRELYSPEN
Roseland
Gorran
ST AUSTELL
*Historical work about Cornwall,
biographies, local history, etc.*

LY-IF PRODUCTIONS
15 Tennyson Avenue
Motspur Park
NEW MALDEN
KT3 6LY
Legends.

THE LYMES PRESS
'Greenfields'
Agger Hill
Finney Green
NEWCASTLE UNDER LYME
ST5 6AA
Tel 01782 750 387

*Poetry written in Europe between
1590 to date.*

Mr Bryan LYNAS
Cami de Sarria 72a
07010 Palma de Mallorca
Spain

Mr C A LYNCH
17 Glendor Gardens
Mill Hill
LONDON
NW7 3JY

Kevin LYNCH
P.O. Box 7
BARNSTAPLE
EX31 1UN
*Publisher of money-making and
spare-time business opportunity
guides. Prices include postage and
packing.
The Small Businessman's
Advertising Guide to Greater
Profits £7.95. Start and Build a
Successful Business by James Carr
£7.95.*

Stanley LYONS
4 the Rise
Shipton Oliffe
CHELTENHAM
GL54 4JQ
Literature.

M PRESS
45 Stafford Road
BRIGHTON
BN1 5PE
Art.

**MSR BOOKS
inc. Rochester Press**
16 Laxton Gardens
Paddock Wood
TONBRIDGE
TN12 6BB

M5 PRESS
Winscombe Farm Studio
WINSCOMBE
BS25 1BT
The Looker Magazine.

MAGONIA
Mr John Rimmer

John Dee Cottage
5 James Terrace
Mortlake Churchyard
LONDON
SW14 8HB
Magazine.

MACH II PLUS
51A Sutton Court Road
Hillingdon
UXBRIDGE
UB10 9HR

MACLAIN PRESS
BCM Box 6732
LONDON
WC1N 3XX
Biography.

MACLEAN PRESS
60 Aird
Bhearnadail
PORTREE
Isle of Skye

MAGAZINES NETWORK
Mary Tee
12 Southcote Road
LONDON
N19 5BJ
*A display and distribution service
for alternative magazines and self-
published books, some of which
have been censored by regular
distribution channels owing to their
controversial content. Send for
details.*

MAGPIE PRESS
1 Hermitage Cottage
Clamp Hill
STANMORE
HA7 3BJW
*The Artist's Book Yearbook 1996-7.
The second compendium for all
aspects of artists books. Copies
available directly or from the
NSPC.*

MAGPIES NEST
Bal Saini
176 Stoney Lane
Sparkhill
BIRMINGHAM
B12 8AN

MAJOR BOOK PUBLICATIONS
The Homestead
Burrator Road
Dousland
YELVERTON
PL20 6NE

MAKE YOUR MARK
71 Goodram Gate
YORK

**MAKING WAVES/BULLS HEAD
GATE**
Anthony Selbourne
P.O. Box 226
GUILDFORD
GU3 1EW
*Poetry imprint which also organises
and publishes art/poetry
exhibitions/portfolios.*

THE MALAPROP PRESS
30 Wiberforce Road
LONDON
N4 2SW

MALCOLM PRESS
18 Princess Way
SWANSEA

SA1 3LW

MALLETT AND BELL
3 College Close
COLTISHALL
NR12 7DT

H. MALTRAVER and T. KAY
P.O. Box 1295
BATH
BA1 6TJ
Architectural salvage.

T D MAN and A BARON
c/o 93a Venner Road
Sydenham
LONDON
SE26 5HY
Tel 0181 659 7713
Poetry and non-fiction. Pro-Forma orders only accepted for single copies. Trade terms for 10 copies or more only.

MANAGEMENT UPDATE
99A Underdale Road
SHREWSBURY
SY2 5EE
Canals. Local Walks.

MANCHESTER F P
Mr Andrew Caesar
Paragon Mill
Jersey Street
MANCHESTER
M4 6FP

MANCHESTER POETS
122 Petersburg Road
Edgeley Park
STOCKPORT
SK3 9RB
Tours, performances, workshops, competitions and anthologies.

MANDEVILLE PRESS
Peter Scupham
2 Taylor's Hill
HITCHIN
SG4 9AD
Fine printer.

MANDRAKE
Mogg Morgan
P.O. Box 250
OXFORD
OX1 1AP
Tel 01865 243671
Specialists in Magick and new writing which is radical and subversive. One of the leading publishers of material which includes Crowley Tantrism Sexology Magical art and the Occult.

MANDRAKE PRESS LTD
Essex House
THAME
OX9 3LS
Tel 0184 421 7567, fax 6420
Works by Austin Osman Spare and Aleister Crowley.

W.S. MANEY
Hudson Road
LEEDS
LS9 7DL
Mediaeval Art.

MANNA PUBLISHING
4 Short Lane
Ingham
LINCOLN
Poetry.

MANNAMEDIA
Geoff Holland
77A Mannamead Road
PLYMOUTH
PL3 4SX
Philosophy.

MANOR ACRE
Mary May
Manor Farm
Collingbourne Kingston
MARLBOROUGH
SN8 3SD
Tel 01264 850251
Series of children's pony stories (8-12 years) involving a disabled girl who takes up carriage driving in her fight for normality. Percentage of all sales pledged to disabled drivers.
"The Will to Win", by Mary May, £6.95
"Piebald is Lucky", by Mary May, £6.95

MANX EXPERIENCE
10 Tromode Close
DOUGLAS
Isle of Man

THE MANY PRESS
John Welch
15 Norcott Road
LONDON
N16 7BJ
"Peaceworks" by Andrew Shelley, ISBN 0 907326X, 24 pp, £3.00 Intellectual yet sensuous poetry in which the insisted-upon details of individual experience are held in often rebarbative contact with the increasingly embattled categories of mind that support shared life, common society.
"The Onion House" by Kate Bass, ISBN 0 907326 35 8, 16pp, £2.50 Poems combining directness with a strong sense of mystery.

MAPLETREE PRIVATE PRESS
Wisteria
The List
Wickhambreaux
CANTERBURY
CT3 1RX
Fine Printer.

MAR MAGAZINE
Flat 1
81 Back Road East
ST IVES
TR26
Eclectic poetry prose and graphics; the editors will publish only what surprises them and contributors remain anonymous. Distributed by New River Project.

MARABY
10 Eastcote Lane
Hampton in Arden
SOLIHULL
B92 0AS
Local Education History.

PETER MARCAN PUBLICATIONS
P.O. Box 3158
LONDON
SE1 4RA
Directories and Handbooks: Art, Music Catalogues: Pictorial Albums and reprints on East and South-East London. Anything else and we're sued.

THE MARCHANTS PRESS
Whispers
Great Oakley
HARWICH
CO12 5AH

MARGIN
The Square Inch
Lower Granco Street
Dunning
PERTH
PH2 0SQ

MARIDIAN PUBLICATIONS
9 Old Pier Street
WALTON-ON-THE NAZE
Children's Fiction

MARINA PRESS
11 Heol Tre Dwr
Waterton
BRIDGEND
CF31 3AJ
Poetry.

MARINE DAY PUBLISHERS
Mr Tony Durrant
64 Cotterill Road
SURBITON
KT6 7UN
Publishers of local history books. Book production managers and typographical designers.

MARISCAT PRESS
3 Mariscat Road
GLASGOW
G41 4ND
Poetry.

MARITIME INFORMATION PUBLICATIONS
147 St. Pancras
CHICHESTER
PO19 1SH
Civil Ships.

A. MARK PUBLISHING COMPANY
Olsover House
43 Sackville Road
NEWCASTLE-UPON-TYNE
NE6 5TA
Music.

MARLBOROUGH BOOKS:
Marlborough Books Wholesalers
6 Milton Road
SWINDON
SN1 5JG
Sport.

MARLON PUBLICATIONS
P.O. Box 3
BECCLES
NR34 0DF
Literature.

MARLOW DURNDELL
18-20 Chapel Street
Titchmarsh
KETTERING
NN14 3DA
Biography.

MARREB
64 Ambler Thorn
BRADFORD
BD13 2DJ
Biography.

MARTELLO BOOKSHOP
26 High Street
RYE
TN31 7JJ
Literary Biography.

MAST PUBLICATIONS
31 Beaufort Gardens
Knightsbridge
LONDON
SW3 1QH
Specialising in books about the gay community with a percentage of profits going to AIDS charities. Also Publishing poetry and short story anthologies.

Raymond MASTERS
129 Park Road
Chandler's Ford
EASTLEIGH
SO5 1HT
General Fiction.

MATRIX PRESS
2 Stafford Mansins
Albert Bridge Road
LONDON
SW11

A. MATTHEW PUBLICATIONS
44 Royal Avenue
Calcot
READING
RG3 5UP
Historical Bibliographies. Bibliographies.

MAVERICK SPORTING PUBLICATIONS
imprint of MIDLANDS MAC (PUBLISHING)
65 St Giles Street
NORTHAMPTON
NN1 1JF
'The Politically Correct Guide to Sex,' explicit sex humour, 63 pp., pbk, ISBN 1-899078-09-6, £4.99.

MAWALANA CENTRE
34 Hollytree Close
Inner Park Road
LONDON
SW19 6EA
Biography.

MAX
c/o Jurgen Wolff
16 Huguenot House
19 Oxendon Street
LONDON
SW1Y 4EH

MAXIPRINT
Kettlestring Lane
Clifton Moor
YORK
YO3 8XF
Snickelways of York.

MAYFIELD PUBLISHING
68 Main Road
Wybunbury
NANTWICH
CW5 7LS

MAYFLOWER ENTERPRISES
54 St. Margaret's Road
Horsforth
LEEDS
LS18 5BG
Music.

MAYPOLE
57 Cowley Road
ILFORD
Tel 0181 554 7258
Fiction, poetry, history, satire, humour.

MAYSDALE BOOKS
63 Fford Glyn
Coed-y-Glyn
WREXHAM
LL13 7QW

M.B.S. PUBLICATIONS
10 Summerbridge Crescent
Eccleshill
BRADFORD
BD10 8BB
Poetry.

SIMON MCBRIDE PRINTS
P.O. Box 31
NEWTON ABBOT
TQ12 5XH

Elizabeth MCDOUGALL
(see E. Warneford)
New Inn Farm
West End Lane
HENFIELD
BN5 9RF
Warneford Family History.

Maureen MCGAURAN
41 Hillhead Crescent
BELFAST
BT11 9FS
Biography.

THE MCGUFFIN PRESS
100 Balls Pond Road
LONDON
N1 4AJ

K.L. MCHUGH
81 Hall Avenue
Aveley
SOUTH OCKENDON
RM15 4LD
Historical Biography.

D. MCLEAN
Forest Bookshop
8 St. John Street
COLEFORD
GL6 8AR
Historical Biography. Biography.

Mona MCNEE
2 The Crescent
Toftwood
DEREHAM
NR19 1NR
Children's Non-fiction.

M.D.E. PUBLICATIONS
16 Hardwick Crescent
SHEFFIELD
S11 8WB
Children's Fiction.

MEADOW BOOKS
Cynthia O'Neill
22 Church Meadow
Milton-under-Wychwood
OXFORD
OX7 6JG
Tel 01998 381 338
*Excellent insight into nursing at the
turn of the century. Picture
reproductions of superb quality of
interest to all especially social
historians.*

MEDIMAGE
Miss S Dehghan
7 Carson Road
BARNET
EN4 9EX
*Specialising in books on gambling.
Current title in print:*

*"The Book of Brtish Blackjack" by
M. Zadehkoochak, ISBN
189772800X, £9.99*

MEDI THEME
Mrs B. Harding
Uplands
Green Road
Skelton-in-Cleveland
SALTBURN-BY-THE-SEA
TS12 2BQ
*Medi Theme is a quartely newsletter
for collectors of stamps and postal
material concerning medicine,
nursing, pharmacy, and dentistry.
Aims to encourage correspondence
and exchanges between collectors.
(Toni Wilson, Editor)*

MEDIUM PUBLISHING CO
1a Clumber Street
HULL
HU5 3RH

MEETING HOUSE PRESS
24 Pitreavie Road
Cosham
PORTSMOUTH
PO6 2ST
Science Fiction.

MELLEDGEN PRESS
F.L.Bannon
71 Thornbury Road
Southbourne
BOURNEMOUTH
BH6 4HU
Tel 01233 623642
*Concerned with the history and
social construction of the various
major industries of the 1st & 2nd
Industrial Revolutions including
alignment & transport development.
Also topographical coverage of the
post 1750 features, UK/Europe/
Australia. Examples of
publications.
"Branch Lines, Links & Local
Connections", £2.99
"A Gazetteer of the Railway
Contractors & Engineers: of Central
Southern England" £3.80. These
two title in The Railway Alignment
Series.
"Coastguard & Preventative",
£3.60. Title in the Poole Bay Series.*

MEMES
Norman Joe
c/o 38 Molesworth Road
Plympton
PLYMOUTH
PL7 4NT
*Once described as 'the
quintessence of the small press
counterculture' (BBR) Memes offers
a challenging blend of
contemporary literature graphics
reviews and comment.*

MEN-AN-TOL STUDIO
Bosullow
Newbridge
PENZANCE

THE MENARD PRESS
8 The Oaks
Woodside Avenue
LONDON
N12 8AR
Tel 0181 446 5571
*In 1993 Menard warned it may be
returning to active publishing after
a phase of relative dormancy.*

MENDIP PUBLISHING
High Street
CASTLE CARY
BA7 7AN

MENTOR STUDIO
399-401 Strand
LONDON
WC2R 0RB
Music.

MERCIA CINEMA SOCIETY
19 Pinders Grove
WAKEFIELD
WF1 4AH
History of Cinema.

MERCIAN MYSTERIES
2 Cross Hill Close
Wymeswold
LOUGHBOROUGH
LE12 6UJ

MERDON MARQUE
11 Swanton Gardens
Chandlers Ford
EASTLEIGH
SO5 1TP
Biography.

MERE PSEUD
Gareth Gordon
P.O. Box 148
BELFAST
BT1
*Magazine providing a voice for
alternative music scene in Belfast
and Ireland.*

MERIDIAN BOOKS
Peter Groves
40 Hadzor Road
Oldbury
WARLEY
B68 9LA
Tel 0121 4 294 397
*A home-based business publishing
4-5 books a year on walking local
guides regional guides and local
history.*

MERIVALE EDITIONS
Peter Sampson
14 Merivale Road
Putney
LONDON
SW15 2NW
Tel 0181 785 903
*Publish prints and portfolios by
contemporary British artists and
illustrators.*

Stanley MERRIDEW
206 Moseley Wood Gardens
Cookbridge
LEEDS
LS16 7JE
*Wharfedale Family History Group
Publications - Whereabouts of
Wharfedale Records £1.80,
Cloggers Daybrook (Henry Gill of
Addingham) £1.80, Conistone MI's
£1.30, Leathley MI's £1.30, Denton
MI's £1.30, Yeadon St Johns MI's
£1.30, posted UK.*

MERRI-MIMES PRESS
21A St Johns Wood High Street
LONDON
NW8 7NG

**MERSEYSIDE ASSOCIATION OF
WRITERS**
12 Aspinall Street
Precot

MERSEYSIDE
Poetry.

MESMERISM
c/o Mark McKay
341 Oldham Road
Middleton
MANCHESTER
M24 2DN

R.R. MESTER
2 Dolanog Villas
MACHYNLLETH
SY20 8AS
Fiction General.

METHOUDINGLE
9 Allard Gardens
Clapham
LONDON
SW4

METRIC OPTIC PUBLISHING
Mr Maats
27 Barclay Square
LONDON
W1X 5HA

METRO ENTERPRISES
48 Southcliffe Drive
Baildon
SHIPLEY
WF17 0HS

**METROPOLITAN: NEW URBAN
WRITING**
John Ashbrook/Elizabeth Baines/
Ailsa Cox
19 Victoria Avenue
Didsbury
MANCHESTER
M20 2GY
*Metropolitan Magazine is
published twice a year, winter &
summer; community arts and
writing. ISSN 1350-3227.
Subscription £4.50 for two issues;
single copies £2.50 + 50p. p&p.*

MEVALYN DEFINITIONS
Vic Baxter
77a Fountain Road
ABERDEEN
AB2 4EA

MEYN MAMRO
Cheryl Straffon
51 Carn Bosavern St. Just
PENZANCE
TR19 7QX
Tel 01736 787 612
*Specialises in books and booklets
on the sacred sites and ancient
ways of Cornwall including earth
energies ley paths Cornish
prehistory and culture megalithic
mysteries and legends and folklore.*

MEZZANINE
Philip Kane
17 Connaught Road
CHATHAM
ME4 5DJ
*Mezzanine was first published as a
co-operative venture, primarily
publishing and promoting the work
of writers from the "North Kent
School". Our horizons have
widened. A literary journal is
planned.
"City's Little Heart", Philip Kane,
pub 1994, ISBN 1899360 00X
"The Industry of Letters: the book of
contemporary North Kent writing".*

Edited by Philip Kane, Bill Lewis & Jim Shean, pub 1996. ISBN 1 899360 02 6

M.H PUBLICATIONS
17 West Heath Drive
LONDON
NW11 7QG

MICAWBER PUBLICATIONS
64 St. Mary's Street
BRIDGNORTH
WV16 4DR
Art.

Timothy J. MICKLEBURGH
Stavelea
Birchcliffe Road
HEBDEN BRIDGE
HX7 8DB
Poetry.

MICKLETON METHODIST CHURCH COUNCIL:
W.A. Warmington
Westington Corner
CHIPPING CAMDEN
GL55 6DW
History of Mickleton Methodist Church.

MICROBRIGADE
74 Lodge Lane
LONDON
N12 8JJ

Judy MIDDLETON
22 Mile Oak Gardens
Portslade
BRIGHTON
BN41 2PH
History of Education.

MIDDLETON PRESS
Easebourne Lane
MIDHURST
GU29 9AZ
Tel 01739 813 169
Starting on a huge programme we are producing a set of 100 unissued, mint condition hard back albums covering former Southern Railways routes and some adjacent GWR lines. The work has taken sixteen years. The titles are by Vic Mitchell and Keith Smith. The offer includes all the long out of print titles and a composite index to all the stations illustrated. The set costs £995.00 - a saving of £100 on current prices. Only available direct from Middleton.

MID KIRK OF GREENOCK
Cathcart Square
GREENOCK
Renfrewshire
Local History.

MIDNIGHT IN HELL
The Cottage
Smithy Brae
KILMACOLM
PA13 4EN

MID-SOMERSET EARTH FIRST
P.O. Box 23
5 High Street
GLASTONBURY
BA6 9DP

MID TRENT HISTORICAL ASSOCIATION
Trevor James
Westminster College

St Peter's College Road
B8 2TE
Tel 0121 327 2709
Rural Housing - An Historical Approach by Bob Machin, Historical Association Publication 1994 40pp £3.95.

MIKE R.L PUBLICATIONS
28 Windermere Drive
Adlington
CHORLEY
PR6 9PD

MILEPOST PUBLICATIONS
39 Kilton Glade
WORKSOP
S81 0PX

Mr Simon MILES
(see also 'Dragonheart')
282 Derby Road
Lenton
NOTTINGHAM
NG7 1PZ
Newsletter 'Archangel' for the congregationalists of William Blake.

(THE) MILITANT
c/o 47 The Cut
LONDON
SE1 8LL

MILITANT PUBLICATIONS
3/13 Hepscott Road
LONDON
E9 5HB

MILITARY HISTORY HERITAGE BOOKS
Robert Downie
95 Hassell Street
NEWCASTLE
ST5 1AX
Tel 01782 723 329
Specialist history and military publications particularly history of Staffordshire Shropshire and Cheshire. New authors wanted. Help and advice available to would be authors living in the region.

David T. MILLER
23 Main Street
PATHHEAD
EH37 5PZ
Art.

MILLERS DALE PUBLICATIONS
Gerald Ponting
7 Weaver's Place
Chandler's Ford
EASTLEIGH
SO5 1TU
Tel 01703 261192
An imprint introduced by Gerald Ponting of Charlewood Press to publish detailed How To... manuals for sale by mail order.

MILLGATE PUBLISHING
48 Hill Carr Road
Rawtenstall
ROSSENDALE
BB4 6AW
Humour.

MILLSTREAM BOOKS
Tim Graham
18 The Tyning
BATH
BA2 6AL
Transport history and architecture.

MILLSTREAM PUBLICATIONS
Tom Porter
Mill Lane
BURLEY
BH24 4HR
Educational. Manual 'Build or Upgrade your Personal Computer'

MILNER AND HILL
3 Duneden House
Somerville Street
CREWE
CW2 7NS
Art.

Peter MIMMS
20 Lonsdale Road
BOURNEMOUTH
BH3 7LX
Were your ancestors labourers? 'Only for life' by Peter Mimms describes the lives of nine generations of his labouring family from 1640 to 1940 in Northants, Beds, Hunts, S. London and Devon, 384pp, 20 illustrations, £19.95. From Bookshops or from the author, see above. ISBN 1 85858 065 X.

MINORITIES RESEARCH GROUP
Dr. E. Ross-Langley
PO Box 1000
ST. ALBANS
AL3 5NY
Tel 01727 52801
Publications in Minorities field: single motherhood; female homosexuality; British expatriates in Spain; high-IQ children. Send for catalogue describing your particular interests: full- length books; short stories; magazines &c.

MINORITY RIGHTS GROUP
Alan Phillips
379 Brixton Road
LONDON
SW9 7DE
Tel 0171 978 9498
Publishes books and reports on human right minority rights and international affairs. Also publish education resources.

MINX PRINTS
Simon Bond
Flat 3
34 Tremadoc Road
LONDON
SW4 7LL

MIRANDA PRESS
28 Fire Station Square
SALFORD
M5 4NZ
Biography.

MODERN RECORDS CENTRE
University of Warwick Library
COVENTRY
CV4 7AL
Tel 01203 524 219
The repository for the archives of the Trades Union Congress 1920-1970 and many trade union archives. Other records held include those of the CBI and its predecessors, motor industry buiness records and the papers of leading Socialists such as Dick Crossman and Victor Gollancz. Send for details of recent titles such as Women at Work and in Society, A Postman's Round etc.

MODERN WELSH PUBLICATIONS LTD
Rev Dr D.Ben Rees
32 Garth Drive
LIVERPOOL
L18 6HW
New title: May we wish you a Good Night in Hospital. 20 page booklet of meditations and prayers designed to help patients. £1.50. ISBN 0901332372.

MOMENTUM
c/o Christine Stace
31 Alexandra Road
WREXHAM
LL13
Magazine for poetry and short stories.

MOMENTUM MAGAZINE
Almere Farm
ROSSETT
LL12 0BY

MONDO COMIX
Lee Davis
35 Manly Dixon Drive
ENFIELD
EN3 6BQ
Tel 01992 651 891
Mondo Comix ... comic book fanzines featuring a mix of super-heroes satire comedy action-adventure horror sci-fi and drama. All writers and artists are aspiring to a professional standard and are allowed to tell whatever style of story they see fit. Mondo doesn't censor its contributors and we consider all comers for possible inclusion in the title.

MONKEY PRESS
36 Richmond Road
CAMBRIDGE
CB4 3PU

MONKSVALE PRESS
14 Monksvale Grove
BARROW-IN-FURNESS
LA13 9JQ

MONOLITH PUBLICATIONS
John Harrison
P.O. Box 241
LEICESTER
LE4 6ZY
Newsletter, donation +SAE, environmental concerns, Stonehenge, UFO's, Arthurian interest, Templars, royal gossip, historical research, conspiracy theory, news, rumour, gossip, knowledge, (dis)information?

MONOLITH/FULL CIRCLE
119 Brassey Road
LONDON
NW6 2BB

MONTAG PUBLICATIONS
6 Minster Avenue
BEVERLEY
HU17 0NL
Specialist history and modern literature including English/ German parallel text publications and art catalogues. Translation work and European market access consultancy undertaken. We assist German authors and small publishers put their work onto the English speaking market.

Malcolm Beresford
MONTGOMERY
26 Cambridge Road
SOUTHAMPTON
SO2 0RD
Stamp Collecting.

MOONDRAGON PRESS
20 Linden Road
BIRMINGHAM
B30 1JS
Poetry.

MOONSHINE
498 Bristol Road
Selly Oak
BIRMINGHAM

MOONSTONE
SOS The Old Station Yard
SETTLE
BD24 9RP
Editors: Talitha Clare & Robin Brooks

Christine MOORE
Whitehorn
Back Lane
Waldron
HEATHFIELD
TN21 0NH
Stockbreeding.

Linda MOORHOUSE
76 Scotforth Road
LANCASTER
LA1 4SF
Peace in Lancaster 1814 — An account of how the Good Old Town celebrated the defeat of France and the exile of Napoleon. It describes the illumination of the town, naming the townspeople and streets and lists the names of the people who subscribed to the subscription for the relief of the sufferers of Waterloo. UK price £3 (includes p&p).
The Opening of Ripley Hospital, Lancaster 1864 — 56 pages of A4 — contains details from the local newspapers about the building and opening of Ripley Hospital.

MOORLAND PUBLISHING COMPANY
Moor Farm Road
Airfield Estate
ASHBOURNE
DE6 1HD

MOORLEY'S PRINT & PUBLISHING
23 Park Road
ILKESTON
DE7 5DA

Laurie MORAN
67 Red Courts
Brandon
DURHAM
DH7 8QN
Local History.

MORAY HOUSE PUBLICATIONS
Moray House College
Holyrood Road
EDINBURGH
EH8 8AQ
Biography. Education. Social Sciences.

MORETO PUBLISHERS
18 Plympton Road
LONDON
NW6 7EG

Political Science.

MORGAN PUBLISHING, LINCOLN
26 May Crescent
LINCOLN
LN1 1LP
Political Science.

MORGAN TECHNICAL BOOKS
R.C. Pickernell
232 Stroud Road
GLOUCESTER
GL4 0AU
General Fiction.

MORIARTY
Mr P Allen
1 Cedar Close
Langley Green
CRAWLEY
RH11 7SB

MORNING STAR PUBLICATIONS
Alec Finlay
14 Clark Street
EDINBURGH
EH8 9HX
Tel 0131 667 7560
Publishers of the Morning Star Folios: letterpress editions featuring one poet and artist in collaboration. Published in editions of 200-350 copies, signed and numbered by the artists.

Morrell Wylye HEAD
Wylye Head
KILMINGTON
BA12 6RD
Photography.

MORRIGAN BOOK COMPANY
Gore Street
KILLALA BALLINA
Co. Mayo
Republic of Ireland
Irish Mythology.

Jeff MORRIS (publisher)
14 Medina Road
Foleshill
COVENTRY
CV6 5JB
MORRIS, Jeff: 'The History of the Blyth and Chambois Lifeboats.' 'The History of the Eyemouth Lifeboats.' Both vols. illus, A5 pbk, £2.50 each incl. p&p. Other titles on same topic by different authors available, ask for details.

Peter MORRIS
9 Malvern Drive
Walmsley
SUTTON COLDFIELD
B76 1PZ
'A Survey of Dickens's Employments'.

MORTAIN BOOKS LIMITED
Mr G H Bransby
43 Sutton Park Road
SEAFORD
BN25 1SJ
Tel 01323 895 112

MOSAIC
c/o NOTTS COUNTY COUNCIL
Trent Bridge House
Fox Road
West Bridgford
NOTTINGHAM
NG2 6BJ

MOSS ROSE PRESS
41 Hardwick Avenue
CHEPSTOW
NP6 5DS

MOTE PRESS
The Courtyard
1 Dinsdale Place
Sandyford
NEWCASTLE-UPON-TYNE
NE2 1BD

MOUBRAY HOUSE PRESS
Tweeddale Court
14 High Street
EDINBURGH
EH1 1TE

MOUNT SANDFORD PRESS
22 Nutgrove Park
DUBLIN 14
Republic of Ireland
History of Scout Troops.

MOURNE OBSERVER PRESS
Castlewellan Road
NEWCASTLE
BT33 0JX
Railway History.

THE MOUSE THAT SPINS
Wharf Mill
WINCHESTER
SO23 9NJ
Publish ‚Thundersqueak', a new clear look at magic and occultism in today's world.

MOVING FINGER
70 Poplar Road
Bearwood
Smethwick
WARLEY
B66 4AN
Literature. Short Stories.

MOVING FOREVER FORWARDS
Miss S Bailey
23 Fairfield Grove
LONDON
SE7 8UA
Sue Bailey writes inspirational verses. Published twice, Sue now has a new range of greetings cards. Also available are bookmarks and verses in frames which make unique and universal presents.

MOVING TARGET
Suite 194
Winifred Villa
68 Northman Avenue
LONDON
N22 5EP

MOWGLI BOOKS
Suite 309
Canalot Studios
222 Kensal Road
LONDON
W10 5BN

MOYLURG WRITERS
Boyle Mill Road
BOYLE
County Roscommon
Republic of Ireland

MOYOLA BOOK
c/o Hill House
Owenreagh
Draperstown
MAGHERAFELT

BT45 7BG
Biography.

MOYTURA PRESS
3 The Dale
Stillorgan Grove
STILLORGAN
County Dublin
Republic of Ireland

M.R.M. ASSOCIATES
322 Oxford Road
READING
RG3 1AD
Poetry.

M S PRESS
P.O. Box 464
BRADFORD
BD8 7SJ

MUILEACH PUBLICATIONS
fao F Langford
Glenleedle
Salen
Aros
ISLE OF MULL
PA72 6JL

MUIRALL PUBLICATIONS
Lane House
Higher Bockhampton
DORCHESTER
DT2 8QH
Poetry, short stories, poem cards, children's poetry and stories.

MULBERRY PRESS
Lionel Barnard
9 George Street
BRIGHTON
BN2 1RH
Dolls House; doll and teddy bear books for collectors. Original works and reprints. Also specialist booksellers in above subjects. Mail order and retail. Book importers. Consultants to other publishers on these subjects.

MULTISCOPE BOOKS
2 Mead Road
TORQUAY
TQ2 6TE
Health and Hygiene.

MULTUM IN PARVO PRESS
6 Chater Road
Oakham
RUTLAND
LE15 6RY
Celebration of Rutland. New book on England's smallest county. 128pp lavishly illustrated in colour. Environment, history, community and arts. Over 80 contributors. Limited, numbered edition. Only 200 copies left. £24 (inc p&p). Cheques payable to 'Celebration of Rutland'.

D.W. MUNNINGS
2A Bedford Place
SOUTHAMPTON
SO1 2BY
Health and Hygiene.

MUNROE BOOKS
1 Chapel Cottages
Kennington Road
ASHFORD
TN24 0TF
Children's non-fiction.

MUSIC IN MINIATURE

38 Northfield Road
BARNET
EN4 9DN
Military History.

MUSLIM EDUCATION TRUST
130 Stroud Green Road
LONDON
N4 3RZ
Education.

MUSTAQIM
146 Whitlock Drive
LONDON
SW19 6SN

L Arthur MYERS
11 Manor Gardens
SAXMUNDHAM
IP17 1ET
Wild silk moths and how to rear them, 75p.

ELIZABETH MYHILL PUBLICATIONS
Farnborough
Sandy Lane
Belton
GREAT YARMOUTH
NR31 9LT

MYSTERIA PRESS
6 Wanderdown Way
Ovingdean
BRIGHTON
BN2 7BX

NAN ELMOTH PUBLICATIONS
J J Morgan
Haberdasher
Shop 28
Chepstow Corner
Chepstow Place
LONDON
W2 4XA
Very short run small personal magazines and fanzines, mostly to do with Tolkien and related interest groups. Contact for the Tolkien Society. Other interests. Costume and textile technology; haberdashery, historical embroidery and design. Photocopy work a speciality.

NANHOLME/ARC PRESS
Nanholme Centre

Shaw Wood Road
TODMORDEN
OL14 6DA

NATIONAL CHILDBIRTH TRUST
Worthing Branch Newsletter
Neil & Angela Rabone
59 Durrington Lane
WORTHING
BN13 2QT
Tel 01903 260483
The Jan/Feb 1997 issue is 68 pps because it covers a wide area. Clearly the topic is 'niche' yet you would be surprised how much they embrace. Really meant for members they welcome donations so you could agree a price for a sample copy.

NATIONAL SMALL PRESS CENTRE
B M BOZO
LONDON
WC1N 3XX
Publishes News From the Centre and Small Press Listings. The Centre's Handbook 1997, publication date 28 June 1997. Send for order forms and details of other services.

NATTA PUBLICATIONS
c/o Energy & Environment
Research Unit
Faculty of Technology
Open University
Walton Hall
MILTON KEYNES
MK7 6AA
Tel 01908 654 638 fax 01908 653 744
Renew On Line & NATTA On Line accessible from EERU site at http://EERU-WWW.open.ac.uk
The Network for Alternative Technology and Technology Assessment publishes the bi-monthly Renew, a state-of-the-art current awareness journal, ISSN 02627221; and books, pamphlets and reports on all aspects of renewable energy developments. NB Distributes remaining back numbers of Undercurrents, the defunct but still seminal journal of AT.

NATURAL FRIENDS UPDATE
15 Benyon Gardens
Culford
BURY ST EDMUNDS
IP28 6EA
Natural Friends is Britain's premier friendship service for vegetarians, and those who care about the world and each other. Updates produced bimonthly (2000 mem bers) containing about 25% text/classified, plus 75% members' ads. Scope for any green/environmental ads.

NATURAL LEISURE
P.O. Box 65
LEIGHTON BUZZARD
LU7 8TJ
The imprint of Naturists. Many titles including 'a super naturist handbook, Who's Where,' by Susan Mayfield, previously editor of Health & Efficiency magazine. Catalogue.

NATURETREK EDUCATION BOOKS
4 Rhodfa Gwilym

ST ASAPH
LL17 0UU

NCVO PUBLISHING
National Council for
Voluntary Organisations
26 Bedford Square
LONDON
WC1B 3HY
Tel 071 636 4066
NCVO publishes a range of practical information and policy books and directories on issues related to the voluntary sector including the best selling 'Voluntary Agencies Directory'. Bedford Square Press series includ e 'Community Action', 'Practical Guides', 'Society Today' and 'Survival Handbooks'.

NdA PRESS
Natalie d'Arbeloff
6 Lady Somerset Road
LONDON
NW5 1UT
Hand-printed limited edition artist's books with NdA's etchings or mixed-media prints and mostly her own texts. Does not publish other people's work. Press established 1974. NdA books are in public and private collections internationally including the National Art Library of the Victoria and Albert Museum.

NEBULOUS BOOKS
12 Raven Square
ALTON
GU34 2LL
Railways.

NEIL MILLER PUBLICATIONS
Mount Cottage
Grange Road
St Michaels
TENTERDEN
TN30 6EE
Tel 01580 764 174
Black Cat Books: Vol.One, Black Cat Tales. 6 horror stories; title pages illustrated. ISBN 095262690X.

NEMETON PUBLISHING
P.O. Box 780
BRISTOL
BS99 5BB
Tel 01272 715 144
Publishing poetry local history and the paranormal since 1985 (aka Carmina). X-CALIBRE is now a thematic series compiling on the theme of poets and poetry for next edition. S.a.e. for details of projects and publications please. Old stock going cheap.

NERUDA PRESS
51 Allison Street
Crosshill
GLASGOW
G42 8NJ
Poetry.

NETHER HALSE BOOKS
John Crisford
Nether Halse
Winsford
MINEHEAD
TA24 7JE
A one-man firm founded in 1980 to publish a village guidebook now in its sixth edition. Publishes owner's

poetry (three titles); local history (two titles) and local biography (one title).

NETWORK EDUCATIONAL PRESS
P.O. Box 635
STAFFORD
ST18 0LJ
Education.

NEVER BURY POETRY
c/o The Derby Hall
Market Street
BURY
BL9 0BN

ADRIAN NEVILLE PRESTIGE
Abbots End
Amesbury
SALISBURY
SP4 7BB

NEW ALBION PRESS
42 Overhill Road
LONDON
SE22 0PH
Collective of self-publishing poets.

NEW ANARCHIST REVIEW
846 Whitechapel High Street
LONDON
E1
Quarterly(ish) 16pp A5 review newsheet with details of anarchist titles currently available in the UK. Available free to alternative bookshops or for a small donation to individuals. Very modest advertising rates.

NEW ARCADIAN PRESS
Patrick Eyres
13 Graham Grove
LEEDS
LS4 2NF
Tel 01532 304 608
Contemporary artist-writer collaborations on landscape and garden issues: poetry and prose with drawings, photographs and watercolours via small books, print portfolios, cards and an annual journal. The New Arcadian Journal, always contextual, comprises lyric celebration, polemic critique or iconographical analysis.

THE NEW ATLANTEAN
20 Ridge Avenue
HARPENDEN

NEW BEACON
7b Stroud Green Road
LONDON
N4 3EN
Books from Africa, Carribean, black Britain and Afro America.

NEW BREED PUBLISHING
Hollywood House
100-102 Woodhouse Road
LONDON
E11 3NA
Paintball Games Management.

NEW BROOM PRIVATE PRESS
Toni Savage
78 Cambridge Street
LEICESTER
LE3 0JP
Small booklets and broadsheets mainly poetry.

NEWBY BOOKS
P.O. Box 40

SCARBOROUGH
YO12 5TW

NEW CAXTON PRESS
Christopher Stevens
Flat Two
11 Clifton Park
Clifton
BRISTOL
BS8 3BX
Tel 01272 738 997
Aims: to produce fiction in traditional and innovative formats, to explore the scope of desk-top publishing, for profit, to encourage and assist other self-publishers.

THE NEW CENTURY PRESS
1 Western Hill
DURHAM
Worthwhile books for literature.

NEW CENTURY FLYER
52 Wimbledon Park Road
LONDON
SW18 5HS

NEW CONSERVATION - POPULATION, RESOURCES, ENVIRONMENT
Publisher & Editor: Peter Berry
Pwllyfan
LLANSADWRN
SA19 8LS
Tel/Fax 01550-777661
E-mail pberry@tacin.co.uk
News, views and current awareness from long established expert in the field of environmental information (see also his ECOBASE in electronics section).

NEW DEATH
Sick of new? (see under old BOZO)

NEW DEPARTURES
Michael Horovitz (editor)
Piedmont
Bisley
STROUD
GL6 7BU
New Departures (organ of the Poetry Olympics) has a few back issues available including multi-signed collectors' items and also copies of Midsummer Morning Jog Log Michael Horovitz's 700-line rural rhapsody with drawings by Peter Blake. Lists sent on request (please send sae or return postage).

NEWDIGATE EDITIONS
8 Newdigate House
Kingsnymphton Park
KINGSTON-UPON-THAMES
KT2 7TJ

NEW DIMENSIONS
1 Austin Close
IRCHESTER
NN9 7AX

NEW ERA PUBLICATIONS
78 Holmethorpe Avenue
REDHILL
RH1 2NL

NEW FUTURIST BOOKS
72 New Bond Street
LONDON
W1Y 9DD
BENNETT, Colin, 'The Entertainment Bomb,' sci-fi or future-shock fiction, 1996, 274 pp., pbk, ISBN 1-

899690-01-8.

NEW GALAXY PRODUCTIONS
Suite 78
Kent House
87 Regent Street
LONDON
W1R 7HF

NEW HOPE INTERNATIONAL
Gerald England
20 Werneth Avenue
HYDE
SK14 5NL
NHI writing showcases poetry; NHI Review is a unique guide to small press productions. £15 for 6 issues (£20 ex-UK) payable to "G. England".
Recent press titles:
"Positively Poetry", ISBN 0 903610 16 7. An international anthology of Little Press Poets. 1970-1995, £5.95 (£10 ex-UK)
"Brigflats Visited",. A tribute to Basil Bunting. ISBN 0 903610 17 5, £3 (£4 ex-UK).

NEW IONA PRESS
Old Printing Press Building
ISLE OF IONA
PA76 6SL
Local Travel Guides.

NEW LEFT REVIEW
6 Meard Street
LONDON
W1V 3HR

NEWMARK EDITIONS
34 Trenchard Close
SUTTON COLDFIELD
B75 7QP

NEW MILLS
Heritage Centre
Rock Mill Lane
VIA STOCKPORT
SK12 3BN
New Mills 1894-1994. Published by New Mills Town Council, 1994. ISBN 0 9521869 2 6, 48pp, 145 illustrations. Described as one of the most ambitious of many publications to mark the centenary of the creation of urban district councils which became parish councils in 1974. Supported by an enormous number of illustrations, the book looks in turn at all of the services provided by the Council over the years. It also provides a useful account of the procedures involved in setting up an elected urban authority in Victorian times. £6.95 including postage.

NEW NORTH PRESS
27-29 New North Road
Hoxton
Hackney
LONDON
N1 6JB

NEW POEMS FROM PORTSMOUTH
(Denise Bennett & Mike Merritt)
6 Algiers Road
Copnor
PORTSMOUTH
PO3 6PJ

NEW PROJECTS
2nd Floor
Openshaw House

Birdshill
LETCHWORTH
SG6 1JB

NEW PROSPECTS POETRY
Prospect House
Snowshill
BROADWAY
WR12 7JU

NEW PYRAMID PRESS
No 1 Arch
Green Dragon Court
Borough Market
LONDON
SE1 9AH

NEW RIVER PROJECT
Bob Cobbing
89a Petherton Road
LONDON
N5 2PT
Tel 0171 226 2657
Border blur of arts activity in movement sound & vision. Publications: Books, cassettes, records; distribution for other publishers; regular workshops for experimental and performance poetry mixed media performances, exhibitions, bookfairs, etc. Write or phone for details.

NEW SPOKES
45 Clophill Road
Upper Gravenhurst
BEDFORD
MK45 4JH

NEWTON PUBLISHERS
Hartfield Road
P.O. Box 36
EDENBRIDGE
TN8 7JW
Mystery Fiction.

(THE) NEW TRUTH
28 Collins Road
Pennsylvania
EXETER
EX4 5DY

NEW WAY PUBLISHING
Spearhead Unit 1
New Life Christian Centre
Cario New Road
CROYDON
Children's Fiction.

NEW WELSH REVIEW
49 Pack Place
CARDIFF
CF19 3AT

NEW WORLD PUBLISHING
The Fairpiece
Mill Road
Gringley-on-the-Hill
DONCASTER
DN10 4QT

NIGHTFALL PRESS
c/o Noel K Hannan
18 Lansdowne Road
Sydney
CREWE
CW1 1JY

NIGHTSHADE PUBLICATIONS
Jackie Askew
P.O. Box 6/F
CHESSINGTON
KT9 1YQ
Vehicle for own self-publishing and

to contact other black-clad creatures of the night and lovers of all things weird and mystical.

Derek NIGHTINGALE
12 Finches Rise
Merrow
GUILDFORD
GU1 2UN
Local History.

NIGHT WRITERS
Hackney Women's Centre
20 Dalston Lane
LONDON
E8

NIMBUS PRESS
Justin Moulder
18 Guilford Road
LEICESTER
LE2 2RB
Fax/Tel 0116 270 6318
Religious publications and drama - for churches/secular.
"Meltdown", Church decline some suggestions for action.
"John Lees - His Lives and Deaths". A play retelling a remarkable incident in British criminal history. (Black comedy.)

NUMBER 9 BOOKS
47 St Georges Avenue West
Wolstanton
NEWCASTLE-UNDER-LYME
ST5 8DF

D. & M. NOBLE
Danar House
27 Longmoor Road
Ashton Gate
BRISTOL
BS3 2NZ
Family History.

NOMADS PRESS
16 Beck Cottage
Digby
LINCOLN
LN4 3NE
Poetry.

NON-PROFIT PUBLISHING
25 Alexandra Road
KINGSTON
KT2 6SD
Publishers of DONORS - The Computer in fundraising magazine.

NORHEIMSUND BOOKS & CARDS
1 Whitney Road
Burton Latimer
KETTERING
NN15 5SL

NORLON PUBLISHING
63 Ermineside
ENFIELD
EN1 1DD

(THE) NORTH (THE POETRY BUSINESS)
51 Bryan Arcade
Westgate
HUDDERSFIELD
HD1 1ND

NORTH AND SOUTH
23 Egerton Road
TWICKENHAM
TW2 7SL
North and South publishes poetry, prose and graphic work by new and established writers and artists.

NOTTINGHAM WRITERS
18 Waterloo Road
Beeston
NOTTINGHAM
NG9 2BU

NORTH-WEST BOOKS
23 Main Street
LIMAVADY
BT49 0EP

NORTHDOWN PUBLICATIONS
50 Albert Road
NEW MALDEN
KT3 6BS

NORTHERN ARTS PUBLISHING
Roper Lane
Thurgoland
SHEFFIELD
S30 7AA
Hobgoblin magazine.

NORTHERN EARTH
10 Jubilee Street
Mytholmroyd
HEBDEN BRIDGE
HX7 5NP
Tel/Fax 01422 882441
*Journal of Earth Mysteries &
related subjects. First published in
1979 under auspices of the
Northern Earth Mysteries Group.
Still affiliated to NEMG, now an
independent quarterly. Single
copies £1.70 includes p&p.
Subscription UK £6.00 p.a.
institutions £15.00; EC £7.50;
elsewhere £10.00. ISSN 0268-
8476*

NORTHERN EARTH MYSTERIES
Mr Rob Wilson
40b Welby Place
Meersbrook Park
SHEFFIELD
S8 9DB
*Magazine investigating the ancient
landscape of the area.*

NORTHERN HOUSE POETS
19 Haldane Terrace
NEWCASTLE-UPON-TYNE
NE2 3AN
Poetry.

NORTHERN VOICES
Durham City Arts
Durham City Baths
Elver Waterside
DURHAM
DH1 3BW

**NORTHERN WRITERS ADVISORY
SERVICES**
Jill Groves
77 Marford Crescent
SALE
M33 4DN
*NWAS specialises in local/family
history, selling mainly through
history societies and mailorder.
Titles: "Piggins, Husslements and
Desperate Debts: a Social History
of North-East Cheshire Through
Wills and Probate Inventories,
1600 to 1760", by Jill Groves, A4,
80pp, 1 map, 1 illustration. £4.50
(including p+p)
"The Demographic History of a
Yorkshire Village: Barwick-in-Elmet,
1700-1900, a case study", by
Pauline Robson, A5, 96pp, 1 map,
illustrations, £5.00 (including p+p).*

NORTH KENT BOOKS
162 Borstal Road
ROCHESTER
ME1 3BB
Tel 01634 403106

NORTHLIGHT
136 Byres Road
GLASGOW
G12 8TD

Pat NORTH
Northdale
ALFORD
LN13 9EY
Stockbreeding

NORTHSIDE WRITERS
134 Farranferris Avenue
Farranree
CORK
Eire

NORTH YORK MOORS
National Park Information Service
The Old Vicarage
Bardgate Helmsley
YORK
YO6 5BP
*Children's non-fiction. Biology.
Railways. Town Planning.*

NORWOOD PUBLISHERS
3 Chapel Street
Norwood Green
HALIFAX
HX3 8QU
School Textbooks.

NOTTINGHAM COURT PRESS
44 Great Russell Street
LONDON
WC1B 3PA

NOTTINGHAM WRITERS
18 Waterloo
Beeston
NOTTINGHAM
NG9 2BU

NOVA PUBLISHING
29 Milber Industrial Estate
NEWTON ABBOT
TQ12 4SG

NOVATA PRESS
3 The Leather House
72-76 St George's Street
NORWICH
NR3 1DA

NOX
15 Oxford Street
MEXBOROUGH

NPR PUBLICATIONS
8 Mendip Court
Avonley Village
Avonley Road
LONDON
SE14 5EU
Tel 0171 639 5407
*The Reid Review publishes short
stories, poems and short plays. The
aim is to publish and promote the
very best of these forms, but the
priority is the encour agement of
new poetry and fiction writing all
over the UK. The Reid Review. A
monthly review featuring the very
best from new and established
writers poetry plays short stories.*

NRB
N R Bradley

91 Hawksley Avenue
CHESTERFIELD
S40 4TJ
Tel 01246 208 473
*Specialist publisher of graphology
hand-writing psychology related
texts .Founded 1987 to promote
research into character/
personality investigation. Also
buyer/seller used books.*

NUIT ISIS
P.O. Box 250
OXFORD
OX1 1AP
Occult.

NUTSHELL PUBLISHING CO.
12 Dene Way
Speldhurst
TUNBRIDGE WELLS
TN3 0NX

OAKLEIGH PUBLICATIONS
METRASTOCK LTD
Unit 7
Cobham Road
Cedar Industrial Park
WIMBORNE

OAKWOOD PUBLICATIONS (WCC)
(see Good Stories Magazine)
23 Mill Crescent
KINGSBURY
B78 2LX

OASIS BOOKS/MAGAZINE
Ian Robinson
12 Stevenage Road
LONDON
SW6 6ES
Tel 0171 736 5059
*Oasis Books founded in 1969
specialises in editions of innovative
poetry and fiction both in English
and in translation.*

OATMEAL PRESS
Alan Harrison
54 Kemsing Gdns
CANTERBURY
CT2 7RF
Tel 01227 760 057
*Committed to increasing public
awareness of the numerous
problem arising from the misuse of*

*food in the home, and the
manipulation of the public mind by
government and the large food and
drink manufacturers.*

OBELISK PUBLICATIONS
2 Church Hill
PINHOE
EX4 9ER

OBERON BOOKS
8 Richardson Mews
LONDON
W1P 5DF
Plays. Theatre.

OCCULTURE
Topy
Station 23
P.O. Box 687
Halfway 687
SHEFFIELD
S19 6UXZ

ODIBOURNE PRESS
Richard Storey
32 High Street
KENILWORTH
CV8 2EU
Tel 01926 57409 (Eves)
*Publisher of all aspects of the
history of Kenilworth and its
immediate locality. Also local
reminiscences and poetry.
Kenilworth's Engineering Age: local
history with a difference. An
illustrated study of many small
businesses, some connected with
the motor industry of nearby
Coventry. £3.95.
* Two 'new' titles are based on the
recollections of Arthur Frodham as
told to Paul Byron Noris.
'Jackender. Memories of a
Kenilworth Man: childhood and
work in the 20th century.' 1995
£3.75
'Kenilworth Town Band.' 1996
£1.75.*

ODINIC RITE
11 Philip House
Heneage Street
LONDON
E1 5LW
Religious History.

ODUN BOOKS
Odun Grange
Appledore
BIDEFORD
EX39 1PT

ODYSSEY
Editor Derrick Woolf
Coleridge Cottage
NETHER STOWEY

OFF PINK PUBLISHING
49a Adulphus Road
LONDON
N4 2AX
Tel 0171 351 5952
*Seeking to fill the gap in literature
concerning bisexuality and related
subjects.*

O'FORTUNA
BCM Akademia
LONDON
WC1N 3XX

O H B
Alan Johnson
Woodman Works

Durnsford Road
LONDON
SW19 8DR

OLD BELMONT PRESS
49 Moorside
SPENNYMOOR
DL15 7DY

OLD BRIDGE MUSIC
P.O. Box 7
ILKLEY
LS29 9RY
Music.

OLD CHAPEL LANE BOOKS
8 Old Chapel Lane
Burgh Le Marsh
SKEGNESS
PE24 5LQ

OLD FERRY PRESS
53 Vicarage Road
TYWARDRATH
PL24 2PH
Tel 01726 813 709
*A recently formed imprint with it's
main interest in maritime affairs,
particularly naval - historical.*

A. OLDHAM
Rhychydwr
CRYMYCH
SA41 3RB
Biography. Caving.

OLD ORCHARD PRESS
The Orchard
5 The Street
Gillingham
BECCLES
NR34 0LH
Welsh History.

OLD POLICE STATION MAGAZINE
80 Lark Lane
LIVERPOOL
L17 8UU

OLD SOD
*Getting equally tired of old? (see
under New BOZO)*

OLD STILE
Frances and Nicholas McDowall
Catchmays Court
LLANDOGO
NP5 4TN
Tel & fax 01291 689226
*New titles:
Land - landscape engravings by
Garrick Palmer & poems. ISBN
0907664342, £125. 240 copies.
The dreamsong of Olaf Asteson
with woodcuts. £150. 140 copies.
p&p £5.
'Lens of Crystal' poems by Robin
Skelton, images by Sara Philpott.
Exploration of the beautiful and
ingenious verse forms of medieval
Wales. The poetry is complemented
by etched and cut linoleum
illustrations. 265 x 192mm, 80pp.
Handset text, printed on special
175g mould-made paper. Fine
binding and slipcase. Limited
edition of 240 copies, each signed
by the poet and artist. £95.00 (plus
p+p). ISBN: 0 907664 39 3.
Also produce a charming
newsletter about themselves, their
activities and their works. Other SPs
might do far worse than copy this
wheeze.*

OLD SWAN WRITERS
Rose Cottage
35 High Street
Wavertree
LIVERPOOL 15

OLD VICARAGE PUBLICATIONS
The Old Vicarage
Reades Lane
Dane-in-Shaw
CONGLETON
CW12 3LL

OLD WEST KIRK
Campbell Street
GREENOCK
Local History.

OLEANDER PRESS
Philip Ward
17 Stansgate Avenue
CAMBRIDGE
CB2 2QZ
Tel 01223 244688
*Celebrating over 35 years of small,
independent publishing.
Oleander's latest:
* Contemporary designer
bookbinders: an illustrated
directory, 224 pp. A5.
* V.J. Prasad: English is a foreign
language. "People who teach
English as a foreign language try
to conceal the woeful fact that
English really is a foreign
language, and has been since the
first howl of Beowulf to the last
shlurp and gurgle of Finnegan's
Wake," a point illustrated by
brilliant comic stories set in Mr.
Gopal's establishment in
Cambridge. 112 pps, A5 format,
ISBN 0900891343, UK £5.95, US
$9.95.*

O'MEDIA
69 Festing Road
Putney
LONDON
SW15 1LW
Tel 0181 788 6109

ONE-OFF PRESS
K. Schubert
85 Charlotte Street
LONDON
SW8 4UD
Art.

ONLY WOMEN
38 Mount Pleasant
LONDON
WC1X 0AP
Lesbian.

OPEN CIRCLE
Hillhead Library
348 Byres Road
GLASGOW
G12
Poetry.

OPEN LETTERS
147 Northchurch Road
LONDON
N1 3NT

(THE) OPEN PATH
5 Kingswood Place
CORBY
NN18 9AF

OPEN TOWNSHIP
Michael Haslam
14 Foster Clough

Heights Bridge
HEBDEN BRIDGE
HX7 5QZ

ORACLE
82 Marine Parade
BRIGHTON
BN2 1AJ
*Oracle was set up to, in the
absence of enlightened response by
the commercial publishing houses,
publish a series of deluxe hardback
books by the now 60 yr old
American poet, writer, critic and
reviewer. Because of no
distribution, Oracle folded after the
one book listed here.(In 1991
Alpha Beat Press published Flowers
of Consciousness by Kaviraj
George Dowden. Down-to-earth
visionary poetry. Introduction by
Sebastian Crevacoer, D.Litt. 107pp
ISBN 0 921720 04 1. £5.00.)
* Great Love Desiderata by Kaviraj
George Dowden with Anne
Dowden - flower illustration. The
very last word on man-woman love
at its greatest in 30 pure abstract
prose aphorisms. 1988 56pp ISBN
0 9513263 hardback £5.95.*

ORANGE BLOSSOM SPECIAL
C. Boxer
Freepost LON226
LONDON
SW8 1BR
*NEW: Quakers & English Civil
War; Romania '89; Science &
Technology in Ancient China.
Latest: Who wrote Shakespeare?
American gangsters.
History: mini info.packs issued
every month except August. Each
looseleaf pack contains a fine
colour plate, prize crosswords and
relevant extract from works of
Montaigne. Annual sub. £25 (11
issues) or £14 (6 issues). Back
numbers include Indians of
N.America, The Risorgimento,
Speculative Booms and Crashes.
For overseas rates, back issues,
contact C.Boxer at above address.*

ORANGE BOX
Simon Spain
59 Mildenhall Road
LONDON
E5 0RT
Tel 0181 985 0852
*Orangebox works with artists to
produce and publish editioned
prints and books. Orange Box also
runs publishing workshops in
schools where children can write
illustrated layout and actually print
their own edition of books.*

ORANGE HERITAGE
c/o McCracken
5 Mansewood Crescent
Whitburn
BATHGATE
EH47 8HA

ORBIS
199 The Long Shoot
NUNEATON
CV11 6JQ

ORCHARD BOOKS
2B Wastie's Orchard
Long Hanborough
OXFORD
OX7 2BA

ORCHID SUNDRIES
New Gate Farm
Scotchey Lane
Stour Provost
GILLINGHAM
SP8 5LT

ORE
7 The Towers
STEVENAGE
SG1 1HE
Poetry and Prose magazine.

ORIEL BOOKSHOP
Peter Finch
The Friary
CARDIFF
CF1 4AA
*Issues all sorts of useful packages
of literature. Send for info.*

ORIFLAMME PUBLISHING LIMITED
Edward Marsh
125 Station Road
MICKLEOVER
DE3 5FN
Tel 01332 510 230
*Publisher. Mainly paperback books.
Now chiefly education for mass
market via W H Smith and direct to
schools. Currently planning US
editions. Some fiction in print: SF/
Fantasy. In current market would
only consider subsidised fiction
deals. No unsolicitores MSS.*

ORINOCO PRESS
41 Oakthwaite Road
WINDERMERE
LA23 2BD
*Local history, folklore, legend, etc.
dealing principally with the
Windermere area.*

ORION PUBLISHING
6 Arcade Chambers
High Street
BRENTWOOD
CM14 4AH
Travel Accommodation.

ORKNEY VIEW
3 Papdale Close
KIRKWALL
Orkney
KW15 1QP

ORLANDO PUBLISHING
Chequers Cottage
Church Lane
Briston
MELTON CONSTABLE
NR24 2LF

ORPHEIS BIBLIA
BCM Orpheus
LONDON
WC1N 3XX
*A dedication to the genius for living
- Literature with a sense of beauty.*

CHRIS ORR PUBLICATIONS
Chris Orr
7 Bristle Hill
BUCKINGHAM
MK18 1EZ
Tel 01280 815 255
*Self employed artist occasionally
publishing books and catalogues
on own work.*

ORWELL PRESS
64 High Street
SOUTHWOLD
IP18 6DN

OSCARS PRESS
BM Oscars
LONDON
WC1N 3XX
'The Vital and Vitalized Oscars Press' - Ian McMillan, poetry review. Specialists in gay and lesbian poetry anthologies.

OSCO
Unit 3-4
Mars House
Calleva Park
Aldermaston
READING
RG7 4QW
Biography.

OSSIAN PUBLISHERS GLASGOW
268 Bath Street
GLASGOW
G2 4JR
Mystery Fiction.

OSTINATO
P.O. Box 522
LONDON
N8 7SZ

THE OTHER WAY PRESS
P.O. Box 130
LONDON
W5 1DQ
Tel 0181 998 1519
Self-help and practical books for the gay community

OTHERWISE PUBLICATIONS
Forge Cottage
The Green
Abthorpe
TOWCESTER
NN12 8QP

OTHERWISE PRESS
111 Blenheim Crescent
LONDON
W11 2JF
Publisher of ALTERNATIVE LONDON (now well-extinct). Other unrelated projects pending, including book on absurd or anachronistic laws. Fluting forever.

OTTER
Chris Southgate
Parford Cottage
Chagford
NEWTON ABBOT
TQ13 8JR

OUTDOOR EVENTS PUBLICATIONS
30 Tudor Manor Gardens
Garston
WATFORD
WD2 7PP
Sport.

OUTLAWS PUBLISHING COMPANY
Margaret Disher
40 Basildon Court
Devonshire Street
LONDON
W1N 1RH
Tel 0171 935 3423
The definitive book on the true-life Just William. By his sister.

OUTLET
Mr Trev Faull
33 Aintree Crescent
Barkingside
ILFORD
IG6 2HD
Magazine.

OVERCOAT PUBLICATIONS
143 Birchfield Road
WIDNES
WA8 9EG
Biography.

OVERDUE BOOKS
37 Melbourne Street
HEBDEN BRIDGE
HX7 6AS
Women writers from the North of England.

OVERSPACE
25 Sheldon Road
CHIPPENHAM
SN14 0BP

OVERTON PRESS
480 Moor Road
Bestwood
NOTTINGHAM
NG6 8UN

OWEN PUBLICATIONS
Bede House
28C Blakebrook
KIDDERMINSTER
DY11 6AP
Historical Biography.

Tuppy OWENS
Box 42b
LONDON
W1A 42B
Tel 0171 499 3527
Safer Sex Books.

OWL BOOKS
27 Queensway
WIGAN
WN1 2JA
Local History. Historical Biography. Sport.

OWL PRESS
P.O. Box 315
Downton
SALISBURY
SP5 3YE
Tel 01725 22553
Small independent book publisher specialising in adult humour and books of interest to The Services.

OWL PUBLISHING
7 Ludlow Drive
ORMSKIRK
L39 1LE
Customs and Folklore.

OWLET BOOKS
'Ballochantuy'
Tunstall Road
Tunstall
SITTINGBOURNE
ME10 1YQ
Educational books for teachers. Junior fiction.

OWNBASE ASSOCIATION
9 Salisbury Road
ANDOVER
SP10 2JJ
Newsletter for people who work at home.

O WRITE
(admin editors)
FCHS Pathways Publications
New Street
Rubery
Rednal
BIRMINGHAM
B45 0EU

OXFIN
Unit one
Paradise Street Business Centre
OXFORD
OX1

OXFORD GRAPEVINE
Box O
34 Cowley Road
OXFORD
OX4 1HZ
Alternative Yellow Pages for Oxford.

OXFORD PROJECT FOR PEACE STUDIES
Belsyre Court
57 Woodstock Road
OXFORD
OX2 6HU

OXFORD POETRY
Magdalen College
OXFORD
OX1 4AU

OXFORD PSYCHOLOGISTS PRESS
Lambourne House
311-321 Banbury Road
OXFORD
OX2 7JH
Education.

OXFORD SCRIBBLERS
c/o Bloomin' Arts
East Oxford Community Centre
Princess Street
OXFORD

OXFORD TRUST
STEP Centre
Osney Mead
OXFORD
OX2 0ES
Architecture.

OXFORD WOMEN'S HANDBOOK
Oxford Univ S U
New Barnett House
28 Little Clarendon St
OXFORD
OX1 2HB

PACSEA
The Martin Centre
6 Chaucer Road
CAMBRIDGE
CB2 2EB

PADDA BOOKS
5 Tilgate Drive
BEXHILL-ON-SEA
TN39 3UH

PANDORA'S JAR
Blaenberem
Mynyddcerrig
Pontyberem
LLANELLI
SA15 5BL

PAGAN ANIMAL RIGHTS
Tina Foooox
23 Highfield South
Rock Ferry
BIRKENHEAD
L42 4NA
Tel 0151 648 0485
Pagan Animal Rights advocates the treatment of the earth and all her creatures with respect. It works on both physical and pychic levels using both normal campaigning methods and meditation and magical techniques. Par Magazine edited by T. Fox and J. Boyd. Quarterly at fire festivals.

PAGAN FEDERATION
BM Box 7097
LONDON
WC1N 3XX
Social Welfare.

PAGAN FUNERAL TRUST NEWSLETTER
BM Box 3337
LONDON
WC1N 3XX

PAGAN LIFE
Irish Pagan Movement
The Bridge House
Clonegal
ENNISCORTHY
Co Wexford
Ireland

PAGAN NEWS
Box 175
52 Call Lane
LEEDS
LS1 6DT

PAGAN PRATTLE
Box 333
52 Call Lane
LEEDS
LS1 6DT
Newsletter which covers the tabloid version of the antics of the Christian right.

PAGES
Mr Robert Sheppard
239 Lessingham Avenue
LONDON
SW19 8NQ

PALAVER PUBLICATIONS
40 Langham Close
Sharples
BOLTON
BL1 7RA
General Fiction.

PALERMO PRESS
33 Burgage
Prestbury
CHELTENHAM
GL52 3DL

Literature.

(THE) PALESTINE POST
P.O. Box 1EQ
LONDON
W1A 1EQ

PALLAS PRESS
S. King
Brookdale
Danyraig Road
LLANHARAN
CF7 0UX
Tel 0443 228 490
*We publish books of local interest.
We also publishj a local free
monthly newspaper 'The Diary'.*

PALLAS ARMATA
98 Priory Road
TONBRIDGE
TN9 2BP

PALLISER PRESS
William Taylor
69 West End Avenue
HARROGATE
HG2 9BX
*Short runs of pamphlets, mainly on
typographical subjects, but
occasionally re-prints of 'street
literature', printed on hand presses,
sometimes on hand-made paper.*

PALMERS PRESS
5 Castle Street
LUDLOW
SY8 1AS

PALTEN PRESS
66 Hayle Terrace
HAYLE
TR20 4XN

PAM PRESS
P.O. Box 35
HASTINGS
TN34 2UX
General Fiction.

PAN CELTIC PUBLICATIONS
P.O. Box 2
KYLE
IV40 8AR
Travel (Scotland).

PANDEMONIUM
c/o Matthew De Monti
42 Kings Lane
Little Harrowden
WELLINGBOROUGH
NN9 5BL

PAPER CASTLE
W Keene
Edco House
10-12 High Street
Colliers Wood
LONDON
SW19 2AE

PAPER DRUM PUBLISHING
12 Sudbourne Road
LONDON
SW2 5AQ
Tel 0171 326 0753

P.A. PUBLISHING COMPANY
Unit 3
Grand Union Centre
West Row
LONDON
W10 5AS
The Knowledge.

PARADINE DEVELOPMENTS
Audley House
9 North Audley Street
LONDON
W1Y

PARANOIA PRESS
Richard Briddon/Kate More/David
Almond
35 Percy Street
MIDDLESBROUGH
TS1 4DD
Tel 01642 224 617
*A small press with local roots and
international interests. Emphasis is
on quality production quality of
writing (several of our writers are
award winning) though our
material is not always mainstream.
We are open to new writers.*

PARFORDWOOD
Parford Cottage
Chagford
NEWTON ABBOT
TQ13 8JR
Poetry.

J. PARKE
c/o Tim Howe (author)
Greenside
Little Kneton
WARWICK
CV35 0DH
Children's Fiction.

PARKE SUTTON PUBLISHING
Hitech House
10 Blackfriars Street
NORWICH
NR3 1SF
Costume.

Ti PARKS
Artists Books
9 the Orchard
Blackheath
LONDON
SE3 0QS
*Small edition and unique artists
books including the famous series
of "Road Print Books". Catalogue -
an artists book in itself - £45. List
available with S.A.S.E.*

PARNASSUS PUBLISHING
Bowes Lyon House
St. Georges Way
STEVENAGE
SG1 1XY
Poetry.

PARRALLEL
7 Rustic Avenue
Southowram
HALIFAX
HX3 9QW

VIC PARRY PUBLISHING
174 Edgwarebury Lane
EDGWARE
HA8 8NE

L. Michael PARSONS
W. Tytherley
SALISBURY
SP5 1NF
History.

PARTICK PRESS
David Hamilton
18 Kirklee Circus
GLASGOW
G12
Fine printer.

PARTIZAN PRESS
Dave Ryan
26 Cliffsea Grove
LEIGH-ON-SEA
Tel/fax 01702 73986
*Military and local history publisher
specialising in C17th & C18th. Also
dealing with political aspects of the
Great Rebellion. We produce 4
magazines covering the period
1450-1820.*

PARTIZANS
Digby Knight
218 Liverpool Road
LONDON
N1 1LE
*Set up in 1978 to publish
information on the world's most
powerful mining company, RTZ.
Lead titles: "Plunder! the Story of
RTZ
Parting Company (Quarterly).*

PASS PUBLICATIONS
11 Baring Road
LONDON
SE12 0JP
School Textbooks.

PASSION PRESS
Sara Burlace/Munni Reddy
c/o 33 Trent Grove Clayton
NEWCASTLE-UNDER-LYME
ST5 4EW
Poetry.

PASSPORT MAGAZINE
Mike Gerrard
5 Parsonage St
Wistow
HUNTINGDON
PE17 2QD
Tel 01487 822 100
*Bi-annual literary magazine in A5
paperback format. Publishes new
international prose. Published April
and October. Has featured writing
from the UK USA Norway India Africa
Yugoslavia Czechoslovakia Japan
China Germany Argentina etc.*

PASSWORD BOOKS
David Parrish
23 New Mount Street
MANCHESTER
M4 4DE
Tel 0161 953 4009
Represents Dedalus Press.

PASSWORD PUBLISHING DESIGN
Peter Simmons
38-40 Exchange Street
NORWICH
NR2 1AX
*Non-profit making service catering
for the voluntary/charity
sector.Design, typesetting, halftone
reproductions, illustration and
camera-ready artwork. Publishes a
number of magazines and
newsletters.*

PASTEST SERVICE
Cranford Lodge
Bexton Road
KNUTSFORD
WA16 0ED
Languages.

PASTIME PUBLICATIONS
15 Dublin Street
Lane South
EDINBURGH

EH1 3PX
*Taste of Scotland Scheme. Fishing.
Sport. Travel in Britain. Travel
Accommodation.*

PATCHWORK PUBLICATIONS
58 New Penkridge Road
CANNOCK
WS11 1HW
Poetry.

PATHFINDER PRESS LTD
47 The Cut
LONDON
SE1

PATHWAYS
Mary Fee
12 Southcote Road
LONDON
N19 5BJ
Tel 01171 607 7852
*A publicity and infomation service
for personal growth and healing;
we publish the Pathways Bulletin,
publicity materials and small
books, which we display at major
exhibitions and in our mailings.*

PATTEN PRESS
The Old Post Office
Newmill
PENZANCE
TR20 4XN
Health Care.

PAUL WATKINS PUBLISHING
Shaun Tyas
18 Adelaide Street
STAMFORD
PE9 2EN
Tel 01780 56793
*Shaun Tyas (trading as 'Paul
Watkins') is an enthusiastic and
informal publisher, interested in
publishing all kinds of history,
biography and humour. Contact
him if these are your areas of
interest. He has a very impressive
catalogue.*

PAULINUS PRESS
12 Blowhorn Street
MARLBOROUGH
SN8 1BT

PAUPER'S PRESS
Colin Stanley
27 Melbourne Road
West Bridgford
NOTTINGHAM
NG2 5DJ
*We publish 10,000-15,000 word
essays mostly on literary criticism.
Royalties paid. 3 new titles
published annually.
Wade, Stephen : "More on the
Word-Hoard: the work of Seamus
Heaney" (£11.95)
Wilson, Colin : "Sex, America and
the Insights" (£7.95)*

PAVELIN
Alan Pavelin
172 Leesons Hill
CHISLEHURST
BR7 6QL
Tel 01689 835 741
*'Fifty Religious Films' a self-
explanatory title is a one-off self-
publishing Venture. It has been
reviewed in Time Out and in 3
religious weeklies. It covers many*

films by great directors like
Bergman Bresson Rossellini and
Tarkovsky
*Fifty Religious Films by Alan
Pavelin. 108pp 1990 ISBN 0
9516491 0 8. £4.95.*

PAVIC PUBLICATIONS
Sheffield City Poly
36 Collegiate Crescent
SHEFFIELD
S10 2BP

PAVILION PUBLISHING
42 Lansdowne Place
HOVE
BN3 1HH
Social Welfare.

Mark PAWSON
P.O. Box 664
LONDON
E3 4QR
*New title: All my rubber stamps.
The first copies of this long awaited
book are now available; 30
hardback copies sewn and bound,
21 x 15cm, 80 pps, edition run
250, pbk - £15, hbk - £45, samples
available on request. Now selling
on other items send for lists.*

PAX CHRISTIE
9 Henry Road
LONDON
N4 2LH

PBN PUBLICATIONS
P. Webb or N. Weir
22 Abbey Road
EASTBOURNE
BN20 8TE
Tel 01323 31206
*Original material transcribed and
printed - of interest to
genealogists and local historians.
All genealogical books.*

PDQ PUBLISHING
FREEPOST
P.O. Box 151
ABINGDON
OX13 5BR
*'Radio Listeners' Guide,' 1996 - 8th
ed., 80 pp, £4.50 (incl. p&p) Why
be deafened by the explosive
number of radio stations, local &
community, nationals such as
Classic FM, Virgin Radio and Talk
Radio? Frequency and location
guide for all radio stations and
transmitters in UK; colour quick ref.
maps; how to get best out of your
radio and improve reception.*

P.E PUBLICATIONS
42 Dalkeith Road
EDINBURGH
EH16 5BS

P.E.P. Ltd.
St Leonard's Mead
St Leonard's Hill
WINDSOR
Berks
SL4 4AL
Tel 01753 852400
*NILES, Alexander, 'Dead Men
Can't Talk,' described in flier as a
'political thriller.' 1996.*

PEACE AND FREEDOM PRESS
Paul Rance
17 Farrow Road
Whaplode Drove

SPALDING
PE12 0TS
*Eastern Rainbow is a magazine
specialising in 20th Century culture
- sci-fi/fantasy/horror fiction,
relevant poetry and art & more
besides.
The magazine now provides one of
the most detailed listings services in
independent publishing.
Send sae/irc for guidelines on
submissions of poetry, prose,
artwork for our paperback
anthologies, magazines and
booklets.
Eastern Rainbow Issue 4, £1.25.*

PEACE NEWS
5 Caledonian Road
LONDON
N1

PEACE PLEDGE UNION
6 Endsleigh Street
LONDON
WC1H 0DX

PEACEWORK PRESS
Bartle Hall
Liverpool Road
Hutton
PRESTON
PR4 5HB
Tel 01772 616 816
*We are an imprint of Barrington
Books, publishing experimental
poetry by new writers. Work often
explores the affect of emotion on
our perception of reality, and is less
political than Barrington.*

PEACOCK VANE PUBLISHING
44 High Street
VENTNOR
PO39 1LT
Food.

PEAK BOOKS
18 St Anstell Drive
WILFORD
NG11 7BP

PEARL PRESS
69 Waldeck Road
LONDON
N15 3EL

PEARL RIVER REVIEW
Kimberly Kelly
Editor-in-Chief
Pearl River Review
P.O. Box 8416
Mobile
Alabama 36689-0416
USA
*A new bi-annual journal of fiction,
poetry, translation and essays from
the USA.*

PEATON PRESS
12 Birkhall Drive
Bearsden
GLASGOW
G61 1DR

PECKHAM PUBLISHING PROJECT
The Bookplace
13 Peckham High Street
LONDON
SE15

PECO PUBLICATIONS & PUBLICITY
Underleys
Beer
SEATON

EX12 3NA

PEEPAL TREE PRESS
53 Grove Farm Crescent
LEEDS
LS16 6BZ
*Radical Third World publishing
house.*

PEEPING TOM
c/o David Bell
Yew Tree House
15 Nottingham Road
ASHBY-LE-ZOUCH
LE6 5DJ

PEERS SCHOOL BOOKS
Michael O'Reagan
11 Warnborough Road
OXFORD
OXW 6HZ
Tel 01865 511518

PEMBERTON PUBLISHING
25 Hunters Rise
BARNSLEY
S75 2JX
Music.

PEN:UMBRA
Mr David Rushmere
1 Beeches Close
SAFFRON WALDEN
CB11 4BU
Magazine.

PEN + KEYBOARD MAGAZINE
David Stern
SQR (Publishing) Enterprise
526 Fulham Palace Road
LONDON
SW6 6JE
Tel 0171 731 5148
*This magazine is probably one of
the smallest publications in the
land, it has the object of being
informative, slightly discurcive and
entertaining. Contributers are
sometimes paid.*

PENDALAY
47 Water Street
Lavenham
SUDBURY
CO70 9RN

PENDRAGON PRESS
Mr Paul Broadhurst
Trebeath
Egloskerry
LAUNCESTON
PL15 8RY
*Publishing the work of Hamish
Miller. But we were suckered in by
John Michell who said why not do
it yourself? We did with 'Sacred
Shrines' - Holy Wells in a de luxe
limited edition. It worked, like the
second book so we caught the bug.*

PENDULUM GALLERY PRESS
Powerfresh
3 Gray Street
NORTHAMPTON
or
56 Ackender Road
ALTON
GU34 1JS
Art. Short Stories.

PENDYKE PUBLICATIONS
Goffeysfa
Methodist Hill
Froncysyllte
LLANGOLLEN

LL20 7SN

PENMARRAN PUBLISHING
60 Argyll Road
Pennsylvania
EXETER
EX4 4RY
Tel 01392 71080
*Publisher of local books, colour
notepaper and colour bookmarks
with ribbons.*

PENMIEL PRESS
Edward Burrett
Full Point
16 New Road
ESHER
K10 9PG
Fine printer.

PENNINE PENS
32 Windsor Road
HEBDEN BRIDGE
HX7 8LF
Cycling.

PENNINE PLATFORM
Brian Merrikin Hill
Ingmanthorpe Farm Cottage
WETHERBY
LS22 5EQ
Poetry.

PENNYFIELDS PRESS
32 Ashville Road
Ashton Gate
BRISTOL
BS3 2AP
(see Avon Poetry News)

PEN PALS
43 Denbydale Way
Royton
OLDHAM
OL2 5TN

PENROVE BOOKS
Christians Warehouses
23 Dockhead Wharf
4 Shad Thames
LONDON
SE1 2NW

PENTAGRAPH PRESS
John Tungay and Sean Russell
Friend
P.O. Box 2757
BRIGHTON
BN7 1PF
Poetry publishing.

PENTAMAN PRESS
Unit 1
Crossland Industrial Estate
Stockport Road
West Bredbury
STOCKPORT
SK6 2BR
Sports.

PEOPLE INTERNATIONAL
P.O. Box 26
TUNBRIDGE WELLS
TN2 5AZ

PEOPLE'S POETRY
Editors Peter Geoffrey/Paul
Thompson
71 Harrow Crescent
ROMFORD
RM3 7BJ
(see Precious Pearl Press)

PEOPLE'S PUBLICATIONS
50 Henslowe Road

LONDON
SE22 0AR
Biography.

PEOPLE AND PLACES
Home Counties region
Rechabite Friendly Society
25e Copperfield Street
LONDON
SE1 0EN

PEOPLE TO PEOPLE
West Midlands Arts
82 Granville Street
BIRMINGHAM
B1 2LH

PEPAR PUBLICATIONS
Unit 26 Southside
249 Ladypool Road
Sparkbrook
BIRMINGHAM
B12 8LF
Poetry.

PEPPERCORN BOOKS
Mrs Judith A White
24 Cromwell Road
ELY
CB6 1AS
*Very small publisher began by
specialising in food-related books.
Aimed at publishing general
subject books including fiction for
as yet unpublished authors. All
enquiries welcome.*

PERCEPTIONS
Temi Rose
73 Eastcombe Avenue
LONDON
SE7 7LL
*Founded in 1982 in Missoula,
Montana, USA. We favour strong
individual voices. Our taste is
ecclectic; the thread is our
fascination with the
transformingresonance of
individual perceptions.
Perceptions is a small, prize-
winning, poetry magazine for the
promotion and development of
women's consciousness of peace
and freedom to be.
Copies: £3.50/$5.00 each
Subscriptions: £10.50/$15.00 for
indivduals, £20.00/$25.00 for
institutions.*

PERDIX PRESS
Walter Partridge
21 The Close
SALISBURY
SP1 2EB
Fine printer.

PEREGINE PUBLISHING
7 Farnham Park
BANGOR
BT20 3SR

PERFECT PUBLICATIONS
BM Perfect
LONDON
WC1N 3XX

PERGAMON CHESS
Railway Road
SUTTON COLDFIELD
B73 6AZ
Indoor Games. Biography.

PERIAKTOS
6 Sandhurst Avenue
IPSWICH
IP3 8DU

PERICLES PUBLICATIONS
48 Newton Road
Mumbles
SWANSEA
SA3 4BQ
*Publisher of poetry, prose,
historical texts etc. Plans to begin
on nautical and Welsh subjects.*

THE PERPETUA PRESS
14 Stanley Road
OXFORD
OX4 1QZ

Bryan PERRETT
Matle Avenue
BURSCOUGH
Near Ormskirk
L40 5SL
Local History.

PERROTT CARTOGRAPHICS
Darowen
MACHYNLLETH
SY20 8NS

PERRY AND PERRY PUBLISHING
16 Pickwick Road
CORSHAM
SN13 9BT
Music.

PERSEVERANCE WRITERS' CLUB
14 Drumbrae Avenue
EDINBURGH
EH12 8TE

PERSIFLAGE PRESS
26 Clacton Road
LONDON
E17 8AR

PERSPECTIVE PRESS
92 Hertford Street
CAMBRIDGE
CB4 3AQ
Education.

PETAL PRESS
2 Longford Wharf
Stephenson Road
Stretford
MANCHESTER
M32 0JT

PETER PRESS
c/o M. Wilson-Smith
59 St. James' Street
LONDON
SW1A 1LD
Poetry.

PETERBOROUGH WILDLIFE GROUP
West Town School
Williamson Avenue
PETERBOROUGH
PE3 6BA
Wildlife.

F. PETERS PUBLISHING
Gatebeck
KENDAL
LA8 0HW
Travel Guide to Lake District.

PEYRERE INDENT
Robin and Hilaire Rimbaud
5 Park Court
191A Battersea Park Road
LONDON
SW11 4LD
Tel 0171 498 3032
*Embracing a joint devotion to art
and books they aim to create work*

which appeals to both the tactile
and intellectual senses. Designing
and printing their own unique
books in extremely limited editions
other projects encompass graphics
music and erotic adventures.

PFC PUBLICATIONS
25 Totnes Close
Devon Park
BEDFORD
MK40 3AX
Poetry.

PHAEDRA BOOKS
Doug Keating
23 Brougham Road
SOUTHSEA
PO5 4PA
Tel 01705 812 100
*Phaedra (Fay-dra) was set up to
help publish innovative writers,
who might otherwise be overlooked
by the short-sighted publishing
giants. We are unashamedly
commercial in approach and proud
of our imaginative presentation of
science fiction, and other genre.*

PHAGPOS PRESS
34 Airlie House
Airlie Gardens
LONDON
W8 7AN

PHILATELIC IMPRINT
12 Holyoake Walk
LONDON
N2 0JX
*Publishers of books for stamp
collectors.*

PHILERGON
57 Green Lane
Chesham Bois
AMERSHAM
HP6 5LQ
Social Sciences.

Carla PHILLIPS
Caley Mill
HEACHAM
Norfolk
01485 572383
*'Herbs from a Norfolk Kitchen',
e.g. how to cook with lavender.*

PHILOSOPHY NOW
Rick Lewis
226 Bramford Road
IPSWICH
IP1 4AS
*A magazine which appears 4
times/yr. It covers all aspects of
philosophy and is aimed at
philosophy students, academics
and amateur philosophers.
Subscriptions £8/4 issues.*

Kathleen M. PHILPOTT
3 King's Drive
Bishopston
BRISTOL
BS7 8JW
Local History.

PHOENIX PRESS
John Fairfax
The Thatch
Eling Hermitage
NEWBURY
RG16 9XR
Tel 01635 200 585
*A poetry press, concerned with
publishing both new and*

established poets. The emphasis in
publication is not only an exciting
poetry but on quality book
production.

PHOENIX PRESS
P.O. Box 824
LONDON
N1 9DL
Anarchist yearbook.

PHOENIX PRESS
Bruce Barnes
19a Marriott Road
LONDON
N4 3QN
*The Press specialises in poetry
publications emphasising a quality
print product and exciting new
poets. Unfortunately the press is not
presently able to consider
manuscripts for publication.*

PHOENIX PRESS
Juliet Atkins
The Rainbow Business Centre
Phoenix Way
Swansea Enterprise Park
SWANSEA
SA7 9EH
*General and academic publisher
on a small subsidy basis. Storage
and distribution available to other
small publishers.*

PHOLIOTA PRESS LIMITED
Josephine Bacon
82 Stonebridge Road
LONDON
N15 5PA
Tel 0171 837 8300
Mainly books of Jewish interest.

PHOTON PRESS
Dr. John Light
The Light House
29 Longfield Road
TRING
HP23 4DG
*Publish only self-generated work.
Light's List of Literary Magazines.*

**PHYSIOLOGY OF A FLY
PUBLICATIONS**
50 Clifford Road
SHEFFIELD
S11 9AQ
Poetry.

PIATKUS BOOKS
5 Windmill Street
LONDON
W1P 1HF

PICKPOCKETS
M.E. Rose
25 St. Mary's Terrace
HASTINGS
TN34 3LS
Tel 01424 714393
*'Pickpockets' are finely produced
pocket-sized books illustrated by
established artists on a variety of
unusual subjects. Especially suitable
as gifts or collectors' items at £1
they still cost less than many
greetings cards and have wide
general appeal.*

PICKS PUBLISHING
83 Greenfields Crescent
Ashton-in-Makerfield
WIGAN
WN4 8QY

PICTURE BOX PUBLICATIONS
New Exchange Buildings
Queens Square
MIDDLESBROUGH
TS2

PIE IN THE SKY PUBLISHING LTD
Markus Kinch
41 Albert Street
AYLESBURY
HP20 1LY

PIG PRESS
7 Cross View Terrace
DURHAM
DH1 4JY
Poetry from the UK and USA.

PIGASIS PRESS
13 Hazely Combe
ARRETON
Isle of Wight
PO30 3AJ
*Publish sci-fi, futuristic zines - also
'Dragon's Breath' newsletter.*

THE PIKERS' PAD
P.O. Box 97
Storrington
PULBOROUGH
RH20 3YZ
*Cheap paperbacks and local
history.*

PILGRIM'S BELL
A.P. Fothergill
7 Janice Drive
Fulwood
PRESTON
PR2 4YE
Tel 01772 719 469
*Tony Fothergill is a retired
insurance clerk and currently the
treasurer at Lune Street Chapel. He
writes: 'Herewith complimentary
copy of the one and only book I
shall be publishing!' No unsolicited
material.
'Avowed Intent' - A Brief
Description of and Short History
About Central Methodist Church
Lune Street Preston by A.P.
Fothergill. A5 32pp illustrations
1992 ISBN 0 9517241 0 9 £3.00
(plus 25p p&p).*

PILGRIM'S PUBLISHING
9 Lyon Street
SOUTHAMPTON
SO2 0LD
Second World War History.

PINE TREE
The Street
Brundish
WOODBRIDGE
IP13 8BN

J PINEWOOD ENTERPRISES
37 Durham Road
LONDON
W5 4JR

Derek PINKERTON
522 Holly Lane
Erdington
BIRMINGHAM
B24 9LY
Cycling History.

PINKFOOT PRESS
Balgavies
FORFAR
DD8 2TH
Military Local History.

PINK PAPER
77 City Garden Row
LONDON
N1 8EZ

PINTSIZE PRESS
49 Essex Street
OXFORD
OX4 3AW
Tel 01865 516 284

PIONEER PRESS
Station House
John Street Central
MERTHYR TYDFIL
CF47 0AW
*Arthur Watkins has studied King
Arthur for more than quarter of a
century and is issuing the results.*

PIPKIN PRESS
19 Charnwood Avenue
Westone
NORTHAMPTON
NN3 3DX

PIRA
Randalls Road
LEATHERHEAD
KT22 7RU

PISCES PUBLICATIONS
Glamorgan Wildlife Trust
Wildlife Centre
Fountain Road
TONDU
CF12 0EH
Travel (Britain).

PIT BULL TERRORIST
The Dollyhead International
c/o 73 Fitzgerald House
169 East India Dock Road
LONDON
E14 0HH

Alice PLANCTON
A J Willis
4 Trinity Street
BRIGHTON
BN2 3HN
*I intended to publish a book of my
own writing but it turned into a four
album set.*

**PLANET - THE WELSH
INTERNATIONALIST**
John Barnie
P.O. Box 44
ABERYSTWYTH

PLASTICS & RUBBER INSTITUTE
27 Cavendish Road
Hazel Grove
STOCKPORT
SK7 6HY
*Developing software for the plastics
industry. Technology publications
for schools.*

PLATEWAY PRESS
Keith Taylorson
P.O. Box 973
BRIGHTON
BN2 2TG
*Plateway Press was formed in 1986
with the aim of producing good
quality books on neglected aspects
of the railway and transport scene
without arbitrary restriction on
cover prices. The imprint was
originally based on Church Road
Croydon on the course of the*

*erstwhile Surrey Iron Railway an
early 'Plateway' providing the
inspiration for our name.*

PLATFORM
Folder 80
c/o Acorn Books
17 Chatham Street
READING
Magazine.

PLATFORM 5 PUBLISHING
Lydgate House
Lydgate Lane
SHEFFIELD
S10 5FH

PLATT CONTEMPORARY ART
The Gallery
The Street
Igtham
SEVENOAKS
TN15 9HH
Art.

**PLAYWRIGHTS PUBLISHING
COMPANY**
Liz and Tony Breeze
70 Nottingham Road
Burton Joyce
NOTTINGHAM
NG14 5AL
Tel 01602 313 356
*A small family firm specialising in
the publication of new plays.
Authors are charge a small reading
fee and the best scripts are printed
in book form and sent out to
libraries in the UK America and
Australia.*

PLEASURE BOOKS
Susan Brett
50 Lakeside
Hightown
RINGWOOD
BH24 3DX
Tel 01425 477 334
*Non-fictional foccusing on areas of
outstanding beauty and interesting
history. Profusely illustrated with
colour pictures and graphics. Easy
reading - highest quality production
and design. Produced by desk top
publishing throughout ensures an
extremely low retail price.*

PLOUGH PRESS
2 Manor Way
KIDLINGTON
OX5 2BD

PLUTO
345 Archway Road
LONDON
N6 5AA
Tel 0181 348 2724
*A radical independent press
publishing academic books in the
social sciences. We publish over a
broad spectrum from the left;
producing about 40 books per
year.*

P.M.G. PUBLICATIONS
165 Jordanhill Drive
GLASGOW
G13 1UQ
Law.

PN REVIEW
208-212
Corn Exchange
MANCHESTER
M4 3BQ

POET AND PRINTER
30 Grimsdyke Road
Hatch End
PINNER
HA5 4PW

POETICAL HISTORIES
27 Sturton Street
CAMBRIDGE
CB1 2QG
*Small pamphlets handwritten,
handprinted, handmade paper.*

THE POETRY BUSINESS
5 Byram Road
Westgate
HUDDERSFIELD
HD1 1ND
*Poetry resource for Huddersfield
and west Yorks. Books under the
imprint Smith/Doorstep. Magazine
'North'. Run workshops and a
poetry bookshop. Mial order and a
library. Too good to be true?*

POETRY & AUDIENCE
Leeds University Poetry Soc
School of English
The University
LEEDS
LS2

POETRY DIGEST
28 Stainsdale Green
Whitwick
LEICESTER
LE6 3PW

POETRY DURHAM
c/o School of English
Univ of Durham
Elvet Riverside
New Elvet
DURHAM
DH1 3JT

POETRY IRELAND REVIEW
44 Upper Mount Street
DUBLIN 2
Ireland

POETRY EXPRESS
Anne Rutter
Juniper
14 Crove Park
LONDON
E11 2DL
Magazine since 1995.

POETRY LIFE
Adrian Bishop
14 Pennington Oval
LYMINGTON
SO41 8BQ
*Poetry Life magazine is now firmly
established as one of the UK's
leading poetry magazines. The
founding principle is to explore the
booming and rich poetry scene in
the UK.*

POETRY LONDON NEWSLETTER
Leon Cych
26 Clacton Road
LONDON
E17 8AR
*Listings of poetry events in the
capital.*

POETRY NOTTINGHAM
Martin Holroyd
39 Cavendish Road
Long Eaton

NOTTINGHAM
NG10 1HT

**POETRY NOTTINGHAM
PUBLICATIONS**
9 Charnwood Avenue
Keyworth
NOTTINGHAM
NG12 5JA
Poetry.

POETRY NOW
4 Hythegate
WERRINGTON
PE4 6ZP
Poetry.

POETRY PROSE PICTURES
52 Wimbledon Park Road
LONDON
SW18 5HS

POETRY REVIEW QUARTERLY
c/o The National Poetry Centre
22 Betterton St
LONDON
WC2H 9BU

POETRY ROUND
c/o The National Poetry Centre
22 Betterton Street
LONDON
WC2H 9BU

POETRY WALES
26 Andrew's Close
Heolgerrig
MERTHYR TYDFIL
CF48 1SS

POLYGON EXPLORER GUIDES
51 East Park Close
Ardwick
MANCHESTER
M13 9SD
Tel 0161 273 4995
*Est. 1988 to produce short runs of
students' 'Map Packs' as a low-cost
record for those involved in Don
Lee's fieldwork in pioneering
footpath routes and urban safaris
in and around the Manchester
region.*

POLYGON RESOURCES
P.O. Box 3
Hedge End
SOUTHAMPTON
SO3 4ZW
School Textbooks.

POMA
'Ellan Beg Vannin'
17 Mendip Drive
BOLTON
BL2 6LQ
Family History.

POMES
(ex Jane Publishing)
Adrian Spendlow
23 Bright Street
YORK
YO2 4XS
Tel 01904 64086
*Poetry societies were reeling with
shock today that poetry is for
everyone! Questions are being
asked in the house 'What's for
tea?'. Yes, poetry is getting vocal -
ordinary people are reading it,
some of them right out loud - join
us.*

POOLBEG PRESS
Knocksedan House
SWORDS
Co Dublin
Ireland

POOLE HISTORICAL TRUST
103 Orchard Avenue
Parkstone
POOLE
BH14 8AH
*Spirit of Poole tells the story of how
the town faced up to its post-war
problems in the years from 1953 to
1963. Available at £13.99
(including p&p) Contains 218pp
and 166 illustrations.
Poole and World War II by John
Hillier, Harold Bennett and Derek
Beamish. Reprint now available.
Price £11.99 plus £3 p&p. The
foreword by Lord Louis
Mountbatten was written a week
Before his murder and is his last
published work.*

THE POPPY AND THE OWL
The Secretary
The Friends of the Liddle Collection
Brotherton Library
University of Leeds
LS2 9JT
Tel 0113 2335566
*The journal of Friends of the Liddle
Collection which is an archive of
personal experience during the 14-
18 War. Full colour reproductions
as well as b&w. £10 pa.*

POPPYLAND PUBLISHING
13 Kings Arms Street
NORTH WALSHAM
NR28 9JX

POPULACE PRESS
Mary Cooke
31 Malmesbury Road
CHIPPENHAM
SN15 1PS

H PORDES
383 Cockfosters Road
COCKFOSTERS
EN4 0JS
Tel 0181 449 2524
*Reprints of Library Reference tools
such as The British Museum Subject
Index 1881-1940; Bibliografia
Hispona-Americana; Canadian
catalogue of books and historical
basics such as L.F.Saltzman's'
English Industries of the Middle
Ages' &' English Industry of the
Middle Ages'; the Shakesperian
dictionary; the complete works of
William Shakespeare in one
volume; etc. Also remainder dealer.*

PORTFOLIO COMMUNICATIONS
c/o Ms Sheila Gimson
27 Emperor Gate
LONDON
SW7 4HX

PORTIA PUBLISHING
Beauchamp Cottage
Abbey Hill
KENILWORTH
CV8 1LW
Tel 01926 58778

POTPOURRI PUBLICATIONS
Charlotte Boggis-Clarke
12 Silver Street
NEWPORT PAGNELL

MK16 OEP
*"'Perpetual Springtime' is a
delicious mixture of stories about
people and places, of poems and
of thought-provoking pieces in a
most attractive magazine of
variety." (from the Foreword by
Canon David Goldie).
Perpetual Springtime: an
Autobiographical Anthology; ISBN
0 904063 26 7; 235pp, £4.99
includes contribution to Newport
Pagnell Church Restoration Fund.*

POWER PUBLICATIONS
Mike Power
Clayford Avenue
FERNDOWN
BH22 9PQ
Tel 01202 875 223
Local interest and pub walk series.

POWERCUT
BM Powercut
LONDON
WC1N 3XX
*Anti-sexist magazine for and by
women and men, seeking to be as
accessible as possible, with views,
arguments, experiences of ordinary
people, plus ace cartoons. Never
academic or boring waffle. Sexual
politics for now: sharp, realistic,
close to home.*

POWYSLAND CLUB
c/o Trewern Hall
WELSHPOOL
SY21 8DT
Historic Local Photography.

PRACTICAL HISTORY
121 Railton Road
London
SE24
*The battle for Hyde Park, ruffians,
radicals and ravers. Setting the
scene for Hyde Park battles,
accounts of riots from 1855-1994.
Free but send A5 s.a.s.e.*

PRAXIS BOOKS
Rebecca Smith
'Sheridan'
Broomers Hill Lane
PULBOROUGH
RH20 2DU
Tel 01798 873 504
*New and reissued titles fiction and
non-fiction. Small but growing. First
title was ambitious but was a big
hit.*

PRECIOUS PEARL PUBLICATIONS
Peter Geofrey Paul Thompson
71 Harrow Crescent
ROMFORD
RM3 7BJ
*Publishes the People's Poetry
Magazine, and the twin once
annual journals, "Romantic Heir"
and the "Cadmium Blue Literary
Journal", specialists in the literature
of the romantic school and
traditional lyrical work.*

PRELUDE
Darren Bentley
74 Monteith Crescent
BOSTON
PE21 9AY
*Music art fashion publication.
Mainly dealing with the extreme*

underground music underground
art underground fashion. A
publication for the deadly 90s.
PREPOSTEROUS PUBLICATIONS
P.O. Box 589
St John Street
CHESTER
CH1 1AA
Tel 01244 831 531 ext 245
*A small publishing company based
in Chester dealing with a wide
range of material.*

**PRE-SCHOOL PLAYGROUPS
ASSOCIATION**
61-63 Kings Cross Road
LONDON
WC1X 9LL
Education.

PRESCOT & WHITSON WRITERS
12 Aspinall Street
Prescot
MERSEYSIDE
L35 5RU

Mike PRESTON MUSIC
The Glengarry
3 Thornton Grove
MORECAMBE
LA4 5PU

PRESTON OTHER PAPER
P.O. BOX 172
PRESTON
PR1 4BU

PREST ROOTS PRESS
P. Larkin
34 Alpine Court
KENILWORTH
CV8 2GP
Tel 01926 592 778
*Seeks to unite a distinctive
contemporary poetry with the best
of traditional fine printing at
affordable prices.*

PRETANI
638 Springfield Road
BELFAST
BT12 7DY

PREVIOUS PARROT PRESS
Dennis Hall
The Foundry
Church Hanborough
WITNEY
OX8 8AB
Tel 01993 881 260
*Previously Hanborough Parrott, PPP
seemed more alluring alliteratively.
Limited editions (100 to 180 copies)
finely printed with a strong
emphasis on illustra-tion. Some
copies hand coloured. Prose,
poetry, drawings and books on
aspects of illustration.*

PRIAPUS PRESS
John Cotton
37 Lombardy Drive
BERKHAMPSTEAD
Fine press.

**PRICE GUIDE PRODUCTIONS AND
PUBLICATIONS**
125 East Barnet Road
NEW BARNET
EN4 8RF
Bibliography.

Mr Do Run Ron PRICE
3 Westhill
Stantonbury

MILTON KEYNES
MK14 6BG
*Defunct officer of moribund SPG.
(see also Prince Chameleon)*

Graham PRIESTLEY
22 Cherry Tree Crescent
BALERNO
EH14 5AL
Fishing.

PRINCE CHAMELEON
Christina Manolsecu
address lost
*Defunct officer of moribund SPG.
(see also R A Price)*

PRINCELET EDITIONS
Annetta Predetti
25 Princelet Street
LONDON
E7 6QH

PRINCIPIA
15 Hillcrest Drive
Slackhead
MILNTHORPE
LA7 7BB

PRINTABILITY PUBLISHING
15 Moorland Close
WOLVISTON VILLAGE
TS22 5LX

BCM PRINTS
LONDON
WC1N 3XX

PRINTWISE PUBLICATIONS
B68 Brunswick Business Park
Brunswick Enterprise
LIVERPOOL

PRION
J Wilson (Booksales)
Lane End Road
Sands Industrial Estat
HIGH WYCOMBE
HP12 4HG

PRIORY STUDIOS
Erik Russell
252 Belsize Road
LONDON
NW6 4BT

PRIORY BOOKS
28 Eccleshall Road
Walton
STONE
ST15 0HA

PRISM PRESS
2 South Street
BRIDPORT
DT6 3NQ

PRIVATE LIBRARIES ASSOCATION
David Chambers
Ravelston
South View Road
PINNER
HA5 3YD
Collectors.

PROCESSED TAPES
1st Floor
22 Lutton Place
EDINBURGH
EH8 9PE
*Badges to order and Chasing
Rainbows 'zine.*

PROMISE PUBLICATIONS
2 Meon Walk

Riverdene
BASINGSTOKE
RG21 2DX
Children's Non-fiction.

**PROMOTIONAL REPRINT
COMPANY**
Harvey's Books
Magna Road
WIGSTON
LE8 2ZH
Children's non-fiction.

PROMOTION MAGAZINE
(see Purple Patch)

PROSPECT PUBLICATIONS
Buckley House
Manston
STURMINSTER NEWTON
DT10 1EZ

PROTEAN PUBLICATIONS
Flat 4
34 Summer Field Crescent
Edgbaston
BIRMINGHAM
B16 0ER
Poetry.

PROUD
Suite 401
302 Regent St
LONDON
W1R 5AL

N.D. PROUDLOCK
181 West Park Drive (West)
LEEDS
LS8 2BE
History of Leeds Tramways.

PROVIDENCE PRESS (WHITSTABLE)
John & Lesley Dench
22 Plough Lane
Swalecliffe
WHITSTABLE
CT5 2NZ
*Self-publishes poetry, short stories
and essays. Original idea to final
product. Other writers published in
'Scriptor'.
New: Vol.6 of Lifelines (poetry
collection) now available, 20 pp.,
£1, ISBN 1872563651.
Scriptor, a new magazine of writing
for the South-East. 72 pps, £2.99,
ISBN 1872563015. Every two
years. Next edition to be published
October 1998.*

PROVIDENCE PRESS
Mr Martin Firrell
90 Victoria Road
LONDON
NW6 6QA

PRYOR PUBLICATIONS
75 Dargate Road
Yorkletts
WHITSTABLE
CT5 3AE

PRYTANIA
126 Bevan Street
LOWESTOFT
NR32 2AQ

PSYCHOPOETICA
Geoff Lowe
Dept. of Psychology,
University of Hull
HULL
HU6 7RX
Tel 01482 465 581

*A magazine of psychologically-
based poetry. Two issues per year,
plus special anthologies.
Established 1980. International
contributors and new writers.*

PSYCHOLOGICAL LIBRARIES
Michael Carr-Jones
P.O. Box 1193
POOLE
BH14 8PT
Tel 01202 739 369
*Distribution to hypnotherapy
psychotherapy association health
education units doctors interested in
alternative medicine.*

PSYSYS LIMITED
Euring, Prof., Dr., A. Sofronion
33, Marlborough Road
SWINDON
SN31 1PH
*"Joyful Parenting", ISBN 09527956
1 2. Deals with pre-natal & post
natal influences.
"The Management of Computing",
ISBN 09527956 0 4. Concerned
with the development &
management of systems & people
in organisations and academia.
"A Town Called Morphou". ISBN
09527956 2 0. Collection of poems
with forceful philosophical
simplicity, metaphysical, romantic...*

P.T.L. PUBLICATIONS
10 Richmond Park
WREXHAM
LL12 8AB
Biography.

PUBLICATIONS UNIT
Department of Adult Education
University Park
Nottingham
NG7 2RD
Tel 0115 951 4427
*The Local Historian's Glossary and
Vade Mecum 2nd Edition, by Joy
Bristow, £8.95 incl p&p.
Sounding Boards: Oral Testimony
and the Local Historian by David
Marcombe, £5.95 incl p&p.
Complete list of Nottingham
University local history titles
available from above.*

PUFFIT PUBLICATIONS
47 South Hill Park
LONDON
NW3 2SS
Music.

PUG e-zine
http://www.pugzine.com/
*Daily Telegraph 10/12/96 rave
review: 'a haul of bizarre features
you'd be hard pushed to find in
print ... engaging graphics and
links to hundreds of underground
Web sites.'*

PULLET PRESS
Penny Berry
Oak Cottage
Lower Road
Middleton
SUDBURY
CO10 7NS
Fine printer.

PULLINGERS
56 High Street
EPSOM
KT19 8AP

Local History.

PULP BOOKS DIRECT
60 Alexander Road
LONDON
N19 3LQ
Tel 0171 494 2479
*Hartnett, P.P. 'Call Me.' An
exploration of the world of contact
ads with the emphasis on sleazy
adventures as he favours the gay
press. £6.99, free p&p in UK. ISBN
1901072002.*

PULP FACTION
Elaine Palmer
60 Alexander Road
LONDON
N19 3PQ
Tel 0171 263 2090
*Pulp Faction is an independent
press specialising in new
(sometimes experimental) fiction.
Publishes regular anthologies
(quarterly) and occasional novels.
"Fission", various inc. Eroica
Mildmay, Nicholas Royle, Jamie
Jackson, Amy Prior.
New: PALMER, Elaine, ed., 'The
Living Room,' May 1996, £6.99.
'Skin,' 20 stories from new writers,
1995, 128 pp., ISBN 1-899571-00-
0, £5.99.
'Technopagan,' themes on media,
music and technology, 1995, 128
pp., ISBN 1-899571-01-9, £6.99.
'Homelands,' living space and
relationships, 1996, 128 pp., ISBN
1-899571-02-7, £6.99.
Unsolicited mss (with sae.)
welcome.*

PULSE PUBLICATIONS
26 Burnside Gardens
Clarkston
GLASGOW
G75 7QS

PUMPKIN PIE PUBLICATIONS
P.O. Box 125
SUTTON
SM1 2DT

PURPLE HEATHER PUBLICATIONS
Richard Mason
16 Rokeby Gardens
Headingly
LEEDS
LS6 3JZ
Tel 01532 740 325
*Founded 1980. Publishers of small
press magazines; individual
collections and audio cassettes of
poetry. Promoters of 'live' poetry/
literature in performance on a
regular basis via Leeds Alternative
Cabaret. 'A major literary and
cultural figure ... ' THE NORTHERN
STAR.*

PURPLE PATCH
8 Beaconview House
Charlemont Farm
WEST BROMWICH
B71 3PL

PURPOSE PRESS
159 Meadowview
DROGHEDA
County Louth
Republic of Ireland
Poetry.

THE PUTNEY PRESS
Richard Nathanson

P.O. Box 515
LONDON
SW15 6LQ
Tel 0181 788 2718
Initially set up to publish and promote 'Walk to the Moon' - the illustrated story of the artist Albert Houthuesen.

PYRFORD PRESS
Marion Malcher
8 Lincoln Drive
WOKING
GU22 8RL
Design and print services provided to authors, everything from typesetting to jacket design, paperbacks and hardbacks produced.
Phone 01932 349 828 for discussion and free quote.
Titles: "Blank Pages- Soviet Genocide against the Polish people", by G.C. Malcher, ISBN 1 897984 006
"Lakeland Family Mystery Trail", by S. Dover, ISBN 1 897984 02 2

PYTHAGORAS PUBLISHING
R Phellas
PO Box 10370
LONDON
NW2 7WE
0181 452 7916
Mathematical texts for student revision.

PYTHIA PRESS
Cecilia Boggis
7 Silver Street
GLASTONBURY
BA6 8BS
Reprints of Rare Writing by Remarkable Women. Our first couple - Olympe de Gouges (The Rights of Women) and Margaret Fell (Women's Speaking Justified) - sold out. Now preparing a new onslaught. Send for details.

QED
John Bibby
1 Straylands Grove
YORK

YO3 0EB
Funmath '96! is the new Mathematics Calender fromQED. We are also booksellers and can get you any book in print.

QI MAGAZINE
11 Wilverly Crescent
NEW MALDEN
KT3 5LN
Qi Magazine published by Michael Tse is both an educational and commercial magazine which promotes understanding of Qi Gong, aspects of Chinese medicine and culture.

QUA IBOE FELLOWSHIP
7 Donegall Square
WEST BELFAST
BT1 6JE
Biography.

QUALM PUBLISHING
John Stoppi
665 Finchley Road
LONDON
NW2 2HN

QUARRY PUBLICATIONS
64 Quarry Avenue
Bebington
WIRRAL
L63 3HF

THE QUARTER-DAY PRESS
18 Fitzwarren Gardens
LONDON
N19 3TP
Original illustrated books in limited editions of forty copies.

QUARTOS MAGAZINE
(see The New Writer)

QUARTZ
Dept of Literature & Languages
Nottingham Poly
Clifton Lane
Clifton
NOTTINGHAM
NG11 8NS

QUAY BOOKS EXETER
Chris Smith
Tuck Mill Cottage
Payhembury
HONITON
EX14 0HF
Quay Books was formed in 1989 to publish "Village Profiles", "The Fourth Wise Man" and in association with Geerings of Ashford "100 Not Out", all titles by Chris Smith. Chief interest local history or fiction of merit.

QUEENSCOURT PUBLISHING
David Cox
1 Queens Court
Kenton Lane
HARROW
HA3 8RN
Queenscourt Publishing is a small-scale imprint for light fiction and poetry.
Titles include: "But Mostly Laughter"; stories by Paul Feakes "Soundings"; poems by Daphne Schiller.

QUEENSCOURT PUBLISHING
S Payne
47 Radcliffe Road
Winchmore Hill

LONDON
N21 2SD

QUEENSPARK BOOKS
Carmel Kelly
Lewis Cohen Urban Studies Centre
68 Grand Parade
BRIGHTON
BN2 2JY
Tel 01273 571 916
Queen Spark is a Community Writing and Publishing group based in Brighton. We believe that anyone who wannts to can be a writer and our aim is to encourage publishing writing by people who do not normally get into print.

QUEST
BCM-SCL Quest
LONDON
WC1N 3XX

QUEST BOOKS
2 Slievenabrock Avenue
NEWCASTLE
BT33 0HZ

QUEST
YUFOS
106 Lady Anne Road
Soothill
BATELY
WF17 0PY

QUESTION PRESS
Maryanne Aytoun-Ellis
'Brookside'
Southover High Street
LEWES
BN7 1HU
Tel 01273 474 893
Young printmaker/sculptor & designer/artist using the intimate environment of books to more fully express, transform & unfold ideas that appear in other areas of their work.

QUIETWORD
Sue
Stable Cottage
EASTON
IP13 0EN
Her introductory letter mentions 'Peaceful Monthly' zine, 'bi-monthly,' 'psychoacoustik quarterly.' Take your pick. 'An occasional seepage onto paper from the weeping spirit .... journal of zebraic trace archaeology fictual faction.' No price. Starting 'end of September ... end of October' 1996.

THE QUILLIAM PRESS
Tim Winter
80 Lamble Street
LONDON
NW5 4AB
Books by and for Britain's largest minority. A unique showcase of muslim cultural and spiritual endeavour.
Knud Holmboe. "Desert Encounter." 218pp. repr of 1936 first ed. ISBN 1 872038 10 7. Adventures of a Danish Muslim in Mussolini's Libya. 1994. Pbk £8.95
Ruqayyah Waris Maqsood. "The Muslim Marriage Guide". 141pp. ISBN 1 872038 11 5. Guidance on marital and sexual problems among British Muslims. 1995. Pbk £5.95

QUIM
BCM 82
LONDON
WC1N 3XX

QUINCE TREE PRESS
116 Hardwick Lane
BURY ST EDDMUNDS
IP33 2LE
Tel 01284 753 228
Following the death of the publisher, J.L. Carr, Quince Tree titles can still be obtained from R.D. & J.M.Carr. Send s.a.s.e. for full list of titles.

QUINCY'S COOKERY BOOK
Ian Dowding
42 High Street
SEAFORD
Tel 01323 95490
A book of recipes from this award-winning restaurant: unusual exciting easy to follow and illustrated with charming drawings.

QUOIN PUBLISHING
The Barn
36A North Road
Kirkburton
HUDDERSFIELD
HD8 0RH

QWF
Jo Good
80 Main Street
LINTON
DE12 6QA
Quality women's fiction magazine, extending the bounds of women's fiction.

R & B PUBLISHING
3 Inglebert Street
LONDON
EC1R 1XR
Tel/fax 0171 837 3854
A new firm specialising in reprints of classic texts. Third title available. Send for list.

RADIO SOCIETY OF GREAT BRITAIN
Lambdo House
Cranborne Road
POTTERS BAR

EN6 3JE
Electronic Engineering.

RAFFEEN PRESS
Union Place
FOWEY
PL23 1BY.

RA HOOR KUIT
14 Linden Close
EXMOUTH
EX8 4JW

RAILWAY CUTTINGS
Tony Hancock Appreciation Society
56 Raddlebarn Farm Drive
Bourneville
BIRMINGHAM
B29 6UW
Newsletter.

RAIN PRESS
David Wells
6 Carmarthen Road
Westbury on Trym
BRISTOL
BS9 4DU
Publishing materials written by the editor/author, in the fields of education. Philosophy and cross-cultural psychology, etc.

RAINBOW
Mr David A Stringer
96 Redhall Crescent
LEEDS
LS11 8DY

RAISING HELL
Box 32
52 Call Lane
LEEDS
LS1 6DT

RALLYMAPS
P.O. Box 11
ROMSEY
SO51 8XX
Old Mapping From the Official O.S. Supplier - 60', 25' and 6' County series. For details of specific archived maps please enclose SAE. Comprehensive book and map catalogue for Local and Family Historians. Send 2 x 1st class stamps mentioning Local History Magazine.

THE RAMPANT LIONS PRESS
12 Chesterton Road
CAMBRIDGE
CB4 3AB

RANNOCH GILLAMOOR PRESS
51 Stepney Avenue
SCARBOROUGH
YO12 5BW
Short Stories.

RATHASKER PRESS
c/o Ryde School
Queens Road
RYDE
Isle Of Wight
PO33 3BE
Illuminations - East & S African writing. Editor Simon Lewis.

RATS CAN READ BOOKS
10 Fox Road
STEVENAGE
SG1 1JD

RATTLER'S TALE
BCM Keyhole

LONDON
WC1N 3XX

RAVEN ARTS PRESS
P.O. Box 1430
Finglas
DUBLIN 11
Republic of Ireland

RAVENCROFT PUBLICATIONS
Haydn House
Castle Street
LLANGOLLEN
LL20 8NY

RAVENSCOT PUBLISHING
Melvin Lyons
Brampton House
10 Queen Street
NEWCASTLE
ST5 1ED
Tel 01782 639109

S A & M J RAYMOND
6 Russet Avenue
EXETER
EX1 3QB
Tel 01392 462158
Raymonds Original Pollbooks - Important sources for local historians and genealogists in facsimile. Volumes forthcoming for London, Westminster, Lincolnshire, Norfolk, Norwich, Somerset, Suffolk and Yorkshire West Riding. Full details from above.
Lincolnshire: a genealogical bibliography. The essential guide for Lincolnshire family and local historians. Price £8.10.
Cheshire: a genealogical bibliography. The essential guide for genealogists and local historians by Stuart Raymond. 2 vols £17.25 incl p&p.
Westminster Poll Book 1774. An essential source for genealogists and local historians, now available in facsimile, price £19.00.

R.B. PUBLICATIONS
Westfield House
Coleshill Heath Road
BIRMINGHAM
B37 7HY
Art.

RCGP [SCOTLAND]
47 Orchard Street
MOTHERWELL
ML1 3JE
Tel 01698 373341, fax: 01698 286801
'Hoolet,' the Scottish Magazine of the RCGP; forum for GPs in Scotland, ISSN 1357-308X.

READ THIS
70 Walstead Road
Delves
WALSALL
WS5 4LX

REDBECK PRESS
24 Airefville Road
Frizinghall
BRADFORD
BD9 4HH
Catalogue of poetry publications.

S REEDER
4 Moor Court
WHITBURN
SR6 7JU
<A Victorian Village School (Mr

Grundy at Whitburn) by Sybil Reeder. A history of education and one remarkable village schoolteacher and his family. 48 pages, 12 illustrations, £2.95 plus 50p postage.

READY RHINO PUBLICATIONS
Tim J. Latham
31 Braemore Close
THATCHAM
RG13 4XP
Shipbuilding History in Barrow-in-Furness.

REAL ART
Malcolm Gibson
'Gilesway'
How Mill
CARLISLE
CA4 9JT
Tel 0228 70415
A bi-annual limited edition publication devoted entirely to visuals. Malcolm Gibson, Andrew Law and James Hall contribute to every issue. Artists are invited to print or make their own editions for inclusion. Other projects include limited edition books and boxes.

REALITY STREET EDITIONS
Ken Edwards
4 Howard Court
Peckham Rye
LONDON
SE15 3PH
Linguistically innovative poetries for the 20th centuries.
Forthcoming in January is "Out of Everywhere", a major anthology of experimental writing by women in Britain and North America.
Recent titles: Fanny Howe: "O'Clock", 104pp, £6.50
Peter Riley: "Distant Points", 64pp, £6.50

REAPER BOOKS
11 Brickley Acres
Eastcombe
STROUD
GL6 7DU
Tel 01452 770 440
Reaper Books is the self-publishing imprint of artist/writer Leo Baxendale, creator of Minnie the Minx, The Bash Street Kids - and latterly The Guardian strip 'I Love You Baby Basil!'

REARDON PUBLISHING
N. Reardon
56 Upper Norwood Street
Leckhampton
CHELTENHAM
GL53 0DU
Family publishing company covering the Cotswold area. Postcards prints driving guides and walking books. in fact mostly anything covering tourism in the Cotswold and nearby counties.

REBEL PRESS
84b Whitechapel High Street
LONDON
E1 7QX
Publishers of anarchist, situationist and related titles.
Main titles: Raol Vaneigen, "Revolution of everyday Life"
Max Stirner: "Ego and It's Own".

RECO-PRESS

22 Goldstone Crescent
HOVE
BN3 6BA

THE RED CANDLE PRESS
M.L. McCarthy, or Helen
9 Milner Road
WISBECH
PE13 2LR
Candelabrium - Poetry magazine of the Traditionalist Revival - one double issue each June.

REDCLIFFE EDITION
68 Barrowgate Road
LONDON
W4 4QU

RED EARTH PUBLICATIONS
Alan McFadzean
7 Silver Street
Marton
ULVERSTON
LA12 0NQ
Tel 01229 64172
Local history; local interest. Anything that falls loosely into this bracket and relates to the north of England - we will publish.

RED GULL PRESS
St Bridgets
Radcliffe Road
HITCHIN

RED HEN PRESS
Shirley Jones
2 Croham Park Avenue
SOUTH CROYDON
CR2 7HH
Tel 0181 686 4178
Shirley Jones publishes her own artist books of etchings aquetints and mezzotints. The accompanying poems prose pieces and translations from Old English are written set and printed letterpress by her on hand-made paper in editions limited to 40 copies.

RED PEPPER
Hilary Wainwright, Editor
3 Gunthorpe Street
LONDON
E1 7RP
Tel 0171-247 1702, fax 0171-247 1695
e-mail:
redpepper@online.rednet.co.uk
Web: http://www.rednet.co.uk/redpepper/
Monthly journal of green and radical Left ideas; check standard ann.sub. with publisher: special offers available to campaigns, currently £6 reduction for members of London Cycling Campaign.

THE REDLAKE PRESS
Ursula Freeman
Brook House
CLUN
SY7 8LY
Tel 0158 84524
Private press producing limited edition hand-made books, mostly poetry. Also hand-printed stationery, ephemera. Formerly The Unidentified Flying Printer.

GR (GEORGE REDMOND) BOOKS
Knotty Lane
Lepton
HUDDERSFIELD
HD8 0ND

RED POST PRESS
Mr Chris Winter
39a Red Post Hill
LONDON
SE24 9JJ
A small press set up to publish independent writing by football supporters.

REDSTONE PRESS
7a St Lawrence Terrace
LONDON
W10 5SU
Tel 0171 221 5219

REDWOOD PUBLISHING
Kelly Pennhaligon
22 Hermitage Road
LONDON
N4 1DE
Tel 0171 312 2717

REDWORDS
31 Cottenham Road
Walthamstow
LONDON
E17 6RP

REID-THOMPSON PUBLISHING
2 Limes Court
Limes Avenue
Mickleover
DERBY
DE3 5DB
Local Social History.

REEVES TELECOMMUNICATIONS LABS LTD
John de Rivaz
West Towan House
Porthtowan
TRURO
TR4 8AX
How to use home computers to draw fractal images. Subscribe to get a free sample copy.

REFLECTIONS
P.O. Box 70
SUNDERLAND
SR1 1DU

REFLECTIONS OF A BYGONE AGE
15 Debdale Lane
Keyworth
NOTTINGHAM
NG12 5HT

REGIONAL PUBLICATIONS
A. Waller
5 Springfield Road
ABERGAVENNY
NP7 5TD
Tel 0187 385 2207
Publishers of Leisure Guides and Specialist Books connected with History and Hobbies Educational.

REID REVIEW
8 Mendip Court
Avonley Village
Avonley Road
LONDON
SE14 5EU

REMI ENTERPRISES
29 Granby Drive
Balderton
NEWARK
NG24 3JD

RENE PUBLISHING
Witham Villa
Cosby Road
Broughton Astley

LEICESTER
LE9 6PA
Poetry.

REPUBLIC NEWSLETTER
P.O. Box 2698
LONDON
W14 9ZT
Tel 0181 8759854
Newsletter of the Republican association. Not the IRA - English non-monarchists.

RESONANCE
London Musicians' Collective
Unit B1
Lafone House
Leathermarket St
LONDON
SE1 3HN
Bi-annual magazine from the London Musicians' Collective covering all aspects of improvised and experimental music. Interviews, feature articles, reviews &c. Current issue comes with a free CD and concentrates on the use of samplers in new music. ISSN 1352-772X. Price £5.00.

RESPONSES
Tony Rollinson
20 Teddler Road
Bridgemary
GOSPORT
PO13 0XP
'Responses' was a series of twelve pamphlet throughout 1991 featuring new work by: Abse Armitage Buck Chaloner Clarke Cobbing Fisher O'Sullivan Sheppard Tabor and others. Their work was `Responded' to and they in turn received a right of reply ... original! Cheques to A. Rollinson.

REVELATION PRESS
Hertford
Mead Lane
HERTFORD
SG13 7AG

REVLOC BOOKS
Y Gilros
Off Vinegar Hill
RHOSLLANNERCHRUGOG
LL14 1EL
Sports.

RHIANNON'S WHEEL PRODUCTIONS
Lyulf Brand
The Cottage
School Road
Finstock
CHIPPING NORTON
OX7 3DJ
Publish Politics, Philosophy, Anti-Culture, Alternative Fiction, Poetry, Art.

RHINOCEROS MAGAZINE
Kevin Smith
Flat 3
90 University Street
BELFAST
BT7
Tel 01232 326 682
Quarterly poetry journal including articles of cultural interest and literary interviews specialising in longer sections of writer's work: long poems sequences etc.

International subscribers & contributors. 100-150 pp b/w artwork.

THE RHINOCEROUS PRESS
24 Manor House Way
BRIGHTLINGSEA
CO7 0QN

RHYME TIME
Allison Magee
Flat 11
Maritime Court
Promenade
SOUTHPORT
PR8 1SP
Quarterly magazine for rhyming poetry, pen pal ads, readers page and list of current poetry competitions; £2 per issue, cheques payable to 'Rhyme Time'; s.a.e for all enquiries and submissions.

THE RIALTO
Editors John Wakeman, Michael Mackmin
32 Grosvenor Road
NORWICH
NR2 2PZ
Tel 01603 666455
'I'm not sure that you want us in SPG Yearbook. We have only one publication.'

John RICHARDS
934 Society St
Lawrence College in Thanet
RAMSGATE
CT11 7AE
Railways.

HEATHER M RICHARDSON PUBLISHING
51 Garden Walk
CAMBRIDGE
CB4 3EW

RICHMOND LOCAL HISTORY SOCIETY
7 Leyborne Park
KEW
Richmond
TW9 3HB
Richmond Boy by Fred Windsor, a fascinating portrait of the beautiful Thameside town as seen by a schoolboy between 1914 and 1933. Illustrations by the author and contemporary postcards. 48 pages. £3.50 plus 50p postage.

Miss G RICKARD
99 Strangers Lane
CANTERBURY
CT1 3XN
Kent Settlement (Poor Law) Records: A guide and catalogue - Part 2: West Kent (Diocese of Rochester) by Gillian Rickard. Catalogues by parish all known surviving settlement records for the Diocese of Rochester, comprising the western third of the pre-1974 county of Kent. ISBN 0-9521828-1-5. 68pp. £4.50 plus 50p p&p inland.
Vagrants, Gypsies and 'Travellers' in Kent 1572–1948. Paperback, 80pp, price £5.00 (£5.50 inc. p&p inland), overseas postage rates on request. A history of travellers in Kent together with a catalogue of records and sources, held in and outside Kent.

Kent Non-Conformists - recent publications: Canterbury Blackfriars Baptist Chapel, births and burials 1780-1836 - a complete transcript, indexes, introduction, £3.90 (incl p&p) - Kent Dissenting Ministers' Declarations 1689-1836. Lists 291 non-conformist ministers, introduction, index £3.90 (incl p&p). Overseas postage rates on application.

JOHN RIDGWAY BOOKS
Miramar
Rowney Green Lane
Alvechurch
BIRMINGHAM
B48 7QF
Frank Sinatra.

RIGHT NOW BOOKS
36c Sisters Avenue
LONDON
SW11 5SQ
Tel 0171 223 8987
Travel books and journals on South East Asia, Thailand, Burma, Laos, Vietnam, Singapore and Indonesia.

P. RILEY
27 Sturton Street
CAMBRIDGE
CB1 2QE
Poetry.

RING O'BELLS PUBLISHING
62 Beechwood Road
SOUTH CROYDON
CR2 0AA
Tel 0181 651 6080

RINGPRESS BOOKS
Spirella Building
Bridge Road
LETCHWORTH
SG6 4ET
Animals.

J. RITCHIE
40 Beansburn
KILMARNOCK
KA3 1RH
Poetry. Religion.

RIVELIN GRAPHEME PRESS
The Annexe
Kennet House
19 High Street
HUNGERFORD
RG17 0NL
Tel 01488 83480
Not just a bookshop but a major poetry imprint. Get lists.

RIVERS ORAM PRESS
144 Hemingford Road
LONDON
N1 1DE

RNLI NORFOLK AND SUFFOLK RESEARCH GROUP
Mark Roberts
4 Paines Orchard
CHEDDINGTON
LU7 0SN
Mark Roberts & Nicholas Leach: 'The 37ft Oakley Lifeboats: a History 1957-1994.' Focuses on design and innovative self-righting system. £5 inc. p&p. Please make cheques payable to 'RNLI Norfolk and Suffolk Research Group.'

ROADS

Gordon Smith
49 Meynell Heights
LEEDS
LS11 9PY

ROBDAWG
David Robinson
200 Belper Lane
BELPER
DE56 2UJ
Tel 01773 824 527
Name the sport or leisure interest (any facet) and hopefully before too long we will have a book out on the subject. Similarly with quiz books and general interest on Derbyshire. Mystery thrillers the publisher's own pet subject.

ROBERTS MEDALS PUBLICATIONS
6 Titan House
Calleva Park
ALDERMASTON
RG7 4QW
Military Medals

Mr David ROBINSON
Robdawg
200 Belper Lane
BELPER
DE5 2UJ
Anything to do with sport and leisure. Run in conjunction with, and as an aid to, sport and leisure consultancy.

THE ROBINSWOOD PRESS
Christopher Marshall
30 South Avenue
STOURBRIDGE
DY8 3XY
Tel 01384 397475
Specialises in educational publications, particularly in remedial education, Steiner education, etc.

THE ROCKET PRESS
Jonathan Stephenson
Millcroft Stables
Berry Lane
Blewbury
DIDCOT
OX11 9QJ
Fine Printer.

ROCKINGHAM PRESS
11 Musley Lane
WARE
SG12 7EN
Poetry. Local History.

RODMELL VILLAGE PRESS
c/o 3 Terrace Cottages
Rodmell
LEWES
BN7 3HL
Local Travel Guides.

J. ROGERS
22 Windermere Avenue
Scartho
GRIMSBY
DN33 3DG
Local History.

Douglas ROME
9 Ellisland Drive
Summerhill
DUMFRIES
DG2 9DZ

ROMER PUBLICATIONS
Hubert de Brouwer & Harry Melkman

Unit 5
Link Yard
29a Spelman Street
LONDON
E1 6LQ
0171 247 581
Romer Publications is dedicated to high quality publishing in the field of raising critical insight into ideologies. Specialises in children's books, law and history
Titles: *"Dominic Dormouse Goes to Town", by Anthony Wall, London (1993), ISBN 0951150863 £4.95 Prize awarded children's book from ex-BBC editor.*
"Fascism Down the Ages: from Caesar to Hitler, by Frank A. Ridley 1897-1994, London (1991) ISBN 0951150820, £4.95 Ridley's incisive analysis of a current phenonema pervading Christian society.

ROOKBOOK PUBLICATIONS
16 Angle Park Terrace
Edinburgh
EH11 2JX

ROSALBA PRESS
55 St Michael's Lane
HEADINGLEY
LS6 3BR

ROSEC PUBLICATIONS
P.G. Rose
135 Church Road
Shoeburyness
SOUTHEND-ON-SEA
SS3 9EZ
"Cruising Guide to Inns and Taverns - Norfolk Broads", ISBN 0 9515467-5-9 River maps/lock sections. Moorings. Distances. Travel and trading times. Beers available. Restaurant facilities. Photograph and description of pub and surroundings.
New Norfolk Broads In Colour, £5.95
Thames - Sonning to Teddington, ISBN 0 9515467-3-2, £4.95 Thames - Reading to Lechlade, ISBN 0 9515467-4-0, £4.95

ROSEDENE PUBLISHERS
Rose de' Rothschild Schwittau
110 New Road
HADLEIGH
SS7 2BP
Tel 01702 551 569

ROSE LANE WRITERS
Flat 2
14 Ramilies Road
LIVERPOOL 18

Malcolm ROSE
The Workshop
English Passage
LEWES
BN7 2AP
Music.

M. ROSE PRESS
4 Gate Street
LONDON
WC2A 3HP
Freelance Artists Directory.

ROSE'S REPARTEE
P.O. Box 339
SHEFFIELD
S1 3SX

Magazine and organisers of event for tvs etc.

ROSLYN PRESS
Jeff Probst
2 Danvers Road
LONDON
N8 7HH
Lead title is the novella "Bachelor Butterflies" by Jeff Probst. "Probst's dystopian vision operates on a personal and, therefore, universal level...a short but strangely compelling narrative". Sunday Times.

ROUGE
BM Rouge
LONDON
WC1N 3XX

ROUNDOAK PUBLISHING
7 Roundoak Gardens
Nynehead
WELLINGTON
TA21 0BX

H. Aubrey ROWE
26 Comforts Farm Avenue
Hurst Green
OXTED
RH8 9DH
Walks Books.

T.H. ROWLAND
4 De Merley Road
MORPETH
NE61 1HZ
Local Travel.

Norman ROWLEY
Blue Gates
Weston
Lullingfields
SHREWSBURY
SY4 2AA
Local History.

ROXFORD BOOKS
Roxford
HERTINGFORDBURY
SG14 2LF
Asian History.

ROXIMILLION PUBLICATIONS
Bishops Park House
25 Fulham High Street
LONDON
SW6
Occult.

ROYAL ACADEMY OF MUSIC
Marylebone Road
LONDON
NW1 5HT
History of Musical Instruments.

ROYAL BOTANIC GARDENS
Kew
Richmond
TW9 3AB
Botany. Children's non-fiction.

ROYAL COMMISSION ON THE HISTORICAL MONUMENTS OF ENGLAND
Karen Jordan
National Monuments and Record Centre
Kemble Drive
SWINDON
SN2 2GZ
High quality publications on the architecture of england from the earliest times to the present day.

Recent titles include: "Medieval Houses of Kent",
"Swindon: the legacy of a railway town",
"Roman camps in England"

ROYAL GREEN JACKETS
RHQ Royal Green Jackets
Peninsula Barracks
WINCHESTER
SO23 8TS
Military History.

ROYAL MILITARY ACADEMY
Sandhurst
CAMBERLEY
GU15 4PQ
Art.

ROYAL SOCIETY OF EDINBURGH
22-24 George Street
EDINBURGH
EH2 2PQ
Mathematics.

RPR PRESS
5 The Oval
Longfield
DARTFORD
DA3 7HD
Anthologies of new poets.

RUBBERNECK
21 Denham Drive
BASINGSTOKE
RG22 6LT
Free magazine, contents about non-establishment performers, writers, musicians etc.

RUBBER STEREOS (AVON) LTD
Station Road
Midsummer Norton
BATH

RUBBER WHAMMY
Christina Lamb
Top Flat
541 Holloway Road
LONDON
N19 4BT
A rubberstamp catalogue pretending to be a fanzine, Rubber Whammy delivers stunning rubberstamps at cheap prices, gobbles up whatever it pleases and spits the semi-masticated remains onto its pages.

RUBICON PRESS
57 Cornwall Gardens
LONDON
SW7 4BE

RUNETREE PRESS
P.O. Box 1035
LONDON
W2 6ZX
Focusses on interaction of past and present, landscape as a sense of place, local history and sustainable futures. Mainly short run reprints.
* Griffiths, Bill: Saxon voices. *Songs, spells and stories read in Old English with brief commentaries in Modern English by a teacher with long experience in adult education. Audio-tape for students and OE addicts. ISBN 1898577048.*
Runetree Dramascripts:
* McKillop, Menzies: The battle of Maldon: 1993, 22 pp., pbk, ISBN 1898577005, £2.00.
* McKillop, Menzies: Columba,

161

Cuthbert, Caedmon: three plays for radio. 1994, 70 pps, pbk ISBN 1898577021, £4.99.
* Gittings, Robert: The makers of violence: a play in two acts. Authorised reprint of original 1951 Heinemann edition with introduction by John Gittings. ISBN 189857703X.

RUNNING HEAD PUBLISHING
R H Spicer
9 Frederick Place
BRISTOL
BS8 1AS
Local history publishing & supplier of indexes.

RUNPAST PUBLISHING
8 Gwernant Road
CHELTENHAM
GL51 5ES

RUNWISE
15 Priory Road
CHICHESTER
PO19 1NS
Poetry.

RUSHMERE PUBLISHING
32 Rushmere Road
Carlton Colville
LOWESTOFT
NR33 8DA

PETER R.D. RUSSEK PUBLICATIONS
Little Stone House
High Street
MARLOW
Cars.

D.S. RUSSELL
8 McGregor Road
LONDON
W11 1DE
Tel 0171 229 3350
Specialist in poetry and experimental fiction.

RUSSELL HOUSE PUBLISHING
38 Silver Street
LYME REGIS
DT7 3HS
Tel 01297 443 948
Catalogues of many titles covering social work. Also handle Ennabler Publications.

RYBURN PUBLISHING
Tenterfields
Luddendenfoot
HUDDERSFIELD
HX2 6EJ

RYDER PUBLISHING
Deborah Ryder
BCM Box 3406
LONDON
WC1N 3XX
Original and exclusive stories of sado-masochism and related erotica.

SA PUBLISHING
Tony Lee
13 Hazely Combe
ARRETON
Isle of Wight
PO30 3AJ
Established 1989. Specialising in sf/horror stories and genre poetry, non-fiction media fanzine, fantasy art and much more! Three magazine titles.

SABOTAGE EDITIONS
Editor: Karen Eliot
BM Senior
LONDON
WC1N 3XX
Aims to compromise leaders and deliver them to contempt. Uses base women to disorganise the authorities and incite the young, ridicule traditions, dislocate supplies, inflict lascivious music, spread lechery, devalue money and be very naughty indeed. To bring all this to pass we publish 'Smile' magazine.

SAINSBURY PUBLISHING
Auldearn Main Street
Bleasby
NOTTINGHAM
NG14 7GH
Chemistry.

ST CLEMENT'S PRESS
24 Stretford Road
Urmston
MANCHESTER
M41 9JZ

ST. IVES PRINTING AND PUBLISHING
High Street
ST. IVES
TR26 1RS
Local History.

ST. JOSEPH'S WORKSHOPS
190 Bag Lane
Atherton
MANCHESTER
M29 0JZ
Language.

Kirk SESSION
St Luke's Greenock
c/o The Manse
50 Ardgowan Street
GREENOCK
Local History.

ST JAMES PRESS
P.O. Box 701
North Way
Walworth Industrial Estate
ANDOVER
SP10 5YF

ST JAMES PRESS
2-6 Boundary Row
LONDON
SE1 8HP

ST JUSTIN
6E Longrock Industrial Estate
PENZANCE
TR20 8HX

Church of ST. MARY SCULCOATES
Parochial Church Council
c/o 16 Spring Grove Gardens
Sunnybank
HULL
HU13 1JZ
Local History.

ST. MARK'S CHURCH, AMPFIELD
c/o 4 Hookwater Close
Chandler's Ford
EASTLEIGH
SO5 1PS
Story of St. Mark's Church, Ampfield.

ST. PETER'S CENTENARY COMMITTEE:
G. Wheeler
Oak Lodge
30 Delahays Drive
Hale
ALTRINCHAM
WA15 8DP
Local History.

Parish of ST. THOMAS OF CANTERBURY
Clergy House
42 Santos Road
LONDON
SW18 1NS
Local History.

SALMON PUBLICATIONS
Paul Salmon
32 Park Crescent
HORNCHURCH
RM11 1BJ
Tel 01708 743 811
Publishers of 'Tradition'; a quarterly publication devoted to traditional custom and culture. Morris Dancing; Arthurian Legend; Green Man; English Bagpipes; Windmills; Regimental History. Some New Age where applicable to traditional matters. Articles welcome but no payment possible at this stage.

SALMON PRESS
Auburn
UPPER FAIRHILL
Galway
Ireland

SALOPEOT
Mr R Hoult
5 Squires Close
Madeley
TELFORD
TF7 5AU

SALVIA BOOKS
4 Logie Green Gardens
EDINBURGH
EH7 4HE

SAMARA PUBLISHING
Samara House
Tresaith
CARDIGAN
SA43 2JG
Zoology.

SAMHAIN
John Gullidge
19 Elm Grove Road
Topsham
EXETER

EX3 0EQ

SAMPHIRE PRESS
BCM Samphire
LONDON
WC1N 3XX

SANCTUARY PRESS LTD
Alan George
Nash House
Fishponds
LONDON
SW17 7LN
Monthly journal: ACTION, for a true union of Europe.

SANDALL OF FROME
Sherwill
Styles Avenue
FROME
BA11 5JN
Local Economic History.

Mr Chris SANDERS
P.O. Box 4AS
LONDON
W1A 4AS
Tel 0171 637 7467
Over the years editor/publisher of many underground newspapers and interventions.

SANDHILL PRESS: SANDERSON BOOKS
Front Street
Klondyke
CRAMLINGTON
NE23 6RF

SANDPIPER BOOKS
D Bent
22a Langroy Road
LONDON
SW17 7PL

SANTA MARIA PUBLICATIONS
8 Queen's Road
MINSTER
Isle of Sheppey
ME12 2HD
Art. Archaeology.

SAREMA PRESS
15 Beeches Walk
CARSHALTON BEECHES
SM5 4JS
Art. Biography.

SAROS INTERNATIONAL PUBLISHERS
48 Aragon Avenue
Ewell
EPSOM
KT17 2QG

SATEB
(see Worker Esperantist)

SATIS
Malcolm Rutherford
14 Greenhill Place
EDINBURGH
EH10 4BR
Tel 0131 447 3587
Poetry pamphlets including translations of contemporary German poetry. Format of 16pp pamphlets cardbound.

SATORI PRESS
149 Bower Street
BEDFORD
Poetry.

SATURN BOOKS

Ardfallen
Green Hill
FERMOY
Co Cork
Republic of Ireland

I SAWICKI & A BURGESS
342 Hartshill Road
Hartshill
STOKE-ON-TRENT
ST4 7NX
Publish 'Get Connected' a
magazine for pen-pal seekers,
artists, writers, etc.

Geoffrey SAUNDERS
22 New Street
KENILWORTH
CV8 2EZ
Education.

MARK SAUNDERS PUBLICATIONS
1 Austin Close
Irchester
WELLINGBOROUGH
NN9 7AX

SAWD PUBLICATIONS
Plackett's Hole
Bicknor
SITTINGBOURNE
ME9 8BA
Second World War.

SAYERS AND CYMBRON
The Garden
Lissington
LINCOLN
LN3 5AE
Travel in Europe.

DOROTHY L. SAYERS SOCIETY
Rose Cottage
Malthouse Lane
Hurstpierpoint
HASSOCKS
BN6 9JY
Short Stories.

SB PUBLICATIONS
5 Queen Margaret's Road
Loggerheads
MARKET DRAYTON
TF9 4EP

S.C.
Stanford Old Farm House
Leinthall
Starkes
LUDLOW
SY8 2HP
Archaeology.

SCARLET PRESS
5 Montague Road
LONDON
N8 2HN

SCARTHIN BOOKS
The Promenade
Scarthin
Cromford
MATLOCK
DE4 3QF

SCEPTIC TANK PRESS
Anna Livia
5 Marine Road
DUN LAOGHAIRE
Republic of Ireland
Humour.

SCHOOL BOOK FAIRS
M Price
5 Airspeed Road

Priory Industrial Park
CHRISTCHURCH
BH23 4HD
Children's Fiction.

SCIAF
5 Oswald Street
GLASGOW
G1 4QR
Travel in Central America.

SCOPE BOOKS
62 Murray Road
HORNDEAN
PO8 9JL

SCOPE INTERNATIONAL LTD
Nicholas Pine
62 Murray Road
WATERLOOVILLE
PO8 9JL
Privacy, freedom, low-profile tax-
haven, second passport, PT
(perpetual traveller) publishers.

SCORPION PRESS
6 Admirals Walk
Portishead
BRISTOL
BS20 9LE
Mystery Fiction.

**SCOTS INDEPENDENT
(NEWSPAPERS)**
51 Cowane Street
STIRLING
FK8 1ER
Poetry.

SCOTTISH CHILD
347A Pilton Avenue
EDINBURGH
EH5 2LE
Crime.

M.G. SCOTT LIMITED
Michael G. Scott
Blo'Norton Hall
DISS
IP22 2JD
Tel 0195 381 354
Individual letterpress printer
designing and printing from all
handset type. Supplier to
Bookshops, Gift Shops &c. of a
series (8) of 'Little Recipe Books',
packets of Bookplates and Jam
Labels, Writing Paper, Bewick
postcards &C.

SCRATCH
Mark Robinson
24 Nelson Street
The Groves
YORK
YO3 7NJ
International poetry plus an
authoritative informative and wide-
ranging review section. Poetry that
counts to more than one or two,
that laughs and rages and knows
the difference. Keywords:
intelligence passion and wit.

SCRATCHINGS
c/o the English Dept
Taylor Bldg
Univ of Aberdeen
OLD ABERDEEN

SCREENTYPE
Vevers
Nightingales
Compton
GUILDFORD

GU3 1DT
Local History.

SCRIEVINS
c/o Willie Hershaw
28 Glebe Place
Burntisland
FIFE

SCRIPTMATE EDITIONS
Ann Kritzinger
20 Shepherds Hill
LONDON
N6 5AH
Biography. Self-publishing.

Hugh S. SCULLION
59 Lancaster Avenue
LONDON
SE27
'Sherlock Holmes Stories -
Politically Correct?'

Alan SEABROOK
Flat 4
56 Marine Parade
BRIGHTON
BN2 1PN
Brighton orientated 'Eye' type
magazine.

SEA DREAM MUSIC
236 Sebert Road
Forest Gate
LONDON
E7 0NP
Books about music, plays, poetry
copyright, antique glass, Chrisian
bias.

DENYS SEAGER CONSULTANCY
10 Jewry Street
WINCHESTER
SO23 8RZ
General Fiction.

SEAGIA PUBLICATIONS
P.O. Box 173
Sliden Street
PORTSMOUTH

SEAGULL ENTERPRISES
Newton Hall
Hall Road
Walpole Highway
WISBECH
PE14 2QE
Parish Registers.

SEARCHLINE PUBLISHING
Searchline House
Bull Lane
CHISLEHURST
BR7 6NY

SEARS
8 Farm Hill Road
WALTHAM ABBEY
EN9 1NN
Local History.

SEASONS COLLECTION
P.O. Box 121
DEAL
CT14 6SL

SECRET HEART
R. Harris
9a Chesterton Road
LONDON
W10
A quarterly magazine primarily
devoted to acoustic music, but open
to many other areas.

2ND RAPTURE
Mr Colin Mulligan
8 Tottenham Close
Ings Road
HULL
HU8 0TN
Maglet for poetry, shorts and
graphics.

**Mr Rufus SEGAR & Ms Sheila
SEGAR**
33 Hamilton Gardens
LONDON
NW8

SELBORNE AGENCIES LIMITED
BCM Zoo Review
LONDON
WC1N 3XX
Illustrated glossy magazine about
zoos

SELECT BOOKS
Rivington House
82 Great Eastern Street
LONDON
EC2A 3JL
Science Fiction. Biography. Mystery
Fiction.

SEMPRINGHAM
11 Augustine's Road
BEDFORD
MK40 2NB

SENECIO PRESS
The Old Drapery
Church Street
CHARLBURY
OX7 3PP

SENTRIES
Chard Street
AXMINSTER
EX13 5DZ
Travel Accommodation.

SEPHTON ENTERPRISES
Lacy House Farm
Charlestown
HEBDON BRIDGE
HX7 6PN
Tel 01422 844 335

**SEPIA
(see KAWABATA PRESS)**
Knill Cross House
Knill Cross
MILLBROOK
near Torpoint
PL10 1DX

THE SEPTEMBER PRESS
42 High Street
IRCHESTER
Wellingborough
NN8 7AB

SEREN BOOKS
Nick Felton
Poetry Wales Press Limited
Andmar House
Tondu Road
BRIDGEND
CF31 4LJ
Tel 01656 767 834
Publisher of poetry fiction
biography drama some history Lit
Crit with a Welsh context. Small
literary house with reps and agents
worldwide Authors include RS
Thomas Minhinnick Curtis Finch
Abse Alun Lewis and many women
poets.

SEVEN ISLANDS PRESS
R.Y. Cook
86 Benedict Street
GLASTONBURY
BA6 9EZ
Tel 01458 832 690
Exploring the ancient origins of philosophy, art and religion.

SEVEN MIRRORS PUBLISHING HOUSE
21 Daleside Avenue
PUDSEY
LS28 8HB
Occult. Poetry.

SEVENTY PRESS
70 South Street
READING
RG1 4RA
Botany.

SEVERNSIDE PRESS
B.W. Wheeler
Severnside
NEWNHAM
GL14 1AA
Letterpress printing facility available up to A2 sheet size. Contact welcomed from private publishers/ similar/interests/ or others with sensible propositions. Proprietor BFMP member with extensive practical experience in letterpress field.

SEVIERS
22A Hampstead Lane
LONDON
N6 4RT
Short Stories.

SEGEULAICHE PUBLICATIONS
Segeulaiche Achnahinich
Plockton
INVERNESS
IV52 8TY

SHADOWFAX PUBLISHING
25 Drysgol Road
Radyr
CARDIFF
CF4 8BT
Health. Psychology. Local History.

Kanta SHAH
17 Hillbury Avenue
HARROW
HA3 8EP
School textbooks.

SHAMAN'S DRUM
Grim
41 Oxford Road
Southport
MERSEYSIDE

SHAPE LONDON
1 Thorpe Close
LONDON
W10 5XL

SHAPES AND STRINGS
121 Ryelands Road
STONEHOUSE
GL10 2PG
Music.

THE SHARKTI LAUREATE
Pamela Constantine
104 Argylke Gardens
UPMINSTER
RM14 3EU
English Renaissance formed the

Sharkti Laureate to proliferate the Renaissance ideal with her SL writing group.

SHARP-CUT
Spencer Hudson
5 Southwood Court
Big Wood Road
Hampstead Garden Suburb
LONDON
NW11 6SR

John SHARP
'Mill Close'
Sandford Manor
Woodley
READING
RG5 4SY
Technology and Manufacturing.

WERNER SHAW
Suite 34
26 Charing Cross Road
LONDON
WC2H 0DH
The Bookdealer Magazine.

SHEARSMAN BOOKS
Tony Frazer
47 Dayton Close
PLYMOUTH
PL6 5DX

SHEBA FEMINIST PUBLISHERS
10a Bradbury Street
LONDON
N16

SHEFFIELD WOMEN'S PRINTING CO-OP
111a Matilda Street
SHEFFIELD
S1 4QF

G SHEPHERD PUBLISHERS
Maggs House
BRISTOL
BS8 1QX

SHERLOCK PUBLICATIONS
Philip Weller
6 Bramham Moor
Hill Head
FAREHAM
PO14 3RU
Specialises in producing journals and monographs concerned with studies of Sherlock Holmes and his times. It is connected with the world 's leading Sherlock Holmes correspondence study group 'The Franco-Midland Hardware Company'.

SHERWOOD FOREST PUBLISHERS
P.O. Box 10
NOTTINGHAM
NG2 3GR
A humorous and useful look at Telecom: British Telecon?

SHERWOOD GAMES
Sherwood House
15 Annesley Road
Hucknall
NOTTINGHAM
NG15 7AD

SHETLAND LIBRARY
Lowe
Hillhead
LEWICK
ZE1 0EL
Local Legal History (Court Books).

SHIELD PUBLISHING
7 Verne Road
NORTH SHIELDS
NE29 7LP

SHIELING PUBLICATIONS
22 Nelson Street
ST ANDREWS
KY16 8AJ

SHILLELAGH BOOKS
257A Ladbroke Grove
LONDON
W10 6HF
Fiction General.

SHIP OF FOOLS
239 Lessingham Avenue
Tooting
LONDON
SW17 8NQ
A press mainly dedicated to the visual work of Patricia Farrell and the texts of Robert Sheppard, and to their collaboratins.

SHIP PICTORIAL PUBLICATIONS
3 College Close
COLTISHALL
NR12 7DT

SHOCKING PINK
121 Railton Road
LONDON
SE24 0LR

THE SHRINKING LAUNDERETTE
26 Howe Park
EDINBURGH
EH10 7HF

SHROPSHIRE BOOKS
Old School House
Preston Street
SHREWSBURY
SY2 5NY

S.I.A PUBLISHING
31 Malden Way
NEW MALDEN
KT3 6EB

SIGNAL
(see The Thimble Press)

SILENT BOOKS
Boxworth End
Swavesey
CAMBRIDGE
CB4 5RA
Tel 01954 32199/31000
Independent publisher established six years. Publisher of high quality beautifully designed and produced books - many illustrated with wood engraving. Gift books community care range and larger format books. Winners of several awards.

Anthony L. SILSON
22 Whitecote Gardens
Bramley
LEEDS
LS13 2HZ
Local History.

SILVER BIRCH PRESS
248A Telegraph Road
Heswall
WIRRAL
L60 7SG
Pictorial Local History.

SILVER MOON BOOKS
64-68 Charing Cross Road

LONDON
WC2H 0BB
Bookshop and publishers of women's topics.

SILVER MOON
300 Old Brompton Road
LONDON
SW5 9JF

SILVER STAR TRANSPORT BOOKS
24 Partridge Close
CHESHAM
HP5 3LH

SILVEY-JEX PUBLICATIONS
14 Chaldon Road
LONDON
SW6 7NJ

SIMANDA PRESS
1 Meriden Road
Berkswell
COVENTRY
CV7 7BE
Local History.

R.E.G. SIMMERSON
36 Wilton Avenue
LONDON
W4 2NY
Language.

A.& S. SIMMONDS
23 Nelson Road
LONDON
SE10 9JB
Maritime Books. Bibliography.

SIMMONS PUBLISHING
37 Lower High Street
WEDNESBURY
WS10 7AQ
Local History.

SIMON KING PRESS
Simon or Angela King
Ashton House
Beetham
MILNTHORPE
LA7 7AL
The Simon King Press publishes poetry and short storiesand prints in letterpress. Titles are usually illustrated with wood engravings or linocuts. A limited amount of printing is undertaken for other publishers. Telephone orders and Mastercard/Visa/Access accepted. Cheques payable to Simon King Press. Send for lists.
* *"Pied Beauty - a selection of poems by Gerald Manley Hopkins", Standard Edition 1/4 cloth £75. Special Edition 1/4 Leather £150*
* *"Night - Fausts' Study" - the opening extract from Goethe's Faust. Sewn in paste paper wraper £45*
* *"Rupert Brooke - the Great Lover", illustrated with 2 wood engravings by Simon King. £20 including p+p.*

Ms Janice SIMONS
17 Kingcup
Pandora Meadows
KING'S LYNN
PE30 3HF
Produces collections of local history material of special interest to genealogists and local histrians. Books currently available include collections of marriage and

obituary notices for the years 1848, 1881 & 1900 taken from the old local press for East Anglia.

SIMPLE LOGIC
Paul A GLover
2 Broadway
NOTTINGHAM
NG1 1PS
Magazine and books covering all aspects of using Atari ST Computers.

SIMPLIFIED SPELLING SOCIETY
39 Chepstow Rise
CROYDON
CR0 5LX
Language.

SIMPLY CREATIVE
246 London Road
Charlton Kings
CHELTENHAM
GL52 6HS
Education.

SIRIUS
P.O. Box 428
DENBIGH
LL16 4AZ

SIXES AND SEVENS
Bruce P Baker
67 Saxbys Lane
LINGFIELD
RH7 6DP
AKA 'The Magic Chameleon' (Charity Jester). Mini-novels, cult sci-fi.

SIXTH DOMAIN PRESS
Rosyda
Mount Pleasant
CROWBOROUGH
TN26 2NF
Facilitating the practical application of natural laws for maifesting harmony and healing within, and between, individuals and nations. Acting as a link between, and debating forum for, Eastern and Western Mystical, occult, and Psychic Research organisations.

SJB PUBLISHING
(see Simon BONLANDS)

SKEEBY PUBLISHING
Hightrees
155 Dukes Ride
CROWTHORNE
RG11 6DR

SKEIN
White Lodge
47 Bisley Old Road
STROUD
GL5 1LY
Poetry.

SKELMERSDALE WRITERS
Library Arts Centre
Shopping Concourse
SKELMERSDALE

THE SKEPTIC
Toby Howard/Steve Donnelly
P.O. Box 475
MANCHESTER
M60 2TH
Tel 0161 748 4628
The UK's only regular magazine devoted to a skeptical view of pseudoscience and claims to the

paranormal. Articles, columns, reviews, humour, letters and much much more!

Hugh SKILLEN
56 St. Thomas Drive
PINNER
HA5 4SS
Second World War History.

SKOOB BOOKS PUBLISHING
15 Sicilian Avenue
LONDON
WC1A 2QH

SKOOBS OCCULT REVIEW
Mrs Caroline Wise
19 Bury Place
LONDON
WC1A 2JH

Ron SLACK
26 Glenthorne Close
Brampton
CHESTERFIELD
S40 3AR
Local History.

SLATERS PHOTOGRAPHIC SALES AND PUBLISHING
7 Malvern Close
Huntington
YORK
YO3 9RP
Entertainment.

Slim SMITH
BM Slim
LONDON
WC1N 3XX
Yes. The graphic novel about an individual voice, including P&P or by dance of life & carpet? Created by the author on the living room is in the wrong typeface. These ones hairdos. The identity of a nasty fake-art. Bab's Rhumba. Mincemeat's Mambo.

SLOUCH
49c the High Street
FALMOUTH
TR11 2AF
Slouch is a comic! It's NOT a zine or a glossy mag. We bring you wulfthing, Elvis porno, Coopers Farm (Aliens talking!!!) plus ads. We are the best comic from Britain - please prove us wrong.

SLOW DANCER
Mr John Harvey
59 Parliament Hill
LONDON
NW3 2TB
Tel 0171 435 5964
Publishes New Poetry by new and established writers; Slow Dancer magazine twice a year, small number of single author pamphlets & occasional books. No unsolicited manuscripts, thanks.

SMALL PUBLICATIONS
151 Norwich Road
Wroxham
NORWICH
NR12 8RZ

SMALL PRESS WORLD
Please note this magazine ended in 1994. Replaced by the publications of the National Small Press Centre qv.

SMITH/DOORSTOP BOOKS
51 Byram Arcade
Westgate
HUDDERSFIELD
HD1 1ND

John Owen SMITH
Oakdene
Beech Hill
Headley
BORDON
GU35 8EG
Poetry. Plays.

J. SMITH'S TADCASTER BREWERY
The Brewery
TADCASTER
LS24 9SA
Local military history.

SMOKE
(The Windows Project)
40 Canning St
LIVERPOOL
L8 7NP

Patrick SMYTH
Marymount
3 North Circular Road
Lurgan
CRAIGAVON
BT67 9EB
Handicrafts.

SNAKE RIVER PRESS
Geoffrey Trenamen
1 Grafton Street
BRIGHTON
BN2 1AQ
Finely printed volumes of poetry illustrated with lithographs, woodcuts, and line drawings personally printed by the artist. The bindings are formally designed and executed by selected craftsman-binders. Write for a list of books in print.

Steve SNEYD
4 Nowell Place
Almonbury
HUDDERSFIELD
HD5 8PB
Prolific writer and producer of bits in print.

SOCIAL INVENTIONS, INSTITUTE FOR
Nicholas Alberry
20 Heber Road
LONDON
NW2 6AA
Tel 0181 208 2853, fax 0181 452 6434
'Encyclopaedia of Social Inventions' edited by Nicholas Albery. 1990. ISBN 0 948826 17 7. 500 best ideas (non-technological) for social change.

SOCIAL ORG.
32 Copley Road
STANMORE
HA7 4PF
Political Science. Religion.

SOFT PENCIL PRESS
29 Douglas Road
Acocks Green
BIRMINGHAM
B27 6HH
Poetry.

SOL PUBLICATIONS
31 Chiltern

Coleman Street
SOUTHEND-ON-SEA
SS2 5AE

SOL
Adrian Green
44 Station Road
RAYLEIGH
SS6 7HL

SORCERER'S APPRENTICE
6-8 Burley Lodge Road
LEEDS
LS6 1QP
Specialist Publishers of limited edition books and monographs on Occult Philosophies, Mysticism, Magick and New Age. Also litature regarding Human Rights and the liberation of minorities from cultural imprinting and philsophical/ religious supremacism.

SORREL PUBISHING
2A Randolph Place
EDINBURGH
EH3 7T
Newcastle Menu Guide. Edinburgh Menu Guide. Aberdeen Menu Guide.

H. SOTHERAN
2-5 Sackville Street
LONDON
W1X 2DP
Bibliography.

SOTTO VOCE PRESS
MAYNOOTH
County Kildare
Republic of Ireland
Plays.

SOUND & FURY ENTERPRISES
8 College Gardens
LONDON
N18 2XR
Tel 0181 803 8952
Began as a 'zine for gaming but went berserk.

SOURCE
109 Oak Tree Road
Bitterne Park
SOUTHAMPTON
SO2 4JP
Journal for Holy Wells.

SOUTH
61 Westborough
WIMBORNE
BH21 1LX

SOUTHGATE DISTRICT CIVIC TRUST
Mr P. R. Hodge
64 Houndsden Road
LONDON
N21 1LY
The publishing arm of a local amenity society, specialsing in the local history of Southgate and district. Current titles include booklets, conservation area guides, maps, postcards and a local history bulletin. Lead titles: Brindle, S. "Broomfield:an illustrated history of the house and garden". Cresswell, H., "Winchmore Hill: memories of a lost village"

SOUTHGATE PUBLISHING
Glebe House
Church Street
CREDITON

EX17 2AF
Education.

SOUTHOVER PRESS
2 Cockshut Road
Southover
LEWES
BN7 1JH
*Good reprints on cookery and
household management.*

SOUTHPORT WRITERS' CIRCLE
c/o 35 Codray Road
Southport
MERSEYSIDE
Short Stories.

SOUTHWELL PRESS
Mrs Jean Baker
Wilton Road
CAMBERLEY
GU15 2QW

SOU'WESTER BOOKS
17 Crestacre Close
Newton
SWANSEA
SA3 4UR

SPACELINK BOOKS
Lionel Beer
115 Holybush Lane
HAMPTON
TW12 2QY
Tel 0181 979 3148
*Publisher of booklets on the
Paranormal. No unsolicited m/s.
Mainly acts as a bookseller and
distributor of books, booklets and
magazines, covering UFOs, crop
circles, earth mysteries and wide
range of paranormal topics.
Several small presses handled:
Ascent Publications, Phoebe Beer
(Devon), Countryside Productions,
Gemini (of Zimbabwe), Deryck
Seymour (Devon), &c. UFOs titles
are main speciality. Publisher of
SPACELINK magazine, TEMS
News.*

SPAREMAN PRESS
65 Sycamore Avenue
NEWPORT
NP9 9AJ
Ranting poet.

P4 SPARES
60 Woodville Road
LONDON
NW11 9TN

SPARTACUS PUBLICATIONS
D. Edwards
8 Shrewsbury Way
Saltney
CHESTER
CH4 8DY
Health and Hygiene.

SPECIAL SORTS PRESS
10A Dickenson Road
LONDON
N8 9ET
Poetry.

SPECIAL TWENTY
1 Fleming House
Portland Rise
LONDON
N4 2PX
Free broadsheet/zine.

SPECTACULAR DISEASES
Paul Green

838 London Road
PETERBOROUGH
PE2 9BS
Journal and distribution of poetry.

SPECTRUM
19 Cunninghamhead Estate
by KILMARNOCK
KA3 2PY

SPEL PUBLICATIONS
45 Crow Hill
BROADSTAIRS
CT10 1HT
Tel 01343 69434
*Talking phrasebooks in French
German and Italian.*

SPELLBOUND CARD CO LTD
23-25 Moss Street
DUBLIN 2
Ireland

SPENDTHRIFT PUBLICATIONS
31 Richmond Road
CAMBRIDGE
CB4 3PP
Poetry.

SPENNITHORNE PUBLICATIONS
1 Bourton Road
Hunts Cross
LIVERPOOL
L25 OPB
*Autobiography of a catholic priest
who worked in South Africa 1959-
69.*

SPIDER PARK
Stanwell Street
EDINBURGH
EH6 5NG

SPIKE PRESS
Avanti Books
8 Parson Green
Boulton Road
STEVENAGE
SG1 4QG
General Fiction.

SPILLER FARM PUBLICATIONS
25 Liskeard Gardens
Blackheath
LONDON
SE3 0PE

SPIRAL PUBLICATIONS
8 Kings Street
GLASTONBURY
BA6 9JY
*Books and booklets on star magik,
meditation, astral travel, higher
consciousness.*

SPIRAL ASCENT
37 Foxlease
BEDFORD
MK41 8AP
*Spiral Ascent takes its name fron
the Edward Upward trilogy of the
same name. Our origins are a clue
to our purpose. We are not 'Arty'
or 'F---y' but come to the aid of the
party!*

SPIRAL SCRATCH
6 Chapel Street
CAMBRIDGE
CB4 1DY

SPOKES MAGAZINE
The Orchard House
45 Clophill Road
Upper Gravenhurst

BEDFORD
MK45 4JH
Tel 01408 583 295
Poetry.

SPORTING AND LEISURE PRESS
Meadows House
Well Street
BUCKINGHAM
MK18 1EW
Sport.

SPREAD EAGLE PUBLICATIONS
3 Upper Clwyd Street
RUTHIN
LL15 1HY
Travel in Britain.

Christine & D. **SPRINGETT**
21 Hillmorton Road
RUGBY
CV22 5DF
Handicrafts and Printmaking.

SPRING HILL PUBLICATIONS
Spring Hill Medical Centre
Spring Hill
ARLEY
CV7 8FD

SPUD
38 Chaucer Road
BEDFORD
MK40 2AJ
*The essential Society for the
Prevention of Unneccessary
(theatre) Directors. Sick of rotten
shows? Now you know who is to
blame and why. Get the
irreplaceable SPUD Introductory
History of Actor-Managers. A
subject about which you know
nothing and care less? Quite. Me
too. But the publication is a treat for
£5.*

SPURGES
22A Picket Piece
ANDOVER
SP11 6LY
Handicrafts.

SPYGLASS: RUPERT BOOKS
59 Stonefield
Bar Hill
CAMBRIDGE

SQUARE ONE PUBLICATIONS
29-31 Lowesmoor
WORCESTER
WR1 2RS

SQR (PUBLISHING) ENTERPRISE
David Stern (Editor)
526, Fulham Palace Road
Fulham
LONDON
SW6 6JE
*"Pen - &- Keyboard magazine".
"Newsletter".*

ST BOOKS
45 Brook Close
EAST GRINSTEAD
RH19 3XZ
Education.

STAG PUBLICATIONS
Thimble Farm
Green Lane
Prestwood
GREAT MISSENDEN
HP16 0QE

STAG PUBLICATIONS
16 Connaught Street
LONDON
W2 2AF
Humour.

STAGECOACH
Avon Cottage
Stratford-sub-Castle
SALISBURY
SP4 6AE
School Textbooks.

Martin Richard **STALLION**
18 Cornec Chase
LEIGH-ON-SEA
SS9 5EW
Bibliography.

STAND MAGAZINE
179 Wingrove Road
NEWCASTLE-UPON-TYNE
NE4 9DA

STAPLE
Donald Measham
Tor Cottage
81 Cavendish Road
MATLOCK
DE4 3HD
*Contract for worldwide distribution
promises development but can as
yet consider only submissions to
first editions series (nominal
reading fee). Poetry & short fiction -
included in Staple Magazine
subscription.
"An Extra Half-Acre" (poetry),
Jennifer Olds
"Women Who Make Money"
(stories) Donna Hilbert*

STARFIRE
BM Starfire
LONDON
WC1N 3XX

STARSHINE BOOKS
P.O. Box 150
CHESTERFIELD
S40 1QH
Children's Fiction.

STATICS (LONDON)
41 Standard Road
LONDON
NW10 6HF
Art. Humour.

David C **STEDMAN**
71A Westward Road
STROUD
GL5 4JA
Booklets - education economics.

ST EDWARDS PRESS
Vine Cottage
Sutton Park
GUILDFORD
GU14 7QN

STEEL CARPET MUSIC
Peter Castle
190 Burton Road
DERBY
DE1 1TQ
Tel 01332 46399
*Mainly folk and traditional music/
tales/lore. Books and tapes. Set up
by Pete Castle a singer/storyteller
to market his material but
expanded to include other artistes*

and related subjects. Free
catalogue and news sheet (sae
appreciated!).

Charmian STEELE
Bluebell Cottage
Upper End
Fulbrook
OXFORD
OX18 4BX
Asian History.

RICHARD STENLAKE PUBLISHING
Richard Stenlake
1 Overdale Street
Langside
GLASGOW
G42 9PZ
Tel 0141 632 2304
*An eccentric independent press
specialising at present in Scottish
interest and transport-related titles.*

STEPNEY BOOKS
Jenny Smith
19 Tomlins Grove
Bow
LONDON
E3 4NX
*Community publishing group
specialising in history and
autobiography of London Borough
of Tower Hamlets*

STEPPENMOLE
49 Gloucester Green
OXFORD
OX1 2DF
Fiction publishers.

STEREO SCENES
22 Rutland Gardens
HOVE
BN3

STERLING PRINT & PROMOTIONS
7 Main Street
AILSWORTH
PE5 7AF
Tel/Fax 01733 380905

STILE PUBLICATIONS
Mercury House
OTLEY
LS21 3HE
Local Walks Books.

STOCKBRIDGE PRESS
16 Danube Street
EDINBURGH
EH4 1NT
Poetry.

STOCKBRIDGE WRITERS
49a Lynham
Whiston
MERSEYSIDE
Poetry.

Peter STOCKHAM
Images
4 & 6 Dam Street
LICHFIELD
WS13 6AA
*Reprint of an English Civil War
Letter.*

**STONE CREEK PRESS
& INKSHED PRESS**
387 Beverley Road
HULL
HU5 1LS

STONEWATER ROWE
Clettwr Cottage

Trer'ddol
MACHYNLLETH
SY20 8PN
Poetry.

STOP MESSIN' ABOUT!
Carl St John
27 Brookmead Way
ORPINGTON
BR5 2OQ
Tel 01689 833 711
*The Kenneth Williams and Sid
James Appreciation Society's
Newsletter. Classic British comedy
bringing together the fans of 'Carry
On' 'Ealing' and Hancock film
shows organised in London.*

STOP PRESS BOOKS
Green Gables
51 The Avenue
Healing
GRIMSBY
DN37 7NA
Humour.

STOURTON PRESS
18 Royal Crescent
LONDON
W11 4SL

John STOW
26A Tregunter Road
LONDON
SW10 9LH
Biography.

STOW'S CLASSICS
Newhaven Fort
Fort Road
NEWHAVEN
BN9 9DL
Historical giftware.

**STRANGE ADVENTURES
PUBLISHING**
Tone Lee (editor/publisher)
13 Hazeley Combe
ARRETON
Isle of Wight
PO30 3AJ
Tel 01983 865 668
*Publishing three genre magazines.
Strange Adventures a monthly
guide to 'fantastic' media. 'News
from the future'. Premonitions bi-
annual SF/Horror stories. All
available by mail order. Please
send sae for further details.*

STRANGE MATTER
Dean Braithwaite
Dept DB
Rhyd-Dderwen
Hebron
WHITLAND
SA34 0XX
The Ruby Book Review.

STRANGE PUBLICATIONS
P.O. Box 66
LIVERPOOL
L69 3PU
Art.

STRANGER GAMES
318 Aldridge Road
Streetly
SUTTON COLDFIELD
B74 2DT

STRANMILLS COLLEGE
Learning Resources Unit
Stranmills Road
BELFAST

BT9 5DY
Children's non-fiction.

STRATA PUBLISHING
P.O. Box 866
13 Rojack Road
LONDON
SE23 2DB
Civil Engineering.

STRATHTONGUE PRESS
Clar Innis
Strathtongue
LAIRG
IV27 4XR

STRAWBERRY PRESS
Paul Nash & Helen Pipe
North Street
Kidlington
OXFORD
OX5 2SQ
Fine printers.

STREET EDITIONS
87 St Phillips Road
CAMBRIDGE
CB1 3DA
*Modern British, U.S., and European
Poetry.*

**STREETLY PRINTING/BEACON
BROADCASTING**
371 Rednal Road
Kings Norton
BIRMINGHAM
B38 8EE

STRIDE
(see TAXUS)

STROUD PUBLISHING COMPANY
Stroud Secretarial Services Ltd
6 London Road
STROUD
GL5 2AA
Poetry.

STUART PRESS
Stuart Peachey
117 Farleigh Road
Backwell
BRISTOL
BS19 3PG
Tel 01275 463041
*Publish books on the period 1580-
1660 nearly 100 volumes. Main
subjects: English civil war, food and
drink, agriculture and living history
topics including medecine, charcoal
burning, costume and sex.
"The Gourmets Guide, 1580-
1660", £5
"17th Century Sex", £2*

STYLUS PUBLICATIONS
181 Long Acre
BOLTON
BL2 6EX

SUBJECT PUBLICATIONS
Beech House
31 Beech Close
BROADSTONE
BH18 9NJ
Music. School Textbooks.

SUCCESS PUBLICATIONS
Robert Burgess
1 Middle Field Road
ROTHERHAM
S60 3JH
*Specialist publishers of trade
directories, "The UK Stamp Shops
Directory", "The 1996 Record*

Dealers Directory" and smal
business titles, "Cash from the
Charts". Write for a free catalogue!

SUFFOLK NOSTALGIA
7 Collingwood Road
WOODBRIDGE
IP12 1JL
Local History.

SUGDEN PUBLICATIONS
Libra Bookshop
West Street
MAYFIELD
TN20 6BA

SULIS PUBLICATIONS
5 Widcombe Parade
BATH
BA2 4JT
Music.

SUMMERS PUBLISHING
22 Ribstock Gardens
Paddock Wood
TONBRIDGE
TN12 6BA

SUMMERSDALE PRESS
Stewart Ferris
127 Maplehurst Road
CHICHESTER
PO19 4RP
Tel 01243 779 327
*Publish books of interest to students
and young people of all ages.*

**SUN AND HARVEST
PUBLICATIONS:**
Sterling Books
43A Locking Road
WESTON-SUPER-MARE
BS23 3DG
Sun Dials, local history of.

SUNK ISLAND REVIEW
P.O. Box 74
LINCOLN
LN1 1QG
*Biannual paperback anthology of
new fiction, poetry, translations,
articals, reviews and graphics from
the UK and around the world.*

SUN MOON AND STARS PRESS
Andi McGarry
Donkey Meadows
Kilmore Quay
WEXFORD
Republic of Ireland
*Specialising in Livres d'artiste and
artist's books on organic themes
love life mountains sea clouds earth
etc. All books are entirely
handmade hard and soft coverings
and in limited editions. Text and
images are original ideas by the
artist.*

SUNRISE PRESS LONDON
34 Churton Street
LONDON
SWIV 2LP
European History.

SUNSHINE ON LEITH PUBLISHING
45 Madeira Street
EDINBURGH
EH6 4AJ

SUN TAVERN FIELDS
Anthony Blampied
P.O. Box 982
LONDON
E1 9EQ

Tel 0171 790 4267
Broken Mirros/Broken Minds: The Dark Dreams of Dario Argento. More film studies and more other stuff. The hugely erotic history of English sex films. Phew.

SUPPORTIVE LEARNING PUBLICATIONS
25 Maes-y-Waun
Chirk
WREXHAM
LL14 5ND
Children's non-fiction.

R.S. SURTEES SOCIETY
Tacker's Cottage
Horn Street
Nunney
FROME
BA11 4NP
Biography.

SURVIVORS PRESS
33 Queensdown Road
LONDON
E5 8NN

SUT ANUBIS
73 Kettering Road
NORTHAMPTON
NN1 4AW

SWAN BOOKS & EDUCATIONAL SERVICES
13 Henrietta Street
SWANSEA
SA1 4HW
Self-publishing of own illustrated small books, bookmarks and picture post-cards. Registered with Welsh Arts Council and West Wales Arts, etc. Illustrated talks given: e.g 'The Ups and Downs of a Small Press.

SWAN HILL PRESS
101 Longden Road
SHREWSBURY
SY3 9EB

SWEENEY MOUNT
SHERBOURNE PUBLICATIONS
Oswestry
SY10 9EX

SWEETHAWS PRESS
Owl House
Pundgate
UCKFIELD
TN22 4DE

SWORDFISH
PO Box 26
CRAWLEY
RH11 7YS
Weird and wonderful zines, rude badges, the best comics, queerzines, loony cult material.

SYCAMORE PRESS
John Fuller
4 Benson Place
OXFORD
OX2 6QH
Tel 01865 56154
Publishing poetry in small editions since 1968.

SYMPHONY
(see Bemerton Press)

SYNDICATION PRODUCTION
38 Mount Pleasant
LONDON

WC1X 0AP
Biography.

SYNFINITY
Michael Law
The Chapel House
Perch Hill
WESTBURY
BA5 1JA

T & J PUBLISHING
P.O. Box 10
TOTNES
TQ9 5GE

TABARD PRIVATE PRESS
Philip Kerrigan
White Timbers
Stokesheath Road
OXSHOTT
KT22 0PS
Fine printers.

TABBY PUBLICATIONS
c/o 66 Nelson Gardens
LEICESTER
Art.

TABLA MAGAZINE
11 Oulton Close
AYLESBURY
HP21 7JY

TABLA POETRY MAGAZINE
Stephen James Ellis
7 Parliament Hill
LONDON
NW3 2SY

TABOR BOOKS
The Barn
All Saint Lane
CANTERBURY
CT1 2AU

TACKMARK PUBLISHING
27 Brookfield Crescent
Kenton
HARROW
HA3 0UT

TAFOL
65 Mardy Street
Grangetown
CARDIFF
CF1 7QW

Mediaeval Welsh Erotic Poetry.

TAG PUBLICATIONS
36 Poole Road
WEST EWELL
KT19 9SM

Charles Grigg TAIT
6 Fambridge Road
MALDON
CM9 6AA
Local History.

Charles TAIT PHOTOGRAPHIC
Kelton St
Ola
KIRKWALL
Orkney
KW15 1TR
Orkney Guide Book.

TAK TAK TAK
Andrew & Tim Brown
P.O. Box 7
Bulwell
NOTTINGHAM
NG6 0HW
Involved in several areas - publishing books (including anthologies and Polish language material) promoting live poetry and music; and producing spoken word cassettes.

TAKE THAT BOOKS
Chris Brown
P.O. Box 200
HARROGATE
HG1 4XB

TALES FROM SLEAZE CASTLE
Dave McKinnon/Terry Wiley
33 Windsor Drive
Cleadon
SUNDERLAND
SR6 7SY
and MORE TALES FROM SLEAZE CASTLE. A wacky sf comic serial: the adventures of Jocasta Dribble and her friend Panda (who rules her own planet) as they tackle weird dimensions, psychotic aliens and split ends.

TALIBAH PRESS
P.O. Box 160
LONDON
SE26 6NJ

TALKING STICK MAGAZINE
Suite B
2 Tunstall Road
LONDON
SW9 8DA

TAMARIND LIMITED
P.O. Box 296
CAMBERLEY
GU15 1QW
Childrens books specialising in ethnicity.

TANTALUS CRIME FICTION
17 Kingsley Drive
Adel
LEEDS
LS16 7PD
Tel 0113 258 9024/Fax 0113 258 6460

TAPE BOOKS
Chris Mitchell
1/L 11 Woodlands Drive
GLASGOW
G4 9EQ

TAPROBANE LIMITED
P.O. Box 717
LONDON
W5 3EY
Our first publication was The Third Sex by Gordon Wilson. It is a book which presents new thinking covering a number of fields: psychology, sociology, evolution theory , 'sex equality', homosexuality, etc.

TARRAGON PRESS
Mr David Summer
Moss Park
Ravenstone
WITHAM
DG8 8DK
Tel 01988 850 368

TARA PRODUCTS
9 Townsend
Quainton
AYLESBURY
HP22 4BP

TARTARUS PRESS
8 Hunterhouse Road
Hunters Bar
SHEFFIELD
S11 8TW

TAURUS PRESS OF WILLOW DENE
11 Limetree Way
Danygraig
PORTHCAWL
CF36 5AU

L. TAVENDER
7 Mark Close
Regent's Park Road
SOUTHAMPTON
SO1 3RZ
Railways.

TAWNJAKE PUBLISHING
156 Station Road
Rainham
GILLINGHAM
ME8 7PR
Health.

TAXUS
c/o Stride
37 Portland Street
EXETER
EX1 2EG
Poetry press.

John B. TAYLOR
36 Fernhill Drive
Stacksteads
BACUP
OL13 8JS
Local History.

Rosemary TAYLOR
5 Pusey House
Saracen Street
LONDON
E14 6HG
Local History.

TAYNTON PRESS
3 Taynton
Burford
OXFORD
OX18 4UH
History of Music.

TCL PUBLICATIONS
A J Tennant
15 Coronation Road
EAST GRINSTEAD
RH19 4AJ

Shipping.

TEARS IN THE FENCE
Sarah Hopkins
Venton Manor
Dartington
TOTNES
TQ9 6DP
Tel 01364 73209
A bi-annual literary magazine of poetry, fiction, graphics, reviews, articles, i nterviews and fun. Concerned to promote women's writing and quality literature.

TEENEY BOOKS
Matbro House
Garston Road
FROME
BA11 1QW
Children's Fiction.

TELLET
Philip Woodrow
30 York Street
BROADSTAIRS
CT10 1PB
Publisher of poetry books. Founded 1996.
First publication; 1996, Philip Woodrow, "Kind of Light".

TEMPLE GROVE/LODGE PRESS
Sevak Gulbenkian
51 Queen Caroline Street
LONDON
W6 9QL

TEMPLE ROCK PUBLICATIONS
The Farmhouse
Cuddesdon
OXFORD
OX9 9ET
Tel 01867 74438
Small publisher of local books.

TEN GRAND MAGAZINE
Lion House Studios
Queens House
12 Queens Square
BRIGHTON
BN1
Magazine for film, tv, comics, music.

THE TENORMEN PRESS/OSTINATO
Stephen Middleton
P.O. Box 522
LONDON
N8 7SZ
A jazz poetry magazine professionally designed with large review section that promotes the links between literature (in particular poetry) and improvised music. We also publish specially designed/illustrated books by creative writing about jazz.

TENTH DECADE
12 Stevenage Road
LONDON
SW6 6ES

TENTH MUSE
33 Hartington Road
SOUTHAMPTON
SO2 0EW

TERMINUS PUBLICATIONS
592a Chatsworth Road
CHESTERFIELD
S40 3JX
Small publishing house catering for the transport enthusiast (train/bus)

and producing A5 books mainly pertaining to the North Midlands/ Derbyshire area.

TERMITE TIMES
c/o Shrewsbury Youth Centre
5 Belmont
SHREWSBURY
SY1 1TF

TERN PRESS
Nicholas & Mary Perry
St Mary's Cottage
Great Hales Street
MARKET DRAYTON
TF9 1JN
Fine printer.

TERN PUBLICATIONS
The Old Post Cottage
Motcombe
SHAFTESBURY
SP7 9NT
History of Hospitals

TERROR FORCE 10
Suite 16
46-48 Osnaburgh Street
LONDON
NW1 3ND

TESEO BOOKS
2 Golders Manor Drive
LONDON
NW11 9HT
Biography.

TETRAD PRESS
Hega House
Ullin Street
St Leonards Road
LONDON
E14

THARSON PRESS
Church Cottage
Morton Hall
Morton-on-the-Hill
NORWICH
NR9 5JS
Military History.

T.H.C.L Books
185 Lammack Road
BLACKBURN
BB1 8LH

THEATRE ACTION PRESS
c/o Department of Literature
University of Essex
Wivenhoe Park
COLCHESTER
CP4 3SQ
Radical theatre books and play scripts originating in Essex University's theatre writer's residency, and the productions of the Theatre Underground Company.

THEATRE SCRIPTS
Upton House
Southey Green
Sible Hedingham
HALSTEAD
CO9 3RN

THE CLIQUE
7 Pulleyn Drive
YORK
YO2 2DY

THEOSOPHICAL PUBLISHING HOUSE
12 Bury Place

LONDON
WC1A 2LE

THE PRESS
53b All Saints Street
HASTINGS
TN34 3BN

THE SYNDICATE
Pettigoe Fair
22 Lansdowne Road
FRIMLEY
Camberley
GU16 5UW

THIMBLE PRESS
Nancy Chambers
Lockwood
Station Road
WOODCHESTER
GL5 5EQ
01453 873716
Journal 'Signal' approaches to Childrens' books. Three p.a. since 1970, also paperbacks.

THINKING EYE IDEAS
13 Fort Street
DUNDEE
DD2 1BS

THIRD HALF
16 Fane Close
STAMFORD
PE9 1HG

THIRD HOUSE
Peter Robins
35 Brighton Road
LONDON
N16 8EQ
Gay fiction in paperback. Check with Gay Men's Press if this address is still valid.

THIRD WORLD PUBLISHING COMPANY
29 Upper Camelford Walk
LONDON
W11 1TU

THIRD WORLD QUARTERLY
c/o Shadid Qadir
188 Copse Hill
LONDON
SW20 0SP
Tel 0181 947 1043

THIS ENGLAND BOOKS
Alma House
73 Rodney Road
CHELTENHAM
GL50 1HT

THISTLE BOOKS
Chiltern Cottage
Gayton lane
WIRRAL
L60 3SH

THOEMMES ANTIQUARIAN BOOKS
85 Park Street
BRISTOL
BS1 5PJ

Kelvin S.M. THOMAS
78 Holcombe Vale
Bathampton
BATH
BA2 6UX
Biography.

William Grenville THOMAS
25 Romilly Crescent

Hakin
MILFORD HAVEN
SA73 3NH
Local History.

THOM PRESS
66 Evans Road
EYNSHAM
OX8 1QS
Short Stories.

Hilary THOMPSON
1 The Quay
Portscatho
TRURO
TR2 5HF
Local History.

THORMYND PRESS
P.O. Box 4
CHURCH STRETTON
SY6 6ZZ

THOROUGHBRED PRESS
Monks Hall
Alport
BAKEWELL

DE45 1LG
New and untried, my attempt at self publishing my first novel.

THORN
M.S.C. Harding and Ed Fairclough
13 Oswald Road
Upper Tooting
LONDON
SW17 7SS
Tel 0181 767 2368
Bi-monthly 32pp pamphlet of esoterica history features images, strange tales, soundbites etc. which reflect the shift from the Newtonian-Descartes paradigm of 17th to 20th centuries to one of transformation and process as described by the increasing understanding of the east by the west.

THORNGATE BOOKS
Thorngate Mill
BARNARD CASTLE
DL12 8QB
Herbs and So On.

THOTH PUBLICATIONS
BM Sothis
LONDON
WC1N 3XX
Esoteric non-fiction.

THREE COUNTIES
59 Dinglewell
GLOUCESTER
GL3 3HP

THREE SPIRES PRESS
Killeen
BLACKROCK
Cork
Republic of Ireland
Poetry.

THRESHOLDWORKS
27 Walpole Road
Tottenham
LONDON
N17 6BE

THROSSEL HOLE PRIORY
Soto Zen Monastery
Carrshield
HEXHAM
NE47 8AL
Journal.

THURSDAYS
70 Poplar Road
Bearwood
WARLEY
B66 4AN

THWARTSEA BOOKS
Suite 11
23 Holland Road
HOVE
BN3 1JF

Brian J. TILEHURST
8 Brickfield Road
Portswood
SOUTHAMPTON
SO2 3AE
Local History.

TIME ENERGY INFORMATION
14 Railway Square
BRENTWOOD
CM14 4LN
Health.

TI PARKS ARTISTS BOOKS
Ti Parks
9 The Orchard
LONDON
SE3 0QS
Tel 0181 852 7246
A fully descriptive and illustrated catalogue of this artist's very unusual artists books, book works and anti books is available price £45. This catalogue is a desirable book work itself. A check list is available with SAE.

'TITANIC' SIGNALS ARCHIVE
30 Eden Vale Road
WESTBURY
BA13 3NY
'Titanic'.

TITCHFIELD PUBLISHING
46 High Street
Buriton
PETERSFIELD
GU31 5RZ

TOAD HOUSE BOOKS
Mole Cottage
17 Prospect Terrace
New Brancepeth
DURHAM
DH7 7EJ
Humour, travel, arts, sociology.

Iain TOLHURST
West Lodge
Hardwick Estate
Whitchurch-on-Thames
Pangbourne
READING
RG8 7RA
A Gardener's Guide to Growing Strawberries Organically.

TOLOUSE PRESS
5 South Drive
LIVERPOOL
L15 8JJ

Kent Lionel TOMLIN
21 Castle Crescent
Castle Bromwich
BIRMINGHAM
B36 9TF
Children's Fiction.

Joseph Tye TOMLINSON
22 The Green
Elston
NEWARK

NG23 5PF
Biography.

TOMPSON PUBLISHING
Oak House
Moor Park
Lower Street
Chagford
NEWTON ABBOT
TQ13 8BY
Children's Fiction. General Knowledge.

TOMVELIAN PUBLICATIONS
3 Scotts Drive
HAMPTON
TW12 2UN
Poetry.

TONGUE IN CHEEK MUSIC
Ian Cheek
55 Albion Street
OTLEY
LS21 1BZ

TOPICAL PUBLISHERS
1 Elm Grove Road
CARDIFF
CF4 2BW
Your Phone Bill - Fact or Fiction?

TOPICAL RESOURCES
4 Brookfield Drive
Fulwood
PRESTON
PR1 4ST

T O P S
The Old Police Station
80 Lark Lane
LIVERPOOL
L17 8UU
The Old Police Station Magazine - poetry.

TOTAL
P.O. Box 284
GLASGOW
G14 9TW

TOUCHSTONE
25 Albert Road
Addlestone
WEYBRIDGE
KT15 2PX

TOUCHSTONE PRESS
12 Portland Place
BISHOP'S STORTFORD
CM23 3SH

TOURNAMENT CHESS
8 Adelina Mews
Kings Avenue
LONDON
SW12 0BG
Chess.

TOWER BOOKS
86 South Main Street
CORK CITY
Ireland

TOWN TEACHER
All Saints Church
Akenside Hill
NEWCASTLE-UPON-TYNE
NE1 2DS

TO YIELD PRESS
Flat Above
4 Wostenholm Road
Nether Edge
SHEFFIELD
S7 1LJ

TRADE AND TRAVEL PUBLICATIONS
6 Riverside Court
Riverside Road
Lower Bristol Road
BATH
BA2 3DZ
Asian Travel. Travel (South and Central America). British Travel.

TRAGARA PRESS
43 Mayburn Avenue
LOANHEAD
EH20 9EY

TRAIL PROJECT
Groundwork House
Bus Station Buildings
Castle Street
MERTHYR TYDFIL
CF42 8BB

TRAMBROOKS
48 Dorrington Road
Cheadle Heath
STOCKPORT
SK3 0PZ
History of Trams.

TRANSLATUM INTERNATIONAL
Mr D S O'Brien
Saithaelwyd Ucha
Carmel
HOLY WELL
CH8 8NU

TRANSPORT PUBLISHING COMPANY
121 Pikes lane
GLOSSOP
SK13 8EH

TRANSVIDEO ENTERPRISES
Old School
Wormshill
SITTINGBOURNE
ME9 0TR
Teachers' resource material for environmental education. "Tree" magazine also printing of flyers etc.

Carolyn TRANT
17 St Anne's Crescent
LEWES
BN7 1SB
Tel 01273 476265
Book publishing in conjunction with 'Silver Studio'.

TRAYLEN
Castle House
49-50 Quarry Street
GUILDFORD
GU7 3UA

TREGATE PRESS
Mary Hopson
Tregate Castle
MONMOUTH
NP5 3QL
Local Religious History. Local History.

TREGENZA STUDIOS
Mr J Ronan
Box 1004
Abbey Place
Mousehole
PENZANCE
TR19 6PQ

TRENDRINE PRESS
Trendine
Zennor
ST. IVES

TR26 3BW
Cornish Flora.

TRIAD ESOTERIC PUBLICATIONS
P.O. Box 134
HORSHAM
RH13 5FG

TRIANGULAR CIRCLE COMPANY
18 Clarence Chambers
39 Corporation Street
BIRMINGHAM
B2 4LS
Travel.

TRIGON PRESS
Roger Sheppard
117 Kent House Road
BECKENHAM
BR3 1JJ
Trigon publishes rference books on books, book collecting and printing.
Our main title is "International Directory of Book Collectors", now in its 5th edition.
Next titles will be "SF Fanzine Index: UK/USA" and "Private Presses"

TRINITY AND ALL SAINTS' COLLEGE
Brownberrie Lane
Horsforth
LEEDS
LS18 5HD
Literature.

TRIP WIRE
Joel Meadows
41 Parkside
Mill Hill
LONDON
NW7 2LN
Tel 0181 906 2650 Fax 0181 959 4192
Comics and music reviews and features.

TRIPLE CAT PUBLISHING
3 Back Lane Cottages
Bucks Horn Oak
FARNHAM
GU10 4LN

TROUBLE & STRIFE
P.O. Box 8
DISS
IP22 3XG

TROUSER PRESS
Anthony Mann
P.O. Box 139
ALDERSHOT
GU12 5XR
Tel 01252 314 585
This 'diary of events' comments on local national and international stories as they occurred personal memories anecdotes and the present day life of the author provide highly amusing observations coupled with thought-provoking and controversial views on serious matters.

TUBA
Charles Graham
Tunley Cottages
Tunley
CIRENCESTER
GL7 6LW
Tuba Magazine (poetry/surrealism) plus poetry books of imaginative kind.

Roy Brian TUBB
13 Elmhurst Road
THATCHAM
RG13 3DQ
Local History.

TUBEWALKING:
World Leisure Marketing
117 The Hollow
Littleover
DERBY
DE3 7BS
Walks in London.

TUDOR SOVEREIGN PUBLISHING
357 Hook Rise
SOUTH SURBITON
KT6 7LW

THE TUFNELL PRESS
Robert Albury
47 Dalmeny Road
LONDON
N7 0DY
Tel 0171 272 4861
*Publishers of books and booklets
on education studies, gender
studies, health education, sociology
and politics.*

TUMI
8-9 New Bond Street Place
BATH
BA1 1BH

Mr Barry TURNER
Town House Publicity
45 Islington Park Street
LONDON
N1 1QB
*Small Press. Also editor of Writers'
Handbook.*

TURNING POINTS
Sabine Kurjo McNeill
21a Goldhurst Terrace
LONDON
NW6 3HB
Tel 0171 625 8804 fax 0171 372
2378
*Turning Points was set up in 1982
to transform consciousness through
lectures, workshops and
conferences. I have always
published my own leaflets and
programmes and eventually the
book Only Connect - The Art and
Technology of Networking for
Personal and Global
Transformation.*

TURNOUT SCOTLAND
Shealinghill
LOCHFOOT
DG2 8NJ
Social Welfare.

TURTLE PUBLISHING COMPANY
2 Rosemary Avenue
BRAINTREE
CM7 7SZ

TV INTERNATIONAL REPARTEE
(see Rose's Repartee)

Thomas Arthur TWEDDLE
M. Lancaster
Parallel Lines
1st Floor
12 Cheltenham Mount
HARROGATE
HG1 1DW
Historical Biography.

TWELVEHEADS PRESS

Chy Mengleth
Twelveheads
TRURO
TR4 8SN

TWENTY-ONE PRESS
745 Barking Road
LONDON
E13 9ER
Social Welfare.

TWIST IN THE TALE PUBLISHING
18 Hind Street
RETFORD
DN22 7EN
Poetry.

TWO-CAN PUBLISHING
27 Cowper Street
LONDON
EC2A 4AP

**TWO MILLIMETRE SCALE
ASSOCIATION**
32 Blount Avenue
EAST GRINSTEAD
RH19 1JQ
Model Railways.

Dave TWYDELL
12 The Furrows
Harefield
UXBRIDGE
UB9 6AT
Sport.

TYNDALE & PANDA PUBLISHING
117 High Street
LOWESTOFT
NR32 1HN

TYNE MUSIC
11 Churchill Street
NEWCASTLE-UPON-TYNE
NE1 4HF

TYPE PUBLISHERS
Unit 367
27 Clerkenwell Close
LONDON
EC1R 0AT
Education.

TYRANNOSAURUS REX PRESS
Keith Seddon, Ph.D.
BM Box 1129
LONDON
WC1N 3XX
Tel & fax 01923 229784
*Specialises in unusual fiction:
gothic, fantasy, and non-category
literature. Not currently looking for
submissions. One title in 1995.
Output limited to one or two titles
per year. Royalties paid.
"Grim Fairy Tales", by Adam
Nicke, illustrated by Jocelyn
Almond.
"House of Gingerbread", by Sheila
Holligon.*

UFO BRIGANTIA
84 Elland Road
BRIGHOUSE
HD6 2QR

UFO DEBATE
40 Stubbing Way
SHIPLEY
BD18 2EZ

UFO TIMES
A. West
16 Southway
BURGESS HILL
RH15 9ST
(See BUFORA)

UK RESIST MAGAZINE
Jake Lagnado
P.O. Box 244a
SURBITON
KT5 9LU
*UK Resist is a 'socially aware'
alternative music magazine with its
roots in the anarchist and punk
movements of the 1980s from rap
to hardcore to political debate on
an almost quarterly basis.*

ULTONIAN PRESS
48 Harberton Park
BELFAST
BT9 6TT

UN-PRESS
Ham Khan & Duncan McCoshan
1 Cholmeley Lodge
Cholmeley Park
LONDON
N6 5EN
Tel 0181-341 9874
*Publishes 'The Journal of Silly,'
cartoon quarterly, anything but silly
in range and variety of visual jokes.
£1 per copy. Superb drawing by
Vlado Palankov in issue no.4. If
you wish to buy original artwork
please phone publisher.*

UNA DEVA
P.O. Box 1177
CHEDDAR
BS27 3UQ
*Publish "O" magazine - fashion,
fetish, fantasies. More than 70
pages of rubber and plastics.*

UNDERSTANDING
(Dionysia Press)
20A Montgomery St
EDINBURGH
EH7 5JS

UNIBIRD
76 Iveson Drive
LEEDS
LS16 6NL

UNICHROME
90 Locksbrook Road
Weston
BATH
BA1 3EN

Travel in Britain.

(THE) UNICORN
P.O. Box 18
HESSLE
HU13 0HW

UNICORN BOOKS
16 Laxton Gardens
Paddock Wood
TONBRIDGE
TN12 6BB

UNICORN PUBLISHING STUDIO
63 Jeddo Road
LONDON
W12 9EE

UNIQUE BOOKS
55 Ventnor Drive
LONDON
N20 8BU
Literature.

UNITY THEATRE NEWS
c/o Lawrie Moore
36 Strathmore Gardens
LONDON
N3 2HL

UNKN
Siobhan O'Rourke
Highfield
Brynymor Road
ABERYSTWYTH
SY23 2HX
Tel 01970 627337
*Founded in 1995 originally to
promote the work of writers
(primarily poets) engaged in the
production of experimental and
marginal text - its core commitment.
Title: "However Introduced to the
Soles!"*

UNPLEASANT BOOKS
Box 32
52 Call Lane
LEEDS
LS1 6DT
Curiosities by Pig Havok.

UNPOPULAR BOOKS
Box 15
136 Kingsland High Road
Dalston
LONDON
E8 2NS
*Ultra Lefties, also distribute Pirate
Productions.*

UN-PRESS
1 Cholmeley Lodge
Cholmeley Park
LONDON
N6 5EN
Tel 0181 341 9874

UPFRONT PUBLISHING
Flat 187
Samuel Lewes Trust
Amhurst Road
LONDON
E8 2DJ

UPSTART CROW PUBLICATIONS
Alistair McCallum
11 St John's Terrace
LEWES
BN7 2DL
Tel 01273 477626
*Publishers of The Shakespeare
Handbooks. Each volume discusses
one play. Invaluable to teachers
and students. Available: Antony*

and Cleopatra, As You Like It, Lear, Macbeth, Twelfth Night. Each £3.99, 40p p&p.

URALIA PRESS
23 Westland Road
WOLVERHAMPTON
WV3 9NZ

URBAN ANGEL PRESS
D.G. Plaiter
13 St Edward's Road
SOUTHSEA
PO5 3DH
Tel 01705 822 146
Plans to produce literature of an extreme nature with minimum sex and violence.

URCHIN BOOKS
Suzanne Andrisson
27 May Road
LOWESTOFT
NR32 2DJ
Urchin Books - publish work by its proprietor Suzanne Andrisson. To date she has shown her prolific abilities by writing books for children consisting of a staggering 139pp. More followed - she pulled her finger out!

UTOPIA OR BUST
Mr Michael Hampton
9 Elham House
Pembury Estate
Pembury Road
LONDON
E5 8LT
Planet X: a poem for tomorrow, 4 pages for 75p.

VACANT HEARSE PRESS
(see ARBOR VITAE PRESS)

VALIAN PUBLISHING
64 Browning Road
Leytonstone
LONDON
E11 3AR

VALIS BOOKS
Nigel Watson
156 Bloom Grove
West Norwood
LONDON

SE27 0HZ
Valis Books publishes a quarterly film magazine "Talking Pictures" along with film orientated books, "Supernatural Spielberg" has been a recent success and a book on "Star Wars" is forthcoming.

VALIS BOOKS
52A Lascotts Road
Wood Green
LONDON
N22 4JN
Subjects: Biography.

THE VAMPYRE SOCIETY
38 Westcroft
CHIPPENHAM
SN14 0LY
Journal "Blood is the Life".

THE VAMPYRE SOCIETY
Ms Carole Bohanan
9 Station Approach
COULSDON
CR5 2NR
Quarterly quality journal. Meetings and film shows.

Michael Arthur VARNEY
c/o D.C. Graphics-Printers
46 Turkey Road
BEXHILL-ON-SEA
TN39 5HE
Local History.

VENNEL PRESS
Richard Price
9 Pankhurst Court
Caradon Close
LONDON
E11 4TB
Poetry from Scotland and other countries illustrated by leading artists. In the Gairfish imprint anthologies of poetry short stories criticism and polemic.

VENTA BOOKS
14 Keith Grove
LONDON
W12 9EZ

VENTURE PUBLICATIONS
11 Shirley Street
HOVE
BN3 3WJ
Publishes a bi-monthly news magazine plus booklets and manuals for freelance writers. Writers Guide Editor G Carroll. Bi-monthly news magazine about markets and media including small press and business journals.

VENTUS BOOKS
Tony Breeze
70 Nottingham Road
Burton Joyce
NOTTINGHAM
NG14 5AL
Tel 01602 313 356
A company formed by Tony Breeze solely for the publication of his own work (see Playwrights Publications Company for publication of other authors).

VERITY PRESS
73 Almshouse Lane
Newmillerdam
WAKEFIELD
WF2 7ST
Second World War.

VER POETS
61 Chiswell Green Lane
ST ALBANS
AL2 3AL

VERTICAL IMAGES
c/o Mike Diss
62 Langdon Park Road
LONDON
N6 5QG

VICTORIA HOUSE PUBLISHING
Selectabook
Folly Road
Roundway
DEVIZES
SN10 2HR
Children's Non-fiction.

VICTORIA PRESS
1 Bank Mansions
Golders Green Road
LONDON
NW11 8LG
Poetry.

VIGIL
Suite 5
Somdor House
Station Road
GILLINGHAM
SP8 4QA

VILLAGE SQUARE PUBLISHING
County Kingsclere
NEWBURY
RG15 8PL
Short Stories.

VILLAGE WRITERS
c/o 34 Church Road
Ballybrack
Dunlaoghaire
COUNTY DUBLIN
Republic of Ireland
Fiction General.

VILLA VIC PRESS
11 Newminster Road
NEWCASTLE-ON-TYNE
NE4 9LL

VINEYARD PRESS
Barnstaple Bookshop
59 High Street
BARNSTAPLE
EX31 1JB
Local History.

VISION SEEKER AND SHARER
Rainbow Publications
P.O. Box 11K9
LEEDS
LS11 8JF
Quarterly defending the rights of native peoples. Incorporating New Diggers of Albion.

VISITOR PUBLICATIONS
Surrey House
Surrey Street
CROYDON
CRO 1SZ

VISUAL ARTS PUBLISHING
82 Sinclair Road
LONDON
W14 0NJ

VITA PRESS
85 Landcroft Road
LONDON
SE22 9JS
Health and Hygiene.

VOLCANO PRESS
P.O. Box 139
LEICESTER
LE2 2YH
Religion.

VOLTURNA & MARSLAND PRESS
52 Ormonde Road
HYTHE
CT21 6DW

VOLO EDITION
66A Ferme Park Road
LONDON
N4 4ED

V.V.L.
POCKLINGTON
'Sunny Dene'
Stain Lane
Theddlethorpe-St-Helens
MABLETHORPE
Poetry.

H.M. WADKIN
Kynance House
Hidding
MELTON MOWBRAY
LE14 3AQ
Local History.

WADSWELL PUBLICATIONS
Haythorne Common
Haton
WIMBOURNE
BH21 7JG
General Fiction.

WAKEFIELD HISTORICAL PUBLICATIONS
19 Pinder's Grove
WAKEFIELD
WF1 4AH
Local history.

WALCOT PRESS
12 St Mary's Gardens
LONDON
SE11 4UD

Charles WALKER
Flat 1
12 Western Place
WORTHING
BN11 3LU
Publish booklets mainly dealing

with the occult, paranormal, UFOs and other mysteries, occasional local history and dolls.

L.G. WALKER
17 Coronation Road
BURNHAM-ON-CROUCH
CM0 8HW
Local History.

WALKAROUND BOOKS
Gayton
Laneside Road
New Mills
STOCKPORT
SK12 4LU

W.H. WALKER AND BROTHERS
Willow Tern
Loudwater
RICKMANSWORTH
WD3 4LD
Historical Biography.

WALKING ROUTES CLWYD
16 Ash Court
RHYL
LL18 4NZ
Walks in Wales.

WALKWAYS
c/o J.S. Roberts
8 Hillside Close
Bartley Green
BIRMINGHAM
B32 4LT
Walks Books.

WALLACE COMMUNICATIONS
Lower Flat
Granco House Street
Dunning
PERTH
PH2 05Q
Local History.

Steven WALLSGROVE
Leycester Court
Leycester Place
WARWICK
CV34 4BY
Local History.

WANDA PUBLICATIONS
c/o Word & Action (Dorset)
61 West Borough
WIMBORNE
BH21 1LX
Tel 01202 883197/889669, Fax 01202 881061
Community publishers.

WANDERING MINSTREL PRODUCTIONS
3 Leah Street
LITTLEBOROUGH
OL15 9BS

WANSTEAD HISTORICAL SOCIETY
81 Warren Road
Wanstead
LONDON
E11 2LU
£1.50 plus 50p p&p.
Wanstead House: The Owners and Their Books by Denis Keeling. Described in East London Record as 'A highly entertaining read - the publication bargain of the year'.

WARATAH BLOSSOMS
P.O. Box 36
340 West Princess Street
GLASGOW
E4 9HF

WARD ENNIS PUBLISHING COMPANY
3 Earsdon Road
West Monkseaton
WHITLEY BAY
NE25 9SX

WAREHAM BEAR PUBLICATIONS
18 Church Street
WAREHAM
BH20 4NT
Children's Fiction.

WARMACHINE
9b Frome Road
Southwick
TROWBRIDGE
BA14 9QB
Fantastic collection of plumbing, wiring, pure mathematics, urine-soaked saffron robes, tales of derring-do, hor wings, leather trumpets, samd soup, Araldite tents, accidents, fighting, lies and provocation (screwdriver not included).

E. WARNEFORD
(See Elizabeth MCDOUGALL)
New Inn Farm
West End Lane
HENFIELD
BN5 9RF
Warneford Family History.

Bernard WARNER
2 Whitemoor Cottages
Loxhore
BARNSTAPLE
EX31 4SR
Travel in Britain.

WARNES PUBLISHING
7 Noel Rise
BURGESS HILL
RH15 8BW
Titles include: "My Research into the Unknown" and "Dogs I Have Known and Loved".

WARREN EDITIONS
28 Ifield Road
LONDON
SW10 9AA

Glyn WARREN
27 The Lakes Road
BEWDLEY
DY12 2QB
Local History.

THE WARTIME COMPANY
Marilyn Ward
4th Floor, Studland House
12 Christchurch Road
BOURNEMOUTH
BH1 3NA
Tel 01212 503902
Publishes The Wartime News which features reminisences from those who fought for peace and the families at home. A non-profit-making quarterly.

WASAFIRI
P.O. Box 195
CANTERBURY
CT2 7XB

WATERMARK PUBLICATIONS (U.K.)
P.O. Box 18
Chiddingfold
GODALMING
GU8 4TP
Architecture.

WATERMILL PRESS
SPA BOOKS
P.O. Box 47
STEVENAGE
SG2 8UH

WATER PRESS
68 Dawes Road
LONDON
SW6 7EJ
Photography.

WATERSHED PUBLICATIONS
Brackley Farmhouse
Gollanfield
INVERNESS
IV1 2QT
Holistic Health.

WATERSIDE PRESS
Domum Road
WINCHESTER
SO23 9NN

WATNAY PUBLISHING
Peter J. Naylor
Ashbourne Business Centre
Shawcroft Centre
Dig Street
ASHBOURNE
DE6 1GF
Tel 01335 300 445
Publishers of local history especially Derbyshire including village histories.

WAVEGUIDE TRAINING & PUBLICATIONS
James Garrod
33 Carter Street
SANDOWN
Isle of Wight
PO36 8DQ
Tel 01983 404342, fax 01983 408058
Jim Garrod has worked in catering since 1964, becoming a major distributor for a world famous microwave manufacturer. His experiences made him aware of the need for clear, readable manuals. With Annemarie Rosier he wrote: Microwave for certain. ISBN 1873437307. 1990, £4.45. New. Garrod, Jim: The caterer's microwave bible, for management staff and students. 1996, 124 pps, landscape format, spiral bound, ISBN 1873373015, £9.95.

WEA
1 Riby Road
Keelby
GRIMSBY
DN37 8ER
Local History.

WEA
Felixstowe Branch
c/o T.A. Cox
7 Constable Road
FELIXSTOWE
IP11 7HL
Local History.

WEA
WEST LANCASHIRE AND CHESHIRE DISTRICT
7-8 Bluecoat Chambers
School Lane
LIVERPOOL
L1 3BX
Education.

WEAVERS PRESS
John T. Wilson
Tregeraint House
ZENNOR
TR26 3DB
Tel & fax 01736 7970
Magazine/book publisher focussing on career change writing and business opportunity. Publishes similar books/manuals and offers book production service.

S.P. WEBB
2 Alderley Court
BERKHAMSTED
HP4 3AD
Library Science.

WELLSPRING
Springside
Bydown
SLIMBRIDGE
EX32 0QB

WELLSPRING PUBLICATIONS
Garden Flat
150 Victoria Road
LONDON
SW4 0NW

WELLSWEEP
John Cayley
1 Grove End House
150 Highgate Road
LONDON
NW5 1PD
Tel & fax 0171 267 3525
Email: ws@shadoof.demon.co.uk
Internet: http://www.inforamp.net/jcayley/wshome.html
Chinese poetry, novels of magic, fantasy and martial arts, essays, avant garde fiction, human rights issues.
Specialist in fine, innovative literary translation from Chinese with truly global reach (see our web site!) No paper catalogue but titles accessible on World Wide Web.

WE PRODUCTIONS
Deucher Mill
YARROW
TD7 5LA

WESSEX AQUARIAN
Josephine Sellers
P.O. Box 1059
STURMINSTER NEWTON
DT10 1YA
Tel 0258 817219
Spirituality & Philosophy. New Age. Alternative Medicine.

THE WESSEX JOURNAL
Peter & Elizabeth Dunn
Court Cottage
West Milton
BRIDPORT
DT6 3SH
Tel 01308 485368, fax 01308 485644
Friendly bi-monthly 'chronicle of the secret heartlands,' spans wide range of interests: nostalgia neutralised by topical comment and wry humour. Single copies £1.75; ann.sub. £13 incl.p&p. ISSN 1358-4596

WEST COL PRODUCTIONS
H Osmaston
Goring
READING
RG8 9AA

Biography.

WEST DERBY PUBLISHING
279 Eaton Road
LIVERPOOL
L12 2AG

(THE) WEST PRESS
48 Ellesmere Road
Benwell
NEWCASTLE-UPON-TYNE
NE4 8TS

Mr William WEST
1 Hawksworth Grove
Kirkstall
LEEDS
LS5 3NB
I publish practical and theoretical writings about my work as a Reichian therapist and spiritual healer.

WESTWOOD PRESS PUBLICATIONS
R. Hollins
44 Boldmere Road
SUTTON COLDFIELD
B73 5TD
Publishers of a wide range of local history and local interest books, plus books for small printers. "The Book of Brum - or Mekya Selfa Tum" "Practical Printers Handbook", the small printers bible.

WESTWORDS
15 Trelawney Road
Peverell
PLYMOUTH
PL3 4JS

WEYFARERS
15 Trelawney Road
Peverell
PLYMOUTH
PL3 4JS

WHARNCLIFFE PUBLISHING
47 Church Street
BARNSLEY
S70 2AH

WHARTON PRESS
74 Hilldale Road
SUTTON
SM1 2JD

W.D. WHARTON
37 Sheep Street
WELLINGBOROUGH
NN8 1BX
History of Windmills.

WHAT THE DOCTORS DON'T TELL YOU
Lynne McTaggart: Editor
4 Wallace Road
LONDON
N1 2PG
Independent monthly newsletter available on subscription only, 'created to lift the lid on modern medicine'. Other publications 'packed with hard-to-get information you just won't see anywhere else.'

WHEEL PUBLICATIONS
144 Leeming Lane South
MANSFIELD
NG19 9BE

WHERE THE HECK IS IT?
No address supplied.

WHITBY OUTPOST
Haggesgate House
Haggesgate
WHITBY
YO21 3PP
Parson's Pence by Noreen Vickers is published by Hull University at £5.75 plus £1.00 p&p. This is a well researched comparative study of 18th century clerical finances in Ryedale and Cleveland, North Yorkshire. Obtainable from bookshops or direct from above.

WHITSLESTOP
Ian Gallacher
Glebelands
Churchtowne
CALSTOCK
PL18 9SG
Tel 01822 833 256
A venture rooted in the West Country. Particularly interested in social and military.

WHITE EAGLE LODGE
Bettine Pickles
New Lands
Brewells Lane
LISS
GU33 7HY
Biography.

WHITE HORSE LIBRARY
Unit 3
Strattons Walk
High Street
MELKSHAM
SN12 6LA
Language.

WHITE ROSE
Nancy Whybrow
14 Browning Road
Temple Hill
DARTFORD
DA1 5ET

WHITE ROW PRESS
Peter Carr
135 Cumberland Road
Dundonald
BELFAST
BT16 0BB
Tel 01232 482 586
Material of (Northern) Irish interest: History, Local History, Folklore.

WHITE TREE BOOKS
49 Park Street
BRISTOL
BS1 5NT

WHITTINGTON PRESS
Lower Marston Farm
Risbury
LEOMINSTER
HR6 0NJ
Fine Printer.

WHITTINGTON PRESS
Manor Farm
ANDOVERSFORD
GL54 4HP
Ceramic Art.

WHITTLES PUBLISHING
Roseleigh House
Latheronwheel
LATHERON
KW5 6DW

WHYLD PUBLISHING
Janie Whyld

Moorland House
North Kelsey Road
Caistor
LINCOLN
LN7 6SF
Specialists in anti-sexist work with boys and progressive issues in education. Mostly teacher/trainer resource materials, eg. "Teaching Assertiveness in Schools and Colleges" and "Using Counselling Skills to Help People Learn". Also multicultural stories with worksheets for use in schools.

(THE) WICCAN
P.O. Box BM 7097
LONDON
WC1N 3XX

WICKED PUBLICATIONS
222 Highbury Road
Bulwell
NOTTINGHAM
NG6 9FE
London History.

A.P.E. WICKHAM
Faith Farm House
Frith Lane
Wickham
FAREHAM
PO17 5AW
Arts (Ceramics).

WIDE BLUE YONDER
107 North Hill
PLYMOUTH
Pl4 8JX

WIDE SKIRT PRESS
Geoff Hattersley
28 St Helen's Street
Elsecar
BARNSLEY
S74 8BH
Aim to publish some good work.

WILDCAT CARDS
P.O. Box 410
SHEFFIELD
S8 9GF

WILDLIFE PUBLISHING
Clive Herbert
67a Ridgeway Avenue
EAST BARNET
EN4 8TL
Tel 0181 440 6314
Publishes local titles on wildlife and the environment in and around London. A new imprint launched in 1989.

WILDLIFE GARDENING MONTHLY
55 Wyndham Road
LONDON
W13 9TE
Magazine.

WILD SWAN PUBLISHING LTD
83 St Margarets Grove
St Margarets
TWICKENHAM
TW1 1JF

WILFION BOOKS
4 Townhead Terrace
PAISLEY
PA1 2AX
Poetry.

Mr Brian WILLIAMSON
46 Wellington Road
NEW BRIGHTON

L45 2NG
Freelance mathematician and poet from Merseyside.

HENRY WILLIAMSON SOCIETY
14 Nether Grove
Longstanton
CAMBRIDGE
CB4 5EL
Newsletter. Literature.

Roy WILLIAMSON
4 Cleevemont
Evesham Road
CHELTENHAM
GL52 3JT
Music.

WILLOW PUBLISHING
Barecroft Common
MAGOR
Newport
NP6 3EB
Sport.

Edward WILMOT
32 Castle Row
CANTERBURY
CT1 2QY
Historical Biography.

Patrice M. WILNECKER
73 Gwynne Road
Parkstone
POOLE
BH12 2AR
Historical Fiction.

David A. WILSON
16 Cragside
Sedgefield
STOCKTON-ON-TEES
TS21 2DQ
Horology.

WILTON 65 PUBLISHING
Flat Top House
Bishop Wilton
YORK
YO4 1RY

WILTS FAMILY HISTORY SOCIETY
Mrs L Williams
7 Chandler Close
DEVIZES
SN10 3DS
Have a small but perfectly formed list of many invaluable local studies including the must-have baptism and burial series for the period 1559 to the mid 19th century. Ask for the catalogue.

WILTSHIRE LIFE
Mark Allen
Visa Publications
Jesses Farm
Snow Hill
DINTON
SP3 5HN
01722 716996
Relaunched in 1995.

WIMPOLE BOOKS
Pip's Peace
Kenton
STOWMARKET
IP14 6JS

THE WINDRUSH PRESS LTD
Windrush House
Main Street
Adlestrop
MORETON-IN-MARSH
GL56 0YN

Green fiction for children - ages 9 and up. Used widely in schools as class readers and ideal for libraries. Distributed also through the Quill Hedgehog Club, which has sprung up and produces a quarterly newsletter for members on environmental matters.

WINDSOR PUBLICATIONS
329 St Leonards Road
WINDSOR
SL4 3DS

WINE SOURCE
393 Ham Green
Holt
TROWBRIDGE
BA14 6PX
Wine.

Peter WINGENT
10 The Dean
ALRESFORD
SO24 9AX
History of Air Transport.

WINGHAM PRESS
Seymour Place
High Street
WINGHAM
CT3 1AB

WINTER PRESS
Simon Curtis
50 Rockbourne Road
Forest Hill
LONDON
SE22 2DD

H E WINTER PUBLISHING
Thorneycroft
Blindcrake
COCKERMOUTH
CA13 0QP
Publisher of Cumbrian and Lakeland History Booklets.

WINTER PRODUCTIONS
Oak Walk
SAINT PETER
Jersey
General Fiction.

Michael WINTON BA PGCE ALA
Eagle Cottage
33A Newmarket Road
NORWICH
NR2 2HN
'Holden's Annual and Country Directory of the United Kingdoms and Wales for the Year 1811.' Facsimile edition, 1996, 8.25" x 4.75", 3 vols, 1,616 pp, 410 places, 210,000 name entries, ISBN 1-898593-14-0; £43.50 + P&P = UK £5, Europe and surface mail £9.50, Airmail £23.00; bound, printed and published to same high standard as his reprints of Pigot and Co.'s directories.

WIRE
21 Lidstone Close
Goldsworth Park
WOKING
GU21 3BG
Poetry Society & Magazine.

WISEFILE
21 Cromford Way
NEW MALDEN
KT3 3BB

WISHING WELL PUBLISHING

P.O. Box 176
HULL
HU9 2PQ

WITAN BOOKS
Jeff Kent
65 Audley Road
Alsager
STOKE ON TRENT
ST7 2QW
Witan Books is a vehicle for the promotion of the works of Jeff Kent, uncensored stories by real authors and anarchy, ecology and co-operation, leading towards the creation of a new society inspired by the model of Anglo-Saxon England.

WITMEHA PRESS
The Orchard
Wymondham
MELTON MOWBRAY
LEICESTERSHIRE
LE14 2AZ

WITNEY ANTIQUES
96-100 Corn Street
WITNEY
OX8 7BU
Art.

WITS END
27 Pheasant Close
Winnersh
WOKINGHAM
RG

WOAD PRESS WOAD
Blue Gate
Burysbank Road
NEWBURY
Berks
Social Sciences.

WOLFS HEAD PRESS
P.O. Box 77
SUNDERLAND
SR1 1EB
A micropress specializing in miscellania, funded mainly by selling aluminium cans for recycling and hanging on grimly in the face of the recession and long-term unemployment. Send us money. "....more entertaining than many expensive books..." John Michellson. "Wearwolf", sporadic magazine, send 2 x 25p stamps for latest copy. "Crop Circles for Fun and Profit" (John Reid) 5 x 25p stamps.

WOMEN'S STAND
Chris George
95B Victoria Parade
Kilburn
LONDON
NW6 6TD
Tel 0171 624 4428
Women's postcards, mugs, tapes, etc. plus independent magazines.

Linda WONG
1 Purcell Avenue
TONBRIDGE
TN10 4DP
Food decoration.

WOOD AND WATER
4 High Tor Close
Babbacombe Road
BROMLEY
BR1 3LQ

One of the oldest established pagan magazines. Goddess-centred.

WOODCRAFT PRESS
152 Hadlow Road
TONBRIDGE
TN9 1PB

WOODFIELD PUBLISHING
Woodfield House
Arundel Road
Fontwell
ARUNDELL
BN18 0SD
Biography. Historical Biography. Children's Fiction. Local History (from the rest of Britain). Humour.

WOOD GARTH PRESS
15 First Avenue
Bardsey
LEEDS
LS17 9BE

WOOD LEA PRESS
Grassendale Lane
LIVERPOOL
L19 0NH

WOODMANS PRESS
(see And What of Tomorrow?)

WOODSTOCK PUBLICATIONS
Spelsbury House
Spelsbury
OXFORD
OX7 3JR

TIM WOODWARD PUBLISHING
23 Grand Union Centre
Kensal Road
LONDON
W10 5AX
Literature.

WOOD WIND PUBLICATIONS
David Hart
42 All Saints Road
Kings Heath
BIRMINGHAM
B14 7LL
Tel 0121 443 2495
Poetry-related publications, not normally publishing actual poetry.

CECIL WOOLF PUBLISHING
Jean Woolf
1 Mornington Place
LONDON
NW1 7RP
Tel 0171 387 2394

Ron WOOLLACOTT
185 Gordon Road
LONDON
SE15 3RT
A Historical Tour of Nunhead and Peckham Rye, by Ron Woollacott, illustrated with black and white drawings, plans and photos. This little book is a must for anyone interested in the history of South London. £2.95 plus 50p p&p from the author, see above.

P. WOOLLER
Walford Lodge
WALFORD
Craven Arms
SY7 0JT
Railways.

WORD & ACTION (DORSET)

43 Avenue Road
WIMBOURNE
BH21 1BS

THE WORD FACTORY
17 Wathen Road
LEAMINGTON SPA
CV32 5UX
Publishers poetry in booklets and on t-shirts.

WORDMAKER BOOKS
Clatleigh House
Little Hyden Lane
Clanfield
WATERLOOVILLE
PO8 0RU
Children's Fiction.

WORDPLAY PUBLISHING
Tony Bowerman
70 Garden Lane
CHESTER
CH1 4EY
Tel 01244 378 927
Specialists in local guides and interpretative literature for the tourism and leisure markets.

WORDS & IMAGES
(see Dragonfly Press and Fern Press)

WORDS AND THE STONES
1st Floor
Scottish Life House
GLASGOW
G2 5TS

WORDSHARE
Keith Ashton
3 Grainsby Close
LINCOLN
LN6 7QF

WORDS MAGAZINE
23 James Collins Close
LONDON
W9 3PU
Quarterly Short Story Magazine published as fundraising effort on behalf of the Childrens Hospice Appeal (reg charity 800485). Sample Copy Free.

WORDS PRESS
Hod House
Child Okeford
BLANDFORD FORUM
DT11 8EH

WORD TEAM
54 Borough High Street
LONDON
SE10 1XL
Local History.

WORDWELL
P.O. Box 69
BRAY
County Wicklow
Republic of Ireland
Irish Archaeology. Irish Prehistory.

(THE) WORKER ESPERANTIST (SATEB)
29 Farrance Road
ROMFORD
RM6 6EB

WORKING PRESS
Stefan Szczelkun
84 Shartsted Street
LONDON
SE17 3TN

An inclusive agency/imprint which promotes self-publications on art and culture by working class people. Sae for list.

WORKING FOR CHILDCARE
77 Holloway Road
LONDON
N7 8JZ
Social Welfare.

WORKING KNOWLEDGE TRANSFER
Brunel Science Centre
Coopers Hill Lane
EGHAM
TW20 0JZ
School Textbooks.

THE WORKING TRAVELLER
Shane Donovan
Compass House
Horsecroft Road
The Pinnacles
HARLOW
CM19 5BN
A quarterly magazine concerning itself with working holidays and budget travel. Contains current job vacancies, articles and a long list of contact addresses.

WORKS PUBLISHING
12 Blakestones Road
Slaithwaite
HUDDERSFIELD
HD7 5UG
Magazine for SF, imaginative fiction, graphics.

(THE) WORKS
122 Clive Street
Grangetown
CARDIFF
CF1 7J

THE WORKSHOP PRESS
Hanna's
Bolford Street
THAXTED
CM6 2PY
Tel 01371 830 366
Books on typography type design and decoration in limited editions of about 170 copies printed and bound at the press.

WORLD MUSICALS
28 Wilsford Green
Egbaston
BIRMINGHAM
B15 3UG
Walks Books for the whole of Britain.

WORLDS END PRESS
Star and Garter Lane
Egerton
ASHFORD
TN27 9BE

WORLD TREE PRODUCTIONS
Umiak Mahoupe
49 Calthorpe Street
LONDON
WC1X OHH
Tel 0171 833 4463
A branch of World Tree Arts Trust which also produces theatre and art exhibitions. We publish two cassettes of Edward Lear nonsense poems set to music. And a collection of short stories.

WORLEY PUBLICATIONS
10 Rectory Road East
Felling
GATESHEAD
NE10

WREN PRESS
22 St Mary's Drive
Pound Hill
CRAWLEY
RH10 3BD

WRITEAWAY
(same address as Windows Projects)

WRITE DRAW PARTNERSHIP
PO Box 41
ELY
Cambridgeshire
01353 662540
Magazine 'Escape' helps entrepeneurs to run home-based businesses.

WRITERS BOOKSHOP
7-11 Kensington High Street
LONDON
W8 5NP
The Small Press Guide 1997 edition. Second outing and smart paperback. A directory of about 500 presses. Leans towards poetry + zines and sf. A very educational survey of the scene is provided by the introduction by Peter Finch. He should know since he manages the Arts Council's bookshop in Cardiff which runs all sorts of schemes to promote small presses. Like any such effort the info changes as it goes to press but so what? Buy your copy direct for £7.99 or get it from the NSPC along with other helpful resource tools. P&p £1.50.

WRITERS' FORUM
John Benton
9/10 Roberts Close
WEDNESBURY
WS10 8SS
"Writers' Forum". Quarterly magazine for new and semi-professional writers. Carries features on the art, craft and business of writing. Does not publish fiction or poetry, (except winning entries to our competitions).

WRITERS FORUM
89a Petherton Road
LONDON
N5 2QT
Tel 0171 226 2657
Experimental poetry and related arts - concrete visual, performance, sound, computer, music, dance, photography, etc.

WRITERS GUIDE
G Carroll
11 Shirley Street
HOVE
BN3 3WJ

WRITERS MONTHLY
Ms Amanda Armstrong
29 Turnpike Lane
LONDON
W8 OEP

WRITERS NEWS LTD
P.O. Box 4
Nairn

IV12 4HU

WRITERS OWN MAGAZINE
121 Highbury Grove
Clapham
BEDFORD
MK41 6DU

WRITERS ROSTRUM
14 Ardbeg Road
ROTHESAY
Bute
PA20 0NJ

WRITING MAGAZINE
P.O. Box 4
NAIRN
IV12 4HU

WRITE SOLUTION
David Weldon
Flat 1
11 Holland Road
HOVE
BN3 1JF
We evaluate and report on book and short story manuscripts. Rewrite. Ghost write etc. We issue reports. Plus, from time to time, a free newsletter.

WRITING ULSTER
Dept of English Media & Theatre Studies
Univ of Ulster
COLERAINE
Co Londonderry
BT52 1SA

WRITING WOMEN
7 Cavendish Place
NEWCASTLE-UPON-TYNE
NE2 2NE

WYRD
187 Wellington Road
Handsworth
BIRMINGHAM
B20 2ES

WYVERN
5 Polly Brooks Yard
Pedmore Road
Lye
STOURBRIDGE
DY9 8DG

XANADU PUBLICATIONS LIMITED
19 Cornwall Road
Stroud Green
LONDON
N4 4PH

XENOS
29 Preband Road
BEDFORD
Tel 01234 349067
Magazine for SF, fantasy, radical departure from the norm.

X PRESS
55 Broadway Market
LONDON
E8 4PH
Spring catalogue 1996 from the outfit which had a Small Press hit with 'Yardie.' Now dozens of titles of interest on black writing also a black kids series.

X-PRESS
Jane Colling
24 Banyard Road
LONDON
SE16 2YA
Tel 071 231 1106
Prints and Postcards. Spot the Dog, Spot Malcom Green. Alphabet Series.

XS-PRESS
Zane Black
Box 12
226 Uxbridge Road
Shepherd's Bush
LONDON
W12 7JD
New press specialising in erotica, s/m, contes cruels, dark fantasy.

YEAR MINUS ZERO PRESS
P.O. Box 71
HASTINGS

YEOMAN PUBLISHING
32 Kingsley Road
KINGSWINFORD
DY6 9RX

YES PUBLICATIONS
Holywell House
32 Shipquay Street
LONDONDERRY

BT48 6DW
Military History.

YESTERYEAR BOOKS
Daniel Young
60 Woodville Road
LONDON
NW11 9TN
*All books A4 size soft cover,
average 96pp, all on British classic
cars, histories, road test or press
publicity collections or buyers
guides, average price £9.95.
Lead titles: "Land Rover 90 & 110
Owner & Buyers Guide 1983-
1990", by James L. taylor, 64pp,
ISBN 1 873078 17 X, £8.95
"Advertising Triumph Sports Cars
1947-1981", by D. Young, 96pp,
ISBN 1 873078 11 0, £9.95.*

Y FFYNNON
c/o The Flat
Plas Llidiardau
Llanilar
DYFED
SY23 5PF

Y.I. PUBLISHING
120 West Street
BRIDGWATER
TA6 7EU

YORE PUBLICATIONS
Dave Twydell
12 The Furrows
HAREFIELD
UB9 5AT
Tel 01895 823 404
*Specialists in football books
normally with an historic theme -
football clubs' histories (current and
defunct) reprints of pre-war football
books etc. Also home video on the
same subjects. Newsletters issued
three times a year.*

YORICK BOOKS
27 Manwood Avenue
CANTERBURY
CT2 7AH

YORKSHIRE ART CIRCUS
Old School
School Lane
Glasshoughton
CASTLEFORD
WF10
*Community publishers of a wide-
range of titles. Roadshow
available.*

YORKSHIRE DIALECT SOCIETY
Hon.Secretary
Farfields
Weeton Lane
Weeton
LEEDS
LS17 0AN
*Est. 1897, encourages study and
recording of dialect; two ann.
publications for members,
publishes wide range of
anthologies of dialect literature.*

YOUNG WOODCHESTER
Ms Alison Flowers
P.O. Box 26
STROUD
GL5 5YF
Tel 01453 832752
"Publishing with a difference."

YUDANSHA PRESS
7 Crossfields Avenue

CULCHETH
WA3 5RS
Sport.

ZANZIBAR PRODUCTIONS
3 Ashfield Close
Bishops Cleve
CHELTENHAM
GL52 4LG
*Offbeat surreal poetry and any
oddities I find interesting, also SF
magazine.*

ZARDOZ BOOKS
20 Whitecroft
Dilton Marsh
WESTBURY
BA13 4DJ
Tel/fax 01373 865371, e-mail
10124.262@compuserve.com
*Also available. Special
paperbacks, pulps and comics.
£12.50.
New title: (published under ZEON
imprint) * Holland, Steve &
Chibnall, Steve - editors: The
mushroom jungle, a history of post-
war paperback publishing. Traces
the emergence of Panther, Corgi,
Pan, etc., col. & B/W, 216 pps,
234mm x 166mm, ISBN
1874113017, £14.95.*

ZED BOOKS LTD
57 Caledonian Road
LONDON
N1 9BU

ZEN ART PUBLICATIONS
Bowmore Gallery
8 Halkin Arcade
Motcombe Street
LONDON
W1P 5DJ
Subjects: Art.

ZEON PUBLICATIONS
(see ZARDOZ)

Neal ZETTER
12 Kimberley Way
LONDON
E4 6DE
*Books of easy-to-read poems,
cynicism, humour, satire - kids love
'em.*

ZODIAC HOUSE PUBLICATIONS
Jan Roberts
7 Wells Road
GLASTONBURY
BA6 9DN
Tel 01458 835 450
*Our Motto: Apocalypse Now! A
giant among small presses. The
flame still blazes and singes! Get
our free catalogue/magazine
which not only lists our titles but tell
you why the press exists. Why do
you exist? Your problem.*

ZOILUS PRESS
Ronn Binns
P.O. Box 9315
LONDON
E17 4UU
*Zoilus Press exists to promote
surreal/comic/experimental fiction
outside the commercial mainstream.
Our authors include Frank Key,
Alison Keller, Charles H. Cutting,
Mac Daly, Elaine Laban and Ellis
Sharp.
Lead titles: Mac Daly & Ellis
Sharpe, "Engels on Video - a Joint
Production", ISBN 0 95220228 2 4,
£6.99, 155 pages (1995); Charles
H. Cuttng, "The Surleighwick
Effect", ISBN 0 9522028 0 8,
£7.99, 277 pages (1994)
New title: Sharp, Ellis: To Watsonia
Feb 1996, 153 pps, ISBN
0952202840, £7.99.
"Sharp is a maddening writer. His
words are well-chosen, his
sentences make perfect sense, his
paragraphs get woozy with non-
sequiturs... seductively interesting
prose that leaves a thicket of
confusion in its wake." Factsheet
Five.*

OTHERS:

061
20 Russell Road
Whalley Range
MANCHESTER
M16 8DL

3:X (Previously ION PRESS 23)
Ion D'Mentiere
95 Old Castle Road
Cathcart
GLASGOW
Tel 041 833 5984
*Experimental Poetry/Prose Illust.
With emphasis on good design. All
desirable limited editions.
Catalogue due, send SAE for info.*

4MATION
14 Castle Park Road
BARNSTAPLE
EX32 8PA
Desk Top Publishing.

4 U
Flat 4
Dorchester Court
2 Colney Hatch Lane
Muswell Hill
LONDON
N10 1BU
*Writing to order. A piece written
and printed just for you. A unique
service. Limited editions of one.
Guaranteed. SAE for details.*

Complete and return the form on page 179 for a FREE listing for your small press!

HELP US TO HELP YOU
Have you spotted a mistake?
Congratulations.

What should you do about it? Stamp and scream? Rage at us? Or do you point it out politely so that we can correct our records and tell others? More of the free service run entirely by volunteers. Which is calculated to work?

"Although I was delighted to see us on the front page I was disappointed to see some fundamental mistakes in both our company name and address, both of which may mean potential customers are unable to contact us. Please note the JENNYWREN is written as one word and our correct address is Ivy Cottage, Blackwell (not Clackwell) Worcs B60 1QJ (not B60 1QT). I would be grateful if you could confirm that you have amended your records and that the corrections will be made on all subsequent publications and perhaps notice could be drawn to this in the next Small Press Listings to inform anyone who may have had difficulties reaching us. I look forward to hearing from you,. Thank you."

"Months ago I submitted a cheque and our details as publishers but you have not included us on this list. This is the second list received and frankly I am disappointed. Why have we been omitted? PSYSYS Ltd, 33 Marlborough Road, SWINDON SN3 1PH."

In both cases we apologise. First case: the errors do not seem bad enough to send your mail astray. Second case: we work our way through the backlog and include entries asap. In both cases you have been given prominence on this page!

Again we remind you the NSPC is an entirely voluntary organisation which receives no grants, funding or sponsorship so its workers receive no pay. They do it because they believe what they provide *helps.*

We hope there will soon be a Centre as there was at Middlesex University 1992-1996. That it will have an office full of equipment and workers – all properly paid. Then we would understand if you were annoyed, however we would not expect so many mistakes!

SAFETY NET
Although we do not plan a new edition of this HANDBOOK this century we provide regular updates every quarter in *Small Press Listings*. We also publish a bi-monthly newsletter, *News From The Centre*. Between them we can mention any errors quite quickly. That seems to us a sensible approach.

WHAT SHOULD YOU DO?
On the facing page you will see 2 copies of our standard form for a free listing. Photo-copy one, fill it in and send it to us. At the back of the book you will find full details about the Centre and a subscription form to our two magazines: *SPL* and *NFTC*. You can subscribe to either or jointly. To show you how this system works we reproduce a facsimile issue of *Small Press Listings* on pages 181 to 184.

WE DO OUR BEST.
PLEASE DO YOURS.
Please don't scribble furiously on your copy of the magazine and send it back to us. We have our own so we can check. Besides you are ruining your copy, wasting it and depriving yourself of information about more than 70 colleagues. Of course if you aren't interested in them why should they be interested in you?

THE NATIONAL SMALL PRESS CENTRE
BM BOZO, LONDON WC1N 3XX

YOUR CHANCE TO GET FREE PUBLICITY FOR YOUR SMALL PRESS

Please enter details of your Press for a FREE listing in the National Small Press Centre publications and return the completed form.

Name of imprint: ....
....
....
....
....

Contact person: ....

Address: ....
....
....
....
....
....
....

Write a **short** description of your Press (30 words max and two lead titles):

Information supplied to the National Small Press Centre will be included in News from the Centre and Small Press Listings, to keep you in touch and help promote your Press. They are available for sale or by subscription from the NSPC.

THE NATIONAL SMALL PRESS CENTRE
BM BOZO, LONDON WC1N 3XX

YOUR CHANCE TO GET FREE PUBLICITY FOR YOUR SMALL PRESS

Please enter details of your Press for a FREE listing in the National Small Press Centre publications and return the completed form.

Name of imprint: ....
....
....
....
....

Contact person: ....

Address: ....
....
....
....
....
....
....

Write a **short** description of your Press (30 words max and two lead titles):

Information supplied to the National Small Press Centre will be included in News from the Centre and Small Press Listings, to keep you in touch and help promote your Press. They are available for sale or by subscription from the NSPC.

SMALL PRESS LISTINGS

The shop window for Small Press publications • Spring 1997

HOW TO BENEFIT FROM SPL.

1 Apart from ordering directly, so cutting out all middlemen, bookshops and distributors, you may wish to find out more about the Presses. Ask for their catalogue.

2 Small Presses see point 1. You can build up your customers at no extra cost. The importance of having a catalogue is obvious.

3 Small Presses - you must remember the cost of p&p. Of course you may want to waive it since you are not giving away 55% to distributors. Please specify when sending info. to SPL

4 Libraries and bookshops – you will learn about Small Presses you never knew existed. SPL is your doorway into their world. If you want to stock any of their publications, or require a catalogue, get in touch directly.

5 Publisher's discount operates in the mainstream. How about some solidarity in the SPs? The customary discount is 33% ie what you expect to allow any bookseller. Bona fides essential.

6 You can read more about some of these Presses in About The Presses in News From The Centre, available from the NSPC.

7 Inclusion in SPL automatically guarantees you an entry in the Centre's Handbook, 1997 edition.

8 Tell us anything useful. Do you accept phone orders? Credit cards? What info. do you find helpful? Send us info about any SP you have discovered. Help each other to help yourself.

9 Deadline for SPL7 (Summer): 22 April 1997.

10 All listings in SPL are free.

AEGIS PRESS
14 Herdson Road, Folkestone, Kent CT20 2PB.
Edited by David Shields, John Rice and Michael Curtis with front cover illustration by Sara Wicks, 'The Scarpfoot Zone' is a major new anthology of poetry by contemporary Kent writers. 35 of the County's leading poets have contributed work in a diverse array of forms, styles and subjects. Included are poems about art, sport, history, travel, love and loss. Many poets chose to write about Kent, a county undergoing immense change. The work both builds on the rich tradition of poetry in Kent and, as we approach the end of the century, points boldly into the future. £5.95 ISBN 0 9519777 3 3

ARBOR VITAE PRESS
BM Spellbound,
London WC1N 3XX.
'A Christmas Ghost Story' by Althea D. Wood.
Limited edition (26 copies) lettered and signed by the author.
Written in 1992 and first aired at a special Christmas reading which took place at Coles farm, Backwell, Somerset in that year. This special edition is for private circulation only, arranged by Arbor Vitae, who also designed the booklet.

AWAY PUBLICATIONS
PO Box 2173, Bath BA1 3TJ
01225 338269
A small independent press specialising in creative fiction and non-fiction. Two titles in 1997.

BIRDS HILL PUBLICATIONS
Maurice Sturgeon, 24 Goldfinch Close, Birds Hill, Chelsfield, Kent BR6 6NF. Tel/Fax: 01689 850859.
'Half A Mo!' by Maurice

Sturgeon. 44pp. £6. ISBN 1 900894009. A collection of stories and rhymes. The anecdotes and accounts relate to true events. The poems were mostly written to amuse, provoke and occasionally infuriate the author's family and friends. Author's acknowledgement of encouragement from Granville Writers. Also available on tape cassette at £5.00.

BLACK ECONOMY BOOKS
Dept. 8, 1 Newton Street, Piccadilly, Manchester M1 1HW
Latest title is 'From Colditz to Bangladesh' a mixture of poetry, story, fairy-tale and graphics with the common theme of Childhood often to do with poverty, misery and the fun found despite all that. 52pp paperback, ISBN 1-901178 00 5, price £2.00. Also have a catalogue of previous publications.

BROADFIELD PUBLISHING
71 Broadfield Road, Manchester M14 4WE
The fourth edition of the Manchester Guide, 'A Year in The Theatre' - of greater Manchester is the biggest and best yet. More pages, more - you name it. Only the price hasn't increased. 'Less than a penny a play.' £6.99. ISBN 0852 1502 3 9

R. BROOMHEAD PUBLISHING
P.O. Box 219, Stockport SK4 1LL
'Robin Hood: ancient poems, songs and ballads.' 356 pp, hardback, £14.99. Please order from your local bookshop or enquire direct from publisher sending SAE.

DALE HOUSE PRESS
John Crook, 18 Keere Street, Lewes, East Sussex, BN7 1TY. Tel: 01273 472007.
'The Ladies of Miller's' by Diane Crook. The book tells the story of two remarkable, eccentric sisters who in 1939 purchased the former home of a miller in Lewes High Street and promptly set about turning it into an

arts centre! With help from nearby Charleston, the two sisters were able to maintain the artistic impetus through the war and went on to set up the influential Millers Press. The book provides an interesting glimpse of pre and post-war cultural life in the area. Price £7.50.

EXTRAORDINARY PEOPLE PRESS
Katherine Butler, Suite 412 Triumph House, 185-191 Regent Street, London W1R 7WB Tel 0171 7343749
'We are a new small press which has just published our first title 'Trans-x-u-all, the naked difference.'
We are dedicated to publishing books by or about 'extraordinary people.' Our publications are non-fiction. Our second book is due out late 1997 on the subject of stage hypnosis.' 'Trans-x-u-all' costs £11.99. ISBN 0 952948 20 6.

EARTHRIGHT PUBLICATIONS
Monica Frisch, 8 Ivy Avenue, Ryton, Tyne & Wear NE40 3PU, Tel. 0191 413 7972. E-mail mfrisch@gn.apc.org
Social, environmental and local issues. Latest publication got splendid review in 'BBC Vegetarian Good Food Magazine.' (Feb. 1997). Attractive distillation of experience by Red Herring which runs a wholefood shop, bakery and restaurant.
Red Herring Workers' Co-op, 'Cordon Rouge: Vegetarian and Vegan Recipes.' 176pp, pbk, illus, ISBN 0-907367-10-0, £7.50(p&p incl.)

THE FRUSTRATED WRITERS SOCIETY
12 Harrisons Court, Myers Lane, London SE14 5JR. Tel: 0171 635 8170
'Peckham Cry' by Janice Cooke. An innovative approach to raising funds for the prevention of child abuse. This is the story of a child growing up in London during the 1950's. £6.99 (post-free). Send a SAE A5 envelope with your remittance.

GERHARD AHN

Bonstorfer Str 7. 29320 Hermannsburg, Germany.
'Letter from the Australian Jungle'.
New European small press. Contact the publisher for more details.

GIEBELS PUBLISHING

10 Martello Manor, Strand Road, Bray, Co. Wicklow, Ireland. Tel. (01) 286 4348. Fax. (01) 286 6737.
Publish 'Evolution in Life Beyond Death' by Henk Giebels. Which promises new insights into evolution beyond Earth from before the Big Bang to the Apocalypse and Beyond.
192pp paperback, ISBN 0-9525980-1-9, Price £8.99.

GORSE PUBLICATIONS

PO Box 214, Shamley Green, Guildford, Surrey, GU5 0SW.
'Pigeon Grounded' a new collection of poems by Pat Earnshaw. Contains a medley of poems in differing styles and content. Signed copies at £6.99 (post free).

HIGNELL'S APPLE PRESS

Susan Campbell (Miss), 550 Berridge Road West, Hyson Green, Nottingham NG7 5JU.
Two titles in print. Send for details.

KERNOW POETS PRESS

18 Frankfield Rise, Tunbridge Wells, TN2 5LF. Tel: 01892 539800. 'Postcards from Occupied Lands' by Bill Headdon is a collection of poetry written from the aspect of exile, wherever exile might be, the land which exists both as concrete reality and the shifting, treacherous quick-sands of memory. £2.95 plus 50p p+p.
'Cornish Links' is an anthology of poems arranged in the context of a Cornish travelogue. £4.95 plus 60p p+p.

Frank KEY

103 Cavendish Road, Highams Park, London E4 9NG
After a two year silence the Hooting Yard calendar returns. All those who have had no idea what day it was can now live again. The 1997 edition rejoices (© M Thatcher) in the title 'Planet of the Crumpled Jesuits.' Mr E informs customers, 'Instead of the usual cack-handed drawings you get a dozen photographs culled from an old encyclopedia, each one doctored and crumpled - or possibly crumpled and doctored.' Each copy is signed, (by whom is not mentioned) numbered and individually dedicated (your decision). For all this you only give money? A simple £5 or cheque to the same value made payable to some 'P J Byrne.'

LANGUAGES INFORMATION CENTRE/CANOLFAN HYSBYSRWYDD IEITHYDDOL

Joseph Biddulph, 32 Stryd Ebeneser, Pontypridd CF37 5PB, Cymru/Wales
Send SASE for this publisher's amazing list with international coverage of languages and dialects you don't often find elsewhere.
'Biddulph's Concise Versemaker: some reflections on traditional English metre, and how to shape it for yourself.' 28 pp, ISBN 0-948565-48-9, £4.00. Postage free in UK. JUST OUT 'Biddulph's Handbook of West Country Brythonic.' This is the quest for the lost Celtic language of South West England. ISBN 1-897999-06-2, UK £4.00. All monies payable to Joseph Biddulph.

LITTLE BIG BOOKS

Number Six, 4th Avenue, Birmingham B29 7EU
Plan the first part of an evolving series of teacher aids titled the 'User's Guide to the Brain' by Peter Scott and Grant Jesse. A net bulletin board will be set up to follow the second stage pilot scheme in Spring. More info from e-mail: ugh@grant-jesse.com

LONG BARN BOOKS

Longmoor Farmhouse, Ebrington, Chipping Camden, Gloucestershire GL55 6NW
Susan HILL, 'Listening to the Orchestra.' Four short stories. Pbk, £3.99

MIDDLETON PRESS

Easebourne Lane, Midhurst, West Sussex GU29. 9AZ 01739 813169
Starting on a huge programme we are producing a set of 100 unissued, mint condition hard back albums covering former Southern Railways routes and some adjacent GWR lines. The work has taken sixteen years. The titles are by Vic Mitchell and Keith Smith. The offer includes all the long out of print titles and a composite index to all the stations illustrated. The set costs £995.00 - a saving of £100 on current prices. Only available direct from Middleton.

MODERN RECORDS CENTRE

University of Warwick Library, Coventry CV4. 7AL 01203 524219
The repository for the archives of the Trades Union Congress 1920-1970 and many trade union archives. Other records held include those of the CBI and its predecessors, motor industry business records and the papers of leading Socialists such as Dick Crossman and Victor Gollancz. Send for details of recent titles such as Women at Work and in Society, A Postman's Round etc.

Jeff MORRIS (publisher)

14 Medina Road, Foleshill, Coventry CV6 5JB
MORRIS, Jeff: 'The History of the Blyth and Chambois Lifeboats.' 'The History of the Eyemouth Lifeboats.' Both vols. illus, A5 pbk, £2.50 each incl. p&p. Other titles on same topic by different authors available, ask for details.

OLD STILE PRESS

Francis and Nicholas McDowall, Catchmays Court, Llandogo, Monmouthshire NP5 4TN.
Tel/Fax: 01291 689226.
'Lens of Crystal' poems by Robin Skelton, images by Sara Philpott. Exploration of the beautiful and ingenious verse forms of medieval Wales. The poetry is complemented by etched and cut linoleum illustrations. 265 x 192mm, 80pp. Handset text, printed on special 175g mould-made paper. Fine binding and slipcase. Limited edition of 240 copies, each signed by the poet and artist. £95.00 (plus p+p). ISBN: 0 907664 39 3. 'Earth Dances' poems by Ted Hughes, images by R.J. Lloyd. Exciting collaboration of painter and printmaker who has made a personal selection of the poet's work for this edition. 317 x 225mm 48pp. Handset text printed on hand-made plant papers. Limited edition of 250 copies each signed by poet and artist. £195.00. ISBN: 0 907664 33 4.

R & B PUBLISHING

3 Inglebert Street, London EC1R 1XR
Tel/fax 0171 837 3854
A new firm specialising in reprints of classic texts. Third title available. Send for list.

RNLI NORFOLK AND SUFFOLK RESEARCH GROUP

Mark Roberts, 4 Paines Orchard, Cheddington, Bedfordshire LU7 0SN
Mark Roberts & Nicholas Leach: 'The 37ft Oakley Lifeboats: a History 1957-1994.' Focuses on design and innovative self-righting system. £5 inc. p&p. Please make cheques payable to 'RNLI Norfolk and Suffolk Research Group.'

SIGMA LEISURE

1 South Oak Lane, Wilmslow, Cheshire SK9 6AR. Tel. 01625 531035; Fax 01625 536800;
E-mail sigma.press@zetnet.co.uk;
also at http://www.zetnet.co.uk/coms/sigma.press/
[Take note of latest advertisement: "WE ARE NOT VANITY PUBLISHERS"]. Mainly local history and folklore; mail order services and FREE catalogue.

SOUTH RIDING

John D. Beasley, 6 Everthorpe Road, London SE15 4DA. Tel/fax 0181 693 9412
Books of quotes and anecdotes for speakers, preachers and writers - and local history books on Peckham and Nunhead. 'Another 500 hundred quotes and anecdotes.' If you buy directly from the press you save £1.00. Send £5.95 post free. 'Handy Hints for Social Writers.' Foreword by Tesa Jowell MP. £3.25 post free.

TRENTHAM BOOKS Ltd

Westview House, 734 London Road, Oakhill, Stoke-on-Trent ST4 5NP; Tel. 01782 745567; Fax 01782 745553
Margherita RENDEL, 'Whose human rights?' (Autumn 1996) 260 pp., 228mm x 145mm, ISBN 1-85856-057-8

WILTS FAMILY HISTORY SOCIETY

Mrs L Williams, 7 Chandler Close, Devizes, Wiltshire

SN10 3DS
Have a small but perfectly formed list of many invaluable local studies including the must-have baptism and burial series for the period 1559 to the mid 19th century. Ask for the catalogue.

WRITERS BOOKSHOP
7-11 Kensington High Street, London W8 5NP
The Small Press Guide 1997 edition. Second outing and smart paperback. A directory of about 500 presses. Leans towards poetry + zines and sf. A very educational survey of the scene is provided by the introduction by Peter Finch. He should know since he manages the Arts Council's bookshop in Cardiff which runs all sorts of schemes to promote small presses. Like any such effort the info changes as it goes to press but so what? Buy your copy direct for £7.99 or get it from the NSPC along with other helpful resource tools.

TIPS
What are your 'bibliographical details'? Some send us publicity material which contains insufficient info. This destroys their chances of selling their publication. Here is the SPL checklist: 1 Imprint. 2 Address. 3 Author. 4 Title. 5 Publication date. 6 Number of pages. 7 Illustrated. 8 Hard/paper back. 9 ISBN. 10 Price and method of payment. 11 P&P. 12 Description.

SPL UPDATE
ODIBOURNE PRESS
c/o Richard Storey, 32 High Street, Kenilworth, Warks CV8 1LZ
The listing in Winter 1996/7 mistakenly mentions a second-hand book as a new title. Two 'new' titles are based on the recollections of Arthur Frodham as told to Paul Byron Noris.
'Jackender. Memories of a Kenilworth Man: childhood and work in the 20th century.' 1995 £3.75
'Kenilworth Town Band.' 1996 £1.75.

Changes of address
• Miss G Rickard, 99 Strangers Lane, Canterbury, Kent CT1 3XN. New list available.
• The Quince Tree Press, R.D. & J.M. Carr, 116 Hardwick Lane, Bury St. Edmunds, Suffolk IP33 2LE. The tel. remains unchanged at 01284-753228

It is with enormous sadness we announce the death on January 31st, of CHRIS CHALLIS. Chris had been a giant of all sorts of creative activity, especially small presses, for thirty years. A mark of this special dedication was seen in the hordes of people from so many interests from all over the world who paid tribute at his funeral. His sudden and unexpected absence will reverberate for ages.

MAGAZINES, PERIODICALS, SPORADICALS, SERIALS, JOURNALS, 'ZINES, COMIX, NEWSLETTERS, BULLETINS, IRREGULAR DROPPINGS
Monitors this issue: Lesley and John Dench, Rose Heaword, Andy Hopton, Hope Pym.

BREAK/FLOW
89 Vernon Road, Stratford, London, E15 4DQ
Idiosyncratic and meticulous underground magazine covering literature, philosophy, dance music, underground resistance &c. Issue 1 covers amongst others Trocchi & Project Sigma, Anti-Oedipus. Price £3.00.

CATALOGUE OF CRAP
Ian Shield, 40 Bingfield Gardens, Fenham, Newcastle Upon Tyne, NE5 2RX
Self-published comic featuring strips entitled "The Skidding Whippet", "Catalogue Woman", "Bonk faced Bishop & His Bouncing Bisexual Boob Bugs" and "Removable Buttock Wolf Boy" amongst others. Price £2.00

CLARINETWISE
Jacqueline Browne, Pengribyn, Cilrehdyn, Llanfyrnach, Pembrokeshire SA35 0AA. 01239 698601

Clarinetwise magazine is a new commercial-looking glossy for the clarinet world. A must if you have anything to do with clarinets. Subs £12 pa. Unclear how many issues this gets you or the price of a sample copy. Ring to check.

CROSS-TALK
Editor Martin Spellman, P.O. Box 803, Harrow, Middlesex, HA3 6UH

An irregular publication which describes itself as 'A Trade Union Zine of Commentary and Analysis for the Communications Industry'. Price 50p per issue or £2.00 for four – payable to M. Spellman.

ELECTRICK SKIZOO
Left Hand Productions, c/o AK Press, P.O. Box 12766, Edinburgh
Anarchist 'zine which has features on the London Psychogeographical Association, Anarchist Computer Net, Anticopyright Network, Survivalists &c. plus listings. No price given.

ESCAPE FROM GRAVITY
Association of Autonomous Astronauts, BM Jed, London WC1N 3XX
The irregular bulletin of the AAA who plan to leave this planet by any means necessary and have a five-year plan to establish a world-wide network of local, community-based AAA groups dedicated to building their own space ships. Send 4 first class stamps for the next 4 issues. Also available 'Here comes Everybody - the First annual Report of the AAA' for £2.50 postpaid - payable to J. Skeet.

EST
Brian Duguid, 41a Bedford Hill, Balham, London SW12 9EY
Irregular music 'zine dealing with experimental/industrial music. Latest issue, No. 7, concentrates on American Minimalist Music (Tony Conrad, Charlemagne Palestine, Rhys Chatham) plus the usual massive review section. Also reviews other publications and provides a directory of suppliers &c. (not all dealing with music). Price £3.00 - payable to B. Duguid.

EVERGREEN
PO Box 147, Waltham Close, Hertfordshire EN7 6BZ. 01992 632250
A bi-monthly maglet whose core function is to be a clearing-house for 'lonely hearts.' It has grown to include extra material such as info about various social activities (at which you can meet) or ideas for presents (which you can give) even odd anecdotes (which you can recount). Display ads offer even wider interests including free internet advertising, good food and home brewe centre, vegetarian society of Ireland and discrimination in sport.

FAMILY TREE MAGAZINE
61 Great Whyte, Ramsey, Huntingdon, Cambs. PE17 1HL
Tel. 01487 814050
Monthly. Single copies UK £1.90; subs. UK £21.50. ISSN 0267-1131

HENRY SWEET SOCIETY
Mark Atherton, 21 Girdlestone Close, Oxford OX3 7NS
The Society was founded in 1984 to promote and encourage the study of the history of all branches of linguistic thought, theoretical and applied, including non-European traditions. They are holding a colloquium at the university of Luton 10-13 September. The above address is for correspondence. Other depts should funnel off. An academic newsletter is produced.

HRAFNHOH
Publisher & Editor: Joseph Biddulph, 32 Stryd Ebeneser, Pontypridd, CF37 5PB Cymru/Wales
Dialects and languages, heraldry and surname studies, mostly in English. Various numbers of Hrafnhoh contain a new Africana supplement, 'Black Eagle,' dealing with the languages, social, economic, religious and cultural life of Africa and its Diaspora. Irregular intervals, 3-4 times p.a. UK £5.25 post incl. Single copies UK £2 post incl. Please make all monies payable to Joseph Biddulph. ISSN 0952-3294

KERNOW POETS
18 Frankfield Rise, Tunbridge Wells, TN2 5LF. Tel: 01892 539800. 'Links' a new poetry magazine to be launched this year is also available from the same address. To

subscribe to the magazine and reserve a copy of the first edition, send £2.25 per issue or £4.50 per year. Please make cheques payable to 'Links'.

KIMBO INTERNATIONAL

Kimbo International, PO Box 12412, London SW18 5ZL
'Lochs magazine is a new quarterly uniting some of the best comedy writers around.' The title comes from Lairds Of Camester Highlanders Society. Vol 1 Issue 1 available. Single copy .90p. Sub special £15 pa.

NATIONAL CHILDBIRTH TRUST
Worthing Branch Newsletter, Neil & Angela Rabone, 59 Durrington Lane, Worthing, West Sussex BN13 2QT. 01903 260483

The Jan/Feb 1997 issue is 68 pps because it covers a wide area. Clearly the topic is 'niche' yet you would be surprised how much they embrace. Really meant for members they welcome donations so you could agree a price for a sample copy.

NEW CONSERVATION – POPULATION, RESOURCES, ENVIRONMENT
Publisher & Editor: Peter Berry, Pwllyfan, Llansadwrn, Dyfed SA19 8LS, Wales Tel/Fax: 01550-777661
E-mail pberry@tacin.co.uk
News, views and current awareness from long established expert in the field of environmental information (see also his ECOBASE in electronics section).

NORTHERN EARTH
10 Jubilee Street, Mytholmroyd, Hebden Bridge, West Yorkshire HX7 5NP Tel/Fax: 01422 882441.
Journal of Earth Mysteries & related subjects. First published in 1979 under auspices of the Northern Earth Mysteries Group. Still affiliated to NEMG, now an independent quarterly. Single copies £1.70 includes p&p. Subscription UK £6.00 p.a. institutions £15.00; EC £7.50; elsewhere £10.00. ISSN 0268-8476

PEARL RIVER REVIEW
Kimberly Kelly, Editor-in-Chief, Pearl River Review, PO Box 8416, Mobile, Alabama 36689-0416 USA.
A new bi-annual journal of fiction, poetry, translation and essays from the USA, Pearl River Review, claims to be the only one of its kind which focuses on biographical articles about contemporary writers.

THE POPPY AND THE OWL
The Secretary, The Friends of the Liddle Collection, Brotherton Library, University of Leeds, LS2 9JT. Tel: 0113 2335566.
The journal of Friends of the Liddle Collection which is an archive of personal experience during the 14-18 War. Full colour

reproductions as well as b&w. £10 pa.

RESONANCE
London Musicians' Collective, Unit B1, Lafone House, Leathermarket St., London SE1 3HN
Bi-annual magazine from the London Musicians' Collective covering all aspects of improvised and experimental music. Interviews, feature articles, reviews &c. Current issue comes with a free CD and concentrates on the use of samplers in new music. ISSN 1352-772X. Price £5.00.

THE SPINSTERS ALMANAC
23 Vaughan Road, Papplwick Lane, Hucknall, Nottingham NG15 8BT
A quarterly for spinners, weavers and dyers. They also produce a booklet series 'Woolgathering' @£2.00 each. There are ten titles so ask for list. Sub to mag £7.50 pa.

SQUALL
P.O. Box 8959, London, N19 5HW

Squall, sub-titled "necessity breeds ingenuity" provides coverage of the squatting milieu and beyond. Protests against the Criminal Justice act, festivals, ecstasy, Job Seekers Allowance, Graffiti, and political theatre have all been featured in recent issues together with coverage of squatting news from around the world. Individual copies £2.20 inc p&p, subscriptions £10.00.

THE WARTIME COMPANY
Marilyn Ward, 4th Floor, Studland House, 12 Christchurh Road, Bournemouth BH1 3NA. 01212 503902
Publishes The Wartime News which features reminiscences from those who fought for peace and the families at home. A non-profit-making quarterly. ISSN 1362-3826.

ELECTRONIC PUBLISHING

CAUSE FOR ALARM
http://www.teleport.com/~richieb/cause/
Online mag monthly. Electronic freedom issues.

COMPUTER PROFESSIONALS FOR SOCIAL RESPONSIBILITY (Berkeley Chapter)
http://www.cpsr.org/dox/program/workplace/index.html
Newsletter.

DESKTOP PUBLISHERS JOURNAL
listserve@DTPjournal.com
or try: http://www.dtpjournal.com/ezine.htm
Free newsletter. Send message. Subscribe.

ECOBASE DIRECTORY ON DISK
Peter Berry Associates, Pwllyfan, Llansadwrn, Llanwrda, Dyfed SA19 8LS, Wales. Tel.01550-777661
New revised version January 1997. Over 10,500 continuously updated records of statutory, voluntary and commercial organisations active locally, regionally, nationally or internationally in environmental field, UK and Ireland. £95 + VAT (50% discount for existing users).

HEART OF ALBION PRESS
bobtrubs@gmtnet.co.uk
Forthcoming publication early 1997 Jeremy HARTE: 'Research in Geomancy - 1990-1994, Readings in sacred space: a bibliography.' Published on floppy disc for reading on any wordprocessor (files in Windows Write format and duplicated in plain ASCII); by using 'Find' specific topics can be readily located in text. On request a print-out can be supplied with disc. Provisional price £5.95 (disc only); £9.95 (disc and print-out)

PUG e-zine
http://www.pugzine.com/
Daily Telegraph 10/12/96 rave review: 'a haul of bizarre features you'd be hard pushed to find in print ... engaging graphics and links to hundreds of underground Web sites.'

STUDENT OUTLOOK
http://www.student.uk.com
Evolving from 'Outlook' hardcopy magazine. 'Student Outlook' now available on web site.

Published by
THE NATIONAL SMALL PRESS CENTRE
BM Bozo, London
WC1N 3XX

HOW TO PUBLISH YOURSELF – IN 26 SIMPLE STEPS

1 Off you go
getting started
what to call your imprint
choosing a business
address
limited companies

2 Making it official
registering on data banks
standard book numbers
standard serial numbers
free listings
Whitakers bibliographic
services
bar codes

3 Basic formal stuff
your legal obligation
deposits to Copyright
Receipt Office
British Library archive

4 Spreading the word
advanced information
sheets
sending out details of
your publication
informing libraries
advertising
publicising your
title

5 About paper
which size?
what is A4?

6 What will you need?
equipment
what's available?
photocopiers
laser and colour printers
silkscreening
do you need a printing press?
metal and paper plates

7 Get the words on paper
materials
electronic typewriters
daisy wheel
dot matrix
photosetting
wordprocessing

8 What's it going to look like?
typesetting
justified text
proportional spacing
typescript
disk compatability

9 Making it pretty
adding pictures and graphics
where to find illustrations
distorting the image
collages
picture libraries

copyright images
computer graphics
CD-ROM clip art
PICT. TIFF and EPS
shareware
wingdings/dingbats
graphics programmes
scanners
freelance illustrators

10 Time to get busy
preparing your artwork
what you will need
paste-up: doing it off screen
layout
scalpels
hot wax
trimming
desk-top publishing: doing it on screen
software
colour separation

11 Printing matters
what are 'shortrun' printers?
binding
appearance
spines
card covers

12 The overall look
designing your publication
basic pamphlets
book jackets

paper quality
handmade marbled paper

13 Safeguarding your work
copyright and the law
do you need it?
does it cost?
how long does it last?
permission to re-use

14 Money matters
royalties
paying your author
do you have to?
how much?
designer's fee

15 What's it going to cost?
calculating a price
mail order discounts
shopkeepers cut

16 Touting for business
selling your publication
what does marketing mean?
what's your market?
selling foreign rights
marketing on the web

17 Telling the world
promoting your publication
launch parties
stunts

press releases
badges
t-shirts
free publicity
directory entries
review copies

18 Paying the price
advertising your publication
how much does it cost?
what's the best medium?
exchange ads
display subscription details

19 Selling from your sitting room
mail order
compiling a list
tips
keeping a data base of customers
data protection
mail shots
catalogues

20 Selling yourself
supplying bookshops
sale or return
retailer's discount
other outlets
planning your sales campaign
Booksellers Association

21 Getting your money back
orders and invoices
retailers terms
postage
book-keeping
statements
late payments

22 Be your own 'rep'
grovelling to the Buyer
choose the right outlet
consulting other presses

23 Out and about
distributors
percentages of the price
sales reports
regular payments
what are they looking for?
importance of presentation

24 The world's your oyster
selling your book abroad
the American market
overseas distributors
the continental market

25 Showing off
exhibiting at Trade fairs
the Centre's Small Press
Fairs on the South Bank
local book fairs
venues
the London Book Fair at
Olympia
specialist fairs
poets convention
Germany's free Mini Press
Fair in Mainz
Frankfurt Book Fair
ABA in Chicago

26 Please can I have some money?
who will help you financially?
awards and prizes
literary grants
lottery money
bodies to approach

HOW TO PUBLISH YOURSELF – IN 26 SIMPLE STEPS

A Rudimentary Guide to Producing Your Small Press Publication (use in conjunction with the RESOURCE DIRECTORY)

This Guide is for those who feel themselves ill-informed about the processes involved in autonomous publishing and are looking for a way in. It is by no means extensive – there are many books on the market that go into greater detail about each aspect of publishing, but the best way to learn about it is by doing it. However, information is never finite. We have updated, amended, modified and revised wherever we could but somebody will always know better. So please share your suprioer knowledge – it benefits everybody. Let us know and we will pass information on in our newsletter, News from the Centre, published every other month. This DIY Guide is designed to be of practical use, and reading it through, taking notes as you do so, may prevent you making many of the mistakes which generally plague the inexperienced self-publisher. Small presses with many years experience may still find something of interest: if you don't, then let us have some of the useful information you've gathered as a small press. Remember too, that one of the services the National Small Press Centre offer is Advice Surgeries. For a small charge you can buy an hour or more of expert advice on all aspects of self-publishing.

1 OFF YOU GO

Getting started ▯ what to call your imprint ▯ choosing a business address

1.0 *Starting your Press:*
Choose a name for your press – an **imprint** you can live with, rather than one you are likely to become stuck with – and decide upon an address to use. If you don't want to use your home address, there are other options available. A **Post Office Box** (located at your local sorting office) can be obtained by filling in the relevant form and paying around £60 per annum. The Post Office allocates the number; you are supplied with an ID card and collect your mail whenever you wish. **British Monomark** (BM) numbers are more expensive. You can choose your own **BM Name** (e.g. 'BM Ken') or if you prefer to be incognito they will allocate you a name or number. Mail can either be collected at regular intervals, or posted on to your current address – which may be useful if you are likely to be in prison, abroad or moving about. A BCM (British *Commercial* Monomark) number is dearer, but is for those who wish put their press on a more business-like basis. British Monomarks, 27 Old Gloucester Street, London WC1N 3XX for details. You can pay an average of £12 per month for an **accommodation address**, these usually sound like a *real* address, instead of a Box Number you might be given a 'suite' or 'flat' number. **Accommodation addresses**: Hold Everything, 162 Regent Street, London W1 (0171 580 4242); The Really Good Business Bureau, 39 South Street, Mayfair, London W1Y 6BB (0171 409 7088); Posthaste, Croydon (0181 688 8144); Flexible Business Services 235 Regent Street, London N3 3LF (0181 343 2316) charge only £2 per week. And **outside London**: Cambridgeshire Accommodation Addresses (01354 677213); and to avoid the tax man? Jersey Addresses, PO Box 436, Jersey JE4 5QY (£25 pm).

1.1 *Limited Companies* can be purchased for £90 from Cosun Limited, 78 Montgomery Street, Edinburgh EH7 5JA (tel: 0800 526421).

2 MAKING IT OFFICIAL

Registering on data bank ▯ standard book numbers▯standard serial numbers ▯ free listings▯ Whitakers bibliographic services▯ bar codes

2.0 *Getting the relevant data:*
If you wish to have your publication circulated outside just a circle of friends, it is a good idea to have it included in the relevant data banks that exist. Use an **ISSN** for a se-

rial, an **ISBN** for your books and pamphlets; and get **CIP** data as well. What are they?

2.1 *ISBN:* International Standard Book Number. **ISBN**s identify publishers, imprint and book title. The LHS digit has weight 10, and the RHS digit has weight 1. Add it all together and divide by 11 and the remainder should be zero. The last digit is the checksum, and may be X or 0 to represent 10 when necessary. If check is 0 then the remainder result can be 0 or 10. The top digit is a language then the next digits identify the publisher. The lower digits are sequential book numbers. Some publishers use sub-fields for their own convenience. Small publishers have larger publisher numbers, leaving less digits for book numbers. Single **ISBN**s are free, and if you are only publishing half a dozen books, there is no need to spend any money: just telephone and they will be supplied there and then. However, if you wish to select your own, you can purchase a list of 100 assigned for your use for £28.20 (1,000 numbers costs £63.45). **ISBN**s are available only from **J. Whitaker and Sons Ltd**, 12 Dyott Street, London, WC1A 1DF (tel: 0171-420 6000). **ISBN**s get your work into bibliographic control systems, 'Books In Print', and 'The Bookseller'. Libraries and shops, which almost all now have computerised accounts, use **ISBN**s for reference, so it is always advisable to obtain one.

2.2 *ISSN:* International Standard Serial Number. Eight figure digit used to identify periodicals and serials. Free service. Obtained from the **ISSN Service** at the British Library, Boston Spa, Wetherby, West Yorkshire LS23 7BQ (tel: 01937 546 958; fax: 01937 546 562). Send description, photocopy of contents pages, etc. for their records and to get the **ISSN** for your serial or journal. Note that any alteration or addition to the title of the serial may require a new **ISSN**. (Libraries and institutions prefer users to print the ISSN on promotional literature as well).

2.3 To have your journal or serial featured in **Current British Journals** (entries on c.10,000 journals) contact: British Library Document Supply Centre, Boston Spa, Wetherby, West Yorkshire, LS23 7BQ (01937-843-434, x6078).

2.4 *CIP data:* Cataloguing-In-Publication data. Allows subscribers to the British Library's bibliographic services to receive advance information about your publications (and to place orders). Formerly provided by the British Library and by **J. Whitaker and Sons Ltd**, this is now provided free by **Bibliographic Data Services Ltd**, 26 Nith Place, Dumfries, DG1 2PN, Scotland (tel: 01387 266004 fax: 01387 265503). **BDS** is an independent, privately-owned company specialising in the creation of high-quality bibliographic data for libraries, book suppliers and the book trade. If you want to join their scheme, call them in the first instance. If you prepare Advance Information Sheets, these should be sent, with dust-jackets and prelims if possible. If you would prefer to fill in the details of your books on pre-printed forms, **BDS** can supply these on request. It is important that you send your advanced information to them as soon as possible; a minimum of three months in advance of the actual publication date. For more information, contact **BDS** directly.

2.5 *Bar Codes:* A familiar item on almost everything we purchase these days, the bar code is the most commonly used means of stock control. For book publishers, they are all but essential, especially when dealing with bookshops, libraries, distributors etc. That unique combination/permutation of lines and spaces between lines, along with a unique sequential number means that your publication can be effectively 'tracked' as required by means of the bar-code being 'swiped' by a special electronic pen or scanner. **Bar-coding** can be achieved in two ways: either by purchasing pre-printed, peel-off labels from a specialist supplier (see resources Directory) or by purchasing the necessary software which integrates with your DTP package and is imported as a 'graphic' in order to be positioned as an integral part of your cover (the rear cover seems to be the favoured location but inside front or inside rear of the cover is acceptable).

For short runs and for cassette cases etc, the peel-off label option is more than suitable but for longer runs of printed matter, the integral printed image is preferred. Whatever you do, don't attempt to draw bar-codes yourself and then scan them in electronically (we've known of people who have tried this with disastrous consequences!). Make the investment and ensure that your products can be located easily, thereby assisting with stock control and sales transactions.

3 BASIC FORMAL STUFF

Your legal obligation □ deposits to Copyright Receipt Office □ British Library archive

3.0 *Legal Deposit:*
Publishers fulfil their legal obligations to the **British Library** by sending one copy of each of their publications to the **Copyright Receipt Office**, Boston Spa, Wetherby, West Yorkshire, LS23 7BQ (tel: 01937-546266) within one month of publication. Other Copyright Legal Deposit Libraries are at **Oxford, Cambridge, NL Scotland, Dublin, NL Wales.** Send 5 copies of each publication to A.T. Smail, 100 Euston Street, London NW1 2HQ (0171-380 0240). In practice the BL etc do not care much about the 'legality' of copyright receipt. It is of advantage to small presses to send publications in, however, with as full information as possible – for archival purposes and so on. The BL is months – years – behind in its cataloguing and is considering not including every published work in its archives: a lobby to insist on proper treatment of small press material is needed.

4 SPREADING THE WORD

Advanced information sheets □ sending out details of your publication□ informing libraries □ advertising □ publicising your title

4.0 *Advance Information:*
Having completed the forms for **Bibliographic Data Services** (see 2.4 above), send details of your publication to some of the book retailers. **NEBS** is Blackwell's New English Book Selection department and may be of interest to small presses dealing with publications likely to be of academic interest: good-quality books primarily intended for the general reader but on subjects of academic interest should not be excluded, but there are other types of book they do not want to be informed about. For full details of their requirements, write to NEBS Dept, Blackwell's, PO Box 185, Oxford, OX1 2ED. In some cases they will order as many as 40 copies of your new titles – which is a good way to launch your publication! Send an **AI** (Advanced Information) sheet to other library suppliers as well: the more pre-publication orders you get the better. An AI is usually an A4 sheet with all the relevant data concerning your product: publication date, ISBN, size, cover type, binding, number of pages, price, author, classification, availability, contact number, ordering details and a few catchy phrases about the content. Library Services UK Ltd. (formerly JMLS or Menzies) have an advance information scheme: they are at Library Services UK, 24 Gamble Street, Nottingham NG7 4FJ (tel: 0115 970 8021; fax: 0115 978 7718). Everett also have such a scheme: contact **W.H. Everett and Son Ltd**, Unit 8, Hurlingham Business Park, Sulivan Road, London SW6 3DU. Finally, a judiciously placed advertisement detailing your forthcoming titles will alert potential customers. Check out some of the magazines that feature in this Handbook. (See also the section below on marketing your books).

5 ABOUT PAPER

Which size? □ what is A4?

5.0 *Paper sizes:*
Unless you have grasped the nettle and wish to publish your work only in electronic format, you will use some sort of paper to circulate your work. Don't know what things like A4, A5 etc mean? They refer to British Standard paper sizes, as follows:
A1: 594 x 841 mm
A2: 420 x 594 mm
A3: 297 x 420 mm
A4: 210 x 297 mm
A5: 148 x 210 mm
Crown 8vo: 123 x 186 mm
Lge Crown 8vo: 129 x 198 mm

Demy 8vo: 138 x 216 mm
Royal 8vo: 156 x 234 mm
A6: 105 x 148 mm
A7: 74 x 105 mm

You'll probably find you are using sizes A3 to A5 mostly if you are printing a magazine, book or booklet. These are the dimensions of trimmed pages. Speak to your printer before purchasing paper yourself (if there is a special paper you want to use) and check that the printer doesn't want untrimmed sheets.

6 WHAT WILL YOU NEED?

Equipment □ what's available? □ photocopiers □ laser and colour printers □ silkscreening □ do you need a printing press? □ metal and paper plates

6.0 *Machinery you might come across and how to use it:*
There are a few machines to which most people will have access: most of these are so familiar and user-friendly as to require no detailed description. Here, however, follows a few hints on their use to the first-time publisher.

6.1 *Photocopiers:* Most people have access to photocopying facilities – either in your own or a friend's workplace, a high street quick printer, community centre, resource centre, library etc. Where a charge is made prices range from 4p-10p per A4 sheet. Machines vary considerably: some will take virtually any paper, others are recalcitrant or produce poor quality copies. You have to find out for yourself by using the machine. The basic 'office' photocopier will reproduce your artwork in line form: the image they print is all of a piece and will reduce fine detail to blocks of black or a single colour. Some photocopiers take cartridges (blue, red, brown, &c): by passing a single sheet of paper through the copier several times, using a different colour each time, you can make fairly lavish covers for a pamphlet, some even resulting in a '3-D' effect. Given the difficulty in registering, choose a design in which the very precise relation of shapes, text, &c on the cover is not especially important. For example, title in black, large

circle in red, small circle in blue, background of yellow spots – elements that need not align precisely, though you'll want your title and name square to the edge of the paper. Your artwork in this instance should consist of four pieces of paper (all the same size – say A4), on each of which you should draw/type/paint/collage – in black – the particular elements.

6.2 *Laser Photocopiers:* State of the art laser photocopiers can reverse out and distort artwork; and can screen photographic images – break the image into tiny dots, enabling clear reproduction. Some are nearly as good as photographic screening – and considerably cheaper. If you are using a printer which uses paper plates (ask them first), the image screened using a laser photocopier will produce results almost as good as if you had used a photographically-screened image, since paper plates are unpredictable when it comes to reproduction of photographs – so you can get away with a laser copy if the quality suits you. For really sharp photographic reproduction you have to use metal plates: ask your printer, who will advise you on the screening of photographs. Never paste an original photograph to your artwork: have it screened first (a photograph of the photograph is taken, using a dot-screen) and then place the screened copy in position.

6.3 *Colour Photocopiers:* Four-colour photocopiers will reproduce any colour artwork – a painting, photograph or slide. Prices range from around 80p-£2 per A4 sheet. It is even possible to have images reproduced on T-shirts for promotional purposes. You can of course do several copies of a small design (A6 size for instance), which can then be cut out and pasted onto the front of your pamphlet. The paper most often used in colour photocopying is such that when the paper is cut a brittle edge often results (though some copiers will take textured Conqueror paper: ask – or experiment). Often, a guillotine will leave a rough edge on colour photocopies, so it is better to use a new scalpel blade to trim the images. Pasting colour photocopies of any size (A5 or bigger) often results in cracks forming on the image, especially if you need to shift it slightly. Use a wet glue or paste rather than a dry glue stick, and smooth the paper carefully from the centre; or use a hot wax roller. It is not possible to colour-photocopy onto thick card; nor to produce double-sided photocopies (since the heat from the machine melts the ink already placed on the paper): however, by fiendish and time-consuming means you can (just) photocopy a black and white text (a poem, say) onto the reverse of a colour photocopy (e.g. photo of the author fire-eating). What you have to do is carefully place an acetate over the colour copy – glue it into position at both ends with a little Pritt – before passing the sheet through the b&w photocopier. You'll make a few errors, but practice will make perfect. When the completed double-sided sheet has been printed, you'll need to trim it. Note that you should do this slowly, a single sheet at a time, and allow the photocopier to cool down between sheets: too much heat will lift the coloured ink off the paper – which can result in some aesthetically pleasing work; but which can also muck up your photocopier.

6.4 *Silkscreens:* With a silkscreen you can produce spectacular results for very little money, but it takes a fair amount of time, patience and skill. Single colour silkscreening is very simple – it gets more difficult the more colours you want to use. There is not enough room here to describe how to go about silkscreening; but there are plenty of books available on the subject (Dover Books publish at least one), and your local arts centre, adult education or resource centre will probably be able to help; or best of all, find a friend who knows something about it. Silkscreens vary in size from those you can use on the kitchen table to large units which will take A1 paper. One of the difficulties in silkscreening a card book-cover using several colours is (as with the monochrome photocopiers) registration. Only practice and patience (and plenty of mistakes along the way) will allow you to overcome this problem. A dust-jacket is an easier option (thinner material), or an image which can be cut out and stuck on the cover.

6.5 *Printing Presses:* Most small presses do not have their own printing press. If you do, you will not need any advice here as to how to use it. For those of us who must rely on commercial printers, there are a few things worth bearing in mind. The first rule is, write down in clear handwriting exactly what you want the printer to do for you – at every stage. Your printer will have many jobs going at once and cannot be relied upon to remember the minute details of your particular job. Always write down your instructions *even if* the printer says (s)he understands.

6.6 Some printers – those using metal plates rather than quick-print affairs – will provide you with layout sheets (which you will usually be charged for). The quick-print printers will expect you to provide **artwork** pasted up to the dimensions of the finished publication (i.e. don't lay out an A5 pamphlet on huge layout sheets and then expect the quick-print printer to trim them). Before presenting your **artwork**, ask the printer you plan to use what you should do and how (s)he wants the copy presented. Ask for a mock-up – so that you can layout the sheets in the correct order for plate-making. Ask about what size grip edge (the area of paper that the printing press grasps and which therefore must be left blank) is required for covers and pages.

Don't be afraid to make an idiot of yourself, and don't wait to feel a fool until after the job is done – **always** ask beforehand if you don't know: it is your money and your publication that is at stake. This cannot be stressed enough.

7 GET THE WORDS ON PAPER

Materials ▢ electronic typewriters ▢ daisy wheel ▢ dot matrix ▢ photosetting ▢ wordprocessing

7.0 *Materials:*
Your text can be prepared at home using a quill, blunt pencil, typewriter, electronic typewriter, dot-matrix, daisy wheel, or any other instrument that will make a mark on paper. You can have your text **typeset** using a desktop laser printer (which uses more or less ordinary paper); or **phototypeset** it at a bureau

(on to bromide – photographic paper – using a hugely expensive piece of equipment such as a Linotronic). **Bromide** produces the best results, but it is more expensive. As always, it depends on your resources and what quality you are aiming for. Don't be put off – or, for that matter fooled – by the so-called 'new technology': **word processing** is quite simple to master, but it does not provide a short-cut to instant results. You (or someone you pay or whose arm you twist) still have to **input** the work: the machine does not do it for you, though such things as spell-checkers do make life slightly easier. Keep copies of all your files and remember while you are word-processing to save files frequently. Don't get carried away and type all night – only to find at dawn that the ten thousand word masterpiece you wish to save is lost because of some inexplicable fault on the machine. Save as you go, stick to small files, and make a habit of making copies of your work.

8 WHAT'S IT GOING TO LOOK LIKE?

Typesetting ☐ justified text ☐ proportional spacing ☐ typescript ☐ disk compatability

8.0 *Typesetting:*
This was the most amazing invention, moveable bits of type, individual letters. It was the Gutenberg revolution. We are passing through a second revolution. Only people who want to use the old techniques 'set' type. Setting type is all done on the desk-top publishing programme of the computer.

8.1 Most people would agree nowadays that a **right-justified text** is better than a ragged edge (verse often doesn't need it, of course). There are still those Luddites who prefer mechanically typewritten text, as being 'uncorrupted' (e.g. numerous New Age Traveller type publications). Nowadays most wordprocessors and many electronic typewriters offer **proportional spacing**: only the recalcitrant will persist in using a typewriter, which is nevertheless still the cheapest way to produce your typescript. However, the public perception is that the work is 'unfinished'

somehow, not a 'proper' publication: the content of a work is appreciated less readily than its form. This is a matter of taste, of course, but consider who your readers are going to be. There are numerous typesetting bureaux which can give you advice: these all want you to come back another time and use them again. They may sell you typesetting software, which enables you to do most of the work at home (coding text, determining page layout, &c) or they may offer you the use of their machines. Ask about disc compatibility if you have a word processor at home. Most bureaux will give you more or less impartial advice. **Laser typesetting** is improving all the time and while the results are not as fine as **phototypesetting**, they are at least adequate. Take care of your artwork: put it in a folder or envelope to keep it clean; if you must roll it up, do so in such a way that the image of the artwork shows on the outside – this means that when you come to pasting up, the artwork does not leap away from the page.

9 MAKING IT PRETTY

Adding pictures and graphics ☐ where to find illustrations ☐ distorting the image ☐ collages ☐ picture libraries ☐ copyright images ☐ computer graphics ☐ CD-ROM clip art ☐ PICT. TIFF and EPS ☐ shareware ☐ wingdings ☐ dingbats ☐ graphics ☐ programmes ☐ scanners ☐ freelance illustrators

9.0 *Illustrations:*
For images, if you are not particularly talented and have no artistically inclined friends, go through old books lying round the house; use an enigmatic photograph or old postcard – or a detail of a picture; produce a collage or montage; get out your Rotring and draw it yourself. Use a jointed metal blowpipe in a pot of ink instead of an air brush. You can buy one for a pound or so at any graphics supplier (perhaps they have a technical name for them). Collage tip: take a black felt-tip pen with a hard, broad tip and very carefully run it across the cut edge of the scraps of paper you are using. This way the ragged edge of the collage elements will not show.

9.1 A useful resource for images is **The Dover Bookshop** at 18 Earlham Street, London WC2 (tel: 0171-836 2111). Dover allow you to use up to ten images from any one of their books (fat volumes of out-of-copyright images on a variety of subjects) in any one of your own publications. The only disadvantage lies in the fact that such images tend to be very widely used and become almost hackneyed. The trick is to select some apposite detail that can be incorporated into your own design. Distort it on a laser photocopier if you like. Regrettably Dover have cottoned-on to this market for their images and consequently prices have shot up in recent years to around the £10-£15 mark for each collection.

9.2 Another possibility, if you've nothing lying round the house, or want special images, is to contact the **British Association of Picture Libraries**, an association of 200 picture libraries and agencies. They have a directory too. Contact them at 18 Vine Hill, London EC1R 5DX (0171 713 1780/Fax: 0171 713 1211.) You must pay a royalty fee for use of Picture Library images. There are also picture agencies which will supply images to your requirements, such as **CLIPART** from Translatum International.

9.3 Note that you can also obtain images from the **British Library** in London; they will charge about £15 for the use of one of their **copyright images**. One problem some people find is gaining access to the B.L. Many people are successfully intimidated by the institution. You should not be put off. The thing to do is knock up some pompous looking headed note paper, type a letter explaining that the bearer of the letter is employed by (name of your press) to research some obscure subject or other (the very obscure is always a good bet); say that it will take at least two years to complete your project; mention that you cannot travel outside London because of work or financial reasons; mention your entire reliability and so forth; and have someone ('the Director of the Press' etc) sign it. Give a couple of references if necessary. Or get a small press colleague to write such a letter: one with academic qualifications is best. Such subterfuge may not be required, but it is more effective than protesting that the B.L. is public property and that it is your right to have a pass.

9.4 *Computer Graphics*: As the **Desk-Top Publishing** (DTP) industry has grown dramatically over the past five years or so, so has the availability of electronic illustrations. Known colloquially as **clip art** (retaining the notion of 'clipping' illustrations from a printed book for the purposes of pasting-up manually), you can now purchase vast libraries of **uncopyrighted images** in black and white or colour for a relatively small outlay. Clip art on floppy disk, whilst still very popular, is rapidly being superseded by art on **CD-ROM**, especially as the latter can hold up to 600-800 times more data, especially useful for memory-hungry colour files.

Thus, tens of thousands of images are accessible if you have a CD-ROM drive, installed as part of your computer set-up (internally or as a peripheral device). But even if you don't, floppy disks, singly or in sets, can provide a fairly substantial library, although not all of the images will necessarily be suitable for you. Before discussing the technical aspects any further, it is necessary to consider the relevance of the images available with regard to your own particular project or overall publishing remit. If for instance, you publish works about transport, then an image library of starbursts, flowers, arrows and Wild-West cartoon characters is unlikely to be of much interest to you. Specialist libraries are available and probably the best way to find these is to study the ads in the computer mags. Send for catalogues and see just what is on offer before parting with your cash. You may have to compromise, if you really are looking for something special.

The images will usually be collated and accompanied by a 'hard copy' reference booklet. For the computer-literate, who will be familiar with the terminology, the files offered will most likely be stored as **PICT**, **TIFF** or **EPS** images. For the uninitiated, PICT files are fairly low quality scanned images, whereas TIFF files which have also been scanned are saved at a higher resolution and consequently better results will be evident on screen and on printing. The problem with both PICT and TIFF files arises when you want to enlarge the image. Too much enlargement will produced jagged 'Lego-like' edges to the image which is unsatisfactory. EPS images, because of the way they are created, do not suffer from this problem. Given the appropriate software, the images can be manipulated and edited. Be careful if you are inverting images; lettering will appear back-to-front and right-hand drive cars become left-hand. Sounds obvious? You'd be amazed at how many people overlook this simple fact!

Look out for any 'freeware' or 'shareware' (the former is often given away with computer mags, while the latter is sometimes distributed on the Internet for instance for a small fee or at the very least, acknowledgement to the author). Some DTP packages contain their own image libraries, with a comparatively small selection to choose from. The drawback with these is that anyone else with the same package will use these images too, thus thwarting your attempts at being original.

With all image libraries, the actual quality of the original drawing should bear close scrutiny. One drawback of the massive 10,000 plus images-on-disk type of libraries is that the drawings are sometimes poor or badly conceived; crudely drawn, unrealistic images are unlikely to enhance your publication, unless you are aiming for that kind of 'image'.

There is no doubt that appropriately selected and positioned 'pix' can make a publication come alive. The choice is yours and the choice is enormous. Your PC will include a **graphics font** in its package of programmes and fonts, modest but versatile and useful such as **Wingdings** and **Dingbats** with symbols, (crosses, blobs, bullets, waving flags, stars, funny faces, pen-nibs, hands and pointing fingers, etc). Or you can buy a **graphics programme** for Windows applications such as **CorelDraw!**. Number 3 is adequate, and gives lots of scope to use their installed range of graphics and symbols, or you can create your own image with pen-strokes, tones and fillings. More elaborate is the newest in the range **CorelDraw 6**, but you require access through a CD ROM slot on your PC. Other similar graphics programmes, such as **WordArt**, and

the equivalent for MACS, are available from **Morgan Computer Co** (0121 456 5565). Their current catalogue lists **Key-Fonts**, a CD-ROM for windows or Mac, of **1,555** of the most popular typefaces, dingbats, symbols and display fonts for £9.99, or **Harvard Graphics** a full package of combined graphics and over 2000 **Clip Art** images with instructions on a 3.5" disk for £19.99. If you have access to a **scanner** to scan pictures and photographs you can **tip them in** to your page-maker programme where appropriate, that is send them from the scanner (or on disk) to be inserted in the slot you have left for them on your layout, with your text **wrapping around** the image.

9.5 Why not come to a deal with a struggling freelance graphic artist? Also, beware of infringing copyright. For information on both contact the **Society of Illustrators**.

10 TIME TO GET BUSY

Preparing your artwork ☐ what you will need ☐ paste-up: doing it off screen ☐ layout ☐ scalpels ☐ hot wax ☐ trimming ☐ desk-top publishing: doing ☐ it on screen ☐ software ☐ colour separation

10.0 *Paste Up.*
This section assumes you won't put everything together on a PC. Your typeset text and finished images are back on the kitchen table. You've got a plentiful supply of coffee, cigarettes, biscuits, snacks, designer drugs – whatever you need to get you through paste-up.

10.1 You'll need a few tools. A **blue pencil** for any marks on your artwork and to write in special instructions for the printer (blue doesn't show up when the printer makes the plates); a **sharp blade** (a surgical scalpel is best, scissors will do for simple jobs); some **glue** (Pritt is 'dry', quite clean; Cow Gum is wet, collects dirt, aerosol cans of spray-mount glue are poisonous – take your pick), or better still some **wax**.

10.2 A **hot wax roller** costs a fair amount – about £50 – but is a worthwhile investment if you plan to do a few publications rather than a one off; or if you plan to do a fairly large job (e.g. a long magazine with plenty of photographs). Wax is clean and it allows you to reposition artwork without damaging it. When you've positioned the artwork, and given it the once over with a roller, wax also gives a smooth, flat surface (excess wax can be removed with **lighter fluid**) – which is important when it comes to the plate-making stage.

10.3 The flatter the surface of the artwork, the better: things like great chunks of typewriter correction fluid and the curling edges of badly glued paper will show up in the plate: the printer will need to erase them, which will cost you more money (often a lot of money: a 64 page magazine every page of which requires touching up, charged at the current union rate, is several times the cost of a wax roller). If you are using a photocopier, this isn't such a problem, of course: there you will want to ensure that the edges of the various pieces of artwork are not visible. Make a good copy of the finished paste-up job and use a photocopier fluid to erase any visible marks.

10.4 When trimming artwork to size and pasting up, it's a good idea to put any rubbish you might generate into a plastic bag, keeping this separate from general household waste. This way, if you find at the end of the paste-up, when you're checking everything is in order, that you have accidentally thrown away something essential – it might be something as minute as a single letter, more probably a line of text that has somehow gone astray – you can recover it without having to wade through discarded teabags, empty cans and other trash.

10.5 *Desk-Top Publishing:* As PCs and MACs become less expensive and more easily available, small presses are turning more and more to producing their publications on screen. Computer software such as **Quark** and **Pagemaker** simply provide you with a image on screen with is the equivalent to a blank sheet of paper. Words are introduced onto this image as prepared text from a word-processing programme (such as **Word for Windows**, **Wordperfect** or **MacWrite**). You

will have imput (typed) your copy on your word-processor, then spell-check, edited and proof-read it ready to import the text onto your prepared layout. You can manipulate, design and size the imported text until it represents the look of your finished book. (The expressions used for preparing your finished pages on computer are the same as if you did them by hand – cutting, pasting, copying, etc.). Finished pages are completed, including headers, footers, page numbers chapter headings graphics and so on. (If you are having colour printing on the cover of your book you can supply your Printer with **colour-separated** pages – one page for each colour. The printer will print one colour then print further colours on top of the first.) This finished artwork is then ready to be supplied to your chosen Printshop for printing and binding to your specifications, either on disk or as originated pages laser or dot-matrix printed. From your word-processing imput text and desk-top published layout the result should be a quantity of finished bound volumes of your publication. Computers with desk-top publishing packages are available from **Morgans** (see above), **Dixons** and the **PC World** chain.

11 PRINTING MATTERS

What are 'short-run' printers □ binding □ appearance □ spines □ card covers

11.0 *Short Run Printers*
The National Small Press Centre is frequently asked: "Can you let me have a list of cheap/ good printers?" First you do not want 'a printer'. If you do you may not be a small press. If you want more than 2,000 copies of your book you are nearing the quantities of a regular publisher. Honestly. For example hardback novels rarely sell more than a few hunded copies. Yes, hundred. There are some small presses who sell more copies of their novels than regular publishers. Honestly. But hardly anybody realises that. Of course if they did the entire business might be re-thought – from both ends! So realise your horizons. At the top end a thousand. At the bottom end it is a

working tip that anybody can shift 200 copies of anything. Once you have got that out of the way you see you are looking for a special kind of printer. One who will take a tiny job like yours seriously. A **Short-run Printer (SRP)**. However you have a tremendous asset. First you are a serial offender. If you publish this means you are more than likely to want more than one job printed. Now if you publish say half a dozen titles, of all sorts, every year you are a welcome customer. Second you are not alone. Turn your question inside out. Once you find your srp you can tell other sps about this paragon. If you are the sort of person who finds something marvellous and keeps it a secret then you deserve boiling in oil. Purely on a selfish level if you attract new customers you will please the srp. You will become a very favoured customer if you not only bring in your jobs but others too. You are making the srp money. He doesn't need to go hunting business or spending money on advertising. He will take more care over your jobs and may offer you preferential treatment. Common sense again. The next most frequently asked question is: "Can you let me have a list of SRPs?"

Yes. But normal common sense applies. It is like going to your town hall and asking them to let you have a list of plumbers, electricians, builders. Sensibly they refuse. They may give you a list but they will qualify it heavily. They refuse any responsibility. They insist it is purely a list, *not* a recommendation. Apart from the obvious pitfalls your job is your job. How can anybody know what you want or what you are like to work with? What do you want the srp to do? Have you done your job? Have you thought through what you want? A printer shouldn't be expected to do this for you. He is in business and can't spend time on discussions. 'Wouldn't it be nice if we had ... ?' He can price your job and he may offer a few tips such as using a slightly different quality paper to get an effect but do not expect him to design your job. Unless you want to pay him huge sums. He will be happy to earn extra money. But will you be happy to pay? You will deserve to be fined for your idleness and stupidity. Which qualities are not the mark of small presses.

11.01 *Binding*

You can avoid proper binding and use the options available to every office. They bind reports in ways that are not meant to last or look pretty.

* There is the strip of hard plastic which holds in A4 pages. Obviously the 'book' will not open fully or the strip will come off. You may wish to produce different editions with different mixtures, a fun product. The strip is really a superior form of filing. These strips are available in black or colours.

* There are ring binders. These hold together by a metal spiral through the sides of the pages. They allow the 'book' to lay open easily. You can buy these ring binding machines, sometimes second hand if you know where to look. You can set up a bindery in your home. This has good and bad points. If you intend to bind a few dozen copies - fine, if you can be bothered. If you intend 100s you face a task. Of course you can always store the loose pages in the proverbial boxes until you have enough orders and then bind the copies. If you have printed 100s of copies you face a lot of work and dreams. Always remember: your time is money too! Think it through. Cost how much you would spend on a proper paperback as against the hidden subsidy of your evenings putting together copies. And the saleability. The end product can never look anything but what it is, not a proper book. Homemade. As with the strip you can turn a defect into an asset with imagination. But do not expect bookshops to put such a product on their shelves. Unless you are blessed with luck.

11.02 *Appearance*

Most people are swayed by the look and feel of the publication. They are not merely rushing for the content. This is why millions of £s are spent on the appearance. They pay not just for the skills of the designers but for their imagination. The design. Not only of the front cover but the whole presentation. Can you compete? You bet! Small Presses lack money, they do not lack imagination. Indeed they may outstrip regular publishers in ideas and ingenuity. Ideas, imagination - the most priceless resource – and you have it. There is no reason for your publication to look amateur. Even if it looks home-made it can entice. If you are imaginative you will have a treasury of possibilities. Years ago I acquired a collection of about 40 titles by one poetry sp. They tried so many ways to disguise the identical basic product, a slim tome of poems. Some of their ideas misfired. This is so helpful because you can see inside the intention and how and why it doesn't work. But some were magnificent. Obviously they hadn't had much money to spend but they had built up until they could afford more than basic. So they used spot colour. But weird colours and in combinations and with colour card. They put a wrap-around paper 'cover' over plain card so the 'dust jacket' had a small flap on which they put blurb. Sometimes they actually had a spine.

11.03 *Spines*
This is the current boundary – bookshops usually reject everything without a spine. Many readers will be preparing to publish poetry magazines. These will be folded sheets of A4, producing an A5 booklet, stapled = stitched. They do not have a spine. A cross between a booklet and a magazine = a maglet. There is no reason for them to lack appeal. (See the remarks above about the poetry sp.) There are other options. A poem does not need a wide page. Therefore there is no need to use A5. Of course this raises other matters. You may hate the idea of throwing away paper! Because we are talking about cutting off the side of the booklet, probably an inch or more, and throwing it away. You may not bother to have the edge of the booklet 'trimmed.' Consequently you save a £ or two but waste many more because your booklet looks scruffy and handles poorly. If you decide to take the plunge and cut off the side this is exactly the same as trimming and should cost the same.

11.04 *The cover*
Even a maglet can have a nice cover. Say a stiff card. There are plenty which come ready made with one side 'shiny.' The printer will ask you your weight preference. Card can be anthing from 110 to 130 gsm. Or you can laminate. This is advisable for paperbacks and can work out under 50p a copy. Again, let us know if you have better tips.

12 THE OVERALL LOOK

Designing your publication ☐ basic pamphlets ☐ book jackets ☐ back covers ☐ paper quality ☐ handmade marbled paper

12.0 *Design/format:*
The design of your publication is not merely a matter of indulging your artistic inclinations: it has an effect on the publication's sales and the response of its readers. By all means try to produce something that satisfies you – but bear in mind the publication's existence beyond the confines of your mind and your circle of indulgent friends – try to imagine what others, those who don't know you and won't know how much effort has gone into your publication, will make of your work.

12.1 *Basic Pamphlet design*: Without a spine, your publication has limited chances in a bookshop. It will most likely be consigned to a rack, which means that only the top third of the front cover will be visible: and it is here that the essential information should be placed. It is no use having the title of an unknown story by a known author here – put the author's name instead! Likewise, don't put the author's name here if it is the issue with which the pamphlet deals which is important. You can create an artificial spine for a pamphlet by using a dust-jacket. You will still have a very thin spine, but it's better than nothing at all. A spine gives you access to that most scarce of resources: a bookshop shelf.

12.2 *Basic book jacket design*: the spine is all important. Reading top to bottom, this is where your basic information should be placed: title, author and (if there's room) name of press. On the back cover (to which every reader turns instinctively) have some explanatory blurb, the **ISBN, bar-code** (if applicable) and price. The front cover is where you can indulge yourself. Providing the basic information is repeated somewhere here, you can do just as you please. The front cover will not be on display for very long, remember: most shops will only have it on show for a few weeks after the book is published, so it may as well be as eye-catching and bright – or as enigmatic –

as possible. If you are using a photograph on the cover, ask your printer about duotones and dot-for-dot printing. For a duotone, the artwork is photographed from two opposing angles: the two plates are used for printing the image, one in black and one in colour. Dot-for-dot printing produces a similar effect. Here the same plate is used. Having printed the image once in black, the plate is very slightly shifted and the image is reprinted in colour.

12.3 *What material do you want to have your work printed on?* The printer will provide you with samples of paper compatible with their machines. These vary from place to place. You can provide your own paper, or your own card for the cover of a pamphlet – but bear in mind the printing machinery might not take to the stock you've chosen. Ask the printer before you commit yourself to ordering vast quantities of unusable paper. Lavish papers (you can buy a few sheets and photocopy onto them) and handmade, marbled, textured papers are also generally available, as is recycled paper. Your printer should be able to provide recycled and/or acid-free paper (made from rags, acid-free does not decay as rapidly as paper made from wood pulp: think of posterity). Ask for it if you want it. For advice and further information on the quality of recycled papers, contact **Earth Matters**, FoE, 26-28 Underwood Street, London N1 7JQ; or **Paperback** (tel 0181-980-2233).

13 SAFEGUARDING YOUR WORK

Copyright and the law ☐ do you need it? ☐ does it cost? ☐ how long does it last? ☐ permission to re-use

13.0 *Copyright:*
Copyright laws do not hugely affect small presses in any practical way. Copyright is broken every day by a vast number of people, businesses and institutions. Almost no-one would pursue a claim against an obscure and impoverished outfit which remains largely out of the public eye. Those with principles will want to credit their source at least, even if

they cannot pay them a substantial amount; only the despicable or lazy will reproduce without permission work by parties similarly unable to pursue their rights. In other words, don't rip off your fellow small presses and others. Pay them what you can – after all, you are paying the printer, the typesetting bureau and so on. Most sympathetic parties will let you use their material, even for nothing, but if you are reproducing a substantial item, have the courtesy to ask first, if you can track them down.

13.1 Further (and precise) information about the sticky and largely incoherent state of copyright is available from **The Patent Office,** Copyright Enquiries, 25 Southampton Buildings, London WC2A 1AR (0171-438 4700). Copyright resides in any original work and doesn't expire until 70 years after the author's death. You do not necessarily have to put the formal copyright sign on your work, though it is done for form's sake. Even if you omit the copywrite sign the work is still copyrighted in the UK, and is thus granted protection in the coutries which signed the **Universal Copyright Convention.** Quoting from other works (a song, for instance) is allowed without payment of royalty fee, etc, if you are quoting for critical purposes or similar (but credit the copyright owner, the publisher in most cases): i.e. if you are not 'in competition' with the actual song, lyric, etc. Fair dealing is mostly a matter of common-sense, but the state of the law is such as to confuse many into parting unnecessarily with money. Don't plagiarise other writer's work. Don't re-cycle chunks without acknowledgement. Read up on the Acts of the Law at the **British Library** if in doubt. The **Society of Authors,** 84 Drayton Gardens, London SW10 9SB, supply a "Quick Guide to Permissions". Help with copyright for small presses is also offered by **Printexpress**, The Old School House, 12 Market Street, Buxton, Derbyshire SK17 6LD and from **Martin Nail** 0171 412 7044.

14 MONEY MATTERS

Royalties ☐ paying your author ☐ do you have to?

14.0 *Payment:*

If you really are in no position to provide a contract and decent royalty, pay what you can, when and if you can. Price your publication so that the writer or illustrator can expect at least a token payment. Give the author some books – not only copies of their own work, but items from your back catalogue and so on as well. If you are the author as well as the publisher, so much the better. The **Society of Authors** will give advise on contracts and produce a guide to "Basic Minimum Fees".

14.1 Paying **designers** to spice up your product is not particularly worthwhile: the cash is better spent in other ways. First, professionals charge fees even bigger than you'd expect; secondly, make your own mistakes, you will learn something useful from them. It is not necessary to overdo your design job. Let the idiosyncrasy shine through, keep it simple – just ensure that it is readable (for other people as well as for yourself: nothing is more off-putting than an illegible text: how are you meant to read the book?). Ultimately, no amount of formal flourishes will disguise a lack of content. Use a bureau or consultancy if you are ignorant of DTP etc. Find one that is reasonably priced and the staff of which you can get on with.

15 WHAT'S IT GOING TO COST?

calculating a price⬚ mail⬚ order discounts ⬚ shopkeeper's cut

15.0 *Pricing your publication:*

Ideally, the retail price of your publication should be at least five times its cost. In practice, a small press usually ends up charging little more than three times the unit cost, allowing them to break even (bearing in mind the bookshop's cut of one third of the retail price). As a compromise – settle for four times the unit cost. When pricing your book, think about who is going to sell it as well as who is going to buy it. The average bookshop will not be particularly interested in making only ten pence on one of your publications: they want to make some money and shelf-space has to be fought for! Then again, if you deal directly with mail-order purchasers, you can afford to be more generous. Think before you underprice or overprice your product. Look around and see what others are charging, ask yourself what you would pay, consider the overheads of the shops you deal with... then decide what to charge.

16 TOUTING FOR BUSINESS

Selling your publication⬚ what does marketing mean? ⬚ what's your market? ⬚ selling foreign rights ⬚ marketing on the web

16.0 *Marketing:*

Not just a buzz word. Rather something to bear in mind from the word go if you seriously want to shift your product (though of course your product may be deliberately unmarketable in which case skip this bit). First, does your press have an identity, a profile, some integrated sales pitch? Leaf through the Handbook – most press names indicate an attitude, an area of concern or interest. Think about how to make some rapid sales of your book: a launch party is a good idea for a start...

16.1 *Market Research* The self-publisher often knows more about a title's market than anybody else – that's why they wrote the thing to fill a gap. Why pass all this hard-won expertise to somebody else? Do-It-Yourself! (see **Questionnaire**).

16.2 *Selling Rights* A very tasty way of making money from your publication is by selling the **Rights** – literally the right for another publisher to reproduce your publication – possibly in another format or language. The small press who is approached to sell his Rights is fortunate indeed. But there is wicked bargaining to be done; the Frankfurt Book Fair each year is held mainly for the purpose of buying and selling foreign book rights and its a real bear pit! **Women in Publishing** 12 Dyott Street, London WC1, offer excellent courses on Rights Selling held on weekends at Book

House in Wandsworth. Price for a one-day course about £35.

16.3 *Web-sites* A popular new concept in marketing magazines and books in America is to create a Web-Site to be accessed on the computer Network. It is possible to create a mini-catalogue on screen, with covers and blurbs reproduced and even include an instant order-form where publications can be mail-ordered at the touch of a button.

17 TELLING THE WORLD

Promoting your publication ☐ launch parties ☐ stunts ☐ press releases ☐ badges ☐ t-shirts ☐ free publicity ☐ directory entries ☐ review copies

17.0 *Promotion:*
A launch party needn't take place in a hotel suite or exhibition hall. Get your local bookshop to lend you some space; hire a room above a pub for a few quid; launch your book with a reading at a local festival (or downstairs in a pub); have a picnic in the park... the possibilities are endless. Try and think of some angle to launch the book: link it up to a contemporary event, a suddenly fashionable notion, go out of your way to be wacky and attract attention. You may be ignored, but people will enjoy themselves and cough up the money. Bully your family and friends into parting with cash there and then.

17.1 Annoy a few journalists. Kick up a fuss. Send out your press release a few weeks in advance and then again when the deadline approaches. Write the press release in easily digestible chunks. Mark it **"Press Release"**, mark at the top of each page in terms of how long the release is (e.g. "1 of 2" at the top of the first page, "2 of 2" at the top of the second); at the bottom of each page write "mf" ("more follows") or "ends" (marking the end of your press release). Try to put as few words as possible in each sentence: never use words of more than three syllables. The average journalist reading the release will want as far as possible to rewrite it (and not necessarily in their own words) in a format that the average

reader can understand straightaway. Include a sentence or two that expresses an opinion or makes a statement in quotation marks (e.g. "It is my second book," said seasoned author Ken, aged 63): the journalist will use this to give the impression that you've actually been interviewed. Your publication will be competing with hundreds of others, so don't expect instant results. It is not easy to get reviews, let alone good reviews. If you can somehow tie the book in with other newsworthy events, enabling a feature article to be written, the result may be very good (for instance, a single article in the Guardian Weekend section on one small press sold 500 copies of a book that had been in print and ignored for several years). Send review copies, dust jackets etc. as well.

17.2 *Promotional items: Postcards, T-shirts, badges* can be manufactured as promotional items linked to your publication, these can also be sold in outlets which would not take books. Record shops and comic specialists are two obvious outlets: many record shops have started to stock books as an extension of marketing badges, postcards, T-shirts, then comics, magazines and so on. Badge-making machines are likely to be found at a local resource centre; or you can have badges made to your design by someone else (consult the **RESOURCE DIRECTORY**). T-shirts can be silkscreened – try an adult education centre or a local silkscreen printer, or one-offs can be done in high street bucket shops. Postcards can range from the very simple (a poem typed onto a sheet of card four times, the card then cut into four) to full colour jobs that you'll need to do in their thousands. Liver and Lights small press recommend **West One Postcards**, Golden House Press, Great Bulteney Street, London W1R 3DD as specialists in printing postcards at good prices.

17.3 *Directories* there are dozens of directories listing small presses (see *Other Organisations*). Make sure your details are included in as many as possible, but if you don't want to receive unsolicited manuscripts or be pestered by poets looking for a publisher, make sure this information is clear in the description of your press. The greatest of all Small Press Directories is included in this book and before each press is included details are first published free of charge in **Small Press Listings** published 3 times a year by the Small Press Centre. It is important therefore that you update your information regularly for amendment on the **Small Press Centre** database.

18 PAYING THE PRICE

Advertising your publication ▢ how much does it cost? ▢ what's the best medium? ▢ exchange ads ▢ display subscription details

18.0 *Advertising:*
Advertising is an additional expense and something of a gamble. You will not necessarily get results: a £20 ad might sell one book; a £5 ad more suitably placed may sell several hundred. Ask around, see where other small presses are advertising, use your common-sense. Keep track of how successful advertisements in various publications have been for you. Let your pals know. Exchange ads with other specialist publishers. Something else to bear in mind is placing other people's ads in your publication, be it pamphlet, book or magazine. These will offset the production costs. Remember to advertise, at the very least, your *own* product in the back of the book or pamphlet. With magazines, make sure that any subscription and advertising details are prominently displayed in each issue.

18.1 *Make the advert readable.* Nothing is worse than an advertisement that looks shabby: it costs very little to produce something decent, yet again and again small presses seem to opt for grotty, third-generation photocopies of ancient artwork. Black on white works best (reversed out is not as eye catching, market researchers suggest): make a clear statement, providing details of what is for sale and who is to be paid. The financial transaction is the whole point of the advertisement, after all. Simply give clear and concise information with, possibly, the aid of a witty or bold catchprase to grab attention.

19 SELLING FROM YOUR SITTING ROOM

Mail order ▢ compiling a list ▢ tips ▢ keeping a data base of customers▢ data protection▢ mail shots ▢ catalogues

19.0 *Mail Order:*
Mail Order is labour intensive and often tedious, but you are cutting out the middle man and can establish a more personal relation with your customers if you so wish. Since book shops are increasingly rigid in their attitudes, and tend to stock only well-established work, mail-order can be especially useful for a small press (or a gang of small presses: team up with a few like minds in your locality).

19.1 First essential is a decent catalogue. Whether you have one title or a hundred your catalogue is your calling card and conveys the image of your press. If your catalogue is messy and scruffy potential customers will imagine your product is the same. It can be as simple or as elaborate as you can afford. The main thing is to list available tiles, including 'back list' if one exists, and their prices and availability. Take a lesson from '60s small press Cokaygne, they didn't have many titles to sell but their home-made, photocopied catalogue, which included smells, tastes, pull outs and push ins and weird wonderfullness, has become a collectors' item!

19.2 When compiling a mail-order list – say you've received two dozen orders for your publication, responses from an advertisement or announcement (remember to keep the addresses) – ask each person on the list to send the names and addresses of five or six of their friends who'd like to receive news of your forthcoming publications. Put a note in your catalogue to this effect. That way, your list of contacts will gradually expand. If you receive no response after a few months from a particular person, just cross them off your list.

19.3 If you keep your list of customers on computer disc – and this applies also to journal subscription lists – you are obliged to tell them so; under the terms of the Data Protection Act 1984, anyone who objects to these details being stored in this way may ask for their particulars to be kept in a written record. For the rules, contact **The Office of Data Protection Registrar**, Wycliffe House, Water Lane, Wilmslow, Cheshire SK9 5AF. Tel: 01625 545745. Fax: 01625 524510. E-mail: data@wycliffewe.demon.co.uk.

20 SELLING YOURSELF

Supplying bookshops ▢ sale or return ▢ retailer's discount ▢ other outlets ▢ planning your sales campaign ▢ Booksellers Association

20.0 *Bookshops:*
With many shops that you visit, you will find that a **Sale Or Return** policy is operational. This is a cross that every small press is obliged to bear. It is justified when applied to magazines and journals limited in their scope by a specific time (e.g. television programme details etc). However, its application has been extended to virtually every publication which the laws of fashion and economics suggest might appear redundant. Its widespread approval by bookshops up and down the country reflects the virtual abandonment of retailers' faith in the publications they sell; and the lack of information about the nature of publications to which the general public has access. Whatever terms are offered, the bookshop will take their percentage, usually 33.3% discount.

20.1 Non-bookshop outlets are also worth considering. While it is doubtful that the local supermarket will be very interested, outlets such as health shops, railway stations, garden centres &c may take some small press items.

20.2 "Are you reaching the right bookshops?" asks the **Booksellers Association**, which can provide peel-off labels of booksellers. They can also provide lists of specialised booksellers (children's; academic; libraries; religious etc). Full details from Booksellers Association of

Great Britain and Ireland, 272 Vauxhall Bridge Road, London SW1V 1BA (0171 834 5477).

21 GETTING YOUR MONEY BACK

Orders and invoices ▢ retailers terms ▢ postage ▢ book-keeping ▢ statements ▢ late payments

21.0 *Invoicing book shops:*
When you receive an order, send the shop an invoice with the books, marking clearly the date, your address and who the cheque should be made payable to; and the **terms of payment** (e.g. "Payment on receipt of this invoice: no statement will follow" or "Terms: 90 days"). Shops will expect a publisher's discount (33%, increasingly often more). It is up to you whether you charge postage (and how much): give maximum reduction for bulk orders (33% post-free), charge more the fewer the items ordered. If a shop orders one copy of a pamphlet costing £1.20, charge them postage as well. It is not your fault if the shop only makes five pence – but do bear in mind that some bookshops are independents too, so "look after our own". Very small orders are likely to be specific requests from customers: the shop offers the service as a courtesy and does not (at least, cannot) expect to make a profit out of such marginal work. Remember to put a flyer for your other publications inside the book when you despatch it – or have some sticky labels printed that urge readers to write for your free catalogue.

21.1 Expect to wait up to several months for your invoice to be paid. Send a **statement** if you haven't received your money after four months or so. The law – a stiff letter couched in legal terms – is a last resort. You will soon establish which shops are likely to be regular customers and which are not. Spread the word about shops that don't pay at all: warn others of their attitude. A good tip that may help small presses owed money is to include the following on your invoices: "As per the advice on late payment from the Minister of State for small firms, after one month from the date of this invoice, we legally require you to add 2 per cent to the total, and a further 2 per cent for each further month's delay in payment thereafter."

22 BEING YOUR OWN 'REP'

Grovelling to the Buyer ☐ choose the right outlet ☐ consulting other presses

22.0 *Repping:*
Telephone the bookshop before you lug your suitcase of products along: ensure that the Buyer is in and will see you. It is no good speaking to the expert in the stationery department if you're trying to shift your philosophical magnum opus. Make an appointment, take along a sample of the work you're dealing with, and try and meet the requirements of the bookshop. It's a lot of work, of course – phoning up, selling the books, calling back with the right quantity, invoicing, etc, etc – but there is often no alternative. Few tasks are quite as soul-destroying – or character-building, depending on your point of view – as repping, but try and bear in mind the bookshop's requirements, not just your own wishes. If a shop thinks (or knows) it can sell a particular product, it will place an order. If the buyer knows the book will not shift, you won't get an order. The buyer is in the position he or she is in because they know – generally – what kind of customer their shop attracts. The best will in the world will not sell a volume of psychic poetry in a shop which specialises in maps or economics. Remember too that while your interest might be Literature or Philosophy or Politics, the buyer's sole interest is Cash Flow. A buyer is more likely to have risen up through the stationery department than to have a degree in English. Try and persuade the buyer, by all means, but try not to be disillusioned if you can't sell your books straightaway. Keep at it.

22.1 Consult other small presses, see how they sell their product. Gang together with like-minded publishers and have one of you do the repping for your area. Bookshops don't

much like having to deal with two dozen small publishers when they could deal with only one central supplier: the paperwork is less, less time is used up. Which leads us onto the next point: you could become a distributor yourself, or...

23 OUT AND ABOUT

Distributors ☐ percentages of the price ☐ sales reports ☐ regular payments ☐ what are they looking for? ☐ importance of presentation

23.0 *Distributors:*
You may wish to have your publication distributed by other parties. It's hard work slogging round bookshops begging them to buy your wares. So much easier if someone else would do it. Ring up and make an appointment, take a few copies along, convince the distributor that you are 'serious'. Do this before official publication, if possible, or at any rate as soon as it is feasible – the distributor will not want to be selling your old stock after you've already been to all the obvious shops. The various established distributors stick more or less to tried and tested products, items they know will sell. A distributor will require a percentage of the price of your publication (between 15% and 25%); they will present you with regular sales reports; and pay you at an arranged time of year (e.g. three months in arrears).

23.1 *What is a distributor looking for?* First, something that will fit into their profile, a publication they think they can sell. Remember every distributor has taken time to establish *their* reputation and credibility with bookshops. They won't jeopardise this for your pet title if it looks dire – hence the importance of presentation. (*Tip* from Counter Culture – see Resources Directory). A useful rule is to put yourself in the buyer's shoes. How patient would you be with somebody incompetently trying to sell you shoddy goods which clearly won't sell and wasting loads of your valuable time? You should be able to ascertain what kind of material they sell over the phone. Suppose the content of your book is apposite, what then? If the distributor is sure it will sell tolerably well, consider the design of the publication and the price. Where sales are more or less guaranteed because the subject is topical, don't ruin the book's chances by making the cover hideous or having the text set in an unsuitable font. If in doubt, have a friendly chat with the distributor and ensure you are not going to scupper the project. A laminated cover will probably be essential, general descriptive text should be readable (in a serif typeface), and the price should give adequate amounts to you as publisher, to the distributor and to the bookshop. If you've no luck, and are therefore obliged to do it yourself, again – why not get in touch with a few other small presses and see if they want stuff taken round the shops at the same time? (Read the article by Jim Lavis in Part 1).

24 THE WORLD'S YOUR OYSTER

Selling your book abroad☐ the American market ☐ overseas distributors ☐ the continental market

24.0 *Overseas distribution and exchange:*
One way of broadcasting your publication is to sell it in the American market. There are a few distributors who are worth contacting: always send a copy of your book and ask for a current catalogue in return: and pass this on to a fellow small press if the distributor does not cater for your product. 'Local' material is very hard to shift abroad, for obvious reasons, and only if it has a very strong political bias of more general application – or if it provides an interesting view of a hidden part of the world – will an overseas distributor be likely to bother with it. America is a vast market compared to Britain, let alone to your home town, but bear in mind that your book, by the time it is shipped to the States, will have to be put on sale at a relatively high price; and that books printed in the USA are anyway a lot cheaper than their equivalent here. So your product will be at a disadvantage: it will be obscure to begin with, and expensive to boot. Don't be put off by such

considerations – but approach the prospect of an overseas market in a sober fashion and don't expect miracles.

25 SHOWING OFF

Exhibiting at Trade fairs ☐ the Centre's Small Press Fairs on the South Bank☐ local book fairs ☐ venues ☐ the London Book Fair at Olympia ☐ specialist fairs☐ poets convention☐ Germany's free Mini Press Fair in Mainz ☐ Frankfurt Book Fair ☐ ABA in Chicago

25.0 *Fairs:*
Fairs are another way to shift products: the Small Press Centre have an annual **Small Press Book Fair** every summer in collaboration with the South Bank Centre in London. The **ALP** run a similar, but smaller, event every year as well – and there are numerous other events. It is worth trying a book fair in your locality or genre at least once, if only to confirm your worst fears.

25.1 If you have the gumption to publish for yourself then you can organise your own fair! John Nicholson, the National Small Press Centre Director who organised the SPG Fairs 1989-1993, offers these tips for small press fairs:

A. Find a suitable **venue,** one which you think is perfect. If it enthuses you then your excitement will help to persuade others.

B. Float the idea on people who you are sure will share your enthusiasm.

C. Widen the **circle of people** who know of the proposed fair. Get their feedback. That will draw them in so their enthusiasm increases the momentum.

D. All of you make a **list** (have a meeting in the pub or each other's houses) of anybody you can think of involved in similar or related activity. This will be the starting point not only of the organisers but of a **mailing list.**

E. Compile another list of **official organisations** and firms who should be interested. You will be surprised how many will be vulnerable, i.e. want to take part."

Enthusiasm is the key but it is not enough. You must create a core of people prepared to work, not just make encouraging noises. Small presses are at a disadvantage in that their resources are limited, so a conviction that the fair is worth doing is essential, as is the organisational ability to attract the book buying public.

25.2 Other fairs. There is an area in the **London Book Fair** (three days at Olympia every March) called the **Small Press Area**. This fair is the British Publishing world's beano involving libraries and bookshops. A stand costs hundreds of £s which indicates their definition of a small press. It means small publisher. Visitors pay £14 – each day, so no browsers! Anyhow exhibitors must not sell books, only rights. So it's not much use to the majority of small presses or the book-buying public.

There are **specialist fairs**: radical and black, women, comics, private presses, poetry, political, anarchist artists books etc. All have flourished for years and you can find out about them by contacting people who participate eg specialist presses or the distributors listed in the **RESOURCE DIRECTORY**.

From this survey you see there are huge gaps which were filled by the **SPG's Annual Small Press Fair**. In 1992 it transcended all the fairs described, including the commercial ones. It transcended publishers because it had the back-up services (listed elsewhere in the Resources Directory) such as DTP studios, illustrators, binders, cheap printers, mailing agencies and distributors. It was this Handbook in 3D. The complete kit in one place for one day attracting more than 4,000 visitors. The potential of the small press phenomenon could be seen at this fair, which will now take place on a more modest scale, each summer in the South Bank Centre, growing annually while maintaining a low level of charges to exhibitors. A small press can do its annual promotion, launch new titles and catalogues, make contacts and deals, get publicity – and sell. This fair is established as a national opportunity without equal for British small presses and will once again become the British date in the world small press calendar.

25.3 Some book fairs to take note of: **Anarchist Book Fair**: books, pamphlets, food, accordion music. Every year, usually late October. Contact: Anarchist bookfair Organisers, c/o 84b Whitechapel High Street, London E1 7QX for details: 0181-533 6936; The **Art-**ists' Books Fair** has become an established. The first two were held in the Royal Festival Hall and outgrew it. The 3rd was held in the Barbican. (Organiser, see **RESOURCE DIRECTORY**). National Small Press Centre and **Association of Little Presses** annual fairs: contact the organisations for full details: addresses in the **RESOURCE DIRECTORY**. The National **Convention of Poets and Small Presses** is a moveable feast and a variable one as it has a dogma: no central organisation, so we can't give you a contact.

There are scattered fairs of the traditional 'let's have a glorified party' sort which take over the upstairs room in a pub and invite everybody and their friends. These can raise enough to pay for the hangover. Then there are the familiar 'readings' fairs where poets read and then sell what they read.

25.4 *International Book Fairs*: only in exceptional circumstances will a small press go to an international bookfair. For many, they are entirely irrelevant but for others they can be useful and the **National Small Press Centre** as a body has determined to represent British small presses at as many as possible, taking NSPC literature along and offering representation for publishers who would otherwise be left out. Attendance at such Fairs costs a lot: several hundred pounds usually, which can only be met by a group of publishers co-operating and presenting their single titles together under the **National Small Press Centre** banner. The results are difficult to gauge, but generally must be considered positive. **The Frankfurt Fair** is the major international fair and occurs every October. **The London Book Fair**, which takes place in Olympia each March, is increasingly an event for remainder dealers and reflects poorly on Britain's attitude to publishing. This trade event attracted only a couple of hundred ordinary citizens – so you cannot expect to sell direct many copies of your books. The so-called 'Small Press Area' is nothing of the kind, and merely offers cramped booths away from the main body of the fair for slightly less than the 5-figure sum you can expect to be charged for a stand in the main hall. The **American Booksellers Association Fair**, in Chicago each year, is far better in terms of organisation and response to small press product. The New York **Small Press Center** fair over 3 days in September takes place on the four levels of the Mechanics Institute Library on 44th Street where the Center is housed. Charges diminish according to the floor on which your table is booked. Sharing is allowed and the fair benefits from having an unusual and fascinating selection of guest speakers throughout the weekend. The biggest small press fair in Europe is held every other year in Mainz, **the Mainz Mini Presse Messe.** The next one is May 1999. Stands are FREE because the event is underwritten by the city, birthplace of Gutenberg, the father of printing. Details from Jurgen Kipp, Mainz Mini Press Archiv, Fischtor Platz 23 , Mainz, Germany.

26 PLEASE CAN I HAVE SOME MONEY?

Who will help you financially? ☐ awards and prizes☐ literary grants ☐ lottery money☐ bodies to approach

26.0 *Prizes, grants, etc:*
Remember, your publication may be eligible for an **award** or **prize**; and you may be able to get a publication financed.

26.1 *Guide to Literary Prizes, Grants and Awards in Britain and Ireland,* compiled by **Book Trust** and **Society of Authors**. From Book Trust, Book House, 45 East Hill, London SW18 2QZ. Tel: 0171-870 9055. This booklet, updated annually, provides addresses of regional arts associations, many of which are able to finance some small press and related activities; and details of prizes and awards available from other bodies. Prizes range from small monetary awards for books contributing to Franco-British understanding to the **Quatrefoil Award** – cash for the author of the book judged to have contributed the most towards an understanding and/or love of oriental rugs – with plenty of others in between.
    * *Scott Moncrieff Prize:* £1,000 awarded annually for best translation of a French text into English, published in the UK by a British

publisher. 20th century texts of literary merit and general interest will be considered. Boost your small press budget by contacting: **Translator's Association,** 84 Drayton Gardens, London SW10 9SB. (Three copies of the work and of the original are required). Some funding and courses for independent projects is also occasionally offered by the Paul Hamlyn Trust. Contact them for details.
    * *Swansea Fund for Small Presses*: apply to David Woolley, Somerset Place, Swansea, Wales, SA1 1SE. (01792 642 584).
    * *Arts Council Of Great Britain*: A source of grants and information including the **Arts For Everyone Express** scheme (A4E) allocating lottery money up to £5,000. Contact The Literature Officer, Arts Council, 14 Great Peter Street, London SW1P 3NQ (0171 333 0100).
    * *Elephant Trust*, P.O. Box 5521, London W8 4WA: was created by Roland Penrose with a view to advancing public education in all aspects of the arts and to develop and improve the knowledge, understanding and appreciation of the fine arts in the United Kingdom. Write for their guidelines if this is your area of interest.
    * *British Book Design and Production Exhibition*: Held annually by British Printing Industries Federation and Publishers Association. Details from 11 Bedford Row, London WC1R 4DX (tel: 0171-242 6904). Numerous **award categories** (General Hardback, Mass Market Paperback, Children's Book, Illustrated Book, Limited Editions, Exhibition Catalogues, &c), reasonable entrance fees, closing date early February.
    * *The Society of Authors* offers grants to "published authors who need funding to assist in the writing of their next book". Details from 84 Drayton Gardens, London SW10 9SB. Tel: 0171-373 6643.
    * *The London Arts Board*, Elme House, 133 Long Acre, London WC2 offers grants to independent publishers. Write for details of deadlines and conditions.

**WHAT ARE YOU WAITING FOR?
GO AND
PUBLISH YOURSELF!**

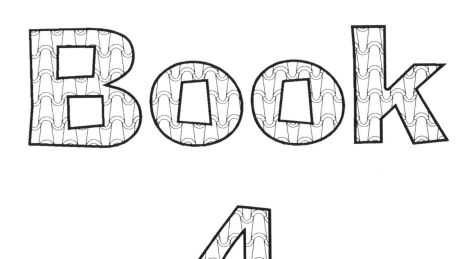

Book
4

Accommodation addresses
Administrative services
Advice and reference, publications
Bar codes
Binding
Booksellers, Libraries suppliers
Campaigns
Directories & Reference
Distributors
Equipment
Exhibitions, Conference facilities
Labels
Letter Press
Mailing services
Marketing
Media
Membership organisations
Merchandise products
Origination: design and setting
Other organisations
Paper (including re-cycled)
Resources (including courses)
Short run printers
T-Shirts
Tools & services
Useful periodicals & publications
Workshops & Resource Centres

Where can I find?

WHAT ADDRESS SHALL I USE? ☞

WHO WILL HELP ME RUN MY BUSINESS? ☞

WHERE CAN I GET ADVICE? ☞

ACCOMMODATION ADDRESSES

Mail boxes; office facilities: day hire; telephone. answering services. Run your business without an office.

1 BRITISH MONOMARKS
Monomark House, 27 Old Gloucester Street, London WC1N 3XX. 0171 405 0463 fax 0171 831 9489

2 CAMBRIDGESHIRE ACCOMMODATION ADDRESSES
01354 677213

3 FLEXIBLE BUSINESS SERVICES
235 Regaent Sttreet, London N3 3LF, 0181 343 2316 charge ony £2 per week

4 HOLD EVERYTHING
162 Regent Street, London, 0171 580 4242

5 JERSEY ADDRESSES
PO Box 436, Jersey JE4 5QY. Charge £25 per month.

6 POSTHASTE, CROYDON
0181 688 8144

7 THE REALLY GOOD BUSINESS BUREAU
39 South Street, Mayfair, London W1Y 6BB, 0171 409 7088

ADMINISTRATIVE SERVICES & INFORMATION MANAGEMENT

They will handle your mail-orders and subscriptions for a fee.

1 ACCESS UNLIMITED
6 Weston Road, Wilmslow, Cheshire SK9 2AN.
'Number 1 in Databases & Networking'.

2 ASLIB
The Association for Information Management, Information House, 20-24 Old Street, London EC1V 9AP. 0171 253 4488 fax 0171 430 0514
Consultancy; training; publications; publisher: *Copyright made easier* by Raymond A. Wall, pbk, 390 pp, £28.00.

3 ALLM SYSTEMS & MARKETING
21 Beechcroft Road, Bushey, Herts

WD2 2JU.
Guides to post codes. Also building and maintaining a marketing database.

4 ASSISTANCE CONSULTANCY AND PLACING SERVICES
P.O. Box 35, Prestwich, Manchester M25 8AX. 0161 798 8830 fax 0161 773 9005
Consultancy: membership services management.

5 ASSOCIATION QUEST
58-60 Rivington Street, London EC2A 3AY. 0171 739 9543 fax 0171 729 4232
Association management services; publishes 'Association Quest' magazine.

6 DEL (DATA ENCODING LTD)
9-11 High Street, Hampton, TW12 2SA. 0181 979 1122.

7 FCC MANAGEMENT SERVICES LIMITED
Federation House, 1 The Briars, Waterberry Drive, Waterlooville, Portsmouth, Hants PO7 7YH. 01705 232 099 fax 01705 232 126

8 HAIGH & HOCHLAND
The Precinct Centre, Oxford Road, Manchester M13 9QA. (0161 273 4156).
Journal subscription services, international university booksellers.

9 UNIVERSAL SUBSCRIPTION SERVICE LTD
Universal House, 3 Hurst Road, Sidcup, Kent DA15 9BA.
Subscription agents and booksellers.

10 R.E.D. COMPUTING LTD
The Outback, 58-60 Kingston Road, New Malden, Surrey KT3 3LZ.
Selling programmes to help you manage: subscriptions, list management, mailsort, reader enquiry etc.

ADVICE & REFERENCE PUBLICATIONS
1 ALEMBIC PRESS GUIDE
Covers the world for private presses: services and contacts, over 300 entries. Invaluable. Third edition special sale price £16 + £2

p&p. 0 907482 42 2 Hyde Farm House, Marcham, Abingdon, Oxfordshire OX13 6NX. 01865 391 391

2 ALTERNATIVE PRINTING HANDBOOK
 (Penguin £3.95) is recommended by Last Ditch. Published 1983 so it will be out of print, but well worth tracking down.

3 BOOK HOUSE
45 East Hill, Wandsworth, London SW18 2QZ. 0181 874 2718
Produce an entire catalogue of relevant titles, Book Publishing Books BPB, gathered from assorted publishers. One-stop shopping. Rivalled only by the mail-order service of the National Small Press Centre.

4 'BOOKSHOPS OF LONDON'
by Charles Frewin (second revised edition March 1997). Two Heads Publishing. £7.99 paperback. ISBN 1 897850 57 3

5 'BOOKSHOPS OF LONDON'
by Diana Stephenson. Went into six editions with the Roger Lascelles imprint but now, alas, o/p. Likely to re-emerge under another imprint? Worth looking for in your library.

6 'BOOKSHOPS OF LONDON'
by Martha R Pease. (fisrt edition in UK 1981. Has re-appeared in USA as a Salem House paperback. $9.95 ISBN 0 88162 294 X

7 COMPLETE GUIDE TO BOOKSHOPS IN THE UK.
Searchlight Publishing. 1994 edition £65.00 hardback. ISBN 1 897864 01 9

8 COMPUTER MANUALS LTD
205 Formans Road, Sparkhill, Birmingham B11 3AX 0121 706 6000
A specialist bookshop willing to advise on the suitablility of books for specific applications.

9 DESKTOP PUBLISHING BY DESIGN
By R.Shushhan and D.Wright, Microsoft Press. 4th edition £37.49 General guide to design. Includes projects for PageMaker users.

10 DIRECTORY OF PUBLISHING
Commonwealth and Overseas. 1997 Cassell and the Publishers' Association (22nd edition 1996). Very useful. The trade bible.

11 EDITING, DESIGN AND BOOK PRODUCTION
By Charles Foster (Journeyman's Media Handbook series) currently only as hardcover £30.00 - takes you through all the stages of publication production.
Pluto (Journeyman) 345 Archway Road, London N6 5AA. 0181 348 2724

12 GETTING IN PRINT, STAYING IN PRINT
Published by HERTIS (now defunct), edited by William A.Forster. ISBN 0 85267 284 5 costs £12.50. At 112pp, this pocket book provides a simple overview for publishers, the trade and librarians of a) the contribution of the electronic manuscrip and b) the rise and fall of the print industry. Still available at this price from Carol Everest, Student Services Faculty, Hertford Regional College, Scott's Road, Ware, Herts SG12 9JF.
NB Bill Forster is now with the University of Hertfordshire Learning Resources Centre 01717 284 681

13 GETTING INTO POETRY
Is a readers' and writers' guide to the poetry scene by Paul Hyland. Price £5.95, ISBN 1 852241 18 7, it is to designed to help the reader in "the jungle of contemporary poetry". Bloodaxe Books, PO Box 1SN, Newcastle upon Tyne, NE99 1SN.

14 A GUIDE TO INDEPENDENT & PRIVATELY PUBLISHED PERIODICALS
G.Carroll, 11 Shirley Street, Hove, East Sussex.
Check it out if periodicals are your area of interest.

15 GUIDE TO PUBLISHING
Proprint, Riverside Cottage, Great North Road, Stibbington, Peterborough, Cambs PE8 6LR 01733 230 797

16 HOW TO BOOKS
David Stewart, 3 Newtec Place, Magdalen Road, Oxford , Oxon, OX4 1RE. 01865 793 806 – fax

01865 248 780

A number of relevant titles: How To – do a newsletter, publish a book, write a press release etc. Even how to survive divorce. The series has plenty of tangential titles. Prices are all around £10. Start with their catalogue.

17 HOW TO PUBLISH YOUR POETRY

Peter Finch (Allison and Busby, 126pp) is written by a widely published poet and bookshop manager, Oriel. Packed with useful advice, remarks and wise saws from many poets, practical hints, plus a thorough bibliography. For the would-be poet, this is an invaluable handbook.

18 ANN KRITZINGER

'Brief Guide to Self-Publishing' (Scriptmate Editions 1991) recommended by Peter Finch. ISBN 0 951376659, was £2.50.

19 LIGHT'S LIST.

1997 is twelfth edition. Photon Press, 29 Longfield Road, Tring, Herts HP23 4DG £1. ISBN 1 897968 31 0. World-wide list of titles, addresses of small press mgazines publishing poetry, short stories etc.

20 LOOKING GOOD IN PRINT

01252 333 575

Roger C.Parker. £21.95. A guide to dtp from USA, with hints on design. Ventana Press/Headway Computer Products.

21 MARKETING FOR SMALL PUBLISHERS

A useful title by Bill Godber (of Turnaround Distribution), priced £9.99. Turnaround Distribution distribute our Hanbook so Bill Godber knows small presses. Pluto (Journeyman) 345 Archway Road, London N6 5AA.

22 THE SMALL PRESS CENTRE HANDBOOK

You are holding it.

23 THE NATIONAL SMALL PRESS CENTRE'S ADVICE BOOKLETS SERIES.

They also do free slips for specialised areas. Send SASE for free details.

24 NEW CAXTON PRESS

Flat Two, 11 Clifton Park, Clifton, Bristol BS8 3BX. 01272 738 997 Produce a manual which has been the bible of many start-up outfits during the 1990s.

25 OLEANDER

17 Stansgate Avenue, Cambridge CB2 2QZ. 01223 244688. Illustrated worldwide directory of contemporary Designer Book-binders £30.

26 PANDOR HOUSE PUBLICATIONS

6 Kelvinbrook, West Molesey, Surrey KT8 1RZ
Tel/fax 0181 979 3060
Small Publishers A-Z, the guide to good publishing by Daphne Macara £6.00 (Angled towards the 'proper' to publish ie do you know what a BS526 is? Do you care?) Comes out of the APN stable – see under Memebrship Organisations.

27 PARADIGM PUBLISHING COMPANY

P.O. Box 3877, San Diego, California 92163, USA. (619)234 7115 fax (619) 234-2607
Publisher: 'Make news! Make noise! How to get publicity for your book!' by Shelley Roberts, $6.00.

28 DAN POYNTER

'Non traditional book markets' (audio cassette) 1993; How To Print, Promote and Sell Your Book - the self-publishing manual. And a host more mauals.
Dan Poynter is one of the giants of the American small press help scene. Get on his list and he will deluge you with leaflets about his range of advice books. Para Publishing, PO Box 8206, Santa Barbara, CA 93118-8206 USA. Or try his web site for details: http:/ /www.ParaPublishing.com/books/ para/360. Contains more than 400 pages of free information.

29 THE PRESENTATION DESIGN BOOK

01252 333 575
Ed. Margaret Rabb. £22.95. For businesses especially. Ventana Press.

30 PRINT – HOW YOU CAN DO IT YOURSELF

By Jonathon Zeitlyn. 1992 £9.99

Also from
Pluto (Journeyman) 345 Archway Road, London N6 5AA.

31 PUBLISHERS HANDBOOK
Published by Grosvenor Press International. Worth looking at in your local library if you want more information. This is a 'trade' publication, 468 pages long, with information on Agents, Design, Marketing Services, Distribution, Sales, etc.

32 STEVE REDHEAD
'Football with Attitude'. Wordsmith 1991
Steve was director of a project at Manchester Poly and claimed to possess a copy of every football 'zine. There is a comprehensive catalogue as an appendix to his book.

33 SCOLAR
Gower House, Croft Road, Aldershot, Hampshire GU11 3HR. 01252 331 511.
An academic press with some specialist titles of interest. 'The Private Presses' by Colin Franklin, 2nd ed 1990. was £30 then. Also 'Spreading the Word: the distribution networks of print 1550-1850'. Edited Robin Myers & Michael Harris. 1990 was £35. Recommended by ADCO.

34 SELLING BOOKS BY DIRECT MAIL
£2.00. A 16pp basic guide to selling books through the mail. Monkey Business Publications, PO Box 184, Colchester CO3 3SL. (see also under Mailing Services)

35 SOME ZINES
The catalogue of an exhibition of the same name held at Boise Stae University. Valuable details of 'American Alternative & Underground Magazines, Newsletters & APAs. A Cold Drill Book 1992. Compiled by Tom Trusky, Dept of English, Boise State University, Boise, ID 83725 USA

36 THORSONS
now part of Harper Collins Publishers Ltd, 77-85 Fulham Palace Road, Hammersmith, London W6 8JB
'How to write a book and get it published'. Susan Curran offers practical advice on getting published rather than publishing for yourself.

37 'THE WORLD OF ZINES'
Mike Gunderloy & Cari Goldberg Janice, Penguin Books 1992. The fruits of the labours of the movers of Factsheet 5 on their retirement. What an introduction.

38 WRITERS AND ARTISTS YEARBOOK
The 97th edition includes a piece by Peter Finch on the self-publishing option. Available in your local library. Published by A C Black, 35 Bedford Row, London WC1R 4JH. 0171 242 0946

39 THE WRITER'S GUIDE TO SELF PUBLISHING
By Charlie Bell (Dragonfly Press, see A to Z) 24pp, £2.25. A little booklet aimed at the amateur writer who wishes to see his or her work in print, containing the usual solid advice, clearly laid out for the beginner.

40 THE WRITER'S HANDBOOK
(Macmillan/PEN), edited by Barry Turner, is described as 'the complete reference for all writers and those involved in the media'. Contributors include Peter Finch.

41 THERE IS A SMALL NEW GENRE OF 'GUIDES' BY PRINTERS ETC.
They are trying to reduce mutual problems by instructing their customers so these little aids are usually free. You can pick up very useful tips.
Full details of addresses see Short Run Printers section below. Biddles, Norman Hardy, Ipswich Book Co., Antony Rowe.

42 LOOK THROUGH THE A TO Z ENTRIES
You will find lots more – Dragonfly, Hi-Resolution, Local History Magazine, Antony North, Words & Images – who offer advice of different sorts.

43 THE BOOKSELLERS' ASSOCIATION
sells labels with the addresses of its members.

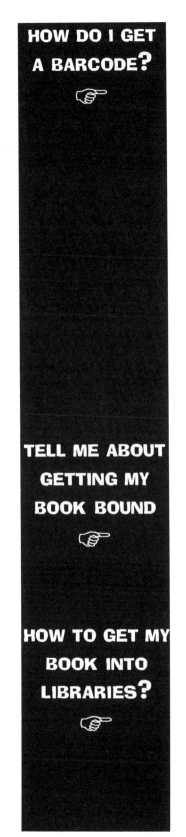

HOW DO I GET A BARCODE?

TELL ME ABOUT GETTING MY BOOK BOUND

HOW TO GET MY BOOK INTO LIBRARIES?

BATCODES

1 BARCODES LIMITED
Vale Road, Portslade, E.Sussex BN41 1GD. 01273 422693.
supplied the barcode for this book. Tom won't treat you like an idiot and will help and advise. Cost is around £17-£20 plus VAT.

2 PEAK TECHNOLOGIES UK LTD.
6 Roxborough Way, Foundation Park, Maidenhead, Berks, SL6 3UD. 01628 508685 Fax: 01628 508687.
Linda will try and blind you with technical jargon. Don't approach Peak unless you know what expressions like "plotted direct onto film" mean… Cost is £13.50 plus VAT.

3 SYMBOL SERVICES
(Div. of Axicon Auto ID Ltd.) Jenny Hicks, Church Road, Weston-on-the-Green, Bicester, Oxon OX6 8QP. +44 (0)1869 351166 fax +44 (0)1869 351205
Shipments are made within 24 hours. They can provide codes in film form or on sticky labels if you suddenly find that, after all, you need a bar code for a book that you already had printed.

BINDING
If you want more binding information contact
The Society of Bookbinders
49 Albion Road, Reigate, Surrey RH2 7SY.

1 CRAFT BOOKBINDING
John Westwood, The Malt House, Church Lane, Streatley, Reading RG8 9HT. 01491 873001.

2 FINE BINDERY
Unit One, Bridge Approach, Mill Road, Wellingborough WN8 1QN. 01933 276 689.

3 CHRIS HICKS BOOKBINDER
64 Merewood Avenue, Sandhills, Oxford OX3 8EF. 01865 69346.
'We undertake binding, repair and restoration work on books of all types and periods. We can also execute short-run work, solander and slip cases, presentation and fine bindings.'

4 JAMES BURN OXFORD
Stanton Harcourt Road, Eynsham,
Oxford OX8 1JE. 01865 880 458.
They make the machines which do those wire spiral 'spines'. You can be your own binder too. If you want your book to look like a Company Report they are the fellows for you. Cheap and cheerful.

5 KADACOURT LTD
Unit 11, Faraday Road, Rabans Lane, Aylesbury, Bucks HP19 3RY. 01296 96192.
Not just binding but all sorts of finishing: shrink-wrapping, recovering, slip cases.

6 PANTHER PRESS
Duckmill Lane, Bedford MK42 0AX. 01234 60176.

7 ROOKS BOOKS
Gavin Rookledge, Gypsy Hill Workshop, 14 Paddock Gardens, Upper Norwood, London SE19 3SB. 0181 766 6398
Prepared to discuss even a one-off commission - if the price is right.

8 SHEPHERDS BOOKBINDERS LTD
76b Rochester Row, London SW1P 1JU. 0171 630 1184
Also make papers and have a shop at the above address so you can view.

BOOKSELLERS/LIBRARY SUPPLIERS
Please note this is a selection. There are many more whose details you can find in the relevant directories.

1 B & M INTERNATIONAL
34 Granvelle Street, Birmingham, W. Midlands B1 2LJ 0121 643 1888
Bookseller.

2 THE BOOKSELLER'S ASSOCIATION OF GREAT BRITAIN
272 Vauxhall Bridge Road, London SW1V 1BB. 0171 834 5477
Trade association for bookshops; sell mailing lists.

3 DELTA INTERNATIONAL BOOK WHOLESALERS LTD
39 Alexandra Road, Addlestone, Surrey KY15 2PQ. 01932 854 776 fax 01932 849 528
Export book wholesaler.

4 W.H. EVERETT & SON LTD
8 Hurlingham Business Park, Sulivan Road, London SW6 3DU. 0171 731 8562 Internet 100064.2777@compuserve.com Fax 0171 371 5870
International bookseller and subscription agent for academic libraries.

5 JMLS LTD
In April 1997 they changed their name to Library Services UK Ltd 24 Gamble Street, Nottingham NG7 4FJ. 0115 970 8021
Library suppliers.

6 JAMES ASKEW AND SON LIMITED
218-222 North Road, Preston PR12 1SY
Library suppliers.

7 B.H. BLACKWELL LTD.
Hythe Bridge Street, Oxford OX1 2ET
Booksellers/library suppliers.

8 THE HOLT JACKSON BOOK COMPANY LIMITED
Preston Road, Lancashire FY8 5AX
Library suppliers.

9 STARKMANN BOOK ORDERING LTD.
6 Broadley Street, London NW8 8AE. 0171 724 5335
Bookseller.

CAMPAIGNS
1 THE CAMPAIGN FOR PRESS AND BROADCASTING FREEDOM
6 Cynthia Street, London N1. Tel: 0171 278 4430 fax 0171 837 8868
Monitors the media and produced a magazine of information and case studies.

2 HANDS OFF READING CAMPAIGN
Oopposed to introducing VAT on publications. Peter Bingle c/o Communications Group, 19 Buckingham Gate, London SW1E 6LB 0171 630 1411

3 JONATHON CLIFFORD
27 Mill Road, Fareham, Hants PO116 0TH
Tel/fax 01329 822 218
Campaigner against Vanity Presses, those publishers who want payment to produce your publication.

4 PRESSWISE
Unit 25, EBC, Felix Road, Bristol BS5 0HE
Campaign for victims of the media.

DIRECTORIES & REFRENCE
1 ALAN ARMSTRONG'S TOP 3000 DIRECTORIES AND ANNUALS 1990/91
Was published by Dawsons. O/P and O/D. However Alan Armstrong runs a service for mailing to libraries.
Alan Armstrong Ltd, Pheasant Coombe House, Hambleden, Henley on Thames, RG9 6SD Tel 01491 577 767

2 THE BOOKSHOPS OF LONDON
Two Heads Publishing, 9 Whitehall Park, London N19 3TS Tel 0171 561 1606

3 CICI DIRECTORY OF INFORMATION PRODUCTS AND SERVICES
Longman, Westgate House, The High, Harlow, Essex CM20 1NE. 'Your key to over 1,500 valuable sources'. Costs £38.

4 THE CREATIVE HANDBOOK
Specialist Marketing Services, Windsor Court, East Grinstead House, East Grinstead, West Sussex RH19 1BR.
The 1996 edition cost £112.

5 DIRECTORY OF BOOK PUBLISHERS, DISTRIBUTORS & WHOLESALERS
Booksellers Association, Minster House, 272 Vauxhall Bridge Road, London SW1V 1BA. 0171 834 5477.
Annual. The 1996 edition cost £43.

6 DIRECTORY OF BOOKSELLERS ASSOCIATION MEMBERS.
Booksellers Association, Minster House, 272 Vauxhall Bridge Road, London SW1V 1BA. 0171 834 5477.
'The essential guide to over 3,300 UK bookshops'. the 1996/7 edition costs £43.

7 A DIRECTORY OF CHILDREN'S WRITERS FROM SCOTLAND
Will help anyone arranging a

I'LL NEED DIRECTORIES & REFERENCE MANUALS ☞

GIVE ME ADDRESSES OF CAMPAIGN ORGANISERS ☞

ABYB 1996 - 97

From the South Pacific Islands to Seriously Absurd with Russian Artists' Books:

ARTIST'S BOOK YEARBOOK

Edited by Tanya Peixoto,
John Bently and Stephanie Brown

ISBN 0 952 3880 6 5   ISSN 1355 - 0187

Contents include:

Book Artists and Education, *Paul Johnson.* Artists Book Exchange, *Patricia Collins.* Northern Stars, *Chris Taylor*. Camberwell Research Programme, *Eileen Hogan.* Seductive Icons & CD Rom, *Susan Johanknecht.* 500 Starting Points for a pub discussion about Book Art, *Les Bicknell.* Two Tate Talks on Why the Book? *Helen Douglas, Telfer Stokes.* Interview with Cathy Courtney, *John Bently.* Special 10 page Insert from JAB USA, *Brad Freeman.* Illiterates, Childishness and the Idaho Centre for the Book, *Tom Trusky.* Dissertation, *Sarah Jacobs.* Biblioklast! Bob Cobbing, *Robert Sheppard.* The Books of Genesis P-Orridge, *Simon Ford.* Seriously Absurd: Here & There with Russian Artists' Books, *Peter Ford.* Daniil Kharms, *Mikhail Karasik.* Material to the event, *Patricia Farrell.* 100 + Useful addresses, *John Bently.* Lists of Books produced by You since 1995. Artists Pages *and other surprises...*

Don't be without it !

Send a cheque for £10 plus £2 p&p U.K, £4 Europe, £5 Overseas, made payable to

Magpie Press

1. Hermitage Cottage, Clamp Hill, Stanmore,
Middx HA7 3JW Tel/fax 0181 - 954 - 0670.

Small Press Center

20 West 44th Street, New York, NY 10036

Small Press Center

A publishing revolution is sweeping the land in the form of a Small Press *movement. Thousands of individual entrepreneurs, using the facilities of short-run book manufacturers, now produce as few as one or two new books a year — operating out of their cellars and garages, keeping alive the tradition of a Free Press in a country which has flourished on free expression.*

The most serious problem faced by the Small Press is marketing. How can people find out about the books that are being produced by the independent press movement? How can small presses reach their audience?

Most book stores will not handle Small Press books because of costly paperwork, shipping, payment, returns, credits. That is why the Small Press Center was born — to provide a not-for-profit common ground where Small Press publishers and their prospective clientele can come together easily, with no commercial pressures. The aim of the center is to aid readers and publishers equally, and thereby contribute in a practical way to the ideals of Freedom of the Press in America.

The Small Press Center offers the following services to publishers:

- **Small press bookcases** where books are placed on year-long display for inspection by the public.

- **Street-level showcase windows**, lighted at night, which may be leased by the month to exhibit books and related materials.

- **An attractive gathering place** which may be rented for book parties or readings.

- **Locked glass case** for display of miniatures and expensive or fragile items.

- **Annual Small Press Book Fair.**

- **Monthly readings** - from small press books, October through May.

- **Annual Exhibit** of small press books in a particular field.

- **Small Press Center Newsletter.**

- **Occasional lectures** on subjects of interest to readers, publishers and would-be publishers.

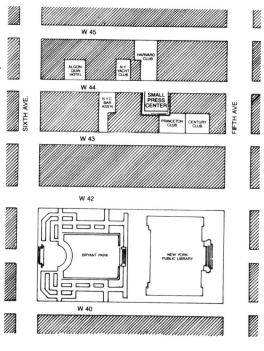

children's book event to find authors, poets or illustrators willing to take part. £2.50.
Scottish Book Centre, 137 Dundee Street, Edinburgh EH11 1BG Tel 0131 229 3663 fax 0131 228 4293

8 DIRECTORY OF PUBLISHING: UK, COMMONWEALTH AND OVERSEAS
Cassel and the Publishers' Association
22nd edition 1996. Packed with information. Use your library.

9 DUSTBOOKS
Len Fulton, Dustbooks, PO Box 100, Paradise, PA 95969, California, USA.
Four huge annual reference books for small presses.
(available from the National Small Press Centre)

10 EUROPEAN SPECIALIST PUBLISHERS DIRECTORY
Free listing for specialist publishers. Gale Research International Ltd, 2-6 Boundary Row, London SE1 8HN. 0171-865 0190. Fax: 0171-865 0192.
(we suspect they have moved but we cannot find them)

11 HOLLIS PRESS AND PUBLIC RELATIONS ANNUAL
24th edition, ISBN 0 9000967 96 X. For PR uses, describing itself as "the source of sources". £64.50.
Hollis Directories Ltd, Freepost RC 465, Sunbury on Thames, Middlesex TW16 5BR.

12 INKY PARROT PRESS
Was the publishing outlet of the Graphics Section of Oxford Polytechnic Design Dept. Compiled a catalogue of Fine Press Printing as part of the Second Conference of Fine Printing which used to be the most comprehensive listing of private printing presses currently available, with details of 185 in the UK plus the most recent Fine Printed publications of 81 of them; plus 23 specialist suppiers of materials and services.
By 1997 Inky Parrot is the independent imprint of Dennis Hall. The Dept has become the School of Art, Publishing and Music, Brookes University, Richard Hamilton Building, Headington, Oxford OX3

OBD Tel 01865 484 955

13 LIBRARY ASSOCIATION RECORD
7 Ridgmount Street, London WC1E 7AE. Tel: 0171 636 7543 fax: 0171 436 7218. The Record is a monthly journal.

14 MEDIA GUIDE
JEM Marketing, Little Mead, Cranleigh, Surrey GU6 8ND. Credit cards 01483 268 888. Produced by The Guardian @ £12. Add £1.50 for p&p.

15 THE NATIONAL SMALL PRESS CENTRE HANDBOOK.
Carries on the trail-blazing work of the Small Press Yearbooks which used to be produced by the Small Press Group. The first edition 1997 is in your hands. Treasure.

16 NEW YORK SMALL PRESS CENTER DIRECTORY
ISBN 0 9622769 4 4 — Price $19.95. New York Small Press Center, 20 West 44th Street, New York, NY10036, U.S.A. (available from the National Small Press Centre)

17 ORIEL'S 'SMALL PRESSES AND LITTLE MAGAZINES OF THE UK AND IRELAND'
is an address list compiled by Peter Finch. ISBN 0 946329 23 0 £4.00 + £2.50 handling.
Oriel Bookshop, The Friary, Cardiff, CF1 4AA. Tel: 01222 395 548.

18 OUTLETS FOR SPECIALIST NEW BOOKS IN THE U.K.
6th edition (1995) ISBN 1 871811 11 2 £15 + 85p p&p. Published by Peter Marcan, P.O. Box 3158, London SE1 4RA.

19 'PRIVATE PRESS BOOKS'
is a worldwide compilation of fine print works. Do an annual and a quarterly. Write for more details. Private Libraries Association, Ravelston, South View road, Pinner, Middlesex HA5 3YD.

20 SMALL PRESS GUIDE
Second edition 1997. A directory of about 500 small outfits, slanted to poetry and sf, some zines. £7.99 add p&p from Writers' Bookshop, 7-11 Kensington High Street, London W8 5NP. Or from the National Small Press Centre.

DISTRIBUTORS

1 A DISTRIBUTION
c/o 84b Whitechapel High Street. London E1 7QX (0181 533 6936). Used to be a venerable supplier of anarchist and related material but we understand from Freedom Bookshop (0171 247 9249) that they no longer distribute however the Rebel Press survives.

2 AIRLIFT BOOK COMPANY
8 The Arena, 1004 Mollison Avenue, Enfield, Middlesex EN3 7NJ (0181 804 0400. Fax: 0181 804 0044).
One of the big three. Deal in Literature, Women's titles, Mind/ Body/Spirit, General: much of it American. Some small press distribution.

3 AK DISTRIBUTION
PO Box 12766, Edinburgh, EH8 9YE (0131 555 5165. Fax: 0131 555 5215).
Stockists of 'the complete range of anarchist and related literature in print in Britain today, from all the publishers big and small, as well as loads of out of print and difficult to find stuff'; including matter from overseas, many zines, titles concerning feminism, squatting, punk, animal rights, ecology, situationism, etc. Write for a full list of titles.

4 ANTICOPYRIGHT POSTER DISTRIBUTION SERVICE
30 Piercefield Place, Adamsdown, Cardiff, South Glamorgan, Wales.

5 BEBC
The Bournemouth English Book Centre Ltd, 15 Albion Close, Parkstone, Poole, Dorset BH12 3YD. (01202 71555. Fax: 01202 715556.) Described as 'a complete distribution service for small publishers'.

6 BOOKSPEED
48a Hamilton Place, Edinburgh EH3 5AX. (0131 225 4950).
Independent wholesaler.

7 BROAD LEYS PUBLISHING CO
David and Katie Thear, Buriton House, Station Road, Newport, Essex CB11 3PL. (01799 540 922)
Publish magazine on Small Holding and Country Gardening. Handle some related titles.

8 CENTRAL BOOKS
99 Wallis Rd, E9 5LN. (0181 986 4854. Fax: 0181 533 5821).
One of the big three. Handle some magazines.

9 COUNTER CULTURE
Pete Gotto, BCM Inspire, London WC1N 3XX (Tel 01823 698 895) Mainly New Age, UFOs etc and counter culture, hence our name! Set up in 1995 'to fill a need for small publishers and self-published authors to reach an audience larger than their local bookshop'. Primarily sell via catalogue, containing some 60 titles including magazines. Fastest growing independent book distributor in UK. Can offer distribution on selected titles in USA.

10 COUNTER PRODUCTIONS
P.O. Box 556, London SE5 0RW. Select mail order of hundreds of small press material, North American anarchist and post-modernist publications, books, magazines, journals and much more. SAE for free catalogue.

11 DS4A DISTRIBUTORS
Box 8, Greenleaf Bookshop, 82 Colston Street, Bristol BS1 5BB. (0117 921 1369)
Punk, anarchist, cds and vinyl.

12 ELEMENT BOOKS DISTRIBUTION
Longmead, Shaftesbury, Dorset SP7 8PL. (01747-51339).
Distributors of books concerned with spirituality, mysticism, psychology, and related 'alternative' matters. Few small press items.

13 GAZELLE BOOK SERVICES LTD
Falcon House, Queen Square, Lancaster LA1 1RN (01524-68765. Fax: 01524 63232).
Describe themselves as a distributor for small publishers and a 'complete marketing service for the UK and Europe'.

14 HIGNELLS APPLE PRESS
Susan, Berridge Road West, Hyson Green, Nottingham NG7 5JU
Trying to set up a mail order distribution for 'zines etc.

15 MARC PAWSON
PO Box 664, London E3 4QR. (0181 983 1738)
Specialises in tiny items with a

I'LL NEED SOMEONE TO DISTRIBUTE MY PUBLICATION ☞

novelty angle, grew out of his own 'publishing' activities.

16 MAGAZINE NET
Magazine Net a new distirbutor for independent magazines whose details have excaped, read about it in News From The Centre.

17 MOMENTA PUBLISHING LTD
Broadway House, The Broadway, Wimbledon SW19 1RH. (0181 542 2465).
Representatives for publishers' specialising in academic, technical and medical works. Yearly fee up front required. Slide package taken round to potential buyers.

18 THE MORLEY BOOK CO.LTD
Elmfield Road, Morley, Leeds LS27 ONN. (0113 538811).

19 NEW SCIENCE FICTION ALLIANCE
NSFA, P.O. Box 625, Sheffield, S1 3GY.
Produce a catalogue of UK Sci-Fi 'zines.

20 PASSWORD (BOOKS) LTD
23 New Mount Street, Manchester M4 4DE. (0161 953 4009 fax 0161 953 4090)
Specialise in distribution of poetry to the booktrade. Before three million shower them with effusions they expect a very high standard of production values from clients. They have Arts Council backing.

21 PAUL GREEN
83(b) London Road, Peterborough, Cambs PE2 9BS UK.
Distributor of imported poetry and poetry related material. Many titles from Canada and USA; some remaindered stock. Also British poetry presses Northern Lights and Micro-brigade. Send off for lists and regular updates.

22 SHELWING LTD
127 Sandgate Road, Folkestone, Kent CT20 2BL (01303 850 501 fax 01303 850 162)
Offer warehousing and mail-outs. Single copy and small press distribution service. Provide estimates.

23 SLAB-O-CONCRETE
P.O. Box 148, Hove, BN3 3DQ. Distributors of 'zines and small press comics. Also publish "Bypass" – the UK equivalent of Factsheet Five.

24 TURBULENCE
BM Box 3641, London WC1N 3XX. Distributors of occultural publications and music.

25 TURNAROUND PUBLISHER SERVICES LTD
Unit 3, Olympia Trading Estate, Coburg Road, London, N22 6TZ. (0181 829 3000. Fax: 0181 881 5088).
One of the big three. Distributors of material, including small press, mostly relating to social issues and issue-politics. Distribute this Handbook.

26 VINE HOUSE DISTRIBUTION
Waldenbury, North Chailey, E Sussex BN8 4DR 01825 723 398 fax 01825 724 158
Comprehensive range for small/ medium size book publishers. Marketing, promotion, mail orders. Warehousing.

Deleted from previous editions ie out of business or we couldn't raise them: New Name Distribution, The Unlimited Dream Company, George Philip Services.

1 COMPUSERVE
1 Redcliff Street, PO Box 676, Bristol BS99 1YN. 0800 454 260. Get on the Internet.

2 GLT PRECISION LTD
Unit 4, Station Road Industrial Estate, Station Road, Market Bosworth, Warks CV13 0PE. 44 0 1455 292633
Sell the machines which print t-shirts and other corporate ephemera.

3 HA OFFICE SUPPLIES
25 Pitfield Street, London N1 (0171 608 36700.)
Specialise in new and reconditioned office machinery, paper, ribbons, &c, &c. Recommended by Bob Cobbing of ALP.

4 HEYDEN & SON LTD
Spectrum House, Hillview Gardens NW4 2JQ. 0181 203 5171. Fax: 0181-203 1027.
Binding machinery. (Also an academic publishing house)

WHAT EQUIPMENT MIGHT I USE?

5 INTERMEDIA GRAPHIC SYSTEMS LTD

Brian Howard, Lewes Business Centre, North St, Lewes, East Sussex BN7 2PE. 01273 478 725. 'Supplier of DTP software, hardware, training and consultancy. Bureau service supplies disk copying facilities, tapes and data cartridges. PC & Apple computers, monitors, scanners, laserprinters &c'.

6 MILES 33

Miles House, Old Bracknell Lane West, Bracknell, Berkshire RG12 7AE. 01344 861 133 fax 01344 860 224
DTP: Pianzhang pagination/page layout software.

7 MORGAN COMPUTER CO.

64-72 New Oxford Street, London WC1. 0171 255 2115
179 Tottenham Court Road, London W1. 0171 636 1138
Offices also in Egbaston and Manchester. Mail order sales. The remaindered store for computers etc. Unbelievable prices if you are not fussy.

8 OPAS LTD

Suite 11, Kinetic Centre, Theobald Street, Borehamwood, Herts WD6 4PJ. 0181 207 2462.
Provide engineering and maintenance service to the typesetting industry. They can supply and service a wide range of office equipment.

9 ORANGE

0973 366 368.
The heavily promoted mobile phone.

10 RANK XEROX (UK) LTD

Business Services, 185 Marsh Wall, London E14 (0171 537 0928)
Also doing compact copiers which sit on top of a desk. The 5009 and 5009RE come about £600 including VAT or nearer £500 without.

11 RM DISPLAY SYSTEMS

PO Box 7022, Hook, RG27 9YQ. 01252 815375 fax: 01252 811 486.
Stands for fairs etc.' Alleviate your exhibition problems by giving them to us.' Good grabber. All sorts of small stuff which you can afford:

those plastic stands for a book which you put on your table at fairs.

12 SHARP

Sharp House, Thorp Road, Newton Heath, Manchester M10 9BE. 0161 205 2333.
Do new cheap copiers eg their Z-20 is small, now lumbering furniture and sells for around £250.

13 SPS BOOK-BUILDER SYSTEMS

Freepost TN1588, Tunbridge Wells, Kent TN3 0BR. 01892 511 110 fax: 01892 514 070.
Supplies complete table top book-producing equipment and technology for Small Presses. Also provides short run book-production bureau service for independent authors.

14 TOP STONE

9 Carisbrook Road, Harpenden, Herts AL5 5QS. Tel/fax 01582 764 510
Specialist suppliers of book display items ie leaflet holders, spinners (the browsers you see in shops), plastic things to prop up your books.

15 TPS (LONDON) LTD

Suite 4 & 12, 27-29 Vauxhall Grove, London SW8 1SY. 0171 735 5353 fax 0171 735 5454
Multilingual dtp fonts.

EXHIBITIONS/CONFERENCE FACILITIES

1 ADVICE TO PUBLISHERS & EDITORS (APE)

112 Bermondsey Street, London SE1 3TX. 0171 378 1579 fax 0171 378 6421
An annual exhibition organised by Norman W. Hardy Printing Group (see Short Run Printers).

2 BARBICAN ARTS AND CONFERENCE CENTRE

Silk Street, Barbican, London CE2Y 8DS
Administration and Enquiries: 0171 638 4141

3 CENTRAL HALL WESTMINSTER

Storeys Gate, London SW1H4 9NH
General Manager: 0171 222 8010

4 CONWAY HALL

25 Red Lion Square, London WC1R 4RL
Hall Manager: 0171 242 8032

WHAT EXHIBITION AND CONFERENCE FACILITIES ARE AVAILABLE?

☞

THE BEST PLACE TO START IS WITH WHO'S WHO IN EXHIBITIONS? 4TH EDITION 1997 £25 PO BOX 229, SUTTON, SURREY SM1 3TP. 07000 XHIBIT (94 42 48) OR VISIT THEIR WEB SITE HTTP://WWW.CM NET.COM/EXHIBIT

WHO WILL DEAL WITH MY BULK MAILING?

WHERE CAN I HAVE LABELS MADE?

LETTER PRESS PRINTERS?

5 FORTE POSTHOUSE ACCOMMODATION
Forte (UK) Limited
Head office: 166 High Holborn, London WC1V 6TT. 0171 836 7744
Weekend event facilities.

6 INTERNATIONAL CHAPTERS
102 St John's Wood Terrace, London NW8 6PL. 0171 722 9560 fax 0171 722 9140
Agency for international fairs.

7 ROYAL HORTICULTURAL HALLS & CONFERENCE CENTRE
Horticultural Halls Ltd.
80 Vincent Square, London SW1P 2PE. 0171 828 4125/834 4333 fax 0171 834 2072
Facilities well known to former SPG.

8 SHOW MANAGEMENT SERVICES LTD
Norfolk House, St James Road, Fleet, Hants GU13 9QH. 01252 811 163 fax 01252 811 024
Organises 'SHOW' events.

9 TANO REA
58 Alexander Road, London NW4 2RY, 0181 203 1747. Arrange events, large and small.

LABELS
1 ABLE LABEL
Steepleprint Ltd, Earls Barton, Northampton NN6 OLS. 01604 810 781.
If you have to make price changes, need distribution stickers etc ask us for details.

2 AVERY DENNISION
Customer Services BDS, Thomas Road, Wooburn Green, Nr High Wycombe, Bucks HP10 0PE. 01628 859 500
As well as conventional formats they offer labels for all kinds of special needs, including those for videos and audio cassettes.

3 ESSEX LABELS
Unit 44k Leyton Industrial Village, Argall Avenue, London E10 7QP. 0181 558 7658
Printed reel to reel label specialists:

LETTER-PRESS PRINTING
TYPOGRAPHY WORKSHOP
Unit 313, 31 Clerkenwell Close,

London EC1R 0AT.
0171 490 4386.
Letterpress printing for small fine editions and prints. Also run courses.

MAILING SERVICES
1 ADDRESSING & MAILING SOLUTIONS
The Maltings, 16 New Road, Ware, Herts, SG12 7BS. 01920 465400, fax 0920 465444. 'The complete mailroom solution.'

2 ADDRESSING SYSTEMS INTERNATIONAL LTD
ASI House, Raleigh Way, Feltham, Middlesex TW13 7BR.
More a seller of equipment than service.

3 A.ARMSTRONG (HAMBLEDEN)
Pheasant's Coombe House, Hambleden, Henley-on-Thames, Oxon RG9 6SD. 01491 577 767 fax 01491 577 568
Shared mailings to libraries on a regular basis. Specialist publishers and booksellers can target libraries under specific subject headings or specific groups of libraries (e.g. all music libraries).

4 BMS LTD
Merlin Way, North Weald Ind Estate, North Weald, Epping, Essex CM16 6HR. 0137 882 4343 fax: 0137 882 4552.
Offer a mailing services for publishers and the direct marketing industry.

5 BPH DATA LTD
Unit 5, Blackwater Industrial Estate, Camberley GU17 9AF.

6 CMC SYSTEMS
CMC Communications Systems Ltd, Northcroft, Oakhill Avenue, Pinner, Middlesex HA5 3DL. 0181 868 4119

7 FLETCHER DATA SERVICES LTD
Federation House, 2309 Coventry Road, Sheldon, Birmingham B26 3PG.

8 HAMILTON HOUSE MAILINGS LTD
17 Staveley Way, Brixworth Industrial Park, Northampton NN6 9TX. 01604 881 889.
They are persistent and send us

batches of their bumf regularly. In their bumf they ask rhetorically 'Why do you keep sending me direct mail?' Well, ignore their answer, note our example. We have noticed them. So that makes their case doesn't it?

9 MACDONALD MAILING
Jim Seehy, 1 Saxon Road, Faversham, Kent ME13 8AR. 01795 536 668.

10 MAILPLUS DIRECT LTD
245/247 Redcatch Road, Knowwle, Bristol BS4 2BR.

11 MONKEY BUSINESS
PO Box 1844, Colchester, Essex CO3 3SL. 01206 752 778.
'How about selling books by Direct Mail'. A booklet by a stalwart of APN (see Organisations). ISBN 1 898030 01 4. £2 + .45p p&p.

12 OUTSET MAILING CENTRE
Cannon Wharf, 35 Evelyn Street, London SE8 5RT. 0171 23x 9923 fax: 0171 231 9951 fax 0171 231 6671
Offer direct mail services.

13 PETERBOROUGH MAILING
25 Harvester Way, Fengate. Peterborough PE1 5UT.

14 PROFORDS ASSOCIATES
01494 766 123 fax: 01494 766 888.
They offer various services incuding producing your stationery. Sell lists of sales contacts etc. There are many categories eg Dept Heads in Local Authorities. Of course you can go into their lists too.

15 SHELWING LTD
127 Sandgate Road, Folkestone, Kent CT20 2BL
01303 850 501 fax 01303 850 162
A mailing house created especially to assist publishers. They offer high-quality shared mailings to library suppliers and booksellers regularly. For further information, please write. They might solve your publicity problems.

MARKETING
1 ACE PUBLISHING
24 Woodlands Drive, Glasgow G4 9DW.

Advertising space sales consultancy; publishes 'Advertising Space Telesales Manual'.

2 ALAN ARMSTRONG LTD
Pheasant Coombe House, Hambleden, Henley-on-Thames, Oxon RG9 6SD. 01491 577 767 fax 01491 577 568
European Database of Libraries: identified by subject interests.

3 LAVIS MARKETING
73 Lime Walk, Headingon, Oxford, OX3 7AD. (01865-67575. Fax: 01865 750079.
Offers comprehensive service packages for smaller publishers, including joint mailings, trade repesentation etc.

4 SPECIALIST BOOKSELLERS
2 Arkwright Road, Reading RG2 0SQ (Fax: 01734 755164).
Annual Touring 'Grey Literature' Exhibition. CHECK IT STILL RUNS!!!!

5 THE ULTIMATE DATABASE COMPANY
97 Valence Road, Lewes, East Sussex BN17 1SJ. (01273 473135).
Publisher's Databank (for marketing research purposes &c).

MEDIA CONTACTS
The Media of press and broadcasting have undergone and are still undergoing huge and frequent changes. Not just in name, address, contact and function but alsoin their very structure. We suggest you refer to regularaly updated reference tools which list such information such as Willings Press Guide and those sections in the Writers and Artists Yearbook (current edition only) and 'The Media Guide': Data base £20, book £12, ISBN 1 85702 491 5, published for the Guardian by Fourth Estate, 6 Salem Road, London W2 4BU.

Broadcasting:
1 BBC RADIO
Broadcasting House, Portland Place, London W1A 1AA 0171 580 4468

2 BBC TELEVISION
Television Centre, Wood Lane,

CAN YOU GIVE ME ADDRESSES OF NEWSPAPERS AND TELEVISION COMPANIES?

WHO WILL HELP WITH MARKETING MY PUBLICATION?

London W12 7RJ 0181 743 8000

3 BSKYB
6 Sentaurs Business Park Grant Way, Isleworth TW7 5QD 0171 705 3000

4 CHANNEL 4
124 Horseferry Road, London SW1P 2TX 0171 396 4444

5 CHANNEL 5
22 Longacre, London WC2E 9LY 0171 497 5225

6 INDEPENDENT TELEVISION
33 Foley Street, London W1P 7LB 0171 255 3000

Newspapers:
1 DAILY EXPRESS & SUNDAY EXPRESS
245 Blackfriars Road, London SE1 9UX
0171 928 8000

2 DAILY MAIL & MAIL ON SUNDAY
2 Derry Street, Kensington, London W8 5TT
0171 938 6000

3 DAILY MIRROR & SUNDAY MIRROR
1 Canada Square, Canary Wharf, London E14 5AP 0171 510 3000

4 DAILY STAR
245 Blackfriars Road, London SE1 9UX 0171 928 8000

5 DAILY TELEGRAPH & SUNDAY TELEGRAPH
1 Canada Square, Canary Wharf, London E14 5DT 0171 538 5000

6 FINANCIAL TIMES
1 Southwark Bridge, London SE1 9HL 0171 873 3000

7 GUARDIAN & OBSERVER
119 Farringdon Road, London EC1R 3ER 0171 278 2332

8 INDEPENDENT & INDEPENDENT ON SUNDAY
1 Canada Square , Canary Wharf, London E14 5DL 0171 293 2000

9 SUN
1 Virginia Street, Wapping, London E1 9BD 0171 782 4000

10 TIMES & SUNDAY TIMES
1 Virginia Street, Wapping, London E1 9XN 0171 782 5000

11 THE EUROPEAN
200 Grays Inn Road London WC1X 8NE 0171 418 7777

MEMBERSHIP
ORGANISATIONS
1 ASOCIATION OF FREELANCE WRITERS
F D Nadin, Sevendale House, 7 Dale Street, Manchester M1

2 THE ASSOCIATION OF LEARNED AND PROFESSIONAL SOCIETY PUBLISHERS (ALPS)
48 Kelsey Lane, Beckenham, Kent BR3 3NE
0181 1658 0459 fax 0181 663 3583
Publishes journal 'Learned Publishing'. Publishing houses rendering services to societies may also become members.

3 THE ASSOCIATION OF LITTLE PRESSES
111 Banbury Road, Oxford, OX2 6XJ. Web Page: http://www.melloworld.com/alp.
An umbrella group for small publishing houses. Established in 1966, it provides support and information for people interested in starting or running small presses. It has over 200 members and through its various publications and listings, provides a useful mail order network. Many members are concerned with creative writing, but there are plenty with a wide range of subjects on their lists. The ALP is a voluntary organisation and its officers are unpaid. Membership currently costs £12.50 for one year.

4 AUTHOR PUBLISHER NETWORK
Nee A.P.E. Is connected to the Society of Authors. It aims at the self-publisher and is a service in the sense of providing advice and back-up. Membership currently costs £15.00 for one year. For membership details, contact Daphne Macara, 6 Kelvinbrook, Hurst Park, West Molesey, Surrey KT8 1RZ

5 BAPA

British Amateur Press Association. Contact: 78 Tennyson Road, Stratford, London E15 4DR (0171 555 2052).

Founded 1890: membership composed mainly of people concerned "with receiving and reading the various amateur publications which BAPA sends out on behalf of the members who produce them". Few members produce magazines: circulation is mainly confined to BAPA members, the publishers not seeking the general public readership.

6 THE FEDERATION OF WORKER WRITERS AND COMMUNITY PUBLISHERS

Tim Diggles, FWWCP, c/o 23 Victoria Park Road, Tunstall, Stoke-on-Trent, ST6 6DX Tel 01782 822 327

'Working to make writing and publishing available to all'.

7 INDEPENDENT PUBLISHERS GUILD

Yvonne Messenger, 25 Cambridge Road, Hampton, Middlesex, TW12 2JL. 0181 979 0250 fax 0181 979 6393

8 INK

87 Kirkstall Road, London SW2 4HE

A newly-formed independent news collective whose members cover many of the issues the mainstream media shy away from. Members include: The Big Issue, The Ecologist, Green Events, (and many more Green titles) New Internationalist, Peace News, Red Pepper, Undercurrents, and so on. http:\\www.ink.co.uk

9 NATIONAL ARTISTS ASSOCIATION

Spitalfields, 21 Steward Street, London E1 6AJ
0171 426 0911 fax 0171 426 0282

Voluntary organisation working to raise professional staus of artists, their rights and working conditions in UK. Work closely with European Council of Artsists.

10 PERIODICAL PUBLISHERS ASSOCIATION

Queens House, 28 Kingsway, London WC2B 6UN.
0171 404 4166. http:\\www. ppa.co.uk

The Publishers' Association of the magazine world,

11 OXFORD GUILD OF PRINTERS

Tom Colverson, 116 Mill Street, Kidlington, Oxon, OX5 2EF. Organise fairs.

12 THE PUBLISHERS ASSOCIATION

19 Bedford Square, London WC1B 3HJ
(0171 580 6321 fax 0171 636 5375).

Is 'an association run by and for its publisher members, and to be eligible for membership you must be a bona fide publisher of books and/or learned journals operating in the UK. The association is primarily concerned with representing the interests of publishers to the UK and foreign governments, the European Commission, and other bodies in the book trade to ensure that publisher's interests are safeguarded, and that the government gives us all possible assistance.' Full details if you think they'll have you.

13 PUBLISHERS PUBLICITY CIRCLE

48 Crabtree Lane, London SW6 6LW 0171 385 3708

Monthly meetings to provides a forum for book publicists to share information.

14 SMALL PRESS GROUP OF BRITAIN LTD.

Defunct. There's nostalgia. Ran from 1988 to 1995. Showed what was possible. A dream fulfilled then wrecked by newcomers. All was not in vain. The memory remains and so it is there to do again. Also a germ was rescued as the National Small Press Centre. Is there a need for a revival?

15 SOCIETY OF AUTHORS

84 Drayton Gardens, London SW10 9SB. 0171 373 6642 Professional association.

16 SOCIETY OF FREELANCE EDITORS AND PROOFREADERS

Administration: Sue King, Mermaid House, 1 Mermaid Court, London SE1 1HR (0171 403 5141) http:/

WHO MAKES THINGS I CAN GIVE AWAY?

☞

/www.sfep.demon.co.uk
Professional association. Annual directory of members' services available to publishers, has close links with Book House Training Centre and Society of Indexders. On BSI Technical Committee BS5261.

17 SOCIETY OF WOMEN WRITERS AND JOURNALISTS

110 Whitehall Road, Chingford, London E4 6DW 0181 529 0886 Founded 1884 to encourage literary achievement and discuss the quality of new writing. Monthly meetings and various social events.

18 ASSOCIATION OF ILLUSTRATORS

First Floor, 32-38 Saffron Hill, London, EC1N 8FN. 0171 831 7377, fax 0171 831 6277.

19 SOCIETY OF YOUNG PUBLISHERS

c/o 12 Dyott Street, London WC1A 1DF

20 UNION OF POETS

Kevin Bailey, 39 Exmouth Street, Swindon, Wilts SN1 3PU
An idea of Kevin's. Did he get it off the ground?

21 WOMEN IN PUBLISHING

c/o 12 Dyott Street, WC1A 1DF
WiP aims to promote the status of women within publishing; to provide a forum for the discussion of subjects of interest and the sharing of information and expertise; to encourage networking and mutual support among women; to offer practical training for career and personal development. Founded in 1979 and now has a worldwide membership of over 500. They welcome all women working in publishing and related trades. Monthly meetings are held on the second Wednesday of each month, at 6.30 for 7.00 pm, at the Publishers Association, Bedford Square, London WC1. All women are welcome. Membership is £20 p.a. (unwaged £15). Entrance charge for non-members is £1.00 (unwaged £0.50).

Gone out of business: Independent Periodicals' Group (replaced by INK).

MERCHANDISE

This is a way of publicising yourself by handing out freebies – key rings, pens, pencils – with your details on them. Start by getting catalogues and you may be surprised. You might actually do such a gimmick.

1 ADLER MANUFACTURING LIMITED

883 Plymouth Road, Slough, Berkshire SL1 4LZ. 01753 696 696 fax 01753 696 217

2 ANGLO CARRIER BAGS

are recycled and recyclable. 01273 323 399.

3 BADGE INTERNATIONAL GROUP

Impress House, Worton Court, Worton Road, Isleworth TW7 6ER. 0181 568 8880 fax 0181 568 2118
Selfit Badge System: personalised badges in about 12 seconds.

4 BAGDA (BRITISH ADVERTISING GIFT DISTRIBUTION ASSOCIATION)

Market Link Publishing, The Mill, Bearwalden Business Park, Wenden's Ambo, Saffron Walden, Essex CB11 4JX. Issue an info sheet 'What's New'.

5 BANANA BADGE CO

Emblem House, Mount Pleasant, Cockfosters, Barnet EN4 9HH
0181 441 9911 fax 0181 440 7771.
Offer info and samples if you phone Sue.

6 BERKSHIRE CHINA COMPANY

298 King Street, Fenton, Stone-on-Trent, ST4 3EN. Put your firm's name on mugs so they sit on the desks of potential customers.

7 OVERSOLVE

Carrier Bags at competitive prices with FREE origination. Orders of above a 1,000. 0115 942 4840.

8 ELLENELL PROMOTIONS

Promotion House, 1B Shrubbery Road, Edmonton, London N9 0QQ. 0181 887 0000 fax 0181 887 0001

9 PRINT & COPY CENTRES

A national chain inside more than 50 superstores such as Office World. A range of petty stuff which is essential if you want that sort of thing. Since they specialise in this speciality they should know what they are doing. Check local Yellow Pages.

10 PROMOTIONAL IDENTITY
The Courtyard, Vine Street, York YO2 1BB. 01904 628 962 fax 01904 612 933

11 REXAM
Essex Business Forms Ltd, Chilton Street, Clare, Nr Sudbury, Suffolk CO10 8QS. 01787 278 444. Membership cards, window stickers etc.

12 TC ADVERTISING GIFTS
Freepost (HA 4771), Uxbridge, Middlesex UB9 6BR. 01895 825 700.

13 WALSH & JENKINS
Queens Croft, 150 Eltham Hill, London SE9 5EA
Offer carrier bags in double quick time. Phone Steve Hunt, The Man, on 0181 859 5721.

ORIGINATION: SETTING & DESIGN
1 AXXENT LTD
The Old Council Offices, The Green, Dachet, Berks SL3 9EH Tel 01753 593 330
Call them for a booklet about their services. They claim to 'do it all from disk to book'.

2 BB BOOKS
Spring Bank, Longsight Road, Copster Green, Blackburn, Lancs BB1 9EY. 01254 49128.
Cheap professional typesetting. IBM electronic composition.

3 COPY ART
Dalby Street, Kentish Town, London NW5 3NQ.
0171 267 8145.
Applemac and Copier facilities, DIY hire, full Internet facilities.

4 CYGNUS MEDIA SERVICES
45 Woodlands Road, Earlswood, Redhill, Surrey RH1 6HB. 01737 768 812.
Offer typesetting, sub-editing, disk conversion and printing.

5 DISNEY DESKTOP
42 Highland Road, Norwich, NR2 3NN.
Offer production of house magazines, brochures &c using DTP.

6 DMZEE MARKETING LIMITED
PCMAC Studio, 24 Grove Place, Bedford MK40 3JJ. 01234 216 016 fax 01234 261 251 ISDN 01234 270404
Pre-press studio: scanning/image-setting/proofing/handwork.

7 HIGH VIEW
Bernard Harrison, Moorland Way, Gunnislake, Cornwall PL18 9EX. 01822 833 500. Fax: 01822 832 500.
'High View undertakes complete in-house design, typesetting, printing, binding and distribution services. The advantages of dealing with a single professional contact in all these fields are obvious and are greatly appreciated by our clients.'

8 HI RESOLUTION
4 Smallbridge Cottages, Horsmonden, Kent TN12 8EP. 01580 211194.
DTP service offering typesetting, consultancy and troubleshooting services. 'People use Hi Resolution because we're fast, friendly and intelligent. For a job with no specification we'll make sensible decisions or if you know what you want that's what you'll get'.

9 ICON GRAPHICS
PO Box 69, Aberystwyth, Dyfed SY23 2EU. 01970 625 205.
DTP, design and layout, direct mail services, promotional services, typesetting, fax services &c.

10 IN-HOUSE TYPESETTING
Temple Press, PO Box 227, Brighton, Sussex BN2 3GL. 01273 679 129. Fax: 01273 621 284.
Low-cost typesetting.

11 JOHN MORIN GRAPHICS
82a Gaffer's Row, Victoria Street, Crewe, Cheshire CW1 2JH. Tel & fax: 01270 211 455.
Typesetting and page make-up on Macintosh computer, scanning also available. Free sample settings, short run printing for magazines

WHO CAN TYPESET & DESIGN MY PUBLICATION?

and booklets at very reasonable rates. Free information pack and advice freely given.

12 LINK UP
51 Northwick Business Centre, Blockley, Glos GL56 9RF. 01386 701 091.
A small desktop publishing team based in the Cotswolds. 'We are concerned with Green and environmental issues, focussing on what is working in the world, instead of always emphasising what is not. We suport Natural Healing methods and Complementary Medicine — realising that they have a part to play in maintaining health. These ideas of welcoming change as a creative opportunity are promoted through our quarterly magazine, also called Link Up. Although this publication comprises the main part of our work we also carry out personal and comprehensive typesetting and general office services.'

13 LONDON PRINT WORKSHOPS
421 Harrow Road, London W10 4RD.
0171 490 4386.
Printing facilities and gallery.

14 G. MCALLEN
Glanrhyd, Llanfair Clydogau Lampeter, Dyfed, Mid-Wales.
Freelance graphics. Specializing in quality design and reproduction'.

15 MCCREADIE PUBLISHING SERVICES
Julie McCreadie, Alexander Russell House, 50 Great Eastern Street, London EC2A 3EP
0171 739 9543 fax 0171 729 4232
Design and production services for magazines and newspapers using latest DTP; planning, launch and marketing of product; multimedia and page design for Internet.

16 NEAL'S YARD DESKTOP PUBISHING STUDIO
2 Neals Yard, London WC2. 0171 379 5113.
'The launderette of DTP'. Machines line the room. Well-established, they offer all kinds of facilities. 'We try to provide highest quality machines and expertise to individuals and small organizations who would not

otherwise have access to such resources'.

17 NORTHERN WRITERS ADVISORY SERVICES
77 Marford Crescent, Sale, Cheshire M33 4DN. 0161 969 1573.
Provide good copy-editing, proof-reading, word-processing and DTP 'at prices small presses can afford'.

18 PRESTON EDITIONS
5 Creek Road, East Molesley, Surrey.
Peter Preston in one weekend typeset and prepared for printing the entire MS of 336 page book. Not bad. Want to know more?

19 REALITY STUDIOS
0171 639 7297.
Offer typesetting and book design for small presses. No job too big or small. Poetry a speciality.

20 REPROPRINT
A commercial chain with branches in Woking, Guildford, Portsmouth, Southampton.
Make initial contact with Ian Burnham, 15 Poole Street, Woking, Surrey CU21 1DY. 01483 740 483

21 ROGER BOOTH ASSOCIATES
18 –20 Dean Street, Newcastle upon Tyne NE1 1PG.
0191 232 8301.
Will give a quotation for typesetting (and printing if required) of your publications. Output at 300 dots per inch on laser printer. Recommended by ALP.

22 TOP FLOOR DESIGN
Lion House, Muspole Street, Norwich NR3 1DJ. 01603 660237.
'An innovative graphic design consultancy that offers a complete service from concept to print, specialising in publishing and editorial design'.

23 TYPEDONE
404 Solent Business Centre, Millrook Road West, Southampton SO1 0HW. 01703 702 681.
DTP Bureau, offering massive typeface range.

24 WORDS & IMAGES
2 Charlton Cottages, Barden Road, Speldhurst, Tunbridge Wells, Kent,

TN3 0LH. 01892 862 395.
Provides publishing services to both professional publishers and to those individuals and organisation who wish to self-publish. Offers book design, typesetting and printing; illustration; editing and manuscript reading; commissioned writing; ghost writing; video scripts; computer tuition. 'We offer quality work, friendly service and reasonable cost.'

25 JOHN YOUE
Knapp Farm, Dunkerswell, Honiton, Devon EX14 0RH.
Book design – conventional and computer aided.

OTHER ORGANISATIONS
1 ASLIB
see under Administration Services and Info

2 AUTHORS' PUBLISHING GUILD
They 'publish and distribute' The Local History Link, a maglet for organisations in the South East. We suggest you contaqct the APG through The Link, David Brown, 2 West Street Farm Cottages, Maynards Green, Heathfield, Sussex, TN21 0DG.

3 BAPLA (BRITISH ASSOCIATION OF PICTURE LIBRARIES AND AGENCIES)
18 Vine Hill, London EC1R 5DX
0171 713 1780 fax 0171 713 1211
Trade association, largest of its kind in the world. Its members between them handle over 200 million images. Publish an annual dierctory of members. Vigilantly promotes the copyright status of pictures.

4 BOOK HOUSE TRAINING CENTRE
45 East Hill, Wandsworth, London SW18 2QZ. 0181 874 2718/4608 fax 0181 870 8985
Courses for book/journal publishing industry; newsletter.

5 BSI (BRITISH STANDARDS INSTITUTION) INTERNATIONAL TRAINING
Head Office: 389 Chiswick High Road, London W4 4AL. 0181 996 7055. Presently no courses, but may revive.

6 EUROPEAN COUNCIL OF ARTISTS
contact through the National Artists Association (qv)

7 HOMING-IN
656 London Road, Milborne Port, Sherborne, Dorset DT9 5DW (01963-250764).
An organisation catering for anyone working from home, including publishers. Newsletter published 6 times a year, meetings, &c.

8 THE INSTITUTE OF PRINTING
8a Lonsdale Gardens, Tunbridge Wells, Kent TN1 1NU
01892 53338 118

9 THE INTERNATIONAL SOCIETY OF COPIER ARTISTS
800 West End Avenue, New York, NY 10025, USA
Founded 1982 as a non-profit organisation to promote the use of the copier as a creative tool. Publishes a Quarterly, houses a slide archive and runs travelling exhibitions.

10 NATIONAL ARTISTS ASSOCIATION
21 Steward Street, London E1. 0171 426 0911.
Also the contact for the ECA, see above.

11 LETTER EXCHANGE
39 Strathblaine Road, London SW11 1RG
0171 585 3783 (Hon Sec Rachel Yallop)
To promote lettering in *all* the technologies. Organises lectures which are held at The Art Workers Guild, 6 Queen Square, London WC1.

12 LONDON COLLEGE OF PRINTING AND DISTRIBUTIVE TRADES
Head of College: Dr Will Bridge, Elephant and Castle, London SE1 6SB
0171 514 6500

13 NATIONAL POETRY FOUNDATION
27 Mill Road, Fareham, Hants PO16 0TH
01329 822 218
Aims to be the national poetry organisation. Advice, information

ARE THERE ORGANISATIONS TO HELP ME?

TELL ME ABOUT PAPER ☞

and a magazine for single low-cost fee. Grants to deserving causes relevant to poetry. Free advice on problems relating to book publishing.

14 POETRY BOOK SOCIETY
Book House, 45 East Hill, London SW18 2QZ
0181 870 8403 fax 0181 877 1615
Promotes books of new poetry through *Choice* offers and 300 title backlist. Publishes *Bulletin* a quarterly. Readings at the Royal Festival Hall. Administers T S Eliot Prize for the best collection of new poems. Operates as charitable Book Club with annual membership fee.

15 THE POETRY LIBRARY
Level Five, Red Side, Royal Festival Hall, London SE1. 0171 921 0943/ 0664.
Located on London's South Bank, the library houses an extensive collection of small press poetry as well as a superb display of small press poetry magazines. The library is also an invaluable resource for finding out about what's happening on the poetry scene generally throughout the UK; competitions, fairs, festivals, readings, publishing events etc. Apply for membership and be sure to get on their mailing list!

16 THE POETRY SOCIETY
22 Betterton Street, London WC2H 9BU.
0171 240 4810 fax 0171 240 4818 fax 0171 2240 4818
Evidently looking "to expand our list of publishers" as they invite you to contact them. Advice and information on all aspects of publishing and poetry. Membership body open to all. Publish *Poetry Review* and *Poetry News* quarterly - info and imagination service. Poetry promotions, educational projects. Administers the annual National Poetry Competition and biennial European Poetry Translation Prize.

17 THE NATIONAL SMALL PRESS CENTRE
Producers of this Handbook. Offer all sorts of goodies which you will read about because they are scattered throughout the book.

None of the wonderful services offered to Poets by all the other bodies. Sorry, we exist for small presses.

18 PRIVATE LIBRARIES ASSOCIATION
Ravelston, South View Road, Pinnet, Middlesex HA5 3YD
International memebrship society. Publications include *Private Library* and annual *Private Press Books.*

19 SMALL PRESS FORUM.
Queenspark Books, Brighton Media Centre, 11 Jew Street, Brighton, East Sussex BN1 1UT. 01273 748248.
Instigated and supported by South-East Arts Literature Department. Runs courses and seminars for small presses based in its region. Has commissioned Queenspark Books of Brighton to compile a database of small publishers in the South-East. Contact them for a questionnaire. For more details on forthcoming activities, contact South-East Arts Literature Department, 10 Mount Ephraim, Tunbridge Wells, Kent TN4 8AS. 01892 515210 fax: 01892 549383.

No longer active (according to Housmans): Federation of Radical Booksellers.

PAPER
1 FALKINER FINE PAPERS
76 Southampton Row, London WC1. 0171 831 1151
A helpful shop.

2 PAPERBACK
Unit 2, Bow Triangles Business Centre, Eleanor Street, London E3 4NP.
Merchant sales: 0181 980 2233; Stationery: 0181 980 5580 fax 0181 980 2399. Also in Birmingham 0121 643 7336 and Sheffield 01742 664416
'The name in recyled paper'. Recyled paper supplier and recycled paper products.

3 PAPERPOINT
Arjo Wiggins Teape Fine Papers Ltd, 83-84 Long Acre, London WC2E 9NJ. 0171 379 6850 fax 0171 379 8046.
Vast range of exciting papers, from poster paper through to thick card.

4 THE PARCHMENT WORKS
Willen Road, Newport Pagnell, Bucks MK16 0DB.
If you want real parchment.

5 JOHN PURCELL
15 Romsey Road, London SW9 0TR. 0171 737 5199.

6 G.F.SMITH & SON
2 Leathermarket, Weston Street, London SE1 3ET. 0171 407 6174. Interesting paper and card (suitable for instant print style printers) and envelopes &c. They will accept fairly small orders (i.e. 500 sheets of A4) and can emboss certain types of card with curious textures. Ask them for a brochure.

7 SVECIA ANTIQUA LIMITED
Robert Latham, Dowding Way, Tunbridge Wells, Kent TN2 3UY. Specialist paper supplier.

PHOTOCOPYING FACILITIES (DIY)
What can we say? We saw no point in mentioning a tiny few who are helpful. Events have overtaken this section. There are hundreds of thousands. We remind you to shop around, some places still offer .05p or below. Check your local Yellow Pages but just keep your eyes open as you go around.

RESOURCES
There is an increasing number of courses at universities and colleges of further education which may be helpful. We mention a few to give an indication: Manchester Metropolitan University, London Institute, London College of Printing, West Herts College, Bournemouth University, Oxford Brookes University, The Robert Garden University, Thames Valley University. While the Small Press Centre was at Middlesex University it set up six different courses, each to run for thirteen weeks, covering aspects of small press activity.

1 ARCHIV SOHM
Heransgeber, Staatsgalerie, Stuttgart, Urbanstrasse 35, 7000 Stuttgart 1, Germany.
In 1986 published a Catalogue 'Fröhliche Wissenschaft' (Happy Knowledge) containing wonderful goodies – and photos of their collection of weird publications – The Beats, FLUXUS, Concrete poetry, underground – they are treading on our heels.

2 CARTOON ARTS TRUST
National Museum of Cartoon Art, Baird House, 15-17 St Crross Street, London EC1N 8UN

3 CENTREPRISE BOOKSHOP
136-138 Kingsland High Street, London E8 2NS
0171 254 9632
Literature Devopment Project and much more besides.

4 THE CONSUMERS' ASSOCIATION
Guide to Earning Money at Home £9.99. Which? PO Box 44, Hertford X, SG14 1SH

5 CREATIVE ARTS COURSES, NORTH CORNWALL
Garmoe Cottage, Trefrew Road, Camelford, North Cornwall PL32 9TP. 01840 212 161
All aspects of writing with published writers.

6 BOOK DATA LTD
Northumberland House, 2 King Street, Twickenham, TW1 0181 892 2272
A new programme beginning Summer 1997 which aims to to provide a massive database of titles in print. More descriptive than Whittakers. Available on CDs. Publishers pay to get listed.
http:\\www.the bookplace. co.uk

7 GREATER MANCHESTER COUNCIL FOR VOLUNTARY SERVICE
0161 273 7451.
Advises on DTP to non-profit groups.

8 56A INFO-BOOKSHOP
56 Crampton Street, London SE17 Near the Elephant and Castle, in South East London. 'We specialise in worldwide anti-capitalist and anti-authoritarian goodies but we encourage small presses to send us catalogues or check the store out. We open Monday, Thursday and Friday from 3 to 7pm.'

9 INTERNET BOOKSHOP
http:\\www.bookshop.co.uk (Has a Whittaker's association). The

PHOTOCOPY SHOPS?

ARE THERE RESOURCES TO HELP ME OR COURSES WHERE I CAN LEARN?

Booksellers' Association tell us there are many more. They suggest you search under 'bookshop'. We know another: Amazon wants to make available every title in print – on the Web.
Amazon. com, 2250 First Avenue South, Seattle, WA 98134, USA. Tel: 1-800-201-7575, Fax 1-800-206 622. Web: http:\\www. amazon.com e-mail listingsbooks @amazon.com

10 IT BOOKSHOP
103-195 Southampton Row, London WC1B 4HH
+44 171 436 9761

11 LONDON INSTITUTE
65 Davies Street, London W1Y 2DA
0171 514 7000.
Umbrella for five colleges (Chelsea, St Martins, Central, Fashion, Camberwell, London College of Printing, qv.)

12 NAPIER UNIVERSITY
The Dunning Library, 10 Colinton Road, Edinburgh E10 5DT. 0131 444 266 ext 2582
The Edmund Clark Collection on printing and printing history is of particular interest to the small independent publisher. Contains more than 5,000 items (mss, journals, woodcuts, typefaces)

13 OPEN UNIVERSITY WEB SITE
http:\\www.Kmiopen.ac.uk
A programme, Knowledge Media Institute, to educate about the new technologies.

14 ORIEL BOOKSHOP
Manager Peter Finch, The Friary, Cardiff, Wales CF1 4AA
Run all sorts of schemes including a subscription to a regular bundle of small press items.

15 PETER STOCKHAM ASSOCIATES
4/6 Dam Street, Lichfield, Staffs, WS13 6AA 01643 264093. *The* Staffs bookshop. Also publish and offer consultancy services to publishers.

16 THE PRINTING HOUSE
102 Main Street, Cockermouth, Cumbria CA13 9Lx
01900 824 984 fax 01900 823 124
Working museum of printing.

17 PUBLISHER HELP LINE
Edward Twentyman Resources, 4 Little Green, Cheveley, Newmarket, Suffolk CB8 9RG
01638 731 332
'The only agency specialising in providing free-lance workers to the publishing industry'. Maintain a register of editors, designers, proof-readers etc.

18 SMALL PRESS AND POETRY ARCHIVE
David Miller, University College London, Gower Street, London

19 ST BRIDE PRINTING LIBRARY
Bride Lane, London EC4Y 8EE
0171 353 4660 fax 0171 583 7073
Covers all aspects of books and printing. Special collections, archives, collection of printing presses and other artefacts illustrating traditional methods of printing and typefounding'

20 SWAN BOOKS AND EDUCATIONAL SERVICES
Salama, 13 Henrietta Street, Swansea, SA1 4HW.
Offer talks on book production by a self-publisher.

21 VANCOUVER SMALL PRESS CENTRE
Opening Autumn 1997. In 1991 the SPG visisted Vancouver and spoke to their Small Press Festival (see cover of this book). Relations were cemented and ideas exchanged. They campaigned as Small Press Action Network, SPAN. They have succeeded. Greetings to the old warriors: Gordon, Kedrick, Sheri D, and all of you. Details from the editor of the Vancouver listings mag Verb: Tom Snyder, 825 Granville Street, #203 Vancouver BC, V6Z 1K9. OR check Broken Pencil's Website: www.interlog. com\-halpen/

22 WEST HERTS COLLEGE
Hempstead Road, Watford, Herts WD1 3EZ. 011923 812 000
Run various courses on publishing and printing, including post-graduate diploma in Publishing.

23 WOMEN IN PUBLISHING
see Membership Organisations
Run about a dozen training programmes each year. Speakers

and course leaders for all Women in Publishing courses are senior professional women from within and outside the book trade. The courses are administered by a small group of volunteers. If you would like to help organise and plan courses, contact the Training Officer. The courses are open to all women. All one day courses are held on Saturdays at convenient London venues, and lunch, coffee and tea are included in the price. All meals plus two nights' accommodation are included in the price of the residential weekend. Cost around £85 (£50 unwaged).

24 WORKING WITH VDUS

(free) or VDUs ab easy guide to the regulations £5. Both from Health and Safety Executive Books, PO Box 111999, Sudbury, Suffolk CO10 6FS

SHORT-RUN PRINTERS

1 BIDDLES

Woodbridge Park Estate, Woodbridge Road, Guildford, Surrey GU1 1DA.
01483 502 224.
Claim to want small press business but no advert in this handbook to tell readers more details.

2 THE BOOK FACTORY

35/37 Queensland Road, London N7 7AH.
0171 700 1000. Fax: 0171 700 3569.
Perfect bound and manual printers/ short runs and reprints. The outfit which printed the SPG's 1994 Yearbook. If you liked that then give them a call and ask for a quote. For more information see their advert in this handbook.

3 BOOKFORCE

The Old Barns, Main Street, Ailsworth, Peterborough PE5 7AF.
01733 230 797 fax 01733 230 751
Printer/publisher; booklet 'Successful Self-publishing with Bookprint', 12 pp., free.

4 BOOKSPRINT

20 Shepherds Hill, London N6 5AH.
Short run printers and binders. Also carry a Brief Guide to Self-Publishing, £2.50 inc p&p. Write to Freepost Booksend, London N6 5BR for this.

5 BRITTON & WALLAND PRINTERS LTD.

Printing Works, 155 New Road (A13), Rainham, Essex RM13 8SH.
01708 558 595 fax 01708 525 925
Specialise in short-run map and booklet work.

6 CROMWELL

Broughton Gifford, Melksham, Wilts SN12 8PH.
01225 782 585.

7 DIGITAL PRINTING CO LTD

Viewpoint House, Nepshaw Lane South, Gildersome pur, Leeds LS27 7JO.
0113 238 0815. Fax 2380794.

8 DOT PRESS

01865-326 611.
Used by WiP. Dot prints stationery and magazines through to four-colour books.

9 E.C.(EDWARD CHARLES) PRINT & DESIGN

10 Hoxton Street, London N1 6NG.
0171 739 6695. Fax: 0171 613 3392.
Recommended by Romer Publications. A company specialising in competitive four-colour origination and printing.

10 EMJAY REPROGRAPHICS

17 Langbank Avenue, Rise Park, Nottingham NG5 5BU.
0115 975 1753.
'A reliable an experienced mail-order, printing and distribution facility.'

11 NORMAN HARDY PRINTING GROUP

Granville House, 112 Bermondsey Street, London SE1 3TX.
0171 378 1579 fax: 0171 378 6421.
Printer group. Holds seminars and organises 'Advice to Publishers & Editors' (APE) annual exhibition and magazine. Consultancy and book production services. Interested in advertising in the next edition of this handbook, probably 2000 AD.

12 HOBBS

Brunel Road, Totton, Hants SO40 3YS.

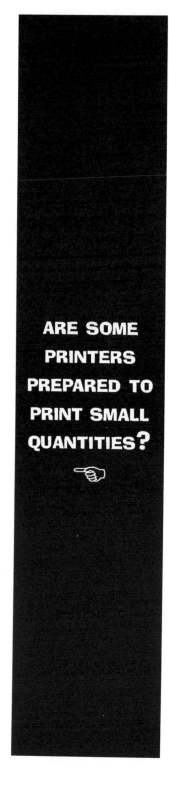

ARE SOME PRINTERS PREPARED TO PRINT SMALL QUANTITIES?

The complete service for Small Presses

INTYPE

can take your Artwork, PostScript disc or typescript and produce professional quality typesetting for 600 dpi laser output on the

DOCUTECH

multiple copies, from as few as 25. Choice of papers. Choice of

FINISHING

from wire stitching to perfect binding and even case binding

COVERS AND JACKETS

on tinted boards, colour printing, laminating.
Suitable for Books, Catalogues, Reprints, Manuals, Reports

Contact us for a flexible and sympathetic approach to your problems.

INTYPE   Units 3/4 Elm Grove Industrial Estate
LONDON LTD Elm Grove, Wimbledon SW19 4HE

Telephone 0181 947 7863   Fax 0181 947 3652   Modem 0181 944 9867

If you are a small Press with **BIG** ideas, then you should phone The Book Factory for a quote! Get the best for your money: best Prices, best Service, best Delivery, best Product.

From 100 to 10,000 copies, Perfect bound
with Laminated multi-coloured covers.

The Book Factory

35/37 Queensland Road • London • N7 7AH
• Tel: 0171 700 1000 •
• Fax: 0171 700 3569 •

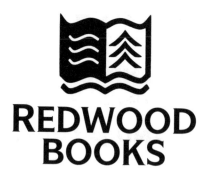

REDWOOD BOOKS

Redwood Books has been manufacturing books for
thirty years and prides itself on the high level
of quality and customer service.

———————•———————

Specialising in short runs we produce books in a variety of styles and
formats for over 350 publishers each year and have a continuing
programme of investment to ensure we provide the fast turnaround
and economic production our customers require.

———————•———————

For a brochure and further information please contact
our London sales office.

Manufacturing Site

Kennet Way
Trowbridge
Wiltshire BA14 8RN

Tel: 01225 769979
Fax: 01225 769050

London Sales Office

22 Bloomsbury Square
London
WC1A 2NS

Tel: 0171 580 9328
Fax: 0171 580 9337

Redwood Books is a division of the Bath Press Group PLC

SHORT RUN PRINTERS

A TEST CASE:

We put our advice into practice when producing this Handbook. We shopped around. We drew up a specs sheet based on the 1993 edition, published Autumn 1993, so we expected there to be changes. We isolated all the srps in the list. We began with a list of 18. We checked the details in the list and decided to double check on some printers. We phoned to ask if their details were correct. We could not get replies or connections to 5. Some addresses seemed insufficient so we checked directory enquiries. This exercise eliminated 5. But as some fell out others came in. We already knew one famous srp who had been lost off the list but who had advertised in the book. As a result of further explorations, tips and referrals we added 9 more. The first working list stood at nearly 30, and 10 were deleted. It does seem strange that in eight years we have only found around 20 srps in Britain. It underlines our suggestion: ask your high street quick print shop.

We drew up a specs sheet and added it to the bottom of a letter to all the srps on our revised list. All received the identical specs in less than a week.

How was the response? Within a week 4 replied. Another 4 replied within two weeks. Two replied to say they could not handle a job like ours. By the end of a month we held 14 replies with 12 quotes. Two others were still trying to cough up, two months later. How did they compare? The first thing is they hardly did. Only some of the quotes gave answers to all our simple questions. The most common practice was to quote for one of the quatities we specified, not all three. This reduced choice inside the printer and prevented an overall view across all printers. One printer sent a rapid follow up letter saying they made an error of £1,000 on one column. Two firms had terriers chasing us. They tried to do the discussion on the phone. We were invited to have a tour of the printworks, at the other side of the country. One firm required two business references before entertaining our job.

Seriously the figures were as expected. Some were more than double, or less than half depending on your temperament. But a consensus did emerge. And two/three front runners for price. The exercise proved worthwhile. We had a ballpark sum, but more importantly we saw the performance and attitude of the contenders.

01703 664 800. Fax 664 801.

13 INSTANT PRINT WEST ONE
12 Heddon Street, London W1.
0171 734 1945.
Very reasonable. Printing of booklets. Recommended by numerous small presses. The editor admits bias since they did a great job on his recent tract (see under BOZO).

14 INTYPE
Input Typesetting Ltd, Woodman Works, Durnsford Road, Wimbledon Park, London SW19 8DR.
0181 947 7863.
'Low cost short run book service. Books, book proofs, reprints, manuals, catalogues, price lists, in-house magazines, fanzines, programmes, on-demand publishing. Runs of 25 up to 1000 copies. Fast delivery, comptetitive pricing, help and advce, price scale on request.' But read their advert for information.

15 IPSWICH BOOK CO
The Drift, Nacton Road, Ipswich, Suffolk IP3 9QR.
01473 711 144 fax 01473 271 412.
Short run monochrome bookwork. Claim to do Small Press work but no advert to tell you...

15 JUMA
Martin Lacey, 44 Wellington Street, Sheffield S1 4HD.
01742 720 915.
Printed 'Small Press World' and other magazines, including many football zines.

17 THE LONDON PRINTING CENTRE
30 Store Street, London WC1.
0171 636 8723
Twin of Instant Print West One (qv) and offering equally speedy, cheap quick printing. Neither can do paperbacks. Offers cheap use of typesetting equipment (at very reasonable prices). Recommended by many small presses.

18 LOOSELEAF
Paul Ford, Pegasus Way, Bower Hill, Melksham, Wilts SN12 6PR.
01225 790 690.

19 NEWBURY PRINTING CO LTD
Newspaper House, Faraday Road,

Newbury, Berks RG14 2AD Tel 01635 43000

20 PDC COPYRIGHT
33 Lower Bridge Street, Chester CH1 1RD.
01244 311 073.
A printer highly recommended by SPG North, from time past.

21 REDWOOD BOOKS
Simon Povey/Tim Sullivan, Kennet House, Kennet Way, Trowbridge, Wilts BA14 8RN.
01225 769 979.
Entering the race in grand style by printing this Handbook. Biased? Naturally. Once you find a sympathetic printer stick with him! Check out their advert for how they present themselves.

22 ANTONY ROWE
Bumper's Farm, Chippenham, Wilts SN14 6LH.
01249 659 705. Fax 01249 443 103.
The first five editions of the SPG yearbook were printed by this firm. They regularly advertised in every edition and exhibited at SPG small press fairs. We had an excellent relationship, not least because so many SPG members used them, so bringing them good business. Times change...

23 SHORT RUN PRINT CO
99/101 Saint Leonards Raod, Windsor SL4 3BZ.
01753 857 349.

24 SOTHERAN,
Freepost, Dept C, Queen Street, Redcar TS10 1BR
Printer & binder. Poetry, memoirs, histories etc. From typescript or computer discs.

25 SUMMERSDALE PUBLISHERS
46 West Street, Chichester, West Sussex PO19 1RP. Tel/fax 01243 771 107
Printing services for other publishers.

26 BPCC/WHEATONS LTD
Hennock Road, Marsh Barton, Exeter, Devon EX2 8RP.
01392 520 222.
Warning! They have changed their emphasis in recent years. Since the last SPG Yearbook they have now moved out of the small press

printing business in favour of data manipulation. If you want this, or know wheat it means, they're the men for you.

UPDATE
Casualties?
We have tried to trace Ennisfield, David Green, Leulex, MS Press, SRP and Wellington Reprographics with no success.

Worth noting?
27 GAMECOCK
Peter Lloyd, 11 Park Road, Rugby, Warwick CV21 2QU.
01788 576 913.
Gamecock is now defunct. It is now The Holbeche Press. Fine printer. Couldn't handle our Handbook.

28 WESET PRINTING SERVICES
G.D.Larkins, 20 Wrotham Road, Barnet, Herts, EN5 4LE.
Tel/fax: 0181 440 7634.
DTP and scanning services by retired typesetter with long experience in hot-metal and monotype techniques.

29 CREATE PUBLISHING SERVICES LTD
Was reccomended by Praxis. Part of Bath Press Group (see Redwood Books – it is their typesetting arm). Book production services for the non-professional print buyer. Riverside Court, Lower Bristol Road, Bath BA2 3DZ. 01225 442 208 fax 0225 421 876

TOOLS & SERVICES
1 ALLADINK
Nick Goodwin, 43 High Strret, Eyemouth, Berwickshire TD14 5EY
018907 50965
Re-inking service for fabric ribbons in cassette-using typewriters and printers. Most types but enquire beforehand if you're unsure if his service matches your machines or cassette. A small but effective way of recycling and cutting down waste. Brought to our notice by Runetree.

2 BHTC DATABASE AND DIRECTORY OFFICE
38 Northcolme Road, London N5 2UU.
Compiling a database on the UK publishing industry, tied to Gale's Directory.

3 BIBLIOGRAPHIC DATA SERVICES
UK Office: 24 Nith Place, Dumfries DG1 2PN, Scotland. 01387 266 004 fax 01387 265 503
Supplies book data to booksellers, library suppliers and bibliographic utilities; CIP services: free to publishers.

4 BRITISH SISALKRAFT LTD
Commissioners Road, Strood, Kent ME2 4ED. 01634 290505.
Ever wondered where to get that cold seal sticky corrugated cardboard for packing books? It's called Cushionwrap and it's from this low profile firm or they'll put you in touch with a local supplier. This is invaluable for those presses doing mail order who have awkward-sizes books to pack. And it is cheaper than many padded envelopes.

5 CASLON LTD
15 Bakers Row, London EC1. 0171 837 3131.
Electric 'handy' wax rollers and wax to use in them. Both rollers and wax are light enough to be posted.

6 CW CAVE & TAB LTD
5 Tenter Road, Moulton Park, Northampton NN3 1PZ. 01604 643 677 fax: 01604 648 542.
Universal filters for PCs are available from Polaroid. Protects your eyes from low frequency radiation. Widely available. For your stockist contact us.

7 CHALLONER MKTG LTD
Amersham, Bucks. 01494 721 270.
Fly Weight envelope stiffener to stop your artwork and publications from being destroyed in the post.

8 DISK CONVERSIONS
9 Wootton Way, Cambridge CB3 9LX. Tel/fax: 01223 363259.
Computer disk translation in all permutations including translation from Amstrad 3" disk. Sliding scale of charges apply depending on work carried out. Also offer technical advice.

9 PETER HUNTER
21 Cooperative St, Coventry CV2 1PT. 01203 682 576.
Bubble-wrap packing available in bulk. Also try your local Yellow

TELL ME ABOUT ODD SERVICES I MIGHT NEED

CAN I GET SOMETHING PRINTED ON A T-SHIRT?

☞

Pages.

10 PAT JOEL PROOFREADING SERVICES
Tel/fax: 01773 856 575.
'A prompt, experienced proofreading service to publishers, printers, industry etc.

11 LITHO SUPPLIES
Unit 10, Brunswick Park Industrial Estate, Brunswick Park Road, London N11 1JL.
0181 368 5999 fax 0181 368 6809
Largest supplier of materials to the printing trade.

12 W. MACCARTHY & SONS
310-326 St James Road, London SE1. 0171 237 1946 fax 0171 252 3286
Make cardboard boxes and containers in short runs. 'Any design you want, well and reasonably priced and in as short a run as you want — which makes them unique' writes Liver and Lights.

13 MAPEJ
Digby James, Meadow View, Quinta Crescent, Weston Rhyn, Oswestry, Shropshire SY10 7RN. 01691 778659 fax: 01691 777638. Offer to provide the solution for transferring data between different disks and operating systems (Amstrad PCW/CPC/BBC/Amiga/IBM/Mac). Also provide Text and mono image scanning. SAE for details.

14 MC SERVICES
111 Hartlebury Trading Estate, Kidderminster, Worcestershire DY10 4JB. 01299 251 413 fax 01299 250 447
Magazine and partworks binder systems.

15 MILLWAY STATIONERY LTD
Chapel Hill, Stansted, Essex CM24 8AP. 01279 812 009.
Recycled products. According to the ALP Newsletter, the cheapest source for stationery etc.

16 RIVAL ENVELOPE CO LTD
50-52 Trundleys Road, London SE8 5JG. 0171 231 5242.
Ask us about your job on our hotline.

17 SENTINEL FOAM LTD
Hart Street, Maidstone, Kent ME16 8RQ. 01622 677 151.
Supplier of padded envelopes.

18 TDP PARTNERSHIP
41 Quarry Road, Old Town, Swindon, Wiltshire SN1 4EW. Tel/fax: 01793 522 497.
Contact: Mandi J.Mathews. Technical Document Presentation specialists, offering dtp and support services for those businesses requiring documentation, technical manuals, promotional material &c. English and foreign language.

19 TEE PUBLISHING
The Fosse, The Fosse Way, Radford Semele, Leamington Spa, Warks CV31 1XN. 01926 614 101 fax 01926 614 293
Publisher: 'Engineering in Miniature', solicits advert space.

T-SHIRTS
We have followed the same principle as we used about Photo Copy shops - there are so many you can use Yellow Pages.

1 AD VENTURE SERVICES
Gambles Factory, Raleigh Street, Nottingham NG7 4FD
0115 962 6118

2 ALEX PHILLIPS PRINTING SERVICES
26 Thurnham Street, Lancaster LA1 1XU 01524 841 286
Absolutely anything printed on a t shirt!

3 DRECKLEY PRINT
John Millett, 2 Carthew Cottages, Newbridge, Penzance, Cornwall TR20 8QJ 01736 66248
Ideas welcomed.

4 FIFTH COLUMN
276 Kentish Town, London NW5
0171 485 8599
Used by the London Cycling Campaign.

5 FLASH PROMOTIONS
Ardennes House, 112 Victoria Dock Road, London E16 1DA
0171 473 1007 fax 0171 473 1077
Process work on dark shirts a speciality.

6 JEN TAIT
2 Baggrave View, Narsby, Leicestershire LE7 8RB UK.
Write for details.

7 MAGIC T-SHIRTS
10-16 Mower Street, Covent Garden, London WC2H 9QD
1071 497 3554

8 MARK CARROLL & CO
45 Barnfield Aveneue, Kingston, Surrey KT2 5RD 0181 546 9606/ 0831 222 727
T shirts printed in colour any logo.

9 OXLEY OF LONDON
1st Floor, The London Pavilion, 1 Picadilly Circus, London W1V. 0171 734 1292

10 STOP
Oxley of London
as above but second floor
0171 494 2425

We can no longer trace Calm Down Puppy.

USEFUL
PERIODICALS &
PUBLICATIONS

You should use these in two ways. Read them to keep informed and to get publicity for your titles. See what they will carry, then bombard them!

1 ARTISTS NEWSLETTER
PO Box 23, Sunderland SR4 6DG. 0191 567 3589.
are interested in small press matters and publish a bi-annual supplement on Contemporary British Artists' Books. They also do a list of handbooks, directories &c for artists, craftspeople and photographers.

2 ALP
Publish a useful newsletter, a twice yearly anthology PALPI and a Catalogue of Little Press Books in Print (see 'Other Organisations' for details).

3 ALTERNATIVE PRESS REVIEW
c/o C.A.L., POB 1446, Columbia, MO. 65205-1446.
From the publisher of 'Anarchy' comes this title to rival 'Factsheet Five', with reviews, articles and features. Recommended.

4 BOOKCASE
W.H. Smith & Son, Greenbridge Road, Swindon. 01793 616 161.

5 BOOKDEALER
Suite 34, 26 Charing Cross Road, London WC2. 0171 240 5890.

6 THE BOOK EXCHANGE
9 Elizabeth Gardens, Sunbury-on-Thames, Middlesex TW16 5LG. 01932 784 855.
'The international journal appraising new books in English'.
Send them your catalogue and ABIs.

7 BOOK MARKETING AGENCY
7a Bedford Square, London WC2. 0171 580 7282.
Publish 'Book Facts'.

8 BOOK MARKETING COUNCIL
The Publishers Association, 19 Bedford Square, London WC1B 3HJ.
0171 580 6321
A trade paper with useful news items and some symptomatically interesting insights into the workings of the trade. ISSN 0264-3219. Various other informative publications.

9 BOOKNEWS
Book Trust, 45 East Hill, London SW18 2QZ.
Listings. If you want to be featured, write to them.

10 BOOKS MAGAZINE
43 Museum Street, London WC1A 1LY. 0171 404 0304.

11 THE BOOKSELLER
Published by Whitakers, 12 Dyott Street, London WC1A 1DF.
0171 420 6000 fax: 0171 420 6103.
The trade's magazine.

12 BOOKSELLING NEWS
154 Buckingham Palace Road, London SW1. 0171 730 8214.

13 BOOKS FOR YOUR CHILDREN
34 Hardorne Road, Edgbaston, Birmingham B15 3AA. 0121 454 5453.

14 BOOKWATCH
7-up Sycamore Place, Hill Avenue, Amersham, Bucks HP6 5BG. 01494 728 232.
National bestseller list compilers for

WHAT MAGAZINES & TRADE JOURNALS WILL BE USEFUL TO ME?

the Sunday Times, Daily Express, Daily Telegraph, The Bookseller, &c. They publish 'Books in the Media', weekly listing of around 1,000 titles linked to tv, radio, films &c. Free helpline service for subscribers. Market research for publishers including weekly retail sales tracking in national sample with option of tv regional breakdown.

15 CASCANDO
PO Box 1499, London SW10 9TQ. 01603 618 058.
National Student Literary Magazine for new student writers.

16 CHRISTIAN BOOKSELLER
Commercial Business Centre, Victoria Street, Rainhill, Merseyside, L35 4LP. 0151 444 2894 fax: 0151 430 7836.

17 COUNTERPOISE
Chris Atton, Dunning Library, Napier University, 10 Collinton Road, Edinburgh EH10 5DT
A new journal for librarians which aims to widen the scope. Published by the Alternatives in Print Task Force of the American Library Association. We are giving you the British contact.

18 EDINBURGH REVIEW
The Editor, Edinburgh Review, Polygon Books, 22 George Square, EH8 9LF, Scotland.
One of this journal's many good features is its interest in small press activity of all sorts and from all countries. Always of interest to small press enthusiasts.

19 THE EUROPEAN BOOKSELLER
15 Micawber Street, London N1 7TB 0171 336 6650 fax 0171 36 6640.
'The magazine for Europe's English language book trade'.

20 FREE PRESS
the bi-monthly journal of the Campaign for Press and Broadcasting Freedom, 2 Cynthia Street, London N1 9JF, 0171 278 4430

21 FREELANCE NEWS
Elvendon Press, Freepost, Goring-on-Thames, Reading RG8 9BR. Quarterly update about freelance scene for publishers. £6.50 subscription.

22 INDEPENDENT MEDIA
Freepost Independent Media, c/o DVA, 7 Campbell Court, Branley, Basingstoke, Hants RG26 5BR. £15 p.a. sub.

23 INDEPENDENT PUBLISHERS GUILD 'BULLETIN'
147-149 Gloucester Terrace, London W2 6DX.
Newsletter from the IPG. Occasionally features items concerning small press activity.

24 LIBRARY ASSOCIATION RECORD
7 Ridgmount Street, London WC1. 0171 636 7543.
Monthly journal.

25 MARKETING EVENT
Haymarket Publications, 174 Hammersmith Road, London W6 7JP
Monthly glossy. Aimed at the trade so very slick and commercial. (A Hezza maga) But check the small display ads in the back for a host of firms offering catoonists/ illustrators, badges, display systems, gifts, carrier bags, biros or tatoos.

26 NEW LIBRARY WORLD
Seaton House, Kings Ripton, Huntingdon. 014873 238.

27 NEWS FROM THE CENTRE
The National Small Press Centre, BM BOZO, London WC1N 3XX. Their bi-monthly newsletter. Sub £6.00 PA. Has a section 'About The Presses'.

28 PRINTING WORLD
Benn Publications, Sovereign Way, Tonbridge TN9 1RW. 01732 364 422.

29 PUBLISHING NEWS
Gradegate Ltd, 43 Museum Street, London WC1A 1LY. 0171 404 0304 fax: 0171 242 0762. Bombard them with your press releases!

30 REFER
Journal of Info Services Group (reference libraries)
The Library Association, Charles A Toase, 6 Watery Lane, Merton Park, London SW20 9AA Tel 0181 540 2619 fax 0181 543 7402

31 SMALL PRESS LISTINGS
The National Small Press Centre, BM BOZO, London WC1N 3XX. Quarterly compendium with multitude of eclectic entries. Essential — either to read or to get a FREE entry. Sub £10.00 PA.

32 WRITERS NEWS
Brunel House, Newton Abbot, Devon TQ12 4YG. 01626 61121. A magazine for writers.

33 FORUM BOOK ART VERLAG
Heinz Stefan Bartkowiak, Körnerstrasse 24, D 22301 Hamburg, Germany.

34 BROKEN PENCIL,
The guide to alternative culture in Canada.PO Box 203, Station P, Toronto, ON, M55 2S7 Canada.

defunct
British Book News, Freelance Writing & Photography, Small Press Monthly, Small Press World …

'Cyber'magazines, accessible via the internet:
1 FEED
cultural monthly
http://www.feedmag.com

2 THE SALON
online arts magazine
http://www.salon1999.com

3 SLATE
Microsoft sponsored webzine
http://www.slate.com

4 WORD
Cybermag of modern culture, upated daily
http://www.word.com

WORKSHOPS & RESOURCE CENTRES
COPY ART PRINTSHOP
0171 267 8145
Macintosh DTP, laser printing facilities. Available for anyone to use, or they'll do it for you. Very competitive. Two photocopiers available, laminating and blade-making equipment. (see below - possibly defunct)

EDINBURGH PRINTMAKERS
0131 557 2479
Open access studio.

LONDON PRINT WORKSHOP
421 Harrow Road, London W10 4RD.
Printmaking: 0181 969 8271; Computers: 0181 969 3247
Professional training, access to facilities for artists, presses, members of community organisations and general public; DTP courses.

LOWICK HOUSE
Nr Ulverston, Cumbria LA12 8DX. Open access studios with litho, etching and screen facilities etc. (check this still exists.)

NORTHERN PRINTMAKERS WORKSHOP
Fish Quay, Northshields. Open access studios with litho, etching, silkscreen etc. Recommended by Liver & Lights.

ORMOND ROAD WORKSHOPS
25 Ormond Road, London N19 4ER. 0181 263 3865.
Excellent screenprinting facilities, dirt cheap, with a very helpful staff, creche facilities, &c. Open access studio with print and ceramic, etching, silkscreen etc.

TRUE PROOF
Unit 52, New Lydenburg Industrial Estate, New Lydenburg Street, Greenwich, London SE10 8NF. (not found in directory so check first) Small run colour photo and repro company.

Defunct as far as we can tell:
Copy Art Printshop and The Union Place Resource Centre. Also check Lowick House, True Proof and the Union Place Centre...

MISSED YOUR CHANCE?
You didn't have an advertisement in this Handbook to inform readers about the service you offer? Lost money? Although this Handbook will last years you shouldn't despair...
•Make sure you keep us informed and be ready to book your advertisement next time...
•Send for our Rate Card for advertising in our regular updates: *Small Press Listings* and *News From The Centre.*

ARE THERE PLACES WITH FACILITIES I CAN USE? ☞

MINIPRESSEN

MMPM

14. MAINZERMINIPRESSENMESSE

Internationale Buchmesse der Kleinverlage und künstlerischen Handpressen vom 8. bis 11. 5. 1997

360 Handpressen, Klein- und Selbstverlage, Literarische Agenturen, Literaturbüros, Galerien, Editionen, Schreibwerkstätten und Zeitschriften aus 14 Ländern stellen aus.

Zum Rahmenprogramm gehören Seminare, Workshops, Vorträge, Literaturbörse, Buchauktion.

Der Katalog zur 14. MMPM ist auch das Verzeichnis von Kleinverlagen und Handpressen 1997/98.

Informationen für Teilnahme, Besuch oder Anzeige im Katalog der Minipresse unter Gutenberg-Museum Mainzer Minipressen-Archiv, Fischtorplatz 23, 55116 Mainz Tel: 0 61 31-12 26 76, Fax: 0 61 31-12 34 88

PLAKATE Zeitschriften Papier BUCHOBJEKTE Bücher Druckobjekte Pressendrucke WORKSHOPS Seminarprogramm

INTERNATIONAL BOOK FAIR FOR SMALL PRESSES
FOIRE INTERNATIONAL DU LIVRE DES PETITS ÉDITEURS

MESSE

THE NATIONAL SMALL PRESS CENTRE

THE NATIONAL SMALL PRESS CENTRE

BM BOZO
LONDON
WC1N 3XX
England

The National Small Press Centre

Independent self-publishers need a centre, a focal point, which coordinates and organises to further their general interests.

Between 1992 and 1996 such a Centre flourished at Middlesex University. Originally set up by the Small Press Group of Britain Ltd it outlived its parent organisation. In 1996 the Centre's Committee and Middlesex University parted on friendly terms so that the Centre could seek a new host organisation and expand its activities.

During the five years of the Centre, and eight of the SPG, invaluable experience was garnered, a wealth of expertise, contacts and information on thousands of Small Presses as well as the back-up services they need. This information is continually shared in the Centre's newsletter, *News From The Centre*, every other month. It is brought together in the Centre's *Handbook* which is the unique reference and resource. The *NSPC* is continually upgrading the quantity and quality of its services, described in this leaflet.

If you feel the NSPC is helping you then why don't you help the NSPC? The Small Press spirit is mutual aid. Help others to help yourself.

What does the National Small Press Centre Committee do?

The *National Small Press Centre Committee* takes further the work begun by the Small Press Group. It continues to raise public awareness of Small Presses and now provides a programme of help and advice. It promotes independent publishers as a whole and is uniquely placed between Small Presses and their back-up services. Through the information published by the *National Small Press Centre* both can benefit commercially.

The campaign

While the campaign for a new Centre continues, the National Small Press Centre Committee is continuing to provide several services in the spirit of the Centre's aim.

What can the NSPC do for you?

•By raising public perception of Small Presses in general the *NSPC* helps you individually.
•By making available information on thousands of Small Presses in Britain and abroad the *NSPC* enables you to contact like-minded people and outfits.
•By supplying information on Services and Resources the *NSPC* enables you to find the help you seek.
•You can keep up-to-date on developments in the world of Small Presses and similar organisations in Britain and abroad.
•By getting an entry in *Small Press Listings* your Small Press and titles will reach libraries, booksellers and the media.
•Our publications keep you in touch and help promote your Small Press.
•Help and advice. Buy a title on the topic you need from our ever-expanding mail-order list. Book an Advice Surgery, send for an Advice Slip.
•*We take your Small Press seriously.*

What can you do for the NSPC?

•Send your details, your proposals, your subscriptions.
•Join in this voluntary work
•Join the campaign!
•*Take your Small Press seriously.*

You can't afford to be left out.

The National Small Press Centre

A self-funding independent organisation relying on voluntary staff.

With its wide experience, contacts and database the *NSPC* can organise or provide:

Exhibitions
Fairs
Talks and lectures
Courses and workshops
Consultancy services for all of the above
Origination service

Make an appointment to consult the *NSPC's*

Reference library
Collection of samples

The Book and Heart
Shall never part

Subscription Form

News From The Centre
(Individual issues and copies @ £1.50)
6 issues per year at £1 per issue
Total price is £6 p.a.

Small Press Listings
(Individual issues and copies @ £3)
4 issues per year @ £2.50 per issue
Total price is £10 p.a.

Money-saving joint offer:
6 issues of News FromThe Centre
and
4 issues of Small Press Listings p.a. for 25% off – only £12

I would like a year's subscription:
☐ News from the Centre £6
☐ Small Press Listings £10
☐ Special joint offer £12
I enclose £ ....
payable to 'Small Press'.

NAME: ....

ADDRESS: ....
....
....
....
....

The NSPC helps The NSPC

The NSPC helps The NSPC

Keeping Informed

Small Press Listings brings together an authoritative record of independent self-publishers and their publications. It is an invaluable reference tool for librarians, booksellers and the media – the *Whitakers* of the world of Small Press publishing. Every quarter it contains full bibliographical details of titles as well as the addresses of the publishers. It does not contain reviews but only descriptive material. There is a reference section with information about services and resources which are essential for Small Presses. *Limited advertising is available.*

More than an information newsletter on the activities of the *NSPC, News From The Centre* contains essential details about the many organisations catering for Small Presses, both in Britain and abroad. As well as short features on ways to increase your effectiveness, *NFTC* has a lively letters column where people seek and give advice. Published every other month *NFTC* provides a unique and eminently readable way of keeping up to date and in touch with what is going on in the world of independent publishing. *Please complete and return a subscription form.*

Resources & Expertise

Through its connections and database, the *NSPC* can put your Small Press in touch with specialists in most areas: proof-reading, editing, setting, formatting, illustrating and graphics, design and cover design, printing and finishing, binding, marketing and distribution, etc. *There is a small fee for this service.*

Book Ordering Service

The *NSPC* Committee has given a lot of thought to which books might best be useful to an independent publisher. Knowing how difficult it can be to find the handbook or resource guide you need, we have come up with a list of essential Small Press reading – including many from abroad, which we can sell to you by mail. Marketing, sales, promotion, publicity, design, proof-reading, illustrating, organising events, etc. publications on these subjects and others are available via this unique service. *Send for a list and order form.*

Origination & Design

Some members of the *NSPC* Committee offer their services and expertise in desk-top publishing, layout, imposition and design to benefit Small Presses. With techniques gained over 20 years, they can help transform raw text into camera-ready artwork, and basic layout into presentable, publishable copy. They will help you create a catalogue from your list of past and forthcoming publications, to make them a viable mail-order item. *Please ask for details and prices of this service.*

Consultancy Service

The *NSPC* also offers a consultancy service to organisations, institutions and educational establishments, etc. These can take the form of hands-on workshops, lectures, illustrated talks, or written proposals. *Let us know the nature of the enquiry and the type of service you require.*

helps The NSPC helps
helps The NSPC helps

Advice Surgeries

The majority of enquiries to the *NSPC* seek advice on how to become an independent self-publisher. The *NSPC* welcomes genuine enquiries about starting up or running a Small Press. It does not offer a publishing service or free advice.The *NSPC* is not an agony aunt for aspiring authors, nor does it replace the functions of publishers by taking on the responsibility for marketing their publications. Instead *NSPC Surgeries* give technical advice on how to run a Small Press. These *Surgeries* are not professional consultancies or agencies, but are a means to share experience, one small press to another. The *NSPC* is staffed by people who run their own Small Presses.

By appointment only.
Tariff: for Small Presses and individuals, £15 per hour or part of an hour.
For institutions, £50 per hour or part of an hour.

Advice Slips

Based on its experience and expertise, the *NSPC* Committee has created a series of *advice slips.* On receipt of a stamped, self-addressed C5 envelope we will be happy to send an *advice slip* on any of the following subjects.

A. Artists books.
B. Getting into print.
C. Helpful organisations.
D. Where to place your poems.
This list is constantly being up-graded and expanded. Look out for further titles.

Handbook

"A novice could end up selling their own books, pamphlets or magazines. It is the perfect way into this 'other world' of publishing." PUBLISHING NEWS
"Strange but wonderful" TIME OUT.

Heir to the legendary Small Press Group *Yearbook,* the new series of *NSPC Handbooks* are invaluable annuals and resource guides. Essential reading not only for Small Presses, but also for the services and the trade: librarians, booksellers, educational institutions, and the general public, who will have a unique access to the world outside main-stream publishing. A world full of wonders and thousands of invisible tiny publications. *Send for an order form.*

Publicity

Every press is offered a FREE chance of publicity in all *NSPC* publications. We ask for the name of your imprint and contact person and address and a short 30 word description of your Small Press. The information supplied is published in *Small Press Listings* and later in the *NSPC Handbook* – this way you keep in touch *and* promote your Press. *Send for a form to complete*

Advertise your latest publication, catalogue, launch or special event in *News from the Centre* and *Small Press Listings* – from linage to full pages. Reach a national audience by advertising in the Centre's *Handbook,* (our advertising team will help with the artwork for a small fee). We also accept advertising from Small Press services – desk-top-publishers, short-run printers, graphic designers, typists, bookbinders, etc. There is nowhere better to reach this unique Small Press market. *Send for a rate card.*